GLOBAL INFORMATION TECHNOLOGY AND ELECTRONIC COMMERCE

Issues for the New Millennium

Editors:

Prashant C. Palvia
Shailendra C. Jain Palvia
Edward M. Roche

Ivy League Publishing, Limited

Global Information Technology and Electronic Commerce
Issues for the New Millennium

Editors:
Prashant C. Palvia
Shailendra C. Palvia
Edward M. Roche

Published by:

Ivy League Publishing, Limited
P.O. Box 680392
Marietta, Georgia 30068, U.S.A.
Phone: (770) 649-6718   Fax: (770) 649-6719

Publisher's Cataloging-in-Publication
(Provided by Quality Books, Inc.)

Global information technology and electronic commerce :
 issues for the new millennium / editors, Prashant C.
Palvia, Shailendra C. Palvia, Edward M. Roche.
  p. cm.
  Includes bibliographical references and index.
  LCCN: 2001118234
  ISBN: 0-9648382-3-0

  1. Information technology--Management.
2. International business enterprises--Communication
systems--Data processing. 3. Electronic commerce.
I. Palvia, Prashant. II. Palvia, Shailendra. III. Roche,
Edward Mozley.

HD30.2.G56 2001   658.4'038
                         QBI01-200976

Global Information Technology and Electronic Commerce:
Issues for the New Millennium

Table of Contents

Dedicated to the cherished memory of our parents:

Dr. C. M. Palvia (a mentor and scholar) who left for his heavenly abode on July 14, 1993

and

Mrs. Lalita Palvia (caring and spirited) who passed away in divine peace on May 17, 2001.

….. Shailendra Palvia and Prashant Palvia

Foreword

Global Information Technology and Electronic Commerce:
Issues for the New Millennium

David Strom

Global Information Technology (IT) has become one of the most critical elements for multinational corporations as they try to expand their markets beyond traditional boundaries and use the Internet to establish new customers and businesses. And global IT can be even more important than the more mundane business functions such as marketing, finance, accounting, human resources, or manufacturing. This is because IT can transform a local business into an international powerhouse in a matter of weeks, if it applied properly and executed well. The stakes involved are high, but so are the benefits.

Electronic Commerce (or e-Commerce) is essentially buying and selling of goods and services using the Internet infrastructure. E-Commerce can be of many kinds – B2B, B2C, B2G, G2C, C2C etc. Successful e-Commerce ventures must result from an optimal mix of value-added products and services and astute marketing strategies. It is also using advertising approaches that exploit the web and search engines to the fullest extent, maintaining continuous high quality customer relationship management, secure and reliable ordering and payment systems, and above all an IT platform along with top notch business applications that support e-Commerce activity on a 24x7x365 basis. Accomplishing all the above is a very tall order. Yet, e-Commerce is an unstoppable bandwagon.

There is no doubt that the convenience of e-Commerce is huge, and that e-Commerce is here to stay and will only get more and more popular over time. Yet e-Commerce – and especially e-Commerce on a global scale, cutting across nations, cultures and currencies -- is still too difficult for most corporations to implement. Getting any kind of online storefront up and running is easy: but getting a good one, with solid service, and one that is easy to use and a pleasure to shop in, is another story entirely.

How can e-Commerce be both so popular and so difficult? That is only one of the many paradoxes that await any student of the subject. My pre-teen daughter has bought and sold items on eBay, and thinks nothing of going online to try to find something, whether it be an article of clothing, a new pop song, or even a horse (she is trying, rather unsuccessfully, to convince me to buy her a horse to ride). My family has spent more money at Amazon.com than at the local bookstore a short walk from our house. And I haven't stepped inside a computer store in years when I can receive most items within a few hours from ordering them online with free overnight delivery.

There are several challenges in the context of global IT and global e-Commerce. This book goes into plenty of detail on all of these issues. First of all is the problem from the customer perspective. Shopping online is still far from where it could be: it is akin to going to any random suburban American mall on the day after Thanksgiving, when stores are crowded and parking is at a premium. And once you fight your way inside the mall, you find that all the stores' signage is gone, and you have to randomly hunt for the right storefront. When you do make it inside the appropriate store, you find that your intended items are out of stock, or only available in the wrong colors or sizes. And even if you do find the right merchandize, you suffer through a long checkout line only to find that they don't take your particular brand of credit card or only deal in some obscure currency.

But there are other problems apart from the customer perspective. Global e-Commerce systems development is a very big hurdle. And the trouble here is that you need to push forward on several fronts, sometimes all at the same time. You need to make changes to the banking network to handle online purchases and returns, integrate online inventory systems to provide real-time status of items, and improve customer-care and support to handle email and web-based inquiries. Any one of these is a big enough challenge on its own, but taken together coordinating all of this work will take lots of expertise and skill and usually a long time to do well.

Finally, there is an issue of gathering mind-share and market share: it just costs plenty of money to develop your brand and take it to the world in cyberspace. Even Amazon.com – arguably the most successful pure online retailer -- can't get everything right: they are now scaling back from being an online department store to focusing on a few departments so that they can become profitable. To date, the company has never made a dime from its operations.

That's unfortunately where we are in mid-2001 for most global e-Commerce situations, and where we will be for some time to come. Hopefully, readers of this book will be able to learn from these challenges and mistakes of the past. Only then will global e-Commerce be able to grow and thrive.

* * * * *

David Strom was the founding editor-in-chief of Network Computing magazine and has written over a thousand articles for numerous computer trade publications. Currently, he writes a weekly series of essays called Web Informant that explore web marketing, e-Commerce and Internet infrastructure issues. Strom is president of his own consulting firm, based in Port Washington, NY. He has lectured on e-Commerce on five continents and is the co-author of Internet Messaging, a book exploring practical applications of corporate email. He can be reached at david@strom.com.

PREFACE

The millennium is here. In the new century, information technology is pervasive not only in service and manufacturing industries but also in government and non-profit organizations, at home and in all spheres of life. Computers with the power of machines supporting entire work groups just a few years ago, are now being carried around in people's coat pockets. Today's "always connected" employee is now a global force for change. Global village is no more a prophecy, but a practical necessity. Businesses that globalize have made history and will continue to do so. The Internet, Worldwide Web and Electronic Commerce have opened up potential for inter-organizational systems and applications never possible in the past. Globalization is now recognized as a compelling force on products such as automobiles, electronic appliances, textiles, computer hardware and software, and many consumer products. Raw materials may be in one part of the world, product and sub-products can be manufactured elsewhere, and the final product sold *everywhere* in the world. Even small and medium sized enterprises (SMEs) accommodate international factors whether it is new customers, human resources, raw materials, or innovative products. Globalization and information technology have in effect converged in synergy to both challenge and benefit businesses, people and societies across the world. The global aspects of IT first articulated by us and a select few in the early nineties are now well understood and accepted worldwide.

In order to address the multiple perspectives and the breadth of the global IT field, we invited proposals from many distinguished scholars and authors for this book. Invitations to write chapters were based on careful screening of the proposals in terms of both quality and relevance. Each chapter is original and was written specifically for the book, and went through a thorough review process and several revisions. The book has twenty-five chapters organized into six sections to maximize pedagogical effectiveness. The first section with four chapters provides the necessary background by way of describing the global IT environment in different parts of the world. The second section has seven chapters and it discusses the strategic, management and business issues related to global IT. Section three has four chapters dealing with international aspects of electronic commerce. The fourth section has six chapters that deal with the various aspects of global systems development and implementation. As international IT outsourcing has witnessed a major growth in recent years, two chapters are devoted to outsourcing related issues. Finally, the two chapters in the last section address operational and infrastructure issues in global information technology management.

Global IT management is here to stay and to stay for good. If anything, most MIS issues would now be viewed through the lens of globalization. In this context, as in our previous two books, this one offers significant value for four groups: students in universities and colleges, educators, researchers, and managers in corporations. It would be a perfect textbook for a graduate level (master's or Ph.D.) course or a junior/senior course dealing with international aspects of IT management. Increasingly, a growing number of business schools have a program in international business or a specific course in international IT; the book is especially designed to meet this need. The book can also be used as a companion text for courses in IS management, advanced IS courses, and executive MBA/MS courses. The book also has considerable value for senior executives and IS managers, as most of the chapters provide practical ideas and mini cases for the global utilization of information technology. Clearly the book will be most useful to educators in incorporating the global dimension of IT in their lectures, and to researchers in pursuing research in the international IT arena. Even if educators are not teaching a specific course in global IT, they are advised to acquire a copy as there is a wealth of information made available concisely in one place. In our view, global IT is where the action belongs, and everyone in MIS should make a special effort to stay current in the field.

So what's new in this book compared to our 1996 and 1992 books on the same subject? The overall theme is the same, e.g. the book focuses on "global information technology" (and by extension global electronic commerce). It discusses issues related to the application of technology in the multinational enterprise, including application development, information technology (IT) management and operations, architecture and infrastructure, as well as IT strategy.

More importantly, this new publication reflects the profound changes that have emerged in the past few years. All chapters are new and provide contemporary knowledge. The first section on global IT environment provides information about important regions of the world. Information technology is now widely recognized as a strategic force; so the entire next section is devoted to business and IT related strategic issues. Another section focuses on global electronic commerce that was virtually non-existent in the mid-nineties. New material has been added to the sections on system development strategies, offshore development, and infrastructure. We have worked hard to ensure that a certain level of maturity in the global IT field is reflected in these chapters. The goal was not only to summarize current experiences, but also to offer managerial insights and foundational perspectives. Two noteworthy new features of the book include a minicase at the end of most chapters and essay-type study questions. Also included is a glossary and index for quick retrieval of important topics.

The editors would like to express their gratitude to the participating authors. Authors, thank you! While we provided coordination and direction for the overall work, it is the individual authors' original work that is reflected in the book. They worked diligently in targeting the chapters to the needs of our readers, presenting contemporary material, and responding to our extensive comments in a timely fashion. We welcome any feedback that will further improve the quality of our work.

Prashant C. Palvia
Greensboro, North Carolina

Shailendra C. Jain Palvia
Long Island, New York

Edward M. Roche
New York City, New York

SECTION - 1

GLOBAL INFORMATION TECHNOLOGY ENVIRONMENT

One of the most common failures in management is to assume that the conditions they are used to in one country will be the same when they reach another. It is common to hear someone say: "IT is the same the world over, it doesn't really make any difference where you are."

To a certain extent this true - certainly many of the computer systems will be the same, and even some of the operating systems. A disk drive works the same in New York City as it does in Hong Kong.

The truth is, it is not the hardware and software the IT manager will find different, but rather the entire social and economic context into which the IT system must operate - different cultures, different languages, different ways of keeping the books, and different management practices - is different. Understanding these differences is a critical success factor in management.

This section presents four chapters designed to heighten your awareness of the international environment in which the multinational enterprise operates. The first chapter discusses how the issues faced by IT management changes from one region of the world to another. It does so by summarizing a series of IS issues studies that have been published over the years. By putting all of this information together, it is possible to see both how issues have changed, and also to identify those issues that have remained constantly important over time. The subsequent three chapters give a more detailed look at three very different regions of the world: Southern Asia, Russia, and finally IT in the Arctic circle.

1

Global Information Technology Management Environment: Representative World Issues[1]

Prashant C. Palvia
The University of North Carolina at Greensboro, USA

Shailendra C. Jain Palvia
Long Island University, USA

James E. Whitworth
Georgia Southern University, USA

ABSTRACT

As an increasing number of businesses expand their operations into international markets, in order to succeed they need to recognize and understand the considerable cultural, economic, and political diversity that exists in different parts of the world. For these reasons, while information technology is a critical enabler and many times a driver of global business expansion, it is usually not applied uniformly around the world. This chapter describes and analyzes the key information systems/technology (IS/IT) issues identified during the last decade and a half in different regions of the world. Spurred by periodic key IS issues studies in the USA, several researchers have done the same for many other countries. This chapter summarizes many of their findings, and provides insights into the various differences and similarities among countries. A model is developed and tested to help understand the nature of the issues and some of the underlying causes.

INTRODUCTION

During the past decade and a half, the world has witnessed an unprecedented expansion of business into global markets. The idea of a "global village," envisioned by McLuhan (1964), has finally come true. At the same time there has been a realization that information technology (IT) has played a crucial role in the race towards globalization. IT has been a critical enabler of globalization in many cases and a driver in other cases. Today, multinational corporations and governments increasingly rely on IT for conducting international business. Therefore, in order to fully exploit the vast potential of IT, it is

---

[1] This chapter is an adaptation and revision of: Understanding the Global Information Technology Environment: Representative World Issues, by Palvia, P. and Palvia, S. In *Global Information Technology and Systems Management: Key Issues and Trends*. Edited by P.Palvia, S. Palvia, and E.M. Roche, Ivy League Publishing 1996, pp. 3-30.

extremely important for corporate executives and chief information officers to understand the nature of the global information technology environment. This chapter provides not only this understanding, but also provides insights into the nature of global IT issues.

Reports of key information system (IS) and IT management issues have continually appeared in the United States. For example, a stream of articles of IS issues in the USA has appeared in the *MIS Quarterly* (Dickson et al. 1984; Brancheau et al. 1987; Niederman et al. 1991; Ball & Harris 1992, Brancheau et al. 1996). A study by Deans et al. (1991) identified and prioritized international IS issues in US based multinational corporations. As technology is assimilated into other countries, researchers have begun to identify IS/IT issues in these countries. Several such studies have appeared recently; representative examples include: North American and European issues (CSC Index 1995), Canada issues (Carey, 1992), Australia issues (Watson 1989), Hong Kong issues (Burn et al., 1993), India issues (Palvia & Palvia 1992), and Singapore issues (Rao et al. 1987). Such studies are perceived to be of value as they not only identify issues critical to determining strategies for organizations, but also provide direction for future MIS education, practice, and research.

A comparison of the cited studies reveals that the key IS issues in different countries vary to a considerable degree. In order to fully exploit IT for global business, it is imperative that the key IS/IT issues of different countries are identified and dealt with appropriately in the conduct of international business. While an examination of IS/IT issues of the entire world is impractical and infeasible, even the data is not readily available, we summarize issues from a few countries selected on the basis of their level of economic development. Four categories of economic development are defined: advanced, newly industrialized, developing (operational), and under-developed. This classification is somewhat parallel to that used by many international agencies (e.g., the United Nations). The countries discussed in this chapter are loosely categorized using this classification.

While some level of generalization is possible based on the countries discussed herein and is intended, we need to clearly point out the limitations. The chapter does not cover the entire world. Only a few countries are surveyed and while they may represent many other countries, they do not represent them all. Second, the classification of a country into one of the above four classes may be disputable, and furthermore, there is certainly a range within each class. Lastly, some countries may simply not easily fit the classification scheme used (e.g., Russia and countries of the former soviet union).

KEY MIS ISSUES IN ADVANCED NATIONS

Advanced and industrialized nations include the United States, Western European countries, Japan, and Australia among others. Key IS/IT issues have been systematically and periodically researched in the United States over the past fifteen years (Ball & Harris 1992; Brancheau et al. 1987; Dickson et al. 1984; Hartog & Herbert 1986; Niederman et al. 1991). Brancheau et al., 1996 compiled a list of key IS issues in USA based on a Delphi study to obtain opinions from IS executives. Rankings from this study are shown in Table 1. While a few new issues have appeared in this list (e.g., business process re-engineering), there is not a substantial departure from the 1991 list of issues reported by Niederman et al. (1991). Also, as reported by CSC Index (1995), the IS issues in Western Europe are very similar to the North American Issues (Tables 2 and 3).

This similarity is also seen in Australian issues (Table 4), Canadian issues reported by Pollard and Hayne (1996) and West European issues reported by Watson and Brancheau (1991). As the 1991 and 1996 issues study by Niederman et al. and Brancheau et al. are well-known, meet methodological rigor, and are widely distributed, they will be discussed below as representative of IS issues of advanced nations.

Table 1: Key Issues In Information Systems Management - USA (1994-95)

Rank	Description of the Issue
#1	Building a Responsive IT Infrastructure
#2	Facilitating and Managing Business Process Redesign
#3	Developing and Managing Distributed Systems
#4	Developing and Implementing an Information Architecture
#5	Planning and Managing Communication Networks
#6	Improving and Effectiveness of Software Development
#7	Making Effective Use of the Data Resource
#8	Recruiting and Developing IS Human Resources
#9	Aligning the IS Organization within the Enterprise
#10	Improving IS Strategic Planning
#11A	Implementing and Managing Collaborative Support Systems
#11B	Measuring IS Effectiveness and Productivity
#13	Increasing Understanding of IS Role and Contribution
#14	Facilitating Organizational Learning
#15	Managing the Existing Portfolio of Legacy Applications
#16	Facilitating and Managing End-User Computing
#17	Using Information Systems for Competitive Advantage
#18	Planning and Integrating MultiVendor Open Systems
#19	Developing and Managing Electronic Data Interchange
#20	Outsourcing Selected Information Services

Source: Brancheau, J.C., Janz, B.D., & Wetherbe, J.C. (1996). Key Issues in Information Systems: 1994-95 SIM Delphi Results. MIS Quarterly, 20(2), 225-242.

Table 2: Key Issues In Information Systems Management - North America (1995)

Rank	Description of the Issue
#1	Aligning I/S and corporate goals
#2	Instituting cross-functional information systems
#3	Organizing and utilizing data
#4	Re-engineering business processes through I/T
#5	Improving the I/S human resource
#6	Enabling change and nimbleness
#7	Connecting to customers/suppliers
#8	Creating an information architecture
#9	Updating obsolete systems
#10	Improving the systems-development process
#11	Educating management on I/T
#12	Changing technology platforms
#13	Using I/S for competitive advantage
#14	Developing an I/S strategic plan
#15	Capitalizing on advances in I/T

Source: The Eighth Annual Survey of I/S Management Issues, 1995. CSC Index Group.

Key Issue Ranks

Complete ranked lists of IS management issues as reported by Branchaeu et al. (1996) are shown above in Table 1. These issues were captured by a three-round Delphi survey of senior IS executives in the US. It should be noted these ranks represent the opinions of the members of the Society for Information Management (SIM) and the survey was actually conducted in 1994/95. The top ten issues from the 1994/95 survey (Table 1) are reviewed below. The review draws heavily from the Branchaeu et al. (1996) and Niederman et al. (1991) articles.

<u>Rank 1. IT Infrastructure</u>: Ranked number 6 in 1991, this issue moved to number 1 in 1994/95. Infrastructure includes such components as organization's diverse computers, telecommunication networks (both LANs and WANs), databases, operating systems, system software, and business applications. A new issue that emerged in the 1991 study, it refers to the development of a sound technology infrastructure that will support business strategy and organizational goals. The appearance of this issue may have again been driven by strategic concerns. A lack of a coordinated strategy for technology infrastructure may have prevented companies from taking timely advantage of business opportunities as they emerged.

Table 3: Key Issues In Information Systems Management - Europe (1995)

Rank	Description of the Issue
#1	Instituting cross-functional information systems
#2	Improving the I/S human resource
#3	Re-engineering business processes through I/T
Tie	Cutting I/S costs (tie)
#5	Creating an information architecture
#6	Aligning I/S and corporate goals
#7	Improving the systems-development process
#8	Educating management on I/T
#9	Organizing and utilizing data
Tie	Changing technology platforms (tie)
#11	Integrating systems
#12	Using I/S for competitive advantage
Tie	Enabling change and nimbleness (tie)
#14	Developing an I/S strategic plan
#15	Connecting to customers/suppliers
Tie	Providing help-desk services (tie)
#17	Moving to open systems
#18	Updating obsolete systems
#19	Determining the value of information systems
#20	Capitalizing on advances in I/T

Source: The Eighth Annual Survey of I/S Management Issues, 1995. CSC Index Group.

Table 4: Key Issues In Information Systems Management - Australia (1993)

Rank	Description of Issue
#1	Improving IS Strategic Planning
#2	Building a responsive IT infrastructure
#3	Aligning the IS organization with that of the enterprise
#4	Promoting effectiveness of the data resource
#5	Using IS for competitive advantage
#6	Developing an information architecture
#7	Improving data integrity and quality assurance
#8	Improving the quality of software development
#9	Increasing the understanding of the role and contribution of IS
#10	Planning for disaster recovery

Source: Pervan, G.P. Results from a study of Key Issues in Australian IS Management. 4th Australian Conference on Information Systems.
September 28, 1993. University of Queensland, St. Lucia. Brisbane, Queensland.

<u>Rank 2. Business Process Redesign</u>: This was a new issue that emerged in the 1994/1995 study and ranked number 2. It was popularized in the United States in the early nineties by Davenport and Short (1990) and Hammer and Champy (1993). Hammer and Champy defined business process redesign/reengineering (BPR) as "the fundamental rethinking and radical redesign of business processes to achieve dramatic improvements in critical, contemporary measures of

performance". The importance of this issue is attributable to the need for major changes in both internal and external processes to adjust to the ongoing massive changes in the environment and the marketplace. According to many, IT is a key enabler in process redesign.

Rank 3. Distributed Systems: This is a new issue ranked number 3 in 1994/95. The importance of this issue has risen dramatically over past years. While centralized and desk-top applications continue to exist in limited numbers, clearly applications offered over local area networks, wide area networks and the Internet are proliferating. The economics of reusable software and making effective use of dispersed computing power make distributed applications far more rewarding than before. They, however, present many challenges including maintaining consistent software versions, maintaining consistent data, controlling joint and global development (Akmanligil & Palvia 2001), and administering large-scale applications.

Rank 4. Information Architecture: This issue moved to 4th place in 1994/95 after having ranked number 1 in 1991. An information architecture is a high level map of the information requirements of an organization. Also called the enterprise model, it provides the overall framework to guide application development and database development. It includes the major classes of information (i.e., entities), and their relationships to the various functions and processes in the organization. The steps included in enterprise modeling include functional decomposition, entity-relationship diagrams, and planning matrices (McFadden & Hoffer 1994). Corporations, by and large, have an acceptable information architecture in place and have even moved into the areas of data warehouses and data mining.

Rank 5. Telecommunication Networks: Ranked number 10 in 1991, this issue moved up to number 5 in 1994/95. Telecommunication systems provide the backbone for an organization to do business anywhere, anytime, without being constrained by time or distance. While the earlier focus in telecommunication systems was on connecting users to a centralized mainframe computer, the renewed emphasis is on providing connectivity between different computing centers and users, who are widely dispersed geographically, and many times globally. Telecommunication networks also need to substantially multiply their bandwidth in order to carry all types of signals: data, graphics, voice, and video. Challenges that face the implementation of telecommunication systems include huge financial investments and lack of common industry standards. Yet, for those who have implemented backbone networks, the rewards have been tremendous.

Rank 6. Software Development: Ranked number 9 in 1991, this issue moved to number 6 in 1994/95. The development of software represents a major expenditure for the IS organization, yet it remains fraught with problems of poor quality, unmet needs, constant delays, and exceeded budgets. At the same time, an organization is presented with more options: in-house development, software packages, and outsourcing. Newer developments, e.g., software engineering methodologies, Internet applications, prototyping and CASE tools, promise to provide much-needed help. However, the organization is further challenged as it has to constantly evaluate new technologies and development paradigms, such as distributed processing, visual languages and object oriented programming. For example, much of the new development is being done using C++ , JAVA, object oriented programming languages, and Internet-based tools.

Rank 7. Data Resource: Ranked number 2 in 1991, this issue has moved down to number 7 in 1994/95. Data has been regarded as a vital resource for an organization, especially for the information systems function and application development for more than a decade now. Data and information are corporate resources, and not in the domain of an individual or a subgroup, but for the benefit of the entire organization. Firms collect massive amounts of not only internal data but also vast amounts of data from external sources, such as customers, suppliers, government and other firms. This data should be properly harnessed and leveraged for optimizing the benefit to the organization. The establishment of large corporate data bases, as well as the emergence of firms specializing in specific types of databases (e.g., Dow Jones, Compuserve, Compustat, Data Resources, etc.) underscores the value of the data resource.

Rank 8. IS Human Resources: This issue moved to number 8 in 1994/95 after ranking number 4 in 1991. Human resources for IS include technical as well as managerial personnel. The factor includes such concerns as planning for human resources, hiring, retaining, and developing human resources. There is an acute shortage of IS talent and rapid technological change – such as the Internet revolution - creates a shortage of specialized skills. For example, Internet specialists, ERP consultants and JAVA programmers are in short supply and in great demand at the present time. Another phenomenon of the last decade having serious implications for human resources is IS downsizing and outsourcing. Organizations have a choice as to which IS functions to outsource to external vendors and which to retain in-house. These decisions have serious strategic implications for the firm.

Rank 9. IS Organization Alignment: Ranked number 7 in 1991, this issue moved to number 9 in 1994/95. The organizational positioning of the IS department within the company has a direct impact on its effectiveness. In the early days of computing, IS was relegated to Accounting or Personnel departments, and had the image of a service/overhead function. While that image has been mostly erased, there are still issues relating to its proper alignment. For those, who view IS as a strategic function, the IS department has moved almost to the top of the organizational hierarchy. Large companies today have positions such as Chief Information Officer (CIO), Chief Technology Officer (CTO) and Chief Knowledge Officer (CKO). Another issue relating to alignment is the question of centralized, decentralized, or distributed IS organization. Technology can effectively support any option; the key issue is that the IS organization should be compatible with the company organization and philosophy.

Rank 10. Strategic Planning: Ranked number 3 in 1991, this issue moved to number 10 in 1994/95. Strategic IT planning refers to IT planning that supports business goals, missions, and strategy. With the role of IT elevated to a strategic tool for obtaining competitive advantage and achieving superior performance, the need for strategic IT planning is of paramount importance. Over the years, organizations have put processes in place to conduct IT strategic planning periodically. Yet, strategic planning remains a thorny issue for both senior IS and non-executives. The rate of technological change requires the ability to develop quick courses of action at economical costs, before they become obsolete. Further exacerbating the situation is rapid organizational change as well as environmental change outside the organization. In spite of the difficulties, this issue has remained one of the top issues in all previous key issue studies.

Other Issues: Collaborative Support Systems and IS Effectiveness Measurement tied for number 11. Entering the key issues for the first time ever, the high ranking of collaborative systems may reflect the popularity of commercial groupware products, distributed and global systems necessitating the use of groupware, and the need for knowledge management in an increasingly complex world. After declining steadily over the past decade, IS effectiveness measurement has increased in rank perhaps due to a renewed interest in cost justification in light of constantly changing technologies and new promises made by countless vendors.

Issues that ranked below the top twelve include understanding the role of IS, facilitating organizational learning, IS for competitive advantage, managing legacy applications, managing multi-vendor systems and the like. It is apparent that the top issues have a strategic orientation, and relate to planning and successful use of emerging technologies in the organization. What is conspicuous by its absence are any references to Internet related issues and e-commerce. This may be explained by the age of the study when the Internet and the Worldwide Web were just beginning to be introduced to the world. However, the management issues described above can be equally applied in the context of the Internet and e-commerce based systems.

KEY MIS ISSUES IN NEWLY INDUSTRIALIZED NATIONS

Several countries have made rapid economic growth in just over a decade. These countries have emerged as the "newly industrialized countries (NICs) " and are now beginning to prosper. While the precise categorization of any country into any class is somewhat contentious, and is also subject to movement over time, countries like Taiwan, Hong Kong, Ireland, South Korea, and Singapore fall into this group. The latest key issue results that are available from some of these countries are included in the chapter. Singapore issues were reported by Rao et al. (1987), Hong Kong issues by Burn et al. (1993), and Taiwan issues by Wang (1994) and Palvia and Wang (1995). The Singapore results are shown in Table 5, and Hong Kong results in Table 6. Once again, there is a certain degree of similarity between these country issues. We discuss only the Taiwan issues as representative of issues of newly industrialized countries, as it is the most recent study of all and one of the authors was directly involved with it.

Key Issue Ranks

The key IS issues in Taiwan were obtained by conducting a survey of senior managers in Taiwan, who were well-versed in technology (Wang 1994; Palvia & Wang 1995). Responses were obtained from 297 managers on a 7-point likert scale on 30 issues. The majority of the respondents were IS executives. A wide range of organizations, both in terms of size and type of business were represented in the study. The ranked list is provided in Table 7. Once again, we focus on the top ten issues.

Table 5: Key Issues in Information Systems Management - Singapore (1987)

Rank	Description of Issue
#1	Measuring and improving IS effectiveness
#2	Facilitating and managing end-user computing
#3	Keeping current with new technology and systems
#4	Integrating OA, DP, and telecommunications
#5	Training and educating DP personnel
#6	Security and control
#7	Disaster Recovery Program
#8	Translating IT into competitive advantage
#9	Having top management understand the needs and perspectives of MIS department (IS role and contribution)
#10	Impact of new technology on people and their role in the company

Source: Rao, K.V., Huff, F.P. and Davis, G.B. Critical Issues in the management of information systems: A Comparison of Singapore and the USA. Information Technology, 1:3, 1987. pp.11-19.

Table 6: Key Issues In Information Systems Management - Hong Kong (1989)

Rank	Description of the Issue
#1	Retaining, recruiting and training MIS/IT/DP personnel
#2	Information Systems/technology planning
#3	Aligning MIS/DP organization
#4	Systems Reliability and availability
#5	Utilization of data resources
#6	Managing end-user/personal computing
#7	Application software development
#8	Information systems for competitive advantage
#9	Telecommunications technology
#10	Integrating of data processing, office automation, and telecommunications
Tie	Software quality assurance standards

Source: Burn, J; Saxena, K.B.C.; Ma, Louis.;and Cheung, Hin Keung. Critical Issues of IS Management in Hong Kong: A Cultural Comparison. Journal of Global Information Management. Vol. 1 No. 4, Fall 1993.p. 28-37.

Table 7: Key Issues In Information Systems Management - Taiwan (1994)

Rank	Description of Issue
#1	Communication between the IS department and end users
#2	Top management support
#3	IS Strategic planning
#4	Competitive advantage
#5	Goal alignment
#6	Computerization of routine work
#7	IT Infrastructure
#8	System Integration
#9	Software development productivity
#10	System friendliness
#11	Security and control
#12	Software development quality
Tie	IS Standards (tie)
#14	Data resource
#15	IS funding level
#16	IS role and contribution
#17	User Participation
#18	Recruit, train, and promote IS Staff
#19	Information architecture
#20	Placement of IS department

Source: Palvia, P., and Wang, Pien. An Expanded Global Information Technology Issue Model: An Addition of Newly Industrialized Countries. The Journal of Information Technology Management. Volume VI, No.2, 1995. p.29-39.

Rank 1. Communication between IS Department and End Users: Communication between these two groups of people is necessary as one group is the user and the other the builder. End users in Taiwan seem to be unable to specify their information needs accurately to the IS group. They also have an unrealistic expectation of the computer's capabilities and expect the IS staff to quickly automate all of their operations. At the same time, IS employees may lack a good understanding of the organization's business processes, and use terminology that end users do not understand. The communication problem between the users and the IS community is further aggravated due to the low level of communication skills among IS graduates.

Rank 2. Top Management Support: Top management support is required as IS projects require major financial and human resources. They also may take long periods of time to complete. As such, the call for top management support is pervasive in the MIS literature. Taiwan is no exception. Top management support was found to be especially important in encouraging the use of microcomputers in Taiwan (Igbaria, 1992). Senior management is expected to demonstrate its support by both allocating suitable budget for the IS department, and by showing leadership and involvement. At the same time, top management support will strengthen the IS department by helping acquire the support of other functional departments. Without strong top management endorsement and support, the IS department would have little chance to achieve its mission.

Rank 3. IS Strategic Planning: IS strategic planning in Taiwan is difficult due to rapid changes in technology, lack of familiarity with IS planning methodologies, inadequate understanding of business processes, short term orientation of firms, absence of successful domestic planning models, top management's unwillingness to provide adequate funding to implement strategy, and lack of top management support for the planning process. Lack of appropriate strategic planning in other countries has had the effect of producing system failures and creating uncoordinated "islands of automation".

Rank 4. IS Competitive Advantage: In the private sector, several retail, wholesale, transportation, and media firms have begun to build information systems that can be utilized to make new inroads, create business opportunities, and enable an organization to differentiate itself in the market place. Even public organizations have made progress. Stories of how public organizations (e.g., a government-run hospital and the administrative office of a village) use IT to improve their administrative effectiveness and reduce the waiting time of clients, have been reported. The aggressive promotion of IT by the government has helped to further raise the IS practitioner's consciousness of the competitive impacts of information technology.

Rank 5. Goal Alignment: The needs and goals of the IS department can often be at odds with the organizational goals. A major incongruence results in potential conflicts and sub-optimization of IS resources. The IS staff is often interested in developing large scale and technically advanced systems which may not meet the needs of the business and the end users. In order to assure goal alignment, senior management needs to clearly communicate the organizational goals, policies, and strategies to the IS staff. In fact, a carefully crafted IS strategic planning process (issue #3) would facilitate goal alignment.

Rank 6. Computerization of Routine Work: In the USA, computerization of routine work (such as accounting functions and transaction processing) was the first priority and was done in the sixties and seventies. Even though, Taiwan is classified as a newly industrialized country, the extent of computer usage in business is far behind that in USA. As a paradox, the production of IT products has had a striking growth in Taiwan, while the businesses themselves have been slow in adopting the technology. In a sense, the IS evolution in many organizations is still in the Nolan's initial stages (Nolan, 1979). For these organizations, automation of routine work (i.e., transaction processing systems) is evolving, yet critical.

Rank 7. IT Infrastructure: In vibrant economies, a responsive IT infrastructure is vital to the flexibility and changing needs of a business organization. The technology infrastructure issue is exacerbated by a combination of evolving technology platforms, integration of custom-engineered and packaged application software, and the rigidity of existing applications. Many Taiwanese organizations are gradually realizing that building an infrastructure, which will support existing business applications while remaining responsive to changes, is a key to long-term enterprise productivity.

Rank 8. Systems Integration: Integration of various system components into a unified whole provides benefits of synergy, effectiveness, and added value to the user. Many IS managers in Taiwan are recognizing the need to integrate the "islands of automation" (e.g., data processing, office automation, factory automation) into an integrated single entity. In the past, the execution of systems integration had encountered great difficulty due to lack of IS standards, insufficient technical ability, and inadequate coordination among functional departments. However, open systems, networks, client/server architecture, and standardization of IT products (promoted by the government) are expected to make systems integration easier in the future. .

Rank 9. Software Development Productivity: Productivity is measured simply by the ratio of outputs to inputs. On both outputs, e.g., the quality and magnitude of software produced, and inputs, e.g., total time to complete a project and the total man-hours, IS has had a dismal record. In interviews conducted during the research process, both IS professionals and end users complained that it takes excessively long to build and modify applications. The speed of development is not able to keep pace with changing business needs. Possible explanations and reasons that were stated include: insufficient technical skills, high IS staff turnover, lack of use of software productivity tools, and inadequate user participation. However, new software technology seems to offer hope, e.g., CASE tools, object oriented languages and visual programming languages.

Rank 10. System Friendliness: Ease of use and user-oriented features are essential to the success and continued use of a software product, as the popularity of graphical user interface (GUI) will testify. Unfriendly and difficult-to-use systems encounter strong resistance from end users at all managerial levels in Taiwan. The development of a friendlier interface is critical not only for the success of the software and hardware vendors, but also for the ultimate acceptance by the end user. Two reasons can be subscribed for the significance of this issue in a non-advanced country. First, the users may be comparatively unfamiliar and untrained in the use of information technology.   Second, a lot of software is imported from the advanced nations of the West and may not necessarily meet the human factor requirements of the host nation.

Other Issues: Issues rated just below top ten included: information security and control, and software development quality. As organizations in Taiwan increase the use of IT for business operations, there is a greater risk of disclosure, destruction, and contamination of data. The high turnover of IS professionals causes great concern for managers that proprietary information may be disclosed to competitors. Probable reasons associated with software quality problems include: lack of business process understanding and technical skills of the IS staff, high turnover among IS staff, and inadequate user participation. Issues rated at the bottom include: open systems, distributed systems, telecommunications, CASE, and experts systems. While these technologies have been introduced in Taiwan, their implementation is in a primitive stage. Also, end-user computing was rated low, as it is not prevalent in the country. However, as employees and the general population acquire greater computer literacy due partly to government efforts, this issue is expected to become more prominent.

KEY MIS ISSUES IN DEVELOPING NATIONS

Countries which can be loosely qualified as developing countries include: Argentina, Brazil, India, and Mexico. These countries have been using information technology for a number of years, yet their level of IT sophistication and types of applications may be wanting in several respects. For example, La Rovere et al. (1996) report that Brazil faces several difficulties in network diffusion. Many of these are caused by lack of integrated policy towards informatics and telecommunication industries, and paucity of quality training programs. Similar obstacles are faced by many of the other Latin American countries. As an example, in Greece, Serafeimidis and Doukidis (1999) describe the lower rate of IT diffusion. With the emergence of many eastern block countries out of closed and guarded environments, and the general trends towards globalization, information is now available about the IT readiness of these countries. Much of this information is derived from individual experiences, general observations, and case studies (e.g., Chepaitis, 2001; Goodman, 1991). Yet, many of them seem to face similar problems.

Russia and several former Soviet Union countries defy a natural classification into any of our four classes. In fact, the World Bank places the former socialist countries in a separate category in and of itself. In their commentary, Goodman and McHenry (1991) described two sectors of Soviet computing: the state sector which included development and deployment of a full range of highly sophisticated computers, and the mixed sector of private, state, foreign and black-marketing activities which were struggling in the sustained use of information technology. Roche (1992) made similar observations. While giant centrally planned enterprises were created that emulated technological developments of the West, little computer equipment was either designed for or used by management and consumers. Thus, while Russia and former Soviet Union countries have made great strides in selected technological areas (e.g., space program, and aerospace industry), the general consumer sector and management have lagged behind significantly in IT utilization. As many reports would indicate, Russian IT issues are therefore characteristic of issues in developing countries. According to Chepaitis (2001), lack of adequate supply of quality information and poor information culture are IS issues reflective of Russia.

A prioritized list of ranked issues based on a systematic study is available for India. We present these results as an example of issues from a developed country.

Key Issue Ranks

The key IS issues in India were obtained by Palvia and Palvia (1992) and were based on data collection from top-level and middle-level Indian managers. These managers either worked directly with computers and information systems, or had been exposed to them by other means. The issues were first generated using the nominal grouping technique and brainstorming, and were then ranked by participant managers in two seminars in India. A fully ranked list is provided in Table 8; the top issues are discussed below. The discussion draws primarily from (Palvia & Palvia 1992) and (Palvia et al. 1992). It should be dated that while the study is somewhat dated, the issues are still reflective of the types of issues faced by developing countries.

Rank 1. Understanding and Awareness of MIS Contribution: An appreciation of the benefits and potential applications of MIS is absolutely necessary for successful IT deployment. There is a general lack of knowledge among Indian managers as to what management information systems can do for their business. The need for computer-based systems is neither a high priority nor widely recognized. Unless the potential contribution of MIS is clearly understood, advances in technological resources are not likely to be of much help. The lack of understanding is partly due to the traditional reliance on manual systems. The ready availability of a large number of semi-skilled and skilled personnel makes the operation of manual systems satisfactory, and prevents management from looking at superior alternatives.

Table 8: Key Issues In Information Systems Management - India (1992)

Rank	Description of the Issue
#1	Understanding/Awareness of MIS contribution
#2	Human Resources/Personnel for MIS
#3	Quality of Input Data
#4	Educating Senior Managers about MIS
#5	User Friendliness of Systems
#6	Continuing Training & Education of MIS Staff
#7	Maintenance of Software
Tie	Standards in Hardware and Software (tie)
#9	Data Security
#10	Packaged Applications Software Availability
Tie	Cultural and Style Barriers (tie)
#12	Maintenance of Hardware
#13	Aligning of MIS with Organization
#14	Need for External/Environmental Data
#15	MIS Productivity/Effectiveness
#16	Applications Portfolio
#17	Computer Hardware
#18	MIS Strategic Planning
#19	Effect of Country Political Climate
#20	Telecommunications

Source: *Palvia, P. and Palvia, S. MIS Issues in India and a Comparison with the United States: Technical Note. International Information Systems Vol. 1 No.2 April 1992.pp 100-110*

Rank 2. Human Resources and Personnel for MIS: Higher national priorities and lower priorities assigned to IS development have caused the neglect of IS human resource development. India is somewhat of an enigma in this regard. In the last several years, India has become a primary location for international outsourcing contracts; yet there is a great demand and shortage within the country for those trained in developing business information systems. While many universities and educational institutes are attempting to meet the burgeoning demand, some of these efforts may be misdirected from an IS point of view. The current emphasis on education seems to be on technological aspects rather than on the application of IS concepts to business needs.

Rank 3. Quality of Input Data: Information systems rely on accurate and reliable data. The age-old adage of GIGO (Garbage In Garbage Out) is well known in MIS, and directly impacts the quality of IS. This issue has also been seen in Russia (Chepaitis, 1994) and other developing countries. While not reported as a key issue in US studies, it appears that developing countries have inferior input data due to several reasons: lack of information literacy and information culture among workers as well as a less-than-adequate infrastructure for collecting data. Some managers reported experiences of excessive errors in data transcription as well as deliberate corruption of data. The underlying causes may be mistrust of and intimidation caused by computer processing, resulting in carelessness, apathy and sabotage.

Rank 4. Educating Senior Managers about MIS: This issue suggests a possible response to the top-ranked issue dealing with the lack of understanding and awareness of the role of MIS in organizations. It appears that senior managers do not truly understand the full potential of information technology. They need to be educated not so much about the technology per se, but more so about its many applications in business. For example, besides transaction processing, IT can be used for building management support systems and strategic systems.

Exposure to such possibilities by way of education and training can provide new and innovative ideas to managers to utilize IT fruitfully. In the authors' opinion, any education must be supplemented with business cases and some practical training.

Rank 5. User Friendliness of Systems: The appearance of this issue in a developing nation may be attributed to several factors. First, the users in a developing nation are generally novices and untrained in the use of information technology; thus they may not be at ease with computer interfaces. Second, much of the software and systems are imported from western and advanced nations. This software is geared to the needs of their people and may not be user-friendly as per the needs and cultural backgrounds of users in the importing nation. A hypothesis can be made that the ergonomic characteristics of an information system are at least partially dependent on the cultural and educational background of the people using them.

Rank 6. Continuing Training and Education of the MIS Staff: The education issue comes up once again, this time in the context of MIS personnel. Rapid advances in technology and a lower level of IT preparedness in developing countries put further pressure on MIS personnel to keep pace with the technology. Another challenge here is to not only provide training on the technology but to be able to do that from a business perspective. Specifically, two of the problems reported were: many current training plans attempt to train a large number of people simultaneously at the expense of quality, and there is a lack of proper training facilities for MIS professionals in business functions.

Rank 7 (tie). Maintenance of Software, and Standards in Hardware and Software: These two related issues were tied in rank. Maintenance refers to fixing and updating production software when there are bugs or new requirements. Maintenance is a problem because of inadequate resources and competition for resources from new applications. Compared to the developed nations, developing nations suffer from an inadequate supply of trained programmers. The problem is compounded if the majority of the software is purchased as packaged software. The maintenance effort is likely to be high if the quality and applicability of the purchased system is low. The quality of a system depends, in part, on the existence and enforcement of hardware and software standards, which brings us to the next issue.

The issue of standards in hardware and software is an important one in developing countries, as much software and hardware (especially hardware) are imported from other countries. The problems of hardware/software standards are a compounded manifold when one is buying hardware and software produced by different vendors in different nations, each with its own proprietary systems. While some international standards exist (e.g. in programming languages and telecommunications); the ultimate challenge will be to develop an exhaustive set of standards, and then to be able to enforce them.

Rank 9. Data Security: An organization's data is a valuable corporate resource, and needs to be protected else it may be abused to the organization's detriment. Data contained in manual systems was not very vulnerable to breach of security due to either unavailability of ready access or inordinately long access times. As a result, many information workers have developed poor practices and habits in data handling. With computerized systems, this attitude can cause severe data security and integrity problems. Newer controls and security provisions, which were unheard of in manual systems, may need to be built which may themselves cause resistance in adoption.

Rank 10 (tie). Packaged Applications Software Availability and Cultural Barriers: These two issues were tied in rank. Off-the-shelf packaged application software provides an inexpensive alternative to in-house development. All around the world, a lot of software is purchased off-the-shelf. An inadequate supply of MIS personnel (an issue discussed earlier) further necessitates an increased reliance on packaged software. While much packaged software is now being made available, there is need to develop more that meets the specific business requirements unique to the developing nations.

Culture plays a role in the application of information technology (Ein-Dor et al. 1993), although sometimes in subtle ways. For example, in one governmental office, secretaries and clerical people were mandated to use word-processing equipment. But as soon as the mandate was removed, they went back to typewriters and manual procedures. Apparently, they trusted their age-old equipment more, and it gave them a greater sense of control. Chepaitis (1994) provides the example of Russia, where people have never gathered, shared, and managed bountiful information. As a result, information is often hoarded for personal gains rather than freely shared or invested.

Other Issues: Issues ranked just after the ones discussed above included maintenance of hardware and alignment of MIS with the organization. Many organizations are getting personal computers, and their maintenance sometimes becomes a problem due to limited vendor presence and delays in procuring parts. Aligning of MIS with the organization is an issue of moderate importance. According to an Indian manager, beyond alignment, the organizational culture and philosophy itself has to change to accept the role of MIS. Applications portfolio is not a major issue as most businesses are in the initial stages of information systems growth and are in the process of computerizing basic operations. For the same reasons, MIS strategic planning was not rated high, and telecommunications was considered not of immediate interest but more a concern of the future.

KEY MIS ISSUES IN UNDERDEVELOPED NATIONS

Underdeveloped or basic countries are characterized by low or stagnant economic growth, low GNP, high levels of poverty, low literacy rates, high unemployment, agriculture as the dominant sector, and poor national infrastructure. While precise categorization is difficult, subjective and arguable, countries like Bangladesh, Cuba, Haiti, Jordan, Kenya, Nigeria, Iran, Iraq, and Zimbabwe may be included in this group. Note that countries may move in and out of a particular class over time. In this chapter, we use two African countries: Kenya and Zimbabwe as examples of under-developed nations.

Key Issue Ranks

The key MIS issues of Kenya and Zimbabwe were reported by Palvia, Palvia, and Zigli (1992), and were based on a study completed by Zigli in 1990. The methodology used in Zigli's study was based on the India study by Palvia and Palvia (1992). The same questionnaire, with minor modifications was used to collect the data. A number of in-depth personal interviews with senior information systems executives were conducted utilizing the questionnaire for data collection and as the basis for discussions. Information was also gathered from local trade publications and other secondary sources.

The computing industry in both countries at the time appeared to be competing in an environment that was strongly influenced by government and lack of "hard foreign currency". The hard currency situation was exacerbated by the virtual absence of indigenous hardware and software production, resulting in an inventory of outdated hardware and software. In addition, IT was accorded a very low priority by the government. As a result, purchases of equipment were being made from wherever possible, leading to mixed vendor shops and associated problems. Given the basic nature of IT adoption in these countries, only seven issues emerged with any degree of consensus. These are shown in Table 9 and are discussed as per the 1990 study reported in (Palvia et al. 1992). Once again, while the study is somewhat dated, the issues represent the concerns of some of the poorest countries in the world.

Table 9: Key Issues in IS Management in Underdeveloped Nations Of Africa (1992)

Rank	Description of Issue
#1	Obsolescence of Computing Equipment (hardware)
#2	Obsolescence of Operating and Applications Computer Programs (software)
#3	Proliferation of Mixed Vendor Shops (hardware and software)
#4	Availability of Skilled MIS Personnel and opportunities for Professional Development for MIS Managers and Non-Managers
#5	Possible Government Intervention/Influence in Computer Market
#6	Establishment of Professional Standards
#7	Improvement of IS Productivity

Source: Palvia, P., Palvia, S., and Zigli, R.M. Global Information Technology Environment: Key MIS Issues in Advanced and Less Developed Nations. In The Global Issues of Information Technology Management, edited by S. Palvia, P. Palvia, and R.M. Zigli, Idea Group Publishing, 1992.

Rank 1. Obsolescence of Computing Equipment: Of greatest concern was the state of obsolescence of most computer equipment. The need for state of the art equipment is urgent and was a critical concern for the IS executives. The current inventory is aging fast and simply does not meet the requirements of most businesses. A major contributing factor is the balance of trade and more specifically, the shortage of "hard foreign currency". These computers were state of the art twenty years ago but no longer. Not much progress has been made in 20 years. In fact, some regression may have occurred. These computers have now gone through two or three iterations of emulation's, and both efficiency and effectiveness have suffered. The shortfall of computer equipment not only affects the private sector but the public sector as well. Overall, national infrastructures of both countries appear ill prepared to advance information technology to bring it to par with the rest of the world.

Rank 1 (tie). Obsolescence of Software: The inventory of software (including operating systems and application programs) is also quite dated. Most of the packages are of the word processor and spreadsheet variety, or their emulations. Only recently have relational databases been introduced into both countries. The acute shortage of "hard foreign currency" precludes firms from purchasing software from overseas vendors, and further leads to exceptionally high rates of software piracy (especially for microcomputers). Major systems development is a rare occurrence. There seems to be simply no concept of integrated business systems, e.g., in manufacturing or in accounting. However, some contemporary software is being introduced on a limited scale. For example, the relational database package Oracle is now being distributed in both countries by local software firms.

Rank 3. Proliferation of Mixed IS Vendor Shops: There are many vendors to choose from within one country, let alone the number of vendors in the entire world. While competition among vendors should raise the quality and reduce the cost of technology acquisition, it may also cause severe problems if vendor selection is not done carefully. Due to lack of coherent policies on part of the government and the firms, many purchases of hardware and software are made on an opportunistic and ad-hoc basis from whatever source and vendor that happens to be available at the time. This has led to the proliferation of mixed vendor shops. Of course, mixed vendor shops have added to the problems of IS management, operation, and maintenance. Mixed vendor shops were seen as a major detriment to efficiency and productivity by a number of firms in the interview sample.

Rank 4. Availability of Skilled MIS Personnel and Professional Development: There is a shortage of people with computing and systems skills. Finding trained personnel and keeping existing information systems people current with the latest advances in IT are vital concerns of information systems managers in these less developed nations. They are too few qualified people, and they are being spread too thin. This issue has implications for the educational system of under-developed nations: they must incorporate education and training in high technology areas, do it fast, and keep their programs constantly updated lest they become obsolete again.

Rank 5. Possible Government Intervention in the Computer Industry: In economies dominated by government control, there is always the risk of government intervention in the computer industry thereby threatening to reduce competition and increasing the probability of a monopoly. While a selected few may benefit from government actions, the larger business community tends to suffer. Such intervention may occur in the form of issuance of import licenses to new, local businesses in an effort to encourage their growth. Unfortunately, these new firms sell their licenses to existing, larger vendors. Both the sellers and the buyers realize substantial profits. Another example of government action is the mandated markups on imported parts and equipment. As a result of these markups (equaling or exceeding 100%), virtual cartels have emerged, and the cost of computers, computer peripherals and computer software have become one of the highest in the world.

Rank 6. Establishment of Professional Standards: The lack of professional standards threatens the entry of non-professionals and untrained people into the MIS field, thereby further aggravating the IS quality issue. Therefore, the professional data processing societies in these two countries are very anxious to gain "official" approval authorizing them to establish or participate in the establishment of standards of behavior and expertise for MIS professionals. The establishment of such standards will go a long way towards the development of better quality IS products. It should also improve productivity, the subject of the next issue.

Rank 7. Improvement of IS Productivity: Productivity is a concern in these two nations as a result of lack of professionalism, lack of access to state of the art productivity tools, and deteriorating hardware and software. In general, the productivity concern seems to extend to all aspects and areas of information systems. Over the last decade, there has been considerable emphasis on productivity in the advanced nations, and serious efforts have been made to enhance productivity (e.g., in the use of fourth generation languages, and CASE tools). However, in the less-developed countries, while being recognized as a problem, productivity appears to take a back seat to often more pressing problems.

Other Issues: The existence of archaic hardware and software and the inability to acquire modern resources have caused an ever-widening technological gap and thereby a loss of competitiveness of the domestic businesses that depend upon such equipment. Erosion of the competitive position of firms was an issue expressed by several local executives. Another issue cited by some executives is the question of the local manufacture of hardware and software. This appears to be a polarizing issue. The foreign-based vendors, as one would expect, oppose the local manufacture, while users and the government favor it. However, software development may be a prime determinant in the evolution of information technology in less-developed nations, as in the case of India and Philippines.

What was equally surprising were the issues not mentioned by the participants. For example, understanding of MIS by senior executives did not emerge as an issue of significant concern. Using IS for competitive advantage is another issue that did not surface in the interview process. In general, the strategic dimensions of information technology do not seem to be as important as the operational issues.

A MODEL OF GLOBAL INFORMATION TECHNOLOGY ENVIRONMENT

In summary, we have presented key IS management issues for representative countries in each of the four classes, and made comments about several other countries. Space considerations prevent us from discussing results from other countries that might be available. For example, key issues not discussed in this chapter, but investigated and available in the literature, include the following countries: Central America (Mata & Fuerst 1997), South Korea (Kim & Kim 1995), United Kingdom (Galliers et al., 1994), Poland (Wrycza & Plata-Przechlewski 1994), Gulf countries (Badrii, 1992), Estonia (Dexter et al., 1993), and Slovenia (Dekeleva & Zupancic, 1993).

In any case, our discussion shows that there are major differences between issues of different countries, and few commonalties. There were more common issues between USA and Taiwan, and fewer between other countries. As an overall impression, it seems that advanced countries are driven by strategic needs, developing countries by operational needs, and under-developed countries by basic infrastructural needs. Based on this observation, Palvia et al. (1992) posited an initial model of country specific MIS issues based on economic development of the country. This model classified countries into three categories based on the level of economic growth. These categories are: advanced countries (e.g., United States, Canada, Japan), developing/operational countries (e.g., India, Russia, Argentina, Brazil), and under-developed/basic countries (e.g., Kenya, Chile, Iran, Nigeria). They acknowledged that the placement of a country into a particular category is subject to some debate, and that countries may change categories over time. Nonetheless, they were able to make some broad generalizations on the nature of IS issues based on economic growth of a nation. According to the model, the level of IT adoption increases from one stage to next, i.e., from underdeveloped to developing to advanced nations. Quite striking are the types of MIS issues at each stage of economic development. In the underdeveloped countries, the survival issues dominate (e.g., the very availability of computer hardware, operating and applications software, and human resources for MIS). In the developing countries, operational issues are paramount (e.g., management's awareness of MIS capabilities, human resource development for MIS, quality of data, standards). Advanced country issues are characterized by strategic needs (e.g., information architecture, data resource management, strategic planning for MIS, organizational learning).

While the Palvia et al. (1992) model appears to be generally sound, the Taiwan study and experience from other countries has led us to refine the model (see figure 1). Another class of countries has been added to the original three-way classification. Several countries have emerged as the newly industrialized countries (NICs) in the last decade and are now prospering. Examples of such countries include Taiwan, South Korea, Hong Kong and Singapore. If we extrapolate the Taiwan issues to NICs in general, then the majority of NIC issues are somewhat unique and different from other classes. To reiterate, representative NIC issues include: communication between IS department and end users, top management support, software development productivity, goal alignment, and security and control. Clearly, most of these issues are above the routine operational and infrastructural issues faced by organizations in under-developed and developing nations. Yet, they are lower in their strategic orientation as compared to the advanced nations. These issues then can most appropriately labeled as "management and control" issues reflective of growing technology adoption. In a sense, the refined "global information technology environment" model is correlated with the Nolan stage model (1979), which posited the need for a control stage to contain and manage the proliferation of IS activities in an organization. The main difference is that our model explains the nature of IT conditions and practices based on economic conditions in different countries.

The addition of NICs into the model is also supported by the "management and control" oriented policies being exercised in these countries. For example, Taiwan, Singapore, and South Korea have one or two government agencies which coordinate and implement explicit national IT plans since the 1980s. These three country governments explicitly promote and manage the production and use of IT products. Computerization is a national goal and essential to maintaining the competitiveness of the national economy in the global environment.

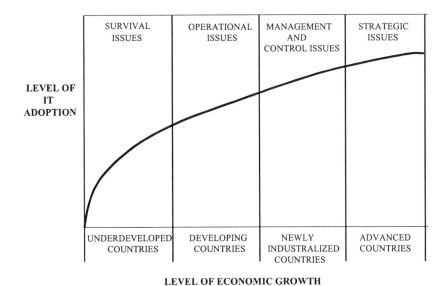

Figure 1: A Model of Global IT Management Environment

The model depicted in figure 1 provides a first attempt in understanding the complex global IT environment. We recognize that there are limitations and other elements may be necessary for a finer understanding of the global IT environment, or the environment of any particular country. For example, the inclusion of Russia and socialist countries under the "developing/operational" country class may be of concern to some. Singapore might also be a special case, as it is not really a country, but a city-state, and has a benevolent ruler form of government. Nevertheless, the above model may be a starting point for an organization considering expansion into other world markets, and attempting to evaluate the role and use of information technology in its pursuit.

Model Validation

An attempt was made by the authors (Palvia et al. 2001) to empirically validate the above model. Specifically, the following hypothesis was examined:

> *There is a correlation between the rankings of IT management issues and the level of economic growth or development of a region/country.*

More specifically, we expect that IT management issues in advanced countries (i.e., with high levels of economic development) will be strategic in nature, and issues in developing/under-developed countries (i.e., with lower levels of economic development) will be more basic in nature. Secondary data for key issues from 16 different regions of the world from previously published studies were used. In order to develop uniformity, the issues were categorized as follows: business relationship, human resources, systems development, quality and reliability, internal effectiveness, end-user computing, technology infrastructure. These are defined as:

Business Relationship. This category includes IT issues that contribute to the business objectives of the firm, and deals with concerns external to the IS department, such as: strategic planning, IT architectures, IT alignment, and data resource issues.

Human Resource. Shortages of qualified IS personnel continues to be a problem everywhere. Furthermore, this issue prevents the full exploitation of IT and may affect other IT management issues. Not surprisingly, this category was judged to be important in many regional studies.

Quality and Reliability. Quality and reliability issues apply to hardware, software, and management of resources. System reliability and software quality standards were notably more important in the developing countries than in advanced countries.

Internal Effectiveness. This grouping includes IS human resources, software development, applications portfolio, and IS effectiveness measurement. Basically, this group of issues focuses internally on the IS function. We separated software development and human resource issues into separate categories of their own, as based on the world environment they appeared to be important in their own right. Issues dealing directly with IS effectiveness, such as: measuring effectiveness, controls, etc. would fit into this category.

End-user Computing. End-user computing (EUC) is pervasive in today's organizations; yet it requires a whole new set of management and organizational strategies compared to mainstream IS management. While EUC and related issues have receded in the background in the U.S., they are beginning to appear among the top issues in other parts of the world.

Technology infrastructure. This group includes such issues as telecommunications, electronic data interchange, IT infrastructure, imaging technology, and distributed systems.

Systems Development. This is a major activity in most IS departments. The development of critical applications is not only necessary for the survival of many organizations, but also for its growth and competitive posturing. Included in this category are such items as concern for better project management and software development productivity.

After the reclassification of data, it was subjected to several types of cluster analysis methods. Details of this process are available in (Palvia et al. 2001). This analysis indicated that the countries are best clustered into three groups based on their issues. The first group was comprised of the most economically advanced countries, the third group comprised of the least advanced, and the second group was somewhere in the middle.

These three groups were labeled: advanced countries, newly industrialized countries, and developing countries. The three issues with highest average rankings for the advanced countries are: business relationship, systems development, and human resource. The three highest ranked issues for the newly industrialized countries are: human resources, end user computing, and business relationship. And finally, for the developing countries, the four highest ranked issues are technology infrastructure, quality and reliability, human resources, and business relationship. In essence, secondary data provides support for the above model. The main difference is that a fourth group of countries with survival issues was not clearly revealed. But that is perhaps due to the lack of available secondary data on the most economically disadvantaged countries of the world.

An Expanded Model

Basic elements of a more complete model for global IT environment are offered in figure 2. Besides, level of economic growth, other factors critical to information technology adoption by firms in a country include its culture and political system. We have already discussed the "economic" variable at length, we discuss the remaining variables below.

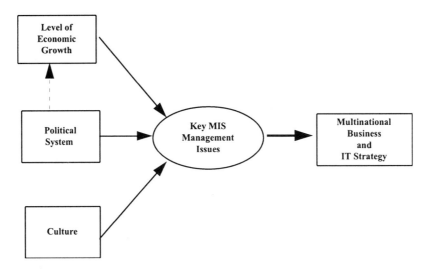

Figure 2: A Proposed Comprehensive Model For the Global IT Environment

Political system: This factor covers a broad spectrum of issues emanating from the political and governance philosophy (e.g., socialism, capitalism, communism, democracy, dictatorship) of a country. The governance philosophy issues may directly or indirectly influence different IT related areas, e.g., transborder data flow restrictions, governmental technology initiatives, privatization trends, enactment and enforcement of standards, technology investments tariffs, and trade and customs regulations. This phenomenon is highlighted by Chepaitis (2001) in her reporting of data quality and information poverty problems in Russia. These problems are exacerbated by the impact of a political system that include control and pressure by the authorities, poor public data stores, and a lack of competitive market experience. Clearly, the political/regulatory practices can have an impact on IS issues. Furthermore, these practices may also affect the economy of the country, as shown by the dotted line relationship in the model. Perhaps this relationship could be a solid line relationship, as lately the political system of a country seems to have a substantial impact on its economic development (this is a tempting inference in light of the crumbling communist regimes of the USSR and East Germany and the embracing of free market philosophies by communist regimes like China, North Vietnam, and Russia).

Culture: This is an often-mentioned factor when globalization of businesses is the subject of analysis. Many of the publications in global IT attempts to analyze the impact of culture. For example, some recent articles include: impact of culture on group support systems (Davison and Jordan 1998), impact on communication technology acceptance (Kwon and Chidambaran 1998). There even have been some studies that suggest that culture may not be a very dominant factor (e.g., Burn and Szeto 1998). Nevertheless, culture remains an important factor in the study of global IT, and frameworks have been suggested that incorporate culture explicitly in the study of global IT (Ein-Dor et al. 1993; Nelson & Clark 1994). The work of Hofstede (1980) is classical in understanding national culture and is being used by IS researchers in their research e.g., Shore and Venkatachalam (1995) analyzed differences in systems analysis and design based on culture.

Multinational Business and IT Strategy: The ultimate purpose for the identification of key IT management issues in a firm is for direction on the formulation of its IT strategy. These issues assist MIS and senior management in the allocation of scarce resources to competing IT priorities. Additionally, we contend that IT issues may also have an impact on the formulation of the overall global business strategy. The traditional model of IT utilization was the cost/service center focus, which is increasingly being replaced by more proactive uses of information technology. For example, Henderson and Venkatraman (1993) proposed the Strategic Alignment Model which identified four dominant perspectives for aligning IT and business strategies. Two of these perspectives regard IT strategy as an enabler in pursuing new or enhanced business strategies.

It is our hope that the expanded model would be the subject of further investigation, verification and enhancement.

CONCLUSIONS

Reports of information systems management issues in different parts of the world are useful to organizations as they begin to plan and implement IT applications across the world. In this chapter, we have presented IS issues for many countries, and have examined the issues in USA, Taiwan, India, and Kenya & Zimbabwe in greater depth. The world is a large place, and attempting to understand the critical issues in every single country, or even selected countries, would be an arduous, perhaps an imprudent task. Instead, we divided countries into four classes, and provided an example in each class. An elementary model for the global IT environment was postulated based on this categorization. We also provided empirical support for the model. An expanded model was proposed as the subject for future inquiry.

While generalizations are fraught with risks, the provision of global IT management model allows practitioners and researchers alike in a preliminary assessment of the criticality of the various IT issues in different regions of the world. In closing, we would like to exhort others to pursue the following lines of investigation:

1. Develop and validate sound models that seek to explain the country issues. A simple model was presented in figure 1. Elements of a more comprehensive model may include causal factors such as: economic growth, national culture, and political system (as in figure 2). At

the same time, evaluate the predictive ability of such models and report on the use of the models for prediction. While descriptive studies are helpful in identifying key issues of individual countries at a given point in time, this is an enormous and time-consuming proposition given the number of countries on the globe and the temporal nature of the issues. However, if the determinants of the key issues are known, then a preliminary estimation of the issues is easier to make.

2. Develop a comprehensive universal instrument and methodology that can be applied globally to identify the key IS issues. This instrument could then be administered simultaneously (or approximately in the same time frame) by a group of researchers in different countries. One of the limitations of previous "key issue" studies is that they have used different questionnaires, different time frames, and different methods to assess the issues. While difficult, this undertaking will be very helpful in obtaining reliable results.

3. Develop specific practical implications and uses of the "key issues" results? How can they be incorporated into the formulation of national policy, international policy, corporate policy and IS policies within an organization?

Mini Case: Use of Information and Communication Technology for Development

The rapid emergence of Information and Communication Technologies (ICTs), and their use in the development context has raised great hopes in developing countries. New tools have become available to promote knowledge industries and to address development problems by improving communication and access to knowledge. Critics argue that despite increasing donor interest and investment in ICT projects little has been achieved. There are claims that in fact the information or knowledge revolution is widening the gap between rich and poor, as a digital divide grows between those who have access to suitable infrastructure and education, and those who do not.

An examination of these issues was conducted in the country of Nepal (land locked between India and China). To begin to answer such questions, field data based on practical experiences and lessons learned is needed. At the outset, a preliminary mapping of current ICT projects in Nepal, and the roles being adopted by Government, NGOs (non-governmental organizations) and the Private Sector was carried out. Data was then collected using (i) a purposive questionnaire based survey among NGOs, (ii) open-ended interviews with key informants from the Government and Private Sector, and (iii) desk based research and personal insights gained from ICT projects.

Results revealed that the potential of ICT for development was constrained by a global and urban orientation in its application. The reason for this bias is partly attributed to the lack of a National Information Infrastructure that reaches rural areas, but there was also a notable absence of critical thinking and application development that related ICT solutions to key problems faced by rural communities. The private sector lacked incentive. The government lacked know-how and resources. NGOs, whilst oriented to working for and among rural communities lacked capacity and know-how and very few NGOs had engaged in projects with an ICT component. Lack of ICT literacy and advocates among and for the rural population resulted in their interests being marginalised.

Some specific observations and facts related to ICT in Nepal are:
1. There is a general lack of policies for ICT development domestically and internationally.
2. Telephone density was less than 1 per 100 in the period 1996-1998.
3. There is huge growth in NGOs working in Nepal. The NGO movement has been responsible for the flow of development funds over which Nepal has little control.
4. A program was initiated to install 1,000 Very Small Aperture Terminals in the Himalayan region by 2002.
5. Plans call for extending the capacity for the use of mobile phones to 50,000 to cover the East West Highway.
6. Vast majority of Internet users are in the urban Kathmandu valley (Kathmandu is the capital). Access to Internet services is extremely low and highly polarized. There is virtually no ICT activity outside Kathmandu and a handful of major towns.

> **Mini Case …. Continued**
>
> 7. Several commercial agencies in Kathmandu now provide web design services. It is estimated that in June 2000, there were 200-300 web istes with the .np suffix – but most customers opt for the .com suffix. Local language material is minimal and most sites have been developed outside of Nepal.
>
> The scarcity of resources available in an LDC, make it vital that lessons are learned about how to qualitatively assess and develop national and project level ICT capacity, in order to promote successfully targeted interventions and appropriate strategies. A preliminary framework called the iCAPACITY framework is proposed, using Nepal as an example. This framework provides a visual indicator of national ICT capacity in terms of content, access, partnerships and overall integration through strategy and policy. This qualitative framework incorporates both local and global aspects of a countries ICT capacity.
>
> Source: Gregson, Jon. "use of Information and Communication Technology (ICT) for Development: A Study from Nepal". *Proceedings of the 2nd annual Global Information Technology Management World Conference*, Dallas, Texas, 2001, Pp. 258.

STUDY QUESTIONS

1. Describe the key IS management issues in advanced countries and the underlying causes for these issues. What other issues you see emerging in the advanced countries in the next few years?

2. Describe the key IS management issues in newly industrialized countries and the underlying causes for these issues. What other issues you see emerging in these countries in the next few years?

3. Describe the key IS management issues in developing countries and the underlying causes for these issues. What other issues you see emerging in these countries in the next few years?

4. Describe the key IS management issues in under-developed countries and the underlying causes for these issues. What other issues you see emerging in these countries in the next few years?

5. Discuss the proposed comprehensive model for global IT environment. Do you agree? Are there other factors may influence the IT environment?

6. Select a country and conduct research into finding its IS management issues. How do your findings compare with this chapter's findings?

7. The following hypothesis was examined: *There is a correlation between the rankings of IT management issues and the level of economic growth or development of a region/country.*
   What did the analysis of data indicate? Explain briefly.

8. Briefly describe several ways that IT can serve as an "enabler" and "driver" of global business expansion.

REFERENCES

Akmanligil, M. and Palvia, P. Strategies for Global Information Systems Development: A Critical Analysis. In *Global Information Technology and Electronic Commerce: Issues for the New Millenium.* Edited by P. Palvia, S. Palvia, and E.M. Roche, Ivy League Publishing 2001.

Badri, M. A. Critical Issues in Information Systems Management: An International Perspective. *International Journal of Information Management.* Vol 12, 1992, pp. 179-191.

Ball, L., and Harris, R. SMIS Members: A Membership Analysis. *MIS Quarterly*, Vol 6, No 1, March 1982, pp. 19-38.

Brancheau, James C., and James C. Wetherbe, 1987. Key Issues in Information Systems Management. *MIS Quarterly*, March, pp. 23-46.

Brancheau, J.C., Janz, B.D., & Wetherbe, J.C. (1996). Key Issues in Information Systems: 1994-95 SIM Delphi Results. *MIS Quarterly*, 20(2), 225-242.

Burn, Janice; Saxena, K B C; Ma, Louis; Cheung, Hin Keung, " Critical issues of IS management in Hong Kong: A cultural comparison", *Journal of Global Information Management,* Fall 1993, Vol. 1, No. 4.

Burn, J.M., and Szeto, C. Information Systems Management Issues in Hong Kong: A Contingency Analysis and Comparison with the U.K. *Journal of Global Information Technology Management.* Vol 1, No 1, 1998, pp. 5-16.

Carey, D. Rating the Top MIS Issues in Canada. *Canadian Datasystems*, June 1992, pp. 23-26.

Chepaitis, E.V. E-Commerce and the Information Environment in an Emerging Economy: Russia and the Turn of Century. In *Global Information Technology and Electronic Commerce: Issues for the New Millenium.* Edited by P. Palvia, S. Palvia, and E.M. Roche, Ivy League Publishing 2001.

Chepaitis, E.V. After the Command Economy: Russia's Information Culture and Its Impact on Information Resource Management. *Journal of Global Information Management*, vol 2, no 1, Winter 1994, pp. 5-11.

CSC Index. *Critical Issues of Information Systems Management for 1995*, Cambridge, Mass. 1995.

Davenport,T.H. and Short, J.E., The New Industrial Engineering: Information Technology and Business Process Redesign, Sloan Management Review, Summer 1990, pp.11-27.

Davison, R. and Jordan, E. Group Support Systems: Barriers to Adoption in a Cross Cultural Setting. *Journal of Global Information Technology Management.* Vol 1, No. 2, 1998, pp. 37-50.

Deans, P. Candace, Karawan, K.R. Goslar, M.D. Ricks, D.A., and Toyne B., "Identification of Key International Information Systems Issues in U. S. based Multinational Corporations, " *Journal of Management Information Systems,* 7(4), 1991, pp. 27-50.

Dexter, A. S., Janson, M. A., Kiudorf, E., and Laast-Laas, J. Key Information Technology Issues in Estonia. *The Journal of Strategic Information Systems.* June, 1993, vol 2, No 2, pp. 139-152.

Dickson, G.W., Leitheiser, R.L., Nechis, M., and Wetherbe, J.C. Key Information Systems Issues for the 1980's. *MIS Quarterly*, Vol 8, No 3, September 1984, pp. 135-148.

Ein-Dor, Philip, Segev, E., M. Orgad, 1993. The Effect of National Culture on IS: Implication for International Information Systems. *Journal of Global Information Management*, Winter: 33-44.

Galliers, R. D., Merali, Y., and Spearing, L. Coping with Information Technology? How British Executives Perceive the Key Information Systems Management Issues in the mid-1990s. *Journal of Information Technology.* Vol 9, No 3, 1994.

Goodman, S.E. Computing and the Resuscitation of Romania. *Communications of the ACM.* Vol 34, No 9, September 1991, pp. 19-22.

Goodman, S.E. and McHenry, W.K. The Soviet Computer Industry: A Tale of Two Sectors. *Communications of the ACM.* Vol 34, No 6, June 1991, pp. 25-29.

Hammer, M. and Champy, J.A., Reengineering the Corporation, Harper Business, New York, 1993.

Hartog, Curt, and Martin Herbert, 1986. 1985 Opinion Survey of MIS Managers: Key Issues. *MIS Quarterly*, Dec., pp. 351-361.

Henderson, J.C., and Venkatraman, N. Strategic Alignment: Leveraging Information Technology for Transforming Organizations. *IBM Systems Journal*, Vol 32, No 1, 1993, pp. 4-16.

Hofstede, G. *Cultural Consequences: International Differences in Work Related Values*, Sage, Beverly Hills, 1980.

Igbaria, M., 1992. An Examination of Microcomputer Usage in Taiwan. *Information & Management*, 22: 19-28.

Kim, Hyo-Seuk, and Kim, JaeJon, Information Systems Management Issues for Korea. Proceedings of the 1995 Korean MIS Conference, 1995.

Kwon, H.S., and Chidambaran, L.   A Cross-Cultural Study of Communication Technology Acceptance: Comparison of Cellular Phone Adoption in South Korea and the United States. *Journal of Global Information Technology Management.* Vol 1, No 3, 1998, pp. 43-58.

La Rovere, R.L., Tigre, P.B., and Fagundes, J. Information Networks Diffusion in Brazil: Global and Local Factors. in *Global Information Technology and Systems Management: Key Issues and Trends*, edited by P. Palvia, S. Palvia, and E. Roche, Ivy League Publishing, New Hampshire, 1996.

Mata, F.J., Fuerst, W.L. Information Systems Management Issues in Central America: A Multinational and Comparative Study, Journal of Strategic Information Systems (6:3), 1997, pp. 173-202

McFadden, F.R., and Hoffer, J.A. *Modern Database Management*, 4th Edition, Benjamin Cummings Publishing Company, California, 1994.

McLuhan, M. *Understanding Media: The Extensions of Man*, McGraw-Hill, New York, 1964.

Nelson, K.G. and Clark T.D. Jr. Cross-Cultural Issues in Information Systems Research: A Research Program. *Journal of Global Information Management*, Vol 2, No 4, 1994, pp. 19-28.

Niederman, F.; Brancheau, J. C.; Wetherbe, J. C. Information systems Management Issues for the 1990s. MIS Quarterly. 1991 Dec; 17(4);475-500.

Nolan, Richard L. 1979. Managing the Crisis in Data Processing. *Harvard Business Review*, vol. 57, no. 2 (March-April), pp. 115-126.

Palvia, P., Palvia, S., and Whitworth, J. Global Information Technology: A Meta Analysis of Key Issues. *Information and Management*, forthcoming in 2001.

Palvia, P. Global Information Technology Research: Past, Present, and Future. *Journal of Global Information Technology Management.* Vol 1, No. 2, 1998, pp. 3-14.

Palvia, P. and Palvia, S. Understanding the Global Information Technology Environment: Representative World Issues. In *Global Information Technology and Systems Management: Key Issues and Trends.* Edited by P.Palvia, S. Palvia, and E.M. Roche, Ivy League Publishing 1996, pp. 3-30.

Palvia, P. C.; Palvia, S. MIS Issues in India and a comparison with the United States. *International Information Systems.* 1992:101-110.

Palvia, P.; Palvia, S. and Zigli, R. M. Global Information Technology Environment: Key MIS Issues in Advanced and Less Developed Nations. In *The Global Issues of Information Technology Management,* edited by S. Palvia, P. Palvia, and R. M. Zigli, Idea Group Publishing 1992.

Palvia, Shailendra; Palvia, Prashant; Zigli, Ronald M., *The Global Issues of Information Technology Management,* Idea Group Publishing,Harrisburg, PA. 1992

Palvia, P. and Wang, Pien. An Expanded Global Information Technology Issue Model: An Addition of Newly Industrialized Countries. *The Journal of Information Technology Management.* Volume VI, No. 2, 1995. p. 29-39.

Pollard, C. and Hayne, S. "A Comparative Analysis of Information systems Issues Facing Canadian Business," *Hawaii International Conference on System Sciences,* 1996.

Rao, K. V. Huff, F. P. and Davis, G. B. Critical Issues in the management of information systems: A Comparison of Singapore and the USA. *Information Technology.* 1:3, 1987.pp. 11-19.

Roche, E.M. *Managing Information Technology in Multinational Corporations.* MacMillan Publishing Company, New York, 1992.

Serafeimedes, V. and Doukidis, G.I. Management of Information Technology Investments in Less Developed Environments: Experience from Greece. *Journal of Global Information Technology Management.* Vol 2, No 4, 1999, pp. 4-22.

Shore, B., and Venkatachalam, A.R. The Role of National Culture in Systems Analysis and Design. *Journal of Global Information Management,* vol 3, no 3, summer 1995, pp. 5-14.

Simon, S. An Informational Perspective on the Effectiveness of Headquarters-Subsidiary Relationship: Issues of Control and Coordination. In *Global Information Technology and Systems Management: Key Issues and Trends.* Edited by P.Palvia, S. Palvia, and E.M. Roche, Ivy League Publishing 1996, pp. 249-275.

Vitalari, N., and Wetherbe, J. Emerging Best Practices in Global Systems Development. In *Global Information Technology and Systems Management: Key Issues and Trends.* Edited by P.Palvia, S. Palvia, and E.M. Roche, Ivy League Publishing 1996, pp. 325-351.

Wang, P. Information Management Systems Issues in the Republic of China for the 1990s. *Information & Management,* vol 26, 1994, pp. 341-352.

Watson, R. T., 1989. Key Issues In Information Systems Management: an Australian Perspective - 1988. *Australian Computer Journal,* 21 (3): 118-129.

Watson, R.T., and Brancheau, J.C. Key Issues in Information Systems Management: An International Perspective. *Information & Management,* vol 20, 1991, pp. 213-223.

Wrycza S., Plata-Przechlewski T., Key Issues in Information Systems Development. The Case of Poland, in: Zupancic J., Wrycza S. (eds), Proceedings of The Fourth International Conference on Information Systems Development ISD'94, Bled, September 1994, pp.289-296.

2

Malaysia's Multimedia Super Corridor:
An Experiment in Employing Information and Communication Technologies for National Development

Roger W. Harris
Universiti Malaysia Sarawak (UNIMAS)

"It can be no accident that there is today no wealthy, developed country that is information-poor and no information-rich country that is poor and underdeveloped".
Dr. Mahathir Mohamad, "The Way Forward - Vision 2020", 1991.

ABSTRACT

In August 1995, Dr. Mahathir Mohamad, Prime Minister of Malaysia, announced Malaysia's Multimedia Super Corridor (MSC) as the centerpiece of a national IT strategy under the Seventh Malaysia Plan (1996-2000). The plan announced the country's intention to "make Information and Communication Technologies the dynamo for growth within all economic sectors." The MSC is intended to leapfrog Malaysia into the information age and to achieve the targets for development set by Dr. Mahathir's Vision 2020, by which Malaysia intends to achieve fully developed status. Malaysia's embrace of ICTs is orchestrated by the National Information Technology Council (NITC), a top-level body that is chaired by the Prime Minister but which consists of a variety of other government ministers, community representatives, industry leaders and academics. The NITC has promulgated the National Information Technology Agenda (NITA), which focuses on ICTs as the engine of growth for the Malaysian economy to achieve fully developed status, through several initiatives, like the MSC.

In this chapter we shall examine the MSC project and attempt to assess its likely impact on the socio-economic development of Malaysia. Firstly, we will briefly describe Malaysia so that the MSC project can be more easily situated within its economic and social context. Secondly, we will describe the main features of the MSC and we will outline the progress of implementation so far. Then we will consider the project within a framework that will facilitate an estimation of its likely impact on national development. Since the MSC is intended to have global impacts, in addition to its national consequences, we will then locate it within an international context, specifically by comparing it with similar ICT-related initiatives in Malaysia's closest competing economies in neighboring countries within South-East and East Asia.

Governments have recognized that success with Information and Communication Technologies (ICTs) is a vital factor for national development in an increasingly global market place. Many countries are now formulating strategies to take advantage of ICTs and to share in the benefits of the information age. Malaysia's Multimedia Super Corridor (MSC) is *an example of how one developing country is "making ICTs the dynamo for growth within all economic sectors." However, some of its Asian neighbors have similar intentions and are challenging Malaysia's bid to create a regionally dominant position in ICT industries. This Chapter describes the MSC and analyses its chances of taking Malaysia into fully developed status and regional dominance, against a background of stiff competition from nations that already have a considerable lead. It concludes by drawing some implications for other developing countries.*

INTRODUCTION

Information and Communication Technologies (ICTs) have assumed a commanding position within the process of globalization and it is now clear that there is a strong link between ICTs and national competitiveness, economic development and social well-being. Success with ICTs has been recognized by governments as a vital factor for national development and survival in increasingly global market places. The American model of Silicon Valley as a catalyst for economic development based on hi-tech products and services is now being emulated by countries as diverse as Spain and Taiwan. In Asia, the economic success stories of the "tiger economies" of Japan, South Korea, Singapore, Hong Kong and Taiwan have been fuelled in large part by their successful use of ICTs, creating what some have termed the East Asian information technology miracle. These countries have experienced remarkable growth rates in the last decade and their industries compete internationally with those of the advanced economies of Western Europe and North America.

Many countries are now formulating strategies that they hope will help them take advantage of ICTs and to share in the benefits of the information age. However, there are a number of important differences between the mechanisms adopted by the East Asian tigers in successfully exploiting ICTs, and it is evident that there is no single formula for national success. For example, the two city-states of Hong Kong and Singapore have adopted markedly different approaches. In Hong Kong, the policy of the colonial government was characterized as one of "positive non-intervention" in economic affairs, and it franchised out core ICT infrastructure creation to the private sector, withdrawing itself to a monitoring function. In contrast, the Singaporean government's approach to ICTs is dynamic and proactive, encouraging the inward transfer of advanced information industry activities from multinational corporations by creating a sound business environment. With small populations, both Hong Kong (6.7 million) and Singapore (3.4 million) lack the huge reserve of technical skills of Taiwan (22.1 million) and Japan (126.2 million). Additionally, the percentage of Singapore's Gross National Product that has been dedicated to Research and Development has been less than half that of South Korea's (pop. 46.4 million).

Yet all of these economies have used ICTs to build national information infrastructures and most have developed national visions for ICTs. Most have targeted the electronics industry as a means of acquiring technology capability, although through the manufacture of different components, with South Korea focussing on DRAM, Singapore on disk drives and Taiwan on flat screen displays and laptop computers. They have also adopted outward looking, export-oriented policies in their desire to catch up with the world's leading economies, and they have adopted national strategies to develop and diffuse ICTs which involve collaboration among government, private and public agencies.

MALAYSIA – AN OVERVIEW

Geography

Malaysia lies just north of the equator in South East Asia. The country is physically divided into West (or peninsula) Malaysia and East Malaysia. The South China Sea separates these two portions. Thailand borders West Malaysia to the north and the island state of Singapore sits off its southern border. East Malaysia, comprising the states of Sarawak and Sabah, occupies the western and northern one-third of the island of Borneo, bordering Indonesia and Brunei. The entire country covers an area of 330,000 sq. km, slightly larger than Norway. Being equatorial, the climate is tropical and the terrain is characterized by coastal plains with mountainous, forested interiors. Malaysia's natural resources include tin, petroleum, timber, copper, iron ore, natural gas and bauxite. Roughly 3% of the country is arable land with a further 12% maintaining permanent crops. Fully 68% comprises forests and woodland.

Malaysia

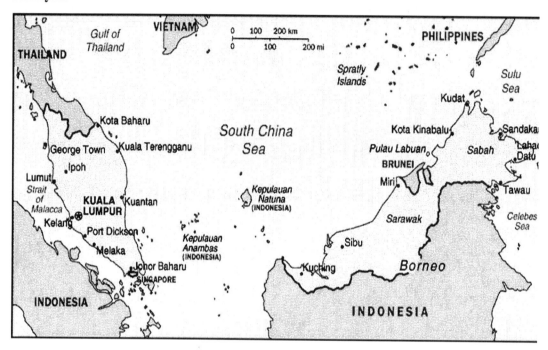

People

The 1997 population was estimated at 20 million, having a life expectancy of 70 years. Malay and other indigenous groups comprise 58% of the population, with people of Chinese origin making up 26%, Indian 7%, and others 9%. The official language is Malay, but English is widely understood as well as a number of Chinese dialects, Tamil, and numerous tribal dialects. Literacy exceeds 83%. Religions include Islam (Malays), Buddhism and Confucianism (Chinese), Hinduism (Indians), Christianity and tribal religions.

Adherence to Islam is considered intrinsic to Malay ethnic identity, and Islamic religious laws, administered by state authorities through Islamic courts, bind all ethnic Malays in some civil matters, such as family relations and diet. It is official policy to infuse Islamic values into the administration of the country, but at the same time, the constitution provides for freedom of religion and the government has resisted pressures to impose Islamic religious law beyond the Muslim community.

The government implements extensive affirmative action programs designed to boost the economic position of the ethnic Malay majority, which remains poorer on average than the Chinese minority despite the former's political dominance. The government maintains that these programs have been instrumental in ensuring ethnic harmony and political stability.

Government

The government is a constitutional monarchy. The Federation of Malaysia was formed in 1963 and is nominally headed by the paramount ruler (king) and a Parliament with two chambers. Most of the 13 states have hereditary rulers but the powers of state governments are limited by the federal constitution. Sarawak and Sabah are self-governing states, with foreign affairs, defense, internal security, and other powers delegated to the federal government. The country's legal system is based on English common law. The chief of state since April 1994 has been Paramount Ruler Tuanku Ja'afar ibni Al-Marhum Tuanku Abdul Rahman and the head of government since 16 July 1981 has been Prime Minister Dr. Mahathir bin Mohamad.

Economy

The Malaysian economy is a mixture of private enterprise and public management. It grew by an average of 9% annually between 1988 and 1996, and this growth resulted in a substantial reduction in poverty and a marked rise in real wages. By 1996, Malaysia had become the world's largest exporter of hard disc drives for personal computers. Malaysia is also the world's largest producer and exporter of edible oil (palm and palm kernel oil) and the world's largest producer and exporter of tropical hardwood logs and lumber. In 1999, foreign investors were continuing to commit large sums in the economy.

By 1995, industry was estimated to make up 45% of the economy, with services at 41% and agriculture at 14%. The rate of inflation in 1996 was indicated by the consumer price index of 3.5%. Manufacturing engaged 25% of the 8 million workforce, agriculture, forestry, and fisheries 21%, local trade and tourism 17%, services 12%, government 11%, construction 8%. Unemployment in 1996 stood at 2.6%. Major industries in Peninsular Malaysia are rubber and oil palm processing and manufacturing, light manufacturing industry, electronics, tin mining and smelting, logging and processing timber. In East Malaysia, the major economic activities comprise logging, agricultural processing and petroleum production and refining.

In order to help position Malaysia economically and socially vis-à-vis its neighbors, competitors and more developed countries, some comparative data is provided in table 1.

Table 1. Comparative Data											
	Malaysia	USA	United Kingd	Thailand	Indonesia	Singapore	South Korea	Hong Kong	Taiwa	Japan	India
Population (Millions)	20.5	270.1	57.6	59.5	209.8	3.4	46.4	6.7	21.9	126.2	1000.8
Exports (US$Billio	$84.6	$625.1	$240.4	$57.3	$49.8	$144.8	$129.8	$180.7	$122.1	$440.0	$32.2
GDP per capita (US$)	$10,750	$30,200	$20,400	$7,700	$3,770	$21,200	$13,700	$26,800	$14,200	$23,100	$1,720
Telephones (Millions)	2.5	182.6	29.5	1.5	1.3	1.2	16.6	4.4	10.0	64.0	12.0
Televisions (Millions)	2	215	20	3.3	11.5	1.0	9.3	1.8	10.8	100.0	50.0
Source: CIA Factbook											

THE MULTIMEDIA SUPER CORRIDOR

The MSC initiative arose out of a proposal made to the Prime Minister and the National Information Technology Council by the consultant firm McKinsey & Company. The proposal asserted that the nation's development strategy, which targeted manufacturing, imposed a ceiling on potential Gross Domestic Product (GDP) far below that which was envisaged by *Vision 2020*. By developing information industries and by leapfrogging into the Information Age, Malaysia's GDP potential would be greatly enhanced, allowing achievement of the country's development targets. The consultants' report indicates that Malaysia can achieve world status in multimedia industries within five years through carefully planned strategies and urgent action, thereby transforming itself into a knowledge-based society and harnessing the power of information as a springboard for socio-economic advancement. The government of Malaysia set up an International Advisory Panel for the MSC, consisting of leading industrialists, consultants and academics from around the world. Its first meeting took place on January 16th, 1997 at Stanford University in California.

The MSC is a 15 by 40 kilometer area encompassing Kuala Lumpur City Center (the nation's capital) and the new international airport as well as a new administrative center, Putrajaya, and an "IT City", Cyberjaya, claimed as the world's first "intelligent city". ("Jaya" is a Malay word meaning "success"). The MSC is intended to "leapfrog Malaysia

---

Box 1. Malaysian Government Description of the MSC

- The Multimedia Super Corridor (MSC) is a gift from the Malaysian government. A gift to technology developers and users seeking to deliver high-value multimedia services and products to customers across an economically vibrant Asia and the World, to Malaysians wanting their country to prosper, and to neighboring countries aspiring to partner with a technology hub.
- The MSC will be the first place in the world to bring together all the elements needed to create an environment that engenders truly mutual enrichment for all kinds of IT/multimedia companies.
- The MSC will bring together four key elements:
    1. A leading-edge soft infrastructure, including highly attractive incentives, unrestricted import of foreign knowledge workers, the world's first comprehensive framework of 'cyber-laws', world's first Multimedia Convergence Act, and a sharper focus on multimedia education.
    2. A world-class IT network consisting of a high-speed backbone, and the most cost-competitive telecommunication tariffs offered to MSC companies.
    3. The Multimedia Development Corporation as a high-powered, one-stop shop that is empowered to ensure that companies interested in the MSC get what they need to succeed by providing information and advice on the MSC, and assisting in expediting permit and license approvals.
    4. A top-quality development in Cyberjaya, Malaysia's first major MSC-designated cybercity designed from the ground up.
- Malaysia welcomes the advent of the Information Age with its promise of a new world order where information, ideas, people, goods and services move across borders in the most cost-effective and liberal ways.
- As traditional boundaries disappear, and as companies, capital, consumers, communications and cultures become truly global, new approaches and attitudes to business are required. Malaysia upholds the virtues of the new world order, believing that the globe is collectively moving towards a "century of the world", a century of world-wide peace and shared prosperity among nations.

into the Information Age" and to achieve the targets for development set by *Vision 2020*. MSC-status companies were beginning to move into Cyberjaya by 1999. Something of the flavor of the project as depicted by Malaysia's national planners can be gleaned from their own description, taken from the project's publicity material, shown in box 1.

A key component of the MSC project is made up of the Flagship Applications, seven national initiatives for IT which are intended to fuel the development of applications by MSC companies. The government describes the Flagship applications as follows:

Electronic Government

A fully computerized operations and service structure that promises a quantum leap in public service – an electronic workflow system for a more transparent bureaucracy, faster processing of applications, clearer accountability, and improved information flow. The Prime Minister's office, for one, will be paperless, procurement will be online, and project implementation will be monitored electronically.

Multipurpose Smart Card

Embedded with a chip or microprocessor, the card will eventually be used both for identification as well as for payment identity card, driver's license, immigration re-entry, medical information, electronic purse, ATM card and credit card. It can be used for EPF (Employee Provident Fund) transactions, voter registration, bill payment, ticket-less air travel, student card, and car park access.

Smart Schools

Aimed at producing knowledge workers who can use Information Age tools and technology to improve productivity. Using technology as the main driving force, the goals are to produce a thinking and technology-literate workforce, democratize education, open doors to enhance individual strengths and abilities and provide all-round development of the individual.

Telemedicine

This will revolutionize the way patients are diagnosed and treated, the emphasis being on smoother and higher quality healthcare. It will enable the future healthcare system to be equitable, affordable, efficient, technology appropriate and consumer friendly. The people will enjoy, among others, both mass and customized health information and education, continuing medical education, teleconsultation and lifetime health plans.

R&D Cluster

This will be the first internationally-focussed R&D zone in Asia, providing the ideal environment for research-driven firms: strong government support, a gateway to the expanding region, growing business opportunities and interaction within a like-minded community. Infrastructure in place already includes the Multimedia University, several other universities, the Malaysian Institute of Microelectronic Systems & Technology Park Malaysia.

Worldwide Manufacturing Web

This will set the ideal environment for manufacturing and manufacturing-servicing companies using multimedia technology to create and deliver value-added services and products to customers around the globe. It will encompass such activities as R&D, design, engineering support, manufacturing control, procurement, and logistics and distribution support.

Borderless Marketing

This is a platform for companies to use multimedia technology to create and deliver marketing messages, customer services and information products to their multicultural and multinational customers. It will break the traditional barriers to doing business: businesses round the clock, reaching customers anywhere in the world and providing messages and services in digitized form. The focus will be on telemarketing, online information services, electronic commerce and digital broadcasting.

Additional features of the MSC include a package of incentives for companies to apply for MSC Status and a number of cyberlaws to remove inhibitors to multimedia applications development. The incentives include; a bill of guarantees from the government; income tax exemption for 5-10 years; allowances on new investments in the MSC; duty-free import of multimedia material; R&D grants for small and medium-sized enterprises; unrestricted employment of foreign knowledge workers; freedom of ownership; and freedom to source or borrow capital globally.

The cyberlaws include; the Multimedia Convergence Act, which will facilitate creation of the communications framework; a digital signature law, which will enable businesses and the community to use electronic signatures in place of handwritten ones; a multimedia intellectual property law, which protects the licensing and royalty collection rights of developers; a computer crime law which defines illegal access and interception of information; a telemedicine development law, which empowers medical practitioners to provide medical services from remote locations; and an electronic government law which allows politicians, public servants and the public to communicate electronically with each other using established and secure formats and standards.

The Multimedia Development Corporation was established in 1996 to set up the MSC, under its executive chairman Othman Yeop Abdullah. By mid 1999, 228 companies had obtained MSC status, including many multinationals, such as Microsoft, Sun Microsystems, Lotus, Lucent Technologies, Nippon Telegraph and Telephone, Oracle, Ericsson, Hewlett Packard, Intel, Siemens, and Fujitsu. Construction of the two new cities of Putrajaya and Cyberjaya has begun and the Prime Minister along with his 800-strong office has already moved in. A Central Incubator Center has also opened, offering management, financial and marketing consultancy services along with low-cost office accommodation. The Multimedia University has opened its doors to the first intake of 3,000 students and a US$32 million venture capital fund has been established to help small and medium sized start-up companies in the MSC (Chin and Heong, 1999).

UNDERSTANDING THE IMPACT OF THE MSC

Two frameworks are used to assist in an analysis and interpretation of the influence that MSC is expected to have on Malaysia's economic and social development. The first is a framework for IT-led development (Dedrick and Kraemer, 1998). The second framework is derived from the World Bank (Hanna, Guy and Arnold, 1995). The two frameworks are complementary, so that their joint use allows for a more insightful analysis than would have been possible using only one or the other.

The framework of IT-led development is shown in Figure 1. It is based on four sets of variables; environmental factors, industry policy, industry structure and IT diffusion. The operation, strengths and interactions between these variables are said to determine the level of economic benefit that a nation can attain from IT. The World Bank framework draws on best practices of industrial countries and suggests broad directions for adapting these lessons to the conditions of developing countries. The lessons include; removing barriers to technology diffusion, designing suitable national strategies, developing human, organizational and governmental capacity, tailoring programs to their context, packaging programs and services to achieve complementarity, disseminating information, and building institutional bridges and intermediaries. The following sections relate the actions and events connected to the MSC to each variable in the two frameworks, and they assess the extent to which the MSC furthers the operation of those variables in contributing to Malaysia's economic development.

Environmental Factors

Malaysia has enjoyed considerable political stability for much of its recent history, which is an

Figure 1. Framework of IT-Led Development (Dedrick & Kraemer 1998)

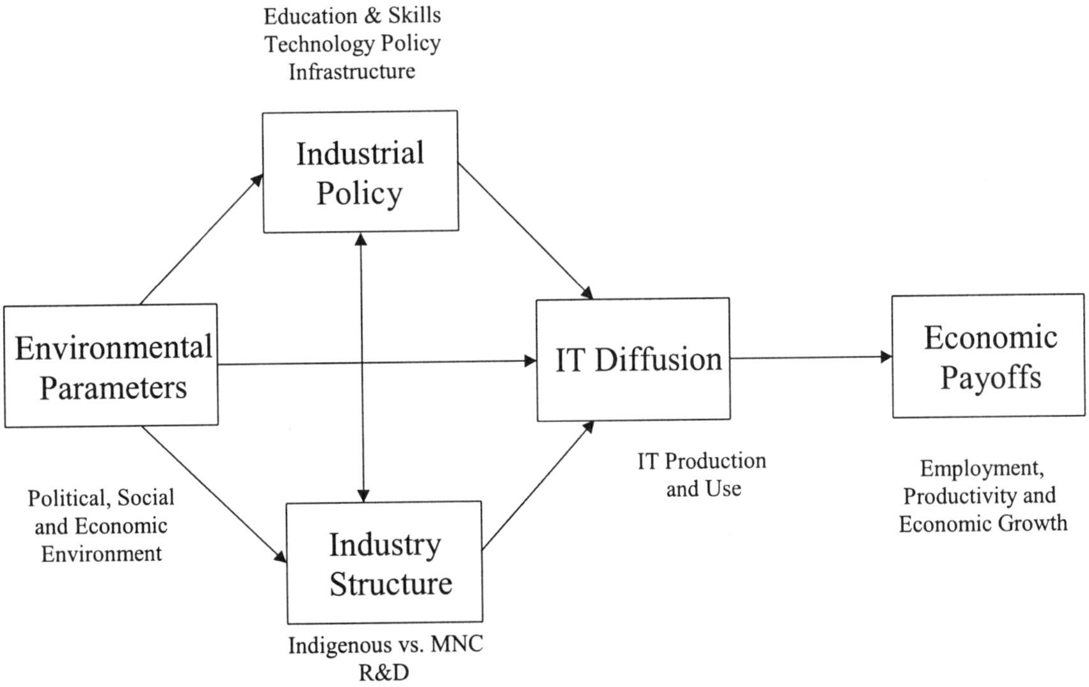

important factor in the development of IT (Raman and Yap, 1996). Despite the economic downturn of the late 1990s that affected the Asian economies, and despite the political disturbances caused by the deposing of the Deputy Prime Minister, Anuar Ibrahim, Malaysia has continued to attract foreign investment as well as maintaining continuity in its development policies. Members of the MSC International Advisory Panel have stressed the importance of continued political stability in Malaysia in maintaining their commitment to the MSC project. As the MSC depends on external investment for its success, political stability is essential. However, observers point out that political stability has been easily maintainable while the economy was growing.

Another consideration from the political perspective is the role of Dr. Mahathir himself. As the dominant figure in Malaysian politics since independence, it is evident that his drive and determination have had a significant impact on the nation's recent economic advancement and on the conception and implementation of the MSC. A potential question arises therefore, with regard to the likely development of the MSC without Dr. Mahathir, who is over 70 years of age and whose position is subject to democratic processes within his party and within the country.

At least three important features characterize Malaysia's social makeup with respect to IT. Firstly, despite the rapid growth of the economy in its transition to newly-industrialized status, half the population of Malaysia still lives in rural areas, according to the 1991 census, and this proportion rises to around 65% for East Malaysia. The implication is that for many Malaysians, IT has little direct impact on their lives, and will continue not do to so for some time yet. At least one observer has highlighted a likely Malaysian "information apartheid" arising between the information "haves" and "have-nots", a condition suffered by the most developed nations.

Secondly, Malaysia's distinctive ethnic and cultural mix serves to moderate the effects of social initiatives and experiments. The social effects of the MSC have to be considered in the light of the economic disparity between the Chinese ethnic community and the others. We cannot yet say that IT in Malaysia will either widen or diminish the disparity between the ethnic communities. But the nation's ambitions for fully developed status make a specific point of creating equal shares in prosperity for all sections of society. With so much hope being pinned on IT for achieving the desired level of prosperity, it would be short-sighted to assume that the development of IT in Malaysia would not be touched by the measures so far employed for favoring the economic development of specific sections of the community. Quite how this might play out has yet to be identified.

Additionally, the use and diffusion of information sometimes raises cause for concern in Malaysian society. Despite pronouncements that the Internet will not be censored, the government has expressed concern about the spreading of rumors. The Star newspaper reported on October 2nd 1998 that four people had been charged with spreading rumors on the Internet, and that the police were closely monitoring the distribution of e-mail. Such actions are indicative of some of the dilemmas which a culture with high regard for authority faces when adopting a technological artifact which originated in a culture which does not have such a high regard for authority.

Rapid economic growth in Malaysia has been achieved as a result of attracting foreign investors to build an IT manufacturing industry. The government, through the MSC, now recognizes the need to ensure widespread internal use of IT and development of software products in order to sustain high levels of growth in support of its target of developed status. However, around 20% of the work force is still employed in agriculture, forestry, and fisheries and slightly more than half the economy continues to be derived from extractive industries. The structure of domestic demand helps shape the diffusion of IT in developing countries and in this respect, the Malaysian economy features some characteristic aspects of developing countries. For example, the absence of the middle-sized enterprise and the existence of isolated islands of sophisticated users. On the positive side, some of the provisions of the MSC demonstrate that the government is coming to terms with its own information and communication needs, and as a large domestic user, this can catalyze a variety of spin-off applications.

Despite the Asian economic crisis, a high level of optimism has been maintained for the MSC. In February 1998, members of the international advisory panel to the MSC expressed confidence in the Malaysian economy and renewed their endorsement of the MSC. Bob Bishop of Silicon Graphics World Trade Corporation said: "The MSC can be the catalyst to pull Malaysia and, possibly the region, out of the economic problems." Dr Mahathir was quoted as saying that with work a year ahead of schedule, "there is really no reason" why the MSC should be postponed. "If there is an impact at all, it has been accelerated." In April 1999, it was reported that under the mid-term review of the Seventh Malaysia Plan, the allocation for

IT, including the MSC, had been almost doubled. However, this may still be insufficient to make a significant impact on the use of IT nationwide. Despite intensifying computer education and training for schools, Dr. Mahathir was late quoted as saying that it was impossible for the government to provide every school in the country with a computer because of the high cost involved.

Industrial Policy

In industrial countries the human, managerial and institutional adjustments to IT have been profound. Manual skills lose their importance and information skills dominate. As technology transforms the economy, national development increasingly depends on the capacity of its people to acquire and apply knowledge.

Education in IT was making some headway in Malaysia well before the MSC project was inaugurated (Siowck-Lee Gan, 1998). The Ministry of Education formulated a Computers-in-Education program in 1989, involving the deployment of locally made PCs into schools. However, this, and other initiatives aimed at computers in education, suffered from a lack of planning direction as well as the absence of a comprehensive plan for teacher training. An IT syllabus within the National Curriculum has now been defined and a number of IT training organizations have established themselves across Malaysia. The government has established a supercomputer research center. It also seems that proficiency in the English language is necessary for assimilation of IT in developing countries. Following a de-emphasis of the English language immediately after independence, the government has since increased its emphasis on English and it is now taught as a second language and is widely used in business.

Despite the continuing efforts to train the population in IT skills, commentators point to a scarcity of intellectual capital in Malaysia with regard to the managerial, entrepreneurial and strategy-formulating knowledge which is required for successful exploitation of IT on a competitive world stage. Whereas a few developing countries have established export industries based on "body-shopping" of software products, Malaysia has yet to establish a critical mass of sufficiently skilled workers to emulate their success. Furthermore, as compared, for instance, to the Indian software industry, which is moving up the value-chain towards software design, Malaysia seems far behind in indigenous creative and entrepreneurial capability to catch up within a foreseeable time frame.

The MSC planners acknowledge the enormous demand for IT skill that is implied by their plans. It has been estimated that the MSC will need 7,000 knowledge workers a year for several years. The Multimedia University, in Cyberjaya, is expected to provide the trained manpower needed by companies operating in the Multimedia Super Corridor. However, it can be expected that a continued and possibly chronic shortage of skilled workers will hamper MSC related developments for some time to come. Government figures indicate that the annual shortfall of 7,000 skilled IT workers during the period of the sixth five-year plan (1991-1995) will increase to a shortfall of 10,000 during the period of the seventh plan (1996-2000). Furthermore, the demand for IT skills from MSC projects is likely to have a centripetal effect, starving non-MSC companies and projects of the skills they need. Dependence on overseas staff will continue for the foreseeable future.

Beyond the development of skills for knowledge workers, there are signs that the government acknowledges the existence of widespread computer illiteracy among the general population, and that such a condition will inhibit the diffusion of IT. Accordingly a number of initiatives, such as road shows and cyber cafes are being instigated. IT is the subject of a pop song, which is often played on the radio. The ultimate success of initiatives to educate the wider public with regard to IT has yet to be determined.

Until the late 1980s, Malaysia's economy was based on its natural resources. In 1988, the government began formulating specific technology policies aimed at encouraging the manufacture of IT products and the increasing use of IT in government. Tariffs on IT hardware and software were reduced. Government itself began using computers more and in 1987 the state-owned telecommunication company was privatized. In 1985, the government had formed the National Committee on Data Processing (NCDP) and in 1987, it began to forge links with the private sector through the National Consultative Committee on Information Technology (NCCIT). The eighties saw major structural and infra-structural changes. The first public network, MAYPAC, was implemented by Telekom Malaysia. In 1981, the National Computer Training Centre (NCTC) was established in the National Institute of Public Administration (INTAN), as a step towards a more effective use of computers in Malaysia. The National Data Processing Committee (JPDN) was formed as the highest authority on computerization in the country. The Science and Technology Policy was formulated in 1986 followed in 1988 by the Computerization Guideline Manual of MAMPU (Management and Manpower Planning Unit).

The establishment of government databases also picked up during the late 1980s and early 1990s. There was also a significant improvement in public counter services, such as a computerized license applications and renewals service of the Road Transport Department at the Post Offices using the dedicated Public Services Network (PSN). Other users of the network include the Police and Immigration Departments. The National IT Council (NITC) was formed in 1994.

The 1990s saw the rapid introduction of new technologies and tools such as the Internet, propounded by MIMOS (Malaysian Institute of Micro-Electronic Systems) through its JARING (Joint Advanced Research Integrated Networking) network, and the proposed Government Integrated Telecommunications Network (GITN) to manage and service the Government computer network and facilities. The use of personal computers proliferated in government and today there is hardly any Government agency without computers. An important effort at integrating and coordinating the use and management of IT was initiated through a Government Integrated IT Services (GIITS) task force, formed in 1996, which has produced various proposals, from a holistic viewpoint, to provide a better management and implementation of IT in the public service. They include the setting up of a Department for IT, looking into the mobilization of personnel, training of end-users, improving career prospect and motivation to IT personnel, better interfacing with private sectors, and developing IT security mechanisms.

The National Institute of Public Administration (INTAN) has embarked on a five-year plan to train 133,500 public personnel in IT, as follows.

1997	1998	1999	2000	2001	TOTAL
944	15,231	39,775	38,775	38,775	133,500

The NCDP was tasked with several functions; formulating a national computer policy, developing a long-term strategy for IT, establishing guidelines for computing in the public sector, promoting a local computer industry, advising government on training and promoting research in computing.

The Malaysian initiatives have parallels in other countries. For example, as early as 1966, French Prime Minister, G. Pompidou initiated the "Plan Calcul" in France, under which the French Research Institute for Computer Science and Control was established. Reporting to both the Ministry of Research and the Ministry of Industry, the Institute is a national scientific and technological research institute active in the following domains:

- basic research
- realisation of experimental systems

- technology transfer
- training through research and knowledge-transfer
- development of scientific international exchanges
- implementation of scientific expertise

Another example is the Brazilian Informatics and Automation Council, which assists the President of the Republic in formulating the country's Informatics policy. This policy is set forth in the Brazilian Informatics and Automation Plan (PLANIN). This is a set of integrated rules and guidelines for the implementation and development of the Brazilian computer industry, with a view to the use and production of goods and services, research and development of activities, and training of human resources. PLANIN also establishes general guidelines for co-operation programs with other countries and the sale of Brazilian products on the international market (Roche, 1990).

The Sixth Malaysia Five-Year Plan (1991-1995) incorporated the nation's first IT program, with the intent of; enhancing managerial effectiveness, improving the productivity of government departments, promoting the availability of information, developing an IT infrastructure and assisting in the creation of an information-rich society. The Seventh Malaysia Five-Year Plan devoted a whole chapter to IT. "With the Seventh Malaysia Plan we move into the Information Age," said Dr. Mahathir.

The development of IT in Malaysia has been paralleled by development of the telecommunication infrastructure. The Sixth Malaysia Plan earmarked US$ 2.2 billion for development of telecommunications with the aim of converting to a fully digitized system by the year 2000. Following the establishment of JARING as the sole Internet Service Provider (ISP), Telekom Malaysia began operations in 1997 and the Government received further applications for the issuance of new ISP licenses from five more fixed line telecommunications operators.

Telekom Malaysia began privatising itself when 14.9% was sold on September 1990 raising US$ 870 million. The second, public offering took place in 1993. Evidence indicates that privatisations extend the reach of the telecommunication network to a larger part of the population. Figure 2 shows the effect of privatisation on growth in teledensity (telephone mainlines per 100 inhabitants) in selected emerging markets, including Malaysia. The indices relate to the year of privatisation, which equals 100, for which the world average is 1985-95.

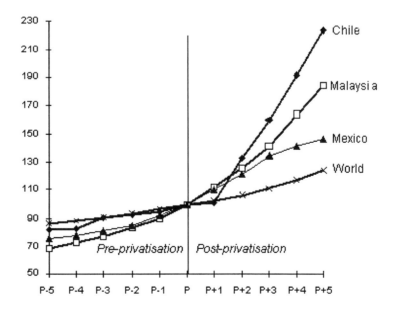

Figure 2. The effect of privatisation on growth in teledensity

Developing Asia is the one region in the world where telecommunication employment is not dropping. A primary reason is the buoyant state of the regional economy that is driving demand for telecommunication services. Trends for operators in Korea, Malaysia, Singapore and Thailand, shown in Table 2, reflect this where employment increased 2.3 per cent a year between 1988-92.

Table 2. Main Telephone Lines and Employees in East Asia, 1988, 1992							
	Main lines		Employees			Main lines per employee	
	1988	1992	1988	1992	Change	1988	1992
Korea Telecom	10,306,028	15,593,454	2,073	59,137	7,064	198	264
Singapore Telecom	938,719	1,169,089	11,620	10,856	-764	81	108
Telekom Malaysia	1,247,687	2,091,578	28,168	29,577	1,409	44	71
TOT (Thailand)	1,005,872	1,790,029	17,956	20,855	2,899	56	86
	13,498,306	20,644,150	109,817	120,425	10,608	123	171

Judging from the rate of growth of Internet subscribers, there is a need for more ISPs. The Government is opening up the ISP licenses to all fixed line operators and it does not plan to restrict the number of licenses awarded. At present, there are some 300,000 Internet subscribers in Malaysia. The Government hopes that with additional ISPs, there would be more competition among the existing and new ISPs, causing the quality of Internet service to be upgraded and improved. Poor telecommunications and unreliable power supplies are common inhibitors of IT diffusion in developing countries. In Malaysia, such problems are largely absent in the urban centers. In the rural districts, though, many villages are without telephone access and electricity. The MSC will have to address this issue if it is to fulfil its promises of equal sharing of the benefits of national development.

IT Diffusion

The electronics industry began in Malaysia in the mid-1970s and came to dominate Malaysian industrialization, with exports reaching US$ 6 billion by 1988, representing 56% of manufactured exports. By 1990, Malaysia was the third largest producer of electronic components and the world's largest exporter. More recently, IT production has moved away from low value added microchips towards the manufacture of complete computers and peripheral devices. Electrical and electronic products accounted for 53% of Malaysia's total export earnings, worth $40 billion, in 1998, up 35% from 1997, according to the Malaysia Department of Statistics. Exports of packaged ICs were up nearly 40% to $10.8 billion in 1998. Malaysian aerospace exports exceed imports for the United States, and the Netherlands. Pharmaceutical exports are similarly high for Switzerland, the United States and Germany. Japan has very high ratios of exports to import in office machinery, computers and electrical/electronics industries, and Malaysia is something of a 'mini-Japan' in this regard showing high exports in both these industries and quite low ratios in pharmaceuticals and aerospace.

Malaysia's manufacturing export-import ratio of 0.85 is on a par with the United States and significantly higher than Australia, but lower than Germany, the Netherlands and

Switzerland. These figures serve to emphasize the critically important contribution of electronics and computing equipment manufacturing to Malaysia's economic and trade performance.

The United States is both a major supplier of high technology goods to Malaysia and a major market for Malaysian-produced high technology goods. In the early 1990s, Malaysia's high technology trade with the United States showed a sustained and spectacular reversal, from a trade deficit of over US$460 million in 1990 to a trade surplus of nearly US$2,400 million in 1994. The biggest share of high technology trade lies in electronics (55.4%) and computers and telecommunications products (30.1%). In both these product categories, but especially in computers and telecommunications, Malaysia enjoys a significant trade surplus with the United States.

During the 1980s, the internal market for hardware, software and services increased fourfold. Internal use of IT grew rapidly throughout this period. In 1997, IT-related spending in Malaysia reached US$1.9 billion. This corresponded with similar growth in the infrastructural components of human resources, telecommunications and research and development. The heaviest users were in the multinational corporations and in the government dominated areas of finance and petroleum. However, manufacturing firms, especially locally owned firms, have yet to fully appreciate the benefits of IT. Additionally, significant internal disparities exist. In Malaysia, only 3.7% of households have personal computers (PCs). Many schools still lack electricity and the telephone penetration rate for rural areas is only 5.5 telephones per 100 people, as opposed to the urban rate of 24.

Industry Structure

The dominance of Malaysia in the manufacture and export of electronic components can be attributed primarily to the incentives offered by Malaysia to attract foreign investors. Several free trade zones with minimum customs formalities have been established and a number of MNCs have taken advantage of the favorable infrastructure and abundant skilled and cheap labor. Their investments have created jobs, encouraged feeder company start-ups, trained skilled staff, transferred technology and opened up international markets.

Table 3 shows recent export values for major commodities and depicts the electrical and electronic products sector as by far the most important.

With regard to the potential for the development of the software industry in Malaysia, some comments about the Indian software industry might provide a useful point of reference as the growth of the Malaysian software industry could take a lesson from that of India. Indian software exports reached US$1,650 million in 1997/98, providing a major contribution to export earning. These exports were dominated by software services, in the form of custom software work, rather than by the export of software products, in the form of packages. Part of their value was accounted for by the explosion of work on the Year 2000 problem, estimated to take up around 40% of the total, with less than 5% of exports coming from packages. Development of software packages in India for export is hindered by unfamiliarity with foreign markets and distance, as well differences in user needs and working environments in the domestic market, alongside a low level of innovation, which do not provide a useful testing ground for the development of products for export. Additionally, advertising and marketing expenses are very high for software products wishing to penetrate new markets.

Another factor of the Indian experience relates to "body-shopping", whereby software development is carried out at the client's site overseas location rather than in India. In 1988, 65% of export contracts was conducted for this type of work. Moreover, the majority of contracts for Indian software involve less-skilled activities like programming, with the more intellectual analysis and design activities remaining with the client. Indian software exports are also dominated by a small number of large concerns that are geographically concentrated in a few cities; Bangalore, Mumbai (Bombay), Chennai (Madras) and New Delhi (Heeks).

Table 3. Major Exports (Malaysian Ringits Millions)			
Commodity	1998	1999 Jan-Feb	2000 Jan-Feb
Rubber	2,343	372	427
Palm Oil and Palm Based Products	19,510	2,899	2,410
Crude Petroleum	9,306	929	2,072
Liquefied Natural Gas	6,349	997	1,842
Timber (Saw Logs & Sawn Timber)	5,469	645	812
Electrical and Electronic Products	185,314	25,435	29,818
Articles of Apparel and Clothing Accessories	8,562	1,213	1,166
Wood Manufactures (Plywood & Veneer)	4,772	662	645
Other Manufactured Goods and Articles	37,192	5,022	6,002

Economic Payoffs

The rate of unemployment in Malaysia in 1996 stood at 2.6%. Apart from the surge in demand for knowledge workers that the MSC is expected to create, eventual effects on employment from MSC activities are hard to predict. Experiences from developed nations suggest a shift in employment from the industry to the service sector as IT encroaches further into public life. Flatter organization structures tend to de-emphasize middle layers of management. Malaysia's ambitions to be a regional player in IT and multimedia imply increased exports of IT products. However, sustainable job creation will only occur if the country is able to effectively transfer capability to indigenous organizations and reduce dependence on MNCs who can relocate to alternative locations when economic conditions change.

In 1996 and 1997, Malaysia's productivity grew at an annual rate of around 5.6%. In terms of contribution to GDP growth, productivity increases contributed 70% in 1997 while employment growth contributed 29%. According to the National Productivity Council, the contribution from productivity was due to the shift towards innovation, high technology, increased efficiency of human resources, and proactive initiatives undertaken by both public and private sectors to enhance productivity. The primary contributor to productivity growth continued to be the manufacturing sector, which contributed 51%.

Internationally, Malaysia's productivity growth of 5.4% for the period 1990-97 exceeded that of seven major countries of the Organisation for Economic Co-operation and Development (OECD), namely Germany (2.7%), Italy (1.6%), the United Kingdom (1.6%), France (1.5%), Japan (1.2%), the United States of America (0.9%) and Canada (0.8%). Among selected Asian countries, Malaysia's productivity growth of 5.7% in 1996 exceeded that of Taiwan (5.4%), the Republic of Korea (2.6%), Hong Kong (1.3%), Singapore (0.7%) and the Philippines (-1.3%).

Some of the differences between developed and developing countries in terms of their rates of IT diffusion include technical and managerial capabilities and government capabilities as user, regulator and catalyst. Management is seen as key to technological dynamism. In this respect, initiatives that are intended to promote productivity at the national level must address the issue of building management capacity. If not just for the sake of achieving break-through improvements in domestic productivity, planners should acknowledge that intensive IT users often become competitive IT suppliers (as in the banking and airline industries). MSC projects, therefore, imply intensive use of "world-class" technology applications, which can be marketed on a worldwide basis. Whilst particular technologies will be heavily implicated in such a process, it will be innovative and entrepreneurial managers who will make it happen.

Similarly, in representing half the domestic market for IT use, government IT planners need to understand their role as national catalyst for the diffusion of IT, and should be prepared to implement innovative applications with far-reaching effects. It is hoped that the electronic government flagship application can serve the purpose of advancing the national IT agenda by catalyzing further applications, such as electronic commerce, within the private sector.

In evaluating the impact of the MSC on Malaysia's economic growth the major consideration is whether the economy can return to the high levels of growth achieved in the 1980s and up to 1996. Also, the likely impact of the 1997/98 economic crisis on the MSC project should be taken into account as well as the longer-term prospects for Malaysia achieving its ambitious targets through further application of IT. Another aspect concerns the extent to which the local market for IT products has been affected by the Asian economic slowdown and the likely effect that will have on the IT manufacturing industry.

Until recently, Malaysia enjoyed several years of strong and relatively consistent growth. For Malaysia to achieve developed status by the year 2020, the country must continue to experience GDP growth of at least 7% per year. In view of the fact that labor costs are rising much faster (about two to one) than Malaysia's productivity, maintaining a GDP growth rate of 7% under normal economic conditions will be difficult. However, with signs of improvement emerging by mid-1999, few observers doubt an eventual recovery. As to the likely impact of the economic downturn on the MSC, government officials have assured the business community that all MSC initiatives are proceeding as planned.

COMPARISONS WITH SIMILAR INITIATIVES

The Malaysian initiative is not altogether unique. Governments from Ireland to Israel are actively involved in trying to encourage and attract IT investment by providing infrastructure, attractive taxation incentives and, most importantly, a well-educated work force with relevant skill levels ranging from technical to research. Regional competition will undoubtedly affect internal developments in Malaysia, and the MSC cannot be excluded from its influence. In particular, Malaysia will face stiff competition from Singapore, Hong Kong, Taiwan and South Korea, and as table 4 illustrates, it is some way behind its strongest competitors in at least one factor, use of the Internet.

Table 4. Proportions of Populations that use the Internet			
USA	22.39%	Taiwan	2.21%
Hong Kong	12.98%	Malaysia	0.67%
Japan	9.15%	Thailand	0.22%
Singapore	3.82%	Philippines	0.11%
S. Korea	3.26%	Indonesia	0.04%

In the following sections we look briefly at Malaysia's Asian competitors in order to assess their challenge in terms of regional ascendancy in ICT industries.

Singapore

Singapore's national IT initiative, known as Singapore ONE, is a national drive to deliver interactive multimedia applications and services to homes, businesses and schools throughout Singapore. The intent is to establish Singapore as an "intelligent" nation. The government is already nurturing the republic's strong points in the computer industry, such as storage device and multimedia product manufacturing, while pushing advancements in less developed local industries like semiconductors and communication products.

Singapore's Economic Development Board (EDB) provides funds to nurture promising entrepreneurs and further IT developments in Singapore will be supported by the Venture fund, the Technology Fund and the Innovation Development Scheme. According to an executive with Oracle, Singapore is ahead of the game, and already has much of what Malaysia is talking about. For example, in July 1998, Singapore's Electronic Transaction Act came into force, providing the legal basis for electronic commerce transactions. Singaporeans can already file their tax returns via the Internet. Nevertheless, set-up costs in Singapore are high compared to Malaysia, which is beginning to attract companies away from the island republic.

In mid-1999, Singapore's government was reported to be drawing up a master plan for ICT that it hopes will drive the country to become the world's second most information-driven economy after the U.S. within three years. The 10-year master plan, which builds on the existing Singapore ONE initiative, maps out strategies for Singapore to become a leader in the use of ICT, as well as a gateway to the Asia-Pacific region and a key node in the global information infrastructure. The minister for communications and information technology describes the country's vision "to transform Singapore into a dynamic and vibrant global ICT capital with a thriving and prosperous Net economy by the year 2010." Such aspirations sound very similar to those of the Malaysian government.

A recent study from market analyst International Data Corp. (IDC) ranked Singapore as the world's fourth most information-driven economy and society after the USA, Sweden and Finland. With extended use of e-commerce, IT-based education, and all public services going online, Singapore can achieve second spot behind USA by 2002, IDC projected.

Singapore's advantages stem for the island-state's responses to its perceived national weaknesses: principally its lack of natural resources. Building on attracting multinational production activities and a high comfort level for foreign companies, Singapore has gone on to intensively cultivate an information industry workforce. Singapore has internalized the production of innovative product lines from abroad to develop a vibrant regional export platform.

From our framework, we can summarize that compared to Malaysia, Singapore is stronger in its environmental factors, mainly as a result of its stronger economy. It also has advantages in greater diffusion of IT as well as education and infrastructure development.

Hong Kong

Like much of its development, Hong Kong's approach to ICTs has been highly laissez-faire. The government franchised infrastructure development to private industry and left ICT development to market forces. The government stepped in only when the market failed as in the shortage of skilled IT professionals. Compared to its regional rivals, the government of Hong Kong was late to formalize a national policy for the development and use of ICTs. However, its strengths as a manufacturing and financial center for the region and in particular, its position as the gateway for foreign firms entering the vast Chinese market, have ensured that its businesses have made extensive use of ICTs. However, manufacturing in Hong Kong has atrophied, due in part to a shortage of IT professionals and a lack of government attention to IT diffusion. Despite this, Hong Kong continues to provide regional leadership in trade, finance and marketing, all of which are ICT intensive, as well as remaining the major center of development for doing Chinese business.

During the 1980s and 90s, Hong Kong's electronic industry declined as manufacturers redeployed their assets into the neighboring provinces of China, where labor is much cheaper. Simultaneously, the economy was transformed from a manufacturing center for relatively labor-intensive consumer goods into a high-tech trading and services center. Consequently, infrastructure development in support of manufacturing in Hong Kong is less developed than in Singapore or Taiwan. However, tertiary education expanded rapidly during the 1990s, increasing the pool of skilled IT workers, and some specialized clusters of advanced ICT use have been built up around niche activities in which Hong Kong excels, such as banking, garments and telecommunications.

Recently, the government of Hong Kong, in partnership with private industry, has announced its Cyberport project to house 30 medium-to-large and 100 smaller companies, specializing in the development of E-commerce related services and multimedia content to support business and industries ranging from financial services to trading, advertising and entertainment to communications. The companies located in the Cyberport will be connected to the world via a broadband optical fiber network. The project will start in 2001 and it has already attracted Hewlett Packard; IBM; Oracle; Sybase; and Yahoo!. The key objective of the Cyberport is to create a cluster of leading edge information technology and service companies and multimedia content creators in Hong Kong.

Returning to the framework, we can see that Hong Kong remains strong in the environment parameters, despite the 1997 change of sovereignty to Chinese rule. Its education policies are showing returns but its technology policies have been late to get started. Its industry structure favors ICT development in a few key areas only, although diffusion of IT has been aided by strength in telecommunications. Industry policy has been strengthened by the Cyberport announcement, although it is too early to judge how this will play out.

Taiwan

The government of Taiwan designated the information industry as a strategic industry as early as 1980 and it has since forcefully advocated manufacturing productivity and technology mastery. By the early 1990s, Taiwanese computer products accounted for 42% of the nation's exports and its computer motherboards made up 67% of the world market. Much of this achievement was due to the government and private sector's strategic pursuits of low costs, productivity and competitiveness in IT products. After encouraging local R&D, the economy is now being steered by the government towards the development of upstream activities, focussing on innovation, strategic alliances and global niche markets (Kraemer et al, 1996).

Unlike its neighbors Japan and South Korea, Taiwan's computer industry consisted of a large number of small manufacturers, which also contrasts with the dominance of MNCs in Singapore's manufacturing sector. Taiwan's polices have been highly diffusion oriented in that technological capabilities have been spread throughout the industrial structure. In contrast to the approach of South Korea, which encouraged large firms to conduct R&D themselves, Taiwan created public institutions to conduct research and to disseminate technology to the private sector. The success that was subsequently achieved was based on the principal of "fast follower." In the 1980s, the open architecture of the IBM personal computer lowered barriers for entry into the computer industry, and Taiwan's manufacturers were able to reverse-engineer the original design to produce low cost computers. Later, they were able to develop their own design and production capabilities to enable them to quickly enter new markets whilst they were still profitable, e.g. notebook computers.

Taiwan has also dramatically transformed its telecommunications infrastructure, introduced ICTs into many of its government functions and its traditional industries and directed indigenous R&D towards new product development and innovation. These developments have been matched by highly focussed educational programs to develop scientists, technicians and professionals for further internal diffusion of IT and for technology mastery. However, Taiwan's installed base of computers lags well behind Singapore and Hong Kong, although it is about twice that of South Korea. Although Taiwan's pool of scientists and engineers doubled between 1984 and 1991, shortages in ICT skills persist, as they do almost everywhere.

From the perspective of the framework, we can see that Taiwan's strength lies in its environmental parameters, its industrial policies and in its industry structure.

South Korea

South Korea's capability in ICTs grew from its aggressive policy of vertically integrating its electronics industry into semiconductors in the early 1980s, when there was a worldwide shortage. This was followed by the acquisition and mastering of technologies for the production of computers and peripherals and the development of telecommunications technology. ICTs have been applied in Korea as a generic technology, with factory automation featuring prominently. The leading role in these developments has been played by the private sector, particularly the large business conglomerates. The government has facilitated ICT development through policies for infant industry protection, directed procurement, preferential financing, human resource development and R&D policies.
South Korea's ICT industry had its start in foreign investments, mostly from USA and Japan, and foreign links continue to be important for technology licensing. The government established a secure environment of predictable macroeconomic policies that were conducive to private sector growth. The government favored the electronics industry from early on and it fostered close relations with selected sectors and firms that allowed it to enforce performance standards. The government has been committed to IT generation and diffusion since the late 1980s, targeting an advanced nation by 2000. IT development plans have directed government funding towards a variety of projects for education, diffusion, R&D and manufacturing.

South Korea's government has consistently shown willingness to evaluate its own policies towards ICTs and to change them in a pragmatic manner. Unlike many industrializing countries that follow inward-looking development strategies, the duration of protection for a given infant industry was limited and government assistance to selected firms was linked to meeting performance standards or to pursuing a strategic intent, such as building new markets or new competencies. Private firms were subjected to strong government pressures to export quickly, in return for favorable treatment. South Korea's strategy now has to switch from one based largely on low-cost mass production of electronic hardware to one involving greater product differentiation and a greater reliance on their own brand names and marketing. Returning to our framework, South Korea exhibits strengths in the environmental parameters, and in its industry structure.

FINDINGS

The Impact of the MSC

In assessing the likely impact which the Malaysia's MSC will have on its national development, few concrete conclusions can be drawn at this early stage. However, by using a standard framework, we can draw comparisons with similar initiatives in other countries, especially those in the same region, and we can speculate on how each of the factors in the framework might influence the outcome of the project. The framework reminds us that the context of any national initiative for the promotion, production or diffusion of ICTs is at least as important as the details of the project itself. In this regard, there are a number of general observations that emerge from the description of the MSC project, and the comparison with other similar ventures:

- Malaysia's choice of ICTs as a means of achieving developed status reflects the experiences of other newly industrializing countries in East Asia, although there are differences in detail between the circumstances and the experiences of each of them.

- Specific targets for the MSC have been publicly proclaimed, i.e., that of achieving fully-developed status by 2020, indicating an unusual degree of confidence in the outcome of a technology-based initiative as well as in the country's ability to sustain the momentum of its development and to resist competition from its neighbors.

- The intended pace of change represents in itself an enormous social challenge, propelling Malaysia from an agrarian colonial existence into world technological leadership in two generations.

- Rarely has so much been put at stake on the basis of so much faith in information technology. Many other countries and major multi-national corporations struggle to articulate such a clear vision for their IT investments as Malaysia's, and few manage to achieve results anywhere near as profound as Malaysia's ambitions. Should those ambitions materialize, there will be lessons for all from Malaysia's experience.

- Other than the need for a massive input into education in order to generate the knowledge workers that will be required to bring the MSC to fruition, little exists in the formal planning pronouncements which could be described as an acknowledgement of obstacles to achievement of the stated outcome. In particular, the social, behavioral and managerial aspects of IT diffusion and adoption, organizational learning and transformation, knowledge dissemination and institutional support receive scant attention.

In further assessing the likely impact of the MSC, two areas are worthy of attention. Firstly, the impact that the MSC will have on attracting foreign investment and promoting Malaysia as a global provider of multimedia products and services in competition with its regional rivals. The second area to address relates to the impact that the MSC will have on the internal development of the nation and its achievement of fully developed status by 2020.

In comparing Malaysia with its neighbors and competitors as a potential regional ICT center, one perspective is provided by the International Data Corporation's (IDC) annual Information Society Index, ranking countries on a variety of dimensions that relate to their information handling capability. For 1998, IDC ranked Singapore in fourth place, behind USA, Sweden and Finland. Other rankings were; Hong Kong, 12th; South Korea, 20th; and Malaysia, 34th. Projected rankings for 2002 placed Singapore in second place with more Asia-Pacific countries joining the upper ranks.

Despite the low ranking, it can be seen that Malaysia has some advantages for foreign firms wishing to establish an Asian regional presence in the ICT industry:

- *Cost*: Most of Malaysia's competitors suffer from higher costs for foreign investors, for space and for skilled labor. This is especially advantageous when Malaysia is compared to Singapore and Hong Kong.

- *Languages*. Malaysia's multi-cultural work force possesses language skills and cultural affinities with Asia's largest markets, as well as a general level of proficiency in English. This furnishes advantages over Taiwan and South Korea.

- *Incentives*. Government incentives for foreign investors are highly attractive, and are additionally leveraged by the low costs of operation. They offer advantageous inducements that are the most comprehensive in the region.

- *Stability*. Malaysia's stable business and political environment makes it potentially more attractive for foreign investment than Taiwan and Hong Kong, where relations with China are a constant source of tension.

There are also some disadvantages for foreign investors, which can be summarized as:

- *Lack of skilled workers.* Although most locations suffer from a shortage of skilled IT workers, Malaysia's shortages are especially acute given the scope and breadth of its plans for IT applications throughout the country.
- *Low diffusion of IT.* Typically, government represents around half the installed base of computers, and the lack of medium-sized firms as well as low rates of usage in the general population limits the scope and range of IT currently in use.

As a factor in the economic and social development of Malaysia, we can see that the MSC has some strong points and some weak points. The strong points are:

- A significant number of world-class companies have already committed to the project.
- The nation's attention has been drawn to the potential for IT as never before, generating a significant cultural adaptation that is now under way.
- Local industries are already benefiting from their association with the MNCs that have agreed to participate, resulting in growth in indigenous capability.
- Increasing numbers of Malaysian nationals are finding professional positions within Malaysia and more are attending tertiary education.

The weak points can be summarized as follows:

- The initial plans for expenditure were drawn up before the Asian financial crisis of 1997-98, so that some slow down in internal investment can be expected.
- Cultural adaptations towards the changes in society and in organizations that will be necessary to achieve the full benefits of ICTs will be hard to achieve.
- The spin-off effects of the MSC to the rest of the country are unclear. In particular, large proportions of the nation still lack a basic infrastructure.
- Development plans will be impeded by the acute shortage of skilled knowledge workers. It is unlikely that attracting foreigners can make up the shortfall.
- Low incomes militate against widespread deployment of computers among households, limiting the potential impact of some of the Flagship applications.

In summing up, there are a few critical measures that can be used to guide our assessment of the MSC. They can be divided into input measures and output measures. Input measures relate to the various activities that make up the project, which must be carried out successfully. Output measures assess the overall effects for the economy and for society in general, especially insofar as they relate to the achievement of developed status targeted by Vision 2020.

Input Measures

The requisite level of investment and participation by major external IT companies must be achieved. Malaysia must be able not only to continue to attract top-line enterprises, but must also be capable of retaining them. Currently, the MSC parades its low start-up and operating costs as major inducements for external investors. The problem with this strategy is that in a lowest cost game, there can only be one winner. Should other nations provide similar facilities at even lower cost, then Malaysia may have to consider implementing exit inhibitors that will reduce the attractions of such alternatives to the multinational corporations that have already established operations in the MSC. Other input related measures relate to the passing of Cyber laws, infrastructure development and the growth of education in IT subjects.

In addition, the flagship applications must achieve the goal of kick-starting the multimedia enterprises that have opened up in the MSC and they must transform Malaysian society in the manner for which they have been designed. Given the catching up that is necessary for Malaysia to be able to describe itself as an information society, these represent considerable challenges. In particular, the level of internal diffusion of IT in Malaysia must be increased by way of technology transfer from the multinational corporations to local companies and to the indigenous population.

Output Measures

Output related measures that have already been targeted by the government include growth in the range of skills in the workforce, improving balance of payments and rising GDP per capita. These factors are fairly easy to measure but it is often difficult to isolate the effects that individual causes have on each of them. Furthermore, given the competitive stance of other Asian countries in promoting themselves as regional centers for ICT industries, another output measure of success relates to the extent to which Malaysia is able to out-shine its regional neighbors. Consequently, account has to be taken of the impact that their ICT initiatives have on their own economies in assessing the effectiveness of the MSC on Malaysia's.

Conclusions and Implications

As a prescription for IT-led economic development, the MSC is arguably the boldest, grandest and most ambitious scheme the world has seen. Rarely has so much faith been pinned on IT as a means for achieving so much i.e., transforming Malaysian society from a developing third-world economy into a fully developed nation. The architects of such a scheme must be admired for their courage and vision. A neutral observer can hardly fail to be impressed by the pace with which the government has pushed through its agenda as well as by the apparent willingness of the rest of Malaysian society to go along with it.

Bill Gates captures the flavor of the public doctrine associated with the MSC in the Malaysian press (New Sunday Times, March 15, 1998).

"Malaysia offers a fine blueprint through the MSC initiative for how a developing country can use technology to move to the forefront of modern industry. All of the technology projects in the MSC initiative involve approaches that I have called the "digital nervous system" and the "web lifestyle". These are ways to use technology to create greater efficiencies in government operations, to serve citizens better, to improve and broaden education, and to help businesses compete globally."

Another perspective is provided by the UK's Guardian newspaper, see box 2. However, some cautionary indicators are required in order to achieve a more balanced perspective. Probably the most public criticism of the MSC appeared in Business Week under the front cover banner headline of "Mahathir's High-Tech Folly" (Einhorn and Prasso, 1999). The article characterized the MSC as "one of the most ambitious state-run projects ever conceived in Asia." It went on to suggest that several of the promised investments by leading international IT companies were unlikely to materialize. This was suggested partly as a result of the Malaysian government's measures to protect its economy from the worst ravages of the Asian economic crisis of 1997/98, and the political unrest provoked by the arrest of the former Deputy Prime Minister, Anwar Ibrahim. The article also drew some comparisons with Malaysia's competing neighbors, such as Singapore and Hong Kong, suggesting that they were better placed economically to attract the overseas investments that will be required by the eventual regional leader in high-tech industries. The MSC responded to the criticism by posting onto its web site allegations of mischievous intent and shoddy reporting, and by outlining the extent of progress so far.

Box 2. Malaysia's Multimedia Super Corridor

"There is something a little bizarre about all this futuristic talk. Just 20 years ago, Malaysia was still an overwhelmingly agrarian country dependent on rubber, tin and palm oil. Then it caught the industrialization bug and transformed itself within little over two decades compared with the 150 years it took Britain. To Western eyes, the super-corridor has moved with reckless, alien speed. For an Asian tiger, it is the norm. The sheer speed of it all can easily lull one into a false sense of expectancy, as if it is all perfectly natural. Hardly. This is happening in a nation still in the process of industrializing, where many of those over the age of 55 live in traditional villages or kampongs, where the education system leaves much to be desired and where there is a desperate shortage of skilled technicians. Malaysia totally lacks the capacity to realize the corridor on its own. Malaysia knows this and that is why it has scoured the world for the companies and techno-brains that can help. If this latest gamble with modernity pays off, as all indications suggest it will, then the ideas that inform it will be progressively applied across the country. Malaysia will move from a rural economy to an information age with little more than a hop step and a jump." .... The Guardian

---

According to opposition leader, Lim Kit Siang, compared to Singapore, Malaysia has been quite slow in realizing the critical importance of IT in enhancing competitive advantage in the global marketplace as well as the quality of life of Malaysians. He refers to the ranking by the International Telecommunications Union (ITU) of 39 nations in terms of their "multimedia readiness", which places Malaysia as 28th behind some of its Asian neighbors such as Japan, Singapore, Hong Kong, South Korea and Taiwan. Lim also makes reference to the possibility of a gap growing between the information-rich citizens of Malaysia and those who will remain information-poor, pointing to the high cost of computers compared to average Malaysian incomes.

Despite the criticisms, there can be no doubting the government's determination to make Malaysia an IT-centric economy. The futuristic concept of the MSC and its seductive rhetoric can be enthralling, to the extent that it is almost heresy in Malaysia to even question the predictions or to seek evidence that they are materializing. Although sometimes touted as a model for development, Malaysia's economy cannot yet be said to have totally moved away from its agrarian basis and its transition to a service-oriented economy, which the MSC implies, has still to be achieved. As has been discovered in other countries, for example Ireland, when MNCs are attracted by tax breaks and other incentives, short-term economic gains can emerge. But the MNCs tend to disappear when the tax breaks run out, sometimes leaving behind little in terms of technology or knowledge. The challenge for the MSC is to ensure that the pressure for short-term improvements is accompanied by measures that can provide for sustained levels of activity and growth.

In the wider context, the development of the MSC carries several implications for developing countries. Firstly, all governments require policies and formal structures for the adoption and diffusion of ICTs within their own countries. In an increasingly networked world, being made more so by the MSC and similar projects, connectivity and participation in the global economy will be key ingredients of economic and social development. As commercial activity becomes increasingly global, those who are not connected to the global network will be shut out. For most developing nations, attracting foreign investors presents the major opportunity for acquiring the technologies that global commerce is becoming increasingly dependent on. Consequently, polices that make a country attractive for foreign investment will be crucial for success.

Although the MSC and the other Asian models mentioned in this chapter grew out of IT manufacturing bases, the essential component of sustainable growth based on ICTs is the extent to which a nation is able to use IT effectively. Malaysia has realized that although the enormous global demand for computers during the 1980s and 90s helped it develop its electronics industry and to expand its economy at consistently impressive rates, a further engine of growth is required in order to accelerate the earlier pace of development and take the nation forward to fully developed status. It is expected that future growth in Malaysia will be derived from its intellectual capacities, which will be leveraged through ICTs.

Finally, despite any misgivings, the association between technology and growth is clear, and as Manuel Castells put it, "the reintegration of social development and economic growth through technological innovation, informational management and shared world development will require massive technological upgrading of countries, firms, and households around the world" (Castells, 1998). The MSC demonstrates how one country is attempting to achieve such an upgrading.

Mini-Case: MSC STARTUPS RE-ENGINEERING BUSINESS

Asia Travel Network (ATN), an MSC web-based travel reservation system, was founded in 1997. It broke even in its second year and moved into profit, targeting revenues of US$3.9 million in 1999. It claims to be the first successful electronic travel reservation company in Asia. With 1,600 clients from 51 countries at its site (www.asiatravelmart.com) it undercuts most travel agencies. Currently, other travel agents make up 80% of ATN's bookings, but CEO Alex Kong predicts that individual customers will soon overtake wholesale purchasers as a result of his US$2.6 million marketing campaign.

JobStreet (www.jobstreet.com) is a web-based recruitment service that obtained MSC status in early 1999. It has 100,000 job seekers on its books and 1,200 employers. The job seekers pay nothing, the companies US$210 per month, matching up to 150,000 positions each month. The company, which was formed by four friends from Harvard, MIT and Wharton, is expanding into the Philippines and Singapore.

Three Malaysians from National University of Singapore obtained a NASDAQ listing for their company MyWeb Inc., three years after coming together to do business. The company offers emerging Internet users the ability to go online using a set-top box for US$180 to work with an existing TV set rather than having to purchase expensive PCs which cost about US$1,000.

Two architects and a former stockbroker launched a web site that offers discount coupons with no expiry date. WWW.e1000.com has signed up 30 retailers ranging from fast-food chains to cinemas to offer discount coupons which users can print out and then redeem at the participating outlets.

STUDY QUESTIONS

1. What is the purpose of Malaysia's Multimedia Super Corridor project? How does it intend to achieve this purpose?

2. What national policies for Information and Communication Technologies should developing countries in Asia implement in order to develop their economies?

3. Describe some of the inhibiting factors within Asian countries that might prevent them from making full use of Information and Communication Technologies for their national development.

4. Some nations are better prepared to enter the information age than are others. Design five national indicators of "preparedness for the information age" and use them to compare and contrast seven Asian countries. Search the Internet for the data you need.

5. Describe some of the differences between Malaysia and the USA and relate them to Malaysia's plans for developing the MSC.

REFERENCES

Castells, M., The Information Age: Economy, Society, and Culture: Vol. III End of millennium. Oxford, Blackwell, 1998.

Chin, J. and Heong, CY., Cyber Czar: Othman Yeop Abdullah's vision for Malaysia's Multimedia Super Corridor, Asia Inc. Vol. 8, No. 8, August 1999.

Dedrick, J. and Kraemer, K.L, Asia's Computer Challenge: Threat or Opportunity to the U.S.? Oxford University Press, 1998.

Eihorn, B. and Prasso, S., Mahathir's High-Tech Folly: The Silicon Valley of East Asia isn't dead, but it is badly wounded, Business Week International Edition, March 22, 1999.

Hanna, N., Guy, K. and Arnold, E., The Diffusion of Information Technology: Experience of Industrial Countries and Lessons for Developing Countries, World Bank Discussion Papers; 281, World Bank, Washington, 1995

Heeks, R., The Uneven Profile of Indian Software Exports, Development Informatics Working Paper Series, Working Paper No. 3, the Institute for Development Policy and Management, University of Manchester, UK. http://www.man.ac.uk/idpm/diwpf3.htm

INRIA http://www.inria.fr/Presentation/historique-eng.html

Kraemer, KL., Dedrick, J., Hwang, CY., Tu, TC., and Yap, CS., Entrepreneurship, Flexibility, and policy Coordination: Taiwan's Computer Industry, The Information Society, Vol. 12, No. 3, 215-249, 1996.

Raman, K.S. and Yap. C.S., From a resource rich country to an information rich society: an evaluation of Information Technology policies in Malaysia, Information Technology for Development, Vol. 7, 109-131, 1996.

Roche, Edward, Brazilian Informatics Policy: The High Costs of Building a National Industry, The Information Society, Vol.7, 1990.

Siowck-Lee Gan, An Overview of Information Technology and Education in Malaysia, Journal of Global Information Management, Vol. 6, No. 1, 27-32, 1998.

Useful links:

CIA Factbook – Malaysia: http://www.odci.gov/cia/publications/factbook/my.html

Business Week: http://www.businessweek.com

Multimedia Development Corporation: http://www.mdc.com.my

MSC News; http://xtremedia.com/asp/msc_mainpage.asp

Malaysia's National Productivity Council: http://www.npc.org.my/report97_1.htm

Malaysia's National Economic Recovery Plan: http://thestar.com.my/archives/neac/welcome.html

New Straits Times (Malaysia): http://www.nstpi.com.my

3

E-Commerce and the Information Environment in an Emerging Economy: Russia at the Turn of the Century

Elia V. Chepaitis
Fairfield University

ABSTRACT

This chapter examines the relationship in emerging economies between the information environment and e-commerce, and surveys cultural and economic factors which influence information resources in emerging markets. The author investigates the state of data communications in Russia: EDI, external business partnerships, the transfer of knowledge based systems, the telecommunications infrastructure, the spread of wireless communications, and the expansion of Internet access. Improvements in business culture and private information environments offer a contrast with a parallel widening of the "digital divide", the gulf between those who have access to computers and the Internet, and those who do not.

INTRODUCTION

Russia's E-Commerce in 2000

This chapter examines the relationship between the information environment and e-commerce, and surveys relevant cultural, political, economic, and social factors which affect the development of robust data and data communications in this decade. These factors include global networks, external business partnerships, the transfer of knowledge-based systems, the telecommunications infrastructures, the spread of wireless communications, and the maturation of domestic business, particularly in the service sector.

What are the prospects for successful e-commerce in Russia's emergent market-driven economy? Like most of Europe, but more severely, Russia lags behind the United States in electronic commerce for three reasons: a lack of capital investment in information technology (IT), inflexible labor markets, and the lack of domestic computer-manufacturers (*Economist,* "Wo ist Goldlilocks?). However, Russia suffers from additional disadvantages which are typical of emerging economies, which Europe does not share: the lack of stable financial practices, an immature telecommunications infrastructure, an egregious lack of security, endemic fraud, and a poor information environment characterized by poor data quality.

Can Russia capitalize on the popular obsession with the Internet and use telecommunications to compensate for systemic problems? Economic failures reduced the GDP by half from 1992 to 1998, and left Russia with an economy smaller than that of the

Netherlands by 1999. Conversely, will economic malaise prevent Russia from exploiting e-commerce to achieve stability, growth, and competitive advantage? The author's thesis is that improvements in data quality are vital for economic well-being and enterprise development in Russia, which must predate e-commerce. Unfortunately, the information environment is so poor in Russia that the emergence of robust data resources will be slow and incremental.

Three confluent but incomplete revolutions began to transform Russia from 1986 to 2000: the transition from a command to a demand economy, the utilization of commercial information, and the spread of information technology (IT), especially telecommunications. The post-Soviet demand for IT and connectivity spawned a massive increase in electronics retailers, board designers, software authors, pirates and legitimate importers. The availability and increasing affordability of personal computers, printers, fax-modems, copiers coincided with unprecedented imports of consumer goods and of uncensored foreign news and contacts. The emergence of the computer as a global communication device produced not only a flood of information from abroad, but also fostered Russians' growing self-image as members of a worldwide wired community. The economic and political elite, as well as entrepreneurs, scholars, artists, and students swiftly sought to cultivate strategic relationships abroad. Interest in business and home computers, and in Internet access, soared in the 1990s, particularly in the larger cities. A 1997 article, "Entangled in the World Wide Web" in *Sputnik* stated that in Moscow, 5,000 users had access in 1995, and 200,000 in 1997 (contrasted with 600,000 in all of Russia). *Sputnik* analyzed the keen interest in the chess match between Gary Kasparov and IBM's Big Blue, and the dependence on computer technology by Yeltsin's heart surgeon. The article stated that the rise in PC sales from 1.2 million in 1992 to 1.6 million in 1997 was driven by hope for web access. Interestingly, 50% of PC sales were for home computing in 1992, and 60% in 1997.

By 2000, mobile phones were mass marketed and a modern GSM network, together with competing Internet Service Providers, emerged in Moscow and Petersburg ("Ivan the talkative", *Economist*; Peron and McHenry). In a decade when most periodicals could not survive financially, newsstand copies of Computer *world Rossiya, Expert Games,* and *Network* sell briskly, and Bill Gates' columns in *Moscow News* covers much-discussed topics such as "How will computer communications affect relationships" and "The Internet and the price of medicine". The ubiquitous availability of Windows-based platforms not only linked Russia to information worldwide, but also provided a nationwide standard interface.

E-mail's popularity soared in the 1990s because it was more reliable than the postal service or faxes, but additional private and public investments in on-line services have been modest, particularly after the financial crisis of August 1998. Even before the crisis, state initiatives, such as the Federal Fund for Electronics Development, founded to foster electronics manufacturing and to improve the telecommunications infrastructure, were ineffectual and under funded (Clarke, 1995).

Prospects for Early E-Commerce

If advanced economies are a model, early e-commerce leadership will first appear in Russia in fields such as retailing, financial services, publishing, reference sites, and software development; the author believes that Russia may be a decade away from this stage. Business to customer applications is constrained by the lack of direct debits from checking accounts or credit cards. At the turn of the century, e-commerce features a proliferation of modest local Web sites from Vladivostok to Voronezh, local service providers, and online commerce in areas such as child adoption, business consulting, job placement, travel and tourism. The role of services increased from 37% of GDP in 1980 to 55% in 1997, and the potential for additional growth in this sector would be massive under optimal circumstances (Morgan Stanley Dean Witter, 1999).

Researchers face significant challenges in assessing opportunities for e-commerce in Russia. A marked increase in online promotions, Web site development, and data communications characterizes the Russian economy, but the impact is, undoubtedly, far less than that of more mature e-commerce in India, the Pacific Rim, the European Union, and, indeed, most of the rest of Eastern Europe. Globally, 80% of global e-commerce consists of business-to-business exchanges; customer e-commerce is modest and concentrated in areas such as travel and tourism, stock brokerage, and publishing ("Dotty about e-commerce?", *Economist*). It is difficult to measure the firmness of strategic plans for this inter-business e-commerce in Russia, although interviews from 1994 to 1998 suggest a huge pent-up demand for connectivity and e-business.

RELEVANCE FOR DEVELOPING COUNTRIES

Information Environments and E-Markets

Although the differences between Russia and most developing countries are profound in geopolitical status, culture, infrastructure, education levels, and natural endowments, Russia shares a salient problem with many emerging economies: because of poor data resources and efficient markets, effective information systems (IS) are scarce, and the promise of e-commerce is limited in the short term, at the least. In Russia and many developing areas, the salient obstacle to networked business is not a shortage of hardware, software, computer literacy, or adequate infrastructure.

In fact, these resources are improving markedly, aided by development policy, private investment, education reform, and foreign assistance and alliances. Indeed, global transfers of communication and information technology (IT) have accelerated: cellular phones, faxes, desktop computers, VCRs, and copy machines are becoming commonplace in urban centers, even in Russian cities where the abacus is still in use. The obstacle to integrated electronic systems is a deep-rooted and neglected problem--poor data quality. Inadequate data quality curtails the effectiveness of electronic, oral and manual systems. In developing countries, concepts of legacy systems can be expanded to include inherited hardware, software, and people, but also data stores. Data quality is affected negatively by inefficiencies and cultural proscriptions left by vanishing and non-viable economic systems, and by distinctive traditional organizational structures, cost constraints, widespread information hoarding or deception, and chronic financial or monetary instability. The author's main findings, summarized in Chart 1, may be used to assess information environments in other emerging economies.

⇒ A pervasive willingness to invest in connectivity for well-defined strategic goals
⇒ A poor information environment for e-commerce
⇒ An inadequate telecommunications and market infrastructure for e-commerce
⇒ Widespread skepticism about the idiosyncratic economy regarding: equity, wealth, and fiscal and monetary policy
⇒ In the short-term, effective transfers of Knowledge Based Systems and other EDI
⇒ The value of a Total Data Quality Management (TDQM) approach to compensate for public data mismanagement and fragmented markets
⇒ Improvements in business culture and private information environments, particularly in the service sector and in small business formation
⇒ Organizational shifts and technology shifts are significant drivers for e-commerce
⇒ E-commerce will broaden the "digital divide
Chart 1: Information Conditions in Emerging Economies: the Russian Model

This chapter will discuss the criticality of data quality for economic development and for electronic markets, the literature and the author's research methods, official and private information resources in Russia, and strategies to improve data quality for economic development.

Data and Information Poverty in Russia

Effective IS and e-commerce in Russia depend on a critical mass of robust data to support business information needs and manage crucial resources for economic development, yet Russia's environment is characterized by deep-rooted information poverty (Chepaitis, 1994). Information poverty can be defined first, as a paucity of useful information, and second, as an endemic condition, the lack of means to acquire the timely, accurate, and complete data needed to create useful information. In economic systems characterized by information poverty, it is difficult to enhance data quality because existing data stores and collection processes are inadequate. Information poverty and data quality are intrinsically linked: the problem is circular and a conundrum.

Since improved information resources precede effective economic development, IS researchers, business enterprises, and public agencies have begun to accept as an absolute priority the amelioration of acute data deficiencies, even if this campaign predates the adoption of IT (Avgerou, 1991). Within both developed and developing economies, a reassessment of data quality provides an occasion to refocus profitably on the definition of data quality within specific organizations. Business re-engineering, quality movements, and global linkages motivated IS researchers to challenge traditional definitions of quality which emphasize only accuracy. In the 1990s, researchers sparked interest in the concept of Total Data Quality Management (TDQM), the concept that data quality is the responsibility of all members of an organization, and they expanded the definition of data quality. TDQM research ranks the degree to which characteristics such as contextual value, interpretability, and accessibility matter to the "data consumer" (Strong, Madnick, Redman, Segev, and Wang, 1994).

In the second generation of e-commerce, it is these components of data quality that determine competitive advantage for virtual commerce in the 2000s *(Harvard Business Review*, November- December 1999). Quality data must not only be accessible and rich but also navigable to attract discriminating consumers; the information environment must provide resources relevant to the task at hand, which can be readily interpreted, accessible to users, and secure against damage and intrusion (Figure 1).

Intrinsic Data Quality
Data have quality in their own right, such as accuracy and freedom from defects

Contextual Data Quality
Relevance and value of the data for the task at hand

Representation Data Quality
Format and interpretability of data

Accessibility Data Quality
accessibility and security of data

Figure 1. The View of Data Consumers: The View of Data Consumers
(Strong, Mad nick, Redman, Segev, and Wang, 1994)

Russian entrepreneurs, foreign partners, and state authorities have low expectations for data improvement, based on their experiences of ubiquitous information shortages. These expectations are significant in Russia because data quality, as presented by Strong and Wang (Figure 1), is in the eye of the "data consumer", and the data consumer in Russia primarily defines data quality as accuracy.

For domestic and foreign enterprises seeking e-business there, an examination of data quality in itself can initiate data enrichment. To improve data quality, existing data supplies and the business environment can be investigated to find: what types of data are unavailable; why are certain desired data uncollected, hoarded, or undervalued; is desired data delivered to the right users in an appropriate format; how relevant are fields for transactions, summaries, and decision making; how reliable and meaningful are temporal field values such as costs and prices; and how critical are data deficits for resource management, productivity, and competitive advantage; is security neglected or problematic?

In Russia, a salient question is: how soon can managers and policy makers develop strategic information resources during turbulent times? How can IS improvement be supported in a period of macro-economic uncertainty and without huge investment in the inadequate telecommunications infrastructure? The business climate is poor but improving, and improved data quality is necessary to enable managers to evaluate emerging options for enterprise development and to establish performance measurements for both the short- and long-term. Capital investments in IS generate cost-effective solutions in other functional areas, such as inventory management. Also, systems development is educative for numerous stakeholders whose experience with quality systems and cross-functional goal-setting may be limited. As a bonus, sharing robust data and successful applications creates an atmosphere of communication and trust. Poor data quality and lack of access can perpetuate culture-based prejudices against sharing information. This prejudice hampers database design and administration, integrated application development, the distribution of telecommunication and information services, and information resource management. Data quality can be enhanced in Russia by not only building on the past, but also capitalizing on discontinuities, revolutionary changes which present striking opportunities for early industry leaders and global partners. A powerful motivation to secure quality data for Russian enterprises is the need to create open, extended, and integrated IS and business systems for survival in a global economy: not only in export industries but also in domestic organizations that cannot compete with foreign imports (Tapscott and Caston, 1993; Castells, 1998; Schechter, 1998).

The author offers three observations: first, whether connectivity is advanced or primitive, seminal data quality improvements in Russia will occur at the organizational level, rather than in the public sector. Second, well-communicated management commitments to data quality are central to effective IS and to electronic relationships, and third, some data collection and processing methods used in advanced economies are not feasible in developing nations but data quality is achievable nonetheless.

LITERATURE

The Information Environment

Palvia and Palvia (1996) identified data quality as a pressing MIS issue in less-developed nations, and Avgerou (1991) and Wilson (1998) emphasize the need to assign top priority to improvements in data quality in economic development, to provide a foundation for information systems infrastructures. A growing body of literature has emerged on information environments and data quality. Two germane approaches to re-engineering and information resource building are Davenport's *Information Ecology* presents research on the critical components of enriched information environments within organizations, and provides portable models and strategies for emerging economies also. Tapscott and Caston claim that information technology (IT) cannot be exploited unless more open, extended, integrated, and flexible organizations are constructed. Paquin's and Turgeon's promotion of a customer-centered approach links quality IS and quality service, and their thesis dovetails neatly with the article by Evans and Wurster (1999) which provides a sound analysis of competitive advantage in the second generation of e-commerce. They focuses on rich and accessible information environments with elegant navigation tools and their thesis is not encouraging for Russia.

Although, no field studies of data deficits or of projects to improve information resources have yet appeared on Russia, numerous authors examined the problem of information scarcities in Russia for almost thirty years, dating from Hard 's *et al* (1967) analysis of the impact of Leninist ideology on econometrics and data management. Brand (1994) discusses the enduring liability of centralized planning on data into the 1990s. Although data quality and information shortages are not the target of his research, Ashland (1995) discusses the twin problems of business integrity and data integrity in numerous areas: official statistics, commodity prices (published by the Moscow Interbank Foreign Currency Exchange), commercial journals, and Russian research institutes.

Interestingly, Aslund finds that public studies sponsored by international groups or relief agencies such as the International Monetary Fund, the World Bank, Organization for Economic Cooperation and Development, and the European Bank for Reconstruction are more reliable than studies conducted by the Russian government. The quality and quantity of foreign data and metadata improved through the 1990s, are improving, as seen in *Russia 1994* by Chamber World Network, published in English with the assistance of the German Chambers of Industry and Commerce; this publication contains a superior business directory and a series of statistics and industry reports intended to assist foreign investors.

Economic Conditions

From 1994 to 1999, foreign studies and online resources flowed *into* Russia; data communications facilitated cooperative research, partnerships, and commercial studies. Nonetheless, primary data on business practices and economic conditions in Russia is scarce and problematic, particularly for comparisons with other emerging economies.For example, in the 1998 *Global Benchmarks: Comprehensive Measures of Development*, Yeung and Mathieson omit Russia from the 108 countries studied since reliable data, even indicators such as GDP or indebtedness, are unavailable. However, a consistently reliable picture of overall conditions and challenges is available through continuously updated references such as *Russia: A Country Study* (Curtis, 1998), which offers a cogent view of the direction and magnitude of change during the past decade. Anecdotal evidence and "war stories", about endemic problems such as miscommunication, misinformation, and unethical information behaviors are ubiquitous (Aslund, 1995; Smith, 1993,1995; Handelman, 1995). Zisk's insightful study (1998) of the behavior of former Soviet enterprises in the new Russia describes systemic obstacles to data collection and dissemination in the transition economy. An outstanding petroleum industry study by Yergin and Gustafson, (1995) describes with some depth the volatility, lack of credibility, and Byzantine complexity in the post-Soviet information environment, as do frequent reports in the Wall Street Journal (Whalen and Bahree, 2000). Gustafson published a broader, definitive description and analysis of the Russian economy in 2000.

A spate of research on management strategies and global competitiveness considers anomalies in market formation (Boycko, Schleifer, and Vishny, 1998; Zisk, 1998). Castells (2000) examined the criticality of Russia's full membership in a networked society of circulating information, capital, and commodities. Chepaitis, who worked in Russia in 1991,

1992, 1994, and 1998, as a consultant and a Fulbright Fellow, described information management and information poverty (1994), data quality (1996), and information ethics (1997, 1999).

Unfortunately, little research has been conducted by Russian scholars, although the popular press in Russia discusses issues such as electronic crime and external information frequently. Investigative journalism in a few periodicals such as the *Moscow Times* features reliable studies of changing business practices and IT, such as a 1998 study of the scope and the affects of software piracy. At the turn of the century, scholars, academic journals, learned societies, and libraries suffer from lack of funding. From 1994 to mid-1998, the author found no relevant publications in the few academic journals housed in the Lenin Library in Moscow or regional repositories in Rostov and Kemerovo.

Because Russia is of such major geopolitical importance, scholars can be expected to develop new lines of research as access and funding improves. However, from the 1990s into the 200s, field studies in Russia are as risky as trade and investment, and nearly impossible for researchers who cannot speak Russian and are not working in supportive industries or institutions. Ironically, the lack of a healthy information environment presents a major problem for research on the information environment itself.

One comparative assessment of IS maturity is noteworthy. In the 1970s, a three-tiered country classification of computer industry development potential by the United Nations divided nations into advanced, operational, and basic levels, and placed the Soviet Union in the second tier, with Hong Kong, Venezuela, Greece, India, Mexico, and others (Palvia, Palvia, and Zigli, 1992). It is clear in the 1990s that Russia has fallen behind those nations.

RESEARCH METHODS AND RESULTS

The author interviewed forty-four Russian and foreign entrepreneurs, managers, policy-makers, and economists from 1991-1995 (Tables 1 and 2), and another thirty in a subsequent study in 1998 (Table 3) with a follow-up in 1999. The subjects in both studies were not chosen at random, but were selected for their experience, information access, and continued availability. The interviews were conducted in a variety of settings, primarily in newly-formed enterprises in three geographic areas: the Moscow and St. Petersburg hub, Western Siberia, and Rostov-Taganrog.

In 1991, 1992, and 1994, the author primarily worked in Siberia, an area larger than the United States with a climate similar to Montreal in most cities, and established numerous contacts, especially in Kemerovo, a major industrial city with a population in excess of half a million people. Kemerovo is the source of significant attention from the central government because of export industries that yield hard currency and because of labor unrest among the coal miners under both Gorbachev and Yeltsin. The standard of living lags behind Moscow and St. Petersburg; Siberians often refer to the imperialism of European Russia and complain that they are treated like colonies, but they, in turn, are biased and occasionally violent toward numerous non-Russians. The author became a social outcast in her apartment building for interviewing a Georgian greengrocer; Russians associate Georgians with organized crime, and the landlady followed a claim that the occupants would be murdered in their beds with an eviction notice. Questionnaires would have been the preferred method of data collection, but these instruments are unwelcome and suspect in Russia, and inhibit open and ongoing communication, since they attract official attention. In fact, many Russians distrust and fear research which identifies individuals or enterprises by name. Interviews had to be conducted with great informality, without tape recordings or extensive on-site note taking, since these inhibited dialog and erected barriers to future contacts (Table 1). Notes often were reconstructed from memory off-site, occasionally after several hours had elapsed, and the author's records and laptop were kept in a secure apartment with a double iron door, due to widespread theft. In 1994, carrying or using a laptop in public made subjects uncomfortable by drawing public attention to the research and interview process, but this was less a problem by 1998. Interviews took place on the street, in computer labs, on airplanes, predominantly in Russian, frequently with the assistance of student interns in Kemerovo and Taganrog.

Table 1. Interviews with Russian citizens (44) (in Palvia, Palvia and Roche, 1996)

Firm/Occupation	Type	Location
GEMMA telecom director	G	Irkutsk
Irkutsk State U. Rector, foreign relations	E	Irkutsk
AG garden tools, management intern	P/S	Kemerovo
ASM air cargo, management intern	P/S	Kemerovo
Chemmash, marketing services, manager	P/S	Kemerovo
Deputy Chief, mayor's office	A	Kemerovo
Development, Junior Achievement, director	A	Kemerovo
EC consultant, lumber exports	C	Kemerovo
Fedorev regional library, operations	A	Kemerovo
Fedorev regional library, acquisitions	A	Kemerovo
GARANT insurance	P/S	Kemerovo
Georgian greengrocer	P/S	Kemerovo
FATA joint venture, industrial tools, sales	G	Kemerovo
Hospital intern/physician	P/S	Kemerovo
Informatics, software development	P/S	Kemerovo
Intourist travel, manager	A	Kemerovo
Kemerovo airport, management intern	A	Kemerovo
Kemerovo city ambulance dispatcher/manager	E	Kemerovo
Kemerovo State University, vice rector	E	Kemerovo
Kemerovo Polytechnic U., Dean of Economics	E	Kemerovo
Knigi bookstore, manager/buyer	P/S	Kemerovo
KROMBANK, deputy manager	P/S	Kemerovo
Kuzbass External Associates, President	G	Kemerovo
Kuzbass Primapolis, shareholding firm, VP	G	Kemerovo
Kuzbassobank, chair, board of directors	P/S	Kemerovo
The Professional, advertising	P/S	Kemerovo
PROMEST, import/export, director	P/S	Kemerovo
Raspadskaya coal, environmental engineer	C	Kemerovo
Restaurant manager	P/S	Kemerovo
Tapes, audio supplies, manager	P/S	Kemerovo
Siemens sales manager	P/S	Kemerovo
Ziminka coal, tools development, manager	G	Kemerovo
Sigma, Russo-Japanese consultant/manager	G	Krasnoyarsk
Moscow Central Stock Exchange, Vice President	P/S	Moscow
Moskva bookstore, sales	P/S	Moscow
Produce farm, privatized sovkhoz, director	P/S	Moscow
Distance education, project director	E	Tomsk
Dom. small hotel owner	P/S	Tomsk
Tomsk radio systems, IS developer	E	Tomsk
Tomsk State U.-Russian-Am. exchange, dir.	E	Tomsk
Siberian Adult Education Academy, dir.	E	Tomsk
YUGANSKNEFTGAS, oil and gas, management intern	G	Tyumen
Kouchat fried chicken rest., manager	P/S	Vladimir
Key A= Public Admin. P/S= goods/services E= Education		
C= Consulting G= Global partners		

Significant variations in attitude according to different occupations, generations, and classes were obvious in three areas: the respectability of business occupations, the value of business education, and, most significantly, the probability that change in the next decade will probably be positive, rather than negative. Interesting strategies for dealing with information poverty emerged. For example, YUGANSKNEFTEGAS, a mammoth oil and gas conglomerate, sent over 1,000 Russians abroad for business education, into environments in which business practice is mature and information resources are not scarce; most will owe years of service to YUGANSKNEFTEGAS and associated enterprises. Kuzbass External Associates also manages foreign business education for scores of interns whose organizations pay all educational costs, plus a commission, in hard currency. A more common strategy, for small enterprises, is to learn to do business with minimal, accurate data until conditions improve.

Table 2. Interviews (1991-95) with Foreign Citizens Working in Russia (12)
(Palvia, Palvia, and Roche, 1996)

Firm/Occupation	Type	Location
Baptist missionary	P/S	Irkutsk
Boston Consulting Group, real estate	C	Irkutsk
Takanabe, Japanese, lumber, President	G	Irkutsk
INL International	G	Krasnodar
Dutch agronomist	C	Kemerovo
Fulbright, Library Science consultant	C	Moscow
Mercedes Benz, German manager	G	Moscow
Sister cities coordinator, U.S. Embassy	A	Moscow
USAID housing rehabilitation, supervisor	P/S	Moscow
Central Asian consultant	C	New York
T.T.E., civil engineering, president	G	
Ohio State joint ventures Ph.D. research	E	
Ohio State joint ventures Ph.D. research		Tomsk
Key: **A** = Public Administrative **P/S**= Products or Services		
E = Education **C** = Consulting **G** = Global		

The participants were asked about four areas: business conditions in Russia, the goals of the organization, their information needs, and their information resources. By and large, except for the largest and most internationalized firms, the respondents expressed caution and modest optimism in all areas. Business objectives highlighted these seven priorities: stability, personal security, cost-control, solvency, and the acquisition of well-endowed partners, know-how, and business acumen. Six factors, which were in general more strategic than tactical, were apparently of secondary importance: growth, quality products or services, customer loyalty, price competitiveness, the acquisition of subsidiaries, and in-house innovation. The author was pleased with the simplicity and logic of responses to the four questions. In general, attitudes and beliefs about contemporary business conditions affected the definition of organization goals, which in turn prompted well-focused examination of information needs and resources.

In addition, a small, group of foreigners working in Russia was also interviewed from 1991 to 1995 (Table 2), using the same four questions, and these interviews yielded significant insights into not only change, but the lack of change in cultural attitudes toward information sharing in Russia. These participants were struck by the lingering effect of the Soviet system, the popular distrust of profits, and widespread attitude that change will probably be for the worse. None had sufficient information resources in Russia, and all revised goals and responsibilities accordingly; most used advanced IT and external data resources, and all but one, the president of T.E.E., thought that the transition to a healthy market economy would require at least twenty years.

From 1996 to 1998, a new set of subjects also stated that they did not have the business data they needed to pursue their business strategies (Table 3). The interviews revealed, not surprisingly, persistent problems with data accuracy, and also access, and interpretability and format, growing in importance and matching the MIT model by Strong, Madnick, Redman, Segev, and Wang (1994) discussed above. Between the 1991 and 1996-1998 interviews, a shift had occurred toward service industries and the perceived urgency of improved information access. The sessions focused on the criticality of not only quality domestic data, but also the attendant need for partners, external data, know-how, and connectivity.

Table 3. 1998 Interviews (24)

Firm/Occupation/Global Partners	Future	Connectivity
TRTU President/G	2	1
Hyundai factory/management/G	1	1
Novotel Manager/G	1	1
Lombard insurance and finance manager	1	1
Ec. Development mayor's office/G	1	1
CEO insurance agency	2	1
EC consultant, shipyard partnership (TACIS)/G	2	1
Taganrog municipal library, operations management	2	2
Rostov regional library, acquisitions	2	1
Chief Pediatrics, Royal College of Surgeons, Rostov/G	2	1
Georgian émigrés/ restaurateurs	3	3
Owner,Samuel Clothes manufacturing and sales	1	3
West computer retail/G	1	1
Chief, Nokia robotics lab/G	2	1
Intourist travel, Rostov manager/G	3	1
DIMIR electronics	2	2
Manager, MSU joint venture/G	1	1
Lobbyist/economist for FTZ in Taganrog/G	2	1
Doninvest/banking-currency exchange/G	1	1
Dean, School of Economics/Business/ G	1	1
Canadian aid workers CLS/G	2	1
Environmental engineer/G	2	1
Medical management software, author	1	1
International liaison, TRTU/G	1	1
Connectivity: 1= critical; 2= somewhat important; 3 = not very important		
Future: 1 = forward; 2 = toward socialist 3 = return to Communism forecast		
G= Global partnerships		

Twenty of the twenty-four subjects stated that linkage was critical, for a variety of purposes: electronic data interchange (EDI), information discovery, marketing analysis, and the acquisition of knowledge-based systems. The subjects ranked six problems as pressing, out of a list of eight, in the following order: access, price, reliability, service providers, content, and flexibility. Security and control were ranked last, by a wide margin.

Three outstanding projects are good examples of the benefits of sustained connectivity in the Rostov region. After Chernobyl, teams of German research arrived with massive medical relief and funding for cancer research. The project evolved into a hugely successful program to increase the longevity of victims of childhood leukemia, and features an ongoing transfer of know-how and other support (Andrenkova, 1998). Second, a Technical Assistance to the Commonwealth of Independent States (TACIS) team, based in the Netherlands, transferred a knowledge-based system on shipbuilding to Taganrog. The contact began as a sister city project, now funded by the European Union (EU). Third, TACIS representatives visit Taganrog frequently and have co-authored Taganrog's application to the Rostov authorities for a free trade zone on the Sea of Azov; TACIS's provided well-documented projections of regional economic benefits (Baalen, 1998).

INFORMATION RESOURCES: ASSETS AND LIABILITIES

The Development of the Infrastructure

The construction of a telecommunication infrastructure in Russia involves: the foundation of commercial utilities, the emergence of competing service providers, affordable flat-rate access, and stable external partnerships. Furthermore, successful e-commerce requires associated industries and secondary services which Russia lacks: freight forwarding companies, customs brokers, credit cards, checking accounts, insurance, and business law for enforceable contracts and unequivocal jurisdiction. The state attempted to reorganize and modernize its communications infrastructure, passing control to regional and local enterprises, mainly joint stock companies. Long distance and international services were given to a new organization, Rostelekom, while the government retained control of satellite transmissions. Russia had only 176 telephones per thousand persons in 1994, mainly concentrated in urban areas (Curtis, 1998). In 1995, 86% of telephones were urban, and more than 10 million potential customers were awaiting installation. Development of the telecommunications infrastructure depends upon foreign investment and joint ventures, but foreign funding lags behind expectations. Notorious contract disputes, the default on foreign debt in August of 1998, and spikes in inflation discourage potential investors, as do delays in privatization and declining national services, from shipping and rail transport to health care and the government's accounts payable (Whalen and Bahree). The government appears unable or unwilling to collect revenues, with dire consequences: "A leadership that cannot tax cannot govern," notes Schecter (176).

In 1998, public transportation, medical, and educational systems operated on irregular schedules, with scant supplies, irregular remuneration for public employees, and ill-maintained equipment. Not only did the prices of communication, transport, education, and health services rise, but investments in the crumbling infrastructure experienced a real decline from 1986 to 1998, as Russian productivity plummeted and inflation occasionally rose to 3 digits. Also, the pricing structure of numerous public utilities and services changed, many were privatized, and delivery was disrupted. Smith (1993) estimates, in his "optimistic" scenario, that several decades are required for stabilization. In this environment, small business formation and commercial communications are impressive in contrast to the embarrassing array of problems in the public sector, including the inability of the government to pay salaries and pensions according to established schedules.

The vigor in the private sector, featuring technological and functional dualism, has a demonstration affect, and enhances self-help movements across enterprises. Visible islands of laptops, clusters of private T1 lines, Internet services, and software shops underscore the dynamism of the private sector, particularly in emerging services such as finance and insurance (Yemelyanenko and Petrov, 1998). The need for external aid and new alliances was accentuated by Russia's economic collapse from 1986 to 1991, followed by declines in productivity, the condition of crucial infrastructures, and traditional services from 1991 to 1997. However, resistance to change steadily eroded in the 1990s with the increased availability of credit, even at interest rates which seem prohibitive in the West. Heavy private and public investments in IT created the widespread impression that "Westernization", through membership in a global commercial community, was inevitable, either along the lines of the United States' or socialist democratic models such as Sweden's (Table 3).

The State and Information

Poor data quality in Russia's developing organizations is an ongoing liability exacerbated by three conditions: the lack of an established business culture, inadequate public data collection, and the continued impact of the previous Soviet system upon information resources. In 2000, the GNP has become a rough approximation, a ballpark figure, after two generations of fiction, double counting, and unexplained anomalies such as endemic shortages in the midst of excess capacity. Authoritarian and non-participatory planning disguised poor data quality and illogical decision-making, unlike any other Western socialist system (Brand, 1994). The Soviet system left unusable data stores, unmeasured social and environmental damage, and imbalances due to repressed consumption, forced savings, systemic underemployment and a widespread reluctance to share information. Incoherence and uncertainty cemented political control in the Soviet era, and were not only tolerated but nurtured: the planning elite did not want economic strategy to be understood and scrutinized, lest individual enterprises use data to achieve autonomy and competitive advantage (Brand, 1994).

Production continued to be over-reported and the GDP overstated by as much as 5% in the 1990s. Although since the collapse of the Soviet economy, there is less secrecy in public data gathering, and biases are more evident, but under Goskomstat (the State Committee of the Russian Federation on Statistics) , data collection deteriorated in the 1990s (Aslund). Entire industries, from automobiles to housing, cannot rely on official statistics in 2000. After state enterprises were auctioned, privatization data became inaccurate when businesses split up, declared bankruptcy, changed their names, hid production, and changed locations frequently to avoid taxation (*Wall Street Journal*, February 9, 2000). A tax man who began work in 1995, Alexander B., told the author that businesses resisted official discovery with force and that a number of his colleagues had been shot at; during the interview, he displayed his new uniform--an impressive greatcoat with highly visible gold braid. One new millionaire, who vacations regularly in Hawaii and Switzerland, a successful banker, exporter, and "consultant" drove the author to his dacha in a Land Rover with bullets rolling on the floor of the vehicle, and was greeted by a bodyguard carrying a shotgun--for protection from bandits, assassins, and confiscatory authorities, he said.

Authorities know that private production continues to be underreported for tax-avoidance and that many enterprises fail to register with national and local authorities to avoid taxes; as many as 50% of private enterprises may be unregistered. Goskomstat fails to collect data on private farming, private housing construction or remodeling, and on most service industries and consumer purchases (Aslund, 1995). Financial and monetary data is especially sparse, a legacy of the perennial neglect of monetary and financial data in the

Soviet era, when the budget, monetary supply, and foreign debt were unpublished. The state has failed to collect critical data on the impact of inflation, bank failures, massive and unrecorded inter-enterprise borrowing, soaring bankruptcies, and privatized assets (Aslund, 1995). Employment statistics are mishandled, relying heavily on samples and on International Labor Organization (ILO) guidelines which are inappropriate for Russia in the mid-1990s (Aslund, 1995; Gustafson, 2000).

In addition, foreign trade statistics are unreliable because of widespread smuggling, bribery, and irregular registration procedures. Interstate trade statistics between members of the Commonwealth of Independent States are especially poor. Similarly, intra-organizational commerce, especially intra-company loans and shared ownership are not tracked (Aslund, 1995).

Finally, managers, academics, and foreign partners frequently complained about irrational government planning in the 1990s, and the inability to secure quality data because of ongoing political shifts, currency devaluation, and sudden changes in taxes, tariffs, and non-tariff barriers. Future costs cannot be calculated because of inflation, unexplained price increases, and interruptions in supply and distribution. Decision makers often refer to the value of business genius and instinct, and use heuristics, trial and error using what little data is available, to achieve ad hoc solutions, but "alchemy" would be a more appropriate term. For example, the cost of shipping coal by rail suddenly increased 26% 1993 in the Kuzbass region. In 1994, bus fares doubled, the free public telephone system was converted to a charge system, and international telephone rates increased 300%, all within periods of twenty-dour hours in Kemerovo. Fluctuating transport and communication costs deeply worry planners and investors in the provinces, and discourage credit, insurance, and other vital support services. Goskomstat has attempted to commercialize information but is under-funded; also, its work has been compromised by parliamentary and government interference, with little adjustment for estimated collection errors (Gustafson, 2000).

The lack of primary data and secondary data from public information stores presents a serious problem for business planners. The author found entrepreneurs in lucrative new industries such as insurance, large appliances, household repairs, personal computer retailing, and commercial remodeling hard-pressed to define problems and opportunities because of widespread information poverty. For example, the Yellow Pages were first introduced in Russia, in Moscow only, in May, 1994. By 2001, moderately detailed city maps, monthly train schedules, and telephone directories appreared in most cities.

Conditions in a museum in Tomsk, a city closed to foreigners until 1991, are symptomatic of official Russia as a whole. The municipal museum houses a large collection of outstanding Western European paintings. The artists' signatures have been obliterated on each masterpiece in the collection; labels placed beneath the priceless paintings read simply: "By a Dutch Master", "By a French Master", "By an Italian Master", and so on. Data which could enhance the value and interest of these holdings exponentially has been mysteriously and crudely painted over; these defacements are symptomatic of a singular and idiosyncratic information environment.

Business Culture and the Private Information Environment

The Soviet experience bequeathed a deep distrust of statistics, a mania for secrecy, and a fear of private data ownership by individuals, lest the data owner seem to be self-serving or subversive. Contemporary businesses still prefer to release minimal data, even to allies, for numerous reasons: for power and leverage, to avoid the tax police, and to maintain a low profile commercially for cultural congruence. Numerous small businesses operate without signs on them or any identifying names, even on sales slips, although this began to change significantly from 1991 to 1999, especially in European Russia. The use of arcane identities such as YUGANSKNEFTEGAS, by a southern Urals oil and gas group, or KEMNAG, for a Kemerovo share-holding group, is common and reminiscent of the Soviet era, but company names often offer even less intrinsic meaning to outsiders.

Pressure by authorities and local mobsters also inhibits easy data sharing between entrepreneurs, consumers, and potential business partners. In 1994, Siemens opened a dazzling electronic and appliance store in Kemerovo, but complied with an "unofficial request" to remove the sign on their storefront. No reason was given to the manager, and an Adidas outlet two blocks away continued to display their logo.

Russian entrepreneurs also maintain minimal accounting data not only because of exorbitant and shifting taxes and fees, but also because of enduring popular resentment of profits. Also, numerous commercial and financial advantages are transitory and optimized by secrecy. In Russia, numerous liquid or scarce assets, such as capital, extra apartments, automobile parts, or luxury items, often are kept off the books, because of fears of confiscation or theft. The private motivation to improve data quality in Russia is sapped also by the short-term imperative to exploit pent-up consumer demand swiftly. Russians concentrate on opening new channels, filling product position gaps, blocking third-party access, protecting internal secrets, and hedging against risk as fast as possible, not on investing in quality resources and products. Since customers often purchase whatever becomes available, fearing shortages and inflation, entrepreneurs have scant interest in thorough data analyses of price, product, promotion, or place. The marked disinterest in market research, personalized advertising, and information ethics is not only a passing phenomenon in the transient *perestroika* era, but also a remaining Soviet cultural bias that advertising is waste, quality is frivolous, and individual codes of behavior are superfluous and disruptive.

A widespread lack of veracity among middlemen and facilitators, and also the temporality of Russian market solutions, reduce the value of private data. Business tactics are often experimental and survivalist, and remarkable discontinuity and metamorphoses in business structure and alliances characterize this revolutionary decade. Business planners and IS designers must deal with poor long-term linear vision and information fragmentation, and lack a critical mass of data which could support durable decision making.

Ironically, entrepreneurs concur vigorously if asked whether enhanced data would reduce the impact of endemic uncertainty and idiosyncratic behavior in Russian markets. For example, an egregious housing shortage often determines where consumers work, travel, and study, and also deeply affects family structure, disposable income, and eating preferences. In many cities, workers, including professionals, cannot be hired unless they can prove that they have secured an apartment. Productivity, labor supplies, and expansion into local markets would be enhanced by data from efficient underground housing markets (Katz and Rittenberg, 1992).

Another cultural prejudice against data sharing stems from the concept that power and position will be eroded if data is shared, a fear found in developed as well as developing countries (Constant, Kiesler, and Sproull, 1994). Data sharing in Russia is related inversely to political and economic dominance: the less information released, the more the dominance of upper echelon managers. Data ownership signifies status and authority in a nation with ubiquitous information poverty.

The impact of gangs and extortionists who dictate the terms of trade also impedes the collection of data on pricing and consumer demand. Organized crime and cartels bully retailers into set pricing, and discounting is also considered suspect and anti-social. In 1993 and 1994, fresh flowers, fruits, and vegetables began to enter Siberian markets twelve months of the year. If bruised, produce is discarded rather than discounted, and garbage bins are filled with wasted food. Produce never is sold at a discount nor distributed to the needy, in areas which had rarely seen fresh food imports prior to 1993, because criminals who control distribution demand uniform prices.

In sum, the vast cultural gap between data handling in OECD countries and those in the CIS affects data quality particularly at the strategic level. Strategic planning and decision making is difficult not only because of economic uncertainty and a lack of business experience, but also because of vestiges of Soviet culture in both the state and private sectors. In addition, although the Internet connects computers all around the world, and every business engaged in e-commerce becomes "international", Russia is ill-equipped at this stage of economic development to handle problems with currency conversion, tariffs, import and export regulations, business regulation, taxation, and languages which are intrinsic to e-commerce across borders. Widespread and rapid small business formation, especially in services, where the legacy and the influence of the state is minimal, may create the optimal information environment for early e-commerce. The capacity to cut costs, improve product quality, reach customers, and create industry value-chains through e-commerce would enable entrepreneurs to leapfrog stages of market development and optimize scarce resources.

TWELVE FACTORS WHICH SHAPE
THE DEVELOPMENT OF E-COMMERCE

Using Russia as a model, twelve salient factors related to market maturity and culture can affect the condition of the information environment. These critical factors limit the emergence and the scope of e-commerce. They include:
1. Unsuccessful and intrusive government planning and regulation;
2. Barriers to entry and dictated pricing in distribution, supply, or production;
3. Clandestine entrepreneurship, black markets, and barter;
4. Singular methods of managerial accounting,(for example, omission of various overhead, depreciation, and maintenance costs, a common practice in Russia);
5. Unanticipated shortages and other tactics that inhibit consumption and disguise demand;
6. Political fear and widespread avoidance of information disclosure and sharing;
7. Inconvertible and unstable currency, nascent financial regulations, and a dearth of financial services;
8. A reluctance to divulge information without compensation or reciprocity;
9. Proprietary attitudes toward data ownership, IT, and IS training, by socioeconomic and political elites, including multinational and foreign controllers;
10. Rigid, hierarchical management styles featuring a marked reluctance to share information or to empower partners or employees through data sharing;
11. Communication behaviors such as a reliance on oral traditions in retailing, or the use of more than one language for business relations and record-keeping;
12. An emphasis on price and availability to the exclusion of quality, which discourages proximity to the customer and attention to preferences and trends;

Wealth, foreign partnerships, and other material and intellectual resources affect data quality also. In Russia, foreign businesses often accept information poverty as part of the high risk of entering the huge untapped market and maintain highly speculative portfolio investments (Browning, 1995). These businesses operate at risk in an environment characterized by weekly currency, regulatory, and competitive shifts, but enjoy the advantages of early market entry.

STRATEGIES AND SOLUTIONS

In Russia, an economy that has never experienced information plenitude, survivalist business practice and fortuitous personal connections are paramount. Data quality which users want is relatively modest, and applications seldom extend beyond operations, transaction processing, summaries, and data communications. E-commerce is increasingly needed for competitive advantage as organizations restructure, democratize, and create alliances, and as exposure to foreign business practices increases. As noted at the beginning of the chapter, most Russians identify data quality with accuracy at present, and this lack of appreciation for added data value reduces widespread interest in both data quality and strategic e-commerce.

However, in developing markets, the negative impacts of culture and historical experience on data quality can be diluted by self-conscious organization-wide culture shifts, quality processes, and technical elegance. Numerous occasions for change arise frequently in these dynamic economies because of shifts in management, financial restructuring, foreign aid contingencies, the initiation of strategic partnerships--all often offer ideal occasions for conversion and reform, although no event intrinsically guarantees quality improvements. Appropriate strategies to improve data quality require a sustained and enlightened effort to capitalize intelligently on moments of change.

IS development may provide an opportunity to experiment with novel business processes, especially if broad partnering can be achieved. IS professionals, business partners, returning Russian management interns, and other allies who work closely with Russian enterprises formulate convincing rationales for investments in data quality. Professional output, cost-cutting, and customer loyalty are central to enterprise prosperity. As electronic data interchange (EDI) creates more intricate coordination between global units, EDI partners can be motivated by positive incentives or threats to improve data quality standards and collection techniques.

Radical market and technology shifts appear to augment the willingness to develop data resources, as long as local priorities are observed. Market information, case histories, or prototypes must be tested locally for profitability and low maintenance costs. In Russia, IS design and conversion through joint application development (JAD) holds promise since many economic units value tactical group decision-making. JAD enhances legitimacy, responsibility, and design skills among participants who are expected to suggest refinements and expansions. The intellectual capital for software development in Russia is vast, since past training in mathematics, engineering, and science was superb. At present, however, domestic programmers cannot compete with the ubiquitous flood of illegal advanced software, and the future for software industry in Russia is in jeopardy (Specter, 1995). Also, formal business education or corporate training is needed to synchronize business planning and JAD.

Creative information strategies can compensate for and, if possible, alleviate poor data quality. An ongoing evaluation of data quality also sustains a focus on those business factors which enhance competitive advantage. Richer data models can be developed as Russia sheds the habits and institutions of a command economy. Domestically, highly competitive and expanding domestic service industries, ranging from automotive repair to waste disposal, are especially receptive to investments in data quality as the means to improve their customer focus (Paquin and Turgeon, 1994). Unfortunately, the prognosis for quality improvement is low in certain industries, even where vast consumer demand exists. In the 1990s, insurance, financial, and healthcare services struggle to achieve stability in Russia.

Nonetheless, in some novel but critical activities, such as auditing air and water quality, radioactivity, or other critical environmental concerns, existing data quality is dangerously poor. Kuzbass External Associates (KEA) request not only tours of waste management facilities when they visit the United States, but also excursions to order or purchase literature on Russia's environmental problems. Many large enterprises, including KEA, sponsor extensive foreign language training and education abroad for Russian students so that English e-Mail and imported periodicals can be understood, to compensate for domestic data shortages in some areas. However, IS cannot succeed in environmental auditing using imported models, techniques and technologies developed in Western firms whose primary objective is compliance with existing regulations (Greeno, Hedstrom, and DiBerto, 1986). Given Russia's massive environmental problems, Russia needs data and decision support which is not intended to keep a firm out of trouble, but to provide the tools for massive damage assessment, policy formulation, and clean-up processes.

Seminal Intellectual Shifts

As Russians gain experience with financial models, market analysis, qualitative measurements, and computer-enhanced processes, a massive intellectual shift is occurring. Before 1986, it was illegal to trade in foreign currency, to own an unregistered copy machine or typewriter, or to make a profit on the resale of manufactured items. The prejudice against business as an honest profession has dissipated as understanding of a demand economy and of business functions spreads (Osipov, 1998).

The prosperity of Finland, as well as the swift stabilization of Poland, the Baltic States, and other former COMECON partners surprised Russians, fueled confidence in market mechanisms, and fed the appetite for IT (Shpakov, 1998). Many citizens have lost faith in the government's ability to arrest the economic collapse, and to identify and attack fraud, shortages and inflation in the free market. By 2000, widespread discontent with governmental ineptitude, fraud and cronyism, and with legal and bureaucratic barriers to entrepreneurship (Urinson, 1998). The impatience with crony capitalism in 2000 encourages self-help movements, movement toward membership in the World Trade Organization, business education, and novel alliances which learn by experience and also research the value of quality information.

Scholars and practitioners only recently began to consider IT transfer as IS turf, have often failed to claim information environments and economic development as IS issues. Unfortunately, IS professionals generally lack experience with e-commerce design and management in multinational environments where robust data is non-existent or not shared. This challenge is central to IS developers for two reasons. First, global information systems in varied information cultures must be developed, since these emergent markets present massive opportunity and valued partnerships in a world of shrinking markets and increasing competition. Second, IS alone provides the pragmatic and integrative functions which make IT and application transfers work.

CONCLUSIONS

A healthy information environment and an adequate telecommunications infrastructure are prerequisites for domestic e-commerce and for global competitiveness in emerging economies. As the economies of the former Soviet bloc and of former European colonies mature and fold into global markets, a migration to e-commerce is pivotal for economic growth, strategic planning, and foreign investment and partnerships. A stable information environment and e-commerce enhances multiple assets: capital, labor, plant, know-how, and inventory. Indeed, these resources are often depleted and ill-managed to compensate for information deficits, turning information resource management (IRM) on its head.

Massive potential for competitive advantage through on-line services exists in new industries, such as financial services, publishing, insurance, delivery services, and consulting. In an information-poor society, the competitive advantage of organization with superior information resources are dramatic: early leadership in value chain management, cost reduction, and product quality through superior organization and streamlined processes. In emergent market economies, consumers soon will be courted and won through improved information services and value-added features: enhanced supply and distribution, superior quality, cost-effective innovation, easy product or service maintenance, clear directions, attractive and durable packaging or casing, and bundled services in areas such as communications, insurance, or finance.

Russians routinely compare their country to the United States, composed of numerous peoples and languages linked by a common political system and one dominant language. However, ideology and ethnocentricity insulated and isolated Russia, and the economic environment is unique. Although rich in natural and human resources, Russia is ill-prepared to exploit either electronic markets or the information age. Improved communications, new industries, and global partnerships may stabilize the economy and create wealth, but many Russians are pessimistic about the benefits of a new economy.

Finally, on the one hand, the advent of e-commerce will probably increase "the digital divide", the gulf between those who have access to computers and the Internet, and those who do not. E-commerce may accelerate the concentration of wealth, deepen class differences, and perpetuate the provincial rivalries and urban-rural bitterness of the 1990s. Resentment in geographic areas that lack adequate telecommunications may increase cynicism and disenchantment with the post-communist system. On the other hand, successful e-commerce will bolster Russia's new identity as global participant rather than an outlaw, and may enable some industries, and small businesses to leapfrog stages of development and achieve strategic advantages.

Mini Case

Russia's GDP was negative for most of the 1990s, and the living standards of the population havedeclined to the level of developing economies. Yet Russia has vast reserves of oil, diamonds, and gold, as well as significant human resources and massive amounts of fertile land. Although Russia's transportation infrastructure is poor, the European Bank for Reconstruction and Development, as well as numerous foreign investors, have been attracted to Taganrog, a city in the southwestern province of Rostov with access to the sea. In Taganrog, the remains of classical Greek trading posts and also of a pre-revolutionary international commercial and banking center still stand.

Yet the shipyards at Taganrog are almost idle. The port is among the finest in Russia, a window to the Black Sea and to the Mediterranean. Peter the Great (1689-1725) developed the deep harbor because this southwestern access to the sea is ice-free longer than any other port in Russia. However, the cranes on the docks seldom operate since exports of weapons, grain, and heavy capital equipment have declined precipitously. By contrast, a flood of imports, mostly consumer goods, arrives continuously by rail from Europe, the Middle East, and Asia: French pate, Danish cheese, Indonesian cookies, Japanese pollock, German glue, Italian pasta. Local producers cannot compete on a price or quality basis with the vast range of imports flooding into Taganrog.

The trade imbalance deepens an endemic recession. Even agricultural productivity has declined since privatization; yet the black soil of the fertile steppe surrounding Taganrog is among the finest in the world. Entrepreneurs, scholars, and city leaders know that foreign investment--bringing know-how, capital, and an improved information infrastructure, is the swiftest means to recovery and long-term competitiveness.

The center of business education, entrepreneurship, joint ventures is the state university. Because the university was a Soviet weapons research center, their telecommunications grid is superior. Outside the university telephone grid, the telephone system is primitive, expensive, and undependable; it is difficult even to get a phone installed.

Mini Case …. Continued

Discussion Questions:

1. Design a strategic information system, including intranets and extranets, for a networked enterprise with foreign partners in Taganrog. What information must be shared?

2. How can this networked enterprises and e-commerce evolve? What obstacles must be overcome? What existing resource endowments can be exploited?

3. List and discuss five major benefits of e-commerce and five major benefits of e-business in this emerging economy. Are there any disadvantages?

STUDY QUESTIONS

1. What political and socio-cultural factors affect information environments? 65-66

2. Why is business trust a central component of successful economic development?

3. What are the leading business opportunities for foreign investors in Russia in 2000? 67-68

4. What is the transfer of Knowledge Based Systems to emerging economies so valuable?

5. What is the "digital divide"? 70

6. Why is the evolution of wireless transmission significant in developing economies?

REFERENCES

Andrenikova, L. (April 27, 1998). Interview on German-Russian program to extend longevity in child leukemia. Rostov, Russia.

Aslund, A. (1995). *How Russia Became a Market Economy*. Washington, D.C. : The Brookings Institution.

Avgerou, C. (1991). Creating an information systems infrastructure for development planning. *Proceedings of the Twelfth International Conference on Information Systems.* New York, pp. 21-259.

Baalen, W. (February 24, 27, 1998). Interviews on TACIS shipbuilding knowledge-based system. Taganrog, Russia.

Brand, H. (1998). Why the Soviet economy failed: Consequences of dictatorship and dogma. In Moldman, M.(ed.), *Global Studies: Russia, the Eurasian Republics, and Central/Eastern Europe*, 6th ed. Guilford, Ct.: Dushkin Press.

Boycko, M., Shleifer, A., and Vishny, R. (1998). *Privatizing Russia*. Cambridge, MIT Press.

Castells, Manuel. (2000). The Rise of the Network Society. Oxford, UK: Blackwell.

Chepaitis, E. (1994). After the command economy: Russia's information culture and its impact on information resource management. *Journal of Global Information Management*, **2**(1), 5-11.

Chepaitis, E. (1999). Ethics across information cultures. In Enderle, Georges(ed.), *International Business Ethics.* Notre Dame: University of Notre Dame Press.

Chepaitis, E. (1997). Information ethics and information cultures. *Business Ethics: A European Review*, **6**(4), 195-200.

Clarke, Peter. (1995). Russia adds electronic muscle. *Electronic Engineering Times*, April 17, 28-30.

Curtis, G.E.(ed.). (1998). Russia: A Country Study. Washington, D.C.: Library of Congress, Federal Research Division.

Denisov, A. (1997). Microsoft seeks a foothold in Russia. Moscow News, October 16-22, 7.

Dotty about e-commerce? (2000). *Economist*, February 26, 24.

Economic crime in Russia. (1995). Delovi Mir, March 20-26, 11.

Entangled in the World Wide Web. (1997). *Sputnik*, December, 68-70.

Evans, P. and Wurster , T.S (1999). Getting real about virtual commerce. *Harvard Business Review*, November – December, 85-93.

Fukiyama, F. (1995). *Trust: The Social Virtues and the Creation of Prosperity*. New York: Simon and Schuster,

Gustafson, T. (2000). *Capitalism Russian-Style*. Cambridge: Cambridge University Press.

Hardt, J.P., Hoffenberg, M., Kaplan, N., Levine, H.S. (1967). *Mathematics and Computers in Soviet Planning*. New Haven: Yale University Press.

Ivan the talkative. (2000). The Economist, January 11, 64.

Morgan Stanley Dean Witter. (1999*). U.S. and the Americas Investment Research Market Watch*. July 9, 15-17.

Palvia, Prashant C., Palvia, Shailendra C., and Zigli, R.M. (1992). Global information technology environment: Key MIS Issues in Advanced and Less Developed Nations. In Palvia, P. C., Palvia, S. C., and Roche, Edward M.(eds.), *The Global Issues of Information Technology Management*. Harrisburg, PA: Idea Group Publishing.

Paquin, B. and Turgeon, N. (1994). *Enterprises de Services: Gestion de la Qualite*. Montreal: Agence d'Arc.

Parsaye, K., and Chignall, M. (1993). *Intelligent Database Tools and Applications*. NY: Wiley.

Perov, E., and McHenry, W. (2000). Measuring the Russian Internet. *Global Information Technology World Conference*. Memphis, Tennessee: p. 192.

Schechter, Jerrold L. (1998). *Russian Negotiating Behavior: Continuity and Transition*. Washington, D.C.: U.S. Institute of Peace Press.

Smith, A.(ed.). (1995). *Challenges for Russian Economic Reform*. Washington: The Brookings Institute, The Royal Institute of International Affairs.

Schneider, G.P., and Perry, J. T. (2000). *Electronic Commerce*. Cambridge, MA: Course Technology.

Specter, I. (1995). Latest films for $2: Video piracy booms in Russia. *New York Times*, April 11, A3.

Strong, D. M., Madnick, S.E., Redman, T., Segev, A., and Wang, R.Y. (1994). Data quality: A critical research issue for the 1990s and beyond. *Proceedings of the Fifteenth International Conference on Information Systems*. New York: pp. 500-501.

Tapscott, D., and Caston, C. (1993). *Paradigm Shift: The New Promise of Information Technology*. New York: McGraw Hill.

Wilson, E.J. III. (1998). Inventing the global information future. *Futures: the Journal of Forecasting Planning and Policy*, 30(1), 23-42.

Whalen, J., and Bahree, B. (2000). How a Siberian oil field turned into a minefield. *Wall Street Journal*, February 9, A21.

Wo ist Goldlilocks? (2000). *Economist,* February 5, 27.

Yemelyanenkop, V., and Petrov, A. (1998). The pirates of the 21st century. *Moscow News,* 4(5), 7.

Yergin, D., and Gustafson, T. (1995). *Russia 2010*. Cambridge Energy Research Associates Report (CERA). NY: Random House.

Yeung, O.M., and Mathiesdon, J.A. (1998). *Global Benchmarks: Comprehensive Measures of Development*. Washington, D.C.: Brookings Institution Press.

Zisk, K.M. (1998). *Weapons, Culture, and Self-Interest: Soviet Defense Managers in the New Russia*. N.Y.: Columbia University Press.

4

IT on the Arctic Circle: A Regional Survival Game

Jaana Kuula
Regional Council of Lapland, Finland

ABSTRACT

This chapter discusses the location issues of the global information technology and software industries. Questions are, what kind of problems IT industries meet in crowded centers, and on which basis these industries could be located elsewhere in a World scale. The chapter introduces Lapland as an example of potential new areas for locating global IT industries outside current production areas. Lapland is located on the Arctic Circle in Finland, and despite of hard living conditions it is producing new innovations in the IT field, and fulfills many of the requirements that international IT and software businesses set for their production. In the article of Wired Magazine (October, 2000) Oulu, the biggest city near the Arctic Circle in Finland, was ranked as the 28. promising high tech center in the World for global venture capitalists. With this position, Oulu was next to Los Angeles, and ahead of cities like Chicago, Singapore and Tokyo. The chapter also introduces two Finnish software companies that have pushed them through to the World market despite of being located near the Arctic Circle, which in general, is not considered as a favorable environment for running IT businesses.

THE CASE OF LAPLAND

Basic Facts About Lapland

Lapland is a fairly large but a scarcely populated area on the Arctic Circle in Finland, in the Northernmost part of Europe. It has 200 000 inhabitants in its 100 000 square km area, and, due to unemployment, especially young and educated people are moving out of there. The nature is extremely beautiful in Lapland, but the climate is hard and distances long. In addition, inhabited centers are separated from each other by many mountains, forests, swamps and lakes. The weather is in average -20 C (0F), and in peaks -40 C (-32 F) in winter, and +20-30 C (65-80 F) in the summer.

In earlier times, Lapland's native culture called sámi people, lived on reindeer herding, but currently tourism is the strongest industry. During the Christmas season, 150 international charter flights come to the Arctic Circle, among them (until the air crash in Paris in summer 2000) direct Concorde-flights from London and Paris. Most of those travelers come to see Santa Claus, but people also write him letters. For example, in 1998 people from 150 countries all over the World sent 600 000 and in 1997 700 000 hand written letters to Santa on the Arctic Circle. Outside Christmas, people come to experience all the four seasons of Lapland. During the sunny spring time, ski resorts are full of international guests, and in the summer people go fishing and carrying out other wild life activities. In the fall people go to the mountains to experience glowing autumn colors, and to the swamps to pick cloudberries, delicate Nordic berries that cost more than 10 USD per kilo.

With native people, unique and vulnerable nature, and hard living conditions, Lapland has similarities with for example Nevada and Arizona in the US, where tourism is the key business, and where the conditions for other industries are not so good. Industries also need to take in respect the vulnerable nature, in Nevada and Arizona because of the hot and dry desert conditions, and in Lapland because of the cold weather, in which forests grow and recover much slower than in a smoother climate.

Due to hard living conditions, and a thin industrial base, currently more people than ever in the history move out from Lapland, and the birth rate has sunk in average 30 %. Now both the government and local authorities need to figure out, what to do with this region that makes one third of the whole country of Finland. The size of Finland is close to Germany, Arizona and Nevada, and almost a half, 44 %, of the area of Australia. At the same time with the depopulation problem in Lapland, government needs to deal with overpopulation in other places, especially in the capital region, where unemployment, crowding, and lack of apartments cause social problems. While Finland is one of the world leader countries in developing and applying information technologies, it tries to create an information society that would help solving some of the Lapland's problems. Also Lapland itself has created a strategy that should connect the region into the international market of IT industries, and support its growing into an internationally recognized center of new media and entertainment businesses.

First of all, the strategy includes starting up new media and information technology industries in the area. These industries are profiled as the 'industry of experience', which refers to digital content production in the fields of entertainment, culture and arts, and to industrial design, that involves 3D product development and rapid prototyping. Second, Lapland is building an advanced information society to support working and living conditions in its rural area, and for offering full public services even despite of the long distances from the centers. Just in the neighborhood of Lapland there also lies Oulu, one of the strongest R&D centers of mobile phone technologies in the World. Oulu is currently ranked as the 28. interesting target for international venture capitalists in the World, and it aims as the World leader city in the 4G technologies in the future. The knowledge and growth of Oulu is planned to be spread into other parts of the Northern Finland as well, and the tool for this is the network of technology centers (called polises) in the area. Each polis has its own profile, and in Oulu Technopolis is of course profiled in mobile technologies. In other parts of Northern Finland and Lapland, polises are profiled in astrophysics, radio signaling systems, electronics, digital content production, telemedicine, etc.

New Media and the Industry of Experience in Lapland

Lapland is putting a strong effort in starting new media and information technology industries in the area, with a profile that is called as the 'industry of experience'. This refers to entertainment, culture and arts, and to industrial design, which involves 3D product development and rapid prototyping. In the entertainment field, Lapland creates virtual reality environments and other offerings for film industries and other fields of entertainment. It is also focusing into more serious fields of digital content production, thus the new digital tv broadcasts will require endlessly new contents in the forthcoming years, and thus the same channel might be used as the major service channel for virtual public services. This includes among other things taxation, and the whole wide area of the social security and welfare system, which in Scandinavia has been broader than in anywhere else in the World.

Lapland wishes to become a serious R&D- partner to Hollywood-based entertainment industries. In other fields of software industries and digital content production, R&D partners are sought especially from the Silicon Valley. The whole business is directed to the global market, even though the whole field is still in the very beginning of serious growth. Some openings are though made on the global market already, especially in the fields of 3D platforms, mobile phone games and platforms, and telemedicine applications. By locating on the Arctic Circle, the University of Lapland is the only university in the 100 000 square kilometer area. It is still very small due to its young age of 20 years, and scarce population in the area. The university was originally focusing on social sciences, law, and the arctic, but in the early 1990's another school was merged with it, which then made a faculty of arts. The faculty of arts, with education in industrial design, textile and clothing industry, and media sciences, now leads the development of new media and virtual reality technologies in the area.

In the beginning of the new Millennium, there are three 3D laboratories at the University of Lapland, two others in two other schools on the Arctic Circle, several in local companies, and a couple under construction for R&D and incubator center purposes. The laboratories are specialized in virtual entertainment environments, 3D industrial product development, digital textile design, 3D programming, and in new media and film making industries. In the incubator center of the university called DesignPark, currently ten companies are growing up, and several are doing business on their own. One of the firms with Lappish roots, Cybelius Software, opened a location in the San Jose incubator center in the Silicon Valley in November 1998, and other firms are encouraged to follow its example. Also, in December 1998, The Ministry of Internal Affairs in Finland nominated the industry of experience in Lapland as one of the twelve national knowledge centers that will be prioritized and supported until year 2006 as the key industrial fields in the country. With this nomination Lapland will receive recognition and funding for its new industries, but much more need to be done for making the new industries flourish in the following years.

The key to the survival of Lapland is information technology and digital content production, because the current leading industry, tourism, can not alone support the population, and because even tourism can not survive without information technology. Also, it is hard to imagine any other field of industry, which could be started in this kind of extreme environment, and whose products could be marketed from Lapland to the global market at a competitive price. The first leading project in this field after nominating the knowledge center of the industry of experience in Lapland was called SAIVO, which name comes from the old Lappish tradition, and refers to a magic lake or to a bottomless well on mountains. For entertainment industries it symbolizes a source of unending new ideas and stories, and in years 1999-2006 the project is aimed at creating new businesses especially in the various fields of digital content production, film making, animation and other entertainment industries. There are three schools involved in running the SAIVO project, and through them elements from the education of masters of arts, engineers in 3D programming, and candidates in film making and other entertainment industries are combined into one and the same program. In addition to tailor made education, the project also has an incubator center program that is focused in the same fields of industries as the education that is given within the SAIVO project.

The Information Society in Lapland

The information society in Lapland is targeted to enable education, business and other key activities in the region, and to make the citizens enjoy living there. In practice, this means creating sufficient infrastructures for business, education and other private and public services, offering wide and equal network services to all people, and generating resources for personal services and other comparable tasks by creating savings in social costs. To mention some examples, there are several regional networks being built all over Lapland. These networks will be offering services both for business, and for private citizens. Additional intranet networks and services have been built also in other parts of Lapland, especially in the biggest tourist areas like in the Levi (www.levi.fi) and Saariselkä (www.saariselka.fi) mountain areas.

Business services are offered also for the North Calotte and Barents region, which refers to the area where the Arctic Circle cuts the area of the four countries of Finland, Sweden, Norway and Russia. Currently two extranet services are being built for this area, the Barents-Extranet (www.barentsnet.com) and Barentsinfo (www.barentsinfo.net). While there are so many different networks and portals in the area, there has been a strong debate of collecting them all behind the same address, www.lapland.fi. Due to competitive reasons, especially private companies have not been willing to join that portal, but as public support is given to that address new actors are slowly coming in. The current appearance of the portal is modest, but it will be developed gradually after having a better commitment from the various actors behind the service.

Also the electronic commerce is one of the key forms of offering services in the information society. In Lapland there are several market places on the Internet, but, so far, none of them is very successful. Current market places are organized in three ways: some of them are simple web stores, some are mediators without instant buying facilities, and some are individual sites for festivals or other attractions that have a physical store at their primary location. The first web store in the area was the MarketWorld (www.marketworld.fi), whose product selection is focusing in Christmas, wild life and leisure time products. Traffic on the site has been satisfactory, but sales hardly cover costs. A younger store, built by applying the same business idea, is found in www.lapland.fi. So far, the product supply in that address has been low, which also means that sales have been weak.

Mediators are, for example, sites in addresses www.laplandfinland.com and www.wildandfree.com. The first of them only offers links to external web stores, and the other is focusing in mediating travelling services. Individual sites with a physical store are found, for example, for the SantaPark Christmas theme park (www.santapark.com), World's largest snow castle (www.snowcastle.net), and for the arctic museum Arktikum (www.arktikum.fi). In general, people in Lapland do not buy much through the Internet, and if they do, they buy through the biggest and well known web sites that are operated abroad or elsewhere in the country. Local web stores do not attract local customers, and so far, neither their sales in other areas are very high. These problems are recognized, and Lapland is trying to create electronic commerce in the way that it will help developing the area, and not only make it poorer by letting people buy most of their products through the Internet outside the area.

For cutting social costs, and for offering better health and social services in the whole area of Lapland despite of long distances, there are telematic services that enable monitoring health and social condition of elderly people from remote. There are also tele-medicine applications through which surgeries in large central hospitals can give special medical help in distant places where only ordinary doctors are available. Also, public services, especially in the fields of health and social care, will be given in cars that are provided with highly qualified medial equipment and strong telecommunication systems. These will be servicing areas, which are most distant from centers, and where the maintenance of physical organizations for public services is too expensive.

Business Examples

Small IT companies' ability to join international businesses is dependent on the businesses themselves, but also on the surroundings of the country in which they are located. In the US, small companies are already a part of a huge home market, but in many other countries there is practically no home market for specialized IT products. Furthermore, if the country is not a member of any of the wide economic areas, firms in that country need not only export their products, but also cross the borders of these juridically defined economic areas. That requires much bureaucracy and additional work from the small firms, and increases the prices of their products. For example, in Finland international business was earlier conducted by government led agreements between different countries, and within those negotiations mainly large firms were able to sign contracts.

After joining the European Union in 1995, Finland was included in the European single market, which made international trade easier. Trading practices, however, change slowly, so there is still not much risk capital in the country, and firms have not learnt to turn to foreign investors either. Businesses also need to learn a new way of becoming international, because since 1960's, firms have carried out international operations step by step by starting from neighboring countries and then by expanding gradually to countries that are psychologically close to their earlier markets. Now the speed of international trade is much faster, and especially IT companies need to move directly to the international market. Even sheltered foreign markets are not possible, thus IT products need already in the beginning to survive competition at the global level. If the country is situated far from its primary markets, also the physical location of the country creates problems for international trade. For example, Finland, which earlier lived from forest and heavy metal industries, has for long suffered from its distant location up in the North, but after first creating successful electronic and information technology industries, it is now able to create international software industries, which in turn are not as dependent on their physical location.

Like the following two business examples show, software industries can be created and run regardless of the geographical distances, but for being successful on the international market, the firms need to have a physical representative on their key markets. The following two software companies have pushed themselves to the international market already in the very early years of their operation. However, if they represented some other fields of industries than information technology and software business, they would not have moved to the international market at this early stage, or at all. Also, if these firms would operate in some other fields of industries, they most likely would have started their international operations from the European market, and not from the North American market.

The beginning of companies like these two has been more like a chance than a result of serious calculation in Finland. There usually is one talented young person, who will start doing something special which then will become a success. This was the case with the Finnish Linus Thorvalds, and the same applies with many other less known business cases. While the technological problem is driving the ambition of some young talented person, the business is not the first thing in that kind of person's mind. However, when that interesting technological problem happens to be a solution into a real problem of other companies, it might become a big business by itself. That, however, needs business skills and funding, and in many cases those are missing, and even good business ideas are left unnoticed. Quite recently, venture capital has been increasing in Finland, and innovations are developed and commercialized more systematically than earlier.

Stonesoft: Stonesoft (www.stonesoft.com) is a Finnish software company, whose main business fields are Internet security and information management. The firm's customers are large manufacturing and service companies utilizing intelligent Product Data Management, Sales Configuration, Document Management and Visual Product Management solutions. Stonesoft both offers its own products, and represents its key partners' products. Key partners are Trend Micro Inc. and Netrex, with whom Stonesoft is offering high quality virus control and firewall systems.

Stonesoft was founded in 1990 to specialize in offering customer unique software solutions to complex business problems. Today the company is one of the most successful Finnish software companies in the global market. Stonesoft is headquartered in Espoo Finland and has offices in cities of Turku and Tampere. Company operates in the USA from its Atlanta, GA located subsidiary, Stonesoft Inc., and San Jose, CA located office. Customers in Asia-Pacific area are served from the office in Singapore. The Swedish subsidiary Stonesoft Ab, locating in Stockholm, was established March 1st, 1999. Stonesoft annual sales growth has been 60-70 % during the last 3 years. Company is listed in the Helsinki Stock Exchange, where the primary and secondary offering (IPO or Offering) to domestic and international institutional investors and to retail investors in Finland was a huge success. It took place on 26.3-29.3.1999, and during that time 27 million shares were subscribed, amounting to some 1000 MFIM. Of the retail offering some 80% was subscribed through the Internet.

Stonesoft first entered the US market after the government of Finland had in 1992 ordered 64 Hornet F-18 fighter airplanes from the United States, and after the US in turn was committed to buy Finnish products worth 3,4 billion USD. These purchases were carried out in various forms, and in one of them, young firms were taken in the General Electric's incubator center in New York to practice foreign trade. Stonesoft then started in that incubator center, and later moved to Atlanta into its own premises. From Atlanta it moved to Silicon Valley in California, and currently it has some other locations around the World as well. Stonesoft's strategic partnership with Trend Micro was published in January 1999, and with Netrex in May 1999.

Cybelius Software: Cybelius Software (www.cybelius.com) develops and markets leading-edge virtual reality tools and concepts based on smart and interactive component technology for 3 D functional virtual product applications in professional E-business. It is a part of a Finnish software company called CCC, which was founded in 1985, and which has operated mainly in the western Europe. Cybelius Software was founded to expand CCC's operation to the US, and it started its operation in Silicon Valley in 1998.

CCC, that has a location also in Lapland, is taking actively part in the regional development in the area. For example, it is assisting to develop IT education in local schools, and it is ready to recruit most of the people who graduate in 3D programming. CCC is also considered as an encouraging example to other young businesses in the software field, because it moved at a very early stage, and with very young people, to the North American market. CCC's subsidiary Cybelius Software though did not start in its own premises, but in an International Business Incubator in San José. The incubator center is partially being financed by the Finnish government through the National Technology Agency Tekes (www.tekes.fi), and that is a new practice in helping Finnish industries to get into the international market.

Cybelius Software's strategy includes, that it has close connections to its home land, that it will be networked with important business partners and organizations like the Web3D Consortium (www.web3d.org), and that it will be seen in public exhibitions. For example, at the Spring Internet World '99 in Los Angeles, Cybelius's TouchMore! 2.0 software won the Best of Show Award in April 1999.

ISSUES IN LOCATING GLOBAL IT INDUSTRIES

In the traditional manufacturing industries, production was usually located near resources. Especially raw materials like mining products, timber and wheat, have earlier dictated the location of primary industries. Nowadays global industries tend to source these materials wherever they can, and original producers get only the lowest price in the value chain. Global industries also locate their production near human resources: Manufacturing industries search for low wages, and in the worst cases even illegal methods like child work are used in developing countries. Also software industries search for cheaper work force, but it is more difficult to find new locations for production, because programming work requires education, and mathematical and technical talent, which is totally different than learning to assemble, carve, paint, knit or sew, as is needed in manufacturing industries.

Programming work has though been located in low wage countries for years, and countries like India, China, Korea, Vietnam and Russia have become important sources for international software industries. These countries have a high population, which among other work force produces more technical talents than smaller countries. Population is, however, not the only reason for locating programming work in these countries. For example in India, the creation of software industries was possible because of technical universities, English language, high population and low wages. Also the government policy must have been crucial, since international investors can not come into the country without the government's permission. Russia is a new comer in this group of countries, because the market was opened for international investors only after the end of the socialist system in the beginning of 1990's. Russia has, however, always had a lot of mathematical and technical talents, so despite of temporary problems with the English language, it was rapidly able to become an important source for international programming work.

The highly populated countries represent the first wave in the international sourcing of programming work. In that respect the policy of global industries seems to be the same as in the manufacturing industries, because the only interest for them is to get the work done wherever it is fastest, cheapest and secured by the high supply of working force. This strategy includes also, that only minimum investments are made and only the routine work is spread into these countries. The real capital is kept elsewhere, and more valuable processes like R&D and marketing are located near the management and markets. While the whole IT industry has become so important in the global economy, it is becoming more difficult for multinational companies to apply the described strategy. By doing subcontracting for international companies, local programming force becomes more skilled, and starts requiring higher wages or carrying out its own business. Also local governments realize the value of the new know how in their countries, and require more cooperation and responsibility from the international industries.

Israel represents another kind of international software production, first, because it is a small country, and second, because international investors have put a lot of money in the area. It has already from the beginning aimed at the creation of its own competitive information technology industry, and it has succeeded to attract powerful foreign investors into the country. Primary reason for that is, though, not information technology itself, but Israel's strategic position on the Persian Gulf, near one of the World's most important oil fields. While the army has a strong position in the country, and while soldiers have a technological education, Israel started to educate retired soldiers into the information technology field. The creation of new IT companies was supported by creating government and private funded incubator centers in the area, and soon also foreign companies like Motorola, Sony and ITT became interested in this area, and started their own business operations in the country. Now the IT business is blooming in Israel, and it is one of the most important exporting articles in the country.

In the US, many important IT industries are located in the Silicon Valley. Due to high competition and high density of IT companies in this small area, the demand for labor is high. Therefore, local labor markets are over heated in the IT field, and firms suffer from the lack of qualified personnel, poor quality of work, over paid salaries, unloyalty of employees, and bad customer service. In the creation of entertaining software, there might also be problems in the innovation process, thus firms tend to lend stories from other cultures for servicing global markets. New businesses also have a capital problem, because – due to high focusing of IT professionals in the area – many new business ideas are introduced daily, and even many of the good business ideas are left without funding. Evaluating and selecting potential business ideas among others also takes time, so, in the area like Silicon Valley new firms need to work hard for getting primary funding from local investors.

The labor problems in the Silicon Valley may be helped by bringing skilled work force from other countries into the area, or having the work done somewhere else. Many of the talented people are, however, not willing to move into a crowded, polluted and hot area with the fear of Earth quakes, and importing new people into the area would also not lower the wage level. Distributing work might be a better solution, and that has been done by directing routine-typed programming work into lower wage countries. In a World scale, this will, however, become more difficult in the future, because the local IT industries become stronger and more demanding, and because the processes of the distributed programming work become more difficult to manage. While also local governments and industries realize the value of the programming work that is being done in their area, they expect from international industries a greater share of the whole software business, and a stronger responsibility and commitment in the economic and social development of the area.

Also the management of the distributed software work is becoming more difficult, because software packages are large and complicated, and have many kinds of different elements. Many parts of these packages are routine kind of programming, but it is a difficult task to divide a large multimedia- or 3D programming work into entities that can be written into a clear program definition, and sent into the other side of the Globe to be programmed by non-English speaking programmers. The management is even more difficult, when the software package includes different elements like sound, moving images, and animation. The whole software must then have a manuscript, and different elements, whether they are done in different locations or not, must be combined into the same piece of work. Programming may then not be the most critical part of the whole job, thus all the different elements need to suit together, and meet the same standards of quality. As a result, high quality programming and technical innovations alone can not make the product sell, if the manuscript is poor, or if the visualization can not keep up the interest of the user.

While software products are immaterial, people are willing to think that, regardless where the software is produced, there are no problems in delivering it anywhere in the World. If deliveries through telecommunications are not possible, software can at least be delivered by ordinary mail. This kind of thinking works for packaged software that users can install and use without professional help and maintenance service nearby. Also cheap prices support this kind of thinking, because, if the purchase appears not to be working, it is not a great loss for the consumer. Due to these reasons, telecommunications and ordinary mail can be used best for delivering cheap consumer products, or small professional products, with which users can manage without additional help.

Larger software packages, especially if they are tailor made, require additional work in addition to deliveries. First, the larger and more complicated software are in question, the more effort is needed for marketing and selling them. Even if all of the needed information would be available on the net, important investments are not usually made that way. Instead, decisions are made after personal negotiations, and on the basis of other things that just the technical features of the software. Second, if the software requires adjusting or tailor made parts, the seller needs to make individual definitions with every user. This is usually done by visiting personally the user's organization. Later on, personal contacts are needed at least for testing the software at the customer's site, and possibly during the whole application process. After the delivery, the software still needs personal support, because users rarely know their software by every detail, and because new users often need guidance in learning to use the system. Software can also fail, although such products will soon disappear from the market.

Due to these reasons, professional software often needs a physical delivery organization, and a local representative on the market. These should carry out local marketing, installation, maintenance and personal support in ad hoc problems. Organizing all that is extremely expensive, and only large software houses can offer that support at once after launching new products on the market. New companies do not have an international organization for marketing and deliveries, so they need to start their business slowly, or by cooperating with a company that already has an international delivery chain.

To summarize, the problems of international IT industries are focused on resources and costs. First, in many centers of IT industries the demand for qualified personnel is higher than supply. That leads to high wages, which software producers try to avoid by distributing programming work into lower wage countries. Highly sophisticated software products, however, require more than just a routine kind of programming, and that kind of skills are available in places that already are highly developed and industrialized, or that are developing at a high speed. Production in these kind of places is more expensive than in less developed regions, and international industries may also be asked to participate in the development of those areas. For example, international companies are expected to make investments, and to help in creating local know how in the area.

Sophisticated and professional software packages also require an international marketing and delivery chain, which is expensive for large software houses, and a real challenge for small and new companies. This makes the international start for new businesses difficult, and larger companies can take advantage of that by buying them out of the market.

In distributing software production into international locations, companies also need to take into account some other things: First, the telecommunication infrastructures and the logistics in traffic and transportation must reach international standards, and the time zone should support distributed production on a 24-hour base. Second, the location must be politically and economically safe. Third, the area needs to be rich in innovation and culture. Fourth, the environment should attract talented people, so that they are willing to move in the area, and to work and rise their families there.

Altogether, the requirements for a potential location for distributed IT industries, the local region should:

- Be located in a world widely logistic area and have fluent transportation and traffic connections everywhere
- Be situated within a time zone that allows 24 hours production in connection with the most important centers of international IT industries
- Have a secure and friendly political and economic environment
- Have highly developed telecommunication infrastructures
- Have a pleasant, safe and attractive environment
- Have a rich and unique history and culture
- Have a high supply of talented and skilled IT professionals, artists and other cultural people
- Have a lot of other kinds of educated people, especially story tellers, writers, artists, movie makers, etc.
- Have low wages
- Have a low taxation rate, and offer other economic benefits for running business there
- Be fluent with the English language.

These requirements are hardly fulfilled in any location in the World, but the more of them are found in a certain country or region, the more likely it is to attract international businesses there.

HOW LAPLAND ANSWEWRS THE REQUIREMENTS OF GLOBAL IT INDUSTRIES

When Lapland is compared with the requirements that global IT industries set for international regions, it appears to be a promising, but an unknown location for practicing IT industries. It has most of the necessary elements to make a good location for industrial production, but the local authorities seem to lack the power to push it through to the international publicity. Also, as the location is not yet known by any of its achievements in the IT field, global industries have not invented it as a potential location for distributing their production.

During the summer 2000 Lapland was receiving international publicity through two innovative software productions, but they are not enough to turn decision makers' eyes towards Lapland. The two Lappish key software products that were presented to the international audience in 2000 were the Adventure Land of Snow and Ice, and the interactive virtual wall in the Finland's pavilion at the World Exhibition of Hannover, Germany in the Summer 2000. The Adventure Land of Snow and Ice is an immersive virtual environment representing a typical Lappish mountain environment in winter scene. The audience may enter that environment through a user interface that in some cases represents walking, or riding a reindeer or a snowmobile. To increase the sense of reality in the winter scene, the show-room itself is a cold laboratory at the same time, so when in the virtual environment it is cold, the temperature in the room is –10 C. The winter effect is strengthened by running the show in the summer, and by moving the show-room into places were it is fairly warm throughout the year. For enabling that the show-room was built into a truck container, in which it was on tour to 12 different countries in Europe during the summer 2000. The tour was started in Helsinki in May, and by September it was traveling through European major cities like Brussels, Paris, Berlin, Hannover (World Exhibition) and St Petersburg in Russia. In the Hannover World Exhibition also another Lappish software product was shown during the summer, thus the University of Lapland produced some interactive animations on the photographic wall scenes of the Finland's pavilion. Simultaneously, the wall reacts on the movements of the viewer, and some of the characters are playing by harmonica a funny old Finnish song called Säkkijärvi's polka. The same tune was also one of the first and the most popular changeable tune in Nokia mobile phones, so foreign people might recognize it by that context as well. Regardless of success in the World Exhibition, international actors may also pay attention to Lapland due to other reasons. One of them is the strong international interest that is currently being paid to Finland due to leading expertise and high diffusion rate of mobile technologies, and due to huge international success of the Finnish leading IT company called Nokia. While being a part of Finland, Lapland may receive international publicity due to same reasons.

The earlier listed criteria for potential locations of global IT industries are fulfilled in Lapland in the following ways.

Logistics and Transportation

Lapland has several airports, which are servicing direct international flights each Christmas. The major airport that is located in the capital city Rovaniemi, exactly on the Arctic Circle, is servicing tight flight schedules daily, and that includes both passenger traffic and air cargo, plus routine military flights. The most direct route around the World for air cargo on the North Calotte area goes through Rovaniemi, so according to the logistics of the air transportation Lapland is an ideal location at that part of the World. Lapland also has good railway and road connections, and a sea port that is open throughout the year.

From Lapland it is an 8 hours' time zone to the United States in the west, and 8 hours to the Far East in the other direction. This means that by locating production units in Lapland, international companies may have 24 hours non stop programming work if they circle the same piece of work from one location to another. The telecommunication infrastructures cover the whole area, so the basic technologies already exist in the area.

Education

There are a lot of highly educated people in Finland, of which a great deal having academic degrees in economic and technological fields, or in more humanistic subjects. The national languages are Finnish and Swedish, but in practice everyone speaks also English because it is being taught from the third class for all children in the comprehensive school. Education is obligatory and free until 16 years of age, and after that people can choose from several kinds of different schools. There are no fees in universities or other schools, so everyone can study as a doctor by paying for teaching materials and living only. Students are though selected into universities, but if one has the talent, good education is available no matter what the economic and social background of one's family is.

In technology fields wages are higher than in average in the country, but internationally compared the wages are lower than in major production areas. This means that locating software production in Finland is reasonable both due to educated people in the area, and due to relatively low wages. In addition to ordinary production, also R&D functions can be located in Finland, because, as the Nokia and several other cases show, Finnish people are technologically innovative, and they also use the technological equipment and applications more than anywhere else in the World. Already from the early 1900's, the diffusion rate of the telephone in Finland has been highest in the World, and until today, practically all households have telephones, TV and radio equipment. Internet access is high and still spreading, and currently a digital-TV system is being built in the country. That should reach every home, but as the system is expensive and so far the content is missing, it is too early to say how well and how fast it will replace the analogical TV. It is very likely that the digital-TV will spread fast, and that it will become the major virtual service channel in each home. Among young and adult people almost everyone has a mobile phone, and the speed of the diffusion has been faster than with any other IT equipment.

Democratic Stable Economy

Finland is a free democracy with a strong and stable economy. Taxation is a little bit higher than in some other countries, but a great deal of it is returned to citizens in forms of the wide social and welfare system, security on streets and homes, free education, caring of the unemployed, etc. Finland is also peaceful and safe country where children may play outside without having adults to guide them, and where in the countryside many people even these days live without locking their doors. The air is clean, and there is still a lot of forest and wild life left in the country. Fresh water is available all over the country, and the drinking water is taken from the public watering system that is coming to each home. There is also bottled water on sale, but it is not actually needed.

Extraordinary History and Culture

Lapland's history and culture are extraordinary, and also cultural offerings are rich in the area. That is though different and smaller than in the international big cities, so people who have always lived in cities may not want to live there. For example, theatre and concerts are available weekly in Lapland, and during the summer some special pieces of opera and other classical music are produced in some very unique locations in the nature. In the cultural life, nature is taken into account, thus during a certain period the sun doesn't go down at all in the summer, and for a similar period of time in the winter the sun does not come up at all. For hearing internationally well known artists, some might sometimes be met in Lapland, but normally one needs to travel elsewhere, for example in Helsinki. There one might here the symphonies of Sibelius, conducted by Esa Pekka Salonen or Jukka Pekka Saraste, or other picccs of music presented by artists like Karita Mattila. In Helsinki one might also meet performers from other countries, for example Pavarotti, Jose Carreras and Placido Domingo, Tina Turner, Tom Jones or Rolling Stones.

SUMMARY

International information technology, software and entertainment industries have a lack of human resources, and their production costs are high. In highly focused areas also their innovation base is narrow, so for servicing different cultures in global markets, they need to distribute their R&D and production. In other parts of the world, regions need to develop, but usually that is hindered because of the missing industrial base, and the lack of knowledge and capital.

Lapland is a part of a technologically advanced and quite wealthy country of Finland, but outside tourism it has practically no basic industries, and due to unemployment, this relatively large area of 100 000 square kilometers that makes a third of the whole country, becomes empty after educated people's moving abroad or into large cities in other parts of the country. During the last few years, Lapland has started to create new information technology based industries in the area, and, due to the region's strong emphasis in tourism, and the local university's strong profile in the new media, virtual reality and other fields of the faculty of arts, Lapland's new industries are called as the 'industry of experience'. Under this title, Lapland is developing especially new media, virtual reality and entertainment industries, but also tourism, and industrial design both in manufacturing, and in textile and clothing industries. As a part of a relatively wealthy country and the European Union, Lapland will have fair resources for developing these new industries, but the most difficult part will be in getting the recognition from the world market. Becoming a meaningful node in the international information technology and entertainment industries requires first creating own knowledge and talent in the area, then making international businesses aware of it, and finally making them willing to invest in the R&D and production in the area. So far, Lapland has only taken its first steps on the international market, and in the cooperation with international partners. The experiences are, however, promising, so there is no reason to cut off the selected strategy.

STUDY QUESTIONS

1. What are the main reasons for large IT industries to distribute their operation in other countries and outside huge urban areas?

2. On which basis do IT industries select their international locations?

3. Describe the capital issues of IT industries, especially in the very early stages of the firms' operation.

4. What kind of growth and internationalization problems do IT firms have in small countries in distant locations?

5. How has the international IT companies' operation in the developing countries changed during the past few decades, and what kind of responsibilities do the industries have in these locations?

6. To your mind, which factors or issues will direct the growth of global IT industries in the following years, and in which directions are these industries heading to?

7. Thinking of digital and virtual content production, what kind of ethical questions do international IT and entertainment industries meet in creating new products to different audiences in different cultures and countries?

REFERENCES

This chapter is written based on the author's personal working experience, research, and discussions with people involved in international business. For more references, please find general literature about regional policies, global business management on IT, etc.

SECTION - 2

GLOBAL INFORMATION TECHNOLOGY STRATEGY AND MANAGEMENT

This section presents seven chapters covering a wide range of issues faced by the IT function in its formation of strategy. It starts with a short essay that points out many of the wrong moves made by IT management in some companies. The next chapter presents a model that can be used to formulate strategic IT options.

Chapter 7 is devoted to how best manage the cultural and other differences between headquarters and the remainder of the enterprise. One recent trend has been the use of IT for creation of ever more complex and efficient supply chains, linking together not only overseas subsidiaries of the multinational enterprise, but also customers and suppliers. Designing, building and maintaining, these types of relationships bring to the fore the complex issues around process engineering in the multinational enterprise. These issues are discussed in Chapter 8. Many companies have found that building world-class infrastructures means little if the supporting business processes are not in place. However, as Chapter 9 points out, when the time comes to re-engineer process through the enterprise, this immediately brings into play what in many cases is an inherent contradiction between headquarters and subsidiaries.

Chapter 10 deals with the issues of transborder data flow. Although it surfaced in the early 1970s, this issue has remained at the heart of much controversy in relationship between host countries and multinationals, and it remains even more important today, particularly as the web and eCommerce allows the easy international exchange of personal information, sometimes without the knowledge from the information is collected. Finally, there is a chapter on how do cope with IT strategy formulation in Russia. In the past, IT operations in Russia have been minimal. However, with the liberalization of markets, greater international cooperation and more joint venture work can be expected, particularly in some heavy industries, such as airframe manufacturing.

5

Avoiding Bad Decisions on the Road to Globalization

Edward M. Roche
The Concours Group, USA

ABSTRACT

Developments in information technologies are giving the multinational enterprise incredible opportunities to build powerful IT infrastructures and intelligent fast-response governance arrangements. Telecommunications continues to show greater cost/benefit improvement than microelectronics; application families such as Customer Relationship Management (CRM) anenterprise resource planning (ERP) are providing integration levels never before obtainable; Application and Business Service Providers (ASP and BSP) are providing considerably more flexible sourcing options than in the past. Nevertheless, in spite of these compelling advantages, firms continue to make bad decisions about globalization. Examples of bad decisions include the use of pseudo-economics [making decisions based on faulty or patently unrealistic assumptions], re-engineering governance in ways that actually make things worse, deciding to consolidate data centers or instances of [major] software dependent based upon unrealistic expectations of network and service performance, as well as adopting meaningless standards and fighting other political battles which even if won yield no benefits. Other persistent difficulties include failing to support innovation in the firm. Taking advantage of the opportunities at hand is best done with a very flexible view of what globalization of IT means for the individual firm.Fast-breaking developments in both applications and infrastructure technologies have given unprecedented opportunities to those multinational enterprises (MNE) wishing to improve how they operate worldwide. But it is always the case that IT leadership in the MNE is able to take advantage of these opportunities?

This chapter discusses first some of the developments that are providing new options for IT. These include [in no particular order] developments in telecommunications, the efficiencies that come from data center consolidation, new possibilities for knowledge management and collaboration of 'virtual' [e.g. geographically-separated] teams, customer relationship management, and the emergence of a much more mature outsourcing industry that can give flexible sourcing of needed IT resources on a scale never before seen in the past. Next, the essay discusses some of the common mistakes and problems present in some MNEs. There include the use of pseudo economics, meaningless restructuring of the IT organization, adoption of 'standards for standards sake', failure to create an innovation engine that will help the firm continually to improve, and a lack of focus on the customer.

Afterwards, we present a series of hypotheses that suggest some of the ways in which the IT function within the MNE might make better use of the technological [and other] opportunities before it.

CARPE DIEM[1]

Telecommunications: In the telecommunications arena, development has been extraordinarily fast. In The Net Effect, published by Sun Microsystems, it is argued that in 1999, developments in network bandwidth overtook those in microprocessor speed. At this rate, it is argued, the total packets being transmitted per second is doubling every 16 months, but the packets/second/CPU is doubling only every 24 months. This represents a triumph of "Gilder's Law" over "Moore's Law", and a confirmation of "Metcalfe's Law".[2] Sun's white paper then goes to describe the wonderful new world this is creating.

Such rapid change in what is possible with the new telecommunications environment translates into opportunities for radical changes in infrastructure and architecture, and for new levels of knowledge management and collaboration among geographically dispersed teams. Working with various customer-facing technologies [such as Customer Relationship Management (CRM) or the Web (internet commerce)] and the databases they create, the stage is set for a powerful innovation engine to power forward the firm, as data that has been held in separate places for so long now can be integrated together, and communicated quickly throughout the world.

Data center consolidation[3] is the end result of taking multiple data centers and moving their applications, data and servers into the same geographical location. This has been popular for years. Even in the 1980s, IBM was able to reduce its data centers serving Europe from hundreds to only 16, and then to even fewer. Provisioning of reliable, less expensive, and responsive telecommunications allows the use of remote processing in ways that end-users become completely unaware of where the computing for their work actually takes place. In addition to servers, the rise of powerful integrated enterprise applications have made it possible to service vast parts of the business from a single instance of software that in the past would require multiple locations. One multinational multi-divisional company I've worked with is consolidating more than 8 instances of SAP (an important ERP) into a single data center in London [running a single instance of the software.

Knowledge management and collaboration are tools used to allow geographically separated persons to work together, and make decisions concerning business operations and strategy. For the multinational enterprise, these tools promise extraordinary benefits by avoiding the difficulty, expense and fatigue of international travel. Doing knowledge management correctly implies that marketing [and other commercial] intelligence systematically is used on a continuous basis by management to improve business delivery to customers. In addition, improvements in telecommunications [e.g. higher speeds, lower costs, faster provisioning of circuits] and robust peer-to-peer architectures have greatly improved the prospects of collaboration on an international scale never before possible.[4] In addition, the growth of open-source[5] technologies continues to lower the entry barrier for experimentation.

Customer Relationship Management (CRM): Technologies now enable the firm to manage customer data, and respond in a completely individualized way, tailoring the business logic [the rules of how the customer is treated] to each unique "touch point" with the customer. The combination of technologies such as email, the Web, interactive chat sessions, traditional computer-telephony integration, mobile technologies such as Wireless Application Protocol (WAP) telephones [or in Japan i-Mode phones], or wireless Personal Data Assistants (PDA), and the soon-to-come growth of wireless video—all of these technologies are making it a competitive necessity for the multinational enterprise to implement a coherent multi-channel architecture for interacting with its customers. If the new channels are not available, business will go elsewhere.

Availability of global customer data plays a critical role in CRM. Some companies make the unfortunate discovery that their customer data is scattered in different data bases around the world. Finding timely data on a single customer is impossible. In response, some have developed systems to allow CRM applications to access data warehouses. This helps make available customer data needed to make decisions (or recommendations)[6]. For the multinational enterprise, this technology enables consolidation of customer data on a global scale. For example, if multinational A is doing business with multinational B in 25 countries, there would be a single instance of B's customer record that would show the total amount of business between the companies. Having access to this type of information has proved to be a serious problem for many organizations and remains a challenge today.

Personalization has been enabled on a global scale. Customers, either individual or corporate, now can be given unique attention on a scale never before contemplated. Examples include special offers, specific non-publicized price schedules, perks, and other services, even including personal news services and home office services [email and calendaring facilities.

Flexible Sourcing

Now more than ever before, the multinational enterprise is able to take advantage of new sourcing options for provisioning of IT services. Some of the major factors include (a) the proliferation of Application Service Provider (ASP) and Business Service Provider (BSP) options, and (b) the continued advance of offshore programming. These developments have yielded greater flexibility for the multinational in sourcing services both for continued operations, for maintenance of legacy systems, and for new systems development.

Application Service Providers make it possible for an enterprise to obtain applications remotely. They are best used when (a) the application being sourced in not critical to the business [For example, one multinational manufacturing company I have worked with is taking all of its Human Resources processing and handing it over to Oracle corporation for processing. They consider their critical systems to be in manufacturing, not in punching payroll for employees.], (b) the growth rate required of IT is high [In some industries, growth rates, particularly in start-up scenarios is projected to be more than 40 per cent per year. In these cases, even if the IT group wished to build the entire infrastructure (and associated applications) itself, it would find it practically impossible to do so due to talent availability constraints. In these cases, going to an outside source that already has the IT capabilities available for rental is the only feasible solution.], (c) time-to-market considerations are critical [Even when funding and talent is available, competitive pressures or other factors may compel the firm to deliver the new application in the shortest possible time frame. In these cases, it is out of the question to wait for months and months for something that can be purchased immediately through an ASP and be made available in weeks. Research has shown that time-to-market considerations are one of the key factors in attractiveness of the ASP model.], (d) skills to build the application may not be available inside the firm, yet there is no budget line to add more staff [In these cases, IT is caught with demands for an application it does not have the resources to provide. There is a risk in hiring new staff for a development effort that may be a fixed duration in time because after the development is completed, it may cost more (than one saved in the first place) to get rid of the employees.] These factors tend to favor the ASP solution.

In the multinational enterprise, sourcing options are even more numerous. There are many ASP and BSP vendors making services available around the world. In addition, given the performance of today's telecommunications network [see above], it is easy to pipeline applications to remote locations that in the past would have been left without service.

Offshore programming, particularly in India, has continued to flourish. The use of these services mushroomed during the Year 2000 crisis, but has continued to grow as the services available there have broadened their appeal and been upgraded to e-Commerce and other "upstream" technologies [such as database conversions]. Most companies are reporting a reduction in development and programming costs of about 20 per cent [from using off-shore services]. One company interviewed said they were skeptical at first, primarily because of the coordination problems posed by having programming teams operating on the other side of the world [from North America]. A few trials, however, quickly demonstrated this concern was a red herring. The programmers in India would work on problems "during the [North American] night" and then send the work back. While the Indian programmers were sleeping, test and quality assurance is done in North America. This cycle repeated, to the benefit of all involved. Another company had spent the past few years paring down its IT costs to the absolute minimum. They had a deep feeling that should there be demands for any more cost reduction, they would be "cutting into the bone". They too have found programming in India to be a viable alternative. Not being able to hire any more persons on staff, the firm is dependent on outside programming resources. On a strictly price comparison basis, the Indian option is one the cheapest.[7]

Some have written about IT in the enterprise becoming more of a "vendor contract management" operation than being responsible for actual delivery of services. I recall sitting on the couch across from the CIO of one of the world's largest and most successful high technology firms. "We expect that within 2 years, more than 85 per cent of all our programming and systems development will be handled by outside vendors." When asked what the remaining persons on staff [inside the organization] were doing with they work, the answer was: "Learning how to manage vendors."

WAG THE DOG

In spite of these great potential benefits of new technologies [and services], leadership in many multinational enterprises frequently make bad decisions one after another. Perhaps, as Professor Clemmons of Wharton suggests, "most bad decisions are made because there is no balance between risk and reward, or risk and punishment [in case of poor decision-making]". Several companies I have worked with have engaged in "globalization programs", but evidently without any clear idea of exactly what is going to be globalized, and how and, perhaps most important, why it is needed.

Below are listed a few of the more common pitfalls companies seem to make. I call this "wag the dog" because in most cases, some false principle or set of assumptions is driving [e.g. "wagging"] the entire IT strategy.

Reliance on Pseudo Economics: Many globalization campaigns appear to be made either without reference to their financial value to the enterprise, or based on assumptions that are so unrealistic as to appear almost laughable. "You need to invest to save money." "The payback period will be long, but it will be worth it." "Our best estimations show a very rapid payoff."

Having spent several years going through IT budgets, and collecting information on what happens with multi-year vendor contracts, one fact seems to be very clear: At the beginning of a project that is more than a year or so long, there is no rational way to determine what it will cost! This problem has come up over and over with vendor contracting, particularly with long- or medium-term systems development [programming] projects, or with outsourcing arrangements of one kind or another. In almost every case, the vendor is locked by default into an adversarial relationship with the customer. Contracts frequently are signed with a generous supply of "escalation clauses" and separate schedules of charges that might occur if the requirements [for the service being rendered] change. [Like compound interest on a credit card,] as these "additional resource compliments" are added into the contract going forward, they begin to magnify the total multi-year cost of the relationship. After a few years of repeated small [incremental] changes, the final cost of the contract bears only the most tenuous relationship with the assumptions of the original cost planning. These extra costs are what the vendor depends on, and what the client hopes to avoid.

In the multinational enterprise, the problem is multiplied by the implicit complexity of some large, geographically separated, and historically incompatible information systems. Companies tend to launch major global campaigns in order to revamp infrastructure—

calculating all the time the promise of vast savings. Yet these savings rarely materialize. Instead, the IT group begins the journey downwards on a long spiral of lengthening project time-lines and untoward consequences. Globalization becomes a type of archaeology expedition in which deeper and deeper layers of incompatible and specialized systems supporting many undiscovered [and critical] business operations and functions are unearthed and brought to light. Eventually the complexity either overwhelms the organization, causing a grinding and painful halt to the program, or, usually under pressure, the IT organization in desperation starts to take what I like to call triage decisions in which systems are sacrificed, but only on the narrowest of criteria. As the impact of these bad decisions start to ripple throughout the organization, the feedback starts to flow up through the business hierarchy to the top. Eventually, IT does not look as good as it did, particularly the corporate "global" IT staff.[8]

Meaningless Restructuring of Governance

Another of the most common mistakes discovered arises when firms make substantial change in the global governance structures controlling how IT is provisioned[9] in the enterprise. One large chemical company had for years given a significant amount of control over IT to each of the different working companies around the world. The company is engaged in business along several parts of a complex international value-added chain starting with extraction and ending up with delivery directly to consumers. Each of the local IT positions was responsible for working directly with the business units they supported—organizations that also paid for the IT budget when things had to be done.

The company then embarked on a "globalization of IT" campaign. A new position of "global CIO" was created. At the same time, the groups that had been operating almost semi-autonomously at the local level were partially trimmed back, with the remaining being forced into a new reporting relationship—in this case, directly into the office of the new global CIO who happened to be moving to a new office in Europe.

The new system put in place was to work as follows: The planning for any new project was now cleared with headquarters, and a centrally-directed process was put into place to standardize IT throughout the enterprise. The rationale behind this restructuring of the governance process was that (a) it would be possible to achieve economies of scale in planning because rather than having planning take place in many different [localized] places, it would be taken "more efficiently" at a headquarters location, (b) it would be easier to control IT costs because they could be "wrapped up" [e.g. consolidated] into a single budget for the enterprise as a whole, rather than have budgetary responsibility handled in many different locations [with inadequate coordination], (c) prioritization [e.g. assignment of capital allocation for proposed projects] would be simplified because all projects could be considered through a single "clearing house" that could reflect on the overall business and how projects supported [or failed to support] the mission, (d) the total number of managers throughout the IT function could be reduced because the small ["elite"] staff at headquarters would be able to enjoy a larger span of control[10].

The real results have been less clear and certainly less compelling. The first problem is isolation of the corporate IT group from the rest of the enterprise. Now the firm finds it is very difficult to maintain a clear line of sight to what is going on throughout the enterprise, because there is not enough of a sophisticated reporting and intelligence-gathering process put in place to draw upon. In consequence, the corporate IT group is forced to rely upon "global" get-togethers in which IT professionals from around the world are rounded up and brought to a single off-site location for 1—2 days to do planning and to discuss initiatives. Theoretically [on paper], this type of arrangement works, but as a practical matter, the corporate IT group is falling out of touch [with reality]. The second problem is that because of the decimation of IT talent at the local levels [cost-cutting, rationalization, elimination of redundancy, etc.], the process of coordination and consultation with the business units in various subsidiaries has started to break down. Many of the experts who did this function in the past have either been transferred to the headquarters operation, or let go, leaving behind more junior persons to handle this function. The result of this is that for any given IT initiative underway in the firm, it is more likely that the course chosen will run into opposition [later on] during the implementation phase when it is "discovered" that many needed [business] requirements are not met [because they were never considered]. The third problem is that although the governance structure for the global IT function has been changed radically, there is virtually no change in the actual underlying IT infrastructure. In other words, the governance system has been changed, but without correlation to any fundamental change in the actual way IT is operated and distributed throughout the enterprise. There is no synchronization or correspondence between the two elements.

When one looks back at the tremendous effort that has gone into changing the governance structure, and the high probability that even poorer results will be obtained, one wonders what the firm was thinking when it undertook this program. What are the prospects? One can surmise that soon it will be necessary to "re-insert" another layer of IT professionals into various more important ["Strategic"] business units in order to serve as a liaison with corporate IT. This will start the long program of partial reversal of the previous changes that were put into place, with so much effort, and with so little effect. In the end, even the IT group at headquarters likely will come under pressure as an "unnecessary overhead" item in itself. The forces that push in this direction will be essentially political in nature (a) they will be stimulated by problems that occur in the business units when IT fails to meet their demands, and yet insists on charging back its budget, (b) then complaints will flow up the chain of command—but through the lines of business not through IT—to a high enough position where they accumulate in a person with high enough power to apply pressure directly against the office of the global CIO.

Standards for Standards Sake

Over and over we have seen IT attempt to set global standards, even when there is little benefit for the firm. In one firm, the global IT group decided they would enforce a single desktop standard worldwide. In order to accomplish this, it was necessary to set up a series of global team meetings with "delegates" from IT groups around the world coming together to a single meeting point. After that, each of the persons was required to return to their "home" area and "sell" the program to the local subsidiary of the MNC. This was necessary because of the substantial amount of investment required [to replace all of the desktops with new ones]. This "selling" and "consensus-building" part of the process took almost 1 year before any real changes began to be implemented in infrastructure [and in the budgeting process]. As approval slowly came, and the provisioning/implementation process started, the company quickly realized that because of local differences in systems [to which the desktop units had to connect] it was impossible to have the me disk image on each machine worldwide. In addition, the process of finding a suitable PC vendor who could provide a consistent level of service world-wide [in each of the MNC locations] took more than another 1/2 year [due to the RFP[11] process], and the best prices the firm could obtain, often were above what individual units could get in their home territories. At the subsidiary level, these actions led to even more confusion [and some resentment].

By the time the roll-out started, the initial design for the desktop system was obsolete, and it was clear that whatever theoretical benefits were counted, quickly would be overcome by difficulties in implementation. The firm then decided to adopt a completely different strategy—it would set a new [and entirely different] global desktop standard. It chose to insist that each desktop would have a browser capable of supporting HTML, java, java script, and XML. So long as the desktop being used supported those technologies, there was now at the local level complete flexibility otherwise regarding choice. As a compliment to this strategy, it was decided all further development would require that all end-user access would be through a web browser—so-called "browser-ware". No one wanted to remember the wasted time and effort of the "desktop initiative".

Failure to Create Innovation Engine

One of the most common complaints I hear from IT professionals is that the IT organization "is creating so much high-quality information about customers, but management does not use it—in fact, they don't even know how to use it". When we make an investigation into the company and the way it works, it is usually the case that the organization has in place no organization that is in charge of knowledge management and strategic use of information.

In order for an organization to use information intelligently about its environment, it must have in place mechanisms that process information. In the best cases (figure 1), it works like a giant "sense and respond" mechanism within the enterprise with several components: (a) sensing mechanisms[12] in place that systematically collect information regarding competitors, customers, and general environmental information [political, economic, regulatory], (b) a storage and knowledge-management system that organizes the information, and makes it easy to access [for members engaged in strategy formulation and decision-making], (c) a decision making and strategy formulation work method that ensures incoming information is processed on a regular basis, and that decisions are taken that transform incoming information and data into specific responses to change [how the firm offers its products and services], (d) a change propagation method, to ensure that once a strategic response is agreed upon, it is acted upon without obfuscation, evasion, or delay, (e) a technology response mechanism, to ensure that any technology work that must be done in support of the new initiative is ready and funded to provide service, (f) a system of performance metrics that are able to evaluate how well the initiative accomplishes what it was intended to do[13].

In the multinational enterprise, putting in place such a feedback-loop mechanism[14] is the only way effectively to ensure that corporate headquarters is able to sense what is going on in the [business] environment and respond appropriately so as to take advantage of any opportunities that might arise. There are several lynchpin technologies that of necessity must be provided by IT to support these activities: (a) comprehensive information [information made available through applications that enable any corporate decision maker quickly to see a complete view of the customer], (b) competitor database [some way to organize incoming information on competitors; using today's technologies, this type of information can effectively be maintained through use of a sophisticated intranet function with a hypertext structure], (c) group decision support systems [these systems allow brainstorming, either in person or remotely, so that groups can take votes, narrow differences of opinion, agree upon prioritization of actions that need to be taken], (d) teleconferencing, "write board", and other geographically distributed mechanisms for "virtual meetings" support [these technologies are difficult to learn at first, but if used systematically can speed-up decision making, and of course help participants avoid tiring international travel], (e) finally, an innovation process needs to be put into place.

Creation of an innovation process involves changes in both organizational practice as well as compensation. Some factors are (a) the use of innovation councils working at different levels systematically to screen ideas, (b) putting in place a reward system that communicates to employees that change and innovation are important,[15] (c) institutionalization of the innovation process [e.g. it is not considered to be something that is working off to the side, attended to primarily by lower-level functionaries; rather it is to be managed and worked on by the business leaders throughout the corporation], (d) top management support [because only the political (and financial e.g. budgetary) power of top management is enough to actually get people to change how they conduct their work.][16]

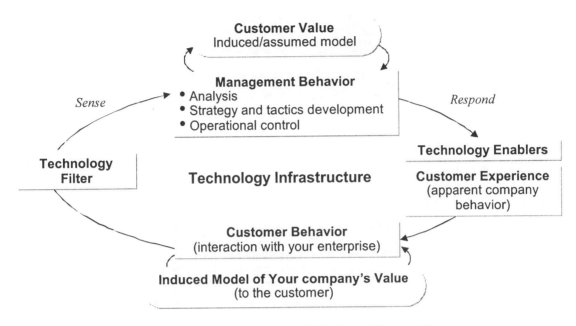

Figure 1: The Sense and Respond Cycle and Innovation

Explanation: Technology intermediates between the enterprise and customer. Some technology filters information regarding customer behavior, and feeds this information to management—part of the "sensing" function. Other technology enables the enterprise to respond to the customer by providing a specific customer experience. The customer interacting with the enterprise creates an induced model of the firm—a positive or negative impression of how beneficial it is to give over its business. The firm also has a model of the customer based on what it thinks the customer values. This model is refined through analysis, then put into action be changing operational control and developing new tactics and strategies to better meet customer requirements.[17]

In many multinational enterprises, however, IT fails to support the innovation process. This leads to a slow-down in decision-making and a retardation of innovation. Line of business managers are never made aware of the possibilities that technology holds for making their work easier, for increasing the amount of collaboration that is possible, and for coordinating how business innovation can take place. One company I have been working with has embarked on a giant program completely to restructure their global information systems. They are proud of the savings it promises. When asked about how the new arrangements will help the company understand what is happening in its various markets, and how to develop a business response to emerging market opportunities, there was a completely blank stare. They had made the mistake that so many others make: defining IT narrowly as a platform to process information. It is of course far more. In today's enterprise, IT is the media for the organization.

Lack of Focus on the Customer

In the age of the Internet and eCommerce, keeping a total focus on the customer and their experience is the only way for firms to operate, and it is the role of IT to assist heartily in this endeavor. In most firms I've worked with, there is always an obligatory "paying of mouth service" to being customer-centric, but little specificity on how this is accomplished. The major element of delivering products and services that are completely focused on the customer include capabilities such as (a) providing personalization of services [ensuring that regardless of how the customer interacts with the firm, they receive a customized experience based on their value to the firm, and on their own preferences], (b) making decisions regarding how the firm develops new products and services dependent upon intensive review of customer preferences, (c) making customer success a key criteria in how people are promoted in the firm, (d) setting up organization of work so that it is directly supportive of enhancing the customer experience [e.g. work is organized according to how it will support the customer experience, and not in the traditional methods, that is 'according to functional areas'], (e) ensuring that allocation of investment capital in IT projects [new systems development] is adjusted around impacts on the customer as the primary [most heavily weighted] criteria in decision making.

In the multinational enterprise, the situation is made more complex because (a) many customers are global in nature [e.g. they have interactions with the firm in many different geographical areas simultaneously, for example through different subsidiaries], (b) in order to maintain coherent customer records a level of data sharing [and auxiliary standardization around data definitions and updating procedures] not known in most organizations is necessary, usually between subsidiaries [or other functional divisions of the enterprise] that in the past have had no incentive or business-logic necessitating sharing and collaboration on customer data, (c) from the point of view of individual subsidiaries, the economic logic of investment in the required collaboration is not clear [e.g. funding for such activities might appear to be a "corporate tax" on individual subsidiaries], (d) the amount of shared information may not be large since the total amount of business to a global customer might be a small percentage of the total business in a particular geographical area [this has the result of raising the cost per application for shared global applications to many times what it costs to provision similar services on a stand-alone basis], (e) account management may become more problematical since account managers in individual subsidiary locations now must be "coordinated" with a global account manager [thus requiring sharing of credit (e.g. commissions) for sales].

In many cases, problems with global customers have compelled acquisition of Enterprise Resource Planning (ERP) systems—some of the largest and most complex international undertakings ever attempted by IT. It is clear that many of these projects were poorly managed, leading to massive cost-overruns, confusion about approaches to take, political fights regarding budgeting and systems design, and in many cases severe failure. In many enterprises, these systems have been implemented, but with mixed results.[18] It is common, for example, for a firm to "standardize" on a set package, e.g. SAP, and then find out that how the package is implemented in different geographical divisions of the enterprise makes more difficult further collaboration between the systems going forward. After a few years, the firm "discovers" a need for further integration across the enterprise, but such further integration poses a daunting challenge because different instances of the software are running in different locations throughout the enterprise. This result has the simple effect of raising up a further notch the complexities in further systems implementation. Again, the pursuit of an ideal global system is botched up [and badly] by poor implementation and coordination across the multinational enterprise. Again, a trend towards "simplification" leads to layering-on of even greater complexity than ever contemplated in the past.

The above are only a few examples of "Wag the Dog" in the multinational enterprise. Globalization often is a tale of untoward consequences. The rapid pursuit of simplification, short-cuts, quick progress, and the like lead inevitably to an even greater slew of problems requiring attention. Bad decisions lead to an even greater headache in the future.

HYPOTHESES ON WHAT WORKS

Perhaps I can suggest a few hypotheses on what works for management of IT in the multinational enterprise.

Movement to Global Product or Customer-based Organizations - Hypothesis

Moving towards a global product organization requires a different IT organization from a customer-based organization. For a product-oriented organization, stronger centralization of IT management and control is preferable. For a customer-based organization, a two-tier IT management and control is preferable with Tier I oriented at serving and coordinating services to global customers [customers with whom the firm is doing business with simultaneously in different regions of the world]; and Tier II oriented at providing local services to smaller [non-global] customers at the regional or nation-state level. For Tier I activities, in cases where there is a single global account representative assigned to a major client, there should be an IT representative counterpart to ensure inter-corporate systems are working smoothly.

How to Rationalize IT in a Multinational Enterprise - Hypothesis

The most effective methods of transitioning to a more global organization involve (a) reduction in multiple instances of major enterprise applications [e.g. SAP]; (b) establishment of a global "coordination layer" composed of "elite" IT executives operating above and across the entire multinational enterprise and reporting into a central location; (c) data center consolidation; (d) adoption of thin client [e.g. "browser-ware"] as much as possible at the end-user level, opening up possibilities for more and eventually all major applications to be pushed back into infrastructure, subject to stronger leverage to achieve economies of scale; (e) rationalization in systems development efforts and narrowing of required internal skills base by winnowing-out of the applications portfolio.

The Role of Leadership - Hypothesis

IT tends to attract strong technologists, but weak non-charismatic leaders not well prepared for global responsibilities. The most effective leadership in IT is grown in organizations that make global thinking and responsibilities an integral part of promotion and compensation. The worst practices in developing IT global leadership skills are (a) setting up politically castrated "international teams" to coordinate global projects, but without any political power or inter-personal connections to be effective; (b) making "international" or "global" a separate organization that falls into a "policymaking" or "coordination" role, but with real decision-making and financial [e.g. budgeting] responsibilities remaining elsewhere, usually in individual business units. The best practices include: (a) picking only the best "elite" [most intelligent, most skilled, most experienced, etc.] IT personnel to work on global issues, and making sure these factors are communicated to all IT personnel so that working on "global" is seen as a substantial reward and personal "mark of excellence" [and change compensation accordingly]; (b) Avoid the "Emperor Model" [cf. The Ming Dynasty (in China) had a policy of sending Imperial governors to states only if they were not from that state (ostensibly so they would have no local connections, and thus remain loyal to the Emperor)], instead try to match local "governors" to areas where they have the greatest amount of familiarity [in cases where a "foreign" governor is "dropped in" to a specific region (or area of work), ensure that counter-balancing decision-making safeguards are put into place by setting up a "back door" informal channel of information reporting.

How to Govern IT in a Multinational Enterprise - Hypothesis

Global management and coordination mechanisms work best when (a) there is a single IT office for the multinational enterprise located in proximity to the corporate headquarters; (b) A "military-like" hierarchical structure is employed [e.g. a General, a Chief of Staff, supporting officers; field commanders, chiefs of staffs for field commanders, supporting officers for field commanders, etc.] with unambiguous reporting structures, clear lines of decision-making authority, and a shared vision of what is to be accomplished. (c) IT has in place a sophisticated knowledge management system that is used on a regular basis as part of standard work procedures and monitors important information such as (i) problems with [internal] customers; (ii) problems with getting agreements on global initiatives [and brainstorming on how to fix them]; (iii) problems with global external partners [e.g. customers or business suppliers].

How to Make Global IT Align with Business Strategy - Hypothesis

The most effective way to manage IT in a multi-divisional [multi-LOB] multinational enterprise is to have a separate CIO [with accompanying staff support] assigned to each LOB. These CIOs also should be members of a Global IT Council responsible for setting policy for the enterprise as a whole. Global policies should be first around overall budgets, with decision-making regarding implementation of the investment funds devolved to each separate CIO. Consolidation of standards [and supporting operating procedures] between different LOB's should be strictly limited to major applications that operate across LOB's. Multi-product firms that attempt to implement "standards for standards sake" are wasting their time.

How to Manage Global Sourcing - Hypothesis

At the most fundamental level, there is little, if anything, different about global sourcing decisions in contrast to similar decisions made on a smaller scale. The only significant differences are (a) vendors need to be qualified as competent to conduct both service and support on a global scale [this tends to limit the choices to a very narrow range of companies], (b) the firm should attempt to take advantage of consolidated global purchasing [pooling together all of the purchases with any individual vendor at a single place in order to get a "volume discount"][19], (c) management of global sourcing contracts [vendor payments; verification of work charged; quality assurance; monitoring of service-level agreements, etc.] requires the establishment of a sophisticated system for sharing information [regarding vendor performance and pricing levels] throughout the enterprise. The best practice is for "global sourcing" to be used only for projects run from global [corporate] IT, and not be used for applications that exist primarily within a specific division or geographical area of the enterprise.

Building an 'Innovation Engine'-- Hypothesis

Companies engaged in rationalizing their global IT infrastructures [through actions such as data center consolidation or reduction in instances of major software systems (and the people supporting them!)] will be more successful [in their continued business operations] if they build an innovation engine for the firm. What is an innovation engine? It is a set of processes [and procedures] within a multinational enterprise that systematically vets ideas for change including (1) development of new goods and services, (2) re-engineering of business processes [particularly at the international level], (3) active collaboration with partners [e.g. other companies, partially-owned subsidiaries, some customers, government agencies, others] in order to re-think the efficiencies of their trans-organizational processes. In order to put in place an innovation engine, leading companies rely on a variety of collaboration technologies [and other practices] to ensure virtual teams can operate effectively on a geographically-distributed basis. For example, as shown in E. Carmel's study Global Software Teams, leading-edge software manufacturers use global networks [and specialized processes and procedures] in order to develop software 'around the clock'.[20] Unfortunately, Carmel's study shows a best practice that is not the norm in most multinational enterprises——but should be. In addition, in order to build an innovation engine, companies need to use a variety of collaborative technologies, not only in software production [the subject of Carmel's study], but throughout the enterprise at the local, regional, and 'global' [e.g. headquarters] levels in order to ensure that ideas for change effectively are used in setting policy and strategy.

In this short essay, I have suggested a few opinions derived from my experiences working with IT groups in multinational enterprises. Perhaps with some of the above hypotheses—they will work for some organizations, but not for others. In any case, one thing is clear: the recent problems with "globalization" in IT have raised more difficult issues that need to be solved, and there certainly is a great deal of research to be done.

STUDY QUESTIONS

1. Define Gilder's Law, Moore's Law and Metcalfe's Law and the "Net Effect". Discuss some of the implications for the multinational enterprise and the way it manages IT.

2. Name several ways in which changes [improvements] in international telecommunications offers opportunities for management of IT in multinational enterprises.

3. What is business intelligence and what are some of the ways in which IT in the multinational enterprise can help obtain and manage it?

4. What is Customer Relationship Management? How does the geographically distributed nature of the multinational enterprise complicate CRM? What types of problems do you think a firm might encounter if it is doing business with the same customer in several different countries at the same time?

5. What role does the Application Service Provider have in the sourcing decisions in the multinational enterprise? Do you think it is a good idea for the firm to depend on outside companies to provide critical IT applications? What happens when something goes wrong?

6. When would a multinational enterprise use an Application Service Provider or an Business Service Provider? When not? Why?

7. Do you think it is practical for a North American or European-based company to hire programmers working around the world in India to do critical programming tasks? What are some of the possible disadvantages to this type of arrangement? Why do you think companies might wish to do this?

8. What are some of the typically mistakes a firm might make when it attempts to "globalize" its IT infrastructure? What about the way it manages IT?

9.   What is governance and why is it so important? Can you give examples of how governance works? What happens when governance does not work correctly? Does the multinational enterprise pose any special problems in governance?

10. How important are standards for information technology in the multinational enterprise? Do you think standards are good? Why? Do you think they might have disadvantages? Why? What type of policy do you think is best for standards?

11. Discuss who should decide on international IT standards and what their criteria for decision-making might be? Why?

12. What is the "sense and respond" cycle? How is it used in innovation in the multinational enterprise? What is being sensed and what are examples of responses that might be made?

13. What are performance metrics and can you discuss how they might be applied in the multinational enterprise? Why is it important for management to pay so much attention to metrics? Do you think constant measurement has any real value for employees, or is it just an unnecessary headache?

14. What is an innovation process and what does it mean for the management and deployment of IT in the multinational enterprise?

15. Can you define what it means to be customer-centric and what technologies might be used to accomplish this? Do you think customer-centricity is primarily an attitude on the part of workers, or do you think something more complicated is involved? What is the role of customer records and why does this create specific challenges to the management of IT in a multinational enterprise?

16. Pick one of the hypotheses in this chapter and discuss the pros and cons of that position.

17. Do you think it is fair for a multinational enterprise to 'outsource' much of its IT-related work to off-shore workers? What about the workers in the country that are being replaced by cheaper overseas workers?

END NOTES

[1] This term is Latin for "seize the day"—it refers to the act of taking advantage of every possibility that presents itself.

[2] Moore's Law describes the exponential growth of microprocessor speed—it doubles every 24 months. Gilder's Law is similar, but is focused on improvements in telecommunications bandwidth. It holds that the growth *also* is exponential, but at a rate of doubling every 16 months. Metcalfe's Law indicates yet another exponential growth factor—it holds that the *value* of a network [of a network to those who use it] increases as the *square* of the number of devices that it is connect to.

[3] There are many examples of different types of data center [and other services] consolidation. For a general discussion, see Coffey, Jeanne O Brien "Serving up consolidation" *Bank Systems & Technology* v37, n12 (Dec 2000): 42-44. For consolidation of data storage, see Dale, David "Storage networking and the data center of the future" *Computer Technology Review* v20, n11 (Nov 2000): 26-27+. For call center consolidation see Hanson, Dave "International call center consolidation: A real-life example" *Call Center Solutions* v17, n10 (Apr 1999):64-70. These [and many similar articles] show how most companies are able to make savings using the consolidation approach. It is clear, however, that such moves are not without risks.

[4] For a detailed examination of the peer-to-peer phenomenon, see Andy Oram (Ed.), *Peer-to-Peer: Harnessing the Power of Disruptive Technologies.* (Sebastopol, California: O'Reilly & Associates, Inc., 2001). Of particular interest to multinational enterprises are vendors such as Groove Networks. Groove makes a groupware system that

works with very robust security, and yet allows a Lotus Notes-type collaboration but without servers, e.g. in a complete peer-to-peer configuration.

[5] Open source software, including its *source code*, is made freely available. This leads to many possibilities for customization. [With proprietary software, the source code is not available, thus making it impossible to make modifications.] Examples include Linux, the Netscape Browser, the Apache Web Server, Sendmail, Emacs [text editor with LISP], and gimp [a graphics editing program]. For details of the open source software movement see (1) Richard M. Stallman, *GNU Emacs Manual* (Thirteenth Edition), (Boston: Free Software Foundation, 1997), especially pps. 461-470 "The GNU Manifesto", (2) Chris DiBona, Sam Ockman & Mark Stone (Eds.), *Open Sources: Voices from the Open Source Revolution,* (3) Eric S. Raymond, *The Cathedral & The Bazaar.* [both published by]: Cambridge: O'Reilly, 1999, and (4) Pekka Himanen, *The Hacker Ethic and the Spirit of the Information Age* New York: Random House, 2001.

[6] "Recommender systems" are used to make product recommendations to a customer. These systems analyze the patterns of customer behavior, and then make recommendations regarding products or services that may be of interest to them.

[7] Over the years, as the IT consulting industry in India has increased its ability to add value, e.g. to provide more sophisticated services to clients, the same was not true elsewhere. Other countries, such as The Philippines in particular, have 'grown' specialized IT services industries around data entry [e.g. *low* value-added services]. In that country, conversion of telephone books [e.g. typing in the names, addresses, and numbers from *printed* telephone books for eventual delivery on CD ROMS or on-line databases], or parts catalogues, etc. has become a major industry.

[8] Do you remember the famous Khrushchev advice to his successor: "I give you two letters. Open the first one when you are in deep trouble. Open the second one when you are in deep trouble a second time." The successor gets into trouble, and opens the first letter. It reads: "Blame the problems on your predecessor". Eventually, he gets into trouble again and opens the second letter [meaning of course that he too soon will have a successor]. It reads: "Write two letters." More than a few CIO's have been in this situation. [Note: This story has been retold in many forms.]

[9] "Provisioning" is a general concept that has its origins in telecommunications. Telecom companies frequently speak of "provisioning circuits"—this of course means installation, planning, testing, and other associated activities. In this chapter, the term refers to the entire process of assessment, planning, allocation of capital, systems development and rollout of new information systems in the multinational enterprise. It is a convenient word that encompasses many separate activities, each of which is complex [in itself] and is composed of many sub-processes.

[10] As measured on a "per manager" basis.

[11] RFP—Request for a Proposal. A document let by an enterprise to various vendors asking for their quotation on a group of products or services to be purchased.

[12] There is no single term for this activity. It is referred to as "environmental scanning", "market intelligence", "corporate intelligence" [which many people joke is a "contradiction in terms"!], "business intelligence", and so on.

[13] A balanced scorecard approach involves not only keeping track of performance measurements, but *organizational learning* as well. See Nils-Göran, Jan Roy and Magnus Wetter, *Performance Drivers—A Practical Guide to Using the Balanced Scorecard.* (Chichester: John Wiley & Sons, 1999).

[14] For anyone interested in the general ideas behind feedback mechanisms, see: Ludwig von Bertalanffy, *General System Theory—Foundations, Development, Applications* (New York: George Braziller, 1968).

[15] In the early days at IBM, employees were given a THINK sign to put on their desk. This was to remind them on a daily basis that their job was not to push paper and engage in routine activity, but rather was to attempt at all times to *think* about how IBM would be a more innovative company.

[16] A good example of this type of leadership was GE corporation under Jack Welch. The Six Sigma program is one of the many processes put into place systematically to foster innovation within GE. The company has built a small university/brainstorming center to do nothing but constantly evaluate how it can innovate in creation and delivery of products and services. The generally conservative and cautious [bureaucratic] behavior of most employees in large enterprises precludes much creative activity unless it is compelled from top management.

[17] Source [for diagram]: E. Roche & T. Novak, *Customerism and e-Business* (Watertown: Concours Group, 2001), used with permission.

[18] For a compelling discussion of Enterprise Resources Planning (ERP) systems, see Thomas H. Davenport *Mission Critical: Realizing the Promise of Enterprise Systems.* (Boston, MA: Harvard Business School Press, 2000).

[19] An example is software license costs. Several companies have reported they were able to find the subsidiary in their organization where the software vendor is providing the lowest licensing cost, then use that contract throughout the enterprise, thus saving a large amount.

[20] Erran Carmel, *Global Software Teams: Collaborating Across Borders and Time Zones* (Upper Saddle River: Prentice Hall PTR, 1999).

6

Strategic Applications of Information Technology
in Global Business: The "GLITS" Model and an Instrument[1]

Prashant C. Palvia
The University of North Carolina at Greensboro, USA

ABSTRACT

Information technology (IT) is now absolutely essential in the conduct of global business in multi-national corporations. A global information system (GIS) provides a new order of world-wide connectivity in the day-to-day, and even minute-to-minute, operational activities of global firms. While the use of technology for operational support and management effectiveness may in some situations be construed as strategic in nature, there are numerous opportunities for many firms to utilize information technology in a clear strategic manner. Anecdotal cases of strategic use of IT for global competitive advantage have been reported in the literature, but how can strategic opportunities for a firm be identified more systematically? This chapter provides a model, called the GLITS model, and an accompanying instrument for the identification of strategic opportunities in a firm, and for the measurement of how IT can be used for strategic purposes. The instrument, while based on a small sample, has undergone extensive statistical testing and exhibits high levels of reliability and validity. Besides obvious practical benefits to global organizations, a validated model and instrument provide the foundation for productive and rigorous research in international/global information systems.

INTRODUCTION

Numerous examples exist and many reports have been published on the use of information technology (IT) for enhancing a firm's competitive position. Explicitly or implicitly, these reports focus on the use of IT to enhance domestic/national competitiveness, i.e., within the firm's own national borders. Nonetheless, as the Landmark MIT study (Arthur Young 1989) predicted, information technology is and would continue to be a vital resource for competing in the global marketplace. Today, many progressive organizations (e.g., American Express,

---

[1]   A previous version of this chapter: "Strategic Applications of Information Technology in Global Business: Using the GLITS Model and Instrument", by Palvia, P. appeared in *Global Information Technology and Systems Management: Key Issues and Trends*. Edited by P. Palvia, S. Palvia, and E. M. Roche, Ivy League Publishing 1996, pp. 510-533. The author acknowledges the assistance of Professor Jim Whitworth of Georgia Southern University in editing and updating the previous version.

Dow Chemical, Federal Express, UPS, DEC, GM, Texaco) consider information technology an essential component of worldwide corporate strategy. However, while there are several anecdotal cases of IT applications for global competitive advantage, the larger American and the world business communities have no validated models for identifying and classifying the strategic use of information technology by global firms.

In this chapter, we provide a model which identifies the various areas for strategic use of information technology in global business, and supplement it with a validated instrument for firms to assess their own use (or potential for future use) of information technology in a global environment. The model and the instrument are extensions of the ones proposed by Mahmood and Soon (1991) in a domestic environment. Throughout the chapter, we refer to the model as the global IT strategic model or the GLITS model. The model was reported in the late nineties (Palvia 1996, Palvia 1997). Specific technologies may have changed since then; however, we believe the nature of IT-based strategic applications and opportunities are still valid and applicable in the new millennium.

With continuous and relentless business globalization, the model and instrument can benefit corporate chief executives and information officers. The model provides a much-needed and validated reference for explicating and measuring the strategic and competitive use of information technology on a global scale. By taking an inventory of the corporate position with respect to each item in the instrument, a firm will be able to identify its own stance in the use of IT for strategic global advantage. A careful examination of the model and instrument components can also point to the strengths and weaknesses in IT applications, and to promising areas for future development. Further research, based on the current model, can lead to the development of a contingency evaluation of the model components based on organizational, industry, and national characteristics. Thus organizations may be able to customize the model to their own unique needs. We will explore the various applications of the model in greater detail towards the end of the chapter.

THE UNDERLYING LITERATURE

There are two streams of literature which have a bearing on the development of the GLITS model. The first of these is the general literature on the use of information systems as a competitive weapon. Such systems, known as strategic information systems (SIS) for competitive advantage, have been developed and studied largely from a national perspective (e.g., Beath and Ives 1986; Wiseman 1985). In the mid 1980s, such systems were billed as one of the ten IT megatrends in the U.S. (Kanter 1985). A few well-known examples of such systems are: American Airlines' SABRE reservation system, Merril Lynch's Cash Management Account, and American Hospital Supply's order-processing system.

Several researchers, led by Michael Porter, have developed frameworks (Porter 1980; Porter and Millar 1985) for the application of SIS. Porter's framework consists of three dimensions for strategic applications of IS: strategic target (supplier, customer, competitor), strategic thrust (differentiation, cost, focus, innovation, growth, alliance), and strategic mode (offensive, defensive). Ives and Learmonth (1984) suggested a 13-stage customer resource cycle for identifying SIS opportunities. Based on the above works, Mahmood and Soon (1991) developed a comprehensive model for measuring the potential impact of information technology on organizational strategic variables and provided a validated instrument. Sethi and King (1994) performed a similar study focusing on the development of measures to assess the extent to which an information technology application provides competitive advantage and Tinaikar and King (1997) analyzed company annual reports for variations in "strategicness" of IT across industries over time.

The above reports examine competitiveness of firms in the domestic arena (primarily in the U.S.). They have generally not been extended to the international environment. The second stream of research relevant for the GLITS model relates to international/ global information systems in general. The early works of Deans et al. (1991), and Ives and Jarvenpaa (1991) explored key issues in managing global information technology in multinational corporations. Specifically, Ives and Jarvenpaa identified business drivers for global IT, which included both operational and strategic variables. Manheim (1992) discussed the various global IT issues as well as strategic opportunities due to technology. Alavi and Young (1992) developed an organizing framework for information technology use in an international enterprise. Porter (1986) probed competitive forces and changes in the international arena; his focus was on general business strategies. Burn and Cheung (1996) studied the information systems resource structure and management in multinational organizations. Gibson (1996) researched information technology planning and architectures for networked global organizations. Wetherbe et al. (1994) discussed fast cycle development enabled by IT as a source of competitive advantage. Several other articles discuss the strategic benefits (e.g., effectiveness, efficiency, responsiveness) attainable by global firms by the use of IT (Cheung and Burn 1994; Nelson and Clark 1994). Several books on global IT (Palvia et al. 1996, Bradley et al 1993; Deans and Kane 1992; Palvia et al. 1992; Roche 1992) discuss the strategic implications of information technology for the global firm.

The above works in domestic SIS and international MIS literature contain numerous examples and recommendations for utilizing IT in a strategic manner in a global firm. These were systematically analyzed and used in developing the GLITS model.

DEVELOPMENT OF THE GLITS MODEL

An overview of the model development process is provided herein; details can be found in (Palvia 1997). Global organizational variables, that information technology may be able to influence, were generated by reviewing the literature (those cited above plus additional works). Mahmood and Soon's study (1991) provided the initial impetus for the identification of variables. Initially, there were a total of twenty seven specific variables plus one overall variable. Seventeen of these were derived from the domestic SIS literature, and were chosen on the basis of their applicability at the global level (e.g., variables like: customers, market, pricing, and flexible operations). Six new variables from the international IS literature were generated (e.g., country requirements, worldwide physical resources, and time zones). Finally, there were four variables that related directly to technology impacts (e.g., coordination, and responsiveness). An additional variable "overall" was created to assess the overall impact of IT. Specific items were developed for each variable (e.g., one item in the "customers" variable is: IT helps serve customers in different countries with different needs). There was a total of 255 items under the 27 variables, and 6 items under the "overall" variable. These constituted the preliminary instrument.

The preliminary instrument underwent extensive refinement. Steps of refinement included: self-examination by the researchers, two-staged pilot test, and the full study. In the full study, an intermediate version of the instrument was completed by thirty six senior executives of U.S. international firms. While the sample size is somewhat small, it was deemed adequate given the exploration of new ground, use of homogeneous sampling method, and level of rigor applied in subsequent tests.

Numerous statistical tests were conducted at different stages. As a result, many items were eliminated, many were modified, many variables were eliminated, and many were regrouped. Validation tests included: reliability evaluation using Cronbach's α (Cronbach 1951), construct validity (Cohen and Cohen 1975), criterion-related validity (Kerlinger 1978), item-variable correlations, and convergent and discriminant validity (Campbell and Fiske 1959). The final GLITS model has 20 variables plus one overall variable. The instrument that captures these variables has 58 items for the 20 variables, and 2 for the overall variable.

Table 1: Cronbach's reliability coefficients for the final 58 item, 20 variable final instrument

	Variable (Variable Code)	# of Items	Cronbach's α
1.	Customers (CS)	3	.7702
2.	Competitive Rivalry (CR)	4	.8976
3.	Suppliers (SU)	2	.9457
4.	Market (MK)	4	.8971
5.	Products and Services (PS)	4	.8280
6.	Economies of Scope (SP)	2	.9586
7.	Internal Organizational Efficiency (EF)	2	.8986
8.	Interorganizational Efficiency (IO)	4	.8632
9.	Business Risk Reduction (BR)	2	.9501
10.	Downsizing/Outsourcing (DO)	3	.9162
11.	Learning Curve/Knowledge Transfer (LK)	2	.9488
12.	Flexible Operations (FO)	7	.9563
13.	Resources (RS)	2	.9660
14.	Government & Country Requirements (GC)	5	.9362
15.	Human Resources (HR)	2	.9031
16.	Alliance and Growth (AG)	2	.8953
17.	Time Zones (TZ)	2	.9020
18.	Coordination (CD)	2	.9468
19.	Integration (IG)	2	.8363
20.	Information Systems (IS)	2	.9730
	ENTIRE INSTRUMENT	58	.9866

The model and the accompanying instrument scored well on all validity tests. Table 1 shows the reliability of the 58 item final instrument as well as the reliability coefficient for each of the updated variables. The reliability of the entire instrument is 0.9866. Nunnally (1978) has suggested a minimum reliability of .80 for basic research and .90 for application. Except for the "customers" variable, all variables have adequate reliabilities. The "customers" reliability is .77, which is only slightly lower than the .80 mark. The 20-variable model and the 58-item instrument, having undergone extensive evaluation and validation, represents significant progress towards the development of a standard instrument for measuring the strategic impact of information technology at a global level. Moreover, the instrument is simultaneously comprehensive and precise.

THE GLITS MODEL DESCRIPTION

The GLITS model is shown in Figure 1, and the instrument in Exhibit 1. The model can be viewed as a 3-level hierarchy. The first and the highest level describes the total strategic impact of information technology on a global business. The second level subdivides the total impact into impact on each of the twenty variables. An organization can therefore identify how IT is being used or may be used in specific areas. Finally, the third level breaks each variable down into its constituent items. At this level, an organization can surmise the specific ways IT can be put to use for global strategic advantage.

Some general comments are offered on the efficacy of the model, followed by a brief description of each variable. First, the model and the instrument are more comprehensive than the domestic model developed by Mahmood and Soon (1991). They had ten variables in their model, and we have twenty. This was expected as we were extending their basic model, developed in the domestic setting, to a global context. Many of the model variables are unique to the global environment and carry a special significance, e.g., physical resources,

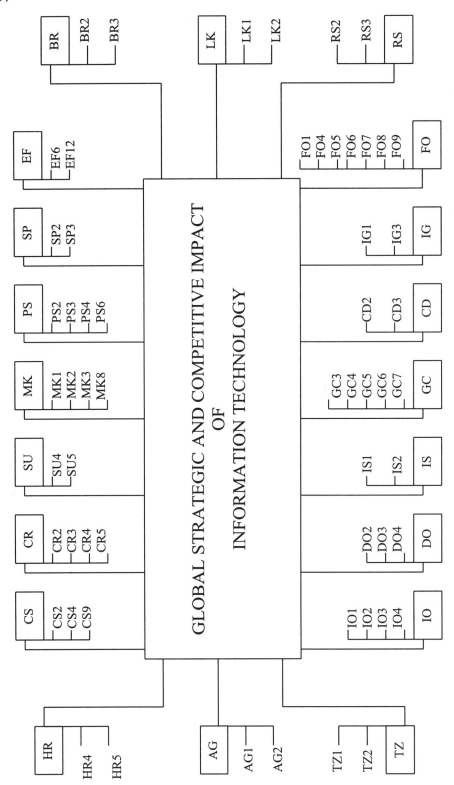

Figure 1: A Model for the Global and Strategic Impact of Information Technology

country requirements, human resources, flexible operations, time zones, and knowledge transfer.

Further, as Emery (1993) commented, in today's global economy, a global organization will be the norm and a domestic firm will be the special case. The model, while developed in the global context, also has relevance for purely domestic firms or those contemplating venturing into the global arena at a later date. The model and the variables for a domestic firm are a subset of the complete model, and can be extracted by simple examination. In fact, firms may choose only the variables that have particular significance for their own unique environment. For example, a firm that is just beginning to globalize its operations, may wish to focus on a different set of specific international variables for IT application, compared to the firm with an extended history of global operations. It is, therefore, possible for one model and instrument to serve the needs of both a domestic and an international organization.

The instrument was completed by executives in thirty six firms. Their responses were used to prioritize the relative impact of IT on each organizational variable. The variable ranks are listed in Table 2. The variables are discussed below in the same order. As a caveat, these ranks require further interpretation and qualification before being generalized to the larger base of U.S. companies or even a single organization for that matter. We are using them merely to facilitate the following discussion.

Table 2: GLITS Variable Ranks

Rank	Variable
1	Customers
2	Time Zones
3	Products and Services
4	Economies of Scope
5	Integration
6	Interorganizational Efficiency
7	Coordination
8	Market
9	Competitive Rivalry
10	Suppliers
11	Information Systems
12	Internal Organizational Efficiency and Effectiveness
13	Flexible Operations
14	Government and Country Requirements
15	Downsizing and Outsourcing
16	Human Resources
17	Learning Curve and Knowledge Transfer
18	Business Risk Reduction
19	Resources
20	Alliance and Growth

Customers

Per our sample, IT has the potential of making a substantial impact on the relationship between the company and its customers. As an inhibiting factor, McFarlan (1984) has stated that information systems can build switching costs so that customers will have to spend too much time and money to change suppliers. IT can increase customer's cost of switching to other suppliers and reduce buyer power. In a more positive and facilitative role, IT can be used to help worldwide customers learn about the company's products and services by making company databases available to them. It can ultimately allow a company to be more responsive to the unique needs of people and customers in different countries by providing relevant information concerning their needs, wants, and preferences (in the form of worldwide customer databases). Another manner to serve customers is by improving customer service. Customer oriented information systems can differentiate products or services through customer service, while simultaneously strengthening customer ties (Learmonth and Ives 1987, Porter and Millar 1985). Customer service stands as the primary IT-driven strategy emerging enterprises should follow to compete effectively globally (Engler 1999).

Time zones

Different countries operate in different time zones creating barriers to the simultaneous conduct of business. Information technology is conquering both time and space barriers in international business. Telecommunication based technologies are permitting communication between two parties at any place and at any time. Not only have such barriers to normal patterns of business been removed, but also new opportunities to conduct business operations during all twenty four hours of the day have been created (McFarlan 1992). For example, while one 8-hour day shift is concluded in U.S.A., work can be taken over by a day shift in a subsidiary in Singapore (while all necessary work-related information is routinely transmitted over telecommunication lines). Another example is in international investments (Ballester and Marcarelli 1992), where there is always someone somewhere around the world trading securities and foreign exchange. While New York City sleeps, Tokyo trades, and London is the bridge between the two.

Products and Services

IT provides opportunities for products and services innovation as well as enhancement of product/service performance and quality. Good examples of products and services enabled by IT include Merryl Lynch's Cash Management Account (Wiseman and MacMillan 1984) and American Express' "Authorizer's Assistant" expert system for credit authorization (Davenport and Short 1990). IT can further facilitate the globalization of a firm's product (e.g., rapid dissemination of information about the product, worldwide sales and service support, etc.). Additionally, it can help coordinate worldwide operations and technologies, such as CIM (computer integrated manufacturing), CAE (computer aided engineering), and CAD (computer aided design) can help build customized products rapidly. Finally, IT can enhance post-product-sale services.

Economies of Scope

Scope economies may be viewed in terms of the synergistic benefits gained through multilateral exchange of resources, competencies and know-how among organizational units or divisions (Teece 1980). Information technology provides numerous opportunities for economies of scope. First, by removing space and time barriers, IT can significantly increase the number of markets a firm can serve in the world with existing financial and human resources. Second, resources can be utilized more effectively. For example, an expertise that exists in one country, can be easily tapped by other locations in the world. Third, operations can be rationalized (Ives and Jarvenpaa 1991), and more products and services can be generated. For example, different subsidiaries may build different parts of the same product or different products based on their comparative advantages.

Integration

Integration is of paramount importance in a global firm; the myriad of activities performed in various countries need to be integrated to produce a unified whole. Integration provides MNCs the opportunity to maximize their total system-wide margins and exploit imperfections in labor and financial markets (Neo 1991). IT allows worldwide integration of activities within the firm as well as with external value-chain business units, e.g., suppliers, distributors, wholesalers, or retailers (Ives et al. 1993). Further, it is a critical resource for building integrated worldwide operations, manufacturing, logistic, and distribution networks. IT also permits the formation of integrated teams that encompass design, engineering, and manufacturing.

Interorganizational Efficiency

Strategic use of IT includes interorganizational applications. Cooperative systems serving the firm and its worldwide customers, distributors, wholesalers, and retailers will have a strategic impact on the firm's performance, efficiency, and competitiveness. Furthermore, they will improve communication and coordination with these external entities (Porter and Millar 1985). Likewise, IT permits communication and formal agreements with other organizations worldwide. McFarlan (1992) provided an interesting example in this respect: an IBM marketing representative, in 48 hours, assembled electronic documentation from around the world from 8 people he had never met to prepare a 200-page, multi-million dollar project proposal for a customer.

Coordination

The essence of coordination is the communication and processing of information (Malone et al. 1987). The number and complexity of the linkages between various units of a global firm increase rapidly (Neo 1991). Information technology provides information systems, information, and the conduits to transport information in order to support, monitor, and control subsidiary operations. Additionally, IT provides control of logistic and distribution activities. The effective, timely, and accurate communication of information between headquarters and subsidiary operations facilitates coordination.

Market

Information technology can be used to alter the market structure in order to gain competitive advantage (Li et al. 1994), and to discover and develop new and profitable worldwide markets (Simon and Grover 1993). Further, IT makes new businesses technologically feasible, and allows a firm to identify worldwide market trends and to focus on product/market niches (Deans and Kane 1992). It helps reduce marketing costs by providing pertinent local market knowledge and sales information, facilitating distribution of the product worldwide and enhancing sales forecast accuracy. As an example of IT's role in this domain, the Internet and the World Wide Web are common place tools used by firms in reaching and penetrating new markets.

Competitive Rivalry

Information technology provides global competitive advantage in several ways. First, it helps differentiate the firm's products and services from its competitors. Second, it enables the firm to make a preemptive strike against competitors (i.e., by introducing new products and services). Third, it helps build customized products rapidly. Fourth, it can mount barriers against less technologically advanced companies wishing to compete in existing markets, or entering into new markets. Fifth, it lets a firm access global markets that were previously inaccessible. Sixth, it can reduce the home-court advantage of local firms by allowing a global firm to make information about its own products and services available readily to local clients. Finally, it can allow the firm to lock in suppliers and customers. In fact, by definition of the GLITS model, practically all variables directly or indirectly lead to competitive advantage. However, this specific variable focuses on items that are directly targeted at competitors. An example of the impact of this variable can be seen in a recent IT diffusion study in China. With the permission to move to privatized banking in China in late 1997, information technology enabled entry into this new market as seen by the surge of interest in upgrading banking computer systems (Mockler et al. 1999).

Suppliers

IT affects the relationship between the company and its suppliers in multiple ways. A global firm may have suppliers from different parts of the world. For example, in almost any automobile manufactured in U.S.A. and Japan, many of the parts are produced in and supplied by different countries. IT not only reduces the company's transaction costs by simplifying the order process but also minimizes supplier's transaction costs by facilitating the purchasing process. EDI is a technology being increasingly used internationally to process customer-vendor transactions (Clarke et al. 1992). IT further increases the bargaining power of the company by increasing the potential number of available suppliers (Bakos and Treacy 1986) and locating substitute products/services on a worldwide basis. Moreover, the monitoring of the quality of products and services can be performed with the use of IT. IT is also used to implement just-in-time manufacturing, which requires close coordination with the suppliers.

Information Systems

Competitive advantages, that were previously even inconceivable, are provided in the global market by special purpose information systems. Besides many of the operational systems discussed earlier, IT can be used to build decision support systems (DSS), executive information systems (EIS), expert systems (ES) and knowledge management systems in other countries (Sauter 1992) as well as build such systems with increasingly global scope. Through the provision of such systems, IT provides rapid and worldwide access to internal and external databases (Deans and Kane 1992; Ives and Jarvenpaa 1991). For example, global EIS (GEIS) can be used to provide quick access to demographic, market, customer, and financial data from other countries (Palvia et al. 1995). On the other hand, special purpose expert systems may provide an opportunity for the inexpensive transfer of technology and expertise to subsidiaries in other countries (Eom 1996). Expert Systems can increase worker productivity because less time is devoted to determining the correct processes to arrive at a decision. At the same time, by helping workers perform higher level tasks, it sets the stage for wider spans of control and can facilitate flattening of the organization and shifting of power and influence within the firm (Motiwalla and Fairfield-Sonn, 1998).

Internal Organizational Efficiency and Effectiveness

While the past use of information technology was to improve the efficiency of the organization, recent efforts have targeted the use of IT to enhance organizational effectiveness. In fact, Keen (1989) observed that the strategic use of IT would provide *organizational advantage* by facilitating the design of adaptive, responsive, and flexible organizations. Globalization involves increased coordination, operation across time zones and locations, increased breadth of activities, time stresses due to geographic dispersion and shortening of planning and delivery cycles, and increasing deregulation. Properly conceived and designed systems can enable a global company to meet such requirements effectively, e.g., the PRISM system at Federal Express Corporation (Palvia et al. 1992). In addition, IT improves the process and quality of decision making in both the centralized and decentralized modes. It can effectively extend these forms of decision-making into the global arena. Furthermore, IT improves strategic planning by providing appropriate data, decision models, and communication facilities to the decision makers.

Flexible Operations

Flexibility in operations provides a hedge against vagaries of the marketplace, e.g., labor shortages or strikes, raw material shortages, strains in supplier relationships, etc. (Ives and Jarvenpaa 1991). Information technology provides requisite flexibility in locating and relocating worldwide operations and in scheduling operations/manufacturing. IT can also be used to support just-in-time inventory and manufacturing systems and allows manufacturing of different parts in different countries. For example, Seagate Technology (Palvia and Lee 1996) manufactures different parts of its disk read-write heads in U.S.A., Northern Ireland, Malaysia, Thailand, and Singapore. Information systems act as the glue holding together the various operations. Finally, IT allows the firm to share facilities across the world and eliminates duplication of effort in various country subsidiaries.

Government and Country Requirements

Information technology is a powerful tool in dealing with government, regulatory, and legal requirements of countries. Sipior and Townsend (1993) provide an example of the use of multimedia technology for training General Electric employees in laws, regulations, and contractual specifications of the U.S. government. Similar systems could me made available for other countries, or perhaps could be part of a global EIS. Software can also be made readily available to automatically decipher differences in accounting and financial practices, currency variations, and language differences between countries. For example, Aiken at al. (1994) have developed a prototype multi-lingual group decision support system which translates the sender's comments into the receiver's language.

Downsizing and Outsourcing

Organizations have used downsizing and outsourcing for cost containment, particularly through the achievement of economies of scale and operational efficiencies. The IT function itself provides opportunities for downsizing and outsourcing, as seen in the classic cases of Eastman Kodak and Continental Bank (Huber 1993). Besides cost control, benefits of outsourcing include: improved financial outlook, control of key operations, return to core competencies, and retention of strategic focus (Lacity and Hirschheim 1993). Globalization dramatically broadens a company's outsourcing options. IT, through its coordination and integration mechanisms, allows a firm to profitably outsource activities to outside firms in its own country as well as other countries. Once again, the IT function itself provides an outstanding example of international outsourcing, where software outsourcing to countries like India, Ireland, and Phillipines have provided savings in the order of 35 to 40%. Private and public international data highways have permitted such collaborations.

Human Resources

Over the last 20 years, the workplace has changed in more ways than we could have ever imagined; the very definition of work is undergoing fundamental redefinition. Increasingly companies, and human resources departments, are examining work process*es,* human capital and knowledge in radically different ways (Greengard 1998). As international outsourcing illustrates, the use of skilled labor (both technical and management) from other countries is being made possible through the application of information technology. Work within the company can be allocated and transferred to specialized or under-utilized employees across the globe. Not only IT allows the transfer of work to other parts of the world, but it also permits distant employees to work together on common tasks (Jarvenpaa and Ives 1994). For example, groupware or collaboration software (such as Lotus Notes) offers the possibilities for geographically dispersed work groups to come together and work on joint projects. This type of software provides the needed elements of communication, coordination, cooperation, collaboration, and control.

Learning curve and Knowledge Transfer

Learning curve effects reflect enhancements in processing, performance and retention capacities by way of increasing knowledge and experience. Information technology accelerates the firm's movement up the learning curve ladder. It permits the rapid acquisition of knowledge about subsidiaries by headquarters personnel (Deans and Kane 1992, Korson and Vaishnavi 1992). By the same token, new business units, especially new subsidiaries, can learn about the core business much more rapidly (Neo 1991). Through systems such as CAD/CAM, multimedia & hypermedia systems, and expert systems, IT helps firms learn about new processes and technologies faster, thus accelerating knowledge transfer (Eom 1996).

Business Risk Reduction

Information technology can also be used to reduce business, market and technical risks. Ives and Jarvenpaa (1991) state that risks associated with currency conversions, multiple global markets, and multiple traders are managed effectively with global IT applications (e.g., applications that provide real time monitoring and financial exposure reporting). They provide examples of a petroleum company which developed a global system for bidding on crude oil contracts, and of a multinational bank which implemented a global risk management system for currency trading. In the international investment arena, IT based information systems are indispensable for the customized design and redesign of global financial products, such as mutual funds, pension funds, and endowments (Ballester and Marcarelli 1992).

Resources

While human resource is important in and of itself and was listed earlier as a separate variable, we pool the remaining global resources that can be leveraged by IT under this category. These resources include raw materials, semi-finished goods, finished goods, and financial resources, and can be procured from any part of the world. Global information systems can coordinate the utilization of joint and scarce resources (Ives and Jarvenpaa 1991). As the earlier example illustrated (Ballester and Marcarelli 1992), financing arrangements for new ventures may actually require raising capital from various financial markets of the world, where the use of IT would be pivotal. In the same vein, quick financial support to host country subsidiaries can be provided through the use of IT.

Alliance and Growth

Strategic alliances are interorganizational relationships in which the partners make substantial investments to develop a long-term collaborative effort (King and Sethi, 1999). Firms can expand by forging partnerships by way of joint ventures, mergers, and acquisitions (Porter 1980). An international firm typically forms strategic alliances with host country partners in order to expedite market entry. An excellent example of this is the automobile parts industry in Japan and U.S.A. Manufacturers in each country have made alliances with part manufacturers in the other country. Interorganizational information systems provide the necessary linkages to reduce costs and to make the alliances workable. As another example, electronic commerce is an important strategy small and midsize companies are embracing to extend globally (Engler 1999). In a Strategic Alliance survey of 2,000 small companies in nine countries, the majority of the respondents had something they called a "strategic alliance," such as technology sharing, licensing agreements, joint ventures, or distribution partnerships. Another growth area is the formation of spin-off companies. The example of the spinoff of Kids "R" Us is well-known, where Toys "R" Us, the number one toy company in U.S.A at the time leveraged its information system's expertise and resources to venture into a new business (Wiseman and MacMillan 1984). International markets present more of such openings, and the "IT ready" companies will be the ones who can move in quickly and capitalize on such opportunities.

PRACTICAL AND THEORETICAL APPLICATIONS

The provision of a comprehensive and statistically validated construct for the strategic application of global IT should be useful to both practitioners and academicians. It forms the necessary base for practical applications as well as for conducting research that is grounded in theory.

Practical Applications

A validated model and instrument for assessing the role of IT in global competitiveness has significant practical value for business organizations. Information technology is vital for an international business' very existence, and it can no longer be ignored from close scrutiny and proper management. The GLITS model and instrument identify the strategic areas for the global application of information technology. Just as the strategic "options generator" developed by Wiseman and MacMillan (1984) provided firms a way to scan opportunities for SIS application in the domestic context, a careful application of this instrument should reveal numerous opportunities to explore information technology on a global scale.

The instrument may be applied in the following ways. First of all, a senior IS executive (e.g., the CIO) or several executives may complete the instrument to assess the *current* impact or use of IT for each of the 58 items. The impact is assessed on a 5-point likert scale, where 1 refers to no impact, and 5 refers to greatest impact. The sum of the scores on all items will provide a measure of the current use of IT in the organization for global strategic advantage. Note that the sum for 58 items can range between 58 and 290. Some guidelines on the range of values for this measure may be developed to indicate what is effective and what is ineffective technology use. Additionally, the executives may complete the instrument a second time, this time assessing the *potential* impact of IT on the 58 items given the organization's internal and external environment. This exercise should yield areas for future application of IT. A careful comparison of the current and potential scores on each item will also allow the organization to identify its IT strengths and weaknesses.

Thus, by taking an inventory of the items contained in the instrument, a firm can determine whether IT can be used at an international level for financial gain or competitive advantage, or for preventing the firm from sliding into competitive disadvantage. Furthermore, the individual variables of the model can be used to separately measure IT's impact on a firm's products or services, economies of scale, optimization of resources, global product, global customer, etc. Based on analysis of the current and potential impacts, a firm can conduct a contingency analysis based on its own unique requirements, and determine the variables of particular relevance to the firm. It can, then, maximize its return on IT investment by focusing on the selected areas.

Another practical application for an organization is to evaluate and monitor itself against industry practices. If industry practices are widely reported or if the instrument is administered to a representative sample of companies in a specific industry, then a particular firm will be able to assess its relative position, and take necessary actions.

Theoretical Applications

While the model provides an initial set of validated and useful variables, there is scope for improvement, as with any model development. Researchers may further refine the model and the underlying construct by using a larger sample, a more focused or a more homogeneous sample, samples from other countries, and using other statistical techniques, such as factor analysis. The current model provides an excellent base from which to seek further refinements.

Another worthwhile research pursuit is to conduct a detailed examination of the specific variables. It may be that some variables are more meaningful for certain firms or industries, and further insights into these variables may be of interest. For example, if "downsizing & outsourcing" is identified as an important variable for a class of firms, specific hypotheses related to it may be formulated and tested in future studies. An illustration of such a hypothesis may be that "IT related global outsourcing is facilitated by heavy investments in telecommunications technology".

Another area of interest is to investigate the relationship between actual organizational strategic performance and global IT competitive impact. A positive relationship between the two should encourage higher IT investment. A detailed analysis could look into which specific elements of global IT variables are correlated with organizational performance, with the implication that these would be the ones that need to be emphasized in terms of investment.

Finally, we recommend that a contingency analysis of the impact variables be undertaken. It seems reasonable to postulate that different variables and items have varying degree of importance to different firms. What are the contingency factors which drive the impact of each variable, and what is the amount of the impact? Some possible factors from the literature are: global organizational structure (Bartlett and Ghoshal 1989), business strategy (Miles and Snow 1978), industry (Deans et al. 1991), firm size, and host country culture (Hofstede 1980). Relationships between these factors and the model variables at present are unknown or speculative; research needs to firmly establish these relationships. For illustrative purposes, some example hypotheses that could be tested are:

Global enterprises (as defined by Bartlett and Ghoshal) would tend to emphasize those IT variables that influence organizational efficiency, where as transnational enterprises would be more likely to use IT to increase management effectiveness. In countries high on Hofstede's uncertainty avoidance scale, global IT variables related to knowledge management would be more likely to be employed than in cultures low on the uncertainty avoidance scale.

CONCLUSIONS

This chapter has provided a comprehensive and concise model and instrument for assessing the strategic impact of information technology in global firms. The model was formulated along the lines of a single-country domestic model (Mahmood and Soon 1991), but was augmented with variables extracted from the international IT literature. While details of model and instrument development are not reported, both were carefully crafted using extensive evaluation and validation procedures. This work represents significant progress towards the creation of a standard global IT impact measurement model and instrument; nevertheless, efforts should be carried out to further refine and extend the model. Furthermore, while the model was developed a few years ago, it still has validity in the new millennium.

The model has practical as well as theoretical and research applications. In terms of practical applications, a validated model provides a much-needed tool for assessing the role of IT use in the global competitiveness of a firm. Senior executives may complete the instrument to evaluate the current use of IT for global effectiveness, as well as assess its future potential. They may further hone in on specific areas of interest. In terms of implications for researchers, the model provides a theoretically grounded initial instrument which can be used to base further research on and to test contingency based hypotheses.

**Mini Case: Expectations and Impacts of a Global Information System:
the Case of a Global bank from Hong Kong**

This is a case study that tells the story of an innovative global banking application, HSBC's Hexagon: what it is, how it came to be developed and how it affected the bank's performance. The article develops concepts about the potential organizational and economic impacts of an innovative product based on a global IS and it uses the story of Hexagon to understand how these impacts might be realized.

Firms have recently been forced, as never before, to view markets and competition globally as rapid trade expansion, reduced trade barriers, and third world political developments have resulted in strategic opportunities and threats. In nearly every industry, multinational firms are under pressure to seek global economies of scale, to build world products, and to tailor products to customers in diverse markets.

The banking industry plays a major role in supporting increased global trade and investment activity. Globally distributed manufacturing and marketing requires that firms finance activities and manage cash among operations across many countries and among many currencies. Banks hope to take advantage of resulting business opportunities, but to do so requires them to build extensive networks of assets and alliances, as well as well-designed global IT infrastructures. This combination of assets may be impossible for all but a handful of the industry's members to assemble.

Here we investigate the use of a global IS to produce a unique IT-based product, made possible by the use of a combination of firm strategy, IT strategy, global assets, and the use of an information system with a global scope. Hexagon is a product of HSBC Holdings, plc, the world's 10th largest bank holding company. Since 1982, HSBC has been developing Hexagon, a proprietary system that allows individual and corporate subscribers around the world to conduct international banking transactions online. HSBC has sought to make Hexagon the firm's 'international bank on a PC,' by providing international cash management, trade finance, and securities services online through an application installed on the customer's PC and connected to HSBC's global banking network. Over the same period HSBC has been putting together a global system of alliances and subsidiaries. This global system allows customers to use Hexagon to carry out banking transactions in nearly every country in the world.

Mini Case .... Continued.

IS research suggests that an innovative global application, like Hexagon, might benefit its firm by affecting performance in several ways. Hexagon is thought to have helped HSBC to realize improved scale and scope economies, improved product value for customers, increased efficiency, improved organizational effectiveness, and competitive advantage. In addition, the firm has been able to offer customers an application with extremely good global coverage. Consequently, it may be the beneficiary of competitive advantage from network externalities because the value of the application to the customer depends on whether it has sufficient scope to satisfy customer needs. The article explores how HSBC used Hexagon to improve its performance in several of these dimensions.

Questions for discussion:
1. What are some of the ways in which Hexagon might have helped HSBC to achieve superior economic performance?
2. Why is it important that an application to support business needs for cash management and trade finance be global?
3. What factors determine whether the benefits provided by Hexagon are sustainable?
4. Could any bank have developed an application like Hexagon?
5. Should a global banking application be different today than it was when the case was written?

Source: Peffers, K. and V.K. Tuunainen "Expectations and Impacts of a Global Information System: the Case of a Global bank from Hong Kong" *Journal of Global Information Technology Management*, 1998, 1:4, 17-37.

STUDY QUESTIONS

1. Describe areas related to the customers where information technology can play a strategic role in global business. Provide some examples.

2. Describe areas related to the suppliers where information technology can play a strategic role in global business. Provide some examples.

3. Describe areas related to the internal operations of the firm itself where information technology can play a strategic role in global business. Provide some examples.

4. What are the differences in the role of information technology in a strictly domestic business versus a global business?

5. Identify the strategic roles of information technology for the four classes of firm structure as defined by Bartlett and Ghoshal.

6. Discuss any changes that you have observed in the strategic role of information technology in global business due to the Internet and expanding ecommerce.

REFERENCES

Aiken, M.W., Martin, J.S., Paolillo, J.G.P., and Shirani, A.I. A Group Decision Support System for Multilingual Groups. *Information & Management*, Vol 26, 1994, pp. 155-161.

Alavi,M. & Young, G. " Information technology in an international enterprise: An organizing framework". In Palvia et al (Eds), *The Global Issues of Information Technology Management*, 1992

Arthur Young, *The Landmark MIT Study: Management in the 1990s*, 1989.

Bakos, J.Y. & Treacy, M.E. Information Technology and Corporate Strategy: A Research Perspective. *MIS Quarterly*, 1986, 10(2), pp. 107-119.

Ballester, G.B. and Marcarelli, E.A. The Impact of Global Information Technology on International Investment Managers and Custodians. in *The Global Issues of Information Technology Management*, eds. Palvia, S., Palvia, P., and Zigli, R. Idea Group Publishing 1992, pp. 356-382.

Bartlett, C.A. and Ghoshal, S. *Managing Across Borders: The Transnational Solution.* Boston, MA, 1989, Harvard Business School Press.

Beath, C.M. and Ives, B. Competitive Information Systems in Support of Pricing. *MIS Quarterly*, 10, 1986.

Bradley, S.P., Hausman, J.A., and Nolan, R.L. *Globalization, Technology, and Competition*, Harvard Business School Press, Boston, MA, 1993.

Burn, J. M.,& Cheung, H. K. " Information systems resources structure and management in multinational organizations." In Palvia et al (Eds.), *Global Information Technology and Systems Management*, 1996.

Campbell, D.T., & Fiske, D.W. Convergent and Discriminant Validation by the Multitrait-Multimethod Matrix. *Psychological Bulletin*, 1959, 50, pp. 81-105.

Cheung, H.K. and Burn, J.M. Distributing Global Information Systems Resources in Multinational Companies - A Contingency Model. *Journal of Global Information Management*, vol 2, no 3, pp. 14-27.

Clarke, R., DeLuca, P., Gricar, J., Imai, T., McCubbrey, D., and Swatman, P. The International Significance of Electronic Data Interchange. in *The Global Issues of Information Technology Management*, eds. Palvia, S., Palvia, P., and Zigli, R. Idea Group Publishing 1992, pp. 276-307.

Cohen, J. and Cohen, P. *Applied Multiple Regression/Correlation Analysis for the Behavioral Sciences*, Lawrence Erlbaum Assoc., Hillsdale, NJ, 1975.

Cronbach, L.J. Coefficient alpha and the internal structures of tests. *Psychometrika*, 1951, 16, pp. 297-334.

Davenport, T.H., and Short, J.E. The New Industrial Engineering: Information Technology and Business Process Redesign. *Sloan Management Review*, Vol 31, No 4, Summer 1990, pp. 11-27.

Deans, P.C., and Kane, M.J. *International Dimensions of Information Systems and Technology*, PWS-Kent, Boston, MA, 1992.

Deans, P.C., Karwan, K.R., Goslar, M.D., Ricks, D.A., and Toyne, B. Identification of Key International Information Systems Issues in U.S. Based Multinational Corporations. *Journal of Management Information Systems*, Vol. 7, No. 4, Spring 1991, pp. 27-50.

Emery, J.C. The Global Organization as the Norm. *Journal of Global Information Management*, Vol 1, No 3, Summer 1993, pp. 3,4,31,44.

Engler, Natalie, Small but nimble, *Informationweek*; Manhasset; pp57-62 Jan 18, 1999

Eom, S. R. Global Management Support Systems: The New Frontiers. in *Global Information Technology and Systems Management: Key Issues and Trends*, eds. Palvia, P., Palvia, S., Roche, E. Ivy League Publishing, 1996.

Gibson, R. "Information technology planning and architectures for networked global organizations." In Palvia et al (Eds.), *Global Information Technology and Systems Management*, 1996.

Greengard, Samuel, How technology will change the workplace, *Workforce*; vol 77, pp78-84; Jan 1998

Hofstede, G. *Cultural Consequences: International Differences in Work Related Values*, Sage, Beverly Hills, 1980.

Huber, R.L., "How Continental Bank Outsourced its Crown Jewels", *Harvard Business Review*, January-February 1993, pp. 121-129.

Ives, B., and Jarvenpaa, S.L. Applications of Global Information Technology: Key Issues for Management. *MIS Quarterly*, Vol. 15, No. 1, March 1991.

Ives, B. and Learmonth, G.P. The Information System as a Competitive Weapon. *Communications of the ACM*, 1984.

Jarvenpaa, S. L. & Ives, B. The Global Organization of the Future: Information Management Opportunities and Challenges. *Journal of Management Information Systems*, Vol 10, No 4, 1994, pp. 25-57.

Kanter, J. Ten Information Systems Megatrends. *The Executive's Journal*, Fall 1985.

Keen, P.G.W., "Information Technology and Organizational Advantage" in *MoIS, Management of Information Systems*, P. Gray, W. King, E. McLean, and H. Watson (eds.), The Dryden Press, Hinsdale, IL, 1989.

Kerlinger, F.N. *Foundations of Behavioral Research*, McGraw-Hill, NY 1978.

King, William R. and Sethi, V.An empirical assessment of the organization of transnational information systems *Journal of Management Information Systems*; vol 15,pp7-28; Spring 1999

Korson, T. D., Vaishnavi, V. K. Managing Emerging Software Technologies: A Technology Transfer Framework. *Communications of the ACM*, Vol 35, No 9, 1992, pp. 101-111.

Lacity, M.C., and Hirschheim, R., "The Information Systems Outsourcing Bandwagon", *Sloan Management Review*, Fall 1993, pp. 73-86.

Learmonth, G.P., and B. Ives, "Information System Technology Can Improve Customer Service," *Data Base*, Winter 1987, pp. 6-10

Li, E. Y., McLeod, R. Jr., Rogers, J. C. (1994). Marketing information systems in the Fortune 500 companies: Past, present, future. *Journal of Management Information Systems*, vol 10, no. 1, 165-192.

Mahmood, M.A., and Soon, S.K. A Comprehensive Model for Measuring the Potential Impact of Information Technology on Organizational Strategic Variables. *Decision Sciences*, Vol. 22, No. 4, Sept./Oct. 1991.

Malone, T.W., Yates, J., and Benjamin, R.I. Electronic Markets and Electronic Hierarchies. *Communications of the ACM*, June 1987.

McFarlan, W.F. Multinational CIO Challenge for the 1990s. In *The Global Issues of Information Technology Management*, edited by Palvia, Palvia, & Zigli, Idea Group Publishing, 1992, pp. 484-493.

McFarlan, W.F. Information Technology Changes the Way You Compete. *Harvard Business Review*, 1984.

Miles, R.E., and Snow, C.C. *Organizational Strategy, Structure, and Process*, McGraw-Hill, 1978.

Mockler,R.J., Dologite, D. G., Yu Chen, and Mei Qi Fang, Information Technology Diffusion in Developing Countries: A Study of China, *Journal of Global Information Technology Management*, Vol 2, No. 4 1999.

Motiwalla, Luvai, and Faifield-Sonn, James, Measuring the impact of expert systems. *The Journal of Business and Economic Studies*; vol 4,pp1-17; Fall 1998;

Neo, B. S. Information Technology and Global Competition. *Information & Management*, Vol. 20, 1991, pp. 151-160.

Nunnally, J.C. *Psychometric Theory*, McGraw-Hill, New York, 1978, p. 245.

Palvia, P. "Developing a model of the global and strategic impact of information technology". *Information and Management*, 32(5), 229-244, 1997

Palvia, P. Strategic Applications of Information Technology in Global Business: Using the "GLITS" Model and Instrument. in *Global Information Technology and Systems Management: Key Issues and Trends*, eds. Palvia, P., Palvia, S., Roche, E. Ivy League Publishing, 1996, pp. 510-533.

Palvia, P., Kumar, A., Kumar, N., and Hendon, R. Information Requirements of a Global EIS: An Exploratory Macro Assessment. Forthcoming in *Decision Support Systems*, 1995.

Palvia, P., Palvia, S., and Roche, E. *Global Information Technology and Systems Management: Key Issues and Trends*, Ivy League Publishing.

Palvia, P., Perkins, J.A., and Zeltmann, S.M., "The PRISM System: A Key to Organizational Effectiveness at Federal Express Corporation", *MIS Quarterly*, September, 1992, pp. 277-292.

Palvia, S., and Lee, K.F. Seagate Technology: Developing Global Information Systems. in *Global Information Technology and Systems Management: Key Issues and Trends*, eds. Palvia, P., Palvia, S., Roche, E. Ivy League Publishing, 1996.

Palvia, S., Palvia, P, and Zigli, R.M. *The Global Issues of Information Technology Management*, Idea Group Publishing, 1992.

Porter, M.E. Changing Patterns of International Competition. *California Management Review*, Winter 1986.

Porter, M.E. *Competitive Strategy: Techniques for Analyzing Industries and Competitors*, Free Press, 1980.

Porter, M.E. & Millar, V.E. How Information Gives You Competitive Advantage. *Harvard Business Review*, 1985, 63 (4), pp. 149-159.

Roche, E.M. *Managing Information Technology in Multinational Corporations*, Macmillan, New York, 1992.

Sauter, V.L. Cross-Cultural Aspects of Model Management Needs in a Transnational Decision Support System. In *The Global Issues of Information Technology Management*, edited by Palvia, Palvia, Zigli, Idea Group Publishing, 1992.

Sethi, V. and King, W.R. Development of Measures to Assess the Extent to Which an Information Technology Application Provides Competitive Advantage. *Management Science*, December 1994, pp. 1601-1626.

Sipior, J. C. & Townsend, J. A case study of General Electric's multimedia training systems. *Information Resources Management Journal*, vol 6, no 4, 1993, pp. 23-31.

Teece, D.J. Economies of Scope and the Scope of the Enterprise. *Journal of Economic Behavior and Organization*, 1, 1980, pp. 223-247.

Tinaikar, R. & King, W.R. Analyzing annual reports for variations in strategicness of IT across industries over time. *Association for Information Systems International Conference* , Indianapolis, IN, 1997

Wetherbe, J.C., Vitalari, N.P., and Milner, A. Key Trends in Systems Development in Europe and North America. *Journal of Global Information Management*. Vol 2, no 2, Spring 1994. pp. 5-20.

Wiseman, C. *Strategy and Computers: Information Systems as Competitive Weapons*, Homewood, Ill, Dow Jones-Irwin, 1985.

Wiseman, C., and MacMillan, I.C. Creating Competitive Weapons from Information Systems, *Journal of Business Strategy*, Fall 1984.

EXHIBIT 1: THE INSTRUMENT

Instrument to Measure Global Strategic and Competitive Impact of Information Technology (GLITS Instrument)

Definition: Information Technology (IT) includes all aspects of computers (hardware and software), information systems, telecommunications, and office automation.

Q1.   From your own firm's point of view, to what extent do you think Information Technology (IT) can do or can assist with the following in providing strategic and competitive advantage over other firms on an international level. Do not be concerned about IT's current role, but its potential role in your firm. Please circle one choice using the following scale.

Scale: 1 = No Extent, 2 = Little Extent, 3 = Some Extent, 4 = Great Extent, 5 = Very Great Extent

Customers (CS)

CS2   Makes the products/services database available to worldwide customers.
CS4   Helps provide administrative support (such as billing, collection, inventory management) to worldwide customers.
CS9   Helps serve customers in different countries with different needs.

Competitive Rivalry (CR)
CR2   Helps to make first/preemptive strike against competitors (i.e., a new product/service).
CR3   Helps the firm provide substitutes before competitors do.
CR4   Helps the firm match an existing competitor's offering.
CR5   Assists in overcoming the home-court advantage of local firms in host country.

Suppliers (SU)
SU4   Helps the firm identify alternative supply sources on a worldwide basis.
SU5   Helps the firm locate substitute products/services on a worldwide basis.

Market (MK)
MK1   Makes new business technologically feasible worldwide.
MK2   Identifies worldwide market trends.
MK3   Discovers and develops new and profitable worldwide market.
MK8   Aids in selling the product in different parts of the world.

Products and Services (PS)
PS2   Enhances product/service performance and quality.
PS3   Allows the firm to bundle more information with products/services.
PS4   Allows the development of new products/services.
PS6   Enhances the after-product-sale services and activities.

Economies of Scope (SP)
SP2   Increases number of markets that can be tapped with existing resources.
SP3   Increases number of countries business can be conducted in with existing resources.

Internal Organizational Efficiency and Effectiveness (EF)
EF6   Improves strategic planning.
EF12   Facilitates organizational change in the firm.

Interorganizational Efficiency (IO)
IO1   Improves communication/coordination with worldwide businesses (e.g., suppliers, wholesalers, retailers).
IO2   Improves communication/coordination with worldwide customers.
IO3   Permits communication/formal agreements with other organizations worldwide.
IO4   Facilitates the making of worldwide financial investments.

Business Risk Reduction (BR)
BR2   Reduces risk by allowing to work with multiple global traders and suppliers.
BR3   Reduces risk by allowing to conduct business in multiple global markets.

Downsizing/Outsourcing (DO)
DO2   Allows to profitably contract/outsource activities to firms in its own country.
DO3   Allows to profitably contract/outsource activities to firms in other countries.
DO4   Allows to consolidate operations all over the world.

Learning Curve/Knowledge Transfer (LK)
LK1   Allows foreign subsidiaries to learn technical and business knowledge much faster.
LK2   Helps the firm to learn about subsidiaries much faster.

Flexible Operations (FO)
FO1   Allows flexibility in locating and relocating worldwide operations.
FO4   Allows the manufacture of different parts in different countries.
FO5   Eliminates duplication of effort in other country subsidiaries.
FO6   Provides for rapid adjustments to the firm's logistics/distribution network.
FO7   Allows the firm to share facilities across the world.
FO8   Allows the sharing of computer software across multiple world facilities.
FO9   Allows the firm to utilize excess capacity in any part of the world.

Resources (RS)
RS2   Assists in procuring semi-finished/finished goods from the most beneficial worldwide sources.
RS3   Allows financing arrangements from the most desirable world sources.

Government and Country Requirements (GC)
GC3   Assists in the advancement and social policy objectives of host countries.
GC4   Helps address accounting/financial/internal control requirements of countries.
GC5   Helps deal with different currencies/physical units of other countries.
GC6   Helps address taxation requirements of other countries.
GC7   Helps address language barriers in other countries.

Human Resources (HR)
HR4   Facilitates the coordination of global research and development efforts.
HR5   Allows to assign work to underutilized employees across the globe.

Alliance and Growth (AG)
AG1   Facilitates the formation of spinoff companies in other countries.
AG2   Permits alliances/acquisitions/joint ventures in other countries.

Time Zones (TZ)
TZ1   Overcomes barriers due to time differences in various countries.
TZ2   Expands the time during the 24-hour day to conduct international business.

Coordination (CD)
CD2   Provides information support to subsidiaries.
CD3   Permits better monitoring and control of subsidiary operations.

Integration (IG)
IG1   Allows worldwide integration of business with suppliers, distributors, wholesalers, or retailers.
IG3   Helps build an integrated worldwide logistics/distribution network.

Information Systems (IS)
IS1   Expedites transfer/development of operational information systems in other countries.
IS2   Expedites transfer/development of decision support/expert/strategic systems in other countries.

Overall (OA)
OA1   Provides an international competitive advantage to the firm.
OA2   Supports the firm in becoming a global business.

7

IT Strategy in
International Supply Chain Management

Barry Shore
University of New Hampshire

ABSTRACT

No area has the potential to affect the competitive business environment more than the internationalization of supply chain management. These relationships between customer and suppliers promise shorter production cycles, more flexible manufacturing strategies, and lower cost production. Benefits from these collaborations, however, can only be realized if several difficult problems are addressed and solved. They include the establishment and management of effective global interorganizational alliances for strategic inputs, the coordination of dispersed production facilities, and the organization of complex logistics operations. Information technology plays a major role in the effective solution of these problems. This chapter explores the emerging developments in international supply chain management and the role of information technology in the development of strategic IT supply chain strategies.

INTRODUCTION

In the last decade of the 20th century, there began to grow an increasing awareness that supply chain management (SCM) was becoming a significant component in the competitive strategy of the firm [Dyer, Cho, and Chu, 1998]. Today, as the new millenium unfolds, supply chain management has emerged as a critical factor in the firms ability to compete.

The objective in supply chain management is to manage the activities associated with the flow of products and services from the beginning of the manufacturing or processing cycle through to the end-user [Handfield and Nichols, 1999]. This suggests that the management of an enterprise is no longer restrained to its internal value chain activities but extends to its suppliers' value chain activities as well. The implications of this broader view are profound and place an unprecedented burden on the role of information technology (IT) in the organization.

STRATEGIC SUPPLY CHAIN DECISIONS

Supply chain decisions are both strategic and operational. Strategic decisions are those that deal with planning issues and generally involve a time horizon longer than a few weeks or a month. They are tied to corporate strategies. Operational decisions are short term and focus on day-to-day activities. They guide the production and manufacture of goods, the storage of goods, and the transportation of goods as well as the flow of and cash among supply chain partners.

There are six major strategic decisions in supply chain management [Walker and Alber, 1999]:

1.   What to outsource
2.   Where to outsource
3.   Where to locate inventory in the supply chain and how much to store
4.   Which transportation mode to use
5.   How to transfer Cash
6.   How do support SCM with IT

The first concern is what components, subassemblies, finished products, or services to outsource. In this step, the process of delivering a product or service is decomposed into independent stages and decisions made to retain the activity within the firm or consider it as a candidate for outsourcing. In the next step, a decision must be made to identify the geographical constraints on the search for trading partners. Can these partners come from all corners of the globe, or must they be located regionally to facilitate coordination and logistics? Closely related to the first two issues is the inventory decision. Inventories can exist at every stage in the supply chain as either raw materials, semi-finished or finished goods. One concern is that as suppliers become geographically dispersed, the tendency is to maintain higher in-process (pipeline) inventories to ensure a buffer between the supplier and focal firm. The transportation mode decision is closely linked to the inventory decision. As faster and more costly modes are chosen, the need for large in-process inventories decreases. Since transportation modes can account for as much as 30 percent of logistics costs, this is an important decision. The next decision must address the mechanism to transfer cash among trading partners. As the geographic distance increases, and as legal, currency and accounting systems are spanned, this process becomes more complex. Finally, decisions must be made about the information system used to link suppliers together. This includes hardware and software platforms as well as the extent to which the information will be shared among partners.

While each of these decisions is critical to the development of effective SCM systems, this chapter focuses on the strategic role that information technology must take in these applications. Furthermore, it addresses the challenges of developing an enterprise-wide system that weaves its partners into a synchronized flow of products and cash for the benefit of the end-consumer.

To begin, this chapter will identify four trends that are having a profound effect on supply chain management. It will then look at one of these trends, information technology, and address the technologies that are having an impact on this field. Next, the cultural challenges imposed by the internationalization of supply chains are addressed. The chapter finally concludes with a discussion of the strategic issues that management must address to develop effective global IT supply chain systems.

TRENDS

Supply chain strategy has been limited in three ways: strategically, geographically and managerially. Strategically it was limited because many organizations placed their emphasis on internal enterprise operations. They struggled to improve their in-house purchasing, manufacturing, distribution, and marketing functions. Integrating these activities with external entities including customers and suppliers received less emphasis.

Geographic scope also placed limits on supply chain management. Trading partners were often limited to the primary or focal firm's immediate region or country. This geographical preference avoided many problems that distance, language, culture, and logistics could introduce [Ein-Dor and Segev, 1992]. Above all, it 'seemed' to ensure better predictability and control over quality, delivery, and even costs.

The third limitation was related to the management of the supply chain. The accepted paradigm was to maintain a competitive relationship between the focal firm and its suppliers. The focal firm is an organization that makes the decision to outsource and chooses suppliers. The challenge to the focal firm was to obtain input at the lowest possible cost and to maintain a competitive relationship to insure that suppliers were 'kept on their toes'. Within that traditional framework, the boundaries of supply chain management were clearly defined. Each supplier planned and controlled its own internal or 'primary' activities including inbound logistics, operations, outbound logistics, marketing and sales, and service. Accordingly each of these suppliers operated independently of each other. They maintained their own practices that often included very different and certainly incompatible information systems. Furthermore, the goals of the suppliers were often in conflict with their customer. Focal firms, for example, generally need to minimize inventory and prefer a 'Just in Time' (JIT) strategy in which suppliers provide appropriate and often small quantities at just the right time. The supplier, on the other hand, prefers to produce in larger economic lot sizes with less frequent shipments and to deliver within flexible target dates. In the traditional framework this conflict often goes unresolved.

Within the boundaries of the trading environment just described, the role of information systems in the supply chain was bounded and somewhat simplified when compared to its role today. Little information was exchanged between trading partners, and the emphasis of the focal firm's IT strategy was, at best, to develop information systems capable of synchronizing its own internal enterprise operations.

Today, many firms still follow this approach, but a dramatic paradigm shift has occurred, especially in large firms. Handfield and Nichols [1994] suggest that three trends have been responsible for this shift. They include globalization, inter-organizational alliances, and information technology. With some modification this list can be expanded to include the following trends: outsourcing, worldwide trading, information technology and electronic commerce, and interorganizational alliances.

In the following sections, each of these trends will be considered.

Outsourcing

Outsourcing occurs when a firm purchases goods or services from suppliers, some of which may have traditionally been supplied in-house. Two categories of outsourcing can occur. In the first, called internal outsourcing, a supplier is chosen from within the same corporation but from a separate division. In the second, called external outsourcing, an independent supplier is chosen. Each category may carry with it a significantly different ability for the customer to exercise control over its supplier, an important issue when developing and implementing IT supply chain systems.

Is outsourcing common? Today, the average industrial firm spends more than half of every dollar on purchased products, and this share has been growing as more firms downsize and outsource [Dyer, Cho, and Chu, 1988]. Suppliers now provide research and development, marketing, manufacturing, information systems services, and human resource services. In a study conducted by Aon Consulting in 1997, they found that nearly 50 percent of the respondents outsource more human resource functions today than they did three years ago and more than 50 percent intend to increase their outsourcing activities over the next three years [Maurer and Mobley, 1999). Yes, outsourcing is common and it is growing rapidly.

Not only is outsourcing increasing in scale but it is increasing in scope. Rather than limited to commodity processes that do not differentiate the firm's product, outsourcing also includes strategic processes that do differentiate the firm's product or service. Choosing which components, sub-assemblies, products or services to outsource can be a difficult strategic decision and has received considerable attention in the literature [Fisher, 1997] [Lacity, Willcocks and Feeny, 1996]. An example of outsourcing a strategic process is the design development and operation of corporate web sites. Many firms have chosen to outsource these activities when confronted with skilled labor shortages, uncertain outcomes, tentative schedules, and high costs.

World Wide Trading

Outsourcing reaches well beyond national boundaries. Focal firms now search all continents to find the most appropriate supplier. The software industry provides an excellent example of this trend. In the 1980's many firms turned to software houses in India for development, conversion, and maintenance of their systems. In the period from 1981 to 1994, software outsourcing to India grew at the rate of 40 percent per year [Heeks, 1996]. While India had the field to itself in the 1980's, suppliers now exist in China, Hungary, Ireland, Israel, Mexico, the Philippines, and Singapore. Choosing a software supplier now means searching the world.

In a Harvard Business Review article, Magretta [1998] provides us with insight into the direction of global outsourcing in an interview with the CEO of Li and Fung, Victor Fung. Li and Fung, located in Hong Kong, is one of the worlds largest trading companies. They rely upon thousands of suppliers around the globe to manufacture and assemble clothes and other consumer goods. In one example, a European retailer places an order for 10,000 garments. Yarn for the garment is purchased in Korea. It is woven and dyed in Taiwan. Zippers are ordered from a plant in China, and assembly of the garment takes place in Thailand. But assembly is scheduled across five factories to meet the customer's need for quick response. Using this complex web of suppliers, Li and Fung can deliver sweaters to European stores in five weeks from receipt of order. This helps the retailer who can now release orders much closer to the market, thereby minimizing the risks that are often taken when orders are released long before goods arrive to be sold to customers.

The practices described in the Li and Fung article underscore the dual impact of outsourcing and worldwide trading. When companies dissect the value chain and search the world for suppliers, both the manufacturer and customer reap the benefits.

Information Technology

Information technology takes on a more central and complex role when production and service activities are dissected and their component parts outsourced throughout the world. Once dispersed, it becomes IT's role to integrate and synchronize these widely dispersed suppliers so that items purchased are received on-time. [Bowersox and Closs, 1996].

Integrating suppliers is itself complex. IT must work with a range of firms that may include suppliers, contract manufacturers, subassembly plants, factory, distribution centers, wholesalers, retailers, carriers, freight forwarders, customs brokers, international procurement organizations, and value-added-network services. Not only are there many different players in this process, but each can be expected to maintain its own island of automation. How can they be connected, integrated, and synchronized? While there is no 'best way', several examples suggest that companies are indeed meeting this challenge.

Hormel Foods Corporation, a multinational manufacturer and marketer of consumer-branded meat and food products, uses supply chain software to integrate its suppliers and optimize its transportation strategy including inbound, outbound and intercompany movements. They link all their carriers to a central logistics-planning center, and have the ability to receive, sort, explore, prioritize loads, and enhance communication with carriers, all via the Internet.

After implementing supply chain software, Motorola Information Systems Group reduced inventory by one-third, eliminated 50% of its warehouse space and cut its order cycle time from six days to one. Hyundai Motor's overseas distributors now receive spare parts almost 10 days faster than before they adopted supply chain management software from GE Information Services.

In all of these examples, the problem of synchronizing dispersed operations would be impossible without a carefully developed information systems strategy. And these strategies require the use of several hardware, software, and telecommunications technologies. Later in this chapter, these technologies will be explored.

Inter-organizational Alliances

One view of customer-supplier relationships, is that the goal of the focal firm is to reduce supplier bargaining power and thereby improve its own bargaining power [Porter and Millar, 1985]. Firms that follow this model invest little in their supplier relationships. This traditional view is often referred to as the arm's-length model of supplier management. It emphasizes independence and competition. Supplier relationships are characterized by short-term contracts, frequent rebidding, low levels of information sharing, low levels of relation-specific investments, and low levels of trust.

In contrast to the arm's-length model is the partner model. Often attributed to the strategy followed by Japanese firms, this model suggests a close working relationship between the focal firm and its suppliers. Studies of firms whose supplier relationships can be placed in this category suggest that more information is shared among partners, interdependent tasks are better coordinated, and investments are made in relationship-specific technology. Furthermore, trust not suspicion characterizes the nature of the supplier-customer relationship [Kumar, 1996]. The downside is that these relationships are costly to establish and maintain, and they constrain the focal firm's ability to switch away from inefficient suppliers. In Porter's terminology, they reduce the bargaining power of the focal firm. What some firms have discovered, however, is that when this model is used, the overall value chain becomes much more efficient as suppliers become full partners and work collaboratively to deliver quality products at the right price and at the right time.

Dyer, Cho and Chu [1998] studied three U.S. automotive firms, two Japanese automotive firms and three Korean automotive firms. What they found was that the arm's-length model prevailed in the U.S. While the research results suggested an arms-length approach, the U.S. firms expressed the belief that theirs was a partnership approach. Apparently, perceptions and reality differed. In Korea, the partner model prevailed. Automotive companies in that country demanded a high degree of supplier loyalty but at the same time engaged in long-term collaborative relationships. The Japanese automakers fell into both categories. Some of their suppliers could be placed in the arm's-length category while those they classified as strategic suppliers, were placed in the partnership category.

Which model is superior? Both are appropriate. To optimize supply chain strategy, the study concludes that suppliers must be segmented into two categories. Strategic partners are those who provide inputs that are typically of high value and play a role in differentiating the firm's products. Buyers should maintain high levels of communication with these organizations, exchange personnel, campaign for relation-specific investments, and make every effort to insure that their suppliers maintain world class operations. Arm's-length suppliers are those who provide commodity inputs that do not differentiate the firm's products and need less integration. How do these categories impact IT? The partner model leads to a relationship that facilitates connectivity, integration, and synchronization. It may be more difficult to achieve these outcomes under the arm's-length model.

INFORMATION TECHNOLOGY IN SUPLY CHAIN MANAGEMENT

Information technology plays a critical role in integrating and synchronizing suppliers and also in connecting supply chain systems with the internal enterprise systems of the focal firm. The development of any strategic plan requires an understanding of these technologies and how they work.

Several technologies are available. Choosing one or a combination of them depends upon several factors including the nature of the relationship, the degree of integration, and the type of data required. These technologies include:

- Postal system and Facsimile (FAX)
- Traditional Electronic Data Interchange
- Internet-based Electronic Data Interchange
- Data Warehousing
- Enterprise Resource Planning

Postal System and Fax

Not more than a decade ago, most interorganizational information traveled through the postal system or by fax [Rosenberg and Valient, 1992], and during that time only essential business-to-business data was sent. These documents included the necessary hard copies to accompany a sale of merchandise and included purchase orders, bills, and invoices. Hard copy dominated, while information technology and telecommunications played minor roles.

Fax or "facsimile" is the transmission of documents by electronic means from one trading partner to another. Using this technology a source document is scanned at the senders location. It is converted to analog data sent over communication lines to the recipient's location. At the receiving end the analog data is decoded and an image printed. Fax has the advantage that the technology is inexpensive, that the public switched telephone network can be used to send the fax, and that this technology is completely independent of the firm's computer information system. Compatibility is therefore not an issue.

While fax machines avoided the interface problems with the firm's computing system, many firms were looking to develop applications that would allow automatic entry into their information system from the sender's information system. Early electronic systems that accomplished this automatic exchange of documents used proprietary formats agreed upon by the two trading partners. But the problem with this approach was that organizations found it necessary to maintain a different set of standards for each trading partner. This burden limited the benefits of conducting business electronically and eventually led to the development of standards called EDI.

Traditional Electronic Data Interchange (EDI)

Electronic Data Interchange (EDI) emerged in the late 1960s and was first adopted by airlines, automobile manufacturers, and shipping companies. Ordering was usually the first process automated, followed by billing and invoicing. During the 1990's the annual growth of EDI was robust and estimated to be 37 percent [Rosenberg and Valient, 1992]. Applications are now found in a range of industries including shipping, retail, grocery, apparel manufacturing, textiles, warehousing, aerospace, chemicals, construction, automotive, financial, electrical and electronics, utilities, health care, petroleum pharmaceutical, metal, paper, entertainment, and higher education [Bower, King, Konsynski, 1990].

The technology embodied in EDI represents a major evolutionary step beyond fax. When a fax system is used, the recipient must manually transfer data contained on the fax into a computer system before the data can be processed. With EDI, data is transmitted in a specific and structured format and entered directly into the recipient's information system without any human intervention. Accordingly, EDI can be defined as the electronic exchange of business documents from one organization's computer to another organization's computer in standard format.

EDI standards are generic and therefore not dependent upon any specific hardware, software, communications system or processing environment. It does require, however, that partners agree upon a common set of standards; have a means for formatting their data according to these standards; and have access to communications media that can send the data between parties. Because EDI standards are generic, many commercial EDI software packages are available.

There are four main components of any EDI system. First are the standards. They define the format of the transaction. Two standards are used, ANSI X.12 and UN/EDIFACT. Organizations may customize these standards within certain guidelines and develop their own implementation conventions.

The second component is the business application that generates the paperwork to be sent over the EDI network. Such applications may include a procurement system, production-planning system, logistics system, financial accounting system, and order management system.

The third component is the EDI gateway. The function of this component is to convert application data into a standard format for sending and receiving messages to and from trading partners. Typically a computer is dedicated to this process and includes software for the EDI translation.

The last component is the communication network. The purpose of this component is to transmit the EDI document electronically to its destination. Several options are available. First, a direct point-to-pont connection can be established between the sender and receiver. In the second option a VAN or value added network supplier is used. These VANs provide proprietary services that will take the responsibility for forwarding the EDI message to its destination. If this alternative is chosen, the EDI encoded message is sent via telecommunications media to a VAN where it is stored and then forwarded to its destination. The user pays a small fee for each message sent

Seagate Technology, a manufacturer of disk drives, has used EDI to integrate its worldwide manufacturing operations. Their manufacturing process, described by Palvia and Lee [1996], begins with a sales forecast that is used to develop a master production schedule extending over several months. The schedule then drives the supply chain all the way down to the lowest levels of planning in the organization. Since many of Seagate's plants are dependent on the components received from plants the next level below, the schedule requires accurate and timely data to ensure effective linkages between plants. Adding considerable complexity to the management of this process is the reliance on the just-in-time concept where component parts and subassemblies are scheduled to arrive just in time for their inclusion in higher level assemblies or finished products. In one example, the plant in Singapore is dependent on three flights daily from Thailand. Components and subassemblies go directly from these flights to assembly lines. In-process inventory is thereby minimized. How does this complex web of suppliers function in an JIT environment? Seagate's IT Director for the Far East comments, "We are very dependent on our IT and on interplant EDI to make all this happen."

Traditional EDI has several shortcomings. Implementation and maintenance costs can be high, thereby limiting the overall market penetration of this technology. The user must first acquire appropriate hardware to run the software. EDI software must then be installed on user machines, and each user must be connected to the focal firm using direct point-to-point telecommunications technology or through a VAN. Many suppliers, especially smaller firms, are unwilling to invest in this technology. As a result, many of a firm's suppliers are not EDI capable and the focal firm must still rely on mail and fax to process some orders. Falling short of 100% compliance affects the focal firm's ability to achieve the benefit from an automated process. These problems notwithstanding, traditional EDI has proven to be very successful in linking customers and suppliers [Jones and Beatty, 1997].

Internet-based Electronic Data Interchange (EDI)

The explosive growth in business-to-business electronic commerce has spawned new types of EDI. Through the use of internet-based technologies, many of the barriers associated with the adoption of traditional EDI have fallen. Internet-based EDI technology relies on familiar and secure browser software technology, operates within a Windows or Windows NT environment on low cost personal computers, and communicates over the web.

Internet-based EDI integrates Internet technologies with EDI. Several alternatives are possible using this technology. In the first, the focal firm maintains an EDI server that performs the same functions as the VAN. Just as in conventional EDI systems, the purpose of this server is to translate the sender's business application to EDI standards and prepare it for transmission via the internet. At the recipient's end an EDI server translates the EDI data to a format compatible with the recipient's business system. The advantage of this approach is that the need for a VAN is circumvented, but its disadvantage is that all users must install and maintain EDI hardware and software at their locations.

Another alternative is service-based Internet EDI. With this technology the focal firm enters into a contract with an Internet-EDI service to host all supplier applications. The service establishes a hub for the system, located on its server. All suppliers and the focal firm are now interconnected through this hub. Using this technology, a manufacturer or retailer and its suppliers can interact with one another through this common site or hub on the Web. They can send and receive purchase orders, order change requests, advance shipping notices, and other structured business documents. All data flowing through the hub is in a standard format and serves to interconnect the business processes of both merchants and suppliers. This also provides the focal firm with the opportunity to closely couple the hub to its existing enterprise business systems. Data coming from suppliers can now trigger the focal firm's internal applications such as production scheduling, shipping, and customer delivery schedules. Often these web-based systems are called Extranets. An Extranet is an Internet system whose access is limited to authorized users. In this case the Extranet is limited to authorized users of the focal firm and its suppliers. Non-authorized users are prevented from access by security systems called firewalls.

With the convenience of browser technology and Internet communications, the cost for suppliers to use this technology is significantly reduced. In addition, industry-standard browsers substantially simplify installation and maintenance of the EDI systems on the Web. Now, with lower costs and simpler systems, focal firms can reasonably expect 100% compliance from their clients.

Another standard in electronic commerce, related to EDI, is OBI. In June 1997, American Express Company and the Internet Purchasing Roundtable (a group of Fortune 500 companies and their leading suppliers) announced the release of Open Buying on the Internet (OBI). This is a standard designed to simplify business-to-business commerce, and brings a standard form and processing style for corporate procurement and requisitioning to the Internet. Currently many firms are using this standard to conduct business-to-business commerce.

The aim of the OBI standard is to make the purchasing of goods through the Internet between businesses easier. It is designed for those seller organizations that maintain dynamic catalogs that present product and price information to the customer. It provides the capabilities to custom make electronic catalogs that meet the buyers needs and also includes search features to help the customer find what is needed. Furthermore, the system provides the opportunity for the catalog to be integrated effectively with inventory and order management system. In addition the system addresses several other issues including the verification that the requisitioner is authorized to make the purchase. OBI is not intended to replace EDI. Most think it will be a complimentary technology used for the purchase of indirect materials such as computer supplies and not for the purchase of production-related supplies. Others feel it will complete well with EDI, especially for smaller and mid-sized companies.

Many companies are already using Internet-based technologies. Mitsubishi Motor Sales of America purchased an Internet based SCM system that changes the way headquarters interacts with its 500 dealers. Using this online system, Mitsubishi can; share forecasts, capture dealer orders, reduce inventory-holding costs, and ensure that dealer's orders are filled on time and on budget.

By capturing demand data in real time and linking this data to manufacturing and inventory systems, Mitsubishi has taken a major step in improving customer service.

Data Warehousing

The process of synchronizing activities between the focal firm and its suppliers requires data sharing. Accomplishing this can be difficult for several reasons. First, software and database systems found in different organizations are usually incompatible. Second, many organizations are reluctant to share data.

One approach to minimizing these problems, and at the same time protecting primary databases from either unauthorized use or the threat of data contamination, is for an organization to develop a separate off-line copy of the database. These separate databases, called data warehouses, are not designed to function in a transaction environment whose responsibility it is to accommodate the second-by-second bread-and-butter transactions of the organization. Instead they are designed as management tools for planning and control purposes. Data in these databases is periodically copied from the central working database and is usually only read by users and not changed. Often these data are aggregated, grouped, and organized specifically for their intended application.

Data warehousing, then, represents one possible tool when very different information systems need to interact with each other to monitor the progress of jobs through the value chain. A supplier, for example, can maintain a data warehouse that includes production scheduling and inventory data that its customer can access to determine the progress and availability of parts and orders.

Enterprise Resource Planning

Enterprise resource planning (ERP) has become the hottest buzzword in the information technology business, and like any buzzword it is often inappropriately applied. ERP is a software system together with integrated databases that take a broad view of the internal and external activities of an organization. Its goal is to develop and integrate the activities within an organization including inbound logistics, operations, outbound logistics, marketing and sales, and service. Furthermore, these systems link suppliers and customers to the primary activities of the focal firm. It promises synchronization of the entire organization.

ERP is an enormously expensive undertaking for many firms, requiring extensive process reengineering, and often taking as many as several years to implement. Unfortunately, the ERP label is applied to many commercial software packages that fall far short of its ideal definition.

In its early stages, ERP focused primarily on a single organization and attempted to synchronize the primary activities within that organization. Even this was an ambitious undertaking, as many of these organizations had developed a collection of incompatible and independent software and database systems. While these original applications were simpler to develop, the eventual price paid was that it was often impossible to relate data from different parts of the organization. Synchronization using timely and relevant data was impossible.

Recently, the scope of ERP has widened to include supply chain management. This extends the reach of ERP's internal focus to include the activities associated with supply chain processes. In one sense supply chain management has become a subset of enterprise resource planning, although some could argue that enterprise resource planning is a subset of supply chain management. Whatever the interpretation, the goal of ERP is to provide a seamless software and database environment that supports the synchronization of all activities from suppliers to the customers.

Wal-Mart is an example of how ERP can extend beyond the boundaries of the focal firm. Together with Proctor and Gamble (P&G), one of its suppliers, they have developed systems for sharing information between firms that address a full range of activities from product supply, logistics, finance and accounting [Handfield and Nichols, 1999]. A state-of-the art information system allows P&G to monitor Wal-Mart point-of-sales data from its retail outlets. Using this data and demand forecasts, P&G takes responsibility for maintaining appropriate stock on the shelves of these retail stores. This vendor-managed inventory system (VMI) provides the timely data to help P&G become more responsive to the sales and marketing of its products while at the same time relieving Wal-Mart of inventory management and control.

It can be argued that the reason Wal-Mart has been effective in extending its ERP is that it has a dominant position in the retail industry and that P&G must comply with Wal-Mart to protect its access to retail markets. Other focal firms may have considerably less leverage. They may not dominate their markets, their suppliers may have many channels through which their markets can be accessed, and their suppliers may be less willing to share data and make relationship specific investments. For them, a seamless and integrated enterprise resource planning system that synchronizes suppliers in an effective supply chain system will be more difficult to achieve.

GLOBAL SUPPLY CHAINS AND CULTURE

While the technical issues of IT, in developing a supply chain system, often dominate management's attention, the opinion of many in this field is that the ability of the information system to meet expectations needs broader consideration. It is not unreasonable to suggest that a universal characteristic of humans, and the organizations in which they work, is that that they resist change. Regardless of the advantages that new methods or technologies can promise, there frequently develops a reluctance to accept the changes that must be made. Indeed much literature has been devoted to this problem and the way in which management can respond to this challenge. But crossing national boundaries seems to impose challenges that are much less familiar. Most mangers and workers seem less prepared to deal with issues of national culture, perhaps because national culture is so ingrained in an individual's behavior.

When people are expected to relate to others and work in ways that conflict with their basic cultural values, the success of a project can be jeopardized just as much as if the problem were a technical one. When this occurs it may be helpful to ask if the methods and procedures imposed by a new application are compatible with the established working patterns of the supplier's management and workforce. If not, then management must be prepared to assume the challenge that these cultural issues superimposed on the universal tendency to resist change. Research into the issues associated with national culture can help in understanding and addressing this problem.

Cultural Dimensions

National culture influences the way that people work, the way people are managed, and the way tasks are designed and even performed. Hofstede (1980) defines culture as a set of mental programs that control an individual's responses in a given context. Parsons and Shils (1951) define it as a shared characteristic of a high-level social systems, while Erez and Earley, (1993) defined it as the shared values of a particular group of people.

Classifying cultures and identifying those dimensions that differentiate cultural behavior is difficult and controversial. One major study, undertaken with the support of IBM and conducted by Hofstede (1980), provides a very useful framework. Utilizing data from 116,000 questionnaires administered in 40 countries he found that national culture could be defined by four dimensions. He identified these dimensions as; power distance, uncertainty avoidance, individualism-collectivism, and masculinity-femininity.

Power Distance is the degree of inequality among people, from relatively equal (small power distance) to extremely unequal (large power distance). Uncertainty Avoidance is the extent to which a society feels threatened by uncertain situations and avoids these situations by providing career stability, establishing formal rules, and not tolerating deviant ideas. Individualism-

Collectivism contrasts a social fabric in which each individual takes care of himself or herself with a social fabric in which groups take care of the individual in exchange for his or her loyalty. Masculinity-Femininity reflects whether the dominant values are associated with the collection of money and things, which Hofstede classifies as masculine, as contrasted with values associated with the caring for others and the quality of life, which he classifies as feminine. Of these four dimensions, power distance and uncertainty avoidance are considered dominant in studying organizations within a particular culture (Hofstede, 1981).

Hofstede work has been criticized in many ways. Some argue that his work implies that these 'common' cultural characteristics should be observable in all organizations within a specific culture. But we know this is certainly not the case, nor was it Hofstede's intention that this be implied. Organizations characterized by high power distance exist in low power distance cultures, and conversely organizations characterized by low power distance are found in high power distance countries. Clearly the range in any culture can be wide. Accordingly, Hofstede's model, and its use in this chapter, is intended to suggest general tendencies observable in a culture; variations are expected. Without the ability to make these generalizations, the development of a simple but useful conceptual framework of culture would be limited.

Culture and Supply Chain Management

How does culture affect supply chain management? The study cited earlier by Dyer, Cho and Chu provides some answers. It concludes that focal firms need to segment their suppliers according to the type of working relationship required. Cultural differences, however, suggest that it may be difficult to expect suppliers from some countries to modify the way they relate to their customers. Can a company in a country characterized as high in individualism find it as easy to engage collaboratively in a partner relationship as it can with an arm's-length relationship? Can a company from a country characterized as high in collectivism (low individualism) find it as easy to engage in an arm's-length relationship as it can with a partnership relationship? If the answer is no, what can be done to help facilitate these relationships?

Consider the difference in supply chain relationships for American, Japanese and Korean automakers described by Dyer, Cho and Chu. American manufactures primarily follow the arm's-length model. The cultural characteristics that describe Americans are high individualism and low uncertainty avoidance (they ranked first in individualism and 43rd in uncertainty avoidance). It would therefore be expected that relationship distances between these focal firms and its suppliers would be high (high individualism) and that frequent bidding and supplier changes would be expected (low uncertainty avoidance). This is exactly what the Dyer, Cho and Chu study found. The opposite would be expected for Korean manufacturers. They ranked 43rd in individualism and 17th in uncertainty avoidance. It would therefore be expected that they would have few suppliers, that these suppliers would be integrated into their planning processes (low individualism), and that they would maintain a reliable and long-term relationship with them (high uncertainty avoidance). Again this is what the study found. While the study suggests that suppliers must be segmented, culture may play a dominant role in what can be expected.

Cultural influences are not limited to relationships. They can extend to the details of the data itself. In high power distance cultures, for example, it is not unusual for workers to be given very little authority and responsibility in the execution of a work task. When an automated information system requires these workers to be responsible for entering job progress and quality control data into an automated system, a longer learning and training cycle can be expected before these workers are comfortable with these added responsibilities.

STRATEGIC IT ISSUES

The success of an international supply chain information system depends upon its strategic plan. As in any strategic plan, the process must take place at the highest levels in the organization and actively involve those affected by its decisions. In large organizations the chief information officer (CIO) plays a critical role.

While the topic of strategic planning has been addressed elsewhere in the management literature, there are several issues that are particularly relevant to the supply chain IT process. They include:

- Number of levels in the supply chain linked through IT
- Degree of integration desired
- Relationship-specific investments expected from suppliers
- Impact from resistance-to-change and cultural differences
- Degree of detail accessed
- Choice between in-house software and commercial software
- Modular Implementation

Number of Levels in the Supply Chain Linked Through IT

Because supply chains can extend to several levels, IT strategy must determine the number of supplier levels that need to be integrated into the corporate IT system. Should integration stop with the first line of suppliers, or should their suppliers also be considered part of the supply chain? Where should monitoring stop? While the Year 2000 problem (Y2K) is now behind us, it does illustrate the dilemma faced when deciding upon the appropriate number of supplier levels that can directly impact the firm's ability to deliver goods and services. By 1999 most focal firms had devoted considerable resources to their own Y2K preparedness programs as well at to their first level suppliers. But in 1999 they began to voice grave concerns about their lower level suppliers, suppliers of their suppliers. If these lower level suppliers would be impacted by the Y2K problem, the entire chain could be shut down. Accordingly, many firms were forced to engage in a last minute effort to ensure that lower level suppliers were compliant. At a minimum, these firms were required to fill out elaborate questionnaires that would uncover possible problems. In some cases lower level suppliers, suspected of not being adequately prepared were dropped as suppliers. While this example addresses an issue that could have had profound impact on the ability of focal firms to operate, it nonetheless suggests that even in less dramatic situations, an effective IT supply chain strategy must consider the implications of limiting IT integration to first level suppliers.

Degree of Integration Desired

Once the number of levels is determined, decisions must center on the degree of integration. Will it be limited to the exchange of trading documents such as orders, invoices, statements, shipping and customs documents? Or, will integration extend to the management and control of the supplier's activities and provide the focal firm with access to production schedules, shop floor information, inventory levels, and shipping schedules [Barrett, 1986-87] [Barrett and Konsynski, 1982].

With increasing frequency, the level of integration is increasing. A good example of this is vendor managed inventories (VMI). Facilitated by the changes in technology and interorganizational alliances, VMI is having a profound impact on the retailing industry. Retail VMI involves a sophisticated information loop that aggregates each store's sales from Point-of-Sales (POS) terminals in order to drive product replenishment schedules. In these systems, suppliers access sales data and these data are automatically integrated with the supplier's enterprise systems to affect master production scheduling, inventory and shipping schedules.

Relationship-Specific Investments Expected from Suppliers

IT strategy is closely tied to the willingness of suppliers to make relationship-specific IT investments. If the supplier is internal to the corporation, an enterprise resource planning system can be implemented across the entire corporation. The 'common systems', used by many Fortune 500 companies have the distinct advantage that they solve the compatibility issue. Using the same systems with similar database structures makes it easier to develop the kind of software that can be used to manage and control the linkages between the focal firm and its internal suppliers. But, when suppliers are external to the corporation, a strategy must evolve that addresses the extent to which these suppliers can be expected to make these investments. Will the focal firm defray some of the supplier's costs? Will outsourcing contracts have to be written over longer periods to ensure that the supplier recoups the cost of these IT investments? Answers to these questions can be difficult to obtain and will depend upon the capabilities of the suppliers and their willingness to make these investments.

The Impact from Resistance-to-Change and Cultural Differences

In most outsourcing decisions that cross national boundaries, the focal firm is best advised to carefully address the consequences of resistance-to-change and cultural differences. If ignored, these issues can seriously impair the transfer of technology, its implementation schedule, and its successful use.

Software systems can affect suppliers in at least two ways. First, the nature of the relationship expected, arm's-length or partner, may be difficult to achieve in some cultures. While many U.S. companies would insist that they follow the partner model of supplier relationships, when compared with partnership relationships in Japan and Korea, Dyer, Cho and Chu classified the U.S. automobile-supplier relationships as arm's-length. It would be reasonable to expect, then, that establishing a partnership relationship in the U.S. may be more difficult, or at least represent different challenges, than establishing the same relationship in Japan or Korea.

The second way cultural factors affect the way people perform is the way in which they execute work related tasks. It may be possible that existing work practices interfere with the methods required by the new software system. IT strategy needs to be sensitive to these problems and address the ways in which these differences can be accommodated.

The Degree of Detail Accessed

Closely related to the issue of integration is the type of data that needs to be collected. If it is determined that an arm's-length relationship for a particular supplier is appropriate, then the type of data that needs to be collected may bounded by the few documents that need to be exchanged. Order data, invoice data, shipping data, and statements may be all that is necessary, and EDI may be sufficient to transfer the data in these documents to the focal firm's information system.

If, on the other hand, integration extends into the supplier's operations, then the focal firm must decide upon the data that are most crucial in synchronizing these separate operations with their own. While the tendency might be to collect too much data, experience suggests that only critical data should be collected. Critical data are a manageable and concise set of data that can be used to monitor and control activities [Rockart, 1979]. Should the supplier's orders to its suppliers be monitored? If the answer is yes, then which data items should be monitored? Should integration extend to the supplier's aggregate production plans, purchasing systems, production schedules, shop floor control systems, and inventory systems? Again, if the answer is yes, which data items should be monitored?

Suppliers, mentioned earlier in the chapter, may be reluctant to share these data with the focal firm. To address concerns about data security, integrity, and confidentiality, data warehouses may prove a very effective away to provide access yet ensure some degree of protection and confidentiality.

Choice Between In-House and Commercial Software

Acquiring the appropriate supply chain management software can take two directions. In the first, the organization buys commercial off-the-shelf software and attempts to change its business processes to conform to those imposed by the software. This approach is faster and less costly than any other and it reduces development risk when the software is purchased from a reliable software vendor with a proven track record. The cost of changing business practices however is highest with this alternative and the cost of implementing these software systems can be from one to ten times higher than the cost of the purchased software. Often these implementation costs are significantly underestimated. At the other end of the spectrum, business practices remain the same, and software is developed to accommodate these practices. Here the development costs can be very high, but disruption to the business is minimized. Many organizations will struggle with these two approaches and settle for something in between these extremes. They may choose commercial software that has some capability for customization to the purchaser's business practices.

Modular Implementation

Supply Chain management and enterprise resource planning systems are clearly ambitious efforts to integrate and synchronize the operations of a firm. But to consider all the individual activities required to deliver goods and services to the customer and at the same time to develop and implement a comprehensive enterprise-wide solution is an overwhelming exercise. For many firms it makes more sense to develop a strategic plan for the entire value chain and then to divide that plan into integrated deliverable modules. Modules are then developed and implemented in a sequence that eventually accomplishes the overall strategic objective of the plan.

For many organizations the first step in a supply chain management IT strategy is to automate billing, shipping and invoicing systems. Care must be taken, however, to ensure that decisions made at this stage are compatible with later stage modules. While the choice may be EDI, many questions need to be answered. What EDI standard should be used? Will we use traditional EDI or Internet-based EDI? With which operating system is the software compatible (Windows/NT, Linux, Solaris, Unix)? With what commercial ERP system is it compatible (Oracle, SAP)? What Internet features does it have? Finally, how do these features constrain the choices that will be made later? While later modules may have already been designed or if some of these modules already exist, then the choice of EDI strategy may be limited. For example, if the organization already utilizes an ERP system developed by Oracle or SAP then it may be preferable to limit the choice of EDI software to those software packages that can be integrated with the ERP system without custom coding.

However the modules are designed, and whatever the sequence of development and implementation, those firms that develop strategic plans to guide these efforts will have an advantage over those whose plans are less organized and integrated.

CONCLUSIONS

Four trends at the turn of this century have had a profound affect on the way in which business is conducted and managed. Outsourcing has made the firm leaner, more focused on its core competencies, and critically reliant on its suppliers. Worldwide trading has greatly increased the range of possible suppliers. Information technology and electronic commerce has provided the means by which focal firms and their dispersed supply partners can organize to meet ambitious schedules that deliver products and services when and where they are needed. Organizational alliances have created a new paradigm that is changing the way firms relate and establish relationships that would have been unheard of not more than a decade ago.

At the very center of these dramatic changes is the Information technology that connects, integrates and synchronizes the far-flung operations of the modern organization. While we know that the objective of these systems is to tie together the customer with all segments of the supply chain to ensure rapid response, this goal is still elusive for many organizations. The technology is available, but implementation must depend upon the willingness of people and organizations to change and the ability to adapt systems to accommodate cultural differences.

Mini Case: CAL

CAL is a South American holding company wholly owned by its central government. They provide purchasing services for clients and are located in Florida to be near the source of many of their suppliers.

The political and economic structure at the present time is such that the economy has a very strong centrally controlled component. Many industries, including most basic industries, are owned by the state. While the government is planning to move from a centrally controlled economy to one that is market driven, current practices are more similar to economies that are centrally controlled.

Basic industries that the government owns and operates include steel, aluminum, mining, forestry and construction. These industries maintain their own management structures, set their own production plans, and operate their own businesses. There is however, one exception.

The state recognized long ago that many of the inputs required by these plants were purchased in the same geographic regions of the world and in some cases different plants used common or near-common inputs. The state concluded that it would be in the best interest of containing production costs to integrate the purchasing for all state owned industry and to coordinate shipping from several regions of the world to a central location in their country.

CAL emerged from the concept of centralized purchasing. Its charter is to provide a "total logistics service package" to its customers. Headquarters were established in the US with other offices in Holland, Japan and Venezuela. CAL role is to coordinate purchasing and shipping activities between their client companies and 1,300 suppliers located throughout the world. Of these 1,300 suppliers, fifty can be classified as strategic while the remainder provide non-strategic products and services.

PURCHASING PROCESS
1. Purchase orders originate in one of the State owned companies and follow several steps:
2. Order received by fax
3. Original order also sent by mail to CAL headquarters in the US.
4. Three potential suppliers identified (This is a state requirement).
5. Requests for quotations sent to suppliers.
6. Quotations received and evaluated in the US.
7. Quotations sent by fax or e-mail to its clients in South America.
8. Clients approve one quotation and return approval via fax or e-mail. All orders over $10,000 require three signatures including the buyer at the clients firm, finance manager, and general   manager.
9. Purchase order sent to supplier via e-mail or fax.
10. Goods sent to US facility where they are consolidated and shipped to clients.

MANAGEMENT OBJECTIVES
The current methods and procedures used to manage the supply chain system were developed to ensure effective execution of orders. Due to these safeguards, CAL has often been criticized for incurring delays in executing orders and delivering them to its customers. Some have complained about the delays while a purchase order awaits the appropriate signatures. Sometimes these delays exceed the quotation's expiration date and CAL must begin the bid process again. But the tradeoff for these delays is considered reasonable and provides management with the control it needs to ensure effective execution of orders. By consolidating all purchasing into one agency they are able to obtain quantity discounts and to consolidate shipments from each region, thereby saving shipping charges. The savings, according to management, outweigh the disadvantages and delays inherent in the system.

Mini Case …. Continued.

INFORMATION TECHNOLOGY

Information technology at the US facility includes two software systems. The first is a commercial package, i installed in 1989-1990, with several upgrades since. It supports the purchasing process from requisition of goods to receipt of goods. It involves requisition entry, quotation processing, vendor selection, purchase order creation, and purchase order verification. The second application is a financial system that includes general ledger, accounts payable, accounts receivable, payroll, fixed assets inventory, and purchasing modules. These information systems are not integrated nor are the systems integrated with CAL's clients. It is necessary, for example, to enter purchasing data manually, when an order from a client is received.

Optical fiber links are used between the US, The Netherlands and Caracas, while digital microwave is used between headquarters, where most of its clients central purchasing offices are located. Dial up lines are used to connect the purchasing facility in Japan.

Louis Sandoval, managing director at CAL, has had the opportunity to observe the dramatic changes occurring in supply chain management in the U.S. In a memo to his boss back home he wrote.

Victor: The changes are dramatic if not revolutionary. I see companies integrating their supply chains using the latest in computer and telecommunication technologies. They send their orders directly into their supplier's databases, and can access these database to see how their orders are coming and exactly when they will be delivered. One company I visited last week even has their suppliers print their own bar codes on products so the receiving process is completely automated. What really surprises me is that many of these companies have better working relationships with their suppliers. They don't seem as competitive as we are. They meet frequently and cooperate more. I am worried that our systems are so far outdated that we will never be able to compete once we open ourselves to sell our aluminum and forestry products on the worldwide market. We need to act now before the world leaves us behind.

His boss wrote him two weeks later.

Louis: I agree with you on some of your points, but don't forget we have the advantage of batching our shipments and saving transportation dollars. This is one advantage we can't afford to loose.

Do we really need to look into our supplier's processes? I can't imagine this would help us very much. We already keep large inventories to prepare us for any problems with their shipments. If they deliver a day or two earlier or we know exactly when they deliver, I don't think this will make any difference. Don't forget we're located half the world away from some of them. We need to keep large inventories just in case.

As for the working relationships that your friends have with their suppliers, I don't buy it. If we're not competitive and squeeze out the last nickel, how can we be competitive with our customers? We have to keep the bargaining power on our side. After all, we are big customers to many of our suppliers.

PERSISTENT PROBLEMS

In general there is very little momentum toward changing current purchasing practices. Meanwhile the staff is kept very busy with meeting the needs of its clients. Just last week they solved a crisis of major proportions. One of the aluminum plants that produces aluminum sheets ran out of steel belting. When the sheets are made they are stacked together and rolled. The belting, wrapped around the roll, holds the roll from unraveling. The US purchasing office was notified only hours before the plant ran out of belting. The urgency of the problem was clear. If the plant did not receive belting within 48 hours, it would have to shut down. Shut-down and start-up costs would be very high. The US office responded to this emergency by finding a supplier with stock on-hand. They then charted a Boeing 747 to pick up the belting and deliver it to its client. While the costs associated with this solution were very high they were lower than those associated with shutting the plant down.

ASSIGNMENT

1. Describe the current purchasing system used by CAL.
2. How does management justify current methods and procedures?
3. How do you think the move toward a more competitive market will affect CAL? What worldwide trends in supply chain management will they forced to address?
4. What type of relationships do they have with their vendors? What other types of relationships are possible? Why might they be difficult to achieve?
5. Develop a strategic supply chain plan for CAL.
6. What problems would you anticipate in carrying out this plan?
7. How would you address these problems?

STUDY QUESTIONS

ı२\   1.   What are the six major strategic decisions in supply chain management?

2.   What factors do you think explain why firms are extending their reach and outsourcing throughout the world?

3.   What is the difference between the arm's-length model of interorganizational alliance and the partner model? Which is preferred? Why might some firms find it difficult to implement one of these models?

4.   Explain why EDI might be an appropriate technology for linking a firm with its suppliers?

ı२५   5.   How does Information Technology help the firm to manage its supply chain?

6.   Describe the different types of data that you think might be useful in managing a supply chain for a manufacturing company.

7.   After attending many trade shows, the Biltmore company was convinced that it would be in its best interest to implement a much more effective supply chain system for its suppliers in the U.S. and Europe. They have hired you as a consultant. They would like to integrate data from their suppliers' purchasing, scheduling, and inventory systems into their own ERP system. Relationship-specific investments by many suppliers will have to be made. They have hired you to consult on the project. The reason you have been hired is that the project has taken much longer than expected to get started. For example, they have just been told by one supplier in France that it is having second thoughts on providing access to their data. This supplier is concerned that access to its data will erode their bargaining power when the contract comes up for renewal in the future. In addition to the data access issue, identify other issues you think need to be discussed. How would you proceed?

8.   You have been hired by a manufacturer of athletic shoes whose customers are some of the largest retailers in the country. While they assemble the shoes in their Miami plant, all of the component parts such as bottoms, uppers and laces are purchased from suppliers in Europe and Asia. Their competitive advantage has been cost, and they have been able to provide a quality athletic shoe to retailers at a very competitive price. Growth has been extremely rapid. You have been asked to provide them with an IT supply chain strategy to take them into the next stage of growth. At present, communication with suppliers is by telephone or fax. Both the manufacturer and its Asian suppliers use very simple information technology. How would you suggest to proceed?

REFERENCES

Barrett, Stephanie S. (Winter 1986-1987). Strategic Alternatives and Inter-organizational System Implementations: An Overview. *Journal of Management Information Systems*, 3(3), 5-16.

Barrett, Stephanie S. & Konsynski, B. (1982). Inter-organizational Information Sharing Systems. MIS Quarterly, 74-98.

Bower, M, J. King & Konsynski,B. (1990). Singapore TradeNet: A Tale of One City, Harvard Business School (9-191-009).

Bowersox, Donald J. & Closs,D.J. (1996*). Logistics Management: The Integrated Supply Chain Process*, McGraw Hill, New Your.

Dyer, Jeffrey H., Co, D.S. & Chu W. (Winter 1998). Strategic Supplier Segmentation: The Next "Best Practice" in Supply Chain Management. *California Management Review*, 40(2), 57-77.

Ein-Dor, P. & Segev, E. (January 1992). End User Computing: A Cross Cultural Study. *International Information Systems*, 1(1), 124-137.

Erez, M. & Earley, P.C. (1993*). Culture, Self-identity, and Work*. New York: Oxford University Press.

Fisher, Marshall L. (March-April, 1997). What is the Right Supply Chain for Your Product. *Harvard Business Review,* 105-116.

Heeks, Richard, (1996). Global Software Outsourcing to India by Multinational Corporations in *Global Information Technology and Systems Management*, Palvia, Palvia, and Roche, Ivy League Publishing, 364-392.

Handfield, Robert B., & Nichols, E.L. Jr. (1999*). Supply Chain Management*, Prentice Hall, 1999

Hofstede, G. (Summer 1980). Motivation, Leadership, and Organization: Do American Theories Apply Abroad? *Organizational Dynamics*.

Hofstede, G. (1981). Culture and Organizations. *International Studies of Management and Organizations*, X(4), 15-41.

Jones, Mary C. & Beatty, R.C. (Fall 1999). EDI Benefits and Compatibility: An Empirical Comparison of End User and EDI Manager Perspectives. *Journal of Computer Information Systems*, 51-54.

Kumar, Nirmalya, (November-December 1996). The Power of Trust in Manufacturer-Retailer Relationships. *Harvard Business Review*, 92-106.

Lacity, Mary C., Willcocks, L.P. & Feeny, D.F. (Spring, 1996). The Value of Selective IT Sourcing. Sloan *Management Review*, , 7(3).

Magretta, Joan, (September-October 1998). Fast, Global , and Entrepreneurial: Supply Chain Management, Hong Kong Style. *Harvard Business Review*, 103-114.

Maurer, Rick & Mobley, N. (November 1998). Outsourcing: Is it the HR Department of the Future? *HR Focus,* American Management Association, 11(75), 9.

Palvia, Shailendra & Lee, K. (1996). Developing and Implementing Global Information Systems: Lessons form Seagate Technology, in *Global Information Technology and Systems Management*, Palvia P, Palvia, C. and E. Roche, Ivy League Publishing, 558-576

Parsons, T. & Shils, E.A. (1951). *Toward a General Theory of Action*. Cambridge, MA: Harvard University Press.

Porter Michael E. & Millar V.E. (July-August 1985). How information Gives You Competitive Advantage. *Harvard Business Review*,149-161.

Rockart, John (1979). Chief Executives Define Their Own Data Needs. *Harvard Business Review*, March-April, 81-93.

Rosenberg, Robert & Valient, S. (July 1992). Electronic Data Interchange – A Global Perspective. *Telecommunications*, 50-53.

Walker, William T., & Alber, K.L. (1999). Understanding Supply Chain Management. *APICS Online Edition*, January, 99(1).

8

Reengineering Global Business Processes:
Challenges and Issues

Choton Basu
University of Wisconsin-Whitewater USA

Prashant C. Palvia
The University of North Carolina at Greensboro, USA

ABSTRACT

Globalization trends have forced companies to contend with several new elements in a highly dynamic business environment. Clearly, the management and operation of organizations in this changing environment test an organization's ability to change. Identification of new markets, increased foreign competition, government regulations, currency issues, availability of technology infrastructure all affect the options for change. In such conditions, organizations are forced to develop global alliances, explore foreign markets, and redesign business processes to support global initiatives. In many cases they have to radically reengineer their business processes and handle resulting changes within the organization. In several cases this reengineering effort may involve multiple organizations, located in different parts of the globe. The ability to successfully transform the business processes of a global organization provides tremendous leverage for organizational growth and innovation. A framework has been developed in this chapter for understanding the salient issues in global business process reengineering. Furthermore, we provide insights into several global business-reengineering projects while incorporating some of the key results from an extensive survey and four case studies conducted during 1999-2000.

INTRODUCTION

The management and operation of global organizations is a challenging endeavor. Numerous issues involving transborder data flows, emerging markets, foreign competition, government regulations, currency issues and technological infrastructure have to be contended with. As subsidiaries and units located in various countries come together to form an integrated organization, the need to address global issues becomes critical for the survival of the organization. Alternatively, the integration can be viewed as a set of problems and decisions consistent with a new business or a radical change of an existing one. One way of accomplishing radical change in a firm is by way of major reengineering of its business processes, whereas a business process is defined as:

> *"...a business process is a set of logically related tasks that use the resources of an organization to achieve a defined business outcome." (Grover and Kettinger, 1995)*

This chapter focuses on the reengineering of business processes in a global organization and issues related to it. The ability to successfully transform the business processes of a global organization allows the company to derive significant advantages with respect to its customers and business environment. In doing so these organizations begin to learn to successfully face radical change to survive in this fast-paced global economy.

During the 1990s, business process reengineering (BPR) quickly became the management philosophy of choice for many corporations. Radical improvements in organizational business processes led to the promise of phenomenal growth in revenues and profitability of several organizations. The fundamental tenet is to view the business as a set of business activities or processes that have clearly defined outcomes, as opposed to the traditional view where the organization is divided by silos with specific assigned functional responsibilities e.g., finance, accounting, marketing, manufacturing. While BPR is complex in domestic organizations, in global organizations, it is not only complex but also has far reaching consequences. Vendor relations, supply chains, resource allocation, organization and national cultural factors, headquarter-subsidiary relations and others make it a challenging task for companies attempting to reengineer their global business processes.

There are several additional factors and dimensions of reengineering efforts of global business processes. Besides the obvious complexities arising from business processes that are global, the effort is further exacerbated by the difficulty of coordinating and controlling the tasks and participants in projects of such magnitude. An incident during the release of Windows NT elucidates the point. The worldwide release of this product by Microsoft was almost held up since the artwork for the product container had been delayed. Interestingly, it was a process problem, since the artwork for the box had been sent to a person who was on vacation. The result – the box failed to reach Manufacturing on schedule. This is an excellent example of the participants of the process being unable to assume ownership of the "whole business process." In another case, a German conglomerate reorganized its integrated manufacturing process and transferred a labor-intensive task to its facilities in Portugal in an effort to reduce cost. Though this is an excellent example of reengineering a process globally, the desired results were far from what the organization had anticipated. After few months the company's production schedule was off and issues of bad quality and delivery delays began to plague the company (Kutscheker, 1994). The managers and workers of the plant in Portugal were unable to perceive the importance of a logical, integrated international manufacturing process. They failed to consider the complete global picture and their roles as participants to this global business process. The Portuguese workers cited language barrier as a major reason for the lack of understanding and commitment to the global manufacturing business process.

With increasing globalization, processes are becoming increasingly complex and global in scope. However, while reengineering research and consulting has continued to expand (e.g., consulting was about 2 billion dollars in 1997), there is hardly any evidence of research, investigation or discourse on the international dimension of business processes. A possible explanation may be the perception that the international aspect does not significantly impact the inherent characteristics of a reengineering project. We contend that this perception is not true or realistic. The author of a study of 51 Swiss and German companies in 1994 states that, "given the complexity, cultural diversity, and the multi-faceted structure of a multi-national corporation, reengineering global business processes, may require additional attention" (Kutscheker, 1994).

This chapter attempts to address this multi-dimensional problem of global business process reengineering (GBR). Specifically, it addresses the following questions:

1) What constitutes a global business process and why is it important to develop reengineering strategies for global processes?

2) What are the key factors that play a significant role in reengineering a global business process?

In order to address these questions, a framework is introduced which captures the various factors and issues related to GBR. The framework provides an appropriate context to discuss these issues as well as the relationships between various independent and dependent variables. The framework was used as a guide in several case studies and a comprehensive survey undertaken by the authors; their results are presented to provide further credence to our claims and statements about GBR.

It is important to note that given the wide variations in reengineering projects, information system (IS) departments, companies, industries, strategies and management philosophies, it is difficult to provide specific universal solutions for all GBR projects. Instead, this chapter would provide generic guidelines and answers based on the literature review, case studies and the extensive survey that was conducted. Some common and key elements of GBR projects would be identified. The chapter is organized as follows. In the next section, we provide an overview of Business Process Reengineering (BPR) in general and discuss BPR success factors. In the following section, we discuss global information technology in general and GBR in particular. A model for GBR is presented next and described in some detail. The findings from the case studies and the survey are presented next. The chapter concludes with some key observations.

BUSINESS PROCESS REENGINEERING

Popularly known as Business Process Reengineering (BPR), this effort involves a total re-examination of a company's all or most prevalent business processes. BPR is about starting over by challenging traditional wisdom and identifying radically new ways of conducting business. Hammer and Champy (1993), the pioneers of the term, define it as "the fundamental rethinking and radical redesign of business processes to achieve dramatic improvements in critical, contemporary measures of performance." Davenport and Short (1990), define it as "the analysis and design of workflows and processes within and between organizations." While the first definition highlights the key words radical and dramatic, the latter definition makes the important observation that the project can be within or between organizations.

The early 1990s was the height of the BPR phenomenon in the United States. A survey of CIOs in 1993-94 by Deloitte and Touche, found that on an average, a CIO had been involved in about 4.4 reengineering projects. Though this period was perhaps the pinnacle of the reengineering phenomenon, the principles associated with it seem to be fairly entrenched in the current management philosophy. In fact, the global BPR survey conducted by the authors (to be described later) indicated that the responding companies had undertaken an average of 5-6 "global" reengineering initiatives in the years 1993-99. However, the Deloitte and Touche survey of 1993-94 also found that the CIOs felt that the outcomes of most reengineering projects fell short of their expectations. Their perceptions, taken in conjunction with the documented evidence of 65% to 70% failure rate of reengineering efforts, make one wonder why reengineering projects are still popular. A quick answer may be the lure of 40 to 100% levels of impact, as evidenced by many anecdotal cases in the literature. On a more profound level, the most appealing aspect maybe the opportunity to rethink "how does one do business." In this sense, the mere prospect of implementing a set of radical, revolutionary ideas to improve various aspects of the business is intuitively appealing.

Caron, Jarvenpaa and Stoddard (1994), provided some insights on reengineering with their longitudinal study of CIGNA Corporation's experience. This was a success story where a number of projects helped the company reduce its operating expenses, reduce cycle times and increase customer satisfaction. One interesting observation was that the learning gained from smaller projects allowed the company to migrate its reengineering efforts to larger and far more complex projects. This learning and willingness to accept a few failures for long term overall success seem to have helped the company achieve overall satisfaction. Thus, reengineering is not as easy as some consultants would like to have their clients believe. There is a substantial learning curve and one must be prepared for a few failures in the beginning.

Reengineering Success Factors

In the nineties, most studies found that a majority of the Fortune 500 companies were involved in some kind of reengineering effort. Some of the same studies also reported a 70% failure rate (Bashein, Markus, Riley, 1994; Klien, 1994; Markus and Robey, 1995). Part of the problem may be the fact that reengineering has become such a popular buzzword that there are too many experts claiming to be know-it-all and promising unrealistic returns. These so-called experts have found willing clients and the ensuing results have been disastrous. Further, a number of projects have been mis-classified under the reengineering category, thus contributing to higher reported failure rates.

There have been several efforts made to understand and successfully implement reengineering projects. In the last 4-5 years of the 1990's era, development of various tools, methodologies, benchmarks, best practices have all contributed to a better understanding of reengineering. Based on a review of past work, a fairly comprehensive list of reengineering success factors is compiled as shown in Table 1. It should be noted, however, that many of these factors are anecdotal and opinion-based and may not have been verified by research.

Table 1: Critical Success Factors for Reengineering

Success Factor	Additional comment
Top management Sponsorship	-Needs to be strong and consistent
Compelling Business Case for Change	-With measurable objectives
Proven Methodology	-Include a vision process
Effective Change Management	-Must address cultural transformation
Securing Business Process Ownership by Line Management	-Pair ownership with accountability
Composition of the reengineering team	-Must encompass both breadth and depth of knowledge
Involvement of employees through communication and empowerment	-Have a plan in place
Ensuring availability of Resources	-Establish resource base on front end of the project
Establishing time limit on the project	-Decide on time frame to avoid over-runs
Establishing relationship between IS professionals and line manager	-Establish internal relationship between the groups
Ensuring Strategic Alignment	-Between project goals and company strategic direction

Adapted from: (Davenport, 1993; Hammer and Champy, 1993; Klein, 1994; Bashien et.al., 1994; Galliers, 1991; Martinez, 1995).

The above list is not all-inclusive. While it is expected that many of these factors are also applicable in a global reengineering effort, there are several new factors to consider in the context of a global business environment. These include issues related to global project costing, global asset allocation, global information technology architecture, sharing knowledge globally; and project collaboration become major issues when the project context is shifted to the global realm. A good example that addresses this reality as well as demonstrates the globalization process is provided below:

Dell entered the retail arena in 1990 by allowing Soft Warehouse Superstores (now CompUSA) to sell its PC's at mail-order prices. Two years later, Xerox agreed to sell Dell machines in 19 Latin American countries. An interesting strategy was also developed in Europe and Asia. For example a customer in Lisbon places a local call that is automatically forwarded to Dell's center in France, which is then, connected to a Portuguese-speaking sales representative. Similar development operations are underway in Asia/Pacific belt (Kalakota and Robinson, 2001).

Throughout the 1990's business process reengineering dominated forefront of management thinking. While this effort at discontinuous change may not be an everyday occurrence in business organizations it certainly led to the transition from an existing functional/silo centered organization infrastructure to a process-oriented, customer centric organization. There is no doubt that all the factors in Table 1 and the previous section contribute in a significant manner to bring about a successful transition but there is need to consider several factors that emerge due to globalization. This may include changes associated with a focused business process such as order-fulfillment or procurement (business process reengineering) or something as vast as enterprise application integration or implementation of an ERP package (leading to business reengineering). The noticeable absence factors related to global dimension, such as culture, technology infrastructure, international legal/political issues and regulations are explored in the subsequent sections.

GLOBALIZATION, INFORMATION TECHNOLOGY (IT) AND CHANGE

During the 1990s, firms continued to explore various strategies to remain competitive in the changing business environment. Mergers, leveraged buy-outs, diversifications, and divestments of business interests have resulted from pressures of intense competition. Among the more recent trends, increasingly easier and more cost effective access to information technology has led to globalization of business operations in order to exploit global markets and gain global competitive advantage. The resultant strategy eventually results in the formation of global alliances, global organizations, and development of inter-organizational systems that span the globe. But even organizations that have adapted globalization as an integral part of their strategy have to continuously adjust to shifts in the business environment due to political adjustments, economic changes, and infusion of new technologies. The formation of new trading blocks in Europe; the North American Free-Trade zone agreement; the trend toward trading blocks in the Pacific and the breaking up of the Soviet Union, all triggered off a series of changes to which businesses had to respond quickly. The escalating global interdependence forces businesses to continuously reassess their goals, strategies, allocation of resources, deployment of IT, and management a complex organization.

As a result of changes in the business climate due to factors discussed above, the demands on a business have changed dramatically. Table 2 below demonstrates some of these radical changes. Clearly the need for change, flexibility, and dynamic organizations holds greater significance in the current business environment than ever before.

Table 2: Past versus Present Changing Demands of Business Organizations

CRITERIA	PAST	PRESENT
Capability	Size and scale	Flexibility
Market Strategy	Low price or high quality	Low price and high quality
Business structure	Middle management	Technology & outsourcing
Management Style	Command and control	Teamwork & empowerment
Competitive Advantage	Sustainable	Increasingly temporary

Source: Anonymous

One of the critical factors that allow a company to pursue such profound changes is information technology. Implementing any global strategy requires a high degree of coordination and control of diverse activities and functions. IT is crucial in supporting such functions. In fact, the use and impact of IT in MNCs has increased manifold in recent years and is expected to continue to rise in the coming years and decades.

With the fast pace of globalization, many business processes are becoming increasingly global in scope. Global businesses processes are inherently more complex and require higher degrees of coordination and control. Nevertheless, the reengineering or transformation of these processes would allow businesses to act swiftly and efficiently. These processes may hold the key for agility and flexibility in dynamic organizations. We review global business processes in the next section.

Global Business Processes

Earlier in this chapter, we introduced some definitions of business process reengineering (BPR). The definition of global business process reengineering (GBR) is consistent with these definitions, except for a few additions. First, a *global business process* is defined as, "any business process that cuts across the borders of *at least* two countries". The reengineering of a global business process, i.e., *Global Business Process Reengineering (GBR)* is defined as: the radical redesign of global business processes, using information technology as an enabler, resulting in organizational transformation of global proportions by impacting organization's structure, strategy, people, and technology dimensions. The key elements embedded in this definition of GBR are as follows:
- radical redesign
- global business processes
- using information technology (IT) as an enabler
- resulting in organizational transformation, and
- affecting several dimensions of the business, such as strategy, structure, people and technology

The new elements included in this definition are the global business process and the resulting transformation of global proportions. This definition delineates global business process reengineering as an effort that cuts across the borders of at least two countries. This requirement essentially forces the company to consider various global issues in addition to factors specific to traditional process reengineering. Among the global issues, Jarvenpaa, Ives, and Pearlson (1996) identified language diversity, geographical distance, regulations of host governments, and coordination across borders, hardware platforms, data structures, and identification of customers as major factors. A comprehensive list of global factors compiled from Deans et. al. (1991) and Jarvenpaa, Ives, Pearlson (1996) is shown in Table 3.

These factors add to the long list of variables that project managers or teams have to face to attempt to reengineer a global business process. Obviously it is a daunting task but many companies have been successful in completing these types of projects. Many types of global business processes have been the targets of reengineering in multinational corporations, but the most popular GBR projects in our experience are related to supply chain management. Additionally, we have seen GBR projects in the areas of global sales reporting, sales forecasting, and global expansion and integrated manufacturing. Clearly there is separation of various business activities such as between sales and service where sales occur during the sales cycle, and service is usually an after-sales activity. In a world of global customers and the need for high level of customer service it is important to break down this barrier. Since customers too often get different answers from the sales and service people, the bottom line is that "service should start before the sale and be present throughout every interaction between the customer and the company" (Kalakota and Robinson, 2001). In the next section, we develop and describe a model/framework for global business process reengineering which includes the important factors that affect GBR success.

Table 3: List of Issues in a Global Business Environment

Environment Dimension	Explanation of Issues
Political/Legal	Issues such as restrictions in transborder data flows, legal restrictions on hardware and software, telecommunications deregulation, tax laws, patents, copyright laws relating to IT, etc.
Technological	Factors such as regulatory strategies, support of company vendors and counterparts in foreign countries, price and quality of telecommunications, data structures, hardware platforms, level of IT sophistication, etc.
Social/Cultural	Factors such as local cultural constraints, language barriers, work habits, work ethics, attitudes, etc.
Economic	Factors such as national infrastructure, exports restrictions, currency exchange rates, cost of labor, wage distribution, and so on.

Source: Compiled from Deans et.al.,1991;Jarvenpaa, Ives, Pearlson (1996)

A FRAMEWORK FOR GLOBAL BUSINESS REENGINEERING

Core business processes cut through the entire organization. The goal of reengineering is to attempt to examine every required functional unit of the organization and make changes in order to make quantum gains. Reengineering of a major process, therefore, can influence and in turn is influenced by many organizational dimensions. Any change, especially one that radically shifts from traditional beliefs and experiences and adopts a horizontal, process view, is bound to present unique challenges. For example, possibilities exist to redefine the roles of functional area personnel, alienating the employees and making structural changes in the organization. In fact, one can expect significant impact on a few or even all of the major dimensions of the organization: the people, the organizational structure and strategy, the technology and the way the organization conducts its operations.

Figure 1 below shows the dimensions of reengineering as conceptualized in the framework by Grover and Kettinger (1995). The variables related to business processes can be categorized into four dimensions: technology, people, strategy and structure. Furthermore, this framework demonstrates that there is an interaction between business processes of an organization and the above dimensions. To emphasize the point, Michael Hammer, the well-known BPR guru states, "In order to make a dramatic progress in reducing costs, increasing productivity and improving quality, an entire organization – not just a portion – must be reengineered." Thus the importance of understanding how highly integrated the dimensions of BPR are in the context of organization change can never be emphasized enough.

We introduce a new dimension for GBR projects: the global dimension. While elements of the global dimension are represented to some extent in the above framework, we contend that the global dimension is so important in and of itself in global projects that it needs to be considered separately and explicitly. Figure 2 shows an extended framework for global business reengineering. The GBR process issues are captured in a broader factor called GBR project profile. Additionally, a dependent variable "GBR Implementation Success" has been added in order to be able to evaluate GBR projects. Additional elements of the framework are: inclusion of key moderator variables and indication of salient relationships between variables. Each of the dimensions/factors of the framework is discussed below in greater detail.

STRATEGY
STRUCTURE
BUSINESS PROCESSES
TECHNOLOGY
PEOPLE

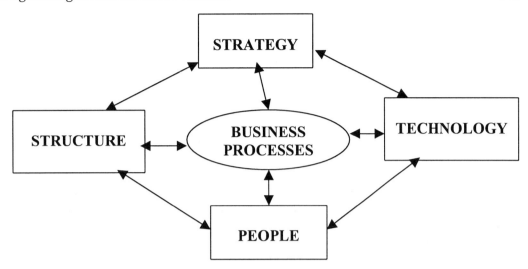

Figure 1: Dimensions of Business Process Reengineering
Source: Grover and Kettinger (1995)

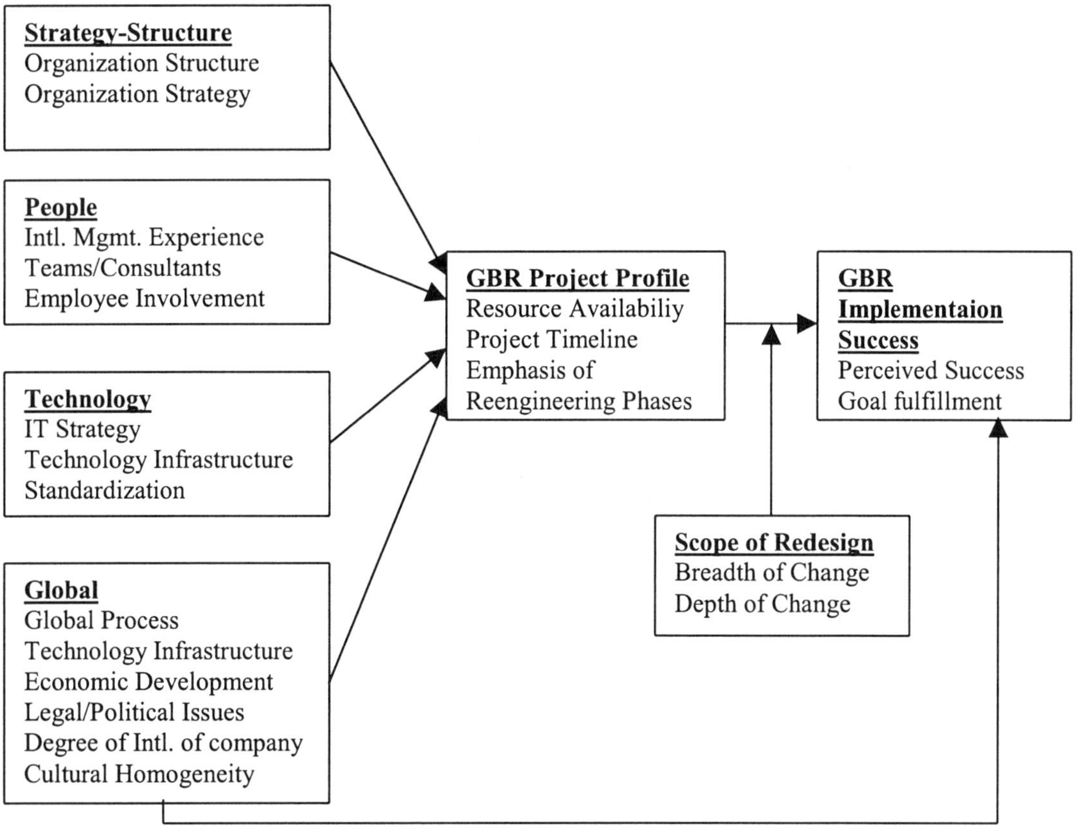

Strategy-Structure
Organization Structure
Organization Strategy
People
Intl. Mgmt. Experience
Teams/Consultants
Employee Involvement
Technology
IT Strategy
Technology Infrastructure
Standardization
Global
Global Process
Technology Infrastructure
Economic Development
Legal/Political Issues
Degree of Intl. of company
Cultural Homogeneity
GBR Project Profile
Resource Availabiliy
Project Timeline
Emphasis of
Reengineering Phases
GBR Implementaion Success
Perceived Success
Goal fulfillment
Scope of Redesign
Breadth of Change
Depth of Change

Figure 2: Framework for Global Business Reengineering

Strategy-Structure Dimension

An organization can be viewed as a social entity that has goals, and makes efforts to achieve these goals within a well-defined boundary. The importance of strategy and structure in an organization lies in the fact that it provides the basis for innovation in most organizations. The deployment of strategies such as vertical integration and diversification are well researched in the strategic management literature starting in the early 1970's. But the shift in the last decade to business processes has been accelerated by the popularity of quality programs (TQM) followed by the strong need for ERP (enterprise resource planning) solutions among larger corporations. Both quality programs and ERP vendors tend to focus on the business processes of organizations. This shift has led to efforts in innovatively changing existing business processes.

One way to view organization strategy and structure is to classify the two dimensions using well-established organizational typologies from the literature. Two such typologies are by Miles and Snow (1978) and Bartlett and Ghoshal (1995). Miles and Snow proposed a theoretical framework to describe alternative ways in which organizations define their market domains (strategy) and construct mechanisms (structures and processes) to pursue their strategies. They classify organizations into the following types: Analyzers, Defenders, Prospectors and Reactors. While prospectors are "first-to-the-market" with new products or services, defenders tend to offer a limited, stable product line and compete primarily on the basis of value. Analyzers pursue a "second-in" strategy whereby they imitate and improve upon the product offerings and reactors respond in areas where they are forced to by environmental pressures. Brief descriptions of these organizations as defined by Miles and Snow are as follows.

Defender: This organization attempts to locate and maintain a secure niche in a relatively stable area. The organization tends to offer a more limited range of products or services than its competitors and tries to protect its domain by offering higher quality, superior service, lower prices, and so forth. It may not be at the forefront of industry developments, and may not pay attention to industry changes that have no direct influence on current operations and concentrates instead on doing the best job possible in a limited area.

Prospector: This organization operates within a broad product-market domain that undergoes periodic redefinition. The organization values being "first" in new product and market areas even if not all efforts prove to be highly profitable. It responds rapidly to early signals of opportunity, and these responses often lead to a new round of competitive actions. However, this organization may not maintain market strength in all areas.

Analyzer: This organization attempts to maintain a stable, focused line of products or services; while at the same time moves quickly to follow a carefully selected set of more promising new developments in the industry. The organization is seldom "first" with new products or services. However, by carefully monitoring major competitors in areas compatible with its stable product-market base, it can frequently be "second-in" with more cost efficient product or service.

Reactor: This organization responds in those areas where it is forced to by environmental pressures. The organization does not appear to have a consistent product-market orientation. The organization is usually not as aggressive in maintaining established products and markets as some of its competitors, nor is it willing to take as many risks as other competitors.

It should be noted that no specific organization type is considered inherently superior. Each organization type has its own strengths and weaknesses. At the same time, each type also manages and functions quite differently from the others.

Another way of classifying organizations is by using the Bartlett and Ghoshal (1995), typology for multinational corporations. Bartlett and Ghoshal have made major contributions to advancing the concept of an international firm structure. Better known as the Bartlett and Ghoshal typology for international companies, it includes the following organization types:

Multinational: The type of company manages its subsidiaries as parts of a larger portfolio of entities. They are sensitive and responsive to various national environments. Subsidiaries are given a high degree of independence and therefore the management style can be classified as – low control and low coordination.

Global: Driven by the need for global efficiency, this type is driven by a high degree of centralized decision making. It views the world as a "unitary world market" (Bartlett and Ghoshal, 1989). Majority of the decisions are made at the headquarters and disseminated to the subsidiaries (Simon, 1996). These companies usually have high levels of control and low levels of coordination.

International: This type relies on transferring and adapting the parent company's knowledge or expertise to foreign subsidiaries. The parent retains control but this influence is less compared to the global type. In addition to exploiting parent company knowledge, these companies are characterized by high levels of control coupled with coordination.

Transnational: This type tries to strike a balance between global integration and local responsiveness. Adaptation is the key and as a result, this type of firm simultaneously displays both centralized and decentralized structure. Transnational MNCs exhibit high degrees of coordination and low degrees of control.

Each of these organizational types inherits strengths and weaknesses associated with its structure. These in turn impact the organization's ability to conduct business and in our case undergo a global reengineering effort. For example, a transnational organization displays certain strong factors for success such as flexibility and learning, but at the same time the coordination of such projects may encounter problems. Though such companies are driven by their goal motivation, the strategy implementation is usually left to each division or unit (Ives and Jarvenpaa, 1991). In essence, the nature of the issues is expected to vary with different organizational strategies and structures.

Global Dimension

The global environment includes all forces external to the organization that exist in the various countries it does business in. The variables in the global dimension can shape the fundamental nature of a MNC's business strategy. The key variables in this dimension are: the global business process itself, technology infrastructure of host countries, economic development of host countries, legal and political issues, degree of internationalization of the company, and cultural homogeneity. We discuss each briefly below.

Global Business Process: The global nature of the process itself is central to the global reengineering effort. It is what in fact distinguishes this work from previous works. The variable raises questions like: how global is the business process, how many national boundaries does the business process cut across and which specific countries are involved? Managing a process across borders is a challenge given the nature of different cultures, work ethic and lack of complete knowledge on part of the managers. While Tractinsky and Jarvenpaa (1995) stated that it might not necessarily require a different set of management skills in a global environment, we argue that as the number of countries involved in the GBR increase, the task of reengineering business processes becomes increasingly complex.

Technology Infrastructure: Due to variations in economic growth and wealth of countries, technology infrastructure and commitment to its development varies substantially. Both the level of technology infrastructure and compatibility of infrastructure between countries would facilitate any technological solution. Among infrastructure issues are computer operating platforms, software, productivity tools, transformation and conversion between applications and so on. Many developing countries that see numerous opportunities to integrate into the global economy and are eager to do so may not have the requisite technology infrastructure. A recent study (Broadbent, Weill, and St, Clair, 1995) found that technology infrastructure within companies plays a significant role on the scope and success of a BPR project. If we extrapolate this finding to the global realm, then technology infrastructure would play a major role in the GBR outcome.

Economic Development: Studies have shown that there exists a relationship between the economic development of a country and its information systems management issues (Palvia, Palvia and Roche, 1996). Less economically developed countries apply information technology to operational level type of work, while developed countries seem to focus on strategic and tactical issues. Given the existence of this trend, it is important to assess whether economic development of a nation has any relationship with GBR implementation success. Furthermore, we can expect to see GBR projects involving countries with similar levels of economic development to have smoother implementation and higher levels of success. Conversely countries with major disparities in economic development would find it difficult to implement reengineering projects.

Legal and Political Issues: Many countries have complex legal and political issues that can seriously impede any reengineering effort by companies located in these countries. For example, several European laws on privacy and information sharing are more restrictive than the U.S. Legal restrictions on trans-border flows and political instability may have adverse effects on the design and implementation of global processes. Similarly, political instability or political climate in countries can impact such projects. It is a well-known fact that IBM and Coca-Cola made the decision not to continue their operations in India due to changes in governmental regulations in late 1960's and early 1970's (MRTP Act 1969 and FERA, 1973). Even political relations with countries such as the former Soviet Union and People's Republic of China can play significant role in any type of global project involving such countries. Ideally, reengineering processes involving countries with similar legal and political philosophies allow for greater flexibility of options for design and implementation.

Degree of Internationalization of the Company: It is reasonable to expect that companies that derive a higher portion of their revenue from foreign sources will be better prepared to handle global projects of this complexity. Companies such as IBM, Hewlett-Packard, Canon, Proctor and Gamble, Goodyear, Hitachi, Microsoft, Siemens have spent substantial effort in the last 2-3 decades establishing a global focus for their products and services. This in turn has led to development of various competencies that make them capable of handling global projects. Such globally active companies have a definite edge over other companies operating on a restricted scale in the global environment.

Cultural Homogeneity: Culture is a very complex issue for managers in global companies. There have been studies where it is reported that national culture explained 50% of the differences in employee attitudes (Hofstede, 1994). While the industrial revolution resulted in an "increasing appreciation of work as a meaningful activity" (Hofstede, 1994), the values of workers and managers vary considerably across nations. Studies have confirmed the above results relating to national culture and attribute the rest of the employee behavior pattern to aspects such as ethnic diversity, gender, race, and age.

International companies that are operating in countries with similar cultures find it relatively easy to transfer their managerial skills between these countries. In contrast, managing resources, people, processes etc. across diversified national cultures that are highly heterogeneous clearly complicates matters. Among major cultural differences, Kirkman and Shapiro (1997) cite Hofstede's concept of power-distance, which is defined as the "degree to which a society accepts the fact that power in institutions and organizations is apportioned unequally".   In addition, people from dominant "doing" oriented cultures emphasize accomplishments, work hard to achieve objectives and maximize work, whereas individuals from dominant "being" oriented cultures stress release, work only as much as required to be able to live, and minimize work" (Kirkman and Shapiro, 1997). Also managers in U.S. based companies may be able to adapt their skills more easily when dealing with situations in European countries than in Japan or India, due to culture disparities.   Clearly, the cultural aspects of the global business process play a significant role in the outcome of the GBR effort and it is reasonable to expect that cultural/social differences between countries involved in the GBR effort will have a bearing on implementation success (Cooper, 1994).

Technology Dimension

The role of technology as an enabler remains at the forefront of reengineering efforts. Davenport and Short (1990) identified technology as a lever or pivot on which most reengineering efforts are based. Broadbent, Weill, and St. Clair (1995), found that technology infrastructure within companies played a significant role on the scope and ability of the BPR project. When the role of IT is shifted to the context of global business environment, several issues and concerns begin to emerge. Some of the primary issues are: strategy of the IT department i.e. centralized vs. decentralized, compatibility of systems and platforms between global organizations, and technology and communications infrastructure within the organization. Each of these are discussed below:

IT Strategy: A controlled and well-coordinated IT strategy is necessary for development, implementation and standardization of information systems in global organizations. For example, the existence of a centralized IT department may enable an organization to forge a cohesive global IS strategic plan and allow a higher level of control over key IS projects. While decentralized strategies have several benefits, there is clearly a dire need for coordination and control for a reengineering project of global proportions.

Compatibility of systems and platforms: Information sharing, business-to-business integration, and information processing are essential to the effective functioning of global organizations. The compatibility of systems across such organizations strongly influences options for any IS application. For example Dow Chemical bought Union Carbide for $9.3 billion in stock and $2.3 billion in assumed debt in mid-1999. While both companies were using an ERP system from the same vendor (SAP AG) the installed versions varied i.e. R/3 versus R/2 or in simple terms client-server versus a more mainframe version. Though this merger resulted in the world's second largest chemical company (DuPont is the largest), it still required hundreds of man-hours of work to resolve the two ERP systems.

Technology and communications infrastructure: The technology and communications infrastructure across global organizations is a fundamental necessity and provide the basis for all technology-based projects. As discussed earlier, some reengineering experts view the role of technology as the key to the success of reengineering.

It must be cautioned however that a well-designed technology solution may not necessarily lead to reengineering success. Technology needs to be an enabler and not the solution itself. There has been strong support for this argument since most companies that ignored the human element failed in their reengineering efforts, in some cases close to 70% failure rates were reported. Therefore, authors such as Marchand and Stanford (1995) have proposed a framework for harmonizing people, information and technology. This leads us to the discussion of the last variable among the independent variables - the people dimension. People play a vital role in every reengineering project. If the people do not adapt to the radical change proposed by a GBR project, the implementation is doomed to failure.

People Dimension

This dimension has emerged as perhaps the most important to the success of reengineering efforts. As mentioned earlier, reengineering represents a new way of thinking about any business and activities within that business. On face value, the focus of reengineering is the business process and the integrated elements of the organization itself. However, in his 1995 book, "Reengineering Management," Champy pointed out that managers have been able to shift the focus of BPR to operational levels of the organization. In other words, BPR has not been allowed to run its full course and managers not only need to support reengineering efforts but also rethink their business activities. The resulting effect is that the organization culture is expected to play a major role in the success of any project involving radical change. Thus technology itself may not guarantee reengineering success. Just as technology is the enabler, the people contribute heavily to the success of the BPR effort. Based on anecdotal evidence through interviews and literature review, the following people-related factors emerged as crucial to success: top management support, international management experience, employee involvement, and formation of global teams.

Almost every study in reengineering has recognized the role of top management support and sponsorship as the key to reengineering success (Hammer and Stanton, 1995; Champy, 1995; Bashein, et.al., 1994; Klien, 1994; Andrews and Stalick, 1994). It is the role of organization leaders to provide the vision, support and sponsorship for reengineering projects that are global in scope. Champy (1995) recommends that this support needs to go beyond endorsement by managers to reengineering of management itself.

Meanwhile the importance of teams and teamwork in organizations are well known and the positive impact of global teams in multinational organizations has also been observed in several cases. Tambrands Inc., a company in White Plains, New York, is an excellent example of a company that successfully completed a global reengineering initiative. Global teams were given the task and this US-European team successfully completed the initiative. The role played by the global team contributed significantly to the success of the global reengineering effort. A similar argument can be made for employee involvement, where employees closest to the business process being reengineered need to be closely involved for a successful reengineering effort.

Degree of international experience of the managers can be cited as a significant factor in the GBR effort. It is quite clear that a manager with international experience will demonstrate a higher ability, tolerance and foresight to anticipate problems associated with any global project and especially one involving radical change of business processes. Clearly this element needs to be considered in a framework for reengineering global business processes.

GBR Project Profile

The Global Business Reengineering (GBR) project profile can be viewed as a group of variables that directly contribute to the execution of the global reengineering project. In other words, these transformation variables capture the dynamics of the change itself. Included are factors such as availability of resources, project timeline, and the relative emphasis at each stage of the reengineering effort. These variables provide insights on the implementation process of the global reengineering project, which in turn lead to the development of critical success factors.

In an effort to capture data on these variables, we used the reengineering stages framework proposed by Teng, Grover and Seong (1998). This framework's goal is to evaluate the "strength of efforts" spent on various stages of the reengineering project. The respondents are provided with an eight-stage framework for reengineering as shown in Exhibit 1 and asked to indicate the strength of effort for each stage. The scale used is 1=very weak and 5=very strong and any stage that is not used is to be left blank. These stages were adapted from the work of Teng, Grover and Seong (1998) and modified to reflect the global focus of research.

In the next section we discuss some issues related to the scope of redesign (a moderating variable) followed by the section of measuring reengineering success.

Scope of Redesign

Teng et. al. (1998) found that reengineering efforts that were more "radical" were found to be more successful. This presented an interesting dilemma in our current research effort. Since global business reengineering is inherently quite "radical," what can we expect to see in terms of implementation success? Is it reasonable to assume that we will find a high level of reengineering success among global projects? In order to address this "confounding" possibility, a measure labeled "scope of redesign" was introduced. The goal was to capture the level of change in two ways – the breadth of change and the depth of change.

Breadth of change was defined as the "number of countries, including headquarters, subsidiaries, suppliers, etc." which were involved in the GBR effort. Additionally, the depth of GBR effort was measured by applying the "dimensions of reengineering" proposed by Andrews and Stalick (1994) that helps identify the level of reengineering that is being attempted. The three levels/layers proposed by these authors are:

- Physical Technical Layer – At this level, the role of business reengineering is to change the process structure, or the technology structure, or the organization structure. These are considered more concrete and thus easiest to change.
- Infrastructure Layer – At this level, the attempt is to change the reward structure, measurement systems and management methods.
- Value Layer – Finally, at this level, the most difficult changes are made, i.e., the organizational culture, political power and individual belief systems.

The Scope of Redesign variable was to give explicit attention to the recognized relationship between the level of change and reengineering success. Once again, the expectation is that most global reengineering efforts would involve change that is remarkably radical due the complexity of the global business environment.

Measuring Reengineering Success

One of the key requirements of any reengineering effort is the measurement of success. Two established ways of measurement in the literature are: (1) comparing the reengineering level of success with fulfillment of goals, and (2) measuring the perceived level of success on a likert scale, such as a 5-point scale (Teng, Seong and Grover, 1998).

The first measure requires the respondents to indicate the "planned level of performance improvement (before reengineering) and the actual level of improvement achieved (after implementation). Then a ratio can be calculated. Some reengineering goals found in the literature include: cycle time reduction, increase in worker productivity, level of customer satisfaction, impact on competitiveness or market share, reduction in the number of defects, and impact on company revenue. The second measure is a rating of the perceived level of success of the reengineering project.

The findings presented in this chapter are based on a survey of strategic and executive level managers who were members of the Strategic Leadership Forum (formerly known as the Planning Forum), an international organization. The survey was preceded by several interviews with executives from large global corporations and followed by four detailed case studies. The next section presents the key findings from this research effort.

Exhibit 1: Global Reengineering Stages

Stage 1: Identification of Global BR (GBR) opportunities
- Establish a steering committee for overall GBR planning
- Secure management commitment
- Align with corporate and global IT strategies
- Identify major business processes with a "business model"
- Understand customers' requirements
- Prioritize processes and select one for implementation

Stage 2: Project Preparation
- Plan for organizational change (e.g. inform stakeholders)
- Organize a GBR team for the selected process
- Train the GBR team members
- Conduct project planning

Stage 3: Analysis of the existing Process
- Analyze existing process structure and flows
- Identify value-adding activities
- Identify opportunities for process improvement

Stage 4: Development of a process vision
- Understand process customers' requirements
- Identify process performance measures
- Set process performance goals
- Identify IT which enables process redesign
- Develop a vision (preliminary sketch) for the redesigned process

Stage 5a. Solution: Technical Design
- Develop and evaluate alternative process designs
- Detailed process modeling (entities, relationships, etc.)
- Design controls for process integrity
- IS analysis and design for the new process
- Prototype and refine the process design

Stage 5b. Solution: Social Design
- Empower customer contact personnel
- Define jobs and incentives
- Develop and foster shared values
- Define skill requirements and career paths
- Design new organizational structure
- Design employee performance measurement schemes
- Design change management program

Stage 6. Process Transformation
- Develop test and rollout plans
- Implement the social and technical design
- Train staff and pilot new process

Stage 7. Process Evaluation
- Monitor performance
- Continuous improvement

FINDINGS

The survey conducted during the latter part of 1999 was mailed to approximately 1000 members of the Strategic Leadership Forum, an international organization. The respondents were selected from a database of the organizational members based on their background and fit with the research topic. Companies included in the list varied from larger corporations such as GM, IBM, Microsoft, Caterpillar, and Citibank to smaller and mid-size companies. However, most respondents associated with these companies were based in USA. The total responses received were 112, of which 89 were usable. While the response rate was a bit low, the absolute number of responses was adequate for the results reported in the chapter. In addition, we supplemented the survey data with four detailed case studies. Note that the focus of the survey was to gather information on all the dimensions and factors of the framework introduced earlier as well as a few additional issues. The primary findings and issues from the study are discussed in the following sections.

Reengineering Stage Effort

Since the stages for global business reengineering (GBR) had been adapted from the BPR study of Teng, et.al., (1998), a comparison was made of the effort for each corresponding stage between GBR and BPR. This comparison is presented in Table 4 below. The average effort for each stage of GBR on a 5-point scale is also indicated.

A remarkable consistency can be observed between the two studies for certain stages of the reengineering projects. The first stage, Identification of Reengineering Opportunities,

Table 4: COMPARISON OF STAGE EFFORTS – GBR vs BPR

STAGES	Average Effort	Study rankings	Teng, et.al rankings
Identification of global BPR opportunities	4.28	1	2
Project Preparation	3.19	7	4
Analysis of Existing Process	3.87	2	1
Development of a Process Vision	3.41	3	3
Solution: Technical Design	3.01	8	6
Solution: Social Design	3.21	6	8
Process Transformation	3.27	5	5
Process Evaluation	3.40	4	7

drew the highest amount of effort and was rated very high for both "domestic" BPR (#2) as well as GBR (#1). Technical design and project preparation were ranked the lowest in the GBR effort, while it was rated low (#6) in the BPR study. Social Design ranking in our study was slightly higher (#6) compared to the Teng study (#8 - lowest rank). This may be a reflection of the awareness brought about by research and experience of companies. Several studies and books have attributed high failure rates of reengineering projects to human and social factors. An interesting observation in the Teng et.al (1998) study as well as our study is the high ratings (# 1 and #2) of Analysis of Existing Processes. This presents an interesting quandary since reengineering is supposed to represent a clean sheet or a radical transformation that ignores existing assumptions and processes. Even Teng's study presented a contradiction: according to them, the likelihood of reengineering success was higher when targeted at social design and process transformation rather than analyzing existing procedures.

The rankings of Process Transformation and Development of Process Vision remained the same in both studies. However, both Process Evaluation and Project Preparation reflected the most difference in the two rankings. These items are discussed further in the discussion section.

The stage efforts findings shed light on how a GBR project unfolds. It is clear, based on the consistency of the two rankings as well as the testimonials provided in the case studies that identification of reengineering opportunities and analysis of existing business processes attract the highest level of effort. The resultant change due to reengineering though "radical" is perhaps a reflection of the efficacy of the existing global business processes. It was evident from the case studies and interviews that global business processes either exist or need to be in place in global organizations. The need for global processes is based on deeply rooted international relationships within and between organizations, which provide strong basis for future GBR projects. This was the case in Compton International and Rovero (two of the companies included in the case studies). Compton was able to rely on its 10-year old relationship with its suppliers to rapidly identify and implement a GBR project.

Critical Success Factors

To gain further understanding of the GBR project, the respondents of the survey were asked to rate the importance of several items related to the success of a reengineering project. This included items pertaining to technology, management, and organizational resources. Table 5 below presents the results of the descriptive statistics on various items critical to GBR success. Note that these are ranks: a lower value signifies that the item is more crucial to the success of GBR.

Table 5: Descriptive Statistics for primary GBR items

Item	Mean (Average)	Median	Rank
Top management support and sponsorship	1.37	1.00	1
High level of employee involvement across the organization	1.88	2.00	2
Ready access to resources to support reengineering	1.88	2.00	2
Compatibility of computer systems and platform across organizations	2.01	2.00	3
Established technology and communications infrastructure	2.15	2.00	4
High involvement of IT in solution	2.24	2.00	5
Importance of centralized IT strategy	2.46	2.00	6
Length of project timeline	2.54	2.00	7
Formation of global teams	3.36	2.00	*8*
Degree of international experience among managers	3.63	3.00	*9*

Please note that the scale used here is 1=Crucial to GBR, 2=Quite important 3=No effect, 4= Not important 5= Negative /adverse effect i.e. lower average implies more crucial to GBR success

Top management support, employee involvement, and access and availability to resources all received high ratings. While none of these items contain any global elements, they are clearly found to be critical for project success in both domestic and global BPR. As the literature would indicate, this is in fact true of most information technology projects, whether GBR or not.

The second set of items, based on ranking all belong to the same underlying group – technology. The technology items were ranked #3, #4, #5, #6. Thus IT is an essential enabler for reengineering projects though social and human factors are key to the implementation of this process change. Items in the technology category: compatibility of computer systems and platforms across organizations, established technology and communications infrastructure, high involvement of IT in the solution, and centralized IT strategy received moderately high ratings between 2.01 to 2.46. In essence, managers clearly recognize that IT is an important element in the global BPR effort.

Interestingly, the items receiving the lowest rankings were: formation of global teams and degree of international management experience. While on "face value", this finding was surprising given that respondents were rating factors influencing the success of "global" projects, there are several possible explanations. First, a high percentage of firms responding to our survey were from USA. This along with the preexisting international experience of managers may have contributed to the above results. This was evident from the case studies where respondents indicated that all their projects had some "global" component. In other words, the extensive experience of the people in such projects did not necessarily require specific international training or global teams. Most of the teams were specialized and were able to successfully execute their share of the overall project. Second, and perhaps the most telling reason is the type of global reengineering effort and the system characteristics. For example, in one case, High Tech Industries was reengineering their global sales reporting/forecasting system. While the project was initiated by the Manager of Global Operations, the team designing and implementing the project comprised of a core group of IT people based in USA. The system was developed centrally and deployed globally after testing it in North America. Apparently, the system did not require much local tailoring. While it is certainly not true that international experience of managers involved is not important, it is most definitely dependent on the type of reengineering project.

Essentially, the management and implementation of these projects came from specific responsibilities assigned to specialized departments. Case studies also identified information sharing between the companies involved as an effective way to ensure success of the project. In the case of Compton International, the highly developed relationship between the company employees and their counterparts in the vendor company added to smooth implementation of the GBR project. There was no formal need for global teams across the two organizations; an informal but dependable structure had already been in place after years of effort. The importance of explicit global teams would be substantially higher if such relationships did not exist or were at infancy stage.

Dimensions: Strategy-Structure, Global, Technology and People

In the strategy-structure dimension, the Bartlett and Ghoshal typology was found to be statistically significant. More specifically, the International organization type received a significant lower success rating compared to the other three types - Global, Multinational and Transnational. However, there was not significant difference in GBR success among the organizations as classified by the Miles and Snow (M&S) typology. We surmise that the International organization type does not provide the high levels of coordination and control necessary for GBR projects. In fact, attempts to transfer/adapt the parent company knowledge to foreign subsidiaries on more ad-hoc and informal basis (as in International organizations) may actually hamper the success of GBR projects. The amount of change is so radical that formal and established relationships may be necessary as in Global and Transnational organizations, e.g., the establishment of an information technology infrastructure. The higher success rate in Multinational organizations compared to International organizations is a bit puzzling, but it may have to do with the nature of the global IT projects (e.g., involving fewer trans-border interactions).

Meanwhile, none of the items in the global dimension were found to be statistically significant. However, this result is not conclusive as this section of the survey resulted in a lower response rate, which did not allow some of the planned statistical analysis to be conducted. Though the survey did not yield much insights into the global dimension, the case studies identified two items from the global dimension as having major impact on global reengineering projects – legal/political issues, and organizational and national culture. Legal and political issues, employee involvement at the global level, and cultural adaptation were all cited as major contributors to the GBR success in these companies. With more experience and bigger samples, we expect several elements of the global dimension to stand out in the GBR effort.

Among the four technology-dimension items, the compatibility of computer systems and platforms in the countries that the organization had operations was found to be statistically significant to GBR success. As per our earlier comment on organization typology, the appropriate amount of control and coordination can have a direct impact on the level of GBR success. Compatible computer systems provide the necessary infrastructure to facilitate this control and coordination. As an aside, the need for appropriate computing infrastructure is also dependent on the specifics of the GBR project as was observed in our results on managers' attitudes toward technology. The above relationship may seem to contradict the earlier finding where technical design stage was ranked last in the amount of effort spent during GBR project implementation. However, the explanation may be that computer systems and platforms are a precondition to the GBR effort; not much can be done about it in any specific GBR project implementation and technical design simply refers to the design based on existing technology. Thus during a specific GBR effort, a reengineering solution needs to be developed using mostly existing technology. As one of the managers in Compton International stated, "Technology is a non-issue, if you have a strong reengineering solution."

As anticipated, the most critical dimension that emerged from the study was the people dimension. Top management support, level of employee involvement, and empowerment were all found to contribute to the success of a GBR project. Case studies also identified that specialized teams are important contributors to the success of GBR implementation. In fact, these factors are generally known to be significant to most reengineering projects and major system development projects. Given that a GBR project is a major undertaking, senior management champions (in terms of time, energy, and resources) and high levels of involvement are absolutely essential to it success.

While the findings in this study provide an interesting mix of results on GBR, it is clear that a multi-faceted topic such as this requires further research and deeper investigation. Nevertheless, the framework and the initial results can be combined to gain an overall understanding of GBR. In the next section, we provide some discussion on GBR in the light of the survey and case studies.

DISCUSSION

The GBR framework introduced in this chapter provides a solid conceptual foundation for understanding the various facets of a global business-reengineering project. The various independent variables among the four dimensions influence the outcome of GBR project as well as the dynamics of project implementation. Factors such as the organization strategy-structure, top management support, availability of resources, employee involvement, project timeline, legal issues and culture were all identified as important in this study. While the results are preliminary due to the exploratory nature of the study, small sample size, and some anecdotal evidence, clearly several insights can be developed and used as the basis for further exploration. Some of the key findings are:

- People Issues such as top management support, employee involvement are critical to GBR success
- Role of global teams may be crucial depending on the level of relationship between organizations involved in GBR

- Technology dimension is important, but is viewed as a relatively easy phase in the overall GBR project. However, compatibility of computer systems does hold major significance in the global context.
- There is a significant difference in the performance of companies as classified by Bartlett and Ghoshal typology. The implication is that certain types of organizational strategy-structure may influence the GBR success.
- Legal and political complexities, clear definition of GBR goals and timeline, and availability of resources are all key variables in GBR success.
- The type of GBR project itself determines the emphases on different factors. There is a need to isolate features that characterize the similarities and differences in global business processes, which in turn may be used to identify the relevant factors in GBR planning and implementation.

The case studies provided a much richer understanding of the GBR process and introduced some new and unexpected issues that had been missed in the survey. The importance of items such as degree and depth of relationship between organizations, and the role of specialized teams were not clearly evident from the survey but were highlighted by the cases. Also, the capacity of managers in large global organizations to handle most global reengineering projects as "any other large project", though initially surprising, made intuitive sense considering their experience and expertise as well as their ability to access specialized teams.

One of the major finding of this study was the degree of similarity between domestic BPR and global reengineering projects. While the explanation that managers in global organizations view most projects as global provides some insight, the high level of consistency in the stages framework of domestic and global projects is also quite insightful. In essence, the global reengineering effort requires attention to the traditional concerns as in any reengineering effort; however, the global dimension adds additional factors and further increases the complexity of the implementation process. Another observation was that with the introduction of new and powerful information technology tools and applications, technology requires the least amount of concern in such projects. The rankings of effort spent on Social Design and Process Evaluation were higher in global reengineering, and perhaps reflect a reaction to past criticism where both items were singled out as primary reasons for reengineering failures. A surprise was the more than expected higher ranking of the Analysis stage in both the current study and the previous study on domestic reengineering projects. This seems to be an apparent contradiction with the reengineering philosophy. Even in the case studies, the respondents indicated that analysis of existing process in many cases was the catalyst for the reengineering effort. In other words, a close examination of the current process provides insights to companies for reengineering opportunities. While the mainstream literature recommends otherwise, this certainly seems to be the current practice. This practice may also be a reflection of what analysts and designers have done for decades, and it may not be so easy to change their ways in a relatively short time.

CONCLUSION

Given the wide scope and nature of global reengineering, it is important to formulate a comprehensive framework for the subject in order to facilitate systematic study and examination. Figure 2, shown earlier, provides a comprehensive GBR framework. The factors identified herein are key to understanding GBR implementation and success. Technology alone is not the answer. As a recent study (Teng, Fiedler and Grover, 2000) points out, that although changes in IT continue at an unprecedented rate, the key to change management are factors such as innovative capacity of the organization and strategy-IS alignment which in turn continue to influence the success of such projects. The same study also recommends the need for future qualitative studies to capture some of the "cultural subtleties" impacting such projects. We agree.

While there is need for further research on this topic, the framework provided in this chapter introduces some key concepts and should serve as the foundation for future studies in the area. Researchers may be able to validate and even extend the framework in the future. This chapter also holds special interest for CEOs and CIOs of major corporations since it is able to provide an operating framework for global process engineering. As businesses continue their quest into the global arena, processes that need to be redesigned are going to be increasingly global in scope. Based on our results, the managers are advised to pay close attention to the people issues, overall organization strategy-structure and the building of dependable relationships with vendors, suppliers and customers. Further, it is anticipated that legal complexities will continue to pose problems in the global reengineering effort and it might be useful to assign responsibility to an individual or a group to address the international legal issues.

Mini Case: Compton International

Compton International is a Fortune 500 company in the business of production of computer related equipment and peripherals. The company has a tradition of performing consistently in the market and is regarded as a major competitor in the industry. The company employs over 60,000 employees worldwide and has sales and support offices and distributorships worldwide. This entails a market comprising of over 100 countries and close to 100 subsidiaries in various forms. In the last three years the company sales has been into several billions of US dollars.

Compton has been involved in over 100 global reengineering efforts in the last 7 years. Given the size and market of Compton, all of their reengineering efforts have some level of global component. Therefore they classify most reengineering projects as GBR. This is probably due to a high level of company revenue from the foreign market (about 50%).

Project environment: The global reengineering project in this case is part of the overall supply chain management process. While the economic development, technology infrastructure, and the political aspects between the countries involved in the GBR project are not an issue, the cultural differences and level of legal complexity do play an important role. In a broader sense, Compton and its primary supplier involved in the GBR effort have completely different management styles due to cultural differences.

Given this environment, Compton decided over ten years ago to take a proactive approach to prevent problems arising from cultural differences. On the insistence of Compton, the two companies (Compton and its supplier) began to foster relationships between the counterparts (personnel) in the two organizations. This relationship was built across organizations down to the staff level. Therefore though cultural differences still exist, the free flow of information between the two organizations helps to alleviate some of the problems.

The business unit that initiated the GBR effort did so under a long-range blueprint. In other words this reengineering effort is part of a much larger ongoing plan.

Project Motivations: The project in this case had multiple goals though the primary ones were – time to market, efficient storage of information, and access to business communications. Among these, the overall motive of time to market is perhaps the most critical item.

Observations from the project: This particular case study is an excellent example of how to implement a successful GBR project. Some of the primary observations from the case study are:
• Legal complexity continues to be a problem – changes in legalities lead to changes that are not easily controllable, thus leading to a more reactive counter-measure.
• The solution undertaken in this GBR project was highly technology dependent which was primarily due to the company's business environment and more specifically the industry in which it competes.

Mini Case .... Continued.

• People issues – requires top management support, formation of global teams but currently involvement of employees across organizations not a major criteria for success. The same thing can be said about international management experience of the managers.
• Stage efforts – the effort in the first few stages of global reengineering such as identifying opportunities and analysis of existing processes were given more effort than solution and process evaluation.
• Consultants – no involvement. Not required due to extensive experience of the people involved in the project
• Benefits of the project were difficult to quantify but qualitatively the project was a huge success
• Success factors – high level of user involvement from Compton especially in the interface design, high-level sponsorship, and existence of worldwide technology infrastructure
• Problem areas – differences in need between the two primary companies in the GBR effort, differences in corporate culture (secretive versus open management styles), and large number of users across multiple functions and entities
• Ongoing issues – changes in organization environment, and problems with training, standards and software licensing fees. These are currently being addressed as an ongoing process

Result: Highly successful implementation of GBR project

*company name has been changed to preserve anonymity.

STUDY QUESTIONS:

1. Based on your reading of the above chapter and other material on reengineering, are you convinced that global business process reengineering requires unique attention? Discuss.
2. Do you agree with the authors definition of the term, global business process reengineering? What modifications, if any, would you propose to make?
3. Identify some of the globalization trends that make projects such as global business reengineering a viable and attractive option for managers in global companies.
4. Do success factors encountered with "domestic" reengineering easily transfer to the global reengineering context? How would you as a manager begin to apply lessons learned in a "domestic" setting to the global environment?
5. Critique the Framework for GBR. Your critique should include a discussion at the dimension level followed by the variables within each dimension. What modifications do you recommend?
6. What could be the possible explanation for the lack of research and interest on the part of academics and practitioners, on the topic of global reengineering?
7. In the case of Compton International, what were the key factors that allowed the company to achieve a smooth GBR implementation? Discuss.

REFERENCES

Andrews, J and Stalick, M. *A Reengineering Survival Handbook*. New York. 1994.

Bartlett, C.A., and Ghoshal, S. Rebuilding behavioral context: Turn process reengineering into people rejuvenation, *Sloan Management Review*, 37:1, Fall 1995, pp.11-23.

Bashien, B.J., Markus, M.L. and Riley, P. Preconditions to BPR Success and how to prevent failure. *Information Systems Management*. 11:2, Spring, 1994. Pp.7-13.

Basu, Choton S. *An Empirical Framework for Transforming Global Organizations through Business Process Reengineering*. (Unpublished Dissertation). University of Memphis. July, 2000.

Broadbent, M; Weill, P. and St. Clair.D. The role of IT infrastructure in business process redesign. *CISR*. WP278. Sloan School of Management. May 1995.

Business Process Change - Reengineering Concepts, Methods, and Technologies edited by Grover, V. and Kettinger,W.J. Idea Publishing Group, Harrisburg, PA, 1995.

Caron. M, Jarvenpaa.S, and Stoddard. D. Business Reengineering at CIGNA Corporation: Experiences and Lessons from the First Five Years. *MIS Quarterly*. 1994. pp.233-250.

Champy, J. *Reengineering Management: The Mandate for a New Leadership*. Harper Business, New York, 1995.

Cooper, R.B., The inertial impact of culture on IT implementation. *Information and Management*. 27:1 July, 1994. Pp.176

Davenport ,T.H. and Short, J.E., The New Industrial Engineering: Information Technology and Business Process Redesign, *Sloan Management Review*, Summer 1990, pp.11-27.

Davenport, T.H. Business Process Reengineering: Where It's Been, Where It's Going. Business Process Change - Reengineering Concepts, Methods, and Technologies edited by Grover, V. and Kettinger, W.J. Idea Publishing Group, Harrisburg, PA, 1995. pp.1-13.

Davenport, T.H. and Stoddard, D.B., Reengineering: Business Change of Mythic Proportions? *MIS Quarterly*, 18:2, June 1994.pp.121-128.

Davenport, T.H. *Process Innovation*, Harvard Business School Press, Boston, 1993.

Deans, P.C., Karawan, K.R., Goslar, M.D., Ricks, D.A., and Toyne, B. Identification of Key International Information Systems Issues in U.S.-Based Multinational Corporations. Journal of Management Information Systems, 27:4, Spring, 1991, pp.27-50.

Galliers, R.D. Strategic Information Systems Planning: Myths, Reality, and Guidelines for Successful Implementation, *European Journal of Information Systems*, 1:1, 1991.pp.55-64.

Hammer, M. and Champy, J.A., *Reengineering the Corporation*, Harper Business, New York, 1993.

Hammer, M., Reengineering Work: Don't Automate, Obliterate, *Harvard Business Review*, Summer 1990, pp.104-112.

Ives, B., and Jarvenpaa, S.L., Applications of Global Information Technology: Key Issues for Management, *MIS Quarterly*, March 1991.pp.33-49.

King, W.R., and Sethi, V. "A Framework for Transnational Systems" in Global Issues of Information Technology Management, edited by Palvia, S., Palvia, P. and Zigli, R. Idea Group Publishing. Harrisburg, PA.1992.

Klein, M.M., The most fatal reengineering mistakes. Information Strategy: *The Executives Journal*., 10:4 Summer 1994. pp.21-28.

Kutschker, M. Reengineering of Businesses in Multinational Corporations. Carnegie Bosch Institute International Research Conference, November, 1994.

Marchand, D.A. and Stanford, M.J. Business Process Redesign: A Framework for Harmonizing People, Information and Technology. Business Process Change - Reengineering Concepts, Methods, and Technologies edited by Grover V. and Kettinger, W.J. Idea Publishing Group, Harrisburg, PA, 1995.

Markus, M.L. and Robey, D. Business Process Reengineering and the Role of the Information Systems Professional. Business Process Change - Reengineering Concepts, Methods, and Technologies edited by Grover, V. and Kettinger, W.J. Idea Publishing Group, Harrisburg, PA, 1995.pp.591-611.

Martinez, E.V. Successful reengineering demands IS/business Partnerships. *Sloan Management Review*. 36:4. Summer, 1995.pp.51-60.

Teng, James T.C., Fiedler, Kirk D. and Grover, Varun. A Cross-Cultural Study on the Organizational Context of Process Redesign Initiatives: U.S. vs. Taiwan. *Journal of Global Information Technology Management (JGITM)*. Vol.3, No.3, 2000. pp.7-31.

Tractinsky, N. and Jarvenpaa, S. Information Systems Design Decisions in a Global versus Domestic context. *MIS Quarterly*. Vol. 19. No.4. Dec, 1995.

9

Cultural Asymmetries Between Headquarters and Foreign Subsidiaries and Their Consequence on the Integrative Role of Information Technology

Barry Shore
University of New Hampshire, USA

ABSTRACT

In an increasingly competitive global market, multinational organizations are under pressure to use "common" information technology systems to integrate the planning and control activities necessary between headquarters and foreign subsidiaries. Successful deployment of these systems however has been challenging. One factor, often difficult to address in a concrete way, is that social systems and work practices be can be very different throughout the world, and since software systems impose a structure on these social systems and work practices, overseas subsidiaries often find themselves confronted with changes that are difficult to accommodate. This chapter will consider these social or 'cultural' influences on the workplace and conclude with several concrete suggestions for managing the process of introducing appellations in cultures very different from the one in which they were developed.

INTRODUCTION

The challenge of managing multinational organizations (Bartlett and Ghoshal (1989) as well as managing the information systems within these organizations (Ein-Dor, Segev and Orgad, 1993) (Roche, 1992) has received considerable attention for over a decade. Because consideration must be given to languages, time zones, currencies, laws, and culture, they are often more difficult to manage than domestic organizations (Shore, 1996).

But world commerce in this new millenium becomes even more complex because it can no longer be assumed that operations throughout world can be left on their own, as many had been in the twentieth century. In this new century a carefully conceived corporate strategy must determine which activities must be centrally planned and or controlled and which are to be decentralized and left under the control of local host organizations (Cheung and Burn, 1994).

The pressure to link strategic activities and thereby centralize strategic processes can be attributed to the drive toward efficiency in an era when most organizations have the knowledge and capability to disperse their operations and distribution facilities throughout the world (Magretta, 1998). With the dramatic increase in overseas operations to take advantage of these comparative advantages, the competitive differentiator for multinational companies is often the ability to manage these far flung operations; those companies capable of managing geographically dispersed operations and providing customers with what they want and when they want it are more likely to achieve and maintain a competitive advantage.

In the twenty-first century, information and telecommunication technology is at the center of any strategy to link these worldwide operations. Without these technologies and their ability to share value chain data from inbound logistics, operations, outbound logistics, and marketing, they will find it impossible to integrate their worldwide operations and compete effectively in world markets.

Sharing through computer and telecommunications systems, however, has increasingly meant that common systems are used. A common system is a computer based application that utilizes the same (hardware and) software platform throughout an organization thereby facilitating the use of the application not only throughout all operations, regardless of geographic location, but also facilitating the use of data for centralized management and control. Using common systems, for example, headquarters in Chicago can set standards for their subsidiaries' planning and control methods and procedures, and they can also check the production schedule in a Malaysian manufacturing plant with that of the production schedule in a South Korean plant to ensure that shipments from these plants to an assembly plant in Hong Kong will include the correct quantity and will be delivered on-time. These common systems are becoming essential to achieving the economies-of-scale and competitive advantage critical in today's worldwide market.

But transferring these technologies to subsidiary organizations located in very different parts of the world can be challenging. A proven headquarters' software package and a detailed implementation schedule are necessary conditions for success, but they are not sufficient.

This is not to suggest, however, that all organizations face these problems. Many efforts to transfer and use an application in foreign subsidiaries experience about the same degree of success or failure, as do transfers to domestic subsidiaries. But problems, often beyond the scope of those experienced at home, frequently plague overseas projects.

In one Fortune 500 organization studied by the author, the full range of outcomes occurred, from total success to total failure. To integrate essential corporate functions, headquarters established a "common systems" group whose purpose it was to implement common sales, financial, and manufacturing applications throughout the world. But several years after this project was initiated only one-third of the worldwide sites were successfully using these applications. Another one-third was still having problems with implementation, while the last third had yet to begin.

Technical factors certainly contribute to these problems: a subsidiary may lack experience with information technology; management may be technically out-of-date; technical support may be unavailable; and the telecommunications infrastructure may be inadequate. But technical factors alone cannot fully explain why problems occur when linkages are attempted between headquarters and subsidiary organizations. What needs to be considered is that these organizations may exist in very different national cultures and that different preferences for IS practices may exist within these cultures. Linkages, which attempt to integrate these geographically dispersed organizations, may therefore be subject to cultural as well as technical failure.

Culture manifests itself in many ways, and many of them may not be obvious to headquarters' management. New systems and applications will almost always change procedures and may change the way workers perform work-related tasks. These new systems frequently change the way workers relate to their superiors, peers and subordinates. In some cultures workers perform tasks under the watchful eye of supervisors; they assume little responsibility and authority for the task. In other cultures considerable responsibility and authority is granted to workers whose responsibility it is produce output that meets specific quality control standards. These differences in work patterns can be traced to many roots including culture, and as such culture becomes one of the variables that needs to be considered in the management process. But it is often difficult for management to attribute these problems to cultural differences, perhaps because culture is seldom adequately understood.

This chapter focuses on the cultural component of these problems. It explores the way in which national culture influences the IS culture within an organization and why the differences between culture may lead to implementation problems. This is done in several steps. It begins by briefly exploring the issues associated with national culture. Next, the role of organizational culture is addressed, and finally the focus is placed on information systems culture. A hierarchy of cultural influences is suggested from national to organizational, and then to information systems; one affects the next. The chapter concludes with several suggestions that, if followed, can help managers cope with the added complexities that naturally occur as information systems are transplanted to other corners of the globe.

NATIONAL CULTURE

National culture influences human behavior and therefore becomes an ingredient in the process of understanding why some efforts to introduce information technology in overseas operations succeed while others fail. Hofstede (1980) defines culture as a set of mental programs that control an individual's responses in a given context. Parsons and Shils (1951) define it as a shared characteristic of a high-level social systems, while Erez and Earley, (1993) defined it as the shared values of a particular group of people.

The influence of national culture on human behavior begins during childhood and is reinforced throughout life (Lachman, 1983; Triandis, 1995). More important to the practice of management is that national culture not only influences our responses in social situations, but as Hofstede found in his research, it also shapes our behavior in organizations.

Classifying cultures and identifying those dimensions that differentiate cultural behavior is difficult and controversial. One major study, undertaken with the support of IBM and conducted by Hofstede (1980), provides a very useful framework. Utilizing data from 116,000 questionnaires administered in 40 countries he found that national culture can be defined through four dimensions. He identified these four dimensions as: power distance, uncertainty avoidance, individualism-collectivism, and masculinity-femininity.

Power Distance is the degree of inequality among people, from relatively equal (small power distance) to extremely unequal (large power distance). Uncertainty Avoidance is the extent to which a society feels threatened by uncertain situations and avoids these situations by providing career stability, establishing formal rules, and not tolerating deviant ideas. Individualism-Collectivism contrasts a social fabric in which each individual takes care of himself or herself with a social fabric in which groups take care of the individual in exchange for his or her loyalty. Masculinity-Femininity reflects whether the dominant values are associated with the collection of money and things, which Hofstede classifies as masculine, as contrasted with values associated with the caring for others and the quality of life, which he classifies as feminine. Of these four dimensions, power distance and uncertainty avoidance are considered dominant in studying organizations within a particular culture (Hofstede, 1981).

Hofstede (1980) also describes four classifications of culture measured by combinations of power distance and uncertainty avoidance. These classifications, depicted later in Figure 2, represent regions or quadrants into which organizations within a specific culture can be placed. The first quadrant, called the family by Hofstede, is characterized by cultures displaying a high degree of centralization (high power distance) combined with a lower level of formalization (low uncertainty avoidance). The second quadrant, called the market, includes cultures which are neither centralized (low power distance) nor formalized (low uncertainty avoidance). The third quadrant, called the machine, is characterized by a high degree of formalization (low uncertainty avoidance) and decentralized power (low power distance). The fourth quadrant, called the pyramid, is both centralized (high power distance) and formal (high uncertainty avoidance). Several of the countries studied are listed in Table 1 together with the quadrant to which they belong.

Table 1: Examples of Countries that can be grouped in Hofstede's Quadrants.

MARKET	MACHINE	PYRAMID	FAMILY
Denmark	Finland	France	Hong Kong
Sweden	Switzerland	Japan	Singapore
Ireland	Germany	Mexico	India
New Zealand	Israel	Greece	Philippines
USA	Argentina	Arab Countries	West Africa
Great Britain	Costa Rica	Korea	Malaysia

Erez and Earley (1993) explain why Hofstede's model has been widely used to study organizations: they contend that it is not only 'approachable', but is sufficiently clear and parsimonious to lend itself to empirical tests. Research which has used this model as a framework includes papers by Kedia and Bhagat (1988), who use it to develop a conceptual model of technology transfer, and Shore and Venkatachalam [1995], who use it to develop a conceptual model of systems analysis and design. However, Hofstede's model has been criticized in at least two areas: one, the model is based on and specific to a single organization (IBM) and hence raises the question of generalizability; and two, the four dimensions used in the study are insufficient by themselves to study all aspects of culture. Addressing the first criticism, Erez and Earley (1993) argue that national culture reflects an individual's core values and beliefs, and it is these values that dominate corporate or organizational culture. They maintain that organizations can, at best, exert influence over an individual's peripheral values and beliefs. Using this argument it is reasonable to suggest that the Hofstede model can be generalized to all organizations throughout the world, not just IBM. To address the second criticism, Hofstede (1991) subsequently introduced a fifth dimension, namely long-term vs. short-term orientation. Others have developed completely different sets of cultural variables while some have added variables to Hofstede's model (Kedia and Bhagat, 1988). Criticisms notwithstanding, the Hofstede model is very useful. Organizations located in a particular country can be placed in their appropriate quadrant, making his model a very practical tool for understanding cultural issues and undertaking cultural analysis.

Hofstede has also been criticized because his work suggests to some that these 'common' cultural characteristics should therefore be observable in all organizations within a specific culture. But this is certainly not the case, nor was it Hofstede's intention that this be the case. Organizations characterized by high power distance exist in low power distance cultures, and conversely organizations characterized by low power distance are found in high power distance countries. Clearly the range in any culture can be wide. Accordingly, Hofstede's model, and its use in this chapter, is intended to suggest general tendencies observable in a culture; variations are expected. Without the ability to make these generalizations, the development of a simple but useful conceptual framework would be limited.

ORGANIZATIONAL CULTURE

Organizational culture can be defined in many ways. Smircich (1983) defines it as the set of key values, guiding beliefs, and understandings that are shared by members of an organization. Schein (1985) defines it as a pattern of basic assumptions that has worked well enough to be valid, and therefore to be taught to new members as the correct way to perceive, think, and feel about organizational problems.

Organizational culture can also be expressed in many ways. Deal and Kennedy (1982) suggest that the manifestation of organizational culture can be placed into four categories, each one can be peeled off like the layers of an onion, until the core values are exposed. They include: (1) symbols, or the words or objects that carry a specific meaning within the organization; (2) heroes, or the persons highly prized as models of behavior; (3) rituals, or the collective activities that are socially essential in an organization; (4) and core values.

Hofstede, Neuijen, Ohayv and Sanders (1990) contend that there is no consensus about the definition of organizational culture. Most authors, they assert, will agree that it is: (1) holistic, (2) historically determined, (3) related to anthropological concepts, (4) socially constructed, (5) soft, and (6) difficult to change. To clarify its definition and introduce empirical evidence to a field dominated by what he criticizes as "in-depth case studies," Hofstede et al. studied ten organizations in Denmark and the Netherlands. He concluded that organizational values are partly determined by nationality, industry, and task. Furthermore, he concluded that while the popular literature insists that shared values represent the core of organizational culture, his factor analysis suggests that the way values affect ordinary members of an organization is expressed through practices. Practices represent what "is" in contrast to values which represent what "should be." Accordingly, an example of a value, in the context of an IS group, might be widespread participation in systems development. A practice would be the inclusion of functional mangers on all major IS development teams.

While Hofstede et al. contend that organizational culture is partly determined by national culture and practices, others place even more emphasis on national culture alone. Erez and Early (1993) argue that organizations do not possess cultures of their own, but are formed as a result of societal cultures. Triandis (1995) suggests that organizations may have a weak effect on an individual's peripheral values, but have no long-lasting effect on core or deep-seated values. Corporate culture may therefore only affect an individual's peripheral values while leaving core values, those learned early in life, intact (Erez and Earley, 1993).

In summary, organizational culture can be defined as a set of shared values, basic assumptions, and practices in an organization. It is historically constructed and difficult to change. While it is generally agreed upon that national culture affects core values established early in life, the influence of organizations may be limited to peripheral values.

INFORMATION CULTURE

The culture within an IS environment can be defined as the set of values and practices shared by those members of an organization involved in information activities including MIS professionals, managers and end-users. Examples of practices in a specific organization might include.
- Exclusive use of Windows environment.
- Extensive end-user involvement during development efforts.
- Commitment to prototyping methodologies in systems development.
- Minimum support for end-user computing.
- Requirement for IS staff approval for all PC purchases.
- Open access by approved vendors to production scheduling databases.
- Restrictions on internet access.

IS culture establishes boundaries for information technology. It determines which practices are acceptable and which are not; which technologies are acceptable, which are not; and which software is acceptable and which is not. Culture influences the process of developing and designing applications and even dictates how we use them (Shore and Venkatachalam, 1995).

Copper (1994) confirmed that IS culture plays a strong role in the IS function of organizations. He found that an IS culture may resist technologies that realign status, power, and working habits, especially when they may violate some of the group's shared values. IS culture, he contends, may be more or less compatible with certain information technologies and to the degree to which it is less compatible, consequences may occur which include, resistance to change, implementation failure, or disappointing results. In another study Davenport et al. (1992) concluded that IS and the information made available from these systems is often used politically, sometimes contrary to the best interests of the organization.

Research therefore concludes that an IS culture does exist and may have profound consequences on performance of the IS function. Indeed the increasing drive toward outsourcing IS activities may be attributed to the fact that the IS culture within an organization becomes incompatible with corporate goals and objectives, and since culture is difficult to change, the option for many organizations is to eliminate much of the IS organization and use outside vendors.

In building a model of IS culture, Cooper uses the competing values framework developed by Quinn and Rohrbaugh (1985). This framework emphasizes the competing tensions and conflicts inherent in groups. They suggested that two major conflicts include: (1) the need for *order* versus the ability to be *flexible*, and (2) the focus on either the demands of the *internal* social and technical systems of the organization versus a focus on the *external* world beyond the boundaries of the organization. When combinations of these conflicts are considered, four cultural archetypes can be defined: survival, productivity, stability, and human relations. The survival archetype is characterized by an organization that is flexible and external. Its leaders can adapt to a changing environment and are willing to take risks in the search for opportunities. The productivity archetype is characterized by an organization that prefers order and is responsive to its external environment. These organizations are very efficient, and nearly all decisions are driven by rational-economic considerations. The stability archetype is characterized by the need for order and internal focus. In these organizations there is a high degree of formalization, and leaders tend to be cautious, emphasizing technical issues. Flexibility and an internal focus characterize the human relations archetype. Emphasis is on informal roles rather than a formal structure, and maintenance of the organization is a primary goal.

Cooper's model is summarized in Figure 1. He associated several *practices* with each of the archetypes. The survival archetypes include such practices as scanning the external environment for project opportunities and inter-organizational linking. The productivity archetype is compatible with applications that facilitate organizational planning, directing and goal setting. Stability archetypes are more likely to emphasize applications that stress measurement and control such as accounting systems, cost-variance reporting, budgeting, and other record keeping applications. Human relations archetypes are compatible with systems that reinforce the social values of its members and provide interpersonal communication and cooperation such as teleconferencing, electronic mail, and group decision support.

In summary, the culture of the IS organization is an important variable in understanding the IS strategy within an organization and the type of practices which the organization follows. It also begins to suggest that transferring technology form one organization such as headquarters to another organization such as a subsidiary will most likely have to confront the integration of differences in organizational culture.

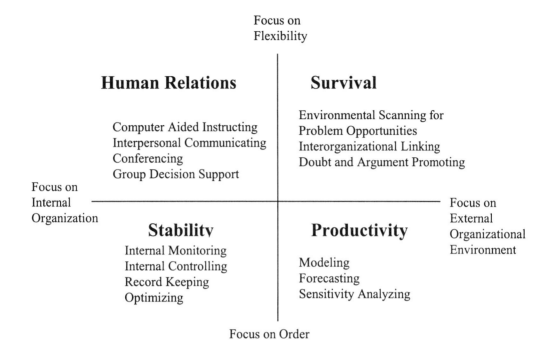

Focus on
Flexibility

Human Relations

Computer Aided Instructing
Interpersonal Communicating
Conferencing
Group Decision Support

Focus on
Internal
Organization

Stability

Internal Monitoring
Internal Controlling
Record Keeping
Optimizing

Survival

Environmental Scanning for
Problem Opportunities
Interorganizational Linking
Doubt and Argument Promoting

Focus on
External
Organizational
Environment

Productivity

Modeling
Forecasting
Sensitivity Analyzing

Focus on Order

Figure 1: Organizational Practices Related to Cultural Archetypes
(Adapted from Cooper, 1994).

INFLUENCE OF NATIONAL CULTURE ON IS CULTURE

To establish a link between national culture and IS culture, it would be useful to determine the extent to which Hofstede's model of national culture can be mapped onto the competing values model as it is applied to IS culture by Cooper. If successful, the competing values model could be used as the basis for an IS culture framework reflecting national culture. Such a mapping, however, is difficult because there is no direct relationship between Hofstede's dimensions of power distance and uncertainty avoidance and the archetypes of IS organizational culture including stability, productivity, survival, and human relations. To some extent, it could be argued that stability archetypes can be expected to occur more frequently in the machine and pyramid quadrants since a stable organization would be expected to be high in uncertainty avoidance. But even organizations in the family quadrant would need to maintain stable organizations in order to protect their "family" structures. Productivity archetypes may be expected to occur more frequently in the machine quadrant, since they emphasize the improvement of efficiency and the reduction of uncertainty. Survival archetypes may be expected to occur more frequently in the market quadrant, since the willingness to take risks is an important component of this archetype. Finally, human relations archetypes might be expected to occur more frequently in the market and family quadrants since formal structures are not emphasized and teamwork is common.

There are at least three problems with this attempt to map culture onto archetypes. First, as suggested by the stability archetype, more than one archetype is likely to exist in each quadrant. Second, the characteristics of each archetype may vary from quadrant to quadrant. For example, in the market quadrant the human relations archetype may emphasize informal structures, widespread participation from end-users, team approaches, and the widespread use of group enhancing technology such as E-mail and decision support systems. But in the family quadrant, human relations may imply strong top-down management emphasizing the maintenance of the corporate family at all costs. The third criticism is that, unlike Hofstede's study, there is no empirical evidence to suggest the feasibility of such a link.

To summarize, national culture can be traced to IS culture, but when Hofstede's national culture model is mapped onto the competing values IS culture model, the results do not suggest a clear association between national culture and organizational archetypes. Rather than use the competing values model, it seems more appropriate to apply Hofstede's work on national and organizational culture directly to IS culture, but still preserve Cooper's approach in which IS practices are identified and placed in quadrants.

IDENTIFICATION OF IS PRACTICES

While one could hypothesize which practices would be most common in each of the Hofstede quadrants, the methodology used in this chapter was to scan the research literature on international IS and place practices, reported in these studies, into the quadrant representing the country in which the study was undertaken. The result of the process is a model, summarized in Figure 2, that begins to build a sense of the prevailing IS culture associated with each quadrant.

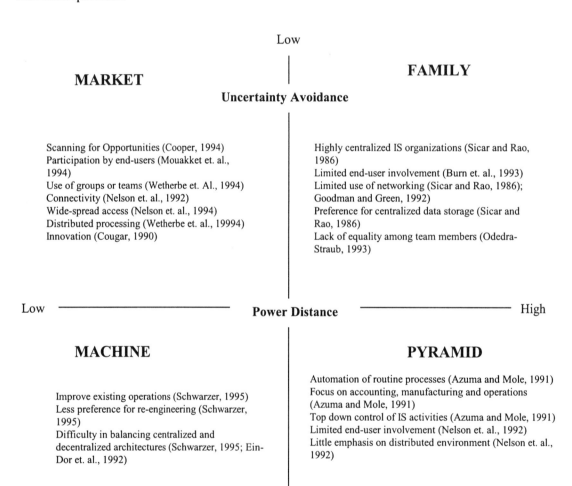

Figure 2: Practices of IS Organizations Classified into Hofstede Quadrants.

The market quadrant includes cultures that are neither centralized nor formalized. Companies placed in this quadrant are likely, as Cooper has suggested, to scan the environment for project opportunities. Mouakket, Sillence, and Fretwell-Dowling (1994) found evidence of end-user participation during the development process in the United Kingdom. Wetherbe, Vitalari and Milner (1994) observed the use of groups or teams in North America. Nelson, Weiss and Yamazaki (1992) reported connectivity and widespread access in the U.S. Wetherbe, Vitalari and Milner (1994) found a reliance on distributed processing in North America, and innovation in the U.S. was suggested by Couger (1990).

The machine quadrant, which includes cultures that are not centralized but highly formalized, is compatible with practices more likely to improve existing IS operations rather than innovate or reengineer. This was the conclusion reached by Schwarzer (1995) in a study of German firms. Both Schwarzer and Ein-Dor and Segev (1992) also suggest the difficult process of balancing distributed and centralized architectures in organizations in Germany and Israel. This struggle can be related to the conflict between low power distance, suggesting the acceptance of distributed architectures, and high uncertainty avoidance, suggesting a preference for centralized data to minimize risks of unauthorized access and fraud.

The family quadrant is characterized by a high degree of centralization but low formalization. A study by Sicar and Rao, (1986) suggests IS organizations in Singapore are highly centralized. Limited end-user involvement was found in Hong Kong by Burn et al. (1993). Sicar and Rao (1986) also found limited use of networking and distributed processing in Singapore, with similar conclusions drawn by Goodman and Green (1992) for the Middle East. Lack of equality among team members was found in East Africa by Odedra-Straub (1993).

The pyramid quadrant is characterized by high centralization and high formalization. Azuma and Mole (1991) in the study of Japanese firms found an emphasis on the automation of routine processes in manufacturing, accounting, and operations. They also found an emphasis on top-down control of IS activities. Nelson, Weiss, and Yamazaki (1992), also studying firms in Japan, found limited end-user involvement and a preference for centralized architectures.

In summary, research on IS practices was entered into Hofstede's quadrants and this new framework then begins to suggest specific practices that differentiate IS cultures found in organizations throughout the world.

INTERACTION OF HEADQUARTERS AND SUBSIDIARY IS CULTURES

While national culture has been shown to influence IS culture, other factors, suggested by Hofstede et al. (1990) also contribute. They may include the competitive environment, business strategy and structure, and portfolio of IS tasks. The competitive environment, even when the same products are sold, may not be perceived in the same way by both organizations. Headquarters may perceive competition as much more intense than its subsidiary or perhaps the reverse may be true. IS strategy and structure also play an important role in the interaction between the two organizations. Global MNCs, because they are highly centralized and treat the world as one market, may require more compliance from its subsidiaries and therefore have less flexible IS cultures. Multi-domestic MNCs, because they see the world as many markets, may have more flexible IS cultures and may demand less in the way of compliance from its subsidiaries. The portfolio of tasks is also a factor in establishing IS culture. For example, an organization that uses simple recording keeping and reporting applications may have developed a very different IS culture than one that uses a broader range of applications from transaction processing to executive support systems. Indeed as the applications move up the information hierarchy from transaction processing to management information systems, decision support systems and finally executive support systems, the role of national culture, organizational culture, and IS culture can be expected to increase as applications respond to environments which become less and less structured. Figure 3 summarizes the way in which these factors influence the development of IS cultures in both the headquarters and host organizations.

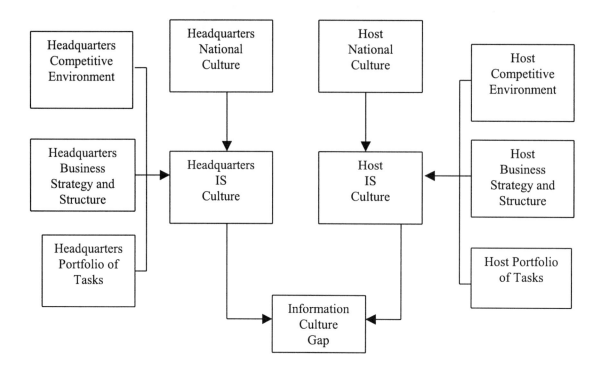

Figure 3: Factors that Influence Organizational Culture Gap

Meyer (1993) suggests that a cultural gap occurs when behavioral asymmetries exist between international work groups. Accordingly, the term IS culture gap, used in this chapter, refers to the asymmetries between headquarters and subsidiary IS cultures.

When common systems are attempted and the IS linkages between headquarters and its subsidiary encounter problems, the presence of this gap may be expressed by headquarters IS personnel in indirect ways. They may complain that the foreign subsidiary: is unwilling to take ownership of the application; doesn't understand the importance of the system; is staffed with people who are 'stuck in their ways'; and doesn't see the big picture. IS management at the subsidiary location, on the other hand, may complain that headquarters doesn't understand that their problems are different, and can't see things from their point-of-view. Often this unproductive cycle occurs with little progress in resolving the real issues that need to be addressed interfere in a successful transfer.

It is undoubtedly difficult to operationalize the concept of a gap and measure its magnitude. Kedia and Bhagat (1988), addressing this issue, suggest that the greatest problems can be expected when applications are transferred between developed and developing countries. Perhaps it is reasonable to suggest that the IS culture gap may increase as the difference between power distance and uncertainty avoidance scores between headquarters and foreign subsidiaries increase.

Figure 2 can be used to establish an understanding of the IS practices which contribute to this gap. Consider, for example, a multinational company with headquarters in France about to introduce manufacturing control software to one of its subsidiaries in the

United States. According to Table 1, France is located in the pyramid quadrant. It is therefore characterized by high power distance and high uncertainty avoidance. The U.S., located in the market quadrant, is associated with low power distance and low uncertainty avoidance. Practices in the pyramid quadrant, summarized in Figure 2, suggest limited acceptance of a distributed environment, top-down control, and limited end-user involvement. Practices in the market quadrant suggest a greater tolerance for distributed processing, widespread access, and end-user involvement. Consider that the new manufacturing application assumes centralized monitoring and control, little end-user involvement, and centralized architectures. If the IS culture of the subsidiary organization in the U.S. strongly reflects the values of the market quadrant, several conflicts are likely to arise. Subsidiary users in the U.S. may react negatively to strong top-down management, which may be expressed in the methods and procedures associated with the new application. For example, in high power distance cultures like France, there may be more restrictions on the freedom given end-users to initiate data entry and schedule changes. Consider also that U.S. participants may expect to take more responsibility for the system, prefer wide access to data, and expect their views on the application to be taken into consideration. For all of these reasons an IS culture gap can be expected to develop.

Attempts may be made to resolve the conflicts associated with this gap. Headquarters may try to influence and change the culture by transferring headquarters personnel to the subsidiary location or by training managers and end-users, or they may choose to ignore the gap and hope that the subsidiary organization will eventually adjust to the demands imposed by the application. Perhaps the subsidiary organization may even make changes in its own culture in an effort to close the gap. Because, as Hofstede contends, culture changes slowly, the gap may close slowly, if at all. Furthermore, the efforts to close this gap will succeed or fail to the extent that core values are respected and left intact. When core values of power distance, uncertainty avoidance, individualism-collectivism, and masculinity-femininity are threatened, conflict between headquarters and the subsidiary may be extremely difficult to resolve.

IMPLICATIONS FOR MANAGEMENT

Several implications can be drawn from this framework and are summarized in Table 2. National culture is a powerful force and affects IS culture and IS practices in organizations. An IS group in a British organization, for example, can be expected to be influenced by British culture, while an IS group in France can be expected to be influenced by French culture. Culture can be measured by many dimensions. Two of these dimensions, which appear related to organization culture, include power distance and uncertainty avoidance. Accordingly, IS practices in the British group may be influenced by the low power distance of the British culture while IS practices in the French group may be influenced by high power distance associated with French culture.

When national culture, IS culture and IS practices at the headquarters operation differ from the culture and practices at the subsidiary operation, an IS gap is likely to occur. The wider the gap, the more difficult it may be to establish effective linkages between these organizations.

IS gaps, however, are easy to neglect. It is easier to blame problems on: technical issues, inadequacy of telecommunications systems, unsatisfactory end-user training, uncooperative subsidiary organizations, and the absence of persons at the foreign subsidiary who might 'champion' the IS application.

Table 2: Implications for Management

1. National culture can exert a strong influence over IS culture and IS practices in organizations.

2. Power distance and avoidance of risk are dimensions of national culture that can be expected to influence these IS practices

3. When national culture, IS culture and IS practices at the headquarters operation differ from the culture and practices at the subsidiary or host operation, an IS gap occurs, and the establishment of effective IS linkages can become difficult.

4. IS gaps are easy to neglect. It is easier to blame problems on: technical issues, local infrastructure problems, uncooperative host organizations, and the absence of persons at the host operation who might 'champion' the IS application.

5. Headquarters must raise culturally sensitive questions with the intent of exploring this potential source of conflict. They must ask how cultural dimensions such as power distance and uncertainty avoidance might affect practices such as end-user involvement, distributed data strategies, networks, user access to data, and teams.

6. Answers to these and other culturally targeted questions must be carefully studied and the temptation to focus solely on the technical issues resisted.

7. The insight gained from these answers must be used to develop a cultural/technical IS strategy for establishing improved IS linkages.

8. IS culture changes slowly. The strategic plan must take this fact into consideration.

9. There can be many benefits to a cultural/technical IS plan: conflict can be reduced; implementation will almost certainly be faster; IS costs may be lower; transfer success rates will increase; and the effective use of the system can be expected to improve.

Management must avoid the temptation to place too much emphasis on technical problems or even 'unsophisticated' end-users. They must address cultural issues directly by raising culturally sensitive questions early in the planning process. "How might the subsidiary culture, which is high in power distance, react to the introduction of a manufacturing system that requires end-user involvement." If the headquarters operation is in a low power distance culture, then end-user involvement, demanded of the subsidiary, may be a difficult request to make.

Answers to these and other culturally sensitive questions must be studied carefully, and the conclusions used to develop a cultural/technical strategy for improving the chances of a successful IS linkage. In most cases this plan must acknowledge that culture changes slowly. Incremental change rather than abrupt change may have a higher likelihood of success.

There can be many benefits associated with a carefully crafted cultural/technical plan. By focusing on these differences and developing strategies to resolve them, headquarters management has the opportunity to: limit conflict, decrease implementation time, reduce costs, improve transfer success, and minimize disappointing results.

CONCLUSIONS

The purpose of this chapter has been to link the role of national culture to the IS culture of headquarters and subsidiary IS organizations. While there has been work done on national culture and organization culture, the influence of national culture on headquarters and subsidiary IS cultures has been ignored. Given the explosive growth in global business, it seems appropriate to add this dimension to the evolving theory of global information systems.

To provide a more concrete framework in which to study the influence of national culture on headquarters and subsidiary IS cultures, this chapter has suggested that the identification of IS practices associated with organizations in a specific culture embodies the values and beliefs of that national culture. Furthermore by grouping these practices into one of four Hofstede quadrants it then becomes possible to predict the nature of the IS culture gap that may be expected, when national cultures are crossed.

While the quadrants into which these practices were grouped were limited to two cultural dimensions, including power distance and uncertainty avoidance, the goal was to keep the conceptual framework as simple as possible, but at the same time robust enough to provide insight. This is primarily a framework that suggests general directions. There will always be examples of headquarters/subsidiary interactions that extend across cultures but experience few problems, and there will be examples of failed alliances within the same national culture. However, the object of the conceptual framework developed here is not to accommodate the full range of possible outcomes but to: provide insight; promote consideration of culture early in the management process; anticipate conflict; and improve the likelihood of a successful headquarters/subsidiary alliance.

Mini Case: Healthcare International Limited.

Bill Horan had just returned from another trip that brought him through Ireland, Korea, the Philippines and Malaysia. As he sat in his London office, he pondered over the frustrations he had encountered. The progress from the plant in Ireland was not hitting any major snags. India was reasonably on schedule. The Philippines were having their problems, but the Malaysians, in particular, were just not getting it. He made a note to himself to begin the process of replacing the managing director in Malaysia.

Healthcare International Limited manufactures and distributes health care products worldwide. They sell through distributors in over 40 countries and carry a product line that includes shampoos, deodorants, cosmetics, and health care products such as vitamins and health-care aids. They manufacture their own products in the UK, as well in plants Horan had just visited. Plants specialized in products, so not all plants produced the same items.

Three years ago Horan was hired to introduce common systems to four subsidiary operations in Asia and Europe. These systems were exactly the same as those used in the UK plant. Until he arrived, the company had basically left these foreign manufacturing and distribution centers alone. As long as they remained profitable, headquarters was pleased. But increasing pressure from competitors demanded that they reign in these operations and begin steps to make them more efficient. Headquarters wanted better ordering systems, better production scheduling systems, better inventory recordkeeping systems, better quality control systems, and better logistics systems. The only answer was to transfer their own software applications to these subsidiaries.

The transfer process was plagued with problems. Horan had expected a few technical glitches here and there, but he was stymied as to why the transfer had proven so much more difficult in the Philippines and Malaysia than when the same systems were installed in the Ireland.

In the Philippines, supervisors were reluctant to take responsibility for using the output of the system. They had trouble making independent decisions and did not feel empowered to keep jobs moving if something got in the way. Traditionally they expected their supervisors to investigate the source of a problem when one occurred or when a schedule began to slip. While he was at the plant, one supervisor fell a day behind schedule because an ingredient was missing; the supervisor was waiting for the manager of production to solve the problem. Actually the ingredient had just arrived and the problem could have been solved had the supervisor simply checked the incoming order database in the new information system. Using that information he could have then expedited the ingredient through

Mini Case …. Continued.

incoming inspection. It should have taken about fifteen minutes to do this! Horan had the sense that managers at this plant just didn't want things to change. What was puzzling, however, was that the managers all seemed willing to take the chance with a new system. They just couldn't make it work.

In Malaysia, the futility of the new system really became apparent. When he accessed the screen to view the in-process schedule he found that the database was inconsistent with the actual progress of the jobs on the production floor. And the more he checked the system, the more he found bad data. The managing director wasn't too alarmed, when Horan confronted him. The director said they were doing the best they could.

In Korea, the problems were somewhat the same. Individual initiative was seldom shown. Workers relied on their supervisors for everything, and expecting them to take responsibility for data entry and use the information systems became a major hurdle. But of even more concern was the fact that many of the Korean managers were very reluctant to change systems. They were comfortable with their old ways and seemed unwilling to make the change that the common system required.

Pondering the events of the last two weeks, Horan got up from his desk and went to see his boss, Joan Williamson. After describing his frustrations with the Malaysian plant, Williamson said she wasn't surprised. " Poor data quality has plagued us since the day we opened there. It seems to be a deep rooted problem," she Continued. "We're just paying the price for the absence of an established business culture in that plant. Maybe we should put someone in there who understands what we need to do and is committed to helping us." "Bill," she continued, "I think the only way is to push through these problem, We need these applications up and running in six months or our effort to integrate these plants is in real trouble."

Questions:

1. Summarize the problems faced by Horan.
2. Do you think that cultural differences are responsible for some of the problems faced by Horan? Explain.
3. Describe the practices that you think would describe the differences between headquarters IS culture in the UK and the IS culture in Malaysia.
4. Which components of the culture gap do you think have influenced the transfer of IT in these subsidiaries?
5. Do you think that Horan and Williamson have recognized that part of their problem can be attributed to cultural differences? If not, Why?
6. What would you advise Horan to do? Would you recommend replacing the Malaysian managing director?

STUDY QUESTIONS

1. Information systems are primarily technical systems that address logical ways of performing tasks. As a result, a headquarters operation need not concern itself with the local environment of its overseas subsidiary organizations in the process of transferring strategic information systems to subsidiaries. As long as the computer application has been designed effectively, and a detailed implementation schedule has been developed, the headquarters operation should expect a successful implementation. Write an essay that comments on this statement.

2. An electronics firm in Denmark is about to open a manufacturing facility in Mexico. They expect the Mexican subsidiary to use their manufacturing software to manage the

operation. With this common system and telecommunications technology, headquarters will be able to access data easily from the Mexican plant and keep on top of schedules and shipments. What advice would you give to management as they prepare to implement their software system?

3. In addition to the practices described in Figure 2, what other practices would you expect to find in these quadrants? Use Hofstede's definition of power distance and uncertainly avoidance and his quadrant model to help you.

4. What are the influences on IS culture and do you think it would be difficult to change the IS culture of a subsidiary organization?

5. The media such as movies and internet technologies has had a remarkable effect on homogenizing the world into one marketplace. The widespread acceptance of movies, music, and products such as those produced by Gillette and Coke; all suggest a convergence of culture. Do you think that the issue of cultural differences will disappear by the middle of this century, and that this will make it easier to transfer common systems around the world?

6. The twentieth century, including the last decade, has witnessed countless examples of racial and cultural intolerance and violence. Some suggest that this is inevitable when deep-rooted differences exist. Does this suggest, as Hofstede has stated, that culture changes slowly, and that the issues of transferring technology into distant lands will be with us well into this new century?

7. Common airline reservation systems are used throughout the world. Why do you think a multinational company with subsidiaries on all continents might find it more difficult to implement common manufacturing planning and control systems than an airline would in implementing a reservation system?

REFERENCES

Azuma, M. & Mole, D. (July 1994). Software Management Practices and Metrics in the European Community and Japan: Some Results of a Survey. *Journal of Systems Software,* 26(1), 5-18.

Bartlett, C.A. & Ghoshal, S. (1989). *Managing Across Borders: The Transnational Solution.* Boston, MA: Harvard Business School Press.

Burn, J., Saxena, K.B.C., Ma, L. & Cheung, H.K. (Fall 1993). Critical Issues of IS Management in Hong Kong: A Cultural Comparison. *Journal of Global Information Management*, 1(4), 28-37.

Cheung, H.K. & Burn, J.M. (Summer 1994). Distributing Global Information Systems Resources in Multinational Companies-A Contingency Model. *Journal of Global Information Management*, 2(3), 14-27.

Cooper, R.B. (1994). The Inertial Impact of Culture on IT Implementation. *Information and Management*, 27, 17-31.

Couger, D.J. (1990). Ensuring Creative Approaches in Information Systems Design. *Managerial and Decision Economics*, 11.

Davenport, T.H., Eccles, R.G. & Prusak, L. (Fall, 1992). Information Politics. *Sloan Management Review*, 53-65.

Deal, T.E. & Kennedy, A.A. (1982). *Corporate Cultures.* Reading, MA: Addison-Wesley.

Ein-Dor, P., Segev, E. & Orgad, M. (Winter 1993). The Effect of National Culture on IS: Implications for International Information Systems. *Journal of Global Information Management*, 1(1), 33-44.

Ein-Dor, P. & Segev, E. (January 1992). End User Computing: A Cross Cultural Study. *International Information Systems*, 1(1), 124-137.

Erez, M. & Earley, P.C. (1993). *Culture, Self-identity, and Work*. New York: Oxford University Press.

Goodman, S.E. & Green, J.D. (August 1992). Computing in the Middle East. *Communications of the ACM*, 35(8), 21-25.

Hofstede, G. (Summer 1980). Motivation, Leadership, and Organization: Do American Theories Apply Abroad? *Organizational Dynamics*.

Hofstede, G. (1981). Culture and Organizations. I*nternational Studies of Management and Organizations*, X(4), 15-41.

Hofstede, G., Neuijen, B., Ohayv, D. & Sanders, G. (1990). Measuring Organizational Cultures: A Qualitative and Quantitative Study Across Twenty Cases. *Administrative Science Quarterly*, 35, 286-316.

Hofstede, G. (1991). *Culture and Organizations: Software of the Mind*. London: McGraw-Hill.

Ives, B. & Jarvenpaa, S.L. (March 1991). Applications of Global Information Technology: Key Issues for Management. *MIS Quarterly*, 33-49.

Kedia, B.L. & Bhagat, R.S. (1988). Cultural Constraints on Transfer of Technology Across Nations: Implications for Research in International and Comparative Management. *Academy of Management Review*, 13(4), 559-571.

Lachman, R. (1983). Modernity Change of Core and Peripheral Values of Factory Workers. *Human Relations*, 36, 563-80.

Magretta, Joan. (September-October 1998). Fast, Global, and Entrepreneurial: Supply Chain Management, Hong Kong Stryle, *Harvard Business Review*, 103- 114.

Meyer, Heinz-Dieter. (1993). The Cultural Gap in Long-term International Work Groups: A German-American Case Study. *European Management Journal*. 11,1, 93-101.

Mouakket, S., Sillence, J.A.A. & Fretwell-Dowling, F.A. (April 1994). Information Requirements Determination in the Software Industry: A Case Study. *European Journal of Information Systems*, 3(2), 101-111.

Nelson, R.R., Weiss, I.R. & Yamazaki, K. (October 1992). Information Resource Management within Multinational Corporations. *International Information Systems*, 1(4), 56-83.

Odedra-Straub, M. (Summer 1993). Critical Factors Affecting Success of CBIS: Cases from Africa. *Journal of Global Information Management*, 1(3), 16-31.

Parsons, T. & Shils, E.A. (1951). *Toward a General Theory of Action*. Cambridge, MA: Harvard University Press.

Quinn, R.E & Rohrbaugh, J. (1983). A Spatial Model of Effectiveness Criteria: Towards a Competing Values Approach to Organizational Analysis. *Management Science*, 29(3), 363-377.

Roche, E.M. (1992). Managing Information Technology in Multinational Corporations. New York: Macmillan.

Schein, E.H. (1985). *Organizational Culture and Leadership*. Jossey-Bass, San Francisco.

Schwarzer, B. (Winter 1995). Organizing Global IS Management to Meet Competitive Challenges Experiences from the Pharmaceutical Industry. *Journal of Global Information Management*, 3(1), 5-16.

Shore, B. (Spring 1996). Using Information Technology to Coordinate Transnational Service Operations: A Case Study in the European Union. *Journal of Global Information Management*, 4(2), 5-14.

Shore, B. & Venkatachalam, V. (1995). The Role of National Culture in Systems Analysis and Design. *Journal of Global Information Management.* 3,3.

Sicar, S. & Rao, K.V. (1986). Information Resource Management in Singapore: The State of the Art. *Information and Management*, 11, 181-187.

Smircich, L. (1982). Concepts of Culture and Organizational Analysis. <u>*Administrative Science Quarterly*</u>, (28), 339-358.

Triandis, H.C. (1995). Culture: Theoretical and Methodological Issues. in M.D. Dunnette and L. Hough, Eds., *Handbook of Industrial and Organizational Psychology*, 2nd ed., Vol. 4, Consulting Psychologists Press, Palo Alto, CA.

Wetherbe, J.C., Vitalari, N.P. & Milner, A. (Spring 1994). Key Trends in Systems Development in Europe and North America. *Journal of Global Information Management*, 2(2), 5-20.

10

Challenges in Transborder Data Flow

Effy Oz, D.B.A.
The Pennsylvania State University, Great Valley, USA

ABSTRACT

Free flow of information is one of the cornerstones of free trade and economic growth. The Internet now connects millions of commercial organizations throughout the world. Ostensibly this huge network could contribute immensely to the welfare of businesses, but there are still technical, political, cultural, and especially legal challenges that make some international transfer of data difficult or simply impossible. This chapter reviews the different types of hurdles, especially the legal ones. We pay special attention to the hurdle between the largest economic blocs, Europe and the U.S. The new European directive on data protection forbids American businesses from using personal data of European citizens the way they use personal data of American citizens. This makes it practically impossible to use such data for marketing and decision making. The chapter reviews the new directive, a sample of data privacy laws, and the efforts to harmonize privacy laws.

INTRODUCTION

The availability of telecommunication networks is vital to the world's economy. In recent years, the Internet has provided the most significant means of communicating information in general, and business information in particular. Technically, the world's business community can collect, maintain, and transfer data as if there were no national borders. Technically, but not legally. In an age when information is so important for the development of new markets, many countries restrict free flow of information between their territories and other countries.

Some countries forbid the transfer of classified data to other countries. They rationalize that information is wealth as are cash and tangible assets. Information has the power to give one country a political and technological advantage over another and, as a result, transfer of data threatens a nation's security. It is legitimate for a government to prohibit foreign access to research and development data, financial information, and other information that may jeopardize economic, political, or cultural interests, or even compromise the nation's sovereignty.

Economists, however, agree that one of the most important conditions for the world's economic growth is the free flow of information. Also, the restrictions on data transfer interfere with the smooth running of multinational corporations (MNCs). The number of these companies is growing fast. For these companies, restrictions on international data flow amount to no less than restrictions of data transfer from one department to another.

What are the issues involved? Fortunately, the standardization issues have been largely resolved in terms of hardware and software. The wide use of Web browsers provides an easy-to-adopt standard for both business-to-business (B2B) and business-to-consumer

(B2C) transactions. Also, as Figure 1 indicates, almost every nation is now connected to the Internet. The few nations in Africa and Asia that are not connected contribute little to the world's economy, and it is expected that they, too, will be connected eventually. In terms of servers making up the network, the world is being fast covered with domain servers, as is evident from Figure 2.

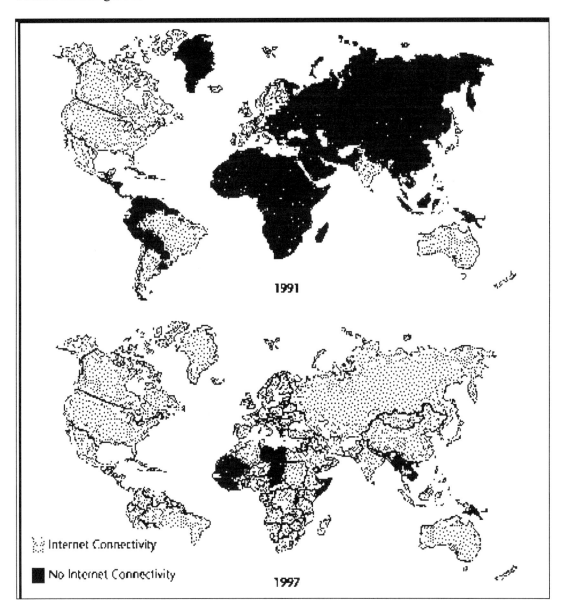

Source: Network Wizards, 1999

Figure 1: The spread of Internet connectivity

The remaining hurdles to free flow of data among countries are mainly legal and political. In the next sections we will discuss the main types of hurdles on the path to truly free cross-border flow of data and information.

THE HURDLES

As shown in Table 1, there are several types of problems that must be resolved. Some are technical in nature, e.g., connectivity, bandwidth, and security. The rest have much to do with cultural, political, and economic interests. The most difficult to overcome are legal issues, which are derived from cultural differences.

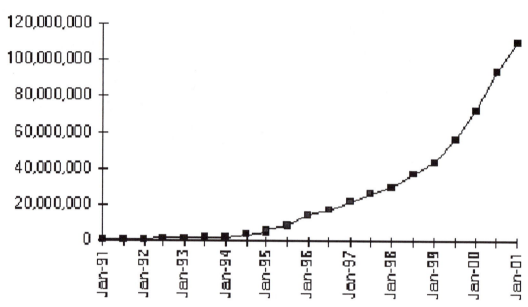

Source: Network Wizards, 1999

Figure 2: *Number of Internet servers*

Table 1: Transborder Data Flow Inhibitors

Connectivity	- A few countries in Africa and Asia not linked - Small number of servers in some countries (e.g., China)
Bandwidth	Narrow bandwidth in many countries (e.g., China and East Europe)
Security	Has largely been resolved
Political Constraints	Government control of Internet access in some countries
Language and Measure Standards	- On-the-fly translation software far from perfect - Distance, weight, address, and date notation: U.S. vs. the world
Cultural Difference	- Fear of cultural imperialism - Colors and icons with different meanings
Legal Issues	- European Union Directive on Data Privacy in disharmony with U.S. practices

Connectivity, Bandwidth, and Security

As Table 1 shows, we are nearing the point when every single country will be connected to the Internet. Obviously, two elements are important in considering connectivity in addition to the fact that there is a link on a nation's territory: the number of servers connected to the Internet's backbone, and the number of organizations and individuals to whom the Net is accessible. Thus, Americans and Europeans have the largest number of servers and people who regularly log on, while China, for example, has a relatively small number of servers, and only about two million of its citizens log on regularly. This number is minute when considering that about 1.25 billion people live in China.

Bandwidth is another issue. Bandwidth is the capacity, or the speed, of telecommunications. When the bandwidth is narrow, the amount of information that can be effectively communicated is small. This becomes a major problem when information in the form of pictures, animation, and sound is involved. To avoid long wait for such information to download, corporations must limit the amount and form of information they would like to transmit. The bandwidth in some nations in Europe and those of African and most Asian countries (notably, China and India) is quite narrow.

The issue of secured links has largely been solved with the advent of strong encryption and the incorporation of such encryption into Web browsers. Public key encryption allows every online user to purchase and provide private data without fear of uninvited deciphering of data by a third party. The strongest encryption software is developed in the United States. The federal government has relaxed its restrictions on the export of strong encryption software (encryption with 64 and 128 bit keys), which may pacify even the most cautious organizations and individuals. Fear of dissatisfactory security has more to do with psychology and culture than with reality.

In addition to these challenges, there is that of translation from Latin-based alphabet sets to other alphabets (e.g., Chinese). The translation itself, as discussed below, is only part of the challenge. Each character is represented by a standard group of eight electrical circuits, called a byte. This is fine for languages with up to 256 (2^8) characters, such as English and other languages whose alphabetic root is the Latin letters. But eight-bit bytes are not sufficient for languages with larger numbers of characters, such as Chinese, Japanese, and Korean. The solution for this is to program computers to use double-byte characters allowing for up to 65,536 (2^{16}) characters. However, if only the servers are programmed to accommodate double-byte characters, while the other systems (such as databases and applications on computers interacting with the servers) work with single-byte characters, the "back-end" systems (those databases and applications) record and return gibberish. Thus, entire systems must be reprogrammed or use special software.

Political Constraints

The Internet has promoted free flow of information more than any other medium of mass communication. However, the degree of free flow of information depends on accessibility. Thus, an individual's ability to communicate depends on the availability of a computer and a server to which that computer is linked. Since much of the Internet's backbone is physical (wires), it is technically easy for governments to control links. Several governments have used their power to control what their citizens can do with the Internet.

For instance, the government of China blocks access of its people to sites that it believes are operated by dissidents. The Singaporan government has blocked reception of Web sites whose contents it considers objectionable. The technical (but not legal) ability of governments to exert such control may diminish when more of the links to the Net are unguided, namely, not through wires, but via satellites. It is significantly more difficult to "choke" communication when one uses a small dish antenna rather than a wired link to a server.

Language and Measurement Standard

The beauty of the Internet and other international computer networks is that they disregard national borders; they are truly an international communication infrastructure. Yet, the world does not speak in one language, literally. It does not take much time for a first-time user of the Internet to realize that English, especially American English, is the dominant language on the

Web. The Internet's language is English. Yet, the number of non-American users of the network is growing faster than the number of American users, and by some forecast is expected to become the dominant group by 2003. Many of these Web users do not read or write English.

Some corporations have taken notice. Their solution is to establish mirror sites with other languages for "local" audiences. For example, Cisco, a world leader in network hardware, established a Spanish Web site for Spanish and Latin American customers, where they can receive general information, maintenance manuals and other information. But translation may be tricky. The company discovered that there is one Spanish word for "router" (a device that routes packets of electronic communication) in Spain and another in Latin America. Since the company wanted to use one Spanish-language site, it had a problem. The Spanish representatives insisted on "their" word, while the Latin American representatives of the company insisted on theirs and did not even know what term the Spaniards used for "router."

Imagine the difficulties of American and European companies in translating all of their information on the Web into Chinese, which they will have to if they want to tap the world's largest consumer market. And while they are at it, they will have to be cautious and use the proper letter set. The Taiwanese use the traditional set of Chinese characters, but people in the People's Republic of China prefer the simplified character set.

Another challenge is how to communicate measurement units, dates, and addresses. While Americans use the English system for distances, area, volume, and weights (inch, foot, mile and their square and cubic notations; and pounds), the rest of the world (including the United Kingdom) has long used the metric system. Companies that wish to do business both in the U.S. and other countries must use both notations. The same applies to dates: people invited to attend a conference on 4/3/2000 may show up on April 3, 2000 instead of March 4, 2000. In the English-speaking world, the order of data in addresses is: number, street, city; in the rest of the world, it is street, number, city. Birth dates, transaction dates, addresses, and other date data must either be stored, or at least displayed in the proper notation to the proper audience.

While there are software packages that translate from one language to another and from one notation to another, the software is far from perfect. Proper translation still requires much human involvement and substantial investment of resources.

Cultural Differences

Information systems are an effective vehicle for communicating cultural ideas and gestures. Since culture is an important ingredient of national heritage, some countries make great efforts to block what they perceive as cultural imperialism. Several years ago, the French government passed a law that forbade the use of non-French words in government owned and funded enterprises, including radio, television, and the educational system. The main purpose of the law was to minimize American influence on everyday life. That law was eventually repelled, but a similar law is still valid in the Canadian province of Quebec: no signs are allowed on the fronts of stores and other establishments which are not in French. Some of the restrictions that China, Singapore, and other countries impose on Internet accessibility have much to do with this fear of cultural imperialism (which almost always means "American cultural imperialism").

Even in countries where free speech is as common as in the U.S., companies setting up Web sites must take care not to offend people of other cultures. Lycos, the company running one of the Web's most popular search engines and portals, launched a Korean version of its portal site in March 1999. The company uses a golden retriever mascot that looks attractive to Americans. But the company discovered that the dog meant something completely different to Koreans: food. Europeans did not like the mascot either. Here are some other examples of cultural differences that Web site designers need to keep in mind:

black has sinister connotations in Europe, Asia, and Latin America; the index-finger-to-thumb sign of approval is a rude gesture meaning "jackass" in Brazil; the thumbs-up sign is a rude gesture in Latin America, as is the waving hand in Arab countries; pictures of women with exposed arms or legs are offensive in many Muslim countries. The important point to remember is that there is no real "local" Web site; if someone who lives in a certain country has access to what a company meant to have as a "local" Web site for that country, that person probably also has access to other Web sites of the company. Those sites, too, must be designed with cultural differences and sensitivities in mind.

Legal Challenges[1]

While many of the challenges involved in cross-border data transfer have been resolved through international agreements, one remains unresolved: respecting different national laws on privacy while conducting international business with very little restriction. Different nations have different approaches to the issue of privacy, as is reflected in their laws. Some are willing to forego some privacy for the sake of a freer flow of information and better marketing. Others restrict any collection of private data without the consent of the individual.

Data protection laws in various countries can be generally described by three different criteria:

1. Whether the law applies to the collection and treatment of data by the private sector (companies), the public sector (governments), or by both.

2. Whether the laws apply to manual data, to automated data, or to both.

3. Whether data protected under the law are only those about human beings, or those about both human and "legal" persons (that is, organizations).

Except for the American and Canadian privacy acts, privacy laws apply to both the public and private sectors; that is, government and private organizations are subject to the same regulation of collection, maintenance, and disclosure of personal data.

Over half of the laws (including U.S. federal statutes) encompass manual as well as computerized record-keeping systems. A minority of the laws apply to legal persons. Denmark, Austria, and Luxembourg are among the countries that protect the privacy of some types of corporations. Countries that support protecting data related to corporations argue that it is difficult to separate data about individuals from data on business activities involving or performed by individuals. This is especially true with respect to small businesses. For example, the financial information of a small business also reveals financial information about the people involved with and/or running the business. Furthermore, a large corporation may unfairly compete against a smaller firm if it has access to the smaller firm's data.

The most important development regarding privacy in recent years was the 1998 adoption of the Directive on Data Privacy by the European Union (EU). The Union includes fifteen West European countries, with a market of close to 400 million consumers. The full title of the EU's directive is *Directive 95/46/EC of the European Parliament and of the Council of 24 October 1995 on the protection of individuals with regard to the processing of personal data and on the free movement of such data.* EU directives are akin to the U.S. Constitution; each member state may formulate its own laws within the framework of the directives. Practically, this means member states may restrict organizations more, and afford more protection than the directive requires, but not less. The EU defines personal data as "any information relating to an identified or identifiable natural person; an identifiable person is one who can be identified, directly or indirectly, in particular by reference to an identification

---

[1]   This section is adapted from *Management Information Systems, 2ⁿᵈ edition, 2000,* by permission from Course Technology, Inc.

number or to one or more factors specific to his physical, physiological, mental, economic, cultural or social identity."

Some of the principles of the Directive are in stark conflict to the practices of U.S. businesses, and therefore severely limit the free flow of personal data between the U.S. and the EU. For example, consider the following provisions, and how they are incompatible with practices in the U.S.:

- "Personal data can be collected only for specified, explicit, and legitimate purposes and not further processed in a way incompatible with those purposes." However, in the U.S., businesses often collect data from people without telling them how the data will be used. Many U.S. corporations use personal data for purposes other than the original one, and many organizations purchase personal data from other organizations, so subjects do not even know that the data are used, let alone for what purpose. Obviously, these activities would not be allowed under the EU Directive.

- Personal data may be processed only if the subject has given unambiguous consent, or under other specific circumstances that the Directive provides. Such circumstances are not required by American laws. In the U.S., private organizations are allowed to process personal data without the subject's consent, and practically for any purpose.

- Individuals or organizations that receive personal data (the Directive terms them as "controllers") not directly from the subject must identify themselves to the subject. In the U.S., many organizations purchase personal data from third parties and never notify the subject.

- People have the right to obtain from controllers "without constraint at reasonable intervals and without excessive delay or expense" confirmation that data about them are processed, information on whom the data are disclosed to, and information on the source that provided the data. They are also entitled to receive information on the "logic involved in any automatic processing of data concerning" them at least in the case of auto-mated decision making. Decision making, practically speaking, means using decision-support systems and expert systems to make decisions on hiring, credit extension, admittance to educational institutions, and so forth. None of these rights is mandated by any U.S. law.

- People have the right to object, "on request and free of charge," to the processing of personal data for the purpose of direct marketing, or to be informed before personal data are disclosed for the first time to third parties or used for the purpose of direct marketing. Furthermore, controllers must expressly offer the right to object free of charge to disclosure of personal data to others. American companies use personal data especially for direct marketing, never tell subjects that they obtain data about them from third parties, and rarely offer subjects the right to object to disclosure of such data to other parties. American companies are very busy collecting, buying, and selling personal data for decision making and marketing purposes. The American approach is that such practices are an essential ingredient of efficient operations, especially in marketing and extension of credit. Thus, this huge discrepancy between the European and American approaches does not allow unrestricted flow of information.

The EU Directive recognizes that countries outside the EU use personal data that are transferred from the EU. It therefore provides that when a "third country does not ensure an adequate level of protection within the meaning of [the Directive], member states shall take the measures necessary to prevent any transfer of data of the same type to the third country." This has created a strange situation: representatives of the EU arrive at least monthly in the

U.S. to monitor American companies that process personal data of European citizens to ensure that the EU Directive on Data Protection is obeyed regarding these citizens. These representatives monitor the information systems of companies such as Visa, MasterCard, American Express and other credit card issuers. Companies that want to do business in EU member states must accept the restrictions of the Directive on their practices. Business leaders on both continents hope that a way can be found to bridge the gap between the two approaches to data privacy, but it seems that a legal solution will not come before a change in culture. Interestingly, the federal government of Canada announced in 1999 that it would initiate changes in Canadian privacy statutes to harmonize them with the EU's Directive.

As mentioned above, the European Directive also limits automated decision making that affects individuals. There is no American law that even addresses the issue, while the EU specifically addresses it in its data protection directive. Article 15 of the Directive is titled "Automated Individual Decisions." It grants every person the right "…not to be subject to a decision which produces legal effects concerning him or significantly affects him and which is based solely on automated processing of data intended to evaluate certain personal aspects relating to him, such as his performance at work, creditworthiness, reliability, conduct, etc."

Automated decision making is done in the U.S. by banks, credit card companies, mortgage companies, employers, and to some extent, educational institutions. The affected individuals may be consumers, credit applicants, employees, job applicants, prospective students, applicants for membership in associations, and people who are evaluated by organizations in other capacities.

Example: The French Law

Members state have had data protection laws that already abide by the EU Directive for a long time. Some of these laws are actually more restrictive than the Directive. Unlike in the U.S., in Europe the collection and maintenance of personal data by the private sector is a highly sensitive issue. In EU countries such activity is restricted. The French Data Processing, Data Files, and Individual Liberties Act may serve as an example of how restrictive such laws may be, relative to the American approach (Coombe and Kirk, 1983). The Law provides:

1. Personal data, i.e. information about an identified or identifiable individual, deserve special protection and should not be stored in an automatic manner (e.g., in a computer) without the data subject's consent.
2. Personal data may be collected only for lawful purposes. Data subjects should be advised about the nature of data collected, the consequences of a failure to supply it, and the intended recipients of the data.
3. A data subject should be able to determine whether an automatic processing system contains information about that subject and, if it does, to gain access to the data and correct inaccuracies.
4. A private enterprise or a public authority processing personal data in an automatic manner must declare the details of the information system to the National Data Processing and Freedom Commission, the regulatory authority created by the Act. The Commission will make the particulars of the system public.
5. Personal data should not be disclosed to unauthorized third parties.
6. The commission is authorized to subject transferred data flow to prior authorization in order to ensure adherence to the Act's underlying principles.

The Act provides protection of personal data which reveal racial origin, political, philosophical, and religious opinions, union membership, and criminal convictions. The National Data Processing and Liberties Commission was established to ensure that automatic processing is carried out in accordance with the law. The French law also requires that any corporation or individual who intends to use a computer for storage and processing of personal data declare its intention to the Commission. The corporation, or individual, must pledge that the processing meets the legal standards. For example, inadequate security controls is a criminal offense on the operator's part. The operator's application for permission to use the automated system must specify:

1. the party making the application and the party empowered to make decisions regarding the processing or, if such party resides abroad, its representative in France;
2. the characteristics, purpose, and type of the processing;
3. the department(s) that will do the processing;
4. the department through which the individual's right of access is exercised and the steps taken to facilitate exercise of that right;
5. the categories of people who, on account of their duties or for the needs of the department, have direct access to the data recorded;
6. the types of data processed, the sources thereof, and the time during which it will be stored, as well as the recipient of the data, or the categories of recipients authorized to receive such data;
7. the linkages, interconnections, or other methods of correlating such data, as well as transfer of the data to third parties;
8. whether the processing is destined for dispatch of data between France and another country.

It is important to note the last provision. Like other governments, the French government realizes that in this day and age it is easy and inexpensive to transfer data to a country whose data protection laws differ from its own. The Commission needs to know the country where the data may be transmitted so it can ascertain that the processing does not violate the French law.

Other member states of the EU have similar laws. Several countries that are not members of the EU, such as Israel, also have laws that are restrictive relative to those of the U.S. Table 2 provides the major elements of data protection laws in 11 countries.

Remaining Obstacles

For the time being, the gap between the U.S. and other countries (mainly EU members) in terms of data protection is quite wide. In fact, there is not even a formal party with which the EU authorities may negotiate this issue, because the U.S. federal government is officially not a party to any communication about personal data held by private organizations. The EU members are not willing to change the principles of the Directive to accommodate countries with less restrictive privacy laws. Their response to protest is: "If you want to do business with us, obey the Directive." As Table 3 shows, several important types of business activities are restricted as a result of the Directive and similar laws in other countries.

Target marketing relies heavily on personal data and profiling. Sorted records allow companies to concentrate their efforts only on those organizations and individuals that are most likely to purchase what the companies have to offer. In the U.S., target marketing has been proven to be a very efficient and effective approach. It has been enhanced tremendously since the Internet was opened for commercial business.

MNCs shuffle personnel, especially executives, among facilities in different countries. Computerized human resource systems are used to select the best candidates for a position in another country. The maintenance and manipulation of a consolidated human resource database are limited or impossible under the laws of many countries.

It is difficult for financial institutions to evaluate the credit-worthiness of individuals from countries that limited transborder data transfer because it is against the law to transfer the parameters used by the institutions to grant credit. Even if this activity were not restricted, the EU restriction on automated decision making on individuals would make the activity either difficult or impossible.

Table 2: Main Provisions of Foreign Data Protection Laws

	Austria	Canada	Denmark Public	Denmark Private	France	Germany	Iceland	Israel	Luxembourg	Norway	Sweden	UK
Scope of Application												
Central Government	Y	Y	Y	N	Y	Y	Y	Y	Y	Y	Y	Y
Province/States	Y	N	Y	N	Ya	Y	Y	Y	Y	Y	Y	Y
Private Sector	Y	N	N	Y	Y	Y	Y	Y	Y	Y	Y	Y
Covers all info traceable to identifiable individuals	Y	Y	Y	Y	Y	Ya	Nb	N	Y	Y	Y	Y
Information collected and/ or processed using computers	Y	Y	Y	Y	Y	Y	Y	Y	Y	Y	Y	Y
Limits placed on personal data collection	Y	Y	Yc	Y	Y	Yd	Y	Y	Y	Y	Y	Y
Personal information must be collected for specified legitimate purpose	Y	Y	Y	Y	Y	Y	Y	Y	Y	Y	Y	Y
Individuals have right of access to inspect personal information	Y	Y	Y	Y	Y	Ya	Y	Y	Y	Y	Y	Y
Sensitive personal details specified (collection only with data subject's knowledge and consent)	N	N	Y	Y	Y	N	Y	N	Y	Y	Y	Y

Key: Y=Yes, N=No

a   Covers information concerning private affairs, such as financial situation of individuals.
b   Covers information on an individual's personal status, intimate affairs, economic position, and vocational qualifications.
c   Collection of personal data limited unless it is "natural part of the normal operations of an enterprise."
d   Personal information collection is permissible if it serves the purpose of a contractual relationship or there is a legitimate interest in (a business) storing it
e   State laws may be enacted that for personal data maintained by the public sector.

Source: Pipe, R. Westin, A.F., *"Employee Monitoring in Other Industrialized Democracies," report prepared for Office of Technology Assessment; Oz, E., Ethics for the Information Age. Wm. C. Brown, Dubuque, IA 1994.*

Table 3: Activities Facing Difficulties

Use of personal data for target marketing
Use of employee data to improve human resource management in MNCs and international hiring
Online crossborder examination of credit-worthiness
Business Electronic Data Interchange (EDI)
Consolidation of financial and accounting information of MNCs

An increasing number of American, European, and Asian companies use Electronic Data Interchange (EDI). The ease of use of Web browsers, and the developing XML (Extensible Markup Language) standard make EDI more affordable and easier to use for many businesses around the world. However, crossborder EDI is limited due to restrictions imposed by data privacy laws.

Finally, MNCs must submit consolidated financial reports. The task would be significantly easier if data privacy and other restrictive laws were relaxed.

CONCLUSION

Although most of the technological hurdles have been removed and the Internet can facilitate freer flow of data across national borders, there are still barriers to such transfer. Connectivity to the Internet, which has become the major means of communication in recent years, is still limited in certain parts of the world. Both the small number of Internet servers and the narrow bandwidth of links in China, India, East European countries, and most of Africa, restrict the ability of business parties to exchange information.

Political restriction on the flow of information do exist. This prevents individuals from receiving not only business-related information, but also educational and entertainment information.

While English is the *Lingua Franca* of the Web, the number of non-English speaking Web surfers is growing faster than the number of English speaking surfers. Companies must pay attention and replicate their sites in multiple languages. They must also provide information such as metrics, addresses, and dates in different formats.

Cultural differences force companies to be doubly cautious about the information they transmit, especially through public networks such as the Internet. Executives mush be sensitive to the customs and gestures of many nations and ethnic groups, not only those within the borders of the country from which they operate.

However, the greatest hurdle to crossborder data transfer seems to be legal. The disharmony of privacy and data protection laws among countries does not allow the free flow of such data, which is vital in marketing, credit granting, and other commercial activities. The greatest gap appears to be the one between the two largest markets: the U.S., which allows private organizations much freedom with respect to personal data, and the European Union, which restricts the collection, maintenance, use, and dissemination of personal data.

Mini Case: A Balancing Act

Unlike many other Chinese entrepreneurs, 31-year-old Wang Zhidong does not count on personal connections in the corridors of China's bureaucracy to promote his ideas. The electrical engineer by training believes that because the Chinese government is becoming increasingly normalized, personal connections are becoming less and less important. The son of a poor teacher in a rural region of this huge nation, he loved computers from childhood. When studying engineering at Beijing University, he became a programming whiz. When he graduated, he decided to exploit the emerging free market environment.

At the age of 24, he teamed up with two partners to found Suntendy, a software company. Two years later he left the partners to start another company. This one attracted the attention of Duan Yong Ji, an investor in Hong Kong. The investor devoted half a million dollars to the new company, Stone Rich Sight

Mini Case .... Continued.

(SRS). The most popular product of the new company is RichWin, a Chinese-language interface for Windows. They sold 800,000 copies of it.

The Chinese government has established experimental zones in which business people are more free to practice capitalism in a manner that is closer to that of the Western world. SRS is located in one such zone in Beijing. (Another notable zone is close to Hong Kong.) Wang's strategy has been to form partnerships with other Web site providers, including state media enterprises. This way, his company can enjoy the fruits of connections with government officials, without directly dealing with them. This is important to him, because he, like many observers, believes that the political environment will eventually change, and he does not wish to be labeled politically when that happens. So far, SRS has succeeded in traversing the dangerous waters.

In 1997, SRS, received $6.5 million in venture capital from U.S. backers. In June 1998, Wang decided to focus his efforts on the Internet. Software piracy in China is commonplace. SRS' Web site was already visited by more than one million per day, giving it the second largest amount of Web traffic of any Chinese-language site in the world. He wanted to take advantage of this fact. In November of 1998, SRS merged with a Californian firm called Sina.com, which had become the most popular site for Chinese who reside outside China. The combined sites, known as Sinanet, get more traffic than any other Chinese-language site.

Political sensitivity to the merger is interesting. Mass media in Hong Kong and Taiwan described the merger as a takeover of a pro-Taiwanese Internet company by a mainland China firm. Apparently, the Chinese government had another perspective, because Sinanet's homepage is blocked in China most of the time. So as not to anger the Chinese government, Sinanet maintains separate home pages for its People's Republic of China, U.S., Taiwanese, and Hong Kong markets. Its plan is to build locally oriented, full-service portals that combine the search index features of Yahoo with the content services of America Online (AOL), all in Chinese.

For the China site, Wang negotiates with many content providers—magazines, newspapers, television stations, and other media. In the future, he plans to charge subscription fees for access to these links. He also wants to add e-commerce and Internet telephony capability to the site. Currently, the bulk of revenue comes from advertising, and most of the advertisements come from U.S. and Taiwanese corporations. Wang is trying to raise tens of millions of dollars from investors to further develop the site.

Source: Ryan, J., "China.com," The Industry Standard, January 25, 1999, pp. 32–38.

STUDY QUESTIONS

1. Consider three world regions: Europe, Asia, and the U.S. What cultural differences cause different attitudes toward protection of personal data?

2. Write an essay on the adjustments that may be made by IS when businesses from the U.S. communicate with business (or units of the same company) from another country due to different standards: date format, length and weight measures, address format, and any other standards.

3. Write an essay on restrictions on Web publishing in different countries. For each country, emphasize what the reason for such restriction is: political, social, or another reason.

4. Research the data protection issues between the U.S. and the European Union. Research recent and pending legislation in the U.S. Is the EU approach to privacy getting closer that of the U.S., or is it the other way around? Corroborate your answer with facts.

5. To alleviate the challenge for U.S. company doing business with European Union (EU) countries, the EU agreed with the U.S. federal government on a "safe harbor" arrangement. Explain what this term means. Visit the FTC site that lists the U.S. companies participating in this arrangement. How successful has the arrangement been? What are the reasons for such success or failure?

6. Some companies seek worldwide business through their Web sites but do not localize sites. What does localization mean in this context? Some companies do a better job with their sites: they "glocalize." What does this mean? Give at least one example of a "glocalized" B-2-C site.

REFERENCES

Coombe, G.,W., Jr., Kirk, S.L., "Privacy, data protection, and transborder data flow: A corporate response to international expectations,' *The Business Lawyer*, Vol 39, November 1983, pp. 33-66.

Oz, E., *Management Information Systems, 2nd edition*, 2000, Course Technology, Inc., Cambridge, MA.

11

Competencies, Capabilities and Information Technology: Analyzing Resources for Competitive Advantage in Russia

Kalle Kangas
Pori School of Technology and Economics &
Turku School of Economics and Business Administration, Finland

ABSTRACT

This chapter argues that the traditional value chain and industry cluster analysis approaches appear to be obsolete for assessing the competitive edge of a firm in the new global information economy. The author proposes the use of a resource-based view (RBV) to identify core competencies and capabilities of a firm, and validates a framework to be used as a tool to analyze them. The proposed approach is utilized to analyze the core competencies and capabilities of a Finland-based firm that trades with Russia and to illustrate the potential role of information technology. The approach stops short of offering prescriptions to develop new competencies; but the conclusions suggest (i) that the framework be developed to provide insights into organizational development over time and (ii) that the role of IT in building new competencies be given more attention by researchers.

INTRODUCTION

Until the 1990's, East-West trade between Finnish companies and Soviet trade organizations was conducted at an inter-governmental level. After the collapse of the Soviet Union, Finnish firms faced new challenges in dealing with the newly independent countries in this region. As far as Russia is concerned, three trends had to be taken into account: (i) social and cultural turbulence, including rising expectations of the people, (ii) the slow and uneven transition from a planned to a market economy, and (iii) the deployment of military technology for civilian use. The political, social and economic turmoil following an era of stagnation drove Russia's business environment and institutions from a strict hierarchy toward slowly evolving market-driven structures. Modern market capitalism, although sought as a goal, appears to be decades away. Russians, after all, are trying to build a market economy system from scratch--an achievement that took the Western world centuries to accomplish.

Turning now to the organization context, businesses--particularly in competitive, more market-driven environments--need to manage their resources efficiently and effectively. This is particularly true for *information* resources. 'Information Resources Management' (IRM), i.e., the design, implementation, management and control of information resources (Reponen et al., 1995; Kangas, 1997), becomes a vital means for business transactions in companies where products and communication become "informated". Operators in the international market often perform occasional one-time transactions through electronic devices with their business partners. In today's digital economy, extensions of the traditional intra-firm value chain (Porter, 1985) concept are emerging. These value chains could be described as customer-centered "wheels of fortune" chains that happen more by coincidence than by plan or design. This means that there is a need to build a one-time value chain for almost every transaction. This chain is ephemeral and dissolves once the transaction has been conducted.

The traditional value chain and industry cluster analysis (Porter, 1985) approaches appear to be obsolete in the new information economy. In a study of a networked global Japanese trading house Viitanen (1998) argues that industry dynamics do not count so much any more in a global network organization. He also says that discussion about centralization and decentralization, i.e. discussion about the structure of the firm, is purely academic, and has no practical value in that kind of organization. It is nonetheless important to understand how firms create and sustain competitive advantage in today's digital economy. New methods of competitive analysis and competence building must be found. Promising approaches in this regard include: (i) the resource-based theory of the firm and its implications for strategic management; (ii) the relationship between organizational learning and competitive advantage; and (iii) the role of information technology in these endeavors. These approaches can also be applied to areas of foreign trade in the newly established and reorganized eastern European economies, where technical capabilities are scarce, costly and of low caliber.

This chapter seeks to address these issues by using the aforementioned approaches. To do this, it:

(i)   Discusses some of the main approaches 20th century to the micro-economic theories of the firm

(ii)   Validates a framework based on the resource-based theory of the firm (Penrose, 1959, 1985, 1995) to best suit the present environment;

(iii)   Discusses implications of the resource-based theory for strategic management, and the relationship between organizational learning and capabilities;

(iv)   Analyzes a case study to demonstrate how a tool based on the resource-based theory can be used to evaluate a firm's competencies. It is shown below how such a tool, initially used to identify such competencies, can then contribute to providing IT solutions to support these competencies.

THEORETICAL BACKGROUND

Background on Theory Testing through a Single Case Study

The discussion here rests on Järvinen's (1999) review of theory testing case research, based on the articles of Markus (1983), Lee (1989) and Cunningham (1997). Cunningham (1997) discusses variations in case studies. However, the most relevant for dealing with the case study in this chapter is Lee's (1989) paper. In the paper, Lee discusses science generally, and the methodological problems arising from studying only a single case. He discusses his scientific method through a review of Markus's (1983) study.

Without going deeper into the contents of the three papers, one main issue arises from Lee's paper; his discussion on science, which emphasizes the Popperian idea that besides the validity of a theory, there are three other requirements in connection with the deductive testing of theories (Järvinen, 1999):

1)   The theory must be logically consistent; i.e., the deductions derived from the theory have to be consistent with each other.

2)   The theory must be at least as explanatory, or predictive, as any other competing theory.

3)   The theory must survive actual attempts of falsification.

All these contingencies will be discussed at the summary of the presentation of case A. Lee (1989) also discusses four problems involved in single case studies. These include:

1)   *Making controlled observations*; these are seldom possible in real world social investigations, where, for example, statistical tests seem to give less information than qualitative methods.

2)   *Making controlled deductions*; although natural science requires these, it is impossible to be sure whether a qualitatively deduced finding is wrong or not.

3)   *Allowing for replicability*; most organizational inquiries are usually one- time phenomena, in which at least part of the attributes constantly change, and thus it is impossible to create exactly the same conditions for replication.

4)   *Allowing for generalizability*; opposite to nomothetic theories of natural science, qualitative single case settings are unique and non-replicable, and thus their generalization is vulnerable.

The above therefore suggests that evidence acquired through qualitative case studies cannot be called a replication of the original test but rather *new* observations of the phenomena under scrutiny.

The above reasoning sets the background for the rest of the chapter. The following discussion concerning micro-economic theories of the firm as well as the case example at the end of the chapter serve to: on the first hand, validate the framework, and on the other hand visualize the practicability of the theoretical the theoretical discussion here.

Some Notions from the Micro-Economic Theory

Two broad outlines of strategic theory development have proved to be useful. The first is strategy formulation research stemming from economics. The second is strategy implementation research, which has its roots more organization theory, sociology and psychology. (Cf. Seth and Thomas, 1994) Of course, strict economic theory and management theory have different research traditions, but it is sometimes worthwhile to combine them. Barney (1996) suggests this. He says that: "Many books and articles seem to adopt the fiction that it is possible to study strategy formulation and strategy implementation independently. This is obviously incorrect. It would be clearly be a mistake for firms to formulate their strategies without considering how they were going to implement those strategie*s*."

The classic Ricardian economics assumed land to be the most important factor of value. However, in the digital economy land does not have that significant a value, nor do most other forms of tangible capital. Dynamic knowledge has They have been replaced by to be the most valuable factor.

<u>The Neoclassical Theory</u>: The neoclassical theory, which is part of the wider theory of value, sees the firm basically as an input/output process. The firm exists for producing end products through combining resources, i.e. through putting together two inputs: labor and capital. The scope and scale is determined by the extent to which the firm owns the rights to the productive services of the inputs (Alchian & Demsetz, 1972).

The neoclassical theory is based on the perfect competition model, which Shepherd (1990, 31) describes as having the following attributes: Perfect knowledge by all participants;

Perfect mobility of resources and participants; Rational behavior by all participants; Stability of the underlying preferences, technology, and surroundings; No nonmarket interdependencies among consumers or producers; Pure competition on both sides on every market.

The attributes above lead to a situation where firms are identical: each firm is equally able to obtain exactly the right input, and an input's price equals the input's marginal productive value to the firm. "Thus the individual firm's ambition to maximize its profits yields a market equilibrium of zero economic returns to each firm". (Conner, 1991; 123) This in turn leads to a zero-sum game in the market, and a static view of competition.

The Bain Type Competition Model: The Bain type competition model involves restraining other firm's outputs. This can happen through exercising monopoly power or by colluding with them. It says that a large firm can exercise monopolistic behavior because they are most likely to control substantial proportions of industry output. The firm's conduct is determined by its industry's structure, as well as by the firm's size and its industry's concentration. Seth and Thomas (1994) therefore call the model the traditional Bain-Mason structure-conduct-performance paradigm of early industrial organization economics. The main difference in the Bain model to the neoclassical theory is that its focus is on the theory of market structure not the theory of price.

Both theories treat the firm as a "black box", and do not discuss firm heterogeneity within an industry, except concerning scale. (Seth and Thomas 1994) In addition, both theories treat the "outside world" very much as given. However, the ontological stances of most contemporary strategy research approaches start from the idea that the firm is surrounded by a variety environmental variables. Of these, some the firm can control, some not. As Seth and Thomas (1994) put it: "An organization is a purposive and entrepreneurial entity with specialized unique resources which interacts with its environment to maintain long-term viability"(p. 167). They say further that "a theory of the firm must be consistent with these elements to serve as a useful backdrop for strategy research" (Ibid.). Put together, the above leads to an idea that neoclassical theory and the Bain type competition model have limited relevance for strategy research.

New Industrial Economics: As already seen above, the traditional industrial economic theories of the firm do not fit very well into strategy research. That is because of their static nature, and their view of environment, which they treat as given. Therefore, other theories have to be explored. Seth and Thomas (1994) suggest that the focus should be turned to the structure and behavior of firms. This, they say, also blurs the boundaries between strict economic theory and the more management-oriented strategic discussion. By that they mean a systematic and rigorous way to analyze the structure and behavior of the firm.

Such a theory is game theory. It offers a mathematical way to analyze competition between competitors, all of whose decisions immediately affect the behavior of other players. During the game, all players have symmetry and completeness of information concerning outcomes. The goal of the game is to maximize individual payoffs. The basic concept of a game is that that all players try to maximize their payoffs through taking advantage of their best strategy. This kind of strategy combination is called Nash equilibrium - "where each player has an optimal strategy such that a unilateral change by any single player cannot possibly improve his/her profit" (Seth and Thomas, 1994: 172)

The game-theoretic models emphasize managerial rationality and motivation. "The profit maximization assumption of these models implies that decision-makers are assumed to be rational and are subject to no uncertainty, i.e. that the environment can be predicted with perfect foresight and managers have unlimited information-processing ability." (Seth and Thomas, 1994: 173) However, Nash equilibrium, and managerial rationality through perfect certainty of the environment, leads to a zero-sum game, where there is no place for the market to grow or to change – through, for example, managerial entrepreneurship. Thus they treat the world as given, and cannot envisage a situation in which all firms in an industry could create competitive advantage simultaneously.

The Behavioral Theory of the Firm: The next theory is the behavioral theory of the firm. It argues that organizations should be viewed as collections of individuals with multiple goals, who operate in a defined structure of authority. (Simon, 1957) Simon claimed that managers have bounded rationality when facing uncertainty, and that behavioral rules replace profit maximizing. One of the rules is called "satisficing", meaning that instead of maximizing profit, the firm tries to achieve a satisfactory level of profit.

An extension of the behavioral theory of the firm is the evolutionary theory of economic change. (Nelson and Winter, 1982) This theory seeks to explain disequilibrium, not the behavior of the firm. The decision-making rules are characterized by certain routines acquired by adaptive memory that is, though, incomplete. These routines involve standard operating procedures, search behavior, and investment behavior. Those firms that select the best combination of routines survive and prosper.

The rule-following and routine-based nature of behavioral theories of the firm suggest their contribution lies more on the operational side, and thus have little to add to the strategic discussion.

Agency Theory: Agency theory of the firm arose from the critique against neoclassical theory, and its failure to consider risks. Such risks involve factors preventing costless diffusion of specialized resources. Those factors involve impediments to information transfer, regulatory constraints, managers' competence, and problems in labor, production factors, or output.

The basic idea behind agency theory is that in corporations, stockholders (principals) delegate decision-making authority to managers (agents). However, the utility function curves of agents and principals diverge. This is because the agents are motivated by their self-interest, while principals aim to maximize their prosperity. This divergence of interests is usually called "agency problem".

Several tools are used to lessen the agency problem. Such tools involve monitoring, bonding, and the design of incentive programs. Agency problems cause agency cost, such as monitoring and bonding cost. However, as managers contribute their human capital to the firm, their stake might be even greater than the shareholders. Therefore, in their own interest, managers are likely to reduce agency costs as well. This leads to an idea that there is no real conflict, and thus that agency costs can be treated only as operational issues. As such, agency theory does not seem to offer any contribution to the strategic discussion.

The Industrial Organization Approach – Positioning: Seth and Thomas (1994) say that the industrial organization (IO) approach advocated mainly by Michael Porter originates from game theory. The industrial organization strategy approach has its roots in positioning in academe and in the work by Boston Consulting Group in consulting. These both in turn have long history in applying military strategy in their frameworks. "In this view, strategy reduces to generic positions selected through formalized analyses of industry situations."(Mintzberg and Lampel, 1999, 22).

As already described above, emphasis is placed on the structure of the industry in which the firm is. The strategy-structure-system triad was a revolutionary discovery in the 1920s. Barney (1986) says the strategy concept in the IO approach has been fundamentally unchanged since it was originally developed by Mason in the late 30s and further by Bain in the 50s. It was a wonderful way to describe big companies, and gave a good mental toolkit to govern and coordinate immense conglomerates. But times changed, and companies that had a clear strategy and structure became more systematic and their actions predictable. As, for example, Ghoshal et al. (1999) say, though, machine-like systems of control are not helpful.

Ghoshal et al. (1999) also note that over and above predictability, another issue also causes problems. Companies are wrapped in the grip of theories, which are part of their problems. Theories have dominated managerial discourse for the whole 20ᵗʰ century, starting from F. W. Taylor's scientific management, up to today. In short, the theory of positioning means grabbing everything oneself and preventing anyone else from doing the same. In order to do this, managers must prevent free competition by all means, and that happens at the cost of social welfare.

Another point in Porter's theory is that it emphasizes competition between industry clusters. (Porter, 1985; 1998; 2001) As long as any cluster has competitive advantage, so have all the firms within that cluster. This however leads to predictable, systematic strategic solutions. On the other hand, though, if all firms enjoy competitive advantage, over whom do they enjoy it?

Transaction Cost Theory: Transaction cost theory, which sees "firms as avoiders of the cost of markets exchange" (Conner, 1991, 130) is said to provide "the market failures framework" (Seth & Thomas, 1994, 180). It originally arose from the early work of the 1991 Nobel Laureate Ronald H. Coase's (1937) critique of neoclassical theory, and more generally the price mechanism and value-based economic thought. In his paper, he emphasized market behavior and the firm's governance structure, in contrast to traditional theories' input/processes of land and capital approach. Coase's general idea was that firms and market are alternative methods for coordinating production, (Conner, 1991), with the firm seen as a chasm (nexus) of contracts.

The production coordination is made by some authority (entrepreneur) who is allowed to direct resources so that costs for operating the market and marketing are minimized. "The firm exists to avoid (economize on) the cost of conducting the same exchange between autonomous contractors". (Conner, 1991; 131) The authority's responsibility is to negotiate contracts so that this becomes possible.

Williamson (1975, 1989, 1993) extends Coase's (1937) idea of the existence of the firm for avoiding cost of using market price mechanism (customary in economics (Williamson, 1993)). He claims that particular attention has to be given to situations with opportunistic behavior. Such situations involve simultaneous occurrence of the following conditions: asset specificity, small number of transactors, and imperfect information. (Conner, 1991; Barney, 1996) "Opportunistic behavior is any action engaged in by an exchange partner, enjoying an informational (or some other) advantage, to exploit that advantage to the economic detriment of others". (Barney and Ouchi, 1986; 19) According to Williamson (1975, 1989), firms exist when all the above conditions are filled, i.e., opportunistic potential is significant.

Ghoshal et al. (1999) have also strongly criticized transaction cost economics. They say that the answer given by the proponents of transaction cost economics to the question "why do firms exist" is that companies exist because the market fails. Ghoshal et al. (1999) say that accepting this is dangerous and leads to an assumption that markets represent some sort of ideal way to organize economic activities.

The transaction cost theory emphasizes static rather than dynamic efficiencies. Static efficiency tries to exploit existing resources as effectively as possible. Innovations creating new options and resources create dynamic efficiencies. In insisting that companies are actually second-rate postures of market mechanisms, the transaction cost view locks companies into the market logic of static efficiency. (Ghoshal et al., 1999; 18)

There is a further problem in applying the transaction cost theory. It does not fit well with strategic management. It is too normative for that. It applies well for designing or examining, for example, state of the art processes. But when it is applied to creating new organizational knowledge, it seems to fail.

The Resource-Based View of the Firm: The theory of the growth of the firm (Penrose, 1955; 1959; 1985; 1995), or resource-based theory (Conner, 1991), was developed by Edith Penrose in the 1950s. Seth & Thomas (1994) see it as part of the theory of value, and a descendant of neoclassical theory. It has also been called the resource-based approach (Mahoney & Pandian, 1992; Robins & Wiersema, 1995), resource-based model (Barney, 1991); and resource-based perspective (Foss, 1998). Penrose (1995) claims that although the analysis in the theory concentrates on industrial firms, it may well apply to other firms too.

Penrose's (1959) original theory notes that in order for a firm to exist it has to grow continuously. She claims that a business firm is both an administrative organization and a collection of productive resources. "The administrative structure of the firm is the creation of the men who run it; the structure may have developed rather haphazardly in response to immediate needs as they rose in the past or it may have been shaped largely by conscious attempts to achieve a 'rational' organization" (Penrose, 1959, 31)

A firm is thus "a collection of human and physical resources bound together in an administrative framework, the boundaries of which are determined by the area of 'administrative coordination' and 'authoritative communication'" (Penrose 1995, 7). She also notes that: "Strictly speaking, it is never resources themselves that are 'inputs' in the production process, but only the services that the resources can render"(Penrose, 1959, 25). The distinction between resources and services is not their relative duration. Resources consist of a bundle of potential services and can, for the most part, be defined independently of their use, while the word "service" implies a function or an activity. This means that the services yielded by resources are a function of the way which they are used.

Bartlett and Ghoshal (1993) describe a large firm's management's reduction from a hierarchical multi-layered structure to an organization of business units with front line managers (manager entrepreneurs). This includes small teams, in touch with customers, and backed up by a layer of middle management in a supportive role. This type of management is based on strongly manipulative but supportive guidance and advice from higher line management. (Penrose, 1995) However, "the very nature of the firm requires that the existing responsible officials of the firm at least know and approve, even if they do not in detail control all aspects of, the plans and operations of the firm" (Penrose, 1959, 45).

External inducements include growing demand of particular products, changes in technology, discoveries and inventions, special opportunities in market positions, as well as changes, which might affect the firm's existing operations. External obstacles include keen competition in markets for particular products, existence of patent rights and other restrictions on the use of knowledge and technology, and entry costs, as well as shortage of resources. Internal inducements arise from the existence of a pool of unused resources and special knowledge. Internal obstacles arise when some specialized types of services are not available in sufficient amounts internally, e.g., managerial capacity or technical skills.

Conclusions from the Above Discussion: All theories, except one, are rather static. They treat the economic world as rather static, and as a zero-sum game, where all the cards have already been dealt. Competition in this kind of static environment is somewhat superficial. Most firms are striving to gain competitive advantages over others; however, only a few enjoy it. Resource-based theory is dynamic and allows firms to keep growing for ever. By implication, an economy can also keep growing for ever.

The strategy-structure-system trilogy was a revolutionary discovery in the 1920s. It was a wonderful way to describe big companies and gave a good mental toolkit to govern and coordinate immense conglomerates. But times changed, companies that had a clear strategy and structure became more systematic and their actions predictable, and machine-like systems of control are not helpful any more. (Ghoshal et al., 1999)

The shift to a new paradigm in the digital economy can only happen through organizational learning, which is enabled only through a dynamic view of the firm and entrepreneurship. From the ones described above, the only theory of the firm to make this possible is the resource-based theory. Therefore, the resource-based management and its concomitants, competence- and capabilities-based management, should be studied more thoroughly in connection with strategy formulations.

RESOURCES AND COMPETITIVE ADVANTAGE

Barney (1991a) claims that whenever identical firms populate an industry, any one firm cannot enjoy sustained competitive advantage. This is also true even if a firm is a 'first mover' (e.g., Lieberman & Montgomery, 1988). It cannot have sustained competitive advantage unless the firms in its industry are heterogeneous in terms of the resources they control. On the other hand, even when the firms in an industry are perfectly homogenous, such firms may collectively be able to obtain sustained competitive advantage over firms in other industries as long as there are strong entry or mobility barriers. Where such barriers do exist, this sustained advantage will be reflected in above normal economic performance for these firms (Porter, 1980). Barney (1991a) assumes that barriers to entry and mobility only exist when competing firms are heterogeneous in terms of the strategically relevant resources they control. The resource-based view thus takes the value chain logic (Porter, 1985) a step further by examining the attributes that resources identified by value chain analysis must posses in order to be sources of sustained competitive advantage.

Barney (1991a) discusses four indicators of a firm's resources that generate sustained competitive advantage:

Value: Can the firm's resources respond to environmental opportunities and/or threats? Firm's resources can only be a source of sustained competitive advantage when they are valuable, meaning that they enable a firm to conceive of or implement strategies that improve its efficiency and effectiveness.

Rareness: How many competing firms already possess these valuable resources? Some strategies require a particular mix of physical capital, human capital, and organizational capital (immaterial) resources in order to be implemented.

Imitability: Are these resources costly to imitate? Imitation can be done through duplication or substitution (e.g., through strategic alliances). Costliness depends on any or a combination of the following issues: (i) whether there is a complex history as to the creation of a given resource; (ii) whether a resource involves numerous 'small decisions' in its creation; and (iii) whether the resources are very complex socially, e.g., involving many stakeholders.

Supportive Organizational Arrangements: Do organizational arrangements support and exploit resources? Within this context, the emphasis is on managerial and organizational resources. Organizational resources include close interpersonal relationships among managers, which in turn enhance mutual trust, reduce monitoring cost and enhance the search for new opportunities.

Barney, in analyzing sources of competitive advantage (1991a), makes two further assumptions that contradict traditional accounts (e.g., industry cluster analysis by Porter, 1985) as to how a firm's resource homogeneity and mobility create such advantage:

(i)   Firms within an industry (or group) may be heterogeneous with respect to the strategic resources they control;

(ii)   These resources may not be totally mobile across firms, and thus heterogeneity can be long lasting.

The implications of these two assumptions are examined in the context of Barney's VRIO framework - Value, Rareness, Imitability, and Organization - as depicted in Figure 1.

Valuable?	Rare?	Costly to Imitate?	Efficiently Organized?	Competitive Implications
no	--	--	No	competitive disadvantage
yes	No	--		competitive parity
yes	Yes	no		temporary competitive
yes	Yes	yes	Yes	sustained competitive advantage

Figure 1: The VRIO Framework
for evaluating the competitive positioning of a firm's resources and capabilities.
Adapted from Barney (1994)

In the case study, this VRIO-framework has been utilized to analyze competencies of a firm, as perceived by its managers engaged in Russian trade. It has to be noted that these perceptions are ex-ante accounts of the present state, and thus they are static. The next section articulates the role of information technology in support of organizational competencies and capabilities.

COMPETENCIES, CAPABILITIES AND INFORMATION TECHNOLOGY

Organizational *competencies* refer to the unique knowledge owned by the firm. Firms are presumed to focus on a few key or core competencies, which they can exploit effectively to their competitive advantage. For Rumelt (1994), the concept of core competencies relates directly to the resource-based framework. As such, the competitive advantage of a firm is determined not only by the industry or environment but also by its possession of unique skills, knowledge and resources (competencies). This can be seen as complementary to market structure analysis, as captured by the seminal competitive forces model by Porter (1990).

In the work of Rumelt (1994), 'corporate core competence'--the concept developed by Prahalad and Hamel (1990)--is taken to include:

1. **Corporate span.** Core competencies span [several] business [functions] and products within a corporation. Put differently, powerful core competencies [can] support several products and businesses.

2. **Temporal dominance.** Products are but momentary expression of a corporation's core competencies. Competencies are more stable and evolve more slowly than do products.

3. **Learning-by-doing.** Competencies are gained and enhanced by work. Prahalad and Hamel (1990, p. 82) say that 'core competencies are the collective learning in the organization, especially how to coordinate diverse production skills and integrate multiple streams of technologies. ... Core competence does not diminish with use ... competencies are enhanced as they are applied and share*d'*.

4. **Competitive locus.** Product-market competition is merely a superficial expression of a deeper competition over competencies. (Rumelt, 1994, p. xv-xvi)

Organizational *capabilities* refer to the firm's ability to *use* its competencies. They represent the collective tacit knowledge of the firm in responding to its environment. Capabilities are developed by combining and using resources with the aid of organizational routines, i.e., those specific ways of doing what the organization has developed and learned. Capability development therefore involves organizational learning. This learning takes place within the context of the firm and is thus path-dependent and firm specific; as a consequence, it is impossible to imitate and may thus create competitive advantage. Core capabilities are thus those that differentiate a company strategically in term of beneficial behaviors that will not be observed in its competitors. Such capabilities evolve from the competitive environment and business mission of the firm through a 'capability learning loop' (Andreu & Ciborra, 1996). As these authors put it: *"Core capabilities clarify their role and scope through acquiring a sense of why they are important"* (Andreu & Ciborra, 1996, p. 112). From the above reasoning, one can conclude that core capabilities are important - or, in Barney's terms, 'valuable' They are firm specific, thus heterogeneously distributed across competing firms, and are path-dependent and thus imperfectly mobile. The consequence of this is that core capabilities are sources of sustained competitive advantage (Andreu & Ciborra, 1996).

Sanchez, Heene & Thomas (1996) posit that as the combining of "internal" and "external" environments is of a systemic nature, it is hard to identify strict borders between the "in" and "out" in the analysis of a specific case In a similar analysis, Sanchez, Heene & Thomas (1996) say that firms can be distinguished by (i) distinctive strategic goals, (ii) strategic logic, (iii) resources available, and (iv) the coordination of resources' deployment. A firm's management processes provide the mechanisms for coordinating and directing its resources under the governance of strategic logic. A firm achieves competence when it is able to sustain coordinated deployment of resources in ways that help it to pursue its goals. This pursuit takes place through the following dual activities, although these do not have to be complementary in all cases:

Competence leveraging: coordinated deployment of resources that do not require qualitative changes in the resources or in the mode of their coordination.

Competence building: acquisition or use of qualitatively different resources or modes of coordination.

It thus follows that competence-based competition is based on:

(i)   Dynamic single loop learning (See e.g., Argyris & Schön, 1978) processes of coordinating and leveraging organizational processes (e.g., current or new market opportunities) into competencies without qualitative changes in existing stock of assets and capabilities (changing only the way of acting, not the underlying assumptions).

(ii)   Dynamic double-loop learning (See e.g., Argyris & Schön, 1978) processes of coordinating and building competencies, with qualitative changes in existing stocks of assets and capabilities (changing the way of acting, as well as the underlying assumptions). In this framework "strategic change within a firm is motivated by managers' perceptions of strategic gaps between their firm's current stocks and flows of assets and capabilities ... and the stocks and flows they believe will be needed to achieve the firms goal's in its competitive environment" (Sanchez, Heene & Thomas, 1996).

The link just set out between competencies, capabilities and single and double loop learning highlights the important role that information technology (IT) and telecommunications (TC) could play in the coordination and learning support (automation) of organizational processes and, by implication, competitive advantage.

The issues involved here are by no means straightforward. Barney (1991), for instance, questions the claim that information systems are a source of sustained competitive advantage. For him, this very much depends on the type of system involved. He contends that machines--be they computers or otherwise--are part of the physical technology of a firm, and usually can be bought across markets. As such, any strategy that exploits just the machines (computers) in themselves is likely to be imitable and thus not a source of sustained competitive advantage.

Mata et al. (1995), in their resource-based analysis, found that out of four attributes of IT--capital requirements, proprietary technology, technical IT skills, and managerial IT skills--managerial IT skills is the only resource that can bring sustained competitive advantage. Keen (1991) comes to similar conclusions, stating that while IT may be a commodity, *IT management* is not--it is the value-added element that *leads to* competitive advantage. Mata et al. (1995) point out, of course, that we cannot consider the other three attributes unimportant, since they may still produce, admittedly temporary, competitive advantage. Mata et al.'s analysis suggests that IT managers should work closely with other managers within the firm to support their information needs. It must be recognized that the information needs of various stakeholders vary in different types of firms depending on the firm's industry, resources and structure.

Mata et al.'s findings suggest two factors that can contribute effectively to gaining sustained competitive advantage:
(1)   Developing methods for strategy generation involving information resources management that emphasize and enforce the learning of these skills across the whole organization.
(2)   Developing shared goals within the whole organization.

Andreu & Ciborra (1996) have also come to similar conclusions in their resource-based discussion, combining IT, organizational learning, and core capabilities development. The author views IT as a central support for routinization and capability learning loops. Moreover, IT is also seen as instrumental in making capabilities become core Andreu & Ciborra (1996, pp. 124-125) also suggest four guidelines if IT is to play a key role in making core competencies and capabilities really count for a firm:

•   *Look out for IT applications that help to make capabilities rare.* An example of this could be the American Airlines computerized reservation system (e.g., see: Copeland & McKenney, 1988), which, at least at the beginning, was unique and thus rare.
•   *Concentrate on IT applications that make capabilities valuable.* Rosenbluth travel agency could be an example of this (e.g., see: Clemons & Row, 1991).

- *Identify capabilities that are difficult to imitate.* This also points to the American Airlines case (Copeland & McKenney, 1988) where systems were complex and thus difficult to imitate.
- *Concentrate on IT applications with no clear strategically equivalent substitutes.* Sometimes certain functionality can only be achieved by means of particular IT applications. Thus IT contributes to the lack of substitution. An example of this could be WWW-pages where the producer has included certain features that can only be viewed on specific browser versions.

Andreu & Ciborra (1996) go on to provide a list of issues where IT-based support for capability creation is feasible. This includes:

- *Supporting the firm's capabilities learning process (capability learning loop).*
- *Supporting the sharing of capabilities.*
- *Facilitating reflection, experimentation and training on routines and capabilities.*
- *Supporting and enabling capability diffusion.*
- *Using IT applications that provide information about the competitive environment.*
- *Using IT applications that disseminate the business mission.*

Having discussed the resource-based view of organizational capabilities and competencies, and how these can be supported by IT, we will now apply the ideas and concepts to analyze the case of Russian trade in this case study.

THE CASE EXAMPLE FOR VALIDATING THE THEORETICAL ASSUMPTIONS

The case that follows reviews perceptions of core capabilities of the Moscow-based office of a Finnish firm. The Finnish company in question is (in Finnish terms) a large multidivisional conglomerate, with subsidiaries, joint ventures and subsidiary companies all over the world. At the time of the study, the corporate turnover was over US$ 10 billion. Although it is diversified in terms of its products, its raw materials differ little across divisional lines. It started its operations in the ex-Soviet area during the "USSR era" of the 1940's. Russian trade forms a considerable part of its total operations, and an even bigger part of its profits. As the Vice President of Russian affairs (Head of the representative office) put it: *"Our turnover here is 20% of the whole, but our profits are about 30%".* The company's headquarters (corporate management and the top management of the divisions) are located in Southern Finland (see Figure 2). Although purchasing and distribution operations are spread around Russia, the only offices are in Moscow and St. Petersburg.

The company is hierarchically managed, with a multidivisional M-form corporation (e. g., see: Williamson, 1975). The official corporate structure is depicted in Figure 2. There are also traces of a matrix structure (e.g., see: Morgan 1989, and an entrepreneurial firm (e. g., see: Mintzberg & Quinn, 1996). The corporate organization involves:

- Divisions, industries or companies within a company, with high levels of independence-- each having subsidiaries all over the world, own strategies, and own specialized information systems covering their worldwide transactions.
- A corporate organization of top management. The corporate organization acts as an umbrella for corporate issues, and provides several support services, such as corporate planning, accounting and finance as well legal. The corporate information systems include common systems, such as accounting, corporate databases and corporate network

architecture for connecting the various individual systems inside the corporation into a network of knowledge nodes (Jarvenpaa and Ives, 1994).

• Different kinds of temporary organizations and task forces (loosely coupled networks, see Orton & Weick, 1990) that utilize temporary formal and informal information systems, complementing the relatively formal corporate systems.

Foreign companies use different approaches to establishing presence in the Russian market. These range from foreign direct investment (FDI) to salesmen traveling in and out of the country. The typical establishment for the size and type of the case company is a representative office. The representative office for a business organization could be compared to an embassy in the area of diplomacy.

The representative office is directly responsible to the Deputy CEO. It has three functions: Servicing, i.e., taking care of various operational matters such as visas, permits, travel arrangements; dealing with legal issues, i.e., dealing with the society, governmental agencies and private institutions; and local accounting. Consequently, the head of the representative office is the only *local* person formally able to represent the company, e.g., sign contracts in Russia with the Russian counterparts. However, in practice, the divisional subsidiaries have complete autonomy from the representative office when it comes to conducting business transactions in Russia. Their business is functionally managed from their respective divisional headquarters in Finland. In practice, contracts are signed between the Russian party and the respective divisional headquarters in Finland, not the representative office.

Background and Description of the Case Company

At the time of the study, in 1994-95, the total number of staff of the company in Russia was about 20-25 people, including service staff (e. g., cooks, cleaners and drivers). The activities were mainly located in Moscow, although there was an office in St. Petersburg (2-3 people). The clerical staff in Russia consisted of the corporate Moscow representative office, totaling about 10 persons, two business unit profit centers, divisional subsidiaries, one of 7 people and the other of 2-3 people.

Method of Data Gathering

The empirical data were gathered through multiple methods consisting of in-depth interviews and observations, primarily at the Moscow offices. Data collection was accomplished between December 1994 and July 1995, in three 2-week visits to Moscow. The interviewees were the representative office staff, the divisional representatives and temporary project staff. The interviews followed a protocol developed by the author. The protocol included qualitative, opinion-gathering questions. Some conceptions were obtained through company documentation or other sources and validated through interviews (or vice-versa). The data collection protocol was used as a guide for the semi-structured interviews. Due to the multiple stakeholder viewpoints, not all the questions were directly applicable to the interviewees' personal involvement.

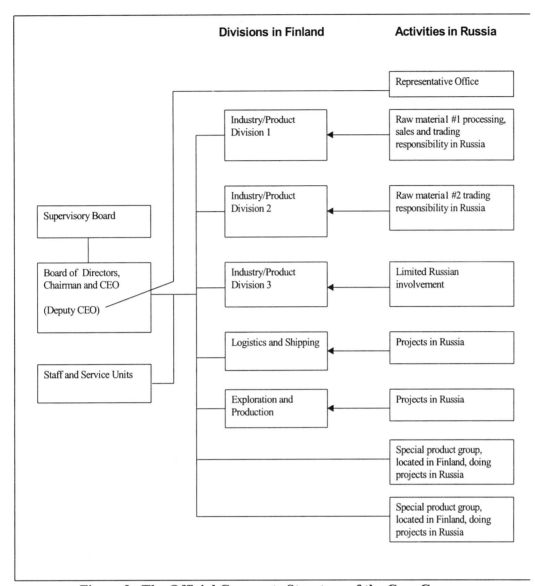

Divisions in Finland   Activities in Russia

Figure 2. The Official Corporate Structure of the Case Company

In addition to the interviews, employee activities were observed. These included the use of computers, electronic communication devices and other non-electronic information devices. The perceptions thus acquired were supplemented and substantiated the company headquarters through interviews with representatives of divisions, strategic units, project management and IS management and through a review of company documents.

All interviews were conducted either in Finnish, German or English. Later, these tape-recorded interviews were translated and transcribed into English. These 50 hours of interviews included 14 people in Moscow, and 18 people in the Finnish headquarters. Additional sources of data consisted of company documents, documentations from several observations and minutes of various meetings. The most important of sources were the tape recorded and transcribed interviews in Moscow. Interview data was further analyzed, and categorized, with the help of a qualitative data analysis software package NUD*IST™. The data obtained from other sources was used to develop an understanding of the company and its processes. The data regarding competencies and capabilities constitutes only a subset of the total data gathered.

The Company's Information Technology Infrastructure

At the time of the study, the Russian offices were located in an office building in central Moscow, with one divisional office (trading) on one floor, and the representative office and one divisional office on another Both floors had a local network to which all the PCs on the floor were connected. All PCs had Windows™ operating system and an MS-Office™ software package. However, there was no connection between the two floors. The head of the representative office gave the following reason: "*We have discussed the connection to be installed, but the landlord does not allow us to draw the cable through the elevator shaft, neither does he allow us to draw it from outside.*" In short, the functional problem was linked to local control over physical space.

The divisional trading office also had a HP-Desk™ connection to the divisional headquarters in Finland. This connection enabled them to send and receive mail messages from their various divisional offices around the world. However, being a trading office they needed current information about the products, their availability and the prices. The system did not allow them to get this information on-line; instead, it was sent daily as an attachment to E-mail messages and then printed out on paper In that way, Moscow was different from all other five similar offices around the globe that were connected directly to the central computer in Finland.

In the beginning of 1995 the corporate LotusNotes™ system was installed in Moscow. The aim was to update the server in Moscow with the data from the corporate server in Finland once every two days. For telecommunications purposes, the representative office had two direct fiber cable lines connecting to the corporate headquarters in Finland. The phone numbers in the Moscow office thus acted as sub-numbers of the headquarters exchange. Calls could be made from Moscow to anywhere in Finland without using the country code.

When staff were travelling in Russia, telephone and telefax were the only means of communicating with the company offices or customers. They could also use cell-phones in the Moscow area, but not elsewhere in Russia. Some locations could be contacted only with telex, as there were no telefax connections available. As a final option, of course, one could always use the snail mail.

Despite its obvious shortcomings, the company personnel in Russia were content with this situation and at the time of the study did not have any great expectations concerning the use of IT and telecommunications. The head of the representative office (VP of Russian affairs) said:

> *We do not have much use for IT and telecommunications in our external communications here. The Russians prefer face-to-face communication. The Soviet era taught the Russians to be very careful of everything they say on electronic media, because they suspect that the 'big brother' is still watching them. On the other hand at least I feel more comfortable when I do not have to communicate the whole day through all kinds of media. I get much more done, when I only have the phone, and a chance not to answer it.*

The Perceived Core Competencies

The Moscow staff were asked during the study to state their perceptions of the company's core competencies in Russia. They were asked to articulate how the company could perform better than its competitors in Russia. Based on the analysis of the interviews, the following 13 issues were identified as core competencies. The researcher's prior knowledge of the company and its environment proved valuable in identifying and conceptualizing the competencies, and then arranging them into appropriate categories. The categories of competencies are presented in Table 1 and described in detail above.

A) Personal/Management Competencies

1. Knowledge of local customs and "action models" acquired from long presence and operations in the area: "*We have some kind of built in knowledge of how to deal with different situations. We never get stuck with our fingers in the mouth.*" (A member of the trading personnel)
2. Ability to work and develop relations at a personal level: "*I know practically everyone who matters something here.*" (Head of the representative office)
3. Corporate reputation: "*We are seen as honest, sometimes too honest.*" (A member of the trading personnel)
4. Advantages of being Finnish/traditions: Forced by geopolitical realities of being an autonomous grand duchy of the Russian Empire during the 18th century and up to 1917 and the geopolitical realities of the cold war, Finnish businessmen and political leaders developed ways to maximize Finland's western technological competitive advantage on the Russian/Soviet market (Berry, 1987). For example, at the beginning of the 1950's Finnish share of the total Russian Western trade was over 50%. "*Our products have a certain 'Finskij' reputation*"; "*Look at geography and history*". (Head of the representative office)

B) Process-Oriented Competencies

5. Long experience in processing Russian raw materials with special specifications: "*We can do it sometimes even better than the Russians themselves, but certainly better than any other Western competitor.*" (Head of the divisional trading office)
6. Special ability, effectiveness and skillfulness in conducting business: "*When a Finn is here long enough he 'Russifies'. Our whole organization is familiar with local customs and can utilize them effectively.*" (Head of the representative office)

C) Logistics-Oriented Competencies

7. Utilization of the long borderline and common rail tracks between Russia and Finland: Finland is the only member of the European Union to have land border with Russia, altogether 1300 km. The rail track width is about 200 mm wider both in Finland and in the ex-Soviet countries than in the rest of Europe. "*Look at geography.*" (Head of the representative office)
8. Strong knowledge of logistics: "*Even Russians often turn to us for their logistics problems. We also arrange transportation for other Finnish companies.*" (Head of the representative office)

Table 1: Assessment of the perceived core competencies based on the VRIO framework

Perceived Competence	Value	Rareness	Costly to Imitate	Organizational arrangements	Competitive implications
Personal/Management Competencies					
Knowledge of local customs and "action models" that the long presence and co-operation in the area has brought	*	*	*	*/-	Temporary/ sustained
Ability for personal level relations	*	*	--	*	Temporary
Corporate reputation	*	*	*	*	Sustained advantage
Advantages of being Finnish, traditions	*	*	*	*/-	Temporary/ sustained
Process-Oriented Competencies					
Long experience in processing Russian raw materials with special specification	*	*/-	--	*/-	Parity
Special ability, effectiveness and skillfulness to conduct business	*	*	*/-	--	Temporary
Logistics-Oriented Competencies					
Utilization of the long border line and common rail gauge between Russia and Finland	*	--	--	--	Parity
Strong knowledge of logistics	*	*	--	*/-	Temporary
Competencies related to the Corporation					
Industry knowledge	*	*	--	*	Parity
Ability to work across divisional lines	*	*	--	--	Parity
Full value chain	*	*	*/-	*/-	Parity/temporary
Extensive marketing chain	*	*	*/-	*/-	Parity/temporary
Special arrangements in monetary transactions	*	*	*/-	*/-	Parity/temporary

* "yes", existing company capability; -- "no", nonexisting or undefinable company capability; */- "yes/no", not possible to define existing/nonexisting company capability

D)   Competencies related to the Corporation

9. Industry knowledge: "*We have been here so long that we know.*" (Head of the divisional trading office)
10. Ability to work across divisional lines: "*Our company is still small enough, and the Russian business is manned with people who get along and know each other.*" (Head of the representative office)
11. Having full value chain: "*We are the only Western company in the industry who has the whole chain from exploration of raw material to product sales outlets here*" (Head of the representative office)
12. Having extensive marketing channels: "*Our people go even to the strangest places in this country.*" (Marketing person)

13. Special arrangements in monetary transactions: "*Instead of money we can also trade with various goods.*" (Head of the representative office)

Analysis of the Perceptions about Competencies

The perceptions about competencies mentioned in the previous section are discussed below both by category/group as well as in the context of Barney's four indicators of a firm's resources that generate competitive advantage.

A) Personal/management Competencies. These include: knowledge of local customs and "action models" acquired from long presence and operations in the area; ability to work and develop relations at a personal level; corporate reputation and advantages of being Finnish/traditions

Value: All the capabilities in this group are valuable, as they are products of long experience in the area, and thus provide good potential for responding to the changing environment.

Rareness: These capabilities can also be regarded as rare, because they are products of long experience and thus firm specific.

Imitability: All the capabilities are costly to imitate, except the ability to work on personal level relations, which probably can be duplicated or bought.

Supportive organizational arrangements: The ability to work and develop relations at a personal level; and corporate reputation are supported by a strong sense of pride and commitment within the firm. As the deputy head of the representative office put it: "*I have been with the firm for 15 years, and always sensed myself to relate to the other people of the firm. That is a feeling that everybody here is proud of.*"

B) Process-oriented Competencies. These include: long experience in processing Russian raw materials with special specification, special ability, effectiveness and skillfulness in conducting business.

Value: Both capabilities are valuable, because they are outcomes of a long experience in the area and good knowledge of the environment.

Rareness: Within the industrial sector of the case company, there are no foreign competitors who can process the specific raw material the way the Finns can, but of course, there are Russian competitors who can. The special abilities to conduct business are outcomes of the long relations between Finns and Russians, and the company in question is the only Finnish firm in its industry.

Imitability: The processing of knowledge can easily be imitated through merging with or acquiring of a Russian company. The special abilities to conduct business are history dependent, socially complex, and consist of numerous small decisions; as such, they are costly and time consuming to imitate.

Supportive organizational arrangements: At the time of the study in 1995 the processing knowledge was dispersed around three divisions, which meant it was not efficiently organized. Today, in 1998, all this knowledge exists within one division, and so the organization supports it quite well. In contrast, special abilities for conducting business such as being able to sort out essential customers and knowing the way to deal with them—having tacit knowledge (Polanyi, 1967)--are dispersed around the organization, and thus cannot be fully supported.

C) Logistics-related Competencies. These include: the utilization of the long borderline and common rail tracks between Russia and Finland and strong knowledge of logistics.

Value: Given the specific historical situation both competencies are valuable at present, but this is changing fast.

Rareness: The advantages of the common border and rail tracks are unique. The knowledge of both Russian and Western logistics is still rare among both Russian and Western competitors, but is also fast becoming more common.

Imitability: Both capabilities are not very hard to imitate, except, of course, the rail tracks. It is possible, however, for competitors in central Europe to develop efficient ways to change the width of the train axles at eastern European border(s).

Supportive organizational arrangements: The geographical knowledge--long borderline-- is not very efficiently supported by the organization--or actually understood by the people at the corporate headquarters in Finland. On the other hand, knowledge of logistics is well understood throughout the organization, and is thus supported throughout the company.

D) Competencies Related to the Corporation. These include: industry knowledge; ability to work across divisional lines; having full value chain; having extensive marketing channels and special arrangements in monetary transactions.

Value: All capabilities listed can be described as valuable as they respond quite well to the opportunities and threats of the environment.

Rareness: Industry knowledge is heterogeneously distributed among competitors because of the current political and economic uncertainty in Russia. An ability to work across divisional lines seems also to be rare for most competitors, which are too huge to be flexible in this regard. This firm is the only western company having full value chain and extensive marketing channels in its industry. Special monetary transactions refer to the ability of the firm to accept payments in the form of products in exchange for raw material across divisional lines (barter system). This is very important in the environment where payments in cash are hard to make, and is very rare among all competitors.

Imitability: Industry knowledge and ability to work across divisional lines can be socially complex, but not very hard or costly to imitate. Full value chain, extensive marketing channels and special monetary arrangements can be imitated in the future, but are, at the moment, socially complex, depend on numerous small decisions and are thus costly to imitate.

Supportive organizational arrangements: The organizational structures and shared views support industry knowledge well across divisional lines. The ability to work across divisional lines varies in different divisions, and is thus not very well supported. Full value chain, extensive marketing channels and special monetary arrangements were organized under different divisions in 1995, and there were quite substantive organizational gaps in supporting them. Today, in 1998, all these competencies are organized under the same division, and are thus better supported. The competitive implications of each of the four attributes in the VRIO framework (Figure 1) are summarized in the last column of Table 1 above.

Prescriptions Concerning Information Systems to Support the Perceived Capabilities

The following section presents the actual and potential role of IT applications in building and leveraging competencies. Some of them are conjectural, and are not directly suggested by the theory presented above. However, they are products of the author's knowledge of IT, understanding of the case organization and his own biases, beliefs and "visions" related to IT potential, all of which came together during the research process.

A) Personal/management Competencies: Most of the capabilities in this section could be supported by a tailored groupware system, examples being LotusNotes™ or ICL TeamWARE™, with applications set up for communication, document sharing and broadcast. Such a system should be open to all parties within the firm associated with Russian trade. It would also allow communication and document transfer among its users, and (the broadcasting capabilities can) provide a free and convenient channel for education that in turn would enhance the feeling of togetherness and assumption of shared goals and meanings within the corporation. The major hurdle to implementation of such a system is the lack of management and IT infrastructure in Russia. As for the management, there is a wide cultural gap concerning modern business perceptions between the Russian and the Western managers. This might involve misconceptions of shared goals, and might even lead to competitive disadvantage. The IT infrastructure in the Russian market involves an environment where technical possibilities are scarce and less advanced or at least their supply is unstructured and very costly. This can hinder efficient use of the suggested system.

B) Process-oriented Competencies: The groupware described above could also support these capabilities. Furthermore, a more technically oriented group support system that coordinates the knowledge and activities of the company's buyers of raw materials *in Russia* and the company's production programmers *in Finland* is essential to the development of the company's competitiveness. Such a system actually exists in Finland. The challenge is extension to Russia where the telecommunication infrastructure is still rather problematic.

C) Logistics-related Competencies: A database, including all details of any logistics operation, could give guidelines for planning and operating logistics. An intranet-type interface to this database with access rights based on need-to-know for relevant parties involved in logistics, trading and production could also make a significant contribution to logistic capabilities. This system also exists in Finland, as a built-in part of the order-processing system where each trading transaction is logged and documented. Again the problem lies in the Russian infrastructure.

D) Competencies related to the Corporation: Most of the capabilities in this section could also be supported by groupware described above. Moreover, there should be an intranet-type access to corporate and divisional special systems, so that anyone needing special information could have access. A company education channel as described in the section on personal/management competencies could be built into the system. One challenge with this kind of application is finding ways to create channels that lead to relevant rather than irrelevant information (Nonaka, 1994).

These four interrelated areas of competencies in the VRIO framework help to identify areas in which information technology can be used to support organizational resources essential to building competencies and capabilities. A group support system cannot support all the capabilities mentioned in the four areas of competencies. It is important, however, that the case company's corporate IT management emphasized the role that the corporate LotusNotes™ could play in distributing documents to various units in the company. Moreover, the trading personnel in Industry/Product Division 1 were about to broaden their system beyond HP-Desk™. Awareness of the potential of IT was present at the time of the research but documentation of the actual implementation falls beyond the scope of this study. The IT system is comprehensive for operations in Finland and should be extended to Russian operations when possible; but the infrastructure realities of the transitional and unpredictable nature of the Russian environment still place limits of this kind of development.

CONCLUSIONS AND SUMMARY

In the methodological subsection three contingencies for testing a scientific theory were presented. These included:

1)   The theory must be logically consistent; i.e., the deductions derived from the theory have to be consistent with each other.

2)   The theory must be at least as explanatory, or predictive, as any other competing theory.

3)   The theory must survive actual attempts of falsification.

The case above deals with the evaluation of perceived core competencies of an enterprise's trade with Russia. We can see from the discussion the importance of applying the VRIO framework, with its focus on the relationship between company competencies and attributes of diversity in the company, both of which contribute to competitiveness.

As shown in the case description, Barney's VRIO framework appears to be appropriate for the evaluation of strategic resources and capabilities. However, the competencies analyzed stop short of indicating how to create new competencies in a dynamic manner. Application of the framework in the case example only provides an ex-post-facto account on the current status of the competencies. As such, contingency 1) seems to hold. Thus, the framework can serve as a tool for the managers of a company to analyze, from time to time, their perceptions of the firms' current competitive edge.

The competing theories were challenged in the theoretical part of the chapter, and the resource-based theory (RBT) was found to be at least as good, or even better than the other competing theories. Thus the VRIO-framework derived from RBT can be at least as explanatory, or predictive, as any other competing theory. Therefore contingency 2) is fulfilled.

The much above average profits (20 % of turnover creating 30% of profits), and the finding of one competence - corporate reputation – is a definite source of sustained competitive advantage, serve as evidence of fulfilling contingency 3).

Capabilities can be developed in at least two ways. They either emerge over time through 'wise' management, with numerous sequences of small decisions made by transformational leaders. Or, they can be purposefully developed through a learning aid of organizational routines, as Andreu and Ciborra (1996) suggest.

The main contribution of the case study in this chapter is the application of a framework to illustrate the direct linking of IT strategy to competitive strategy. Building on the traditional Porter approach and using the resource-based view does this. This offers new insights into the value-adding process. Another contribution is the linkage between theory and practice, which is rare in research within the field of competence-based competition and resource-based theory. The main limitation is that the analysis and prescriptions have not been validated with the interviewees, nor have they been empirically tested. The model can remain static, and of limited value for a company in the future, unless there are follow-up studies.

The study suggests that a longitudinal series of snapshot studies can help managers to create knowledge of the directions into which the previously perceived competencies are moving and to gain awareness of the emergence of new competencies. The role of IT in building new competencies should be integrated into these longitudinal studies.

STUDY QUESTIONS

1. What is the relevance of the theory of the firm in the discussion concerning strategic management?
2. What is the link between the theory of the growth of the firm and competence-based competition?
3. What is the role of information technology and organizational learning in building and leveraging competencies?
4. What is the role of information technology in the analysis through the VRIO-framework?
5. How can a theory or a framework be tested and validated through a single case study?
6. Which are the drawbacks in testing and validating a theory or a framework through a single case study?
7. Why do the industrial organization approach, positioning, and the transaction-cost theory not fit well in the discussion of strategic management?

REFERENCES

Alchian, Armen A. & Demsetz, Harold (1972). Production, Information Cost, and Economic Organization. In: (1996) *The Theory of the Firm*, Ed. By Mark Casson, 92-110. Elgar: Cheltenham (Originally in *American Economic Review* LXII, 777-95).

Andreu, R. & Ciborra, C. (1996). Organizational learning and core capabilities development: the role of IT. *Journal of Strategic Information Systems*, 5, 111-127.

Barney, J. B. (1986a). Types of Competition and the Theory of Strategy: Toward an Integrative Framework. *Academy of Management Review*, 11(4), 791-800.

Barney, J. B. (1986b). Strategic Factor Markets: Expectations, Luck, and Business Strategy. *Management Science*, 32(10), 1231-1241.

Barney, J. B. (1991a). Firm Resources and Sustained Competitive Advantage. *Journal of Management*, 17(1), 99-120.

Barney, J. B. (1991b). Special Theory Forum: The Resource-Based Model of the Firm: Origins, Implications and Prospects. *Journal of Management*, 17(1), 97-98.

Barney, J. B. (1994). Bringing Managers Back. In J. B. Barney, J. C. Spender & T. Reve (Eds.) *Does management matter?: on competencies and competitive advantage*. Lund: Institute of Economic Research.

Barney, J. B. (1996). *Gaining and Sustaining Competitive Advantage.* New York: Addison-Wesley:

Barney, Jay B. and Ouchi, William G. (1986). Basic Concepts: Information, Opportunism, and Economic Exchange.. *In Organizational Economics; Toward a New Paradigm for Understanding and Studying Organizations*. Ed. By Barney, Jay B. and Ouchi, William G., 18-71, San Francisco: Jossey Bass Publishers

Berry, M. (1987). *American Foreign Policy and the Finnish Exception*. Helsinki: Societas Historics Finlandiae.

Coase, Ronald H. (1937). The Nature of The Firm. In (1993) *The Nature of the Firm; Origins, Evolution, and Development.* Ed. by Oliver E. Williamson & Sidney G. Winter, 18-74, New York: Oxford University Press (originally in *4 Economica N.S.)*

Conner, K. R. (1991). A Historical Comparison of Resource-Based Theory and Five Schools of Thought Within Industrial Organization Economics: Do We Have a New Theory of the Firm?, *Journal of Management*, 1991, 17(1), 121-154

Cunningham, J. Barton (1997). Case Study Principles for different type of cases, *Quality and Quantity*, 31.

Ghoshal, S. & Bartlett, C. A. (1990). The Multinational Corporation as an Interorganizational Network. *Academy of Management Review*, 15(4), 603-625.

Ghoshal, S., Bartlett C. A, and Moran, P. (1999). A new manifesto for management. *Sloan management review*, Spring, 40(3), 9-20

Hamel, G. & Heene, A. (Eds.) (1994). *Competence-Based Competition*, Chichester: Wiley.

Hamel, G. & Prahalad, C. K. (Eds.) (1994). *Competing for the Future*. Boston, Ma: Harvard Business Press.

Jarvenpaa, S. L., & Ives B. (1994). The Global Network Organization of the Future: Information Management Opportunities and Challenges. *Journal of Management Information Systems*, 10(4), 25-57.

Järvinen, Pertti (1989). *On Research Methods,* Opinpaja: Tampere

Kangas, K. (1997). Case of a Finnish Multinational; Coordination Mode and a Resource-Based View to Core Capabilities. *Proceedings of the 1997 Information Resources Management Association Conference*, May 20-22, Vancouver, BC, Canada, 61-68.

Keen, P. W. G. (1991*). Shaping the Future*. Boston, Ma: Harvard Business School Press.

Lee, Allen S. (1989). A Scientific Methodology for MIS Case Studies. *MIS-Quarterly*, 13(1), 33-50

Lieberman, M. B. & Montgomery, D. B. (1988). First-Mover Advantages. Strategic Management Journal, 9, 41-58.

Mahoney, J. T. & Pandian, R. (1992). The Resource-Based View Within the Conversation of Strategic Management. *Strategic Management Journal*, 13, 363-380

Markus, M. Lynne (1983). Power, Politics, and MIS Implementation. *Communication of the ACM*, 26(5), 430-444

Mata, F., Fuerst, W. L. & Barney, J. B. (1995). Information Technology and Sustained Competitive Advantage: A Resource-Based Analysis. *MIS-Quarterly*, 19(4), 487-506.

Mintzberg, Henry - Lampel, Joseph (1999). Reflecting on the Strategy Process. *Sloan Management Review*, Spring, 21-30

Morgan, G. (1989). *Creative Organization Theory, a Resourcebook*. London: Sage Publications.

Nelson, R. R. and Winter, S. G. (1982). *An Evolutionary Theory of Economic Change*, Cambridge: The Belknap Press

Nonaka, I. (1994). A Dynamic Theory of Organizational Knowledge Creation. *Organizational Science*, 5, 1, Feb., 14-37.

Orton, J. D. & Weick, K. E. (1990). Loosely Coupled Systems; A Reconceptualization. *Academy of Management Review*, 15(2), 203-223.

Penrose, E., T. (1959). *The Theory of the Growth of the Firm*. Oxford: Basil Blackwell.

Penrose, E., T. (1985). *The Theory of the Growth of the Firm Twenty-Five Years After*. Uppsala: Acta Universitatis Upsaliensis, Studia Oeconomiae Negotiorum 20.

Penrose, E., T. (1995). Preface (3rd edition). *The Theory of the Growth of the Firm.* Oxford: Oxford University Press.

Polanyi, M. (1967). *The Tacit Dimension*. London: Routledge & Kegan Paul.

Porter, M. E., 1985, *Competitive Advantage; Creating and Sustaining Superior Performance*. New York: Free Press

Porter, M. E. (1990*). Competitive Advantage of Nations*. London: MacMillan.

Porter, Michael E. (1998). Clusters and the New Economics of Competition. *Harvard Business Review*, November-December, 77-90

Porter, Michael E. (2001). Strategy and the Internet. Harvard Business Review, March, 62-78

Prahalad, C. K. & Hamel, G. (1990). The Core Competence of the Corporation. *Harvard Business Review,* May-June, 1990, 79-91.

Prahalad, C. K. & Hamel, G. (1994). *Competing for the Future*. Boston, Ma: Harvard Business School Press.

Reponen T. (1993). Information Management Strategy - An Evolutionary Process. *Scand. J. Mgmt.*, 9(3), 189-209.

Reponen, T., Auer, T., Pärnistö, J. & Viitanen, J. (1995). *Tietoresurssien johtamisstrategia kilpailukyvyn välineenä*. Turku: Publications of the Turku School of Economics and Business Administration, Series C-8.

Robins, J. & Wiersema, M. F., (1995). A Resource-Based Approach to the Multibusiness Firm: Empirical Analysis of Portfolio Interrelationship and Corporate Financial Performance. *Strategic Management Journal*, 16, 277-299

Rumelt R. P. (1994). Foreword. In G. Hamel & A. Heene (Eds.). *Competence-Based Competition.* Chichester: Wiley.

Sanchez, R. & Heene, A. (1997a). Reinventing Strategic Management: New Theory and Practice for Competence-Based Competition. *European Management Journal*, 15(3), June, 303-317.

Sanchez, R., Heene, A. & Thomas, H. (Eds.) (1996) *Dynamics of Competence-Based Competition; Theory and Practice in the Strategic Management.* Exeter: Pergamon.

Seth, Anju - Thomas, Howard (1994). Theories of the Firm: Implications for Strategy Research. Journal of Management Studies, 31:2, March, 165-191

Shepherd, William G. (1990). *The Economics of Industrial Organization*. Third Edition, Englewood Cliffs: Prentice Hall

Simon, H. (1957*) Administrative Behavior*. New York: Macmillan

Stalk, G., Evans, P. & Shulman, L. (1992). Competing on capabilities: The new rules of corporate strategy. *Harvard Business Review*. March-April, 57-69.

Viitanen, J. (1998). *The Information Management Strategies in the Global Network Organization*. Turku: Publications of the Turku School of Economics and Business Administration, Series A-6.

Wernerfelt, B. (1984). A Resource-based View of the Firm. *Strategic Management Journal*, 5(2), 171-180.

Williamson, O. E. (1975). *Markets and hierarchies: Analysis and Antitrust Implications*. New York: Free Press

Williamson, O. E. (1989). Transaction Cost Economics. In: *Handbook of Industrial Organization*, Ed. by Richard Schmalensee and Robert D. Willig Volume I, 137-182, New York: North Holland

Williamson, O. E. (1993). Introduction. In: *The Nature of the Firm; Origins, Evolution, and Development,* Ed. by Oliver E. Williamson & Sidney G. Winter, 3-17, New York: Oxford University Press.

SECTION - 3

GLOBAL ELECTRONIC COMMERCE

The use of the Internet for data communications has greatly simplified building international networks, including networks that connect enterprises together. The future for the multinational enterprise is one of a ``networked world'' in which multiple partners compete and cooperate together in ``industrial networks''. The term ``electronic commerce'' has come to represent the process of conducting trade via transactions carrier through the Internet.

For the multinational enterprise, the challenges are great. The spread of the Internet is highly uneven around the world - some countries have high penetration rates, others are just beginning to scratch the surface. Another issue that repeatedly comes up is the inconsistency of legal and regulatory regimes around the world. In the absence of a consistent ``rules of the road'', it is difficult for the multinational enterprise to build a coherent policy.

This section presents several chapters to address these issues. The first is a general overview of eCommerce issues. It focuses on the role of advertising and the middlemen functions in the growth of eCommerce and suggests how these factors necessitate strategic changes to adapt to growing global electronic markets. The second chapter illustrates how national and cultural differences pose specific challenges to the multinational engaged in eCommerce. It also includes a study of five firms in the book retailing industry and shows how business-to-consumer (B2C) eCommerce is providing both challenges and opportunities for these companies. The third discusses these issues within the context of small and medium-sized enterprises (SMEs). It presents a framework for the analysis and design of global information infrastructures with the organizational context of SMEs. The final chapter is a case study from northern New Zealand, and it discusses the role of eCommerce in supporting tourism. An additional theme of this chapter is the difficulties of technology transfer to culturally different environments - something that any multinational enterprise should keep in mind as it makes assumptions regarding where to place its IT resources.

12

Global e-Commerce: An Examination of Issues Related to Advertising and Intermediation

Shailendra C. Jain Palvia
Long Island University, USA

Vijay K. Vemuri
Long Island University, USA

ABSTRACT

The Internet is rapidly changing how we communicate, earn, learn, entertain and do business. The speed at which the Internet has adapted to conduct business transaction is simply mind-boggling. In a short period of five years, a number of dot com companies were formed, generated memorable excitement in the investment community and then went out of business during the year 2000-01. The key to the survival of the e-Commerce companies is their ability to quickly adapt to the sweeping changes in Internet technology, consumer preferences, government regulations, and global alliances. For the future, we need to project and think about the most likely changes to occur. In this chapter, we concentrate on the role of advertising and the middlemen functions and how they are evolving with the growth of electronic commerce. Electronic commerce is radically affecting the advertising function. The Internet technology is allowing companies to monitor advertising effectiveness better and also to utilize reimbursement schemes pegged to actual results. Our analysis suggests that the prediction of disintermediation due to e-Commerce may just be a hype. The role of middlemen is evolving: in some sectors the role is disappearing, in others it is expanding, and in yet others newer intermediaries are forming to facilitate the demands of electronic commerce. We discuss the implications of and necessary strategic changes to adapt to growing global electronic markets. Finally, we articulate a few factors critical to the success of global e-Commerce.

INTRODUCTION

Internet Explosion

The use of the Internet has been exploding exponentially during the last decade. In the middle of 2000, in the US, 122.7 million people ~~are~~ were connected to the Internet and this figure is expected to grow to 197.2 million by 2003[1]. Growth in Internet access is not limited

---

[1] An International Data Corporation estimate. For these and other statistics provided in the chapter, refer to The Industry Standard, a news magazine of the Internet economy. Many interesting Internet

to the US alone, the worldwide growth is also phenomenal. By 2003, it is estimated that 500 million people will have access to the Internet[1]. Statistics suggest that e-mail usage is now ten times greater than postal mail[2]. According to Jupiter Research (2000), the number of Internet connected users in the 19-49 age group is expected to grow from 54.5 million users in 1999 to 84 million by 2005. Number of households online is expected to increase to 80.2 million in 2005 compared to 45.4 million at the end of 1999. The number of websites in the world as of April, 2001 is nearly 1.5 billion.

The Internet was originally conceived for rapid access and dissemination of research for US military use. Over the years, the World Wide Web (WWW) has been developed to be a pool of human knowledge -- ranging from architecture, astronomy, and biology to telemedicine, video-conferencing, and zoology -- accessible from anywhere by anybody at anytime. The Internet can be easily deployed for sharing information among multitude of business parties along the global supply chain. Intranets use Internet technology to inexpensively and easily share organizational data across a private network. Extranets (or extended intranets) connect companies with their suppliers and customers using again the Internet infrastructure – WWW and browser software.

Productivity Paradox and Investments in Information Technology

At a firm level, it is well known that investment in information technology (IT) is justified due to benefits it provides. Investments in computers and IT can reduce costs, streamline business processes and improve efficiency. Information technology investments can also provide strategic advantage. For the economy in aggregate, however, the benefits of investments by businesses in information technology are less clear. In the past, many skeptics questioned the broad-based productivity gains due to investments in information technology. Robert Solow, a Nobel laureate in economics, once commented: "You can see the computer age everywhere except in the productivity statistics."[3] Federal Reserve economists Daniel Sichel, and Stephen Oliner also once expressed similar concerns[4]. The lack of productivity gains in macroeconomic statistics, despite heavy investment in computing and telecommunication technology, was puzzling and the phrase "productivity paradox" was added to the economic jargon to refer to this puzzle (Brynjolfsson and Hitt, 1993.) The Productivity Paradox, in a nutshell, is the puzzling lack of observation of productivity gains in macroeconomic data, despite heavy investment in IT by firms. While the debate over macroeconomic effects of IT continued, investments in IT have been steadily rising in both absolute amounts and as a relative share of corporate spending. During the 1990s, spending on the computing and telecommunication hardware alone quadrupled. The proportion of spending on the hardware during the 90s went up from 29 percent of all spending on business equipment to 53 percent[5]. In the recent years, the effects of increased investment in IT on the economic growth of the US economy are becoming clearer. The 1997 US census data estimates that almost one-third of US economic growth is due to IT. The following table (Table-1) summarizes their findings. The Productivity Paradox is resolved by newer evidence that suggests that investments in IT have a long gestation period and the payoff occurs after the necessary changes in human skills and organizational structure occur.

---

commerce statistics can be found at http://www.thestandard.com in the "metrics" subsection of the "research" section. http://ecommerce.mit.edu maintains extensive collection of e-commerce statistics.

[2] NetWork Commerce Adevertisement, The Wall Street Journal, Novemebr 8, 2000: C17.

[3] New York Times, April 14, 1999, p. A1.

[4] New York Times, April 14, 1999, p. C14.

[5] *Ibid.*

Table 1: Contribution of IT to Real Economic Growth[6]

YEAR	REAL ECONOMIC GROWTH	INFORMATION TECHNOLGY INDUSTRY CONTRIBUTION	PERCENTAGE OF GROWTH DUE TO INFORMATION TECHNOOGY
1994	4.2%	0.8%	19%
1995	3.3%	1.0%	30%
1996	3.5%	1.2%	34%
1997	4.7%	1.3%	28%
1998	4.8%	1.3%	27%
1999	5.0%	1.6%	32%

It has been established that Information and Internet technologies, besides improving productivity, provide opportunities for companies to gain strategic advantage, open up new markets, streamline business processes, and coordinate activities with its business partners. In his testimony before the Joint Economic Committee of the US Congress, Federal Reserve Board Chairman, Alan Greenspan said, "innovations in information technology ... have begun to alter the manner in which we do business and create value, often in ways that were not readily foreseeable even five years ago[7]." As an example of increases in business efficiencies, he says, "the recent year's remarkable surge in the availability of real-time information has enabled business management to remove large swaths of inventory safety stocks and worker redundancies, and has armed firms with detailed data to fine-tune product specifications to most individual customer needs."

GLOBAL e-COMMERCE

The 1993 decision to replace government funded NSFNET backbone with many commercial Internet backbones gave impetus to its commercialization, opening up a new distribution channel providing direct access to the consumers, supplementing traditional marketing channels for the evolving global electronic commerce. Internet is basically a *global* infrastructure connecting thousands of telecommunication (TC) networks around the world. To exploit this worldwide network for one or some countries will be suboptimal. The *first phase* of Internet's use for sharing wealth of information stored on globally distributed databases has been very successful. The success of the *second phase* of B2C e-Commerce transactions (besides B2B transactions which have been used in the form of EDI or private networks for almost 15 years) is critical for the survival and sustenance of the Internet.

Global electronic commerce can be viewed as the buying and selling of information, products, and services via computer networks spanning the entire globe. A catalyst for the growth of global electronic commerce is moving the procurement process to the Web through the use of electronic exchanges and marketplaces. The reengineering of the procurement process has simplified, automated, speeded up and reduced costs of B2B transactions. The extent of growth of global e-commerce can be traced to the growth of Web B2B technology platform providers that make the global e-commerce possible. Commerce One, a leading B2B solution provider, operates the world's largest B2B community called Global Trading Web (GTW). GTW connects 58 independently operated B2B portals each designed to serve a

---

[6] Statistics derived from Bureau of Census data for 1994 to 1997 by Commerce Department. 1998 and 1999 figures are estimates. IT industries are the firms that supply goods and services that support IT-enabled business processes, the Internet and e-commerce.

[7] Testimony before the Joint Economic Committee, U.S. Congress, June 14, 1999.

specific region or industry. The rate of transactions on GTW has exceeded one trillion dollars annually (Mottl, 2000). Using open platform and extensible Markup Language (XML), Commerce One enables any company to buy and sell products to the buyers directly.

An Example

To understand the impact of transformation of businesses due to the Internet, let us take the example of the banking industry. More than 95% of top US banks do already have full service Internet banking sites. Before the 1970s, traditional banks allowed customers to deposit or withdraw only in a specific bank or its branch. In the 1970s, ATMs and banks alliances broke the barriers between bank-to-bank services. The 1980s were the time of telebanking with telephone touch buttons used as remote terminals for money transfers including bill payments. From the mid 1990s onwards, banking required only a few clicks from the PC terminal. International Data Corporation estimates that by the end of year 2003, over 32 million people in the USA will be banking from PCs (Kirkpatrick, 2000). Internet sites will essentially become Internet bank branches. Internet branches will increasingly allow consumers to easily check the balances in their accounts, transfer funds among accounts, order electronic bill payments online, apply for loans, trade stocks or mutual funds from anywhere at anytime. According to Jupiter Communications, by 2005, the number of households paying bills online will exceed 40 million (K. Thomas, 2000). Netbank.com is the largest bank operating solely on the Internet offering lending, investing and high interest checking services since 1996. Its customers can plan for retirement using IRAs and other types of investment accounts, conduct online trading, obtain home mortgage, obtain car and business loans, get a line of credit, get an ATM card, get a Visa credit card, and obtain free online bill payment services (Deitel et al, 2001).

Some Statistics

According to International Data Corporation (a market research company), the worldwide e-commerce revenues will grow to $623 billion ($291 billion in US alone) in 2002, up from $41 billion ($31 billion in US alone) in 1998. According to Jupiter research (Spring, 2000), teenager spending online will escalate from $129 million in 1999 to $1.2 billion by 2002. According to Forrester Research, the United States is expected to spend $1.4 trillion online by 2004. Comparison with other countries highlights the much talked about Digital Divide: in 1999, online shopping was offered by only 26% of Canada's 200 largest retailers whereas 50% of America's biggest stores offered some form of e-Commerce (Rickefs, 2000); at the beginning of the year 2000, only 13% of Europeans used the Internet at home, whereas 43% of Americans had home access (Baker and Echikson, 2000); the Indian parliament passed the path breaking Information Technology bill in the year 2000 to finally pull down the remaining shackles of e-Commerce and Internet while retaining a crucial provision to hit hard on cyber crimes (Nanda-A, 2000); between 1996 and 2000, the number of African countries with Internet access increased from 11 to 51 (83, DD, p.374); according to the Computer Industry Almanac (2000), 14% (of which 29% from home) and 40% (of which 51% from home) of the populations of Japan and USA respectively use the Internet; Indian tourism ministry's website registered 1.7 million hits during the first 4 months of the year 2000 (Anbarasan, 2000). According to statistics provided by eMarketer 2001 (Pearl, 2001, Translator), Internet users as percentage of adult population in the Asian countries Singapore, Australia, Taiwan, Hong Kong, South Korea, Japan, China, and India were 36.2, 26.3, 22.8, 19.7, 17.9, 16.2, 0.9, and 0.3 respectively. According to the same source, B2B revenues for India were expected to jump from US$0.11 billion in 2000 to US$5.42 in 2004, and B2C revenues were estimated to jump from US$0.01 billion in 2000 to US$0.67 billion in 2004. According to Gartner, the vast majority of Internet bank users, 21.6 million merely checked accounts online; only 6.6 million used services such as bill payments online (Hechinger, 2001). According to Gomez Advisors, active web bankers (defined as those who use the web at least once a month) have a median income of $57,800 compared with $44,800 for non-web bankers (Hechinger, 2001).

Global E-Commerce can be of six types: Business to Business (B2B) utilizing mostly the extranets developed to build alliances with suppliers and customers; business to employees (B2E) utilizing almost exclusively the intranets developed using the existing Internet technology; business to customer (B2C) utilizing the Internet; and business to government (B2G) and Customer to Government (C2G) utilizing the Internet and consumer to consumer (C2C.)

Business to Business (B2B)

The traditional methods of mail, phone, fax and courier services are no longer adequate for a company to conduct business with its suppliers, customers, distributors and other value chain partners. These traditional methods of transactions are slow, expensive and prone to errors. Use of the Internet for transactions with other businesses is widely known as B2B (Business-To-Business) and is a fast growing segment of electronic commerce. Electronic commerce between businesses is not a new concept. It began almost twenty years ago, when a few businesses, including some mass merchandisers, began to restructure their procurement processes by linking with their suppliers through computer networks. These early networks, utilized electronic data interchanges, or EDIs, which were expensive and closed to outsiders. The inexpensive and global cost effective access to the Internet has now made it the preferred medium for business to business transactions. The growth in B2B transactions is exceeding the wildest expectations. The estimates of B2B transaction volumes are revised upward frequently. Forrester Research (Boyle, 2000) estimates this business to grow from $109 billion in 1999 to $2.7 trillion in 2004. In June 2000, Jupiter Communications estimates the B2B spending at 346 billion in 2000 and a staggering six trillion by 2005 in the US alone. Gartner Group predicts $403 billion will change hands via online B2B transactions in the year 2001, and they expect the number to climb to $7.3 trillion by 2004 (Microsoft website). The projected B2B growth in Asia-Pacific, Western Europe, and Latin America are even more dramatic. Not only has B2B e-Commerce struck roots in India, sites like Indiamarkets.com launched in December 1999 are providing relevant infomediary type services to small and medium size enterprises (SMEs) across over 140 product categories (Nanda-B, 2000). The excitement over B2B is mainly due to its potential in improving operational efficiencies and integrating supply chains. In the global context, B2B can be either intra-organizational i.e., between the headquarter office and foreign subsidiaries or among foreign subsidiaries (manufacturing plants, warehouses, marketing/sales offices) or inter-organizational i.e., between different organizations across national borders worldwide.

Extranets are revolutionizing the interactions and transactions between organizations. Before the open architecture of extranet technology, linking the product supply chain required expensive, and proprietary networks that were custom developed to connect heterogeneous platforms and networks. Electronic data interchange (EDI) used during the last two decades provided limited automation of transactions between organizations. High costs of implementing EDI made its implementation beyond the reach of smaller and medium-sized companies. Advances in Internet technology are making the automation of inter-company transactions less expensive and affordable to almost all organizations. The Internet provides cheap and universal connectivity, http and ftp provide the standards for data transfer, browsers provide the consistent user interface, and TCP/IP protocols provide the ability to connect dissimilar computing systems. Extranets enable companies to extend boundaries of the organization to reach suppliers, business partners, consultants and customers. Extranets enable an organization to streamline its operations and make just-in-time supplier relationships possible. The uses of extranets are extensive – they can improve customer service, reduce operating costs and increase revenues.

Electronic commerce is providing opportunities for sales automation and self-service purchases. In addition to providing self-service, B2B storefronts enable the partners to check and track existing orders. Order returns, adjustments, service requests, and field service scheduling are also handled by many storefronts. In addition to reducing the cost of selling, storefronts enable the business to concentrate on channel relationships and selling strategies. In many industries (automotive, electronics, energy, food, chemical, construction), B2B exchange sites have emerged to allow manufacturers, wholesalers, retailers, and end consumers to buy, sell, and barter over the web. For example, an automobile exchange site (www.covisint.com , www.istarxchange.com , www.autovia.com) can give an automobile manufacturer access to hundreds of suppliers, each competing for its business, potentially leading to lower prices and/or better services.

In the global context, Asian countries have also entered the B2B fray. Hongkong's www.studiodirect.com allows small retailers to buy like the big guys by aggregating orders from multiple sources; China's www.alibaba.com since starting in 1999 has grown into a trade portal connecting small buyers and sellers of products ranging from Uruguayan sheep to emu fat and looks forward to getting revenues from online advertising and from hosting websites of its 425,000 members; America's Meet www.China.com connects suppliers in China with buyers worldwide and holds hands through an entire trade (McFarland, 2001).

Business to Employee (B2E)

Based on a survey done by Watson Wyatt Worldwide[8], Business-to-Employee e-Commerce using *intranet* represents internal communications (and some transactions) that eighty percent of all companies in USA are using as the primary method for delivering human-resource services to the employees, up from fifty percent in 1998. Intranet-based B2E communications keep everyone up to date, especially in this information age where workers are globally dispersed. Examples of how companies are exploiting this technology are: General Electric revamped its intranet in 1999, the number of hits jumped from a couple of thousand a week to 10 millions a week. Employees can create a personalized page where they can read industry-specific news or check the weather. They can also download tax forms and review benefits information. Furthermore, an online marketplace offers discounts on GE appliances, Dell computers and other products. AT&T, thorough their intranet, helps its employees manage their benefits, check their 401 (K) plans and make investment changes. Company news is also updated each day. Hallmark Cards in Kansas City, Mo., posts the cafeteria menu, employee newsletter, and job-training resources on the intranet. Texas Instruments is rolling out a program that will let new hires access the intranet before their first day on the job, getting them up to speed before they start. The site includes a concierge service that will plan vacations, run errands, and help to pick doctors from the health plan. American Century Investments uses its intranet for classified ads and information on competitors. Employees can submit any question to be answered on the intranet. In the global context, the above approaches make utmost sense since the various organizational units and their employees may be in any part of the world. As mentioned above, this mode of e-Commerce is mostly information exchange at this time, but includes transactions including signing up for medical, dental, life, disability insurance which results in automated deduction from the payroll; buying of company products at significant employee discount; issuance of coupons and

---

[8] Stephanie Armour, USA Today, March 20, 2000.

bargain prices for employees with allied organizations (Prudential does it for its employees with Staples, House Cleaning Services etc.).

Business to Consumer (B2C)

Online retailers (Business to Consumer) signify the first imprints of structural changes in business due to electronic commerce. The first wave of online retailers received enthusiastic response and gained instant recognition. For certain products (like books, computers), brick-and-mortar retailers may become extinct and will be replaced by click-and-portal[9] retailers. A substantial proportion of computer software, books, videos, and DVDs is now being sold by online merchants including amazon.com, CDNow.com, and buy.com. In fact, it is hard to find a bookseller without an online sales outlet. An Internet-based presence has become the norm rather than an exception. The excitement over electronic commerce is evident from the incredible market capitalization of the electronic retailers (increasingly being termed e-tailers). For example, Amazon.com with a total loss of more than $1.2 billion loss since its inception in 1995, commands a market capitalization of $5.3 billion (on 02-02-01), rivaling well-established industrial giants. The enthusiasm for B2C is understandable. According to Forrester Research, online buying is expected to jump from $20.3 billion in 1999 to 184.5 billion in 2004. Giga Information Group Inc. predicts U.S. B2C sales to grow from an estimated $25 billion in 1999 to $152 billion in 2002 and $233 billion in 2004. (Microsoft website). The eBay site epitomizes several auction sites (in addition to sites that search other auction sites) to pinpoint the lowest prices on an available item. The Internet user can assume the role of either a seller or a bidder (and buyer if his/her bid goes through). As a seller, you can post an item you wish to sell along with its minimum price and a deadline for closing the auction. As a bidder, you may search the site for the availability of the item you are seeking, view the current bidding activity and place a bid if so desired. There also exists a reverse-auction model that allows the buyer to set a price that sellers compete to match, or even beat (Liquidprice.com).

Business to Government (B2G) and Government to Consumer (G2C)

B2G (and G2B) means conducting of transactions between Business and Government, while G2C (and C2G) refers to doing transactions between the Government and the Citizens of a country. B2G is a rapidly growing sector of e-commerce and improves efficiency in dealing with the federal, state and local governments. Increased access and reduction of paperwork can be achieved through customizing B2B technologies to suit interactions with the Government. In addition, many portals are emerging to streamline government procurement processes and sale of surplus resources of the government. The enthusiasm for B2G commerce is understandable – the US federal government alone accounted for 31 million procurement transactions amounting to over $200 billion in goods and services. Even with small transaction fees, online transaction facilitators have much to gain in expediting the transactions between businesses and state, local and federal governments. In 1999, total B2G transactions, including procurement, at the state and local level were about $800 billion. In contrast, citizen-to-government (C2G) transactions (including filing of electronic tax returns) amounted to $500 billion in 1999[10]. G2C does wonders for the IRS in distributing tax forms, an expensive and logistically cumbersome activity. In the past and even now, an army of

---

[9] Internet-based portals where relevant hyperlinks are available to be clicked to get the information a user wants about almost anything – weather, sports, travel, specific products and services etc. A portal is a cyber-door for a user serving as a customizable home base from which he/she does searching, navigating, and other web-based activity.

[10] Wall Street Journal, April 4, 2000.

workers from form pullers, envelope stuffers, label addressers to   mail-room deliverers process mail-in requests for tax publications at an average cost of $3 per request against less than a penny for handing a single Web request (Gomes Lee, 2001).

Many companies are formed to facilitate business to government transactions. FedBid.com[11] is the first web-based market for B2G transactions. At its site a government purchaser can shop with government purchase cards, much like a consumer with her credit card. In addition, the site facilitates reverse auctions[12] where the sellers compete to supply the government's procurement needs at the lowest cost. FedCenter.com[13], the largest electronic marketplace for exclusive use of government buyers, simplifies the government procurement process. The federal government is also taking initiatives to streamline and simplify government purchases. The U.S. General Services Administration built buyers.gov[14], a site for private buyer reverse auctions, reverse auctions of pooled orders and online shopping.

Consumer to Consumer (C2C)

Napster, a free consumer-to-consumer music swapping service, epitomizes this kind of business over the Internet. Napster provides a search capability for songs, chat capability for users to communicate in forums of like interest and an audio player. Napster has been at the center of much controversy since its inception in May, 1998 from players involved in the music industry - notably, the Record Industry Association of America (RIAA), and the heavy metal band, Metallica. The issue at hand is -- is Napster responsible for the copyright infringements that occur amongst its users even though Napster itself does not host any of the infringing audio files. The 9th U.S. Circuit Court of Appeals in San Francisco ruled against Napster and made trading of copyrighted music using Napster unlikely to continue. The court battles are expected to continue and it may take some time before the legality of sharing copyrighted material is resolved. The protections for Internet service providers provided by the Digital Copyright Millennium Act, coupled with the relative anonymity and ease of distribution afforded by the Internet are likely to make prevention of copyrighted material next to impossible. According to a recent web-based unscientific poll, 52% people would not support paying a price for the Napster service, whereas 40% said they will be willing to pay a price, if the price was right. Auction sites like eBay also promote C2C business by allowing individuals to place their products on the site for auction. Online newspaper sections of Want Ads also promote C2C business by listing products individuals want to sell or list houses individuals want to rent or sell.

Global Issues

When a website is created to conduct e-Commerce, a business can potentially reach every Internet user in each nook and corner of the world. Reaching customers all over the world requires addressing legal, language, currency, taxation, and cultural differences around the globe. The following is a summary description of these differences:

Cybercrime: When a copyrighted work on a computer in one country is accessed in another, which country's copyright laws should be applied? Privacy protection standards are stricter in Europe than USA – whose standards should apply when sharing information created in one

---

[11] http://www.FedBid.com

[12] Reverse auctions are Request For Quotes where the potential suppliers bid to supply the needed products or services. The buyer purchases from the lowest bidder.

[13] http://www.FedCenter.com

[14] http://www.buyers.gov.

country and accessed in another? Governments must determine whether an e-Business that maintains a website is subject to the laws of all countries from which the site can be accessed. For example, in May 2000, the destructive ILOVEYOU virus was spread via e-mail to computer systems around the world. Although the virus led to billions of dollars in damage around the world, the suspected Phillipine citizen could not be prosecuted for lack of applicable laws in his home country. Globally adopted laws must address cybercrimes such as copyright infringement, cybersquatting (illegal use of trademarked names in website addresses), cyber terrorism, violation of privacy rights etc.

- Per recommendation of the American Bar Association (www.abanet.org), there is a need to form a "global online standards commission" to mediate and govern Internet and e-Commerce related disputes among countries.

- The World Intellectual Property Organization (www.wipo.int) set up by United Nations primarily deals with cybersquatting disputes.

- The Organization of Economic Cooperation and Development (www.oecd.com), a forum for its 29 member countries, suggests increasing the scope of its jurisdiction to include collecting data related to computer-related security breaches and supervising the creation of national policies on digital certificates (Grande, 2000).

- After three years of research, the Council of Europe (www.coe.int), composed of 41 countries (with additional representatives from Canada, Japan, south Africa and the U.S.), released in 2000 a draft of the world's first international treaty relating to cyber crime (Deitel et al, 2000, page 343). The treaty mandates that all signatories will establish laws prohibiting unauthorized access of computers, interception of computer data, and exchange or possession of equipment used in hacking.

Global Market Exploration: Although the Internet provides easy access to customers and suppliers worldwide, technology alone cannot eliminate other barriers – legal, language, and cultural. Evolutionary approach is recommended i.e., start with one or two most promising international markets and make further expansion decisions based on this experience (McCollum, 2000). Such opportunities can be identified by reviewing the access logs of a site from foreign domains (Tapper, 2000). When deciding on a market, factors such as the number of people online, Internet usage growth rates, per capita income, existing competitors in the product or service arena of a country, host government's restrictions on imports and other factors must be considered. Two useful sites for learning about foreign markets are www.glreach.com and www.idiominc.com. Note that smaller, less obvious markets are sometimes better choices for marketing specific products. For example, Russia is predicted to be a strong emerging market for golf supplies (Deitel et al, 2000, page 345). Even though, geographical location of a websites' host should be logically immaterial, some governments require it to be registered and hosted in their own countries. Registering a domain name for a company in foreign markets can help a company avoid cybersquatters and problems obtaining an appropriate domain name later. For information on registering foreign domain names, visit www.iana.org and for registering, visit the largest global registrar of domain names, www.netnames.co.uk. Considering that India's software outsourcing revenues are second only to USA, e-commerce activity and revenue has been disappointingly small, estimated at half of even China's low level of online sales. One major reason is that most of the country's two million or so Internet users are in offices or Internet cafes compounded by the fact that

Indian offices themselves are not immune from the country's telecommunications problems (Pearl, 2001, Lost in the Translation).

Internationalization and Localization: *Internationalization* means restructuring the software so that it can process foreign languages, currencies, date formats, and other variations around the world (Schwarz, 2000). Unicode (www.unicode.org), a 16-bit encoding system that assigns a unique code to almost every character in every language (with still room for future new characters or symbols), enables computer systems to handle ideographic languages like Chinese, Japanese, or Korean. . www.rediff.com India Ltd., the only dotcom company to raise money in the U.S. stock market so far and patterned after www.yahoo.com , was faced with a dilemma, when many shoppers reported they could not find what they wanted through the site's search engine (Pearl, 2001, Searching for Solutions). The problem was that the standard e-Commerce software that Rediff was using couldn't handle Indian-English differences like substituting "trousers" for "pants." Another interesting example (Pearl, 2001, Searching for Solutions) is about the use of shopping cart technology by Rediff – just 4% of web surfers visiting Rediff's site put something into their cart, and 93% of those moved on without buying. This figure, the so-called drop off rate, is between 60% and 80% in other countries. The higher drop off rate can be attributed to the use of shopping cart, which is an easy metaphor in the U.S., but a rarity in India's much smaller shops. This article went on to emphasize that, not only is the number of shoppers much smaller than in the U.S, but also the market is more complex – e.g., dividing up its Indian pop music and traditional music selections by region and style resulted in no fewer than 300 categories.

Localization results in translation and cultural adaptation of a website's content and presentation (Deitel et al, 2001, p. 346).   Services like www.transparentlanguage.com, www.alis.com, www.logos.it, and www.babefish.altavista.com offer translations into different languages. Providing information in more that one language is key to conducting business globally; according to Forrester Research, consumers are three times more likely to purchase products or services from a website presented in their native language (Deitel et al, 2001, p 347). When considering the layout of a foreign language website, you should be aware that translation into European languages can expand English text up to 40% in length, whereas translation into some Asian languages requires slightly less space than English text (Yunker, 2000). Also, colors are viewed differently by world's diverse cultures and religions. While creating a website for the Chinese audience, include red, which signifies celebration and good luck in Chinese culture. While Americans commonly connect green with money, other countries may not. Blue is viewed positively in almost all cultures. For foreign audiences, it is important to avoid American slang, idioms etc. IKEA's foreign websites demonstrate localization (Deitel et al, 2001, p. 351). IKEA has created 14 localized sites for different national markets, including one for Italy (www.ikea.it) and one for Saudi Arabia (www.ikea.com.sa).   IKEA has included photographs of young women in pajamas and bathing suits on their Italian website. However, for Saudi Arabia, IKEA markets the site as a place for "good values and fun for your family" and contains photos of a man in Arab clothing shopping with his son (Lagon, 2000). Bazee.com India Inc. started in 2000, an Internet auction site modeled after eBay inc.; localization was deemed necessary (Pearl, 2000, Lost in the translation, R12). Indians tend to equate auctions with bankruptcy liquidations. Initially, Bazee started holding live auctions in shopping malls to promote the idea. Now, it is setting up "exchange centers" in different cities, where the seller and the winning bidder can complete their transaction in person.

There is a danger in overdoing localization. Scania AB, global truck and bus manufacturer, had allowed the company's array of websites around the world to be developed independently, with no common identity, design, or structure (Dorsey, 2001). Based on recommendations from Tridion BV, a 3 years old Dutch start-up, Scania's 12 corporate websites as well as those of its approximately 30 importers and several thousand dealers, were updated to project unified branding. This was achieved by using an XML written software DialogServer which not only allows content managers to centrally update multiple websites, but also automatically translates websites into different local languages.

Payment Systems: According to Cyber Dialogue, Inc., approximately 88% of the $53 billion dollars spent online in 2000 in USA was paid with credit cards (Crocket, 2000). Contrast that with Europe – only approximately 30% of Europeans have credit cards, and many feel uncomfortable revealing credit card numbers over the telephone or Internet (Mullen, 2000). Credit cards are rare in developing countries, because of infrastructure and trust issues. Cash on delivery (COD) is likely to be a more feasible option in Europe. According to Mullen (2000), DirectDebit™ is likely to be available in Austria, Belgium, the Netherlands, Switzerland, Luxembourg, Sweeden, and the United Kingdom, besides Germany at the present. DirectDebit enables electronic debits from European customer's bank accounts to be sent to merchant's bank accounts for a small fee. Few Indians have credit cards, and e-shopping sites avoid credit cards because the country does not have good verification systems. One Bangalore-based site, www.fabmart.com came up with its own currency called "Fabmoney," sold in Internet cafes (Pearl, 2001, Translate). Given India's low labor costs, delivery companies pick up cash at one location and deliver the gift to another location for about $1 to avoid the credit-card problem.

Legal and Taxation Systems: The relative ease with which e-Businesses can buy and sell internationally is a major advantage, but it makes violation of import and export laws much simpler. Selling and distributing animals, plants, products made from endangered species, arms and explosives, toy guns, Viagra, weapons of any kind, pornographic material, items related to the nazi era, certain software, certain nuclear technology are prohibited to be exported or imported by certain countries (Tapper, 2000). E-Businesses should also investigate international tax laws as they apply to Internet sales. In many countries, including all members of the European union, a value-added tax (VAT) is also added to all goods sold to consumers. Companies like www.mycustoms.com and www.worldtariff.com help in computing international taxes and other fees for global businesses.

Learning Curve or Quantum Leap?: In the past, it has been theorized that laggard companies and countries have to go through the same learning cycle as the leader companies and countries. Given the speed with which knowledge transfer can occur in today's age of global IT and Internet – it is no surprise that we have witnessed leapfrog computing in countries like India and China. Both countries, for example, essentially skipped mainframe and minicomputer ages and leap forged into the PC and networking age. Same phenomenon seems to be working in the arena of e-Commerce. First, "it took the U.S. seven or eight years to learn that Internet sites needed direct revenue from surfers, here we've learned it in six months," says Dewang Mehta, executive Director of the National Association of Software and Service company based in New Delhi, India (Pearl, 2001, R12, Lost In the Translation). Harsh Roongta, creator of www.apnaloan.com in India patterned after www.lendingtree.com in the U.S., found that Indian web users would drop out if he followed Lending Tree's practice of promising responses by e-mail within one business day. That was too long for his skeptical users, who are used to instant responses on the Internet. Mr. Roongta had to convince banks to share enough information with Apnaloan and authorize it to give loan quotes while the users were still logged on.

ADVERTISING IN GLOBAL e-COMMERCE

Forrester Research has predicted that the Web, which accounted for less than 1% of retail sales during 1998, will account for 6% in 2003. According to Jupiter Research, revenues from online advertising are expected to reach $13.3 billion by the year 2003 (Mulcahy, 2000). Most terrestrial merchants want to transform themselves as fast as they can into cyberspace merchants. For example, even though Barnes & Noble was and is the largest physical bookstore chain, they have lost market share to Amazon.com when it comes to e-commerce. The same thing is true with Toys-R-Us. Since they missed the e-commerce bandwagon, e-toys had dug in prior to the Christmas season of 1999 and were able to beat Toys-R-Us. However, during the year 2000 Christams season, e-toys were not able to achieve their sales targets. Tower Records, the No. 2 conventional record retailer missed the boat, and is working hard to improve a site that lags far behind many other music sites like CDNow.com. This section describes the different Internet based advertising approaches that have emerged in the last five years. Based on actual examples and some published articles, we conclude that the Internet is truly becoming a catalyst for a radical shift in the way advertising of products and services is being done and will be done in the future.

The promise of the new technology itself is creating confusion regarding what results to expect from web advertising. The possibilities of collecting information about the viewers of the ads, feasibility of immediate action by clicking on hyperlinks and the ability to track visits and sequence of clicks are placing unrealistic expectations of results due to web advertising. In traditional print and TV advertisements, advertisers are content with exposure of their ads but with web advertising advertisers are expecting click-throughs and sales leads. Traditional media has established Nielsen's ratings, and circulation audits. Established institutions exist for evaluating effectiveness of traditional advertising media. Similar institutions are emerging for electronic advertising.

The future of web advertising may involve rethinking of advertising strategies. Simply transferring the print copy or TV commercial to the Internet may not be sufficient. Advertisers need to be creative to exploit the unique features of the Internet. Not surprisingly, the merchants that market only on the Internet are the first to realize the benefit of cooperative advertising. A search for information not only gives the web pages of interest but also links to related sites such as Amazon.com and CDnow.com. What is the nature of advertising on the world wide web? Is it the same as using the print medium, radio, and television? Or has it changed in a way that is fundamentally different than in the past? The Internet as an advertising medium is very different from magazines, radio, and TV where the written or unwritten rules are known to all. Some striking differences between traditional and web-based advertising are described below.

Contents Driven Advertising

Increasingly contents of editorial and news items determine advertisements rather than advertisements being independent (Hansell and Harmon, 1999). Stretching it a little further, sometimes the contents of the editorial and news items are determined by the sponsors of the underlying advertisements. "Advertising is being woven into the very fabric of the WWW...there is an advertising influence on most of the contents web surfers see." Examples are Johnson & Johnson baby powder being recommended by BabyCenter.com site, El Cholo restaurant (restaurants are rank ordered based on the size of the displays on their Internet sites) being recommended by Mexican Restaurants section for the LosAngeles.com site. Traditionally advertising and feature articles or news items have been independent, not so in the case of Internet based advertising. Amazon.com has been found to recommend books from publishers who paid for the favor. On the Internet, web surfers avoid paying subscription fees for information they seek, so the money to be made is from advertising products and services and ultimately selling them. Search engines like Yahoo also favor sponsors e.g., clicking on Travel Agent would lead one to Travelocity.com (instead of Travelocity's competitor Expedia.com), an affiliate of the AMR corporation, which has paid to be the official travel service of Yahoo. Many news websites provide hyperlinks (advertisements) to one or more books from Amazon.com or Barnesandnoble.com related to the topic of the news item. It is clear that advertising is becoming more context-based i.e., linked to the thought processes of a reader and a prospective customer. Hyperlinking has unleashed several new and creative global alliances.

Payments Tied to Performance

Another important distinction between traditional and Internet-based advertising is that advertising payments from the latter can be and are increasingly being based on the transactions that ensue from specific hyperlinks (Hansell and Harmon, 1999). With this approach, there is a real danger to the traditional journalistic independence, because of the potential commercial influence. Some sites try to draw a line e.g., CompareNet which offers shopping guides to products ranging from electronics to cars maintains independence and objectivity on "what to buy", but the section on "where to buy" is for sale to advertisers, who bestow financial incentives on CompareNet for the favor. The Federal Trade commission's bureau of consumer protection has established a group to watch for "deceptive" advertising on the Internet. According to this group, there is a real need for standards to evolve for the Internet as they exist for television or radio or the print medium. However, Mr. Schuler of America Online argues that the Internet is self-policing and there is no need for more regulation or more disclosure. CNN and MSNBC have started tying advertisements of books from the online store of Barnes & Noble to the topic of the news stories and collecting a commission for each book sold from these ads (Hansell, 1997). Is this strategy merely exploiting the hyperlinked nature of the WWW by offering readers a new dimension in easy and relevant shopping or is it compromising with the fundamental independence of news reporting thus losing the confidence of the readers. More and more merchants like Barnes & Noble are willing to pay their advertisers like MSNBC and CNN, only when the ads produce results. It is predicted that such transaction-driven ads will account for the lion's share of advertising revenue (Hansell, 1997). An individual's PC-screen is becoming his/her window to the world and the hyperlinked files are weaving a web of information that is simply mind-boggling. Since the Internet is in its infancy and electronic commerce is exploding, advertisers and publishers are inventing a set of rules that are very different from those in the print or the broadcast medium. Instead of saying that the lines are getting blurred between news and advertising, we can say that we are creating a new paradigm that is neither editorial nor advertising. The bookseller or the travel agency does not see itself as merely buying advertising space or links but a partner with the various news and information sites. The publishers are invariably given instant access to data about book titles or travel agencies that are hot on other sites. In this hyperlinked WWW community, there is a real danger of the surfers wandering around from one site to another and not being able to focus on a topic.

Meta Advertising

All potential customers do not necessarily learn about an online business's products and services on the web (links and banners on other companies' websites and registering your website with search engines and directories). There is a mix of traditional advertising (newspaper, magazine, radio, television, films) that can be exploited to send the message about a company's online presence. Once the customer visits a website, then it can promote and advertise its products and services in a big way and in detail. So, essentially, these traditional advertising options can be looked upon as advertising for advertising i.e., meta-advertising. Others might look upon online advertising as just another option besides traditional advertising options.

FTD, Inc. www.ftd.com spent heavily initially on television commercials and print advertising – its marketing budget for the fiscal year ended June 2000 was $42.9 million or 44% of total revenue (Coleman, 2001). FTD.com Inc. finally began to heed advice from several sources that FTD name already had more than 95% brand recognition among consumers – a legacy of its 90-year old parent, floral giant FTD Inc. By Mother's day of 2000, FTD.com pulled the plug on meta-advertising thorough TV and print media slashing its marketing budget by 50% to $17-20 million. Finally, in the third quarter of 2000, the company posted profit.

According to Richtel (1999), www.hotjobs.com had revenue of $4 million during 1998, but in late January 1999 they spent half of that amount in a 30 second ad during the Super Bowl. This was a high stake ad. Did it work? After the game, the site which lists about 17,000 jobs was so overwhelmed that many visitors were unable to enter it. The competitors of Hotjobs.com are www.monster.com , www.areermosaic.com , and www.careerpath.com. The amount of money spent on advertising for e-Businesses during Super Bowl 34 in January 2000 was approximately $135 million (Eliot, 2000).

Latecomers have a lot to lose in this age of Internet based advertising. Table-2 shows the top 25 websites, their reach and the number of unique visitors in June 2000[15]. Companies trying to catch the Internet-based merchandizing can choose a three-phase strategy: Advertise, accept orders, and receive payments. Some companies only advertise on the Internet, while others advertise as well as accept orders online, while some exploit the full potential of Internet by implementing all three phases on the Internet.

Value Velocity versus Visual Virtuosity

The bedrock principle of Website design is that viewers value velocity over visual virtuosity (Kaufman, 1999). Photographs and elegant colorful images are minimized to avoid unnecessary downloading time. Most websites allow for text to appear before images appear (allowing for image borders to appear along with the text) to maintain the interest of the surfer viewer. Such gulag-style design standards are anathema to retailers who have spent years cultivating upscale images (Kaufman, 1999). However, there is a cultural twist to this. Members of a polychronic culture like those in the Arab world may be less likely to hold negative attitudes toward download delays than those from a monochronic culture such as in the US (Rose and Straub, 2000). Velocity of navigation enhances shopping interest and motivation. Web retailers like Amazon.com observe the "three click rule" meaning that a shopper can get to the product she wants within three clicks of a mouse. In addition to simplifying access to desired products with three clicks, purchasing the selected products can be simplified with few clicks. Amazon pioneered the use of 1-click ordering – a customer with an account with Amazon can complete an order with a single click of the mouse.

Measurement of Advertising Effectiveness

Making decisions about advertising medium and form is undoubtedly based on advertising effectiveness. A simple measure of advertising effectiveness is the exposure generated by the advertisements. For traditional media, well-established measures of advertising effectiveness exist. For print media, Audit Bureau of Circulation, among others, verifies circulation. Viewer reach and advertising effectiveness of television programs are measured by AC

---

[15] Based on PC Data Online survey of 120,000 home Internet users.

Nielsen ratings, which are then also used for establishing advertisement rates. The measurement of effectiveness of Internet advertising is relatively new and requires modifying traditional measurement techniques. The following two approaches are currently being used for measuring Internet advertising effectiveness.

Table 2: Web Traffic to Popular Websites

Rank	Website	Reach[16]	Number of unique visitors[17] (000)
1	Yahoo	60.7%	49,404
2	AOL.com	51.2%	41,725
3	MSN.com	48.2%	39,244
4	Passport.com	36.3%	29,573
5	Microsoft.com	36.3%	29,567
6	Geocities.com	34.7%	28,247
7	AOL Propreitary	33.6%	27,335
8	Altavista.com	24.8%	20,237
9	Lycos.com	24.1%	19,659
10	Netscape.com	21.6%	17,606
11	Ebay.com	21.5%	17,535
12	Excite.com	21.4%	17,400
13	Angelfire.com	19.9%	16,174
14	Amazon.com	19.6%	15,923
15	Tripod.com	18.4%	14,994
16	Ask.com	18.1%	14,728
17	Iwon.com	17.3%	14,109
18	Doubleclick.com	15.9%	12,979
19	Real.com	15.2%	12,403
20	Bluemontain.com	15.1%	12,318
21	Speedyclick.com	15.1%	12,274
22	Americangreetings.com	14.8%	12,088
23	Freelotto.com	14.8%	12,084
24	Looksmart.com	14.4%	11,729
25	Zdnet.com	12.9%	10,474

Server-based: Every user of WWW leaves an electronic trail of visits made to different websites. The trail of visitors can be logged, stored and analyzed. Server log files provide extensive usage information. The data collected in the logs include the operating system and browser of the web surfer, number of clicks, time of visit, and where visited from. Although it seems that the Internet log solves the measurement problem, the process is imperfect. For security reasons many websites utilize a proxy server to connect the clients to the real server. A proxy server intercepts and evaluates client's requests for a particular service and decides which to pass on to the real server and which to drop. To speed up processing information requests, proxy caches are used. Some client requests are satisfied by the information stored in the proxy caches and therefore these requests never reach the real server. Widespread use of proxy caches are making server-based measurements difficult if not impossible. The server log-based measurement of web traffic includes international traffic as well as traffic generated

---

[16] Reach %: This is a simple division of the Unique Users divided by the total estimated population viewing the web during the reported time period.

[17] Unique Users is the number of web-active individuals who visited a particular site or web property within a given time period. Each visitor is represented only once as a unique user.

by American surfers. *The data generated is anonymous giving little information about the demographics of the user.* Due to inexpensive collection of visitor information and their journey through the site with clicks, server log analysis remains a useful measurement tool.

Surfer-based: Alternatively advertising effectiveness can be measured by observing consumers' surfing habits. Nearly 40% of a web site's traffic originates overseas. Surfer-based measurement avoids measurement of international traffic by utilizing a panel of American users. Relevant Knowledge[18] has 10,000 members and their web surfing habits are sent to the company. Media Metrix[19], on the other hand, uses a panel of 30,000 and their web usage is stored on the user's computer and automatically mailed to the company every month. Surfer-based measurement is becoming widely accepted and measurement methods used for broadcast media are increasingly applied to measure Internet user habits. In the year 2000, Nielsen Media Research started Nielsen//NetRatings[20] with 110,000 panelists to measure Internet audience habits in real time.

Reimbursement Schemes

Traditional media has established formulas for advertising reimbursements. Internet advertising provides additional opportunities for fine-tuning reimbursements. The tracking ability on the Internet provides a richer set of reimbursement schemes potentially configurable to meet the objectives of the advertisers. Unlike traditional advertising, reimbursement scheme for Internet advertising can be based on actual results e.g., sales volume generated by the advertisement. Results-based reimbursements enable advertisers to optimize their advertising budgets in ways not imaginable in the past. The following reimbursement schemes are popular for Internet advertising.

Cost per Thousand (CPM) Click-through: CPM is a method used for payments to traditional media such as magazines and TV advertisements. In the web adaptation of CPM results in charging a designated fee for every 1000 people who visit the website on which your banner ad is located. If the company hosting your banner ad has 50,000 visitors per month, your ad will cost 50 times the CPM rate. This payment plan was considered by Proctor and Gamble with a combined advertising budget of $3.3 billion. (Taylor, 1996).

Pay-Per-Performance: The fee for this method includes pay-per-click, pay-per-lead, and pay-per-sale. Pay-per-click results in the payment to hosting site (the site hosting a banner ad) based on the number of click-throughs to the company's site from the banner ad. Pay-per-lead means that the company pays the hosting site for every lead generated from the ad. Fore example, Garden State Life Insurance pays $10 per lead to its advertisers for generating request for information by filling in forms (Snyder, 1998). Pay-per-sale means that the company pays to the hosting site fore every sale resulting from a click-through.

Content-Sharing and Web Linking: Many innovative and targeted approaches to web advertising are emerging. Advertisers such as bookstores and music shops are linking their advertising to search engines. A user's search not only results in other websites but also the appropriate ad by the advertiser with pricing and delivery information. Affiliates programs are used by many e-retailers to link their commerce site to millions of music or literature fans' personal webpages. For example, dozens of fan pages of Roger Waters, formerly of Pink

---

[18] http://www.relevantknowledge.com.

[19] http://www.mediametrix.com

[20] http://www.nielsen-netratings.com

Floyd, not only gives information about the musician and the body of his work, but also enables the surfer to buy CDs from the e-retailer affiliated with the fan's web page. Such innovative and performance-based advertising is unimaginable using traditional media.

Fixed Fee for Providing Hyperlinks to an Advertiser: Based on ranges of number of visits or hits per week or per month to a website that provides advertiser's hyperlinks, a fixed fee is paid to the owner of that website. The fixed fees may be based on number of hits or number of eyeballs to an advertiser's website from a host website.[21]

Not all advertisers are happy with the costs and advertising effectiveness of Internet. Some complain about the high cost-per-thousand (CPM) on websites. A Jupiter communications study reports $12 CPM for TV, compared to $20 for websites (Boyce, 1998). However with better understanding of customer response to Internet advertising, rates are expected to stabilize to a level where Internet advertising is more cost-effective and targeted.

Search Engine Strategies

Search engines are the vertical portals that lead 8 out of every 10 web visitors to a specific web site. About fifty percent a typical web surfer's time is spent in searching and 29% of web surfers give up in frustration not able to find what they are looking for. Not finding needed information is not due to lack of available information, but, rather paradoxically, due to abundance of information. Each webpage is a potential target of a search engine's search. Also, there are 12 main search engines, including Altavista, Askjeeves, Excite, Google, Lycos, and Yahoo. Registering with as many search engines as possible and by submitting keywords and information geared towards the ranking strategy of each search engine will improve the chances of a website being found. Most search engines (bots, crawlers, spiders) take a proactive stance and crawl through the HTML code of websites looking for keywords (especially repetition of keywords) or other search-engine ranking criteria. Search engine ranking is important to bring new visitors to a site. Most web surfers do not look beyond top three, top seven, or top ten ranked sites. How do search engines rank websites? Some examples from Deitel et al (2001) are:

- Altavista sends out crawlers that find sites and adds them to Altavista's index. The crawler follows hyperlinks from the sites it finds and adds more URLs to its index. So, if many web pages link a site, that site is more likely to be found. Altavista will find a site, even if that site is not registered.

- For free registration on Lycos, a site is required to submit a URL for each page of that site as well as a contact e-mail address. Lycos then sends spider to that site and in 2-3 weeks, that site is entered into Lyco's catalog.

- To register with AskJeeve's knowledge base, it requires an e-mail with the site's URL and short description. Human editors visit the website to check for conformance to certain guidelines including quick load time, regular updating of contents, and free features without requiring user registration. There are additional guidelines for e-Commerce sites including security requirements, customer service and credibility.

- If a site is not already listed on Yahoo, the potential site should find an appropriate category in the Yahoo! Directory to list the site. The site name, URL, and a short description of the site are needed to for a listing on the Yahoo directory.

---

[21] Eyeballs means number of visits from a unique user, whereas hits means number of total number of visits including multiple visits from same users.

- Google does not index every site submitted. It requires only the submission of a site's main page, since its crawler called the *Googlebot* will be able to find the rest of the pages as it searches all possible links. Google ranks pages by the number of connections between websites, with the theory that the more the connections to a site, the more popular and useful the site. This is different compared to other search engines that use META tags and site descriptions as a method of ranking. Recently, Google has started indexing millions of Portable Document Format (PDF) files, which average more tahtn five tiems as many words, compared with pages constructed in HTML (Fleishman-A, 2001).

There are also metasearch engines which aggregate results from a variety of search engines. Two examples are metawcrawler.com and framesearch.net. It is important to provide text-only alternative in the website, since surfers with physical disabilities and low bandwidth connections prefer text-only access to websites.

Global Issues

Extracted from the website http://www.the-net-effect.com/articles/multiculture.html, the following ads exemplify the errors or gaffes that happen when a message in one language is translated into another language.

- The American slogan for Salem cigarettes, "Salem-Feeling Free", was translated into the Japanese market as "When smoking Salem, you will feel so refreshed that your mind seems to be free and empty".

- When Parker Pen marketed a ball-point pen in Mexico, its ads were supposed to have read, "it won't leak in your pocket and embarrass you". Instead, the company thought that the word "embarazar" (to impregnate) meant to embarrass, so the ad read: "It won't leak in your pocket and make you pregnant".

- The Coca-Cola name in China was first read as "Ke-kou-ke-la", meaning "Bite the wax tadpole" or "female horse stuffed with wax", depending on the dialect. Coke then researched 40,000 characters to find a phonetic equivalent "ko-kou-ko-le", translating into "happiness in the mouth".

- The popular ad campaign for the dairy board which asks you "Got Milk?" had to be dropped in Mexico after it was discovered that the Spanish translation meant literally "Are You Lactating?"

- Hunt-Wesson introduced Big John products in French Canada as Gros Jos. Later they found out that in slang it means "big breasts".

Also, American advertising tactics such as "hard sell" are despised in other cultures. It is also illegal to use foreign languages when advertising in France or to directly mention competitors when advertising in Germany. The sending of unsolicited commercial e-mails (even with opt-out provision) or Spam, is restricted in many countries. In addition to evaluating cost-effectiveness of various advertising options, a company making advertising decisions should also consider cultural and legal appropriateness of the advertisements.

Privacy Issues

Privacy issues are increasingly becoming very important in determining what data companies can collect, summarize, sell or use for advertising in different countries and cultures. For example, Federal Trade Commission (FTC) charged that Geocities was sharing customer data such as education level, marital status, and income with marketers, in violation of company's own privacy policy. New privacy laws and regulations in Europe are forcing companies that do business in Europe to pay attention to privacy policies. Dr. Ponemon, the head of PriceWaterhouseCooper's privacy practice, estimates that about 80% of companies do not comply with their own privacy policies. Based on Dr. Ponemon's recommendation, www.expedia.com switched from an opt-out policy (users received e-mails with special offers unless they opted not to receive e-mails.) for e-mails to users to an opt-in policy (proactively sign to receive special offers through e-mail) for e-mails. Both IBM and Earthlink named Chief Privacy officers to emphasize the importance of privacy issues; and some companies are now turning to the P3P technology (Platform for Privacy Preferences) to streamline their privacy practices (Petersen, 2001).

Paradigm Shift or Old wine in A New Bottle?

An individual's PC screen is becoming his/her window to the world and the myriad of hyperlinked files are weaving an extraordinary web of information. Since the Internet is in its infancy and electronic commerce is exploding, advertisers and publishers are inventing a set of rules that are very different from those in the print or the broadcast medium. Instead of saying that the lines are getting blurred between news and advertising, we can say that we are creating a new paradigm that is neither editorial nor advertising. The bookseller or the travel agency does not see itself as merely buying advertising space or links but as a partner with the various news and information sites. The publishers are invariably given instant access to data about titles or travel agencies that are hot on their sites. The following table captures the fundamental differences between Internet-based advertising and traditional advertising.

Table 3: Comparison of Internet and Traditional Advertising

Criterion	Traditional Advertising	Internet-based Advertising
Advertising versus Contents	Advertising driving contents	Contents are increasingly driving advertising
Use of hyperlinks	No hyperlinks	A network of hyperlinks
Timing of viewing	View when broadcast or printed	View on demand
Measurability of Effectiveness	No or little information on exposure. Based on sample data.	Complete information on hits. Based on population data.
Control over Exposure Time	Exposure time determined by advertiser with the exception of print medium	Exposure time determined by web surfer
Interactive or not?	Advertising is non-interactive	Can be interactive by including chats with experts
Image – Upscale or Relevant	Preference for upscale image	Preference for relevant information fast
Payments versus Effectiveness	Advertising payments are not tied to actual advertising effectiveness	Advertising payments are increasingly being tied to to actual advertising effectiveness
Focus on Target	Limited target advertising	Many ways to promote target advertising

INTERMEDIATION IN GLOBAL e-COMMERCE

Like the industrial revolution, the information revolution and more specifically the Internet revolution -- which makes electronic commerce possible -- affects consumers in a fundamental way. While the industrial revolution made a wide array of products available and affordable, the information and Internet revolution has primarily improved quality, service, price and speed of delivery. The World Wide Web provides a platform for a paradigm shift in how commerce will be conducted globally in the future. The easy accessibility of vast amounts of information on the Internet may fundamentally alter the channels of distribution of products and services. Several researchers have predicted the elimination of middlemen in the distribution channels of the future. (see section 4.3 for details).

Anticipated Changes in Market Structure

Due to the rapid increase in the volume of transactions through electronic commerce, there is an immense interest in predicting changes in the structure of economic activity. Empirical analysis is severely hampered by the lack of data availability. Electronic commerce is expected to change industry structures in a fundamental way. Prices, distribution of profits, strategic interactions between market participants, organisational hierarchies, transaction costs, value chain compositions and barriers to entry are some key economic variables likely to undergo rapid changes. The analysis of the impact of electronic commerce on market structure is difficult and prone to errors (Wyckoff, 1997). A conceptual analysis based on economic models, however, has the potential of yielding refutable hypotheses concerning the impact of electronic commerce on market structure. The extant conceptual analyses include 1) search cost analysis (costs buyers pay to obtain information about product availability, characteristics and prices), 2) product characteristic analysis and 3) transaction cost analysis (thinking, planning, bargaining and contracting costs among economic agents).

Electronic networks provide fast and inexpensive information about products and services, their availability at a point in time, and their current prices. The reduced search costs incurred by buyers is expected to have great influence on market structure. Bakos (1991) draws on economic theory of search costs to make predictions of changes in market efficiency and competitive behavior -- reduction in search costs due to electronic markets is expected to lower prices, transfer wealth from the sellers to the buyers, and improve efficiency in commodity and differentiated product markets. Bakos (1991) anticipates electronic markets to be a critical component of economic infrastructure. Bakos, further, states that the implementation of electronic commerce will not necessarily result in sustainable advantage.

Economic theories of organizations identify either hierarchical authority structures (hierarchies) internal to the firm or market mechanisms (e.g., price adjustments based on supply and demand) to coordinate transactions among participants in a firm's supply and distribution chains. Malone, Yates and Benjamin (1987) analyze the effect of product characteristics on the choice of hierarchical authority structures and market mechanisms for coordination. Past experience has shown that information technology will reduce the cost of coordinating transactions and will also enable the coordination of economic activity thorough market mechanisms. They argue that 1) asset specificity (investments made for a specific client), and 2) complexity of product description (extent of information needed to describe product attributes), are the determinants of selection of hierarchical authority structures or market mechanisms. High asset specificity and high complexity of product description favor hierarchical authority structures as a coordinating force. Low asset specificity and low complexity of product description favor markets as coordinating mechanism since, reliable information will be available to attract sufficient number of buyers. They further identify roles of informational technology for 1) communication, 2) electronic brokerage, and 3) integration. All these roles of information technology are expected to make increased use of markets as coordinating mechanism in the value chains. Wyckoff (1997) uses intangibility of products or services as the determinant of changes in distribution channels. He predicts that selling products or services such as travel and ticketing services, entertainment, financial services and computer software will be most affected by the growth in electronic commerce.

Search cost analysis predicts changes in market structure due to the reduced costs incurred by the consumers in the electronic marketplace. Transaction cost analysis, however, predicts changes in market structure due to lower coordination costs of the participants in the distribution and supply chain. According to the transaction costs theory, if transaction costs are high, it will be economical to conduct the transactions through hierarchies within the firm rather than through market mechanisms. Williamson (1985) recognises that if investments are specific to economic agents (asset specificity), bringing transactions from the market into the firm through vertical integration is warranted. Malone, Yates and Benjamin (1987) argue that the reduction of transaction costs due to electronic commerce will shift economic activity from internal hierarchical structures to market mechanisms (e.g., we would expect a diminished role of vertical integration in supply and distribution chains). By predicting a shift towards market-mediated transactions, transaction cost analysis implies an enhanced role of marketing intermediaries in electronic commerce.

How reliable are predictions of changes in market structure due to the increasing use of electronic commerce? It is too early to make empirical evaluations because of limited availability of data. According to Lee (1998), recent evidence from Japanese used car auctions suggests that prices are higher in the electronic marketplace than in traditional marketing channels. He further points out that these findings do not necessarily contradict the prediction of reduced prices in electronic markets. The increase in price may be offset: by the improvement in convenience to the buyers, sellers, and intermediaries; and by the improved confidence in quality of the relatively new models of used cars that are auctioned.

Next, we will analyze the functions of marketing intermediaries and make predictions about how these intermediaries will evolve in the market place dominated by electronic commerce. Unlike the previous analyses, we will utilise functional analysis, that is, identify the functions performed by marketing intermediaries, and make predictions based on how electronic commerce is equipped to perform these functions. By disaggregating the functions, we are able to identify the products and services that will experience rapid evolution of marketing channels. The next section articulates research issues that will be explored in subsequent sections.

Intermediation, Disintermediation, or Hypermediation?

In the future commerce dominated by the World Wide Web on the Internet, many predict the demise of traditional marketing channels and foresee a direct channel in the flow of goods and services from manufacturers to consumers. Notably, Tapscott (1996) argues that 'middleman functions between producers and consumers are being eliminated through digital networks' (p. 56). This process of elimination of middlemen due to direct online channels is termed *disintermediation*. Roche (1996) recognizes the possibility of major changes in distribution channels due to electronic commerce. However, he surmises that '[t]he age of electronic commerce might bring to an end the intermediate enterprise.' (p. 436). Benjamin and Wigand (1995) analyse the effect of electronic markets on the value chains of a company and conclude that 'electronic markets lower coordination costs for producers and retailers, lower physical distribution costs, or eliminate retailers and wholesalers entirely, as conusmers directly access manufacturerers.' (Roche (1996), p. 62). The concept of disintermediation has gained considerable support in the popular media, trade journals, and industry magazines. Extensive evidence supports the dwindling role of middlemen in bringing the buyers and sellers together and affecting the sale of goods and services.

However, the disintermediation hypothesis is based mostly on anecdotal evidence (see next section) alone and not subject to systematic analysis. We will analyze the role of, the functions provided by, and the efficacy of utilizing traditional middlemen. Then we will discuss how electronic commerce and digital networks are equipped to fulfill various functions provided by traditional middlemen more efficiently. With this understanding of efficiency gains, we are able to make predictions of how marketing channels will evolve in the age of electronic commerce. By analysing various functions provided by traditional middlemen we will be able to make predictions about the product and industry characteristics that will lead to the greatest impact of electronic commerce on marketing channels.

Anecdotal Evidence Supporting Disintermediation

Considerable anecdotal and empirical evidence exists to support the disintermediation process. Airline ticket sales, book sales, computer sales, auctions, and sale of securities by discount brokers are often cited as examples of fundamental sweeps to come in bringing providers and consumers of products and services closer in the information age. Travelocity, an online travel service provider, barely two years old, is experiencing weekly sales of $3 million. While Microsoft's Expedia is not far behind with $2 million weekly sales (Wilson, 1997). The projections of online sales by travel agencies is even more impressive. They are expected to grow from $126 million in 1996 to $1,579 million in year 2000 (Thompson, 1997). These impressive gains are having an impact on earnings of travel agents. The commissions earned by traditional travel agents have been reduced. In 1995, traditional agents earned 10 percent commission on the tickets they sold. With the advent of online sales of airline tickets, commissions have diminished to 8 % or $50, whichever is lower. The survival of many traditional travel agents is in doubt. The number of travel agents in the United States is predicted to dwindle from the current 32,000 to 15,000 in one year (Wilson, 1997).

Some discount security brokers have experienced a rapid increase in online commerce. Charles Schwab, a discount brokerage firm, opened 80,000 online accounts within a short period of starting online brokerage. It is currently adding 12,000 to 15,000 new accounts a week. Within six months of initiating online brokerage, 30 percent of its trade was Web based (Tadjer, 1997).

Within two years of its online inception in 1995, Amazon.com, generally acknowledged as a pioneer in exploiting the new marketing channel, grew to 300 employees and 2.5 million book titles (Hogan, 1998). Not yet profitable (Vizard, 1997), Amazon.com has posted impressive sales of $121.7 million in the year 1997 (Electronic Advertising and Market Report (EAMR), 1998). The popularity of Amazon.com is transforming the marketing channels utilized in book sales. Traditional booksellers such as Barnes and Noble have also started selling books online since May 1997.

Computers and peripheral sales are also experiencing substantial growth in online sales. Dell Computers' success on the Web is impressive -- its Web sales are reported to go over $4 million a day. NECX, a leading computer reseller, generated $35 million in revenues last year, and is currently averaging $5 million per month (EAMR, 1998).

Book and computer (re)sellers are not the only beneficiaries of growth in electronic commerce. 1-800-Flowers, a leading flowers and gift retailer, generated 10% of its total revenues of $32 million through electronic commerce. Onsale.com[22], a leading Web based auctioneer, had $75 million in revenues in 1997, - about an 800% increase in sales from 1996 (EAMR, 1998).

Above anecdotal evidence leads many to believe that electronic commerce will dominate the future by providing a direct link between the manufacturers and consumers and *eliminate* or reduce the layers of middlemen. In the subsequent sections, we provide a systematic analysis of the role of middlemen in the distribution channels, the services they

---

[22] In 1999, merged with Egghead.com. See the following case for strategic implications of the merger.

provide, and how Internet commerce may affect and obviate their role in moving the products and services from manufacturers to consumers.

While many dotcom companies failed in 2000, airline sites drew a record number of visitors by giving them what they want – bargains. Revenue from airline tickets sold online rose 85% from 1999 to $8.7 billion in 2000. The airline gains came at the expense of their fiercest online competitors – travel agencies (Rewick, 2001). This article goes on to assert that airlines have been reaping huge savings – about $100 million in 2000 alone – basically by saving travel-agency commissions that average 5% of ticket's cost and by using e-mail to trim mailing and printing costs.

Intermediation in Traditional Marketing Channels

We will review the role of middlemen in traditional marketing channels and discuss the essential functions they provide. Industry and product characteristics determine the number, functions, and roles of middlemen. Generally, exporters, importers, brokers, manufacturer's agents, wholesalers, jobbers, retailers, distributors, elevators, auctioneers, and commission merchants are considered middlemen. Industry, product, and service characteristics determine which of these middlemen are utilized in the distribution of a particular product or service. Wholesalers and retailers are common across most distribution channels.

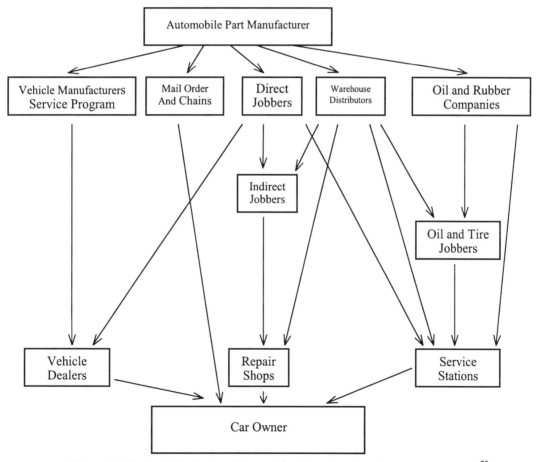

Figure 1: Typical Marketing Channel for Distribution of Automobile Parts[23]

---

[23] (Adapted from C.N. Davidson, "The Marketing of Automotive Parts, Michigan Business Studies, Vol. 12, Number 1, 1952, p. 652, University of Michigan, Ann Arbor).

Figure 1 illustrates the complexities of marketing channels used in the automobile parts industry. Other industries such as groceries and pharmaceuticals have their own particular needs for distribution channels.

Traditional Intermediary Functions

The middlemen perform a variety of functions in facilitating transactions between ultimate buyers and sellers. The following list discusses some important services provided by middlemen.

1. **Communication, coordination and Exchange Costs**: Middlemen reduce the number of communications and exchanges needed in the delivery of goods and services. Here we will use wholesalers as an example of how the middlemen will reduce cost of communication and exchange. For exchange between four manufacturers and three retailers, without a wholesaler, 12 exchanges are required. With the incorporation of a wholesaler into the marketing chain, the number of exchanges are reduced to seven. In general, exchange between m manufacturers and n retailers, without the aid of wholesalers, requires m * n exchanges, while a single wholesaler will reduce the number of exchanges to m + n. The efficiency gains in transaction and communication costs are even higher if transactions with numerous consumers are considered.

2. **Assortment of Products**: Middlemen, especially retailers, by carrying a variety of products, provide consumers with convenience in shopping. By eliminating the need to visit many shops for comparisons, retailers reduce shopping time and enable consumers to purchase goods and services closely matching their preferences for attributes, quality, and price.

3. **Warehousing and Distribution**: The movement of products from the manufacturer to the retailer consists of complex routing and storing decisions. Manufacturers are not well equipped to deal with the complexities of network routing and warehousing decisions to ship products to numerous consumers. Middlemen enable decentralization of complex network and warehousing decision problem into smaller, more manageable problems. Middlemen specialize in solving logistical complexities and relieve the manufacturer of these complexities. They contribute to the efficiency and cost reduction of the marketing chain by exploiting the favorable bulk rates offered by transporters of goods.

4. **Financing and Risk Sharing**: The provision of goods and services involves many uncertainties, including demand uncertainties. Inclusion of middlemen partially relieves the manufacturer of many uncertainties. Most products are sold (in contrast to consignment) to middlemen by manufacturers. This ready market for the output relieves the manufacturer of tying up funds in inventories. The sale of output to middlemen provides indirect financing to the manufacturers. In some cases, middlemen provide funds for financing manufacturers' operations. As a part of the marketing chain, middlemen, at least partially, shield the manufacturers from the risk of manufacturing, marketing, and distribution functions. For example, the risk of less than expected product demand is, at least partially, absorbed by the wholesalers, retailers, and manufacturers.

5. **Product Promotions**: Sales promotion is an effective tool to generate faster response in sales than through advertising. The combined expenditure on sales promotions in the U.S. is about $85 million in 1985 and it is about twice the combined advertising budget of that year. In addition, increase in sales promotions outpaces increases in advertising budgets. In trade promotions (push promotion), promotional efforts are directed to the marketing

channel partners rather than the consumers (pull promotion). In the U.S. typical trade promotion budget exceeds consumer promotion budgets. In trade promotions, marketing intermediaries are an essential part of the promotional strategy. In highly competitive product markets characterized by proliferation of brands, marketing channel members provide an important service.

Selling products without the involvement of marketing middlemen is not an entirely new phenomenon. To sell their products, many companies have experimented with vertical integration of marketing channels. Sherwin-Williams sells paint directly to consumers in about 2,000 retail outlets. Hart, Shaffner, Marx has about 200 retail outlets to sell its own clothing. Gap and other fashion clothing lines use direct retailing to reach consumers. However, direct sales to consumers is not the predominant paradigm for moving products from manufacturers to consumers.

Emerging Intermediation Trends in e-Commerce

Despite the well-publicized evidence of disintermediation, electronic commerce is not eliminating the need for middlemen. Electronic commerce is transforming the marketing channels into new configurations best suited for the new information technology. A manifestation of the disintermediation process occurs when manufacturers or service providers utilize electronic commerce to sell products and services directly to the consumers. However, there is a need to analyse some of the anecdotal evidence cited earlier supporting the emergence of disintermediation. Amazon.com is selling books on the Web without utilizing traditional retailing facilities. Yet, Amazon.com is really an online retailer of books fulfilling an important function of the middlemen in transferring books from publishers to the readers. Online travel agents, Travelocity and Expedia, also provide centralized access to fares, schedules, and reservations much like traditional travel agents, but exploit the unique features of electronic commerce.

To discuss how electronic commerce is transforming marketing distribution channels, we present the following seven cases. There is a common thread running through them. The role of middlemen and marketing distribution channels is evolving to exploit the particular features of electronic commerce. We also argue that newer institutions are emerging to fill the newer needs brought by electronic commerce.

1. Cisco Systems: Cisco Systems, the worldwide leader in networking for the Internet, provides networking solutions to build a unified infrastructure for large enterprises, service providers, and small/medium sized businesses. Cisco Systems may not have received as much coverage in the popular press as other success stories of electronic commerce, but it is the world's largest electronic commerce site with $10 million in sales every business day. Between September 1996 and September 1997, the percentage of orders received through electronic commerce went from 4 percent to 36 percent. The annual online sales during the fiscal year 1997 were $2.734 billion compared to $30 million during the previous fiscal year (Cisco Fact Sheet, 1998). Cisco Systems' adaptation of business systems and practices to the emergence of electronic commerce is a interesting case study to gauge the evolution of electronic commerce. Cisco Systems has the network technologies and transaction processing capabilities to implement innovative strategies to exploit electronic commerce opportunities effectively.

Cisco Systems perceives electronic commerce as more than just electronic catalogs and order and transaction processing systems. It uses the Web as a platform to forge efficient relationships with suppliers and distribution channel partners. Rather than replacing the traditional supply and distribution channel partners, Cisco is providing direct access to its manufacturing systems, so the channel partners can track inventories, engineering changes, shipment status, and other information in near-real time (Moad, 1998). Cisco embraced the Global Networked Business model to implement innovative tools, systems, and innovative approaches to share information with diverse company stakeholders: suppliers, distributors, customers, and employees. The Global Networked Business model will improve information sharing with the company's stakeholders in a networked environment. By using Cisco Connection Online (CCO), Internetworking Product Center (IPC), Partner-Initiated Customer Access (PICA), and direct link to manufacturing resource planning system (Cisco White Paper Series, 1998), Cisco opened the corporate information infrastructure to its key constituents. Cisco estimates a cost savings of $360 million a year, while improving customer/partner satisfaction (Cisco Fact Sheet, 1998). Cisco leveraged growth of electronic commerce by optimizing information flows between its channel partners rather than replacing the channel partners. *This example does not support the disintermediation hypothesis.*

2. Wal-Mart: In September, 1997, Wal-Mart Stores Inc. purchased an EC system from Sterling Commerce to set up an e-Commerce and EDI network with the retailer's non-US suppliers and trading partners. The initial goal was to create a network of 500 trading partners, each with access to purchase orders and invoices. Wal-Mart keeps a tight rein on its EDI relationships within the US, but has had problems working in countries such as Argentina, Brazil, China, Indonesia, and Mexico which have their own EDI standards. In June, 1998, Wal-Mart expanded its system to reach smaller suppliers. It purchased a system called Trusted-Link Express from Harbinger. This system allowed Wal-mart to automate business transactions with its suppliers that were not EDI capable. Those suppliers were then able to exchange purchase orders and invoices electronically over the Internet. This Internet-based client/server system enabled Wal-mart to extend its EDI program to its entire trading community without requiring its smaller trading partners to implement EDI translation software. Instead, the suppliers could use the Client software to receive purchase orders and send back invoices simply by filling out an easy-to-understand form. All required information on the purchase order automatically appeared on the invoice, eliminating any transcription errors and improving supplier's productivity. Before purchasing the system, Wal-Mart made sure that the server was fully integrated with Wal-Mart's existing EDI infrastructure and translation software.

3. Office Depot: This world's largest seller of office products, implemented EDI and EC long before others in the field. It operates over 600 retail stores, 23 delivery warehouses, and 3 national telecenters, and has approximately 32,000 employees. It is the industry leader in total sales, which totaled $4.95 billion in the first 3 quarters of 1998. Office Depot continues to expand internationally with 37 retail stores in Canada and 43 joint ventures and licensing agreements in other parts of the world. Office Depot pioneered EDI in the office supply industry in 1989 as a means of automating the process of sending purchase orders to suppliers. Later on, EDI was combined with point-of-sales barcode scanning. Now, with integrated logistics management, direct EC marketers can bypass store-based intermediary retailers like Office Depot and source products directly from the manufacturers and route them directly to customers – perhaps via a distribution point that allows for custom assembly of products for individual customers (mass customization).

4. Michelin North America, Inc.: Michelin is a multinational tire manufacturer with 1996 sales of over $13.9 billion. Michelin, contrary to prognostication of future of electronic commerce, is forging a closer relationship with its tire dealers. In 1997 it designed an extranet, Bib Net, for the use of its 1,700 independent dealers (Wrenden, 1997). The Bib Net helps the dealers to check inventory, order tires, and perform claims processing. Future plans include expanding the capability of Bib Net to allow dealers to combine orders placed on different days and process delivery/receipt information. *Michelin North America, Inc. is another example of effective coordination of functions of middlemen possible through improvements in network technologies.* Michelin surveyed its dealers' needs in the design and implementation of the Bib Net.

5. Security First Network Bank: This Internet bank topped on overall score (ease of use, customer confidence, on-site resources, relationship services, and overall cost) among twenty Internet banks (gomezadvisors.com). Security First Network Bank, the branchless offering from Royal Bank Financial Group of Canada, opened its "doors" in October 1995. Customers can apply for and manage deposit accounts and credit cards, access unlimited transaction history for checking and savings accounts, and perform a range of routine service requests through the Web interface. This quarter, however, saw the end to the bank's 6% interest checking account promotion, although customers that signed up before April 15 will continue to receive the promotional rate through November. SFNB made news this quarter when its parent company bought Prism Financial Corp., which in the coming months should bolster the bank's loan and line of credit offerings -- products currently available only to residents of Georgia and Florida are not supported by the Web interface. **Key Benefits** include SFNB's account management platform that supports online access to checking, savings, CDs and credit card balances, as well as unlimited transaction history. Interest rates and fees are competitive, even for a branchless offering, and the bank now reimburses up to four ATM fees charged by other banks. **Key Shortfalls** include SFNB's site being not as easy to use as the sites of some of the other Internet banking leaders. For instance, some functions relating to the bank's credit card offering, including transfers from checking accounts to credit cards, are buried in the "edit account" area of the site instead of the more intuitive "transfer" area. The bank has yet to integrate the brokerage offering of sister company Bull & Bear.

6. Transaction Processing Vendors: This case demonstrates that growth in electronic commerce may produce new intermediaries performing functions uniquely suited to electronic commerce. Transaction processing vendors such as CyberCash, Inc., ICVerify, Inc., Internet Billing Co., and LittleNet L.L.C. link commerce sites to credit card companies and lending banks are experiencing a doubling of transaction volume every quarter (Kerstetter, 1998.) These middlemen of electronic commerce handle credit card transactions for Web sites, communicate with lending banks, and approve the credit card for the merchant site in real time. In addition, they provide value added services such as fraud detection. This case is consistent with prediction by Bakos (1991) about expanded role of information intermediaries. *The growth of online transaction processing vendors contradicts the disintermediation hypothesis.*

7. Integration of Logistics in Supply and Distribution Channels: Freight companies such as UPS and FedEx have expanded role in their electronic commerce. Their function goes beyond shipping goods from warehouses to consumers. The freight companies are becoming an integral part of supply chains and distribution channels. Delegation, or out-sourcing of supply chain and distribution logistics to the freight companies, is an emerging trend. UPS is increasingly involved in supply chain and distribution logistic management. Its DockMerge service coordinates delivery of goods to the consumers. It synchronizes the delivery of system units, keyboards, and monitors from different suppliers for delivery to the consumers (Wilder, 1997). Customer tracking systems of UPS and FedEx add value to the transportation service and improve customer satisfaction. UPS is going beyond the traditional functions of freight companies and becoming involved in inventory management, facility planning, warehousing, and order processing (Payne, 1997). Globalization of commerce will add additional functions to the freight companies. Complexities of custom regulations, and collection from international customers will open up opportunities for freight companies to become closely aligned with their customers and become an important component of the supply chain and distribution channel. *The integration of logistics into core business functions illustrates the evolution of the role of middlemen.*

Global Issues

In the global context, factors of importance are: cost-effective distribution infrastructure in and shipping costs from/to host countries. *If focusing on globalization efforts in a small number of key countries*, it is usually more efficient to ship goods from local distribution centers than from the home country (like USA), since package delivery companies like UPS and Fedex charge much more in other countries (Deitel et al, 2001, page 354). Sometimes it is better to utilize national companies like British Post Office (www.postoffice.co.uk) , or the Deutsch Post office (www.post-ag.de) . In India, several national and regional private courier companies have successfully captured significant package delivery market. *If choosing to do business in a large number of foreign countries*, a volume deal from a well established like UPS (www.ups.com) or Federal Express (www.fedex.com) or DHL at www.dhl.com (covers almost all countries of the world from Albania to Zimbabwe) is highly recommended. InterShipper (www.intershipper.com) provides free service to compare the shipping price and arrival times of eight different shipping companies according to specific package's weight and destination (Deitel et al, 2001, page 355). The name of the game is effective global logistics supply chain management.

Hypotheses Postulation for Future Research

The above analysis clearly indicates the sweeping changes taking place in distribution channels due to the increase in electronic commerce. The disintermediation hypothesis, however plausible, will not obliterate the need for middlemen. Some of the traditional functions performed by middlemen may be eliminated in electronic commerce, but not all of the functions. For example, there are no institutions in electronic commerce to replace financing and risk sharing service provided by wholesalers and retailers. Newer institutions will emerge to fill the unique need for middlemen in electronic commerce. Purely information intermediaries, and transaction processing vendors (CyberCash) will evolve to fill the unique demands of electronic commerce. Greater integration of supply chain and distribution channel management into the core business functions is another trend. Some contend that electronic commerce, rather than reducing the need for intermediaries, is enhancing reliance on them to complete transactions. Even a small purchase over the Web may involve content providers, affiliate sites, search engines, portals, Internet service providers, software developers, and others, all of them sharing in the proceeds of the sale. The term hypermediation is coined to describe the phenomenon of increased number of intermediaries participating in the electronic sales.

Based on the above analysis, the following hypotheses can be postulated for future research:

1. The number of layers of intermediaries will decrease across all industries. This reduction will take place first in the industries in which the role of the middlemen is limited to facilitating communication and exchange between buyers and sellers. In the industries where the middlemen provide other important functions, reduction of layers may occur, but not as rapidly.

2. The reduction of layers of intermediaries will take place more rapidly in the service industry than in the manufacturing sector. The logistic and distribution function is minimal in the service industry. Typically, capital requirements in the service sector are lower than in the manufacturing sector. Due to low levels of capital investments, the service industry relies less heavily on middlemen for financing and risk sharing support.

3. The diminishing role of middlemen will depend on product and service characteristics. Reputed brand name products and services will have greater advantage in direct sales and diminish the role of middlemen. A similar effect will take place for the products and services whose attributes can be easily communicated to consumers.

4. Products and services that rely heavily on promotions, especially pull promotions, will be slow to adopt electronic commerce as the dominant channel. As of yet, there are no comparable mechanisms to substitute product promotions in electronic commerce.

5. Newer forms of intermediaries will emerge to fill the demands of electronic commerce. Their role will be limited. Further, ease of entry and low investments needed for entry of these new intermediaries will be numerous and face a competitive market.

6. Logistics and distribution will become an important part of the core functions of a business. The role of freight companies will be expanded from transporters of goods and services to an integrated component of business operations.

This section analyzed the viability of the "disintermediation" hypothesis. By analysing the functions provided by marketing intermediaries, we are able to make predictions about the evolution of marketing channels which will be dominated by electronic commerce in the future. Our analysis suggests that some functions of the traditional marketing intermediaries are efficiently performed by electronic markets, while others are still performed more efficiently by traditional intermediaries. The marketing intermediaries who primarily facilitate information exchange will be eliminated by electronic commerce. Real estate brokers, travel agents and auctioneers primarily facilitate exchange of communication, and our analysis suggests that electronic commerce is better equipped to execute this role. Some marketing intermediaries, especially retailers with considerable market power, are a crucial component of product promotions. Electronic markets have no mechanism to execute product promotions. It is too premature to predict the demise of these marketing intermediaries. As predicted in the literature (Bakos, 1991), we observe new institutions of electronic intermediaries to exploit the unique needs of electronic markets.

EMERGING CRITICAL SUCCESS FACTORS FOR GLOBAL e-COMMERCE

Despite the extraordinary potential of e-commerce, many obstacles remain: Lack of trust among transacting parties, lack of access to computers and the Internet, limited capability to make payments electronically, lack of interoperability among applications, and lack of standards. Most e-tailers do not ship overseas due to the complexities of customs, tariffs, currency exchange, and shipping. These impediments may remain for the foreseeable future. The vast majority of Internet websites cater to English speaking audiences and e-Commerce is still in its infancy catering primarily to businesses and consumers in America. Although only 8% of the world's population are native English speakers, 78% of all websites and 96% of all e-Commerce sites are presented in English (Dietel and Dietel, 2000, p. 364). E-Businesses will have to become global in their reach, as more and more Internet users in future will be from the non-English speaking regions of the world.

Global e-commerce, for its survival and sustenance, depends on the following two basic pillars, five building blocks, several classes of services (like B2B and B2C described earlier), multiple BPR initiatives, and technology enabled customer relationship (trust) management.

- Two basic pillars -- (a) globally accepted and enforced public policy that includes legal, privacy, and tariff issues within and across nations, and (b) technical standards for electronic documents including multimedia and network protocols.

- Five building blocks -- (a) information superhighway infrastructure, (b) multimedia content and network publishing infrastructure, (c) messaging and information distribution infrastructure, (d) common business services infrastructure, and (e) e-commerce applications including supply chain network management, video on demand, online marketing, home shopping, and remote banking.

- Several classes of services as discussed earlier -- B2B, B2E, B2C, B2G, G2C, and C2C.

- Multiple Business Process Reengineering (BPR) initiatives to change the basic structures of supply chain management in the context of electronic hierarchies and electronic markets.

- This relationship is fostered by the capability of the Internet technology to allow collection of data on customer's behavior, preferences, needs, and buying patterns. Armed with this critical information, businesses can set prices, negotiate terms, tailor promotions, add product features, and in general customize its entire relationship with that customer.

History has taught us that new technology or innovation does not necessarily translate to the demise of the old technology, they simply continue and co-exist. For example, film theaters did not die when TV and VCR became pervasive, radio did not die with the introduction of TV, wired telecommunications did not die when wireless telecommunications caught on. In the same vein, click-and-portal business does not mean the end of brick-and-mortar business. In fact more and more brick-and-mortar businesses are providing the ability to click and transact business – this is what the industry calls the brick-and-click option. It may mean, ordering or perhaps even paying over a network, but collecting goods and engaging in after-sales support services with the business's physical store.

In a short period of roughly five years a number of dotcom companies were formed, generated considerable excitement in the investment community and went out of business. To succeed during these periods of rapid transformations, businesses need to quickly adapt to the sweeping changes. The survival of a company may depend on how quickly it can correctly predict the changes and make necessary adjustments to its strategies. Based on our observations we identified the following factors as critical for success in the era of global electronic commerce.

Critical Success Factor 1: Complement High Tech with High Touch

The opportunities to automate selling process with high technology and Internet connectivity does not imply losing touch with customers. A successful electronic commerce implementation exploits high technology to enhance bonds with its customers. Although the temptation may be strong to cut costs in the short run by turning websites into an equivalent of automatic vending machines, the move is sure to fail. A website, no matter how well conceived, cannot compete with face-to-face interactions.

Many companies are realizing the need for supplementing e-commerce sites with physical presence or human interaction. For example, in mortgage lending, only about 2% of all mortgages are made online (Barta, 2001). Many online loan companies are tweaking their sites to make them more customer-service oriented. Customers prefer the convenience of online lending with physical branches that can be visited when customers want personal attention. LendingTree, the industry leading intermediary for mortgage loans, has now made customer-service representatives available all day and weeknights. Successful online mortgage lenders are replicating the offline experience in terms of access to information and customer service. Gateway computers, a fierce competitor of Dell computer, has also resorted to putting a human face, by supplementing its distribution channel with Gateway Country Stores. Online retailing companies like Ashford.com have realized that their online operations require the same merchandizing knack as a physical store – in effect, the Internet is a better vehicle for buying, but the physical store is better for shopping. In the cosmetics business, shoppers prefer to buy online, but value the ability to return wrong shades or scent products to a physical store. In the spirit of providing human touch, Digiscents Inc., a California maker of hardware and software for emitting scent online, envisions people clicking on a beauty website and sniffing samples of perfume or mixing their own floral fragrance (Nelson, 2001). As described under the subsection of Internationalization and Localization, www.Bazzee.com in India had to include the human component of having exchange centers in India to close the deal emanating from online auction (patterned after eBay).

Critical Success Factor 2: Globalize Operations, but Segment Geographically to Localize Service

Though the basic premise of Internet is to perceive the world as a global village, in reality differences around the world abound. Even though, there are global products and global customers and global suppliers, promotional material and campaigns have to be adapted to local culture, language, tax regime, pricing structure (based on custom duties, value added taxes, local competition). Even though money is money is money, currencies and payment mechanisms and preferences differ in different parts of the world. Time Zones must be considered when providing interactive customer service. Dell computer maintains 38 different sites catering to different countries and regions contributing to its much growth outside U.S.A. By comparison, its competitor Gateway computers lags behind in this arena. Examples of Ikea, Rediff, and Yahoo, as described earlier also support the importance of this critical success factor.

Critical Success Factor 3: Simplify and Expedite Transaction Process

Hyperlinks can bring a customer to a commerce site with a few mouse clicks and also can take her away from the site as easily. The web is creating shoppers with short attention spans. If the ordering process is complex and involves prolonged navigation through the web site, the shopper may be lured away from the transaction. For example, PayPal's initial sign-up process required users to click through seven screens – the company discovered that with each new screen, 25% of the users dropped off (Gomes, 2001). Using simple mathematics, that would result in only 17% of the original potential customers remaining. In the international context, it would be disastrous to have to go through seven web pages (amazon.com) in India, where Internet connections are shaky (Pearl, Searching For Solutions, 2001). Simplicity and ease of use are important design considerations in a commerce site design. The use of three-click rule and 1-click ordering are some of the successful design features that are effective.

Critical Success Factor 4: Foster Trusting Relationships with Customers

Trust is the magnetic force that pulls the customers to a business. We continue to patronize a physician, a hair stylist or a hardware store based on the confidence we have in their advice and how much we trust their expertise and competence. The electronic commerce replaced the human face with graphical user interface in interacting with the customers. The usual cues that build trust relationships such as facial expressions, voice inflections, and personality traits are absent in online transactions. In commerce over the network, it is critical that customers trust privacy policies and security measures to safeguard personal information. A single breach of trust may forever break a robust relationship. Due to the absence of physical cues in building a relationship, customers need unambiguous guarantees about privacy and security of personal information. Privacy policies regarding sale and exchange of mailing lists must be made available on the main page to build trust. Assurances regarding safety of personal information including credit card numbers, address and telephone numbers must be unambiguous, guaranteed and easily available to establish trusting relationships. In the spirit of enhancing trust, eBay made the most significant policy change – it moved away from allowing buyers and sellers to rate each other regardless of completion of any transaction; some disgruntled users were attempting to sabotage the reputation of others with unsubstantiated negative comments; now they require that all Feedback be connected with specific transactions (Wingfield, 2001). Brand awareness and brand loyalty also bring in confidence and trust. Brand loyalty can continue from the past offline presence of a business or must be earned through continued excellent product and after sales service. In the spirit of fostering trust, several merchants (e.g., Expedia travel site) are now switching from the thrust upon opt-out to the proactive opt-in for e-mail promotion campaigns; IBM and Earthlink named chief privacy officers whose primary role will be to safeguard consumers' privacy preferences (Petersen, 2001).

Critical Success Factor 5: Reinvent with Focus on Convenience, Information, Intermediation and Pricing Strategies

Creating and sustaining competitive advantage in the hyper-competitive online world is extremely important. One needs to start with the kernel of a good idea and then continuously reengineer and reinvent. For example, PayPal is positioning itself to be the online answer for all sorts of small cash-transfer needs – every 24 hours, PayPal handles more than 100,000 transfers, worth upward of $7 million (Gomes, 2001). United Airlines knows the kernel of its business – to fly passengers nationally and internationally, but its initial website was a dismal failure. So, United had to reinvent itself (at least on the web) – from the first screen users see, they can now perform three most common tasks – check the status of a flight, search for air fares, and monitor frequent flyer miles. Amazon.com and eBay.com, the two big success stories in the arena of e-Commerce must owe their success to their philosophy of constantly changing their websites to add convenience and provide more relevant information to their customers – current or potential. Amazon.com's uses "discovery tools" based on collaborative filters technology (software that recommends merchandise to customers based on past purchases) to limit the merchandise displayed from among 20 million items on its database (Wingfield, 2001). More recently, amazon.com has added a feature called Page You Made – it deciphers your desires based on items a surfer clicks on.   E-Bays's Personal Shopper e-mails potential bidder anytime new items that match a user's personal wish list; Item Watching lets buyers keep an eye on all of the auctions that they're interested in – but haven't yet bid on; convenient payment mechanisms through Billpoint.com and PayPal.com (Wingfield, 2001). Several pundits had predicted the downfall and even demise of the package deliverers like Fedex, UPS, U.s. Postal Service, and Airborne. But they reinvented their businesses to include moving information electronically by launching zap documents over the Net in a secure form (UPS and U.S. Post Office); launching eCourier service (Airborne); UPS, getting into the logistics supply management business, now manages the spare-parts and service parts network of Comapq Computer Corp. in North America; Fedex headquartered in Memphis, TN, moved a semiconductor warehouse of Koninklijke Philips Electronics from California to Memphis in order to improve customer response times for urgently needed high-tech components; essentially, these once-upon-a-time package movers are exploiting their huge weapon – their enormous, well-oiled delivery systems (Brooks, 2001). Internet platform provides the merchants the superb capability to set dynamic pricing – adjusting the price in miniscule amounts frequently (since the menu costs of the clerk running through a store with a pricing gun need not be incurred). This concept is what the economists call, first-degree discrimination, an idealized pricing strategy, charging exactly what the market will bear (Hamilton, 2001). Finally, intermediation or disintermediation strategy must be used prudently in keeping with the times – there is a lot of shakeout going on right now among the dot com companies, the ones bowing out are mostly infomediaries. For example, PriceLine's stock has nose dived, Travelocit is not doing that well either. Why? The airlines are coming back with a vengeance and selling airline teickets directly to the customers at a price better than what he intermediaries can offer. Finally, involve value chain partners in creative ways to add value to customers.

Critical Success Factor 6: Get Yourself Found Often and on the Top

Eighty percent of the times, web surfers rely on search engines to find what they are looking for. Furthermore, another 80% do not look beyond the first 10 sites found by a search engine. Thirty percent of web surfers give up their search in frustration. Clearly, it is critical for an online business' success that it be found by potential customers. So, what do you do, you register your site for free or for fee with major search engines like AltaVista, Yahoo!, Lycos, Ask, Google. Also, it is important to understand the search engines' algorithms to rank order websites that are found based on surfer specified search criteria (mostly look for keywords in HTML tags on the first page of a website and specially look for repetition of keywords). Some search engines rank order websites based on their popularity, which itself is determined by how many other sites link to your site. One way is to be part of a web wheel; a grouping of similar websites that agree to cross-reference each other for the greater good of the virtual community (Huff and Wade, 2000).

Critical Success Factor 7: Plan Technology to Evolve for Transactional e-Commerce

e-Commerce websites can be categorized as: static, interactional, or transactional (Huff and Wade, 2000). We add another level -- Full Blown (a Portal). *Static* is, in effect, an electronic version of a paper brochure; *Interactional* is updated and provides a degree of interaction with your customers e.g., the opportunity to e-mail to company officials; *Transactional* provides full online commerce capabilities of buying and selling; and finally, *Portal* goes beyond Transactional in providing all kinds of information and links – weather, travel, phone directory etc. The technical challenges in moving up this hierarchy are substantial; it is roughly 10 times more difficult and costly to operate the next higher level of website. The challenge is to determine what level of website you envisage implementing initially and what will be your progression strategy (scalability) in future, if any. You are damned if you start at too high level of technology and you are damned if you do not – there are pros and cons to starting at a higher level of e-Commerce solution. So, must get the right technology (e-Commerce solution). Once you get it, we are all aware of the problems of implementation, so implementation must be done right (that is the second right). The second right refers to appropriate acquisition option (rent versus buy); appropriate security management; appropriate backup and recovery strategy to ensure close to 100% uptime. Once eBay site notoriously went dark for almost 22 hours in June 1999 and then again one 11-hours outage in January of 2001 and that is just not acceptable anymore (Wingfield, 2001). Some web hosting companies offer dedicated servers (ensures no interruption of service to customers) and co-location (Deitel et al, 2001, page 64). Co-location services provide a secure physical location for a business' server hardware; dedicated Internet connections; and protection from power outages, fire, and other disasters.

Critical Success Factor 8: Prepare for m-Commerce

In Europe, especially in Finland, accessing Internet and corresponding via e-mail on the mobile phone, is pervasive. Doing e-Commerce transactions over the mobile phone in Europe and Japan is also becoming increasingly popular. In the United States, the use of mobile phone to access the web is growing rapidly. A number of companies like www.airwave.com, www.globaldigitalmedia.com, www.mobilestar.com, www.surfandsip.com, www.homerun.com, www.wayport.com,are offering wireless Internet access for laptops and hand-held devices in public places like airports, hotels, and stores (Fleishman-B, 2001). Touted as m-Business and m-Commerce, wireless e-Commerce will have significant implications for both B2C and B2B transactions. According to a study by International Data Corporation, m-Commerce in Europe is likely to reach over $30 billion by 2004 (Baker, 2000). In the B2C arena, customers are currently using mobile devices for news, sports scores, e-mail, for trading stocks and making some purchases. In future, consumers will use these devices for frequent small transactions; in the B2B marketplace – company databases, ordering systems, and billing systems will enable ordering and billing to be conducted remotely (Deitel et al, 2001, page 155). Echoing similar initiatives at other Internet companies, amazon has started a project called Amazon anywhere that lets customers purchase books from cellular phones and persona digital assistants (Wingfield, 2001). A well planned e-commerce infrastructure should include a planned upgrade path to accommodate impending m-commerce. Retrofitting an e-commerce site to enable mobile access in a haphazard fashion is bound to result in difficulties. Scalability (as mentioned in the previous critical success factor) concerns should include not only accommodating changing transaction volumes, but also technologies such as mobile commerce that are expected to emerge soon.

SUMMARY AND CONCLUSIONS

Almost all aspects of human endeavor have been or are getting affected by the use of Internet-based information exchange and e-Commerce. We provided statistical and anecdotal support to the far-reaching changes that are taking place and are expected to continue to take place. The pace of adaptation and the rate of growth of electronic commerce have no other comparisons that any of us might have experienced during our life times. Electronic Commerce has transformed the nature of relationships among businesses, governments, employees, citizens, and consumers. The so-called productivity paradox due to mass scale deployment of information and Internet technologies has been proved wrong.

The world of ours has a strange way of accommodating diversity. Something new does not necessarily mean the demise of the old. When TVs came into prominence, people predicted the demise of radios. That did not happen. When satellite telecommunications technology came into prominence, there were predictions about the abandoning of microwave, coaxial cable, and twisted wires as telecommunications media. That also did not happen. When VCRs came, there were predictions about the end of movie theaters. That also did not come true. The same conclusion can be drawn about the emergence of e-commerce.

E-commerce will not in any way result in the disappearance of the traditional commerce. The click-and-portal (online) economy can only be sustained if supported by adequate brick-and-mortar (offline or traditional) economy.

This chapter has described the different Internet based advertising approaches that have emerged in the last five years. Based on actual examples and some published articles, we conclude that the Internet is truly becoming a catalyst for a radical shift in the way advertising of products and services is being done and will be done in the future. The possibilities of collecting information about the viewers of the ads, feasibility of immediate action by clicking on hyperlinks and the ability to track visits and sequence of clicks are placing unrealistic expectations of results due to web advertising. The future of web advertising may involve rethinking of advertising strategies to accommodate the new paradigm that is emerging.

We analyzed the prediction that marketing intermediaries will be eliminated in the electronic markets. We concluded that this prediction is not valid and the role of marketing intermediaries is evolving to facilitate transactions in the electronic markets. In some sectors, newer intermediaries that did not exist in pre-electronic markets, are emerging.

Since Internet by definition is global, throughout the chapter, we have articulated cultural, language, legal, taxation, privacy, and other issues that differ from country to country.

Mini Case: Egghead.com

In 1984, Egghead, Inc., a personal computer (PC) software and hardware reseller, was founded with one software store in Bellevue, Washington. By 1994 Egghead grew to be a major computer retail chain with annual sales over $778 million and operating nearly 200 company-owned and operated stores. The customer base included businesses, government agencies, educational institutions, and individuals. The retail sales to individuals was through small shops in strip malls staffed by knowledgeable salespersons.

Despite the record sales in 1994, problems were looming in the horizon. The competition from computer and office superstores, consumer electronic stores, and mass merchandisers was fierce. Preloading and bundling of software with PC purchases reduced the demand for software. The effect of twin pressures of reduced demand and increased competition is swift and decisive. The profits declined from $15 million in 1992 to a loss of over $500,000 in 1994. Many software publishers started to sell directly to end users, further eroding Egghead sales.

Egghead began first of its transformations by moving into to online sales in 1995. Due to its mounting losses, in January 1998, Egghead announced a change of its name to Egghead.com, Inc. and shifting of its business emphasis to Internet commerce. As part of this transition, Egghead closed all of its remaining stores in its retail network and became Internet only store. It expanded its product offerings to include consumer electronics and consumer goods. It operated three shopping formats to attract a broad base of customers and to satisfy a variety of budget needs by offering a wide selection of competitively priced products at different points in their product life cycles. The three shopping formats are Egghead Superstores, Egghead SurplusDirect and Egghead Auctions. The following condensed income statements show the result of this transformation.

Mini Case .... Continued

Fiscal Year Ended

	April 1, 1995	March 30, 1996	March 29, 1997	March 28, 1998	April 3, 1999
	(in thousands, except per share data)				
Consolidated Statement of Operations Data:					
Net sales:					
Online.....................	$ --	$ 149	$ 1,408	$ 59,737	$148,721
Retail.....................	434,021	403,692	359,307	233,342	--
Total net sales..........	434,021	403,841	360,715	293,079	148,721
Cost of sales:					
Online.....................	--	95	1,159	52,016	134,341
Retail.....................	361,567	334,484	303,092	205,159	--
Total cost of sales.......	361,567	334,579	304,251	257,175	134,341
Gross profit.................	72,454	69,262	56,464	35,904	14,380
Selling and marketing expenses:					
Online.....................	--	29	382	10,118	34,722
Retail.....................	54,256	59,210	56,970	38,453	--
Total selling expenses....	54,256	59,239	57,352	49,219	34,722
General and administrative expenses.....................	19,594	23,257	24,065	18,847	16,084
Depreciation................	7,363	7,569	7,352	5,809	4,560
Restructuring	--	--	15,597	19,500	--
Operating loss..............	(8,759)	(20,803)	(47,902)	(57,471)	(40,986)
Other income, net(1)........	3,362	2,652	3,729	2,940	6,563
Loss from continuing operations before income taxes.....................	(5,397)	(18,151)	(44,173)	(54,531)	(34,423)

In yet another transformation, in November 1999 Egghead.com merged with Onsale.com, an Internet auction company paving way for creation of Web auction giant. Its refocused business strategy is to create a Web superstore, increase market awareness, customer loyalty and brand recognition, broaden existing offerings, build international customer base, and deliver compelling value. However, annual loss for 1999 was over $150 million.

Despite mounting losses, Egghead.com has a positive outlook towards the future. Approximately $1 billion of merchandise is sold on the web site in 1999. Egghead.com has approximately three million unique visitors each month. By the end of 1999, three million people are registered to bid or buy, including more than 325,000 new registrants in the fourth quarter of 1999.

Questions for discussion

1. Evaluate the transformations of the company from Egghead, Inc., a software retail store to Egghead.com, an online auction house.

2. A recent advertising campaign of Egghead.Inc. boasts "since we closed our doors, store traffic has increased 611%." Explain what is meant by the advertising slogan.

3. What are the strategic implications of the company's merger with OnSale.com.

4. Comment on the future of Egghead.com.

STUDY QUESTIONS

1. Critique the assumption: "Technology is the answer to all business problems."
2. The movie Field of Dreams' maxim, "if you build, they will come," may not be appropriate for developing a successful Internet retail business. Discuss what an entrepreneur may have to do to build an electronic commerce site besides setting up a website?
3. Levi Strauss, a successful clothing company, built a sophisticated e-commerce site in 1994. After operating the site for a few years, Levi Strauss ceased selling its products at the website. Discuss how selling goods at a website may affect relationships with existing distribution channel comprising of wholesalers and retailers? Discuss why the prices of shoes are no lower at the Nike website than at any brick-and-mortar stores. (Hint: Channel Conflict.)
4. Some suggest that electronic commerce rather than eliminating intermediaries is creating more intermediaries. They coined the term hypermediation to describe this phenomenon. List and discuss all potential parties receiving payments when you complete one click shopping at Amazon.com
5. "Worldwide E-Commerce: It's More Than A Web Site," quips a headline in Information Week on May 8, 2000. Discuss the issues to consider and how to resolve them in fulfilling retail sales to overseas customers.
6. Critique the assumption: "All of the industry leaders and gurus are on e-business bandwagon; if its good for GE, it must be good for us."
7. Advertising is advertising is advertising -- what difference does the medium make? Critique this statemnt in the context of commonalities and differences between traditional advertising and Internet-based advertising approaches.
8. What global considerations are important in designing websites to sell products and services worldwide?
9. In the context of closing of several dot com companies during 2000-2001, please describe critical success factors for existing and new start-up Internet-based companies.

Activity: Visit as many websites of Fortune 500 companies as your time permits and track the proportion of companies that provide information in languages other than English. Also, note the importance of non-US activities in overall operations of the firm. Write a short paragraph reflecting on your observations.

REFERENCES

Anbarasan, E. (2000). Indian Tourism enters e-Business Age, *News India*, June 23, 2000.

Baker S. (2000). Goliath vs. Goliath: In the Battle for Europe's Mobile Web, the Small May Not Last, *Business Week*, 29th May 2000, pages 152-154.

Baker S. and Echikson W. (2000). Europe's Internet Bash. *Business Week*, 7 February, EB42.

Bakos, J. Y. (1991). A Strategic Analysis of Electronic Market Places, *MIS Quarterly, 15*, 295-310.

Barta Patrick (2001). On the House, *The Wall Street Journal*, 02-12-01, R16.

Bollier, D., Rapporteur (1998). *The Global Advance of Electronic Commerce.* Colarado: The Aspen Institute.

Benjamin, R. and Wigland, R. (1995). Electronic Markets and Virtual Value Chains on the Information Superhighway. *Sloan Management Review, 36,* 62-72.

Berryman, Edward R (1997). Web Commerce: Be Prepared. *New York Times*, Oct.

Boyce, R. (1998). Exploding the Web CPM Myth. *Advertising Age, 96, n. 5, Feb.* 2, 1998, 17.

Boyle M. (2000). Anyone Up For a B-to-B Business-plan Bandwagon? *Revolution*, August, 8.

Briggs and Hollis (1997). Advertising on the Web: Is there response before click-through?, *Journal of Advertising Research, 37, n. 2,* March-April 1997, 33-45.

Brooks, Rick (2001). Outside the Box, *The Wall Street Journal*, 02-12-01, R20.

Brynjolfsson, E. and Hitt L. (1993). New Evidence on the Returns of Information Systems. MIT Sloan School, Cambridge, Massachusetts.

Cisco (1998) 'Fact Sheet'.

Cisco (1998) The Global Networked Business: A Model for Success, White Paper Series.

Coleman Calmetta (2001). Pruning Costs. *The Wall Street Journal*, 02-12-01, R30.

Crocket R. (2000). No Plastic? No Problem, Business Week E.Biz, 23 October 2000:18.

Deitel H.M., Deitel P.J., and Steinbuhler K. (2001). *E-Business and e-Commerce for Managers*. Prentice Hall.

Dorsey James M. (2001). The Fixer, *The Wall Street Journal*, 02-12-01, R12. Electronic Advertising & Market Report (1998) New Exclusive EAMR Survey: Leading Marketers generate $7.03 billion in 1997, January 13, 12, no. 1, p. 1.

Eliot S. (2000). Not X'es, Not O's, It's the Dot-Coms that Matter: Marketers Suit Up for a Costly Race for Recognition, *The New York Times*, 28 January 2000: C1.

Erwin, B., M. and Johnson, J. (1997). Business Trade and Technology Strategies, *Forrester Research Report*.

Fleishman-A, Glenn A (2001). Google Extends Search Engine's Reach to a Popular File Format, *The New York Times*, 02-22-01, G8.

Fleishma-B, Glenn B (2001). The Web, Without Wires, Wherever, *The New York Times*, 02-22-01, G1, G7.
FIX IT

Gomes L. (2001). Fix IT and They will Come. *The Wall Street Journal*, 02-12-01, R4.

Grande C. (2000). Crime Leaves Websites Rushing to Fill the Breach, The Financial Times, 19 October 2000: 10.

Hamilton, D. (2001). The Price Isn't Right, the Wall Street Journal, 02-12-01, R8.

Hansell Saul (1997). News-Ad Issues Arise in New Media, *The New York Times*, December 8, 1997.

Hansell Saul and Harmon Amy (1999). Caveat Emptor on the Web: Ad and Editorial Lines Blur, *The New York Times*, February 26, 1999.

Hogan, M. (1997) You Can Make Money on the Web, *PC World, 7, n. 7* July, 15, 1997, 190.

Hechinger John (2001). Check It Out, *The Wall Street Journal*, 02-1-01, R28.

Huff S. L. and Wade M. (2000). Critical Success Factors for Electronic Commerce, *Cases in Electronic Commerce,* Irwin McGraw-Hill, 2000, 450-461.

Kaufman Leslie (1999). Playing Catch-Up at the On-Line Mall, *The New York Times*, February 21, 1999.

Kerstetter, J. (1998). Middlemen Cash in on Growth, *PC Week Online*, March 9.

Kirkpatrick K. (2000). Banking On the Net, *Computer Shopper*, May 2000, page 189.

Lagon O. (2000). Culturally Correct Site Design, *Webtechiques*, September 2000:51.

Lee, H. G. (1998). Do Electronic Marketplace Lower the Price of Goods?, *Communications of ACM, 41,* 73-80.

Malone, T., Yates, J. and Benjamin, R. (1987) Electronic Markets and Electronic Hierarchies, *Communications of the ACM, 30,* 486-497.

Mccollum T. (2000). Foreign Affairs, *The Industry Standard*, 7 August, 2000:175. FIX IT

McFarland Sofia (2001). B2B Squeezed, *The Wall Street Journal*, 02-12-01, R28.

Moad, J. (1997). Forging Flexible Links, *PCWeek*, 14, 74-75.

Mottl, J.N. (2000). Commerce One: A place where anyone can play; *InformationWeek, 788,* May 29, 2000, 92-94.

Mullen T. (2000). Service Aids Selling to Europeans, *Internet Week* 17 July, 2000: 13.

Mulcahy S. (2000). On-line Advertising Poised to Explode; Lern Ropes Now. Mass High Tech, February, 4.

Nanda-A, Antara, "India throws open e-Commerce Gates, *News India,* May 26, 2000.

Nanda-B, Antara, "B2B Infomediary Indiamarkets targets SMEs, *India Post*, June 16, 2000.

Nelson Emily (2001).On the Right Scent. *The Wall Street Journal*, 02-12-01, R18.

Payne, J. (1997). Contract Logistics is Now Strategic, *Electronic Buyers' News 1087*, December 8, 1997, 34.

Pearl Daniel (2001). Lost in the Translation. *The Wall Street Journal*, 02-12-01, R12.

Pearl Daniel (2001). Searching for Solutions. *The Wall Street Journal*, 02-12-01, R12.

Petersen Andrea (2001). Private Matters. *The Wall Street Journal*, 02-12-01, R24, R31.

Rewick (2001). Flying High, *The Wall Street Journal*, 02-12-01, R36.

Richtel Matt (1999). Big Stakes in On-Line Job Listings, *The New York Times*, February 14, 1999.

Rickels R. (2000). U.S. e-Tailers Expand Efforts North of the Border, *The Wall Street Journal*, 31 January, 2000: A21.

Roche, E. (1996). The Multinational Enterprise in An Age of Internet and Electronic Commerce , in Global Information Technology and Systems Management Key Issues and Trends, Palvia, Prashant, *et al* (eds.) 424-440.

Rose G. M. and Straub D. W. (2000). Download Time Attitudes in the Arab World and the US: A Cross-Cultural Study in E-Commerce, 1st Global Information Technology Management World Conference, Memphis, TN, p. 147.

Boyle M. (2000). Anyone Up For a B2B Business Plan Bandwagon? *Revolution*, August, 2000:8.

Saul H. and Amy H. (1999). Caveat Emptor on the Web: Ad and Editorial Lines Blur, *New York Times*, February 26, 1999.

Saul H. (1998). News-Ad Issues Arise in New Media, *New York Times*, December 8, 1998.

Schwartz, E. (1997). *Webonomics*, New York: Broadway.

Schwartz H. (2000). Going Global, *Webtechiques*, September 2000: 54.

Snyder B.(1998). Pay-per-lead Makes Inroads as Online ad Pricing Method, *Advertising Age, 69,* March 30 1998, 41.

Tadjer, R. (1997). Web's Value Assessed Many Ways, *CommunicationsWeek, 667,* June 9, 53.

Tapper S. (2000). Is Globalization Right for You? *Webtechniques,* September 2000:26.

Tapscott, D. (1996). *Digital Economy,* New York: McGraw Hill.

Taylor, C. (1996). P&G talks Tough on Web: Said to make offer on pricing that ad sellers wish they could refuse, *MediaWeek, 6,* April 22.

Thomas K.(2000). Millions Turn PCs Into Personal Tellers, *USA Today,* 3 October, 2000: 3D.

Thompson, G. (1997). Driving Down the Freeway of Web Commerce, *HP Professional, 6* June, 11, 9.

Vizard, M. (1997). I-Commerce May be a Tough Sell After All, *InfoWorld, 36,* p.3.

Wilder, C. (1997). Delivery Goes Digital, *Information Week, 649,* September 2, 274-277.

Williamson, O. (1985). *Economic Organization,* New York: New York University Press.

Wilson, T. (1997). Online Services Squeeze Travel Agencies, *InternetWeek, 695,* December 22, 1997, 20.

Wingfield (2001). The Giants. *The Wall Street Journal, 02-12-01, R6, R14.*

Wrenden, N. (1997). Good Deal for Michelin Dealers, *InformationWeek, 653,* Oct. 20, 98-100.

Wyckoff, A. (1997). Imagining the impact of electronic commerce, *The OECD Observer, 208,* Oct/Nov, 5-8.

Yunker, J. (2000). Speaking in Charsets," *Webtechiques,* September 2000: 62.

13

The Role of Culture in Global Electronic Commerce

Michelle L. Kaarst-Brown
University of Richmond, USA

J. Roberto Evaristo
University of Illinois, Chicago, USA

ABSTRACT

This chapter has three main parts. In the first part, we provide a broad understanding of the global trends in Internet Commerce, including statistics that illustrate trends in Internet usage around the world. The second section focuses on key national and cultural influences on these trends and how they explain the differences in Internet commerce in different countries. The third section illustrates how five firms in the book retailing industry around the globe reflect these differences in business-to-consumer (B2C) Internet commerce.

INTRODUCTION

Although electronic commerce activities have been an important part of organizational telecommunications strategies for almost two decades (Roche, 1991)[1], the commercialization of the Internet in the early 90's has brought electronic commerce from backroom telecommunications strategies to public attention. The retail industry in particular has jumped onto the Internet bandwagon to market everything from books and clothing to fine wine, real estate and sports cars. Not surprisingly, the lack of geographical restraints provided by Internet commerce has extended retailing possibilities into international markets. The assumption that a "globally accessible website" means global markets is widely encouraged in television advertisements, but may be a false assumption if you are trying to run or develop a business. English may be assumed to be the language of commerce, but for many countries, it is a sign of foreign cultural contamination. Even when English is the dominant language in a country, Internet usage may be affected by other factors at the national and regional levels. Local knowledge and cultural practices play an important part in how new technologies, including Internet technology, are adopted. An understanding of national differences provides insights into the marked disparity in Internet usage and Internet commerce at the consumer level. In this chapter, lessons for Internet retailers seeking to reach local and global consumers are drawn from the book retailing industry, using examples from the United States, England, Burma, Brazil, and Ireland.

GLOBAL INTERNET USAGE AND ELECTRONIC COMMERCE

As recently as two years ago there were plenty of articles in the trade press claiming that retail was not quite ready to take over the Internet. Notwithstanding these strong positions, the

Christmas of 1998 was dubbed the first E-Christmas by the press, with the percentage of sales through the Internet becoming significant for the first time. The Christmas of 1999 further highlighted the significant role of the Internet to retail business. Forecasts for growth are constantly been revised upward. Predictions (Thompson, 1999) for the business-to-business (B2B) electronic commerce volume in 1999 were in the order of $110 billion, more than double the 1998 figures, yet more recent predictions suggest growth of B2B sales to reach *$1.3 trillion* by 2003 (Greenspan Report, May 6, 1999). Similar rates of growth are also forecast for Internet retail, although business-to-consumer (B2C) retail volume is estimated to be less than 20% of total global electronic commerce. An earlier forecast suggesting that Internet retailing figures would reach $7 billion by the year 2000 were surpassed before the end of 1998. Forecasts now project that on-line retail sales will exceed $80 billion by 2002 (Greenspan, 1999).

For the consumer, the Internet plays an important role in B2C transactions at three levels:

1) On-line shoppers who purchase products over the Internet and pay on-line.
2) On-line shoppers who purchase products over the Internet but then pay through phone, mail or fax.
3) On-line shoppers who use the Internet for research but then purchase big-ticket items at physical locations.

Cyber Dialogue estimated the impact of the Internet on 1998 consumer spending to exceed the mere $11.0 billion in on-line sales that were ordered and paid for on-line. Their figures indicate that an additional $15 billion in sales were ordered on-line but paid for off-line, and that another $51 billion off-line orders were influenced by the Internet (Thompson, 1999). NUA Internet Surveys provide current information on best estimates of the number of on-line users by international zones (Table 1).

Table 1: World Wide Internet Users as of June 1999[2]

World Total	*170 Million users*
Canada & USA	102.03 Million users
Europe	42.69 Million users
Asia/Pacific	26.97 Million users
Latin America	5.29 Million users
Africa	1.14 Million users
Middle East	.88 Million users

These numbers are only somewhat useful, as they do not illustrate the percentage of households that are users or any comparison to population size. When this comparison is included, it is very clear that there is much deeper penetration of electronic commerce – both in absolute and relative numbers – in North America and Europe. Not only do the United States and Canada occupy a larger absolute share of the Internet world, they also have a higher level of Internet participation on a per capita basis. According to Greenspan (1999), relative to population, the United States, Canada, the Nordic countries, and Australia have at least *twice* the level of Internet access so far achieved by the United Kingdom, Germany, Japan, and France (Figure 1). Furthermore, despite the growing globalization of electronic commerce, there are indeed marked differences in Internet retailing among nations. The difference in Internet purchase behavior reported above is related to more than PC usage or Internet availability. Internet commerce varies widely, even among those countries with stable telecommunications infrastructures and higher levels of disposable income. The differences can best be understood by reviewing a complex set of national characteristics that define the global Internet culture.

UNDERSTANDING CULTURAL UNIQUENESS – A MULTI-LEVEL FRAMEWORK

There are a variety of factors that influence willingness to conduct business on-line. Although there are several cultural frameworks that seek to categorize national cultural differences (Hofstede, Neuijen, Ohayv, & Sander, 1990; Shore, 1996), it is our belief that a broader range of interacting technological, political and cultural factors must be considered when studying national differences related to global electronic and Internet commerce. As noted by Dr. Pasquali, former Deputy Director General of UNESCO:

> *"A national culture is not the touristic total of stones, heroes, folklore and fashions which characterize, roughly speaking, the national stereotype, but the synthesis of a spiritual legacy of a national community. As a common and global patrimony, it includes all the concrete and abstract values which define and characterize it." (Source: Smith, 1980:64)*

Nations are unique on a number of levels, ranging from individual level purchase preferences and concerns about security to national telecommunications infrastructures and regulatory issues intended to enhance or protect a country. Geography and weather may also play a role in the historical development and diffusion of distance technologies such as radio, television and now the Internet. It is the complex *interplay* of many levels of cultural, political and technological issues that influence Internet commerce activities and result in distinct subcultures of Internet consumer within and across nations.

Table 2 summarizes some of the levels and factors that should be considered when assessing the role of culture in global electronic commerce.

Table 2: The Role of Culture in Global Electronic Commerce

Levels	Representative Factors
International/Cross-national Level	• World Trade Organization (WTO) International Trade Policies • Historical Political Barriers (war or alliances, e.g.: EEC) • Currency exchange
National Level Issues	Language Geography/Weather Emphasis on Regional versus National Technology Infrastructure • Legislative/Legal Framework (cross-border data flows; content rules) • Censorship to protect National Identity
Regional/Industry Level Issues	• Infrastructure Support Industry Legislation and Protection Competitive Structure (alliances & information sharing versus direct competition Type of industry: Commodity versus Customized
Firm Level Issues	Leadership strategies for role of Internet Organizational Culture
Individual Level Issues	Socialization (gender issues; social practices) Security Issues • Product Availability • Income • Relative Costs of On-line access and Internet Access • Idiosyncratic Preferences

The following provides examples of each of these levels and factors in action around the world. Additionally, these factors not only interact within levels but also across levels.

International/Cross-National Issues

At the international level, we are dealing with interaction of nations – in other words, cross-national issues. To understand the cultural elements of these issues, we can turn to historical bodies that represent negotiated order by these countries over long spans of time, at the history of war or alliances, and also at differences in currency valuation.

The *World Trade Organization (WTO)* was formed in 1995 to replace the General Agreement on Trade and Tariffs (GATT). The WTO provides the foundation for the international Trading System. It oversees the administration and functioning of the multi-lateral trade agreements and rules governing international trade. In preparation for the November 1999 meeting, governments asked for proposals from local business on gaps in current legislation (for instance, the Canadian Electronic Commerce Strategy). Of particular concern to the WTO and participating organizations are the following:

1) To what degree do WTO Trade agreements cover what is typically meant by electronic commerce activity, and what adjustments, if any, are required?
2) As national policies and international frameworks for global electronic commerce mature, is there risk that new barriers or impediments to trade will arise?

These trade agreements are subject to their own historical development and also to the *historical political barriers* of the countries participating. This too becomes part of the culture of Internet commerce. Past and present political, ethnic, religious or economic differences may have both short and long term impact on trade between countries. Even today, there are countries that refuse to do business with other countries because of such deep differences. It is too early to tell what the effect of Internet availability will be on long standing grudges or specific trade barriers to cross-national commerce activities.

Currency is often not thought to be a cultural issue, but it is certainly a reflection of national trade issues within an international marketplace and also of the valuation placed by other countries on goods and services provided by those countries. Countries without a hard currency have struggled to become established in international trade and will continue to struggle even with the advent of Internet commerce. Currency creates a barrier to trade and can create a perception that one's currency is not as good as another. Ask a Canadian how they feel about going across the border to the United States to pay almost double the price for the same goods. They will be quick to point out that at one time their own currency was valued *higher* than the American dollar. Canadians are more likely to sign-on to Chapters.ca[3] (a Canadian on-line book retailer), than to Amazon.com. Not only can they pay in the currency of their own country bit they also reduce delivery expenses and avoid possible customs charges.

The Euro will greatly facilitate a full range of electronic commerce and Internet retailing in Europe and may well assist in breaking down other cultural barriers. A common currency permits price comparisons, makes billing easier, and avoids currency exchange difficulties that can inhibit trade between nations. As an example, by early 1999 more than 400 on-line stores operated in Italy, in comparison to only 13 in 1997 (Tagliabue, 1999).

Trade policies, political barriers or alliances, and currency are not alone in reflecting cultural issues in global electronic commerce.

National Level Issues

At the national level, there are many characteristics that can define or influence the Internet culture. Among these are language, geography and weather, an emphasis on regional/local versus national technology infrastructure, the legislative and legal framework (such as cross-border data flows, content rules), and censorship to protect national identity.

Language has long been accepted as a potential barrier between peoples of different countries. Many countries, such as Canada and Kuwait, require that food products be labeled in the official languages of the country (for example: both English and French in Canada and Arabic in Kuwait). This inhibits the free flow of goods into countries, even when they participate in global barter or when goods can be easily ordered via the Internet. In support of Internet commerce, the rate of growth of non-English language material available on the Web is increasing. Cisco Systems [4], a leader in electronic commerce, sells its networking products to a worldwide market and offers its website in over twelve languages.

Forecasts suggest that by 2003, more than half the content on the Internet will be in a language other than English, up from 20 percent today (Greenspan, 1999). There are also ongoing technological developments that will improve translation services (by people and machines), and new browsers that recognize characters of different languages. These changes will greatly expand the amount of content usable by the entire worldwide Internet citizenry.

Geography and weather are also part of the national culture and shape many of the values and behaviors of a people. Moderate temperatures may encourage use of easier means of attaining goods. Extreme temperatures may encourage indoor activities. As an example, Kuwait has the highest recorded temperatures for any populated area in world, as well as experiences frequent sandstorms. Internet Cafés in Kuwait offer a welcome source of air-conditioned activities (Wheeler, 1998). Many Internet Commerce businesses advertise their services as saving time and avoiding *weather*, as is the case with Peapod Grocer in California. In Australia, 42 percent of those already involved in Internet shopping expect to do their grocery shopping on-line[5].

The future role of Internet Commerce can also be gleaned from the historical adoption patterns of other distance technologies that may have been used to overcome geographical barriers. Geography has long been accepted as a significant factor in cultural formation and technology adoption. It impacts innovation and development policies throughout countries. The catalog business was originally developed as a means of reaching consumers outside the normal physical retail area. Internet commerce may be more acceptable in countries where the barriers of distance and weather have long been a challenge.

Horvath and Daly (1989) conducted an analysis of Sweden and Canada and how trade and industrial policy closely mirrored the goals of social policy and geography. Although both countries are rich in natural resources, Canada is much larger and its population much more geographically dispersed. In comparing its industrial and social policies with those in Sweden, it becomes obvious that Canada has historically supported technologies that upheld goals of geographical integration. Among the countries with the highest Internet usage and growth of commercial sites, we find the USA, Canada, Australia, and New Zealand. Australia and New Zealand have historically turned to technology to ease the demands of terrain and geographical barriers. Private radio education, advanced distance education using software programs, and flying doctors accessible via short-wave radio, have been an accepted part of their electronic culture for generations.

Regional/local versus national infrastructure development also reflect a country's cultural challenges and focus. The current website on "Electronic Commerce" provided by the Canadian Government[6] has a strong national focus that encourages Canadians to present a united Internet front so that the entire country can benefit from new national and global Internet opportunities. Significant expertise and financial support are offered to encourage electronic commerce among small business and entirely wired communities. The socialistic policies of the Canadian government are intended to encourage unity and integration across provincial boundaries. Electronic commerce has been embraced as a means to achieve this and further global trade expansion.

This approach to national integration versus regional control may also influence infrastructure development (Angehrn and Meyer, 1997). Examples of different approaches are found in the banking industries of Canada and the United States. In Canada, there are a handful of national banks. This means that the ATM networks established national-reach networks early on, permitting customers to access their accounts from anywhere in the country. In contrast, the United States has a strong municipal and regional banking system. It is only in recent years that collaboration among banking organizations in the U.S. has permitted statewide, national and international network access for customers. For some regional banks, international account access is still fraught with currency difficulties as noted from the authors' recent interview with an MBA student just back from an exchange-semester abroad.

> *"I took 600 francs from my American bank account. When I tried to access my account later that day, the transaction was refused. When I finally called back to the U.S., I was told that I had exceeded my limit of $500 U.S. dollars per day. I tried to explain that 600 francs was only about $100 U.S. dollars but she said the system didn't know that."*

The orientation toward integrated versus differentiated regional infrastructure may also significantly influence the Internet infrastructure and support. The Norwegian government is trying to encourage its citizenry to go online with Internet based Public Administration Services (The Open Group). Geography is only part of the Norwegian government's motivation, sharing with Canada the problem of a small, widely dispersed population. In addition, their intent is to help develop a national network infrastructure that will aid firms throughout the country as they become more active in the European Union. Using government resources, they hope to maximize the use of the latest market developments in technology and service. According to a case study by The Open Group (1999):

> *"With the Public Sector Network, Norway leads the world in creating a national, Internet-based infrastructure to administer public services and improve government operational efficiency. The country's proactive steps guarantee the construction of an effective, supplier-independent and flexible national on-line resource."*

The *legislative and legal framework of nations* is both a reflection of cultural values and will also influence what subsequently becomes legitimized within the country. Legislation and legal policy have an impact on businesses and on individuals as they pursue electronic commerce activities. That is clearly the case when countries address the thorny problem of taxing electronic commerce activities that occur over the Internet. Australia's approach, for example, has been to avoid taxing any transaction that occurs exclusively over the Internet. This decision avoids the question of how would Internet transactions be inspected or taxation enforced. However, this decision does not apply to any transaction in which one of the components is physical – for instance, the purchase of a computer. Although, in this case, most of the transaction can be completed over the Internet, the actual delivery is physical and therefore incurs taxes. A similar problem has occurred in the U.S. regarding sales tax on mail order transactions. A different decision was originally reached: sales taxes did not apply to any transaction that crossed a state boundary, regardless of whether it included a physical component.

The degree to which personal information and corporate information is protected may be as much a cultural issue, as it is a legal one (Hofstede et al, 1990; Walczuch, Singh, & Palmer, 1995). In fact, the countries that first enacted privacy laws were frequently those with the smallest power-distance among individuals, presumably because this equal distribution of power increased the value of privacy. Moreover, countries where individualism was more highly valued tended to value the dignity of the individual more, and therefore also enact more privacy laws (Walczuch et al, 1995). France has always been particularly protective of employee data and personal information about customers. The United States, however, is much less so with a growing market in list selling. For example:

"There has been a huge rise in the number of online companies - now two-thirds - which tell site visitors that their data, including addresses, names, e-mail addresses and personal likes and dislikes may be used for marketing purposes" (Lillington, 1999).

Privacy issues and list selling has extended into major concerns about unsolicited emails and faxes, and consumer data gathering over the Internet without the consumer's knowledge (Lillington, 1999; M2, May 21 and August 16, 1999; New Media Age, June 24, 1999).

Another legislative aspect of culture is reflected in content rules. Content rules are different from rules about cross-border data flows on firm or personnel information. Some countries have very specific policies to control entry of foreign content or the amount of national content required in various types of media or product offerings. Censorship to protect National identity may be a concern in non-English speaking countries such as China, as well as in English speaking countries such as Canada. In some countries where there has been considerable political unrest, ethnocentric concerns about content extend to the point where individuals are imprisoned for possessing technologies that might enable outside contamination. For example, in Burma (also known as Myanmar) it is illegal to own a fax machine due to concerns about cultural contamination and what might be deemed inappropriate comments against the current military regime. Leo Nichols, a Burmese businessman and honorary consul for Norway, died in prison some years ago while serving a three-year sentence for possession of one (Barron, 1999).

A group of journalists in Burma – the Reporters San Frontieres (RSF) – criticized their own country as being an "enemy of the Internet." They included in their "Top 20 Internet enemies list" countries such as Azerbaijan, Kazakhstan, Kyrgyzstan, and Tajikistan in central Asia and the Caucasus. In the Middle East and Africa, they highlighted Saudi Arabia, Iran, Iraq, Syria, Libya and Tunisia, along with Sierra Leone and Sudan. Cuba, Vietnam, China and North Korea were also sited as being excessive in their censorship and control over Internet activities.

"On the pretext of protecting the public from 'subversive ideas' or defending 'national security and unity', some governments totally prevent their citizens from gaining access to the Internet," says RSF. "Others control a single Internet Services Provider (ISP) or even several, installing filters blocking access to websites regarded as unsuitable and sometimes forcing users to officially register with the authorities." (Barron, 1999)

All of these national issues will shape the national Internet culture, and will impact Internet resources and use.

Regional/Industrial Issues

The Internet culture of a nation is also influenced by what happens in different parts of that country (within a region) and at the industry level. Infrastructure support, industry legislation and protectionism, the competitive structure of an industry, and even the commodity nature of an industry may encourage or discourage both generic electronic commerce strategies and B2C Internet retailing. Sackmann (1991, 1992) found that occupational influences such as professional training and affiliations may have a strong influence on the knowledge sets and types of technologies people are exposed to.

Local *infrastructure support* is extremely relevant for the success of electronic commerce. Focusing on the telecommunications industry of specific areas of a country may identify gaps in infrastructure support. Regions facing a shortage of hosts or Internet Service Providers, or even lacking telephone lines for customers to access the Internet, will clearly be behind the curve in adopting Internet commerce. Another significant infrastructure issue is the delivery system. Poor postal service in countries such as Italy, and the high cost of private delivery services, impede growth of Internet retailing (Tagliabue, 1999).

An infrastructure issue specific to individual industries is whether they are extremely fragmented and independent or well coordinated with good formal and informal educational and communication structures to encourage adoption of new methods. The lack of Internet adoption within one region of a country, or by an industry in general, will restrict business participation in the global electronic commerce market and may inhibit later entry due to a lack of expertise with an increasingly sophisticated medium. Combined with a lack of Internet infrastructure, lack of local industry adoption and skills also likely means that customers are restricted to local producers and will not be among those surfing the net. This in turn further discourages adoption by businesses within an industry or a region.

It is in these situations where an outsider or new entrant can also shake things up. The book retailing industry is generally segmented into a cluster of thousands of small, independent retailers, a group of dominant regional retailers, and a handful of national distributors. In the U.S., a new entrant to book retailing – Amazon.com – challenged the industry, but also paved the way for Internet retailing for even the smallest independent bookseller. The American Booksellers Association (ABA), the national trade association, finally decided to assist its members by offering a web-based electronic commerce product, bringing both expertise and infrastructure support to their industry.

Another issue is the amount of *protectionism* a country is willing to extend to certain types of products, regional development efforts, or industry sectors. Protectionism can be expressed in extraordinary taxation over a certain period of time or incentives for manufacturing development in certain regions of a country. One example of protectionism was Harley Davidson (U.S.) lobbying for extra taxes to be levied on large sized Japanese motorcycles so that they would have time to become more competitive. However, even before these taxes were supposed to be phased out, Harley Davidson felt that they were ready for the competition and the taxes were brought back to the original level. In Italy, the European Economic Commission carefully assessed the implications on both local and distant book-selling activities when Mondadori of Italy and Bertelsmann of Germany wanted to merge to better serve the Italian book market. The Commission's initial concern was that a stable competitive structure be maintained (Commission of the European Communities, 1999).

The *competitive structure* that has evolved in an industry, perhaps because of government roles, may also influence the Internet culture, sometimes in unexpected or inconsistent ways. Industries with a history of firm collaboration and strategic alliances among them would seem more inclined to work together in electronic commerce initiatives. The insurance industry in the UK – known as the London Market – turned to Internet products to permit faster sharing of information among underwriters at different firms. The fact that many of these firms shared the risk on the same large projects has historically encouraged information sharing. The Internet was a natural extension of this.

In Italy and Mexico in particular, there is the concept of industrial districts, or a large set of small organizations, all producing either similar or complementary products (Rabellotti, 1997). Part of the reason this arrangement has been so successful is the ability of the stakeholders to share information about the availability of idle capacity. They can also share information on orders that may enter the system, often through the services of an intermediary, or the *impanatore* (Kumar, van Dissel and Bielli, 1998). Interestingly, even though such structure would suggest that this might be an extremely fertile test bed for electronic commerce, this has not yet proven to be the case. Cultural traditions in the conduct of business decreased chances of adoption. One key issue was that face-to-face meetings, a mainstay to their business practices for centuries, was not captured in the new systems.

Monopolistic, government operated, or industries with much government protection may have more or less freedom to pursue Internet strategies, as noted under the influence of

National pressures. In Brazil, during the opening of the telecommunication market to foreign operators, a well laid out explanatory website was put up by the then monopoly holder, with the objective of making the privatization process as competitive and as transparent as possible. Typical information in those pages included usage statistics about customers in the different geographical areas in which the country had been divided for the purpose of bidding for telephony services (Evaristo, 1998) as well as forecasts of potential telephony demand. Therefore, although the site was being used only for informational purposes, it clearly impacted the overall privatization process of telecommunications in Brazil, including the final bidding values for the regional concessions.

Typically, *industries* focus on *commodity or customized (or highly customizable)* products. When customized products are also of high cost, like a Ferrari, it is less likely that they will be successfully sold through the Internet. Instead, firms use the Internet to provide information about these high end products and promote awareness. On the other hand, commodity-like products, even of high cost, can be successfully sold over the Internet. A good example is the sale of good quality used cars, sold in Internet auctions in the U.S.[7] or the retailing of books and music CDs around the world. In the latter case, these high volume, low transaction cost items are ripe for Internet retailing. The amount of personal interaction in different industries is the key to Internet Commerce. Industries with commodity products may be quicker to try to take advantage of Internet commerce than "custom-product" firms who have traditionally relied on personal contact for their orders. This may be the case even though the Internet provides an opportunity to distribute niche products to a broader audience. Product customization usually requires prior knowledge of the customer, including identity. As will be noted under personal preferences, many customers are hesitant to disclose information and will even avoid sites that require them to identify themselves (Financial Times, March 15, 1999).

The complex interaction of these regional and industry characteristics creates a unique culture for each industry. While newcomers may challenge the old cultures, established firms and new firms alike cannot help but be influenced by these factors and the customer base that has grown to accept them.

Firm Level Cultural Issues

Even within an industry, the values and orientation of leaders, as well as the collective organizational culture, will reflect in a firm's unique orientation toward risk and technological innovation (Deal & Kennedy, 1982; Sackmann, 1991, 1992). *Organizational culture* has been linked to everything from personnel policies and practices (Gordon, 1985; Hofstede et al, 1990) to leadership strategies on the role of Internet (Cronin, 1996; Westland & Clark, 2000).

The cultural impact on global electronic commerce of *a leader and her or his strategies* can be significant. As noted in the following quotation, some leaders are convinced that Internet commerce is the road to the future, while others are still waiting to see where the profits are.

> *"What's my ROI on Electronic Commerce? Are you crazy? This is Columbus in the New World. What was his ROI?" (Andy Grove, chairman of Intel, as cited in Westland & Clark, 2000.)*

A large number of organizations involved in Internet retailing have seen their share price skyrocket after very successful IPOs. Interestingly, most of these organizations are not able to show any profit, and many (including Amazon.com) are reportedly still losing money with every sale. In fact, the more they sell, the more they loose. However, the innovative strategies that these leaders have shaped for their organizations have created new markets or new services which could not be offered before the advent of the Internet (Cronin, 1996).

They are betting that their particular offering will be a hit (and so are the investors). Other leaders have resisted not only the Internet, but also computers (for example, Christina Foyle of Foyle's Bookstore).

Organizational culture can also vary tremendously and it can affect the way an organization tackles electronic commerce, even with supportive leaders that encourage use of information technologies (Kaarst-Brown & Robey, 1999). Some organizations have pursued virtual operations, drawing heavily upon electronic communications and transactions both internally and with the public. Many multi-nationals locate customer service operators in different time zones in order to extend the times service is available, without actually having to employ somebody to work the "graveyard shift". As these organizations pursue cheaper business-to-business (B2B) operations via secure Internet transactions, they are also more likely to utilize business-to-consumer (B2C) Internet options.

Businesses may vary in what they offer their customers or potential customers via the Internet. Dell[8], for example, moved from a catalog orientation to full Internet retailing, allowing customers to obtain quotes and order their computer via the Internet. Virtual Vineyards[9] exists only in a website and sells wines and gourmet foods. Hewlett Packard[10] has a system widely admired for providing excellent post-sales support to customers. FedEx[11] allows customers to user the Internet to track shipments. American Airlines[12], Travelocity[13] and Trip.com[14] all offer on-line reservations and ticket purchases that tremendously increase the convenience and timelines for their customers. While firm strategy is used to describe what each firm has done, the value and emphasis placed on different activities or aspects of the value chain may be inherent to the culture of the particular firm. Furthermore, organizational culture may also influence the timing of the adoption.

What is common to all of the above firm examples is that their organizational cultures or their leaders reflected an orientation of risk taking and technology innovation, similar to many of the early firms noted for their excellence (Deal & Kennedy, 1982)

Individual Level Differences

A discussion of individual level differences and their impact on electronic commerce could include dozens of factors. Demographic differences are often aggregated to provide meaningless averages on income and other demographics. When considering global electronic commerce, individual level factors such as income and literacy or socialization result in choices that very much reflect the culture of the people. We would like to focus on only a few elements that have been specifically linked to Internet usage or purchase behavior. These include socialization (gender issues, social practices), concerns for security or privacy, preferences for product availability, income and literacy, and quite simply their own idiosyncratic preferences for use of various communications media. It should be noted, however, that individuals interact and make choices within the context of their geographic regions and nations.

At the individual level, we find differences across countries *in socially acceptable ways for different genders to interact.* In much of Northern Europe and North America, it is perfectly acceptable for a young woman to openly carry on conversation with a young man. In parts of the Middle East, this behavior would not only be unacceptable, but also it would be punishable. On the other hand, electronic commerce and telecommunications can come to the rescue of terminally lovesick young individuals. A common practice in conservative Saudi Arabia is for young males to carry an extra cellular phone that they drop in the lap of the female they are interested in talking to. A little while later, the phone rings and the connection is made. Interactive chat is the dominant Internet service in many countries that restrict direct contact between non-related men and women. In a study of Internet use in Kuwait, the general consensus among researchers is that 95% of Internet use is for chatting, both to enable business transactions between genders and also for personal interactions among the country's youth (Wheeler, 1998).

Gender issues may also impact web features and design or preferences for certain sites. There has been research that shows that different cultures and genders enjoy certain combinations of colors more than others do. Similarly, there are also variations in preferences for the type and amount of graphic content in web pages (Roberts & Hart, 1997). Use of the Internet is now – at least in Western Cultures – less dominated by males than in the past. However, sites that cater more to a specific gender are not yet widespread, except perhaps as a function of content.

Concerns about privacy and security can also be a socially constructed concern. Beyond the technological issue of Internet security via encryption and other means is the psychological security issues associated with electronic communication. What we in North American refer to as privacy may be deeply rooted in security concerns for some peoples. In Kuwait, for example, there is great concern that information communicated via the Internet might find its way into the wrong hands.

"No one wants to talk on the record or to be quoted. The idea makes people scared or nervous. Only those who are elite feel they can speak freely and openly." (Wheeler, 1998)

Such fears may significantly impact the use of electronic communications technologies, including the Internet, as well as the features of websites. Something as simple as a feedback mechanism or e-mail link on a website may be threatening to some and yet expected by other consumers. Freely giving basic information required for purchasing might be considered acceptable within a country, but sharing this information outside of local boundaries may be perceived to be fraught with risk. In Argentina, the majority of Internet users are in the top socio-economic group, but reportedly 70 percent of those who use the Internet have *not* made on-line purchases due to concerns about giving out personal credit card information on-line.

Product availability or lack thereof, may significantly influence the desirability of other sources. In a study of on-line purchases in Arab countries, almost half of those surveyed indicated that the driving reason for preference of on-line products was their non-availability in the consumer's local market. Interestingly, in the Arab market, price was not reported to be a dominant consideration (Source: NUA Surveys, August 1999).

Income levels and affluence, combined with literacy, have a bearing on individual choices for Internet usage. As noted by Greenspan (1999):

"The "digital divide" between certain groups of Americans increased between 1994 and 1997, resulting in a widening gap between those at upper and lower income levels, and between both Blacks and Hispanics as compared with Whites. Rural areas lagged behind urban and central cities with respect to rates for online access... Similarly, throughout the world, lower income countries have lower rates of Internet access when compared to the higher income countries... In Mexico, a nation of close to 100 million, for example, only about 1 million people have access to computers and only 10 percent of those presently access the Internet".

In fact, one of the concerns in the United States today is that Internet access diffused more rapidly among those with higher income levels and varies widely among various demographic groups and geographic areas.

The level of literacy combined with income also impacts purchase choices at the individual level. The Brazilian government is working to increase literacy, distributing over 100 million books to the country's 34 million primary school students. Illiteracy is an important cause of the country's low reading rate: 14.7 percent of Brazilians older than 15 are illiterate. People who are unable to read or who retain little disposable income are unlikely to seek Internet access, let alone become experienced purchasers of on-line products.

Putting these various individual level considerations together, the result is that relative costs for Internet access vary widely, both in real terms and in relation to income. Reports suggest that unlimited Internet access can be obtained for as low as 12 USD/month in the U.S. In some underdeveloped countries, the cost might be as high as $5 USD/hour, with much lower personal income levels. In a perverse way, the places where individuals might benefit most from Internet commerce may actually be the most expensive and therefore, the most inaccessible for the majority of the population[15]. Some firms are adapting to these limitations in order to cultivate the "get-off-line-quick" users. Boxman, a CD retailer out of Sweden has taken an opposing position to firms such as Amazon.com who try to provide customers with interesting content, graphics, and personalized purchasing suggestions. Instead, Boxman has been very effective in adapting their website to the customer who is concerned about line costs. Its home page is graphically very poor but is fast, interactive, and makes it easy for customers to make purchases by offering both credit card payment or invoicing option (Giussani, 1999).

Finally, *idiosyncratic preferences* need to be considered in Internet Commerce, as any marketing textbook will tell you. For example, the most likely determinant of future behavior is prior purchase behavior. Similarly, experienced users are more likely to buy on-line. As we have seen in this overview of different levels and factors, the challenge for business it to understand enough about global cultural differences to be able to identify where the most likely users will be found and where new users will likely emerge. To complicate this challenge is the fact that the interaction between factors at multiple levels creates a complex Internet culture that is, in fact, a web of diverse sub-cultures.

In summary, major differences in social systems, concerns about privacy and security, literacy, income distribution, and personal preferences interact with differences in national infrastructure and tax systems that influence the relative cost of Internet access and the amount of discretionary income available for entertainment or purchases. Delivery infrastructures and costs impact whether on-line goods reach the intended consumer. The nature of trade tariffs, barriers to imports, and competitive policy also have an impact. These multi-level national differences help us understand the diverse consumer cultures in which we find different levels of adoption and usage of the Internet and other communication technologies.

The following section provides some examples of how one worldwide industry has been shaped by these factors. Interesting to note, even firms in the same industry in the same country have chosen different approaches. The complex interplay of multi-level cultural influences also becomes evident as we see examples from different countries.

CULTURAL UNIQUENESS, ELECTRONIC COMMERCE AND BOOK RETAILING

Book retailing has for centuries been basically a retail business like any other. Some stores were segmented based on topic such as "mystery" or "text book" (like a boutique) while others tried to have large in-store inventories across a diverse range of subjects. Typically the larger inventory bookstores were full-price stores that catered to convenience and availability, like an expensive department store. Others tried to keep mainstream inventory and special ordered anything else.

Book retailing, like most industries, also faces unique competitive pressures. One of the problems facing book retailers is the large variety of titles in print. It is virtually impossible to keep more than a small portion of these in stores. Space and inventory carrying costs are the major limitations. This challenge was addressed by some firms through special order services, mail-order bookstores, as well as "book-of-the month" clubs. These initiatives flourished in the 80's and early 90s', appealing to a cost-conscious buyer who was willing to wait for their books. However, there was still the problem of reaching the central bookstore location either via a toll free call or mail. Immediate feedback about availability as well as general browsing was somewhat difficult.

This scenario opened extraordinary possibilities with the advent of electronic commerce via the Internet. Book retailing has received increasing media attention suggesting that this industry can not only benefit from electronic commerce via the Internet (Del Prete, 1996; Borenstein et al, 1996) but may also be transformed by Internet retailing. Book retailing is a high transaction volume industry. Amazon.com was among the first Internet-based firms in the U.S. book retailing industry to go public and to go global, but there are many other international firms, including Chapters.ca in Canada and BarnesandNoble.com. As of 1999, Germany, whose 80 million population makes it the largest market in Europe, had more than 1200 on-line stores that sold books. Its book sales per capita rivaled those in the U.S. (Tagliabue, 1999).

The existence of Internet commerce has strong implications for how people interact. Culture both affects this interaction and, in the long run, will change because of this interaction. The cultural impact is particularly felt when you look beyond the economic transaction to the social interaction that occurs not only throughout the transaction, but also "instead of" the transaction. For example, Many North American and UK bookstores have evolved their strategies to include playing a role in the social structure of the local or regional community.[16] In addition to more traditional "meet-the-author" sessions, book signings and story sessions, we are seeing bookstores such as Books-a-Million, Borders, and Barnes & Noble hosting art exhibits, singles groups, and sharing their space with cafés and restaurants. These same stores are trying to create the impression of social proximity in their websites as they reach out to both local and distance customers.

The following examples illustrate the wide range of approaches taken by book retailers in how they use – or don't use – the Internet to address the complex dynamics of national and global differences in national customers. Examples are drawn from the U.S., U.K., Burma, Brazil, Italy, and Ireland. Each of these examples was selected because it highlights how individual book retailers have interpreted and responded to the complex electronic commerce environment in their own unique ways.

Amazon.com (U.S.A.) – Global Internet Commerce[17]

Amazon.com, widely publicized as the "Earth's Biggest Bookstore", is a fully Internet-based retail operation. Established in 1994 by Jeff Bezos, they went public in 1997 with a reported customer base already spanning over 100 countries. Amazon.com relies heavily on mail and courier delivery infrastructure services to delivery its product. About one third of its 1.5 million offered titles are shipped from a central warehouse in Seattle, WA. The majority of the other titles are special ordered from two main suppliers or distributed from one of two European warehouses, established in 1998 in Britain and Germany. Amazon's mission has been driven by Bezos' belief that "...by serving a large and global market through centralized distribution and operations, online booksellers can realize significant structural cost advantages relative to traditional booksellers" (Prospectus, 1997, 10K, p.3).

Jeff Bezos, founder and CEO of Amazon.com, believed that there were tremendous first-mover advantages to starting up as a wholly Internet-based firm, despite the risks of an immature Internet market. Amazon.com's organizational culture and innovative strategy can be directly attributed to its leader's global vision and the entrepreneurial people who join the Amazon.com team. Amazon believes this risk-taking orientation had led to "a pre-eminent position among on-line retailers". This is despite being neither the cheapest nor the fastest on-line bookseller. Although they are acknowledged as being among the first Internet-based book retailers, it has been a costly investment for Amazon.com to establish a brand presence.

Amazon.com's web services seek to provide a full range of content related to books, their availability, reader's reviews, as well as a variety of search capabilities. With no physical retail outlet, its website has become the company's image to the world.

As Amazon.com has not been profitable since its inception, some have gone so far as to suggest that this lack of profitability is in part due to the huge front-end investment required to build its image   of credibility and reputation as an efficient, low cost provider. Yet, Amazon's strategy seems to be paying off in local *and* global business. On-line consumers in Arab countries have been estimated to spend over USD95 million on electronic commerce in the twelve months ending June 1999. Eighty-two percent of these expenditures were made at international sites, with Amazon.com being among the most popular international site (NUA surveys).

Amazon.com has widely advertised itself as being a global retailer, but at the time of this book, its website was only available in English. The majority of its publications are also in English, although it seeks to change this with the new distribution centers in Europe. It will be interesting to watch whether Amazon.com's global popularity remains as the growing number of international sites cater to their own national clientele or offer sites in multiple languages. Bezos is determined to keep Amazon.com and his team of entrepreneurs in the lead of global electronic commerce.

Foyle's Bookstore at Charring Cross (U.K.)[18] - Low-Tech Cultural Icon

Christina Foyle (1911-1999) is remembered both for her eccentric style and unique management approach. Foyle's Bookstore was established in 1904 by Miss Foyle's' father, William, and her uncle, Gilbert. Even though Ms. Foyle did not officially take over operations of the bookstore until approximately 1963, Christina Foyle created a unique competitive position for Foyle's with the launch in 1930 of Foyle's Literary Lunches. These lunches helped to keep the firm solvent in the 1930's and continue to play a role today in publicizing the bookshop as a unique entity even in this era of chain stores and Internet booksellers. Foyle's lunches have included speakers ranging from Roger Moore to Margaret Thatcher, Bertrand Russell, and Ethiopian leader Haile Selassie.

At one time, the Charing Cross Road location in London housed more than 30 miles of bookshelves. The strong impact of a leader on the culture and practices of an organization is well illustrated at Foyle's. Despite a somewhat inefficient and confusing result, Ms. Foyle strongly resisted the use of computers. "She preserved the store's eccentric layout – books filed by publisher, not author – and accounting practices, and refused to install computers." (The Herald, June 12, 1999). Foyle's did not offer their customers a more efficient personalized service, but a rather unique – if often times frustrating – experience. Richard Donkin, a journalist for the London Financial Times, wrote about Foyle's unusual success and recounted his own experiences of hunting fruitlessly for a book. When he asked one of the assistants if they had the book, she replied that she didn't know. "Surely it must be catalogued," he stated. He reported that the assistant just laughed.

Her obituary in the Glasgow Herald reports "Christina Foyle, *Bookseller*, born January 30, 1911; died June 8, 1999". Her identity and her shop at Charing Cross became an important part of the UK's literary community made up of writers, publishers, and readers. Not only had Ms. Foyle resisted the trend toward Internet book selling, even a customer lamented "Of course it needs to change. It is changing, but somehow, 10 years from now if I find a Foyle's on every street corner or if I search the booklists on Foyles.com, I will hang my head in despair." As a bookstore, Foyle's became more than a bookstore, a cultural icon.

Innwa Bookstore (Burma) – An Off-line Cybercafe Enters the Digital Economy?[19]

Even bookstores in Burma are feeling the pressure to enter the digital economy, but they must do so within the constraints of a military-run government that tightly controls information content. Innwa Bookstore was given permission to open the country's first "cybercafe". The Innwa Cybercafe is, however, perhaps the world's first and only cybercafe without Net access. Instead of accessing the Internet, customers use CD's that have passed the military junta's stringent censorship. "Customers may also use the multimedia computers for word-processing or other tasks - during periods of the day that are free of Rangoon's regular electricity black-outs. They are also invited to register for the unavailable Internet access", reports MyaBuzz, a local newsletter.

Innwa's book list is also subject to approval by those that control the national publishing network and imports. Still, it sees a potential to differentiate itself by creating the illusion of being part of the electronic community.

Brazil Publishers Aim for Youth Market Via Fair Not Internet[20]

Brazilian book publishers have a hard time reaching the relatively small segment of the population that can afford a product that on average costs about one seventh of the minimum monthly salary. In fact, about 90% of the 5,500 municipalities in Brazil do not have even one bookstore. Therefore, many publishers and book retailers are focusing on the upper middle class, and in particular, on the area which shows the highest demographic promise: adolescents and younger children. Upper middle class adolescents have considerable disposable income available, and affluent parents want to give the best possible education to their children, lavishing money both on cultural and youth literature. As an example, 1.2 million books were sold at the Biennial Book Fair in May 1999. The fair had over half a million visitors and focused on children and adolescent sectors.

The book fair is a relatively new attempt to reach and entertain a growing market. In the past, the better bookstores just kept a large inventory, including books in Portuguese (the native language) and in other languages. This inventory was much larger and varied than the average U.S. bookstore. But that approach is not common anymore, particularly because of the critical problem of carrying costs for extensive inventory. As a result, most imported books are not readily available in Brazil.

This situation creates an extraordinarily promising market for electronic commerce. Given the limited and widely dispersed demographic market within Brazil, Internet commerce could enable a lower cost approach to reaching the maturing (literally) consumer. The wise Internet retailer in Brazil could take a lesson from the national publishers, identify the country characteristics, and focus on growing with the population as younger readers become ongoing book consumers. Although most of the on-line orders are still being placed at U.S. or European websites, it seems that the market is ripe for a Brazilian Internet book retailer.

Mondadori and Bertelsmann Book Club Merger[21] - Distant Selling in Italy

At the level of international trade policy, the European Commission took an interesting position when authorizing the merger between Mondadori (Italy) and Bertelsmann (Germany). Despite the European Economic Community (EEC), the Commission had concerns about national protection of Italian industry and fair competition within the book retailing industry. They concluded, "there is strong competition from both existing and potential book distribution channels such as bookstores, supermarkets and the Internet. The Merged entity is therefore not expected to become dominant on the Italian book retail markets and thus not impair effective competition in Italy". In addition to considering the total retail market for books in Italy, the Commission also focused specifically on the narrower market of distribution of books through "distant selling", including book clubs, mail order, Internet sales, and other forms of selling via correspondence. A focal point of their analysis was whether the new merger would simply steal existing business from traditional Italian bookstores or actually grow the book retailing market in Italy. The Commission realized that if Italy did nothing, the country's book retailing industry risked losses to outside on-line firms. By permitting this merger between Mondadori and Bertelsmann, the Commission acknowledged the risk of other start-up firms – specifically Internet firms – but also the fact that even a small loss of volume is enough to turn a profitable store into an unprofitable one. The merger also allows Mondadori to benefit from Bertelsmann's prior Internet expertise.

In addition to trade policy and national trade constraints for the industry, another condition holding back both book clubs and Internet purchasing of books in Italy is the delivery channel. Regrettably, as noted earlier, the Italian postal service is not regarded as the most reliable. The newly merged company still has to address this infrastructure challenge.

Waterstone's and Yahoo! - UK & Ireland Join Forces[22]

Waterstone's, once owned by Christina Foyle, seems to have decided that joining forces with Internet service providers might be a safer move than either resisting the forces for Internet Commerce, or waiting for someone else (like Amazon.com) to trample one's turf. In addition, they are trying to overcome access barriers such as high on-line costs. Going beyond simply offering Internet purchasing, Waterstone's has established a strategic alliance with Yahoo! UK and Ireland to provide *free instant access* not only to Waterstone's online bookstore but also to the whole Internet – with no subscription fees.

Waterstone's is using this strategic alliance to extend its offering to customers, while working hard to maintain the image of personalized, in-store service that its customers have come to expect of a high street retailer. At Waterstone's online customers can take advantage of invaluable recommendations from Waterstone's team of specialist booksellers, reviews of new books, special offers, (including Waterstone's now legendary Book of the Month), and regularly updated information on events and highlights in the literary calendar. The Waterstone website also allows their customers to access Booksearch - a unique specialist service set up to search out books no longer in print. Other personalized services include a service for collectors to built up their book collection with Signed First Editions – an exclusive club for Waterstone's customers featuring a choice of over 120 of the year's best fiction and non-fiction, signed and dated by the author and delivered to your own home.

Waterstone's approach has been to remain true to the firm culture while overcoming the national barriers created by high Internet access costs. The bottom line is hopefully the retention of the Waterstone customer base and growth of a new segment of the local market.

CONCLUSIONS

So, where does Internet commerce fit within a global economy and cultural context? There is no doubt that electronic commerce is here to stay. Moreover, it seems that its impact in the world economy is going to be even bigger and faster than expected. The only question is how this impact will occur differently in diverse global locations. The same apparent conditions do not appear to generate the same results. Australia has among the highest Internet penetration and yet individuals report to be uncomfortable with Internet purchasing. A portion of Argentina's population has significant disposable income, but is similarly reserved. Arab countries are restrictive in their social culture, have a strong income divide among classes, and yet those individuals with resources are heavy purchasers on the Internet – including at Amazon.com. Brazil has a similar divide and yet the book retailing industry has to pursue other alternatives to increase book sales. In the UK and Ireland, firm culture may segment the market between a die-hard literary culture and a cost-conscious consumer.

The examples provided in this chapter suggest that indeed there will be differences in the global Internet Culture. The chapter has provided a multi-level framework to help businesses assess how, where, and why these differences will manifest themselves – but the intent is only to provide a range of issues to be considered. The Internet has created a network that transcends time and place, but whether it can overcome national differences is still to be seen. The variety of multi-level variations of different nations will influence not only the availability and use of the Internet but also preferences for local products over global ones, even those available on-line.

**Mini-Case: The American Booksellers Association (ABA) provides
Web Access to their Members**

The American Bookseller's Association (ABA) is a trade association that represents over 3000 independent booksellers in the United States. In the spring of 1999, the ABA launched "Booksense.com", an electronic commerce product for its members. The goal of Booksense.com is to permit national branding and marketing via an Internet presence. Using focus groups, the ABA developed a website development product to address the basic needs and goals of their members. To avoid overwhelming their busy and often non-technical members, they established a three phase role-out of the electronic commerce product. The initial version released in mid-1999 provided a template for basic store information. Later versions linked the stores to a national database that would allow customers of even the smallest independent store to have access to over two million titles.

Some of the ABA's members have already experimented with websites. A pilot survey completed by the authors discovered that several of the ABA's members already had experience with websites. The owner of a small, specialty bookstore focusing on African-American titles, shut its website down after three years of operation. "The site was removed after 3 years because it generated $300.00 in total sales. We may put it back up for advertising only."

Another firm, the Tattered Cover Bookstore, has two locations in Denver Colorado, but is developing an international reputation for the number of titles in one location – and its unique store environment. It is popular with locals as well as visitors to Denver, and is recommended to tourists for its ambiance, fireplaces, café's, and the four star restaurant in one of their locations. The owner hires people who "like people and like books".

The Tattered Cover also had their website up for about 4 years. Although management was unwilling to disclose specific revenue figures, they reported that their website was a profitable source of new sales and that many of their international visitors continued to stay in touch via their website. What draws customers back, however, may well be the memories of the quality in-store service and the delicious almond-cherry pie at The Fourth Story Restaurant.

The ABA's goal is to provide the smaller bookstores with resources, infrastructure and expertise. The ABA is optimistic that their new electronic commerce product will help the small bookstore compete more successfully against the larger chains and wholly internet-based retailers such as Amazon.com.

Discussion Questions:
1) What are your predictions that the availability of web expertise and a national book database will encourage an increase in independent book retailers using the Internet to reach their customers? What cultural factors might inhibit or encourage the development of an Internet presence among the ABA's members?
2) Will an Internet presence likely increase global sales for local and regional book retailers? Why or why not?
3) Would the ABA's strategy of providing a template for their members' likely work in other countries such as Italy, Norway, the UK or Kuwait? Why or why not?
4) What role do you think the in-store environment plays for different countries? What factors might make a difference?

STUDY QUESTIONS

1. What are the key determinants of global electronic commerce adoption? What additional factors might influence Internet retailing and purchasing?
2. What are the main issues at the individual level that affect the adoption of Global Electronic Commerce?
3. We usually think of electronic communications or commerce as supporting international operations. How might the local geography of a country support the use of electronic commerce strategies? Provide three examples.
4. What are some of the challenges facing retail business today that may be overcome through electronic commerce strategies?
5. Why is the Internet different from other types of distance technologies, such as the telephone or fax machine?
6. Why has Internet retailing become popular for bookstores?
7. How has Internet retailing challenged the role of bookstores and forced changes in their roles and strategies?
8. Do you think wholly Internet-based book retailers, such as Amazon, are more likely to succeed at Internet retailing in foreign countries than physical retail firms in those countries that also have websites? Why or why not?
9. Do you think all book retailers with websites that enable Internet retailing of books will eventually attract international audiences? Why or why not?
10. Do you think Amazon.com will ever replace the smaller, community bookstore? Why or why not?

REFERENCES

Angehrn, A.A. & Meyer, J.F. (1997) "Developing Mature Internet Strategies: Insights from the Banking Industry." *Information Systems Management*. Summer, pp. 37-43.

Barron, S. (1999) "An Enemy of the Net Strikes Back", *The Irish Times*. 23 August. City Edition. Computer Crimes Section, page10.

Borenstein, N.S., Ferguson, J., Hall, J., Lowery, C., et al, (1996) "Perils and Pitfalls of Practical Cybercommerce." *Communications of the ACM*. (June, 1996) Vol. 39(6), p.36-44.

Commission of the European Communities. (1999) "Commission authorises the merger of the Italian book-clubs of Mondadori and Bertelsmann". *RAPID*. Press Release 99/260. 26 April.

Cronin, M.J. (1996) *The Internet Strategy Handbook*. Harvard University Press. 296 pages.

Deal, T. E., & Kennedy, A. A. (1982). Corporate Cultures: The Rites and Rituals of Corporate Life. Addison-Wesley.

Del Prete, D. (1996) *"Booksellers test cyberspace marketplace."* Marketing News. (January 15, 1996) Vol. 30(2).

Evaristo, J. Roberto (1998) "The Impact of Privatization on Organizational Information Needs: Lessons from the Brazilian Telecommunications Holding Company" *Information, Technology and People*. Volume 11, Issue 3.

Financial Times (London) (1999) "Surfing among the sharks: How to gain trust in cyberspace", Section: Survey – Mastering Information Management, p.5. 15 March.

Giussani, B. (1999) "Nordic Anti-Amazon Thrives on Keeping it Simple" *International Herald Tribune (Nuilly-sur-Seine, France)*. 11 February. Pg. 6.

Gordon, G. G. (1985). "The Relationship of Corporate Culture to Industry Sector and Corporate Performance". In R. H. Kilmann, M. J. Saxton, R. Serpa, & Associates (Ed.), *Gaining Control of the Corporate Future* (pp. 103-125). Jossey-Bass.

Greenspan, A. (1999) Report on "The Emerging Digital Economy II". Federal Reserve Board Report. 6 May.

Horvath, D.J. & Daly, D. J. (1989) *Small Countries in the World Economy: The Case of Sweden - what Canada can learn from the Swedish Experience.* Halifax, NS: The Institute for Research on Public Policy

Hofstede, G., Neuijen, B., Ohayv, D. D., & Sander, G. (1990). "Measuring Organizational Cultures: A Qualitative and Quantitative Study Across Twenty Cases". *Administrative Science Quarterly, 35,* 286-316.

Kaarst-Brown, M.L. & Robey, D. (1999) "More on Myth, Magic and Metaphor: Cultural Insights into the Management of Information Technology in Organizations" (1999) *Information, Technology and People,* Vol. 12(2).

Kumar, K., Van Dissel, H. G., and Bielli, P. (1998) "The Merchant of Prato -- Revisited: Toward a Third Rationality of Information Systems*" MIS Quarterly,* Vol. 22(2) June.

Lillington, K. (1999) "Spam spiders roam the Web collecting addresses" *The Irish Times CITY EDITION.* Business Section, pg. 57. 16 July.

M2 Presswire (1999) "Elron launches product to protect organizations from email misuse, abuse and spam." 16 August.

M2 Communications Ltd. TELECOMWORLDWIRE (1999) "The US Federal Trade Commission Takes SPAM Case to Court" 21 May.

New Media Age (1999) "Users blame ISPs for SPAM" Section: Trends, pg. 21. 24 June.

NUA surveys. Available WWW URL: http://www.nua.ie/surveys

Palvia, P.C., Palvia, S.C., & Roche, E. M. (Editors) (1996) *Global Information Technology and Systems Management: Key Issues and Trends.* Ivy League Publishing.

Rabelloti, Roberta (1997) *External Economies and Cooperation in Industrial Districts: A Comparison of Italy and Mexico.* New York: St. Martin's Press.

Roberts, S. C. & Hart, H. S (1997) "A Comparison of Cultural Value Orientations as reflected by Advertisements Directed at the General US Market, the US Hispanic Market, and the Mexican Market." *Journal of Marketing Theory and Practice,* Vol. 5 N. 1, pp. 91-99.

Roche, E.M. (1991) *Telecommunications and Business Strategy.* Chicago, IL: Dryden Press. 512 pages.

Sackmann, S. A. (1991). *Cultural Knowledge in Organizations: Exploring the Collective Mind.* London: Sage.

Sackmann, S. A. (1992). "Culture and Sub-Cultures: An Analysis of Organizational Knowledge" *Administrative Science Quarterly, 37,* 140-161.

Shore, B. (1996) "A Conceptual Framework to Assess Gaps in Information Systems Cultures Between Headquarters and Foreign Subsidiaries." In Palvia, P.C., Palvia, S.C., and Roche, E. M. (Eds.) *Global Information Technology and Systems Management: Key Issues and Trends.* Chapter 9, pp. 191-208.

Smith, A. (1980) *The Geopolitics of Information: How Western Culture Dominates the World.* Oxford Press. 192 pages.

Tagliabue, J. (1999) "Europeans Begin to Shed Resistance to On-line Shopping." *International Herald Tribute (Neuilly-sur-Seine, France).* 29 March. Pg. 13.

The Open Group. Case Study on Norwegian government available at WWW URL: http://www.opengroup.org/comm/case-studies/norway.htm)

Thompson, M. J. (1999) "Only Half of Net Purchases are Paid for Online" The Industry Standard. 1 March. Available at http://www.thestandard.com/metrics

Walczuch, R., Singh, S. & Palmer. T. (1995) "An analysis of the cultural motivation for transborder data flow legislation", *Information, Technology and People*, Vol. 8(2), pp. 37-57.

Westland, C. & Clark, T. (2000*) Global Electronic Commerce: Theory and Cases*. MIT Press, Forthcoming

Wheeler, D.L. (1998) "Global culture or culture clash: new information technologies in the Islamic world – a view from Kuwait" *Communication Research,* Vol. 25(4), pp. 359-377.

---

[1] Roche's strategic opportunities included the provision of value added services, rapid market penetration, reducing time required for various activities, providing superior customer services, operating a distributed business, reducing inventory costs, reducing operating costs, delivering innovative services, and linking strategic alliances.

[2] Source: NUA Internet Surveys, June 1999 Available at http://www.nua.ie/surveys/how_many_online/index.html

[3] Chapters is a Canadian book retailer with a strong on-line presence. Located at http://www.chapters.ca

[4] Cisco Systems is found at http://www.cisco.com

[5] Source: NUA Surveys, Aussie Net Shopper, July 7, 1999.

[6] Canadian Government Site on Electronic Commerce and Global Issues. "Canada and the Next Round of WTO Negotiations". Available WWW URL: http://e-com.ic.gc.ca

[7] Manheim auto auctions found at http://www.manheim.com/.

[8] Dell can be found at http://www.dell.com

[9] Virtual Vineyards can be found at http://www.virtualvin.com

[10] Hewlett Packard can be found at http://www.hp.com

[11] FedEx can be found at http://www.fedex.com

[12] American Airlines can be found at http://www.aa.com

[13] Travelocity can be found at http://www.travelocity.com

[14] Trip.com can be found at http://www.trip.com

[15] Costs in many countries may include the local call (which is rarely billed at a flat rate as it is in the U.S.) plus the timed access price from the ISP. This means that in such countries the total cost for both the telephone call and Internet access time is severely limiting.

[16] Sources: 1997 and 1998 10K and 10Q Prospectus Data for Amazon.com Inc., Books-A-Million Inc., Barnes & Noble Inc. Available from Disclosure found at http://www.disclosure.com

[17] Adapted from the following sources: Disclosure 1997 and 1998 10Q and 10K data and NUA surveys. Available at http://www.disclosure.com and http://www.nua.ie/surveys

[18] Adapted from the following sources. "Christina Foyle – Bookseller", The Glasgow Herald, June 12, 1999, pg. 22; Obituary: Christina Foyle, by Ian Norrie for the Independent (London, UK), June 11, 1999, pg. 6; and Richard Donkin's "Rewrite the Rule Book: Management Gurus could learn from Christina Foyle's eccentric style", Financial Times (UK), Friday June 18, 1999.

[19] Adapted from "An enemy of the Net strikes back" by S. Barron, The Irish Times, August 23, 1999, City Edition, Computimes Section, pg. 10.

[20] Adapted from "Brazil: Book Publishers looking to New Generation of Readers" by Maria Osava. Global Information Network Interpress Service, May 14, 1999

[21] Adapted from the following sources: "Press Release from the Commission of European Communities, April 26, 1999, RAPID, and "Europeans Begin to Shed Resistance to On-line Shopping", by J. Tagliabue, International Herald Tribute (Neuilly-sur-Seine, France), March 29, 1999.

[22] Adapted from "Take home UK's favourite bookstore and discover a route to the web". M2 Communications Ltd. Presswire, March 25, 1999.

14

A Framework for the Management of Global
e-Business in Small and Medium-Sized Enterprises

Emmanuel O. Tetteh
Edith Cowan University, W. Australia

Janice M. Burn
Edith Cowan University, W. Australia

ABSTRACT

The World Wide Web (WWW) provides unique opportunities for small and medium-sized enterprises (SMEs) to build effective global infrastructures in at least three ways. First Internet-based infrastructures are relatively cheap; requiring significantly reduced capital investments over proprietary networks. Second, they provide an ever converging and rich environment for effective business networking and inter-organizational process management. Third, they provide SMEs with access to a greatly expanded consumer market through electronic business. In order to exploit these advantages in a global strategy, the SME needs to adopt an entirely different approach to management that can enable it to deploy an extensive infrastructure network based on shared resources with other firms. This chapter presents a framework for the analysis and design of global information infrastructures within the organizational context of SMEs using Internet-based information technologies. Central to the framework is the transformation of the key attributes of an SME environment through a virtual organising perspective. The framework is supported by a number of case examples of SMEs in the global context. It provides a new perspective to strategic infrastructure management in SMEs and to electronic business research.

INTRODUCTION

SMEs in a Global e-Business Context

Much of the literature on global information systems is based on the experiences of large firms with huge capital resources to support extensive IT infrastructure development (Palvia and Palvia 1996, Cavaye, et al. 1998, Niederman, et al. 1991, Jarvenpaa and Ives 1993, Dean and Kane 1992). Most smaller firms have limited human, financial and technological resources and thus have limited access to global markets. Yet the SME[1] sector is generally recognised as

---

[1] SMEs (sometimes referred to in this chapter as small firms) are defined in this chapter as firms with less than 500 employees. In the literature, SMEs are variously classified based on a wide range of criteria including number of employees, sales turnover, size of capital assets, etc. The most popular criterion is the number of employees (NOE) on company's payroll. Most national accounting systems

a window of opportunity for rejuvenating mature industries, creating new and innovative markets, and achieving rapid economic growth through employment generation and wealth creation in all economies (ISPO 1998, OECD 1993, Kaplan, *et al.* 1997). Web-based business is an extremely attractive option for most SMEs, especially given the huge publicity and support provided by governments to push growth in the sector. Also, the unique features of small firms namely, flexibility of operations, relatively simple organizational structures, entrepreneurial culture and high propensity to engage in business networks can be advantageous in the electronic marketplace. The availability of the Internet and World Wide Web (WWW) technologies provides unique advantages for SMEs to build effective global infrastructures in at least three ways. First, Internet-based infrastructures are relatively cheap; requiring significantly reduced capital investments over proprietary ones. Second, they provide an ever converging and rich environment for effective business networking and inter-organizational process management. Third, they provide SMEs with access to a huge mass of consumers through electronic business (e-business).

Kaplan *et al.* (1997), like many others, endorse the view that small businesses offer some of the best options for making meaningful productivity gains in the global marketplace through the exploitation of enhanced technological competencies. Mastery and effective deployment of Internet technologies in enterprise-wide infrastructures is certainly critical in the global e-business environment. In most of the e-business success stories, Amazon.com and CDnow.com, to name but two of the most celebrated, the underlying factor has been the installation of networked information and technologies and the exploitation of enhanced information competencies. These online firms have experienced phenomenal growth in size, market value and performance within the space of less than five years.

A key lesson from these success stories is that in order to achieve competitiveness and profitability in the electronic marketplace, SMEs must of necessity extend their environments by exploiting the capabilities of online infrastructures to supporting virtual operations that span wide geographical locations and multiple time zones.

An SME may achieve this without acquiring the traditional measures of large size, namely large employee base, vast capital resources, and extensive investment in conventional networking technology. New information and communication technologies -- especially the Internet -- together with innovative business strategies offer opportunities for SMEs to extend their scope of operations, enhance their competitive status, and improve their performance.

Growth in Global e-Business

Electronic business (e-business) refers to business conducted over electronic networks and encompasses supply chain management, production, commercial transactions and distribution (e-commerce), and strategic management processes. Business on the Internet is booming and attracting all sizes of companies. A review of the diverse estimates of the growth of e-business points to significant increases in global online activity in the next few years with the highest activity in the USA. On a global scale, business-to-business e-commerce, estimated at US$5.6 billion in 1997, is projected to reach US$268 billion in 2002. Also business-to-consumer e-commerce is expected to rise from US$1,8 billion in 1997 to US$26 billion by 2002[2].

In the US for example, 23% of adults (i.e. 44 million people) are estimated to use the Internet regularly (Strader, et al. 1999). Online banking activity by US households using PCs

---

would defined SMEs as those with NOE within the range of 1and 500. These may be further sub-classified as of micro with NOE < 5; small-sized: 5<NOE<20; and medium-sized: 20< NOE< 500. The sub-classification may be further modified on the basis of industry sector. For example, in the manufacturing sector the NOE of a small-size firm may be in the order of 200 as compared with about 20 for a similar category in the services sector.

[2] 1998 e-Commerce Report [online], in the eMarketer (21 May 1998), www.iw.com/daily/stats/1998

is expected to triple by 2004 from 7 million at the end of 1998 to more that 24.2 million (Dataquest, Inc.)[3] Dataquest Inc, estimates that more than half (13.7 million) of the 24.2 million PC banking consumers will be paying bills online in 2004.

Research by International Data Corporation (IDC) also points to a substantial online activity outside US (especially Western Europe) with almost 60 percent of the worldwide online population coming from outside the US[4]. This group is expected to contribute nearly 46 percent of global e-commerce spending by 2003, representing an increase from 1998 levels of just 26 percent. Electronic commerce spending in the Western European region is predicted to grow at a compound annual growth rate of 138 percent from US$5.6 billion in 1998 to US$430 billion by 2003. The IDC also reports that in the Asia/Pacific region (including Japan) Internet users will almost quadruple, from 21 million in 1998 to over 81 million by 2003 – representing a projected rise in e-commerce spending from US$2.7 billion to US$72 billion. Such huge activity raises critical issues for managers in all businesses. Some of these are reviewed in the next section in relation to global oriented SMEs.

Challenges of the e-Business Environment

Unfortunately going on-line for most SMEs presents major hurdles and requires a strategic appreciation of the dynamics of the Web and the building of capabilities for managing their information infrastructure. The online environment is subject to rapid changes both in industry structure and the technologies that underpin the Internet. The real-time inter-network presents the challenge of managing diverse time and geographical locations of global clients and partners. There are stringent requirements to produce and deliver very high quality products to consumer communities who increasingly demonstrate greater levels of sophisticated demand due to improved access to information about product alternatives. To stay competitive in the online environment, the ability of the SME to continuously identify strategic partners and manage its relationships with them to maximise its business value is a major success factor. It is also important to be able to manage the characteristics of the electronic marketplace.

Many international studies have also highlighted other issues associated with the adoption of the Internet as a medium for doing business by SMEs (Poon and Swatman 1997, OECD 1998, CIRCIT 1998, Ng, et. al. 1998, O'Connor *et al.* 1997, Kurbel and Teuteberg 1998). These studies point to some of the common characteristics of SMEs with respect to adoption levels, challenges, and general benefits from online infrastructures. While there appears to be a lot of enthusiasm about the Internet and electronic business, these current studies show that it is the minority of SMEs who are reaping significant benefits from the Internet. The majority of SMEs employ the Internet as a basic communications facility using it as a cost-effective alternative to the more traditional means (e.g. fax and telephone) of communication with partners or customers. The reasons for the relative low level of use include: uncertainty about benefits, low level of technological expertise, low commitment of owner/manger, poor understanding of the dynamics of the electronic marketplace and their inability to devise strategies to leverage online infrastructure for profit (Igbaria, et al., 1998; Fink, 1998).

These challenges are not helped by the general lack of clearly defined frameworks for analysis of the entire process of strategy building, implementation and management with respect to this emerging global information economy. This chapter attempts to address the problem by providing a holistic framework for the study and design of global information infrastructure within the organizational context of SMEs. With such analytical tools and specific e-business strategies SMEs could and should capitalise on the opportunities offered in

---

[3] http://www.internetnews.com/ec-news/article/0,1087,archive_4_179891,00.html accessed 25 August 1999)

[4] http://www.internetnews.com/ec-news/article/0,1087,4_189121,00.html, accessed 25 August 1999

the electronic marketplace. The framework is supported by a number of international case studies centred on successful on-line SMEs. Critical success factors are identified and an agenda is provided for future research into this area.

DEVELOPING INFRASTRUCTURES FOR GLOBAL e-BUSINESS

Internet Based Infrastructures

An Internet-based information infrastructure may be described as a three-tier model of technologies, systems and business applications (Tapscott, et. al., 1998), namely:

Level 1:Base technologies – these include the underlying open-systems network platforms and devices supporting multi-environment integration and interoperability of systems across groups, organizations, industries, and regions. Examples are internet-based network equipment and connections, network printers and scanners, and domain server computers. Base technologies also include routers, wide area networks, the Internet backbone, firewalls, and communications controllers.

Level 2: Network systems, server technologies, and applications development utilities – these are the building blocks for electronic business applications and facilities. Generally, components at this level deal with network and process management, digital imaging and security management aspects of the infrastructure. Process management tools at this level form the basis of developing collaborative features into supply chain manage applications for e-business.

Level 3: e-Business applications and solutions – These include routine enterprise system management and web authoring programs (e.g. Microsoft FrontPage); client interactive communication and information management applications (e.g. Netscape Communicator and Microsoft Explorer browsers); applications for online shopping and ordering (e.g. Cart32, http://www.cart32.com); secured payment facilities (e.g. Digicash), transaction certification programs (e.g. SET™, http://www.setco.org/), and product delivery tracking programs. There is a growing market for complete e-business solutions, which provide a flexible and scalable environment for developing an internet-based infrastructure to support e-business. Examples of these are IBM Net.commerce and WebSphere Suite (http://www-4.ibm.com/software/webservers/).

Competitive advantage is associated with the third level of infrastructure deployment. This is because as the underlying technologies and systems mature, relatively cheap and effective resources in the first two levels become affordable to most businesses. Indeed in the near future, real competitive performance will be linked more and more to strategies employed by firms to manage the third level systems rather than the mere ownership of them. For a global oriented SME, these strategies must be targeted at the transformation of the firm's environment through the functionalities associated with the Internet environment. These may be understood from two interrelated views of the Internet, namely:

- As an inter-organizational system (IOS) platform
- As the marketspace.

Each of these perspectives reveals potential benefits and contributions to the global strategy of the online SME. It is important to appreciate how these functionalities can be brought together to create a winning strategy for any particular business.

Internet - An Inter-Organizational System (IOS) Platform

The Internet provides a platform for building flexible, adaptive and innovative organizational formats. The Internet's open systems architecture allows the SME to achieve a high level of integration of its enterprise-wide infrastructure by building on the installed bases of PCs, digital assets and competencies of clients, suppliers, partners and others on a global scale. With the growth in powerful applications such as the Extensible Markup Language (XML) and portal systems, online businesses can manage their entire value chain activities over integrated platforms. XML, which is a further improvement on the Hyper Text Markup Language (HTML), provides a common protocol for accessing and processing diverse forms of electronic content. It also provides a convergence of client-server computing and electronic publishing, enabling businesses to exchange intelligent information over the Internet. Portal systems provide unified browser-based environments for live access to critical customer information from multiple and disparate enterprise data sources, such as front- and back-office systems. For example, a portal application can enable employees to anticipate customer needs, build stronger customer relationships, improve customer service, and increase revenue-generating opportunities.

Indeed, designing an infrastructure on the Net, allows the SME to focus on only a core set of information technology (IT) equipment, tools and personnel to support its operations. This can lead to huge savings in IT investment and management costs. The core assets and resources may be distributed across wide geographical regions. Thus the cost of transactions with clients and partners can be significantly reduced leading to improved profit margins. Also, the increasing simplicity and familiarity of the user interfaces and online applications mean that employees, clients and other stakeholders can learn quickly and participate in knowledge creation and development of end products.

Internet - The Marketspace

The Internet effectively simulates an electronic marketspace through its ability to intermediate among market players and to integrate diverse markets. As a *marketspace* it can reduce search costs and thereby enhance the efficiency of inter-organizational transactions. Specifically, it has the capacity to lower the marginal costs of electronic business processes, reduce the criticality of many intermediaries and enable the efficient handling of large volumes of transactions leading to superior cost/performance for the business. (Bakos 1991, Benjamin and Wigand 1995). However, these functionalities are not equally available to all businesses across all industries. Palvia and Vemuri (1999) point out that the extent of disintermediation (i.e. the process of removing the role of middlemen) will depend on product and service characteristics. They project that information intensive businesses, especially the services sector, will witness a reduction in layers of intermediaries as compared with those in manufacturing industries. Also there is increasing recognition of the emergence of new forms of intermediaries which seek to exploit the emerging niches in the electronic marketspace (Hagel & Singer, 1998). Thus it is critical for the global oriented SME to articulate its current and future business directions and to analyse how these relate to developments in the electronic marketspace. This will allow it to choose the appropriate business model, infrastructure configuration and an effective management strategy.

In the next section we present a broad framework for managing an internet-based information infrastructure that facilitates the achievement of extended market access and competitive performance of a global oriented SME. A number of case examples will demonstrate how this online infrastructure can facilitate the extension of the scope of operations of the SME, especially in:

- managing core organizational activities which may now be dispersed over multiple geographical sites
- mediation of the co-operative efforts between business partners and other stakeholders
- management of the client community

- development of a consistent global image of business and products.

The cases also reveal that to be successful, an online enterprise needs a strategy that aligns its business logic or model with its infrastructure configuration on a continuous basis.

FRAMEWORK FOR STRATEGIC MANAGEMENT OF ONLINE SMES

Strategic Framework

Figure 1 below describes the broad framework for managing a global e-business strategy within an SME context. For the online SME a useful perspective to adopt in managing its global orientation is the virtual organising perspective which emphasises the management of values associated with the electronic market environment through the innovative use of its online infrastructure. The core elements of the strategy are :

- Organizational system re-definition, ie. choice of a business model to align the strategic objectives with its business activities as well as the electronic market environment
- Transformation of the scope of business of SME
- Virtual infrastructure management.

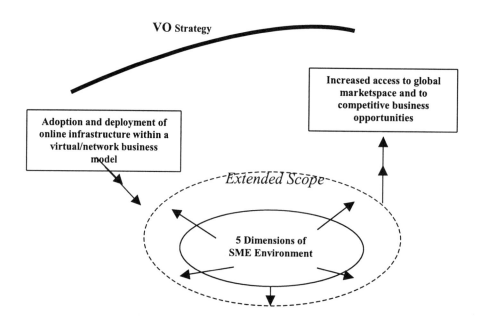

Figure 1.   Internet-enabled transformation of business scope

In the following sections, brief description of each of the elements is provided.

The Virtual Organising Perspective

Many writers highlight the feature of virtuality associated with electronic mediated work processes, virtual organizations and products (Venkatraman and Henderson, 1998; Grenier and Metes 1995, Tapscott, *et al.* 1998). These authors suggest that in order to benefit from the new electronic mediated markets, firms must adopt new organizational forms based on the virtual organising perspective. Virtual organizations are those that employ extensive networked information infrastructures to attract resources and manage a value chain that transcends organizational boundaries, geographical regions and time zones. Such firms deal in products, which lend themselves to a virtual market, namely mass-customised goods and services produced and deliverable anywhere, anytime and in any variety (Davidow and Malone 1992, Boudreau, *et al.* 1998).

The concept of organizational virtuality is a characteristic of the firm's entire environment. It defines *the perception of globalness* held by its stakeholders about the business scope with respect to its presence, processes, products and relationships. It is associated with features such as flexibility of operations, responsiveness to market changes, agility in the management of inter-firm relations and other linkages within industry. The exploitation of these valued features through the strategic management of a global infrastructure platform can enhance the perception of an extended scope of business even though in reality the enterprise may be operating with a limited physical scope. In other words, the firm may be able to project itself and its products as being available at multiple locations and in varied time zones.

Choice of Online Business Model

An online business model is a generic organizational format adapted to the electronic market environment and emphasising the use of Internet-based information infrastructure to do business. There exists a wide spectrum of online formats that may be broadly categorised under three generic online business models (table 1).

Table 1: Online Business Models

ONLINE BUSINESS MODEL	FEATURES	EXAMPLES
Virtual Face e-Shop	• Provides an extra space for presenting organization and products to a wider market. • Usually involves a single enterprise • Limited commitment to common business goals in relationships with others	**Harris Technology** **Boots Online** **Hawaiian Greenhouse**
Virtual Alliance	• Involves a number of firms sharing resources and competencies to develop some product offering. • Site may represent the common interface for the group or may place different emphasis on a focal firm while providing visibility to the alliance • Significant use of online infrastructure and e-Commerce technologies • Cross reference to sites of participating firms	**SCB Co-op** **LAA**
Virtual Community E-MALL PORTALS	Represents an electronic marketspace involving a large number of firms and grouping of other online models	**Best of Italy** **Sofcom**

Each category may have sub-classifications, which can only represent generalised descriptions with significant overlap. For example portals and electronic malls may both be described as virtual communities since both represent a collection of wide variety of services and service providers working as a community. The unique feature of virtual communities is that they provide a sense of a uniform marketspace to all players including manufacturer, service providers, suppliers, and customers.

Virtual Face

In its basic format, the enterprise usually exists as a single business entity with some online presence primarily to advertise itself and its products. The business may also be organised around the virtual face model as the primary point of access to their entire business and products. Harris Technology, Sydney and Boots Online, Melbourne, are typical examples of online SMEs employing the virtual face business model to enhance their competitive performance. While Harris Technology targets the Australian national market in computer related products, Boots Online is a global oriented SME selling to world wide markets. Both businesses have witnessed substantial growth in sales and profit margins within two years of going online. In an elaborate form of the virtual face model, as in the case of Harris Technology, the SME may undertake extensive business activities online, including sourcing of resources and services, communication and collaboration with other firms, and the management of its customer base. This will usually require a significant re-definition of business processes to enhance the information processing aspects and to ensure a high level of integration and interoperability with the stakeholder environment. Another requirement will be the development of enhanced online information management skills in employees.

Virtual Alliance

An SME employing this model participates in a cluster or group of autonomous businesses both online and offline, and organises its core operations and offerings around the shared resources, competencies and markets that the group create. An example of this type is SCB Co-op, Scotland. The strategic advantage of the online infrastructure is to provide a cost-effective collaborative medium for pooling critical resources to achieve the objectives of individual participants. In the case of SCB Co-op the online infrastructure has enabled very small traditional Scottish breweries to market their products under a common label across the UK and globally. Leading Agents in Australia (LAA) is another example of a virtual face business model. Even though each member of the alliance maintains an elaborate website, their alliance is not uniformly represented online as a single site. The main gains of the online infrastructure for the group is fast access to information that they share about regional opportunities. Also extensive referrals to each other provide potential clients and visitors to their sites an assurance of dealing with a well connected group of professionals in the Australian real estate market. This increases trust in their services and can be a source of competitive advantage.

Virtual Community

The third generic category of online business model is the *virtual community*, which is a large collection of firms in the online market, including other stakeholders such as customers and government agencies. In that environment the focal SME is highly integrated with those of others and its separate existence is hardly discernible to stakeholders of the community. Examples of a virtual community are portal services such BOI (Best of Italy) Srl. and Sofcom.com.au. In both examples, the virtual community owner supplies and manages the online infrastructure on behalf of participating SMEs. This reduces the need for substantial investments in technology and infrastructure management. Participant enterprises can concentrate on selling their products. On the other hand clients are offered a one stop access to a wide range of goods and services and at reduced prices due to the relativly low cost associated with marketing and distribution channel management for the vendors.

TRANSFORMATION OF SME ENVIRONMENT

S-M-A-L-L Attribute Model

Central to the global strategy of the online SME is the virtual transformation of five key dimensions (or attributes) of the SME environment. These attributes, which capture the scope of business operations of the SME, are:

- Size/value of assets and resources
- Market coverage and product mix
- Activities and processes,
- Linkages and relationships within environment, and
- Locational diversity/scope.

The attributes focus on those aspects of the SME that impact on its ability to reach wider markets; access extensive resources; enhance, diversify and integrate its activities; manage collaborative engagements with others; and deal with temporal and locational diversity issues. By gaining a wider market the SME is placed in a favourable position to enhance its competitive performance estimated as a composite measure of a number of performance variables including value of sales, profits, enhanced global image, increased market access and broader customer base. Leveraging the online infrastructure can lead to an extension of the dimensions of the SME to varying degrees. The extent of transformation depends on the fit between the firm's business model, its strategic direction and the appropriate infrastructure management strategy. Table 2 provides detailed descriptions of each attribute and the associated organizational variables. For any SME, relative values can be assigned to each of the attributes using a set of discrete values {Low, Medium, High} on a qualitative estimation scale.

Virtual Infrastructure Management

The extent of contribution from the infrastructure will depend on the information intensity of the business value chain (Moreton & Chester, 1997; Porter & Miller, 1985; Venkatraman, 1994). According to Moreton & Chester (1997), the information intensity of the value chain derives from four related factors: nature of partnerships internal arrangements, nature of market or industry, and the product offerings. The analysis of the information processes in each of these factors would reveal the aspects of the business that may be transformed by leveraging the online infrastructure. These factors also provide the basis of virtual infrastructure management by seeking continuously to enhance the alignment between these factors while increasing the firm's ability to work with them across multiple sites and time zones.

Employing an adaptation of Henderson and Venkatraman's strategic alignment model, Figure 2 shows the interaction of the SME's strategic objectives, information infrastructure and its relevant business environment. The firm seeking to leverage its information technology infrastructure must work out a close fit between these three aspects. In general, the strategic objectives of an online SME will relate to seeking increased access to wider markets and resources through extension of its environment. The firm's infrastructure (based on Internet technologies) and its industry environment (i.e. electronic business) present a virtual market environment. Thus it becomes critical to identify and exploit those features of the infrastructure that facilitate and optimise virtual values in the business chain. The strategy for alignment and exploitation of the online infrastructure to achieve increase virtuality may be described as a Virtual Infrastructure Management (VIM) strategy.

Table-2: S-M-A-L-L - Key Attributes of SME Environment

Size (S) Number of employees Number of branch offices Value of assets Annual turnover of Business Investments in IT	This attribute can be defined in terms of number of employees, sales turnover, and assets, etc. It may also include the size or investment in infrastructure. The adoption and management of a successful online infrastructure strategy may result in an increase or decrease in size.
Market (M) Share of market (value of sales) Product mix (variety and novelty) Number of states/ regions covered	This attribute describes the firm's share of the market and the number and variety of products. By developing an online presence it is possible to extend it markets and reach out to a wider customer base. It is also possible to develop new products and offerings based on exposure to opportunities made available to the firm on going online.
Activities and Processes (A) Nature of activities Information intensity of activities and Products Level of electronic mediation Changes in products/ processes	Application of online infrastructure can lead to increased integration and enhanced efficiency of processes. The infrastructure can also support re-engineering of business processes and to enhance the value added. New opportunities can emerge innovative products may be developed through the application of the infrastructures.
Linkages (L₁) Number of strategic <u>partners</u> Nature of partnerships/networking (regularity, permanence) Type of contractual arrangements	This attribute refers to relationships and co-operative arrangements, which span the firm's internal and external environment. Also implied here is the frequency of forming and breaking links with others.
Locational Diversity (L₂) Spread of regional/ international branches Range of time zones Extent of asynchronous working	This describes the geographical spread of sites from which the firm's core operations are conducted. It also involves the diversity of time zones that the enterprise can effectively manage. With an online infrastructure individual or small groups of employees may work from wider geographical locations and/or diverse time zones without establishing branch offices. On the other hand the online infrastructure may allow concentration of total workspace.

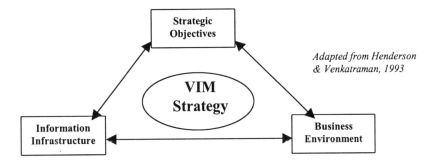

Figure 2: Alignment of objectives, business environment and

Based on the above discussions on virtual organising, an effective virtual nfrastructure management strategy would include among others the following aspects:

- Develop components of the infrastructure that add value to the business chain
- Install networking features -- e.g. to facilitate collaborative effort and linkages among stakeholders
- Use of infrastructure to develop virtual values of process, products and image - e.g. through customer interaction with web-site content including product information, use of graphics for retention and encouragement to re-visit, cultivate value for virtual products
- Cultivate information skills and virtual culture in customers - e.g. through the web site tutorial, development of virtual communities (e.g. newsgroups, chatlists, forums)

The following cases illustrated various aspects of the infrastructure management to extend the business environment of online SMEs and how this leads to enhanced market performance.

CASE STUDIES

All of the following case studies are based on extensive website assessment and secondary data sources and were selected as examples of SMEs who have successfully exploited the Internet infrastructure to enhance their global operations and performance.

Boots Online[5]

Boots Online is an example of a global SME employing the virtual face model. The company is the online shopfront of Stitching Horse Bootery, a small business established in 1977 as an authorised retailer of R.M. William brand of boots, leatherwear and travel accessories. The Melbourne based company established the online shopfront in 1995 with a total investment of AU$ 3,000. The company's strategic goal in going online was to market the best of Australian boots and leatherwear to a worldwide market. With a staff of only 4 people this company has transformed itself from a local agent of a renowned product to a global business with over 15 percent of total sales from online customers. Over 95 percent of its online customers are located overseas. Boots Online has reaped significant benefits from its online strategy. Within a year of establishing an online presence the company achieved huge increase in sales (15%) with six additional sales per week. It makes about $1,500 worth of online sales per week and

---

[5] Company's performance details are as quoted in Phillips, M. (1998) Successful e-Commerce:10 case Studies to Show Small Business How to Profit from Online Commerce, Bookman, Australia

total company sales of AUD75, 000 are projected to double in one year. Profit margins on online sales have increased due to reduced inventory costs. Also the company has seen an increase in customer satisfaction over the period. <www.bootsonline.com.au>

Hawaiian Greenhouse, Inc

Hawaiian Greenhouse, Inc.[6] is a family owned business located in Pahoa on the island of Hawaii. The installation of an online infrastructure has resulted in a remarkable transformation of the business scope and led to increased profitability. The company, established since 1965, has been growing anthuriums and other tropical flowers and foliage and shipping them worldwide. Traditionally it has thrived on growing large crops and selling to a small group of wholesale customers who in turn market them worldwide. The effects of globalisation and intensifying competition from many other growers in the region have prompted the company to rethink its business logic. Focusing on retailing as a more lucrative sales channel, the company set out in 1997 to exploit the capabilities of the Internet to increase its sales volume and expand its customer base, while keeping its operational costs to a minimum. It started by automating its order fulfilment, accounting and customer-tracking functions with an IBM e-business solution based on Lotus Notes and Lotus Domino application environments. Since then, the company has developed a fully functional web-enabled shopfront based on the Lotus Domino.Merchant. There has been a complete transformation of core business processes. As recalled by the manager of the company "When we first started, we were manually doing all the work orders, message cards, labels and so on ... At present, the online infrastructure supports a simplified and fully automated sales and distribution process." In less that a year of building the virtual shop front, Hawaiian Greenhouse's e-business has grown tremendously. Currently, over 1,400 customers visit its site each month, generating 10 to 15 percent of the company's new orders. The company makes $350,000 worth of retail business today compared to the $175,000 when it was operating as a wholesale business. Also it expects to double retail sales within another year Other performance improvements include: 100% annual growth in retail sales, 100% ROI in 18 months, 10-15% revenue from online orders, 50% reduction in processing time, and improved customers services. The business plans to add new products to its portfolio including the possibility of marketing products of their competitors on its site: <www.hawaiian-greenhouse.com.>

Harris Technology (HT)

Harris Technology is another Australian SME, which has transformed its scope of operations from a metropolitan base in Sydney to cover the entire Australian market through its online business. HT is computer technology reseller established over 11 years ago and listed as on of Australia's top 100 fastest growing private companies for five consecutive years. The company online shopfront has yielded significant benefits increased sales and share of the computer equipment retail market. In its first year of going online the company made $1 million in e-business and another $3 million in its second year. HT currently employs about 80 staff all of whom are actively involved in the use of the online infrastructure. The online site was designed, built and managed by an in-house team. The company considers its web site to be a great success: "Our Web-presence has been so successful for us that we believe almost any business would benefit from a well presented Web-site."

---

[6] Case features on IBM e-Business website < http://www.software.ibm.com/solutions/internet/G325-4070-00.htm> last accessed August 1999.

The web site is designed around the QUIDS (Quotations Inventory, Distribution, and Sales) [7] database. The QUIDS database was written in Microsoft FoxPro and contains over 30, 000 products and 6000 customer entities. It enables tracking all aspects of HT business including sales, serial numbers and bills of material and profitability. The interesting feature of HT's online system is that the QUIDS database is common to all its key stakeholders. Suppliers and customers see the same information (pricing, stock availability, images and text) as seen by HT staff. For example, Tech Pacific, the company's main supplier, shares its stock availability and pricing with QUIDS each day via the Internet. Customers also interact with database's inventory in the same way as employees make queries to the system. Web pages are generated upon request by assembling data elements associated with each product (e.g. images, texts, downloadable drivers and sites links).

Using the integrated environment of the website, HT's employees can manage electronic transfer of stock and ordering information from all key stakeholders of the company (i.e. manufacturers, distributors, resellers, and end users). The facility also enable clients to scan product information, make orders, as well as track the process of delivery. Bank cheques, telegraphic transfer, and major credit cards can be used to make payment. Another interesting feature of the website is the "live show room" which provides real-time snapshots of HT's physical showroom. <www.ht.com.au>.

Scotland's Craft Brewers Co-operative[8] (SCB Co-op)

SCB Co-op is an online SME made up of six Scottish SMEs and a bottling plant. The co-op was formed to deliver global sales and marketing functions for the participant enterprises that specialized in traditionally brewed Scottish beers in Lugton, Scotland. The distinctive feature of SCB Co-op is that all its beers are traditionally using Scottish malt with no artificial additives. The Co-op was formed to pool the limited resources of individual SMEs to create a winning business image and a competitive product brand. Products of members are promoted under the Scotland Craft Brewer Cooperative brand name to large UK supermarkets. The Co-op's strategic objectives in going online are access global markets, expand regional market share, create jobs and increase revenues. Through the web site the Co-op has achieved significant performance growth that would have been difficult to achieve through conventional marketing strategies. Products of the Co-op have been submitted to the Canadian Liquor Board for sampling. As a result of online strategy, SCB Co-op is forecasted to create 75 new jobs within a year and then build a brand name to rival better known traditional brewers on a world scale.

In order to overcome the lack of technical skills and financial resources for developing an online infrastructure, the Co-op chose the IBM HomePage Creator service, which enabled it to establish the working website at a very low cost within a few days. The simplicity and low cost has made it possible for SCB Co-op to concentrate on its core operations of co-ordination and the participant SMEs and developing a competitive global brand.

The site features product information, nutritional information and recipes and links to some its major partners. One of the major business partners is ASDA, which is one of Britain's large supermarket chains. The Co-op's site integrates seamlessly with that of ASDA. Clients in Britain, or those planning a visit may also purchase the Co-op brand from any of the 31 ASDA stores across UK. The ASDA website features an innovative search engine, Store Finder, for locating any ASDA store by entering name of your location. Search results provide lists of nearby ASDA stores with details about address (including telephone and fax) , distance

---

[7] Details about the QUIDS system are described in Lawrence, E. (1998). Setting up a Shopfront, in CCH Australia Ltd., E-Commerce HandBook, Australian Print Group.

[8] Secondary data on case obtained from Chappel and Feindt (1999). Analysis of E-Commerce Practice in SME, ESPRIT Project KITE, <http://kite.tsa.de>

from central location, and a map. All these extend the infrastructure commanded by SCB Co-op in developing its global marketing strategy. <ww.lugton.co.uk>

Leading Agents of Australia (LAA)

Leading Agents of Australia (LAA) is an example of a virtual alliance where participating firms maintain their independent web sites. There is no common site representing their common interests as in the case of SCB Co-op, UK. LAA is a network of nine autonomous real estate SMEs operating across different states in Australia. Two key participating companies are Acton Consolidate Ltd., Perth and Patrick Dixon Real Estate, Brisbane. Acton has a total of seven branches across the Perth Metropolitan Area and is one of the leading firms in the Western Australian real estate market. The other partner firms also enjoy significant market shares in their respective state markets. The members of the network share a common business philosophy namely: "commitment to the highest ethical standards and excellence in client service". While each partner firm maintains autonomous business strategies for developing their competitive, they join effort when it comes to making a deal in other states. For example, partners sharing market information and competencies. It is clear that nature of the industry place a part in choosing the collaborative strategy. In the real estate industry local information and knowledge about products are crucial in making a good deal. As stated on one of the affiliates' websites these firms "are leaders in their respective markets and the interchange of property listings brings numerous qualified inter-state prospects" to their various operations. In relation to the management of their online business, the various partners maintain business links within the real estate industry and also with IT and e-Commerce development companies. For example, Acton Consolidated, reports a strategic alliance with The Globe.com.au and Spin Technologies in the development of their website, ActonNet.

Sofcom

Sofcom, is a Melbourne company acting as an electronic intermediary, which provides, in addition to other online content publishing, a virtual shopping mall for about 60 virtual storefronts. Sofcom may be described as an example of a virtual community. Members of the community engage in extensive linkages with each other and with a host of e-business service providers through Sofcom. The mall advertises over 4835 products in about 60 stores. There are ten categories of stores including: Apparel; automobile;, business services; computers and electronics; gifts and collectable; home design; perfumery and jewellery; entertainment. Other electronic market services and facilities provided by Sofcom to its virtual community are: business information, Internet directories publishing, websites/shop hosting, links to the Australian stock exchange, business newsletter and advisory services.

Sofcom has an extensive online infrastructure to support its product lines and to manage the virtual stores of other businesses. All transactions at Sofcom pass through Sofcom's SSL secure server. The site offers an online Store Builder facility for potential online storeowners. The facility takes potential store owners step by step through the process of setting up a storefront at Sofcom and doing business online. There is a flat charge of AU$ 40 per month for stores available to the public and selling. Potential storeowners may develop and test run a store for free. <www.sofcom.com.au>

DISCUSSION AND CONCLUSION

Table 3.1 presents a mapping of online processes from the perspective of both clients and focal SMEs to the key infrastructure components employed in delivering each functionality.

Table 3.2 summaries the case examples of business scope transformation resulting from the successful management of internet-based infrastructures in a number of online SMEs.

Table 3.1: Mapping of on-line transactions to key infrastructure components

PROCESS/ ACTIVITY	Description Client/Stakeholders	Focal Online Enterprise	KEY INFRASTRUCTURE COMPONENTS
Information Search & Data transfer	View/ scan web pages, navigate multiple and widely distributed sources, submit request for information, exchange information.	Capture and process online activity of visitors, develop profiles of products, and stakeholders.	• Browser/ navigational software • Client/product profile database servers • Search engines • data capture/transfer utilities • Multimedia communication facilities • Web authoring software
Selection & Customisation	Make choices, configure according to preferences, sample products, fill shopping basket.	Provide product options and offer samples, provide tutorials on product and services, cultivate customer interest in products.	Shopping cart software Multimedia presentation software
Order placement & Fund transfer	Fill out order form, provide details of credit/ debit card, give details of preferred delivery location and date.	Provide secure environment for online shopping and trading with partners, enable use of certificates and authentication procedures.	Software for secure online ordering and authentication procedures Invoicing & Billing applications Negotiation and Trading software for business-to-business processes
Product delivery	Online tracking of package delivery	Provide use of tracking software Manage relationships with couriers services contractors online.	Package Tacking software (e.g. DHL and FedEx tracking systems)
After Sales Activities	Visit web-site to find out about product usage, upgrades and other offering, Join user communities to discuss product quality and service needs	Develop feedback mechanisms on product quality and client support, provide upgrade details, information on new offers create or sponsor product user groups.	E-mail filtering software Chatlist and newsgroup management software
Online Advertising	-	Gather and present advertising information from multiple sources, monitor responses to advertisements.	Branding and banner advertising applications
Work flow management Business relationship management	-	Automated co-ordination of activities of employees and partners across distributed locations and time regions.	Network management utilities, Process management/ monitoring systems

Table 3.2: Application of *SMALL*: Transformation of SME Environments

Online SME	Transformation of Attributes				
	Size	Market	Activities	Linkages	Locational diversity
Boot Online	Reduced physical assets, inventory and warehousing facilities, Reduced need to recruit more personnel to manage global clientele.	Expanded market coverage local to global, increased sales from international clients, Potential to develop new products in tourist information and hotel reservation.	Increased simplicity, flexibility and automation of sales and distribution.	Increased linkages supporting services providers (e.g. ISP and software companies, courier services- DHL).	Increased diversity, can now supply to many international destinations, can also manage a global client base in different time-space locations.
Hawaiian Greenhouse	Reduced need to recruit more personnel, reduced need for many branch offices.	Direct retail instead of through wholesalers, potential for new products and diversification.	Automation of entire sale and distribution process, increased flexibility and market responsiveness and efficiency.	Relationships with courier services and e-business solution providers (Datahouse & IBM).	Able to reach a worldwide market without need for regional branches. Can supply to customers in any region/ time zones without difficulty.
Best of Italy *Sofcom*	Expanded effective size of business, infrastructure and resources as a group of companies.	Huge collection of diverse Italian products, worldwide coverage, prospects to develop other products e.g. *Happy Gift.*	Increased flexibility and efficiency through automation and enhanced information management.	High and diverse links and business relationships among many participant firms, business services providers, e-commerce solution providers. Also alliances with major global companies such as FedEx and Western Union.	Although each of the participating SMEs continues to operate in their traditional localities in Italy, their products and services are available worldwide through the virtual marketspace at BOI site.
SCB Co-op *LAA*	Increase in effective size through pooling resources, and products of group of seven SMEs.	Extended access to market from local to national and global, development of competitive global brand.	Effective co-ordination of group of SMEs, enhanced efficiency and cost savings in marketing/ distribution of individual products	Development of strong business relationships among participant SMEs, effective management of business relationships with some of the major service providers (e.g. ParcelForce) and distribution channels (e.g. ASDA).	Concentration of group operations to virtual location, ie web site of Co-op. Operations of Co-op can enjoy the benefits of extended diversity even though participating SMEs still operate from their traditional localities.

In all cases, there is a common thread linking the strategic intents of the enterprise to go online and the choice of infrastructure components. While not all made explicit commitment to extend all the attributes defined in the framework, analysis shows that these were consistently modified directly or indirectly as a result of the application of the online infrastructure. Also, the benefits from virtual transformation of business scope always led to significant improvement in competitive performance even where it was not easy to quantify.

This chapter has outlined a framework for analysing an online SME based on the concepts of virtual organization and global information technology management. The *S-M-A-L-L* framework describes five dimensions of the business that may be transformed with the strategic application of information technology. These are the size of resources, market coverage, activities and processes, linkages and locational scope. Effective extension of the SME's environment along these dimensions should increase its access to resources and opportunities and enhance its ability to compete in the global market. The transforming factors are the firm's chosen business model, the technological infrastructure and the virtual infrastructure management strategy. Also corporate vision of the future, top management commitment, nature of business, level of adoption of /expertise with IT are relevant to the virtual infrastructure management approach to the global strategy of online SMEs.

Mini Case: Starting An Online Business

This case presents a typical situation that faces many young entrepreneurs as they plan to enter the electronic business industry. Mostly, they are motivated by the popular stories about the phenomenal performance of some of the start-up online companies like Amazon.com which have grown to become large global businesses through innovative exploitation of online infrastructures together with winning business management strategies. There are however very important issues to deal with in developing an online business. Particularly, strategies to develop the appropriate organizational infrastructure and manage it successfully represent a critical input. In this case question, you are given the chance to apply the principles outlined in this chapter to help these entrepreneurs start right towards a successful global online business.

* * * * *

Charles Evans and Dell Peterson are two young MBA graduates aspiring to develop an online business, which will eventually offer products worldwide. The company, which is yet to set up a website, hopes to develop a niche business in business consulting services for Australian tourism and hospitality companies.

Dell, an immigrant from Netherlands, studied Finance for her MBA degree and is currently employed in a home finance company in Adelaide. Her employer is a national company with branches in all the states of Australia. As a financial analyst her work involves regular interaction with the various branch offices both through electronic communications systems as well as planned meetings every quarter in one of the states.

Evans currently works with an international organization in the IT consulting business in Australia. His job includes researching e-Commerce solutions for SMEs. Having studied computer engineering and information systems for his first and second degrees respectively, he feels he has the background expertise to develop a global SME based on the Internet. Product offerings of the company would include electronic market research, infrastructure management solutions and business alliance brokering. Evans is keen to learn about the appropriate strategies with respect to aspects such as the business location, number of branch offices across country, IT equipment and online infrastructure, and the types of alliances to form to in order to make his business successful. He is also interested in developing a business value chain that is effectively aligned with the chosen industry and the electronic market environment from beginning.

They plan to run the business from Melbourne, Australia where, in their estimation, there exists a vibrant e-commerce industry and therefore cheaper access to Internet resources. They also planned to work with a team of about eight persons, mainly with background in information systems, technology management, and finance. They intend to recruit a couple of others for routine administrative support. In the bid to get going, Evans has already applied for a website address with the

---

Mini Case .... Continued

international Internet registrar, InterNic. This means that very soon the company must decide on a web hosting service provider with the possibility of providing a total e-business infrastructure solution.

Discussion Questions

1. Briefly outline the opportunities in the chosen industry for the prospective enterprise.
2. What opportunities can the company take advantage of in developing some Internet presence and later exploiting some online infrastructure as part of its routine business?
3. State with appropriate examples the key issues associated with an online business in the chosen area, specifying what must be considered as core competencies of the start-up firm.
4. Using the five attributes of a typical SME, discuss the relative merits of (a) double the proposed number of staff, (b) having employees working from locations in three states: WA, SA and ACT, and (c) increasing the number and complexity of business relationships within industry.
5. What Internet technologies and systems would you recommend to form the core of the start-up business. What are some of the foreseeable developments in infrastructure as the business grows.
6. What will you advise as the minimum level of information management competence of any future employees of the company?
7. What should form the strategic reasons for joining or forming any alliance with other business?
8. How will these reasons change in the near future and in the long term?
9. What are the key lessons from the Harris Technology and Boot Online companies for the new enterprise?

REFRENCES

Benjamin, R., and Wigand, R. (1995). Electronic Markets and Virtual Value Chains on the Information Superhighway, *Sloan Management Review*, 36, 62-72.

Boudreau, M., Loch, K.D., Robey, D., and Straud, D. (1998). Going Global: Using Information Technology to Advance the Competitiveness of the Virtual Organization, *Academy of Management Executive*, 12 (4), pp. 120-128.

Bakos, J.Y. (1991). A Strategic Analysis of Electronic Marketplaces, *MIS Quarterly*, September, pp. 295-310.

Cash, J.I. and Konsynski, B.R. (1985). IS Redraws Competitive Boundaries, *Harvard Business Review*, March/April, 1985, pp. 134-142.

Cavaye, A., Mantelaers, P., Wander van de Berg, and Zuurmond, A. (1998). Towards Guidelines for Development and Management of Transnational Information Systems, *Australian Journal of Information Systems*, 5(2), p.13-21.

CIRCIT, (1998). Small Business and Electronic Commerce, *Policy Research Report* No. PRP-44, by Singh, S. and Slegers, C., Centre for International Research on Communication and Information Technologies (CIRCIT), Melbourne. http://www.circit.rmit.edu.au/publics/smxsum.html#Small

Davidow, W. H. and Malone, M.S. (1992). The Virtual Corporation: Structuring and Revitalising the Corporation for the 21st Century, HarperBusiness Press, New York.

Dean, P.C., and Kane, M.J. (1992) International Dimensions of Information Systems and Technology, PWS, Kent.

Fink, D. (1998) Guidelines for the Successful adoption of Information Technology in Small and Medium Enterprises, *International Journal of Information Management*, 18 (4), pp. 243-253.

Henderson, J.C. and Venkatraman, N. (1993) Strategic Alignment: Leveraging Information Technology for Transforming Organizations, *IBM Systems Journal*, 32(1), pp. 4-16.

Hagel, J. and Singer, M. (1998). *Net Worth: Shaping Markets when Customers Make the Rules*, Harvard Business School Press, Boston, USA.

Igbaria, M., Zinatelli, N., and Cavaye, A.L.M. (1998). Analysis of Information Technology Success in Small Firms in New Zealand, *International Journal of Information Management*, 18 (4), pp. 103-119.

ISPO, (1998).Accelerating Electronic Commerce in Europe, URL:http://www.ispo.cec.be/ecommerce/aece2.htm

Ives, B. and Jarvenpaa, S.L. (1991). "Global Information Technology: Key Issues for Management", *MIS Quarterly*, 33-49.

Jarvenpaa, S.L., and Ives, B. (1993). Organising for Global Competition: The Fit of Information Technology, *Decision Science*, 24(3), 547-580.

Kaplan T.E., Johnson, I.W., Pearce, G.C., and George, G. (1997). The Strategic Role of Communication Technology in Small Business: Where We Are and Where We Should Be Going", *American Business Review*, January, pp. 86-91.

Konsynski, B.R. and Karimi, J. (1993). On the Design of Global Information Systems, Bradley, S.P., in Hausman, J.A, and Nolan, R.L. (eds) *Globalisation, Technology and Competition: The Fusion of Computers and Telecommunications in the 1990s*, Harvard Business School Press, Ma. USA.

Kurbel, K. and Teuteberg, (1998). The Current State of Business Internet Use: Results From an Empirical Survey of German Companies, *Proc. of the 6th European Conference on Information Systems*, Aix-Marseille III, France.

Grenier, R. and Metes, G. (1995). *Going Virtual: Moving your Organization into the 21st Century*, Prentice Hall Computer Books, New Jersey.

Moreton R., and Chester, M. (1997). Transforming the Business: The IT Contribution, McGraw Hill, London, UK.

Ng, H, Pan, Y.J., and Wilson, T.D. (1998). Business Use of the World Wide Web: A Report on Further Investigations, *International Journal of Information Management*, 18(5), pp. 291-314.

OECD, (1998). A Borderless World – Realising the Potential of Global Electronic Commerce, Ottawa, October. Organization for Economic Co-operation and Development http://www.oecd.org//subject/e_commerce/index.htm

OECD, (1993). Small and Medium-Sized Enterprises: Technology and Competitiveness, Organization for Economic Co-operation and Development, Paris, France.

Palvia, P., and Palvia, S. (1996). Understanding the Global Information Technology Environment: Representative World Issues. In P. C. Palvia, S. C. Palvia, and E. M. Roche (eds.), *Global Information Technology and Systems Management: Key Issues and Trends*, Ivy League Publishing.

Palvia, S. C., and Vemuri, V. (1999). Distribution Channels in Electronic Markets: A Functional Analysis of the Dis-intermediation Hypothesis. *Electronic Markets*, 9(1&2), 118-125.

Poon, S., and Swatman, P.M.C (1997). Small Business Use of the Internet: Findings from Australian Case Studies, *International Marketing Review*, 14(5), pp. 385-402.

O'Connor M., Bentley, J., and Calvert, C. (1997). Small Business and the Internet: An Exploratory Survey, *8th Australiasian Conference on Information Systems*, pp. 251-259.

Porter M.E. and Millar, V.E. (1988). How Information Gives You Competitive Advantage, *Harvard Business Review*, 66 (4), pp. 149-160.

Sieber, P. (1998) Organizational Virtualness: The Case of Small IT Firms, in Sieber, P., and Griese, J. (eds.), *Organizational Virtualness, Proceedings of the VoNet -Workshop*, April 27-28, Bern, Simowa-Verlag.

Tapscott, D., Lowy A., and Ticoll, D. (1998). *Blueprint to the Digital Economy: Creating Wealth in the Era of the E-Business*, MacGraw-Hill, USA.

Tetteh, E.O. (1999). From Business Networks to Virtual Organisation: A Strategic Approach to Business Environment Transformation in Online Small and Medium-sized Enterprises. *Proceedings of the 10th Australasian Conference on Information Systems* (ACIS'99), Wellington, New Zealand, Dec. 1999, pp. 980-992.

Venkatraman, N. (1994). IT-Enabled Business Transformation: From Automation to Business Scope Redefinition, *Sloan Management Review*, Winter.

Venkatraman, N., and Henderson, J.C., (1998). Real Strategies for Virtual Organising, *Sloan Management Review*, 4, pp.33-48.

15

E-Commerce and Community Tourism

David Mason
Victoria University, Wellington, New Zealand.

Simon Milne
Auckland University of Technology, Auckland, New Zealand

ABSTRACT

Tourism is often put forward as a way of helping rural communities to escape the poverty trap. In practice the development of viable tourism results in incurring costs and receiving benefits. While both households and businesses may benefit economically it may be difficult to attract the 'elusive tourist'. Residents must also deal with the negative socio-cultural and environmental impacts that are often associated with the industry. While technology may offer the potential to assist communities in solving some of these dilemmas, its use and acceptance, even amongst willing participants, is unpredictable. This chapter describes a project to build an e-Commerce solution in a poor rural area in Northern New Zealand and the methodologies developed and then utilized. We show that technology transfer in this context is problematic, and that it is the methodology which is important, not the technology itself.

INTRODUCTION

There are communities around the world which have been bypassed by progress. Rural communities in both developing and developed societies often share intractable problems of low education, limited capital bases, inadequate infrastructure, chronic unemployment and high emigration. These communities do, however, often have a major asset – attractive and pristine environments, sometimes combined with unique ways of life.

While tourism represents a potential avenue through which to benefit from these environmental and cultural resources, it is not a simple industry to break into (Brohman 1996; Harrison and Price 1996). Tourists want to experience pristine nature, but only if there is the infrastructure to support their needs. This leads to a paradox: tourists won't come unless the facilities are there for them, the facilities can't be built until there are tourists to pay for them (Brown 1998).

There is also the very real problem of how a small community with few resources and limited business infrastructure can get itself noticed. And even when they have created a tourist industry it is often owned and controlled by people from outside the community. If the tourism industry is to perform effectively for communities it must not only generate long term economic benefits, but must also mesh with the needs and desires of local people and not destroy their quality of life (Mowforth and Munt 1998; Milne 1998).

In this chapter we look at how the Internet and e-Commerce may help communities improve the potential of tourism to generate local benefits while also overcoming some of the limitations associated with the industry. In particular we focus on the ability of these technologies to enhance local ownership and control over tourism development. We begin with an overview of e-Commerce's broader impact on tourism and then move on to define community tourism, discussing its characteristics and potential. The discussion then focuses on the role that e-Commerce can play in enhancing the performance of community based tourism. Using a case study drawn from the North Hokianga region of New Zealand we discuss recent attempts to create a community developed and controlled web-site and present the reader with a sense of the strengths and weaknesses of adopting 'web-raising' methodologies. The chapter concludes with a review of some of the key themes raised by our research. We also present a mini-case that presents similar issues, but in the setting of Canada's eastern Arctic.

TOURISM & E-COMMERCE

E-Commerce and the Internet have had a significant impact on the travel industry - perhaps more so than on any other sector. Companies of all sizes are rushing to gain a presence on the Internet. Governments are implementing policy frameworks to foster IT adoption by the industry, and tourists everywhere are beginning to see the potential for new technologies to improve their ability to make travel plans.

Recent research by Jupiter Communications shows that over two-thirds of online consumers in the US report having used online travel sites to research travel products and destination information. According to Jupiter's latest projections, online travel sales in the US exceeded $3.9 billion in 1999, and are expected to grow to $11.7 billion by 2002. It is estimated that air travel will continue to dominate the travel products sold online, representing more than 80 percent of the online travel dollars. However, as online car and hotel bookings continue to climb, that share will fall to 60 percent of what promises to be a $16.6 billion market in 2003 (Jupiter 1999).

The literature on tourism and the Internet focuses on a number of ways in which the industry is benefiting from the adoption and development of e-Commerce (see Buhalis and Schertler 1999, v):

- *Knowledge management and marketing.* In addition to reducing communication and transaction costs the Internet is also changing the shape and nature of traditional global distribution and marketing systems in the tourism industry (Milne and Gill 1998; Buhalis 2000a). Technology also opens up new horizons for data mining, and market segmentation (Buhalis 2000b)

- *Changing consumer behaviour through information technology.* While it is difficult to quantify the Internet's ability to shape consumer perceptions and decision making processes it is clear that the Internet is already a force to be reckoned with in molding visitor behaviour (Beirne and Curry 1999). The Internet also provides a vital (and unparalleled) set of information to support consumer choice and the development of information management skills.

- *New product development.* The Internet offers the industry improved possibilities for price differentiation based on personally tailored products and also enables greater networking between disparate elements of the industry. In simple terms the Internet improves the ability of the tourism industry to provide a flexible array of product choices. In effect the tourists themselves have a greater opportunity to create their own 'customized' packages. Even though dollar spending continues to grow, online travel businesses will not see significant customer growth unless they create online product offerings that simplify the purchasing process and exceed the value of traditional offerings.

- *Disintermediation.* There is a growing interest in the impact of the Internet on components of industry (Palvia and Vemuri, 1999). This is especially the case in the tourism industry where travel agents have previously acted as intermediaries between the industry and the consumer. Some commentators have predicted the demise of the travel agent unless skills are upgraded effectively (McNeill, 1997). Nevertheless, despite falling commissions and increased competition, travel agents have conceded only one percent of the US online travel market in the past two years (Jupiter 1999).

- *Labour market impacts* Several commentators are now beginning to focus more closely on the impact that the adoption of the Internet and e-Commerce strategies can have on labour use, training regimes and service quality delivery in a broad range of tourism sectors (see Milne and Ateljevic 2001).

- *The empowerment of small and medium enterprises through IT* . There is an expanding body of work dealing with the potential for e-Commerce to 'level the playing field' for smaller businesses that have difficulty accessing traditional tourist distribution channels (Buhalis 1999). It is also clear that the data-mining potential of e-Commerce holds great benefits not just for larger firms but also their smaller counterparts (Schertler and Berger-Koch,1999, 26).

While there is plenty of 'hype' about what IT can do for various elements of the tourism industry, it is still not easy to find comprehensive descriptions and reasoned analyses of the key issues associated with the adoption of new information technologies. In particular there are gaps in our knowledge about how the Internet and tourism will mix in less developed settings where telecommunications infrastructure and human capital bases are limited. At the same time we know relatively little about how e-Commerce may alter the ability of community based tourism products to reach the elusive tourist and how it may, in turn, shape visitor behaviour to cater to local needs.

E-COMMERCE & COMMUNITY TOURISM

Definitions of community led tourism cover a wide spectrum from "giving an opportunity to local people to become involved in the decision-making process" (Tosun & Jenkins 1998, 110), to: "producing a tourism product that the community as a whole wishes to present to the tourism market" (Murphy 1985, 37). In simple terms community tourism focuses on community as an integral part of providing a tourist experience that:

- Respects traditional values
- Generates economic benefits for the host population
- Is socially acceptable
- Is authentic
- Is ecologically sound
- Is politically viable

This can only be achieved by listening to the needs of communities. A focus on local decision-making in tourism planning began to emerge in the tourism literature in the late 1970s (Gunn 1979). Murphy (1985, xvi) explains that community is the obvious place to start the analysis and planning of tourism because the local people who are involved in tourism activity:

"represent the industry's shop floor, where visitor and host meet, where its impacts are felt most keenly, and where the hopes of corporate and government planning will lie."

In recent years the argument that community-based approaches to tourism development are a prerequisite to successful and sustainable tourism development has become almost a mantra among researchers (Taylor 1995, Din 1997, Tosun and Jenkins 1998).

It is possible to discern two main sub-streams in the way in which 'community' has been analysed in this literature. One considers local residents as largely passive forces in the development process (Britton 1996). In this case the community is seen to be 'serving' the industry's needs rather than vice versa. The other approach emphasizes local agency, and sees communities and their constituent members playing an active role in determining tourism's outcomes (Drake 1991, see also Taylor 1995). This approach views communities as being capable of planning and participating in tourism development, of making their voices heard when they are concerned, and of having the capability to control the outcomes of the industry to some degree. Murphy (1988) argues that if host communities can define the types of tourism they wish to attract and would like to accommodate over the long term they can shape the type of industry that is most appropriate to their needs. As Midgley (1986,2) notes:

"Participation is not only one of the goals of social development, but an integral part of the social development process."

Din (1997) comments on the fact that while tourism researchers and planners often support the idea that tourism should benefit the community, they do not explain how to mobilize local involvement. Perhaps most importantly there are few clear indications as to how the views of different stakeholders can be communicated effectively to interested parties, including tourists.

The key challenge facing communities that wish to turn to tourism as a source of economic development is how to fine tune tourism product development and marketing strategies to meet the changing needs of the consumer. At the same time there is a growing need to create a *sustainable* industry - one which will maximise economic benefits without alienating local people through cultural insensitivity, limited economic returns or adverse environmental impacts (Getz and Jamal 1994; Milne 1998).

Small firms and communities face systemic problems in gaining access to the mainstream tourism distribution system. Accessing large scale computer reservation systems is usually prohibitively expensive (Milne and Gill 1998). International airlines, package holiday companies and major hotel chains have difficulty in integrating with and serving small enterprises because they immediately lose economies of scale. The small operators are often left with no alternative but to market themselves independently. The traditional channels are advertising, posters, brochure drops and listing with tourism authorities. All of these are either expensive, limited in reach and flexibility, or of questionable value. As a result of these difficulties increasing numbers of small tourism firms (and to a much lesser extent communities) are turning to the Internet as a marketing tool.

E-Commerce and the Internet are in many ways ideal for small communities (Schon et al 1999; Gurstein 2000). For the first time there is an easy way to build a locally owned media presence, capable of attracting and servicing tourists and of forming the basis of a coordinated tourism product. The Internet has several key elements that make it an important alternative to traditional marketing approaches for community tourism development:

- Web sites are flexible, the images and text they present can be changed easily and quickly.

- Internet sites provide an international presence.
- The Internet makes customer relations easier and more individualised.
- It decentralises and democratises access to the customer.
- The customer can make better decisions through more precise product information.
- There are cost savings in distribution, service, marketing and promotion. Revenue prospects grow correspondingly.
- The number of Internet users is growing rapidly and the demographic profile of users (wealthy, well educated) is of interest to communities that wish to attract free independent travelers.
- Partnerships between tourism agencies can be nurtured more easily.
- Web sites have the potential to reflect community aspirations more effectively than many traditional marketing approaches.
- The process of developing a community web site offer an effective way to foster cooperation and networking between different players in the local tourism scene.

Clearly the Internet has potential. How can that potential be turned into a reality? Primary obstacles are the limited IT skills of community members, and little (if any) money to purchase the expertise (Bruce, 2000). The remainder of this chapter looks at how these obstacles have been overcome in one particular community.

THE NORTH HOKIANGA CASE

Maori communities throughout New Zealand are turning to tourism as a source of economic development. While there are several examples of successful Maori-owned and community controlled tourism operations, they are usually situated on the main 'tourism circuits'. Those communities and businesses that lie off the 'beaten track' face a number of challenges in tapping into the tourism industry (Page et al 1999).

This case is focused on empowering a remote grouping of Maori communities with few resources and very limited IT skills to build a manageable tourism marketing and development tool. The strategy is to build an Internet presence that will advertise the region, handle enquiries, take bookings for the few local tourist facilities available and allow the people to actively pursue appropriate market segments. The web site is to be a foundation, rather than an end in itself, aimed at creating the nucleus of a self sustaining industry owned and operated by local people. The objective is to build a tourism centered web site based on a high level of local participation. What the community wanted was a web site which reflected the community's values, not the developer's values.

The Context

The communities of North Hokianga sit on the Northern shore of the Hokianga Harbour – a twenty kilometer long body of water which is one of the largest harbours in the Southern hemisphere. The whole area is thickly forested with kilometer after kilometer of lush, green canopy. Massive golden sand-dunes tower over the entrance to the harbour (Mitchell and Park, 1998).

The population density is very low, even by NZ standards, and the inhabitants are mostly people of Maori descent, the indigenous people of New Zealand. In addition there is a sprinkling of European residents who one way or another never got around to leaving. The population consists of the very young and the old, with young adults moving away to the cities. The general level of education is poor, few people having completed secondary schooling, and with no tradition of educational attainment. There is, therefore, very little technological knowledge to build on (Singh 1997).

North Hokianga is the sort of place where everyone knows everyone else, there is a strong sense of community tradition, and close links to the land. There is no manufacturing of any kind, and the only extractive industry is logging. There used to be an active dairying industry, but the removal of national farming subsidies saw that die out in the mid 70s.

Most people now eke out a subsistence living from small farm holdings made up of cows, chickens and horses. For the last two generations this has been supplemented by welfare grants and, in some cases, a growing reliance on the sale of locally cultivated marijuana. Few people are today in 'professional' occupations or are self-employed, and few people have jobs in 'tourist compatible trades' (for example, restaurants).

The level of income most people receive is low – less than US$10,000 annually. Nevertheless, while the people are not well off, they live comfortably and enjoy what some would be regarded by some urban dwellers as an idyllic rural quality of life. However, change is threatening the status quo. There is a determination in New Zealand politics to stamp out long term welfare dependency. Attitudes among and towards Maori have changed from their being victims of a colonial history to an expectation that Maori will take control of their own destiny and stop seeking government assistance. At the same time the government has accepted that there are past wrongs to redress and has started to negotiate multimillion-dollar land claim settlements for tribal groupings.

Unfortunately, the people of Northern Hokianga are unlikely to see much from these settlements. They are, by and large, still in possession of their ancestral lands. The lands and forests are communally owned, according to Maori custom, and are regarded as an inviolate resource to be preserved for future generations. Any change has to be sustainable and agreed by community consensus.

The tourism industry offers great potential for the North Hokianaga. The main tourist attractions of the region are centered on forest trails, sandy beaches, water activities and cultural experiences. One of the clear strengths of the area is the fact that Maori culture is quite intact. Studies have shown that Maori cultural heritage is one of the main attractions for overseas tourists. There are a few tourist facilities but these are all owned by individuals or families and have no strong capital base. Very few people have the capital to start even a small tourism project, such as a bed and breakfast or transport service (Henry and Pryor, 1998). It also probably means that people do not have sufficient capital to wait 3-5 years before small-scale tourism business becomes profitable.

The problems facing North Hokianga as it attempts to turn to tourism as a source of economic development can be summarised as:

- How does a community control the nature, pace and marketing of tourism development so that local needs are met?
- How can it reach and attract tourists and inform them clearly about what they can expect to find?
- How can tourism be more effectively linked to the surrounding economy?

Implementing a Participative Internet Site

The methodology we adopted was designed to address these issues through community participation and organic growth, mediated by e-Commerce technology. Participatory approaches have much to offer the policy-making process as they "enable local people to share, enhance and analyze their knowledge of life and conditions and to plan, act, monitor and evaluate" Chambers (1997, 102). They are a way to give people a voice, enabling them to express and analyze their problems and priorities. Used well, participatory approaches can generate important and often surprising insights contributing to policies which better serve the needs of local residents and communities (Zazueta 1995; Redclift 1995). More fundamentally, they can strengthen the understanding of those in authority and begin to change attitudes and agendas (Chambers 1993).

Participation has also been a widely used component of computer systems design and has a rich literature cataloguing its success and failures (Checkland and Scholes 1990, Avison and Wood-Harper, 1990). The methodology used was one we have developed from experience with similar situations in other parts of the world. It lies firmly within the burgeoning literature on community informatics (Gurstein, 2000; Loader et al 2000)

Phase One
Seek Permission
Measure Need

Phase Two
Demonstrate Possibilities
Build 'Pride in Place'
Establish Capability
Develop Joint Plan

Phase Three
Prototype Web Site
Transfer Skills
Iterative Development
Transfer Ownership

The methodology is intended to be spread over a 2-3 year period of time. There is intense activity in each phase, with interaction and participation of the community, and then long periods away from the community when the developers prepare for the next stage.

Phase One: To learn what the Hokianga communities did or did not want in the way of tourism, a survey of community preferences was carried out in August and early September, 1997 by the James Henare Maori Research Centre from Auckland University (Singh 1997). An attempt was made to survey each household in the community. In total, 219 households answered. This is over half of the total number of households identified by the surveyors, and exactly half of the total identified in the 1996 Census.

North Hokianga residents are generally very much in favour of having tourists in their midst, as long as numbers are controlled. This is interpreted first from the fact that over 75% answered they preferred tourists to spend 'much time' visiting Maori, while only four people answered they wanted tourists to spend 'no' time getting to know the Maori residents. In addition, almost 85% of respondents said residents would be friendly to tourists, and over 60% did not think meetings would get boring after awhile. In the open-ended question on benefits, 33 people mentioned making friends and meeting people from other nations.

North Hokianga Maori are also quite in favour of visitors doing 'touristy' things while visiting the area. Residents were asked to say 'yes' or 'no' to a list of 20 tourist activities, with 'yes' meaning the activity would be good for the community. The results were startlingly positive. With the exception of 'mass tourism' all of the other activities were considered favourable by at least 60% of respondents. Nine of the twenty activities received a 'yes' answer from more than 90% respondents.

Respondents asked for community based tourism which is based on, and above all which respects, Maori values. Some options were ruled out immediately. The populace do not want mass tourism, or coaches running through their villages, nor hamburger stands on the beaches. Nor do they want to dress up in 'native' costume and get photographed.

Primarily what people want are jobs and income. The tourism the people want is small scale in nature and tightly controlled. Maori life revolves around its social institutions, including respect for seniority, communal assets, shared responsibility, and action by consensus. The people are clear that they do not want to have to lie to the tourists, to show things that are not authentic parts of Maori culture. The Maori will only accept sustainable tourism that does not adversely affect the environment. Most of the area that would be open to tourists is part of the NZ conservation estate, and any proposals would also have to pass scrutiny by the environment agency.

Taking all the responses together, it was interpreted that the Centre had the necessary community support to proceed with tourism development. However, because people clearly expressed different opinions in different communities, it was vital to ensure that all tourism projects were implemented at a scale appropriate to the community. If an overall project was proposed for the whole of North Hokianga, it would probably not be accepted by certain communities, and therefore might not be sustainable. Developing different components of tourism in each community is a good idea anyway because it expands the types of experiences tourists can have and reduces competition between businesses.

Phase Two: Phase two consisted of holding public meetings in a communal hall to which every stakeholder was invited. Local business owners, people who had registered for a small business course at a local community college, and local notables were particularly targeted. The first meeting was scheduled over two days in June 1998 to allow time for a full exploration of the issues.

The main issue was to raise awareness of what we were doing. We also hoped to be able to show the community that we were not outsiders trying to impose a solution, but genuinely trying to address their concerns. The group meeting also encouraged actual and potential operators to meet and consult informally, and to motivate them by showing the strength of public support.

This phase of the research was also aimed at getting joint agreement to a schedule for the work and to have locally respected persons affirm in public that they endorsed the plan. The method used was to first show a demonstration of the Internet. This had been carefully set up in advance to show how their area was currently being featured on various web sites. Many of these were amateur efforts, some were official tourism sites and some were tag-ons from various hotels and guesthouses outside the area. As expected, the audience was appalled at how their region was being displayed and 'used' by 'unauthorised' sources.

For more than half the audience, this was the first time they had seen the Internet in action. So our next demonstration was to show how a nearby region had set about promoting itself and showed them how you could buy souvenirs, book a room, inquire about activities and so on. This effectively demonstrated the possibilities of the Internet and caught the interest of the group.

The next step was to move the group towards some sort of action agenda, so that they could make a start on building an Internet site that would serve their needs. We started by facilitating a group meeting, challenging participants to define what was good about their region and what things would be of interest to a visitor. After and hour or so there was a general agreement, to some people's surprise, that there actually was a great deal of potential for tourism, and that the opportunity was there if only they chose to take it.

The second day was aimed at getting the local business people to see if they could come up with a way of working together. We did another facilitation on the theme of how could they handle a visitor who arrived at one of their member's operations with no set itinerary. Quite soon viable plans were devised for handing on the visitor to related operators, and discussions were held about how a notification system could be put in place to ensure all visitors were fully serviced.

This process gradually caused a change in attitude of the operators who realised that their own best interests would be served by acting jointly and that no one operator could expect to succeed in isolation. We then called together the whole group and again set up our portable computer and projector and demonstrated examples of high quality tourism sites on the Internet. We showed them a site map and explained how this could work to act as a common focal point for a joint tourism venture.

The strategy was to set up a Welcome page that would give visitors a single point of contact for tourism in the North Hokianga. The site would consist of two complementary parts. One part would be a cultural welcome designed to attract the independent traveler. It would emphasize the history, culture and uniqueness of the area and its people. The other part of the site would be an operator oriented guide about: what to do, where to stay, how to get there etc. It would list every tourist operation and act as a classified directory. Both parts would be complementary in that they would be able to give the browser access to tourism information, brochures and so on and allow the user to register their interest or book activities directly.

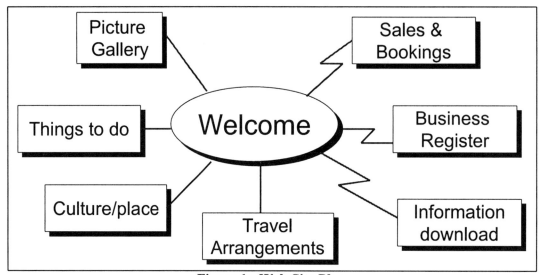

Figure 1: Web Site Plan

It was made clear to the community that the success of the site depended on them providing the text and pictures to go on the page, and that this was the only way they could guarantee that the site would be an authentic reflection of their lifestyle. To encourage this we arranged a group session where people first challenged each other to come up with things that could be featured on the web site, and then broke into small groups to write down the ideas and produce a page plan. The final step was to get agreement on who would take responsibility for making sure the material was gathered and forwarded to the web programmers. This step was very fruitful, with ideas we had never considered, such as listing famous people who came from the region, or secret locations only know to the locals.

By the end of the session we had a viable page plan for an Internet site (figure 1) which was unique to the region and which had been, and would be, written by the local people. As an unexpected bonus, the deliberations of the local business owners had gone so well that they formed an official North Hokianga Tourism Association and voted in officers and a constitution. This was a remarkable event given the failure of all previous attempts to build cooperation. The researchers left the meeting with high hopes and a promise that the web page material would be forwarded shortly. Overall, phase two of the methodology appeared to have been a great success, almost certainly because of the catalytic effect of the e-Commerce technology.

Phase Three: In phase three the methodology calls for the developers to build the new tourism site and take it back to the community for approval and comment. After necessary amendments, the site is implemented and goes into production. The idea is that as the site gets used, visitors attract more and more businesses in a 'snowball' effect. However, the transition from phase two to phase three did not work as planned in the Hokianga project. The follow on from Phase two was disappointing. Although the community was enthusiastic and people promised lots of relevant information, only a few hand written pages were actually produced, and even then only after much prodding. In retrospect, this should have been expected: producing written material is difficult, especially for people unused to expressing themselves in writing. The only really useable information came from a few of the small businesses. We therefore had to reevaluate and redo phase two.

We decided to return to the community and try a different approach. We built a prototype web site with what little content we had. This consisted of the pages sent by the community plus a number of photographs taken by the research team. We were able to create an Internet site based on the agreed plan, creating pages with the headings but without the content, indicating what the site would look like when built. In addition we were able to create a picture gallery from our own photographs. For the second visit we demonstrated their new community web site and showed what we had done and what more was possible.

Although the site was light on factual material and generous on photographs, this turned out to be an advantage. People loved seeing places they recognized and this re-affirmed their commitment to the project. Paradoxically, the written material caused problems almost immediately.

We had asked participants to write about what made their region unique, and what would interest visitors. Among the material supplied were suggestions that visitors could gather shellfish and cook it on the beach, a bit of local color was also added about how local teenagers drive up and down the beach on weekends in old cars for amusement. This led to protests from the people living near the beach that they were not going to allow outsiders to take 'their' food, and that the bit about the cars had to be removed from the site or the beach would become a racetrack. Another page included a review of the origins of local Maori place names. This too caused disagreements among people who held differing interpretations of past events.

As part of our revised phase two strategy we incorporated the concept of 'web raising' into our methodology. Web raising is the digital equivalent to a barn raising -- a community working together to create a collective asset. A web raising is a community event where neighbors share experience and skills to help empower one another in the creation of web documents. We learned about this concept from the Los Angeles Community Network (LACN, 1998) and decided to adapt the idea to meet our own needs.

Members of the research team took with them portable computers, tape recorders and a scanner. Community members were encouraged to bring themselves and family photos, documents, genealogies, cultural artifacts and other icons of their lifestyle. The turnout was high, and many items were produced for inclusion on the site. The team scanned in the objects and images, and interviewed the people, either recording their stories on tape or typing the words directly into a laptop. In this way we gathered an immense amount of material in a very short time. The result was a 'self image' of what the group believes defines their collective identity, and how they want the rest of the world to see them. We believe this was the first time this innovative technique has been used in an e-Commerce methodology. We left behind an enthusiastic community carrying with us a lot of information and prepared to build the first instance of the real site.

Authenticity and Participation

When we finally embarked on phase three and started building the web site we quickly realized that the material from the web raising was not going to be useable immediately. In asking what people thought were important in their lives, we forgot that people have interests that not everyone shared. One contributor had insisted on scanning in dozens of photographs associated with a religious movement. Another had proudly produced gory pictures of pig hunting which may be disturbing to certain visitors. Another aspect concerned the accuracy of the reminiscences and stories about the region's origins and history. Local people are not historians, and no one seemed competent to distinguish myth from fact. In a project where authenticity is a fundamental requirement, this was clearly a problem. It seems clear that the goal of authentic representation of the community on a web-site is very difficult to achieve. The following key issues have been raised by the research.

Content: A traditional community is unlikely to be able to spontaneously generate content themselves. The temptation then will always be for the developers to supply what is missing in order to make progress, and thus put forward their own viewpoint, not the community's. On the other hand if you persevere with eliciting information from the community, someone is going to have to exercise editorial control of the material and thus the image presented. In exercising editorial choice some groups are inevitably going to feel excluded.

Acceptability: Getting agreement on a 'look and feel' acceptable to everyone can be a problem.

Risk: There are also major problems with trying to implement a tourism e-Commerce strategy that involves everybody. The North Hokianga area has an economic history that has led, at present, to widespread unemployment and reliance on income support. The situation is that some people live reasonably secure lives within this system, which allows them time for involvement in community and social activities. Moving out of the system by starting up a tourism business could be very risky, economically, and could be very disruptive to their own lives and to the people who depend on them.

Commitments: Many locals spend up to fifty hours a week in support of group social and cultural activities. The upshot is that people are already busy, even though they are not employed full time, and change can be difficult, particularly when government reduces the safety net for people who go out on a limb to set up a business. This makes it much more difficult to motivate such people for the long term.

Cultural Values: There is another cultural dimension that must not be overlooked. Tourism is essentially an information-based industry. Maori often have considerable scepticism and discomfort about the use of personal information because of the way it has tended to be used in the past, without the Maori's knowledge or permission. As a consequence, Maori have become very distrustful of giving out information. (Te Puni Kokiri 1993, 7)

Rewarding Efforts: Opening communities to tourism represents integration with the wider world and inevitably brings social change. Not everyone can contribute equally or will be effected equally. This means monitoring frameworks should be set up along with the development of tourism businesses, so that negative impacts on individuals are controlled. There is a need to balance individual rewards from efforts put into tourism with community needs. It is also important to maintain local control even if there is a need to bring outsiders with appropriate skills in to ensure the businesses stay profitable.

Measurement: Measuring the success of the Northern Hokianga initiative means establishing suitable benchmarks. Besides measuring the more usual things like the number of visitors or revenue generated, there are unique qualitative issues to be considered. First, there are a multiple agendas in community tourism. The benefits for a community may be quite different from a profit oriented European company and results may have to be judged differently. Any evaluation of success or failure must take into account the capture and enhancement of local knowledge, increased indigenous skills and the preservation of indigenous culture. Second, a community must understand not only the benefits that IT can bring to business but also how to use them effectively. Thus evaluation requires an analysis of how successful the training of local talent was as well as the amount of local content that was generated. Simply measuring cash flows will not be enough.

THE DUAL INTEREST COMMUNITY MODEL

A tourism Internet site has two components, the e-Commerce which enables the site to service the visitors, and the content, which builds the desire to visit. Of the two the simplest component is the e-Commerce functionality - there is nothing particularly challenging about implementing a booking form or an on-line guest book. The programming and implementation are entirely under the control of the developer. The difficulty is always in generating fresh, unique and relevant content. This cannot be provided by the developer, it has to come from within the target community.

The only group in the community who are motivated long term to make the web site a success are the local businesses. They are the ones who will see an immediate benefit from a successful marketing site and who can be expected to take an ongoing interest in its upkeep. On the other hand, they alone cannot be allowed to determine the site image, since the interests of the operators will never coincide exactly with the interests of the wider community. There is always going to be conflict between the community which provides the infrastructure, and the operators who although part of the community, exploit it for private gain. There has to be a methodology which recognizes and builds on this duality of interests. Our research with the Hokianga community has led us to develop a new model for ensuring a vibrant e-Commerce tourist site (Figure 2).

This model is a refinement of the earlier methodology which now treats the community as composed of distinct groups. Phase one is unchanged. Phase two is similar but recognizes and targets two different groups. The initial objective is unchanged: to get the agreement and commitment of the whole community to an Internet strategy leading to a tourism product. When this is achieved the developers set up two consultative panels drawn from the community. One is a monitoring body, a web owners' panel which scrutinizes the pages of the site, ensuring they are culturally acceptable and conform to local mores. The second group consists of local operators (both existing and potential), who will set up the commercial side of the site. These people are much more like the normal commercial clients of IT developers - their needs are easily specified, their measures of success can be stated in advance, and they have clear goals. This gives the developer an unambiguous users' statement for building an e-Commerce site which satisfies a definite need. These operators can be relied upon to produce factual, trade oriented material and to keep the material up to date. The community panel will have the opportunity to comment and criticize the presentation and format of this material and will therefore ensure that it is in keeping with the community's values and image. The two panels will ensure a dialogue between the business interests and the community interest in that businesses develop their web presence so that they can make a living, but the community still feels in control of these pages.

An examination of existing tourism web pages all over the world shows that too often the above two aspects are not in balance. While the Internet can provide local people with the potential to influence the images and information being presented to the public, very few sites appear to actually reflect communities' needs and interests. Where the site serves mostly the commercial interests, authenticity can be lost, and in many cases there is more than a suspicion that it is the programmers' needs and values that are being presented (Mason, 1999). For example, traditional ecological knowledge is rarely incorporated into tourism sites. It is essential that communities have direct input into web site development process otherwise they run the risk of placing the construction of 'place' into the hands of outsiders.

On the other hand, where the site does not service local businesses directly, it is too easy for tourism web sites to become collections of online brochures, rather than actual e-Commerce tools. This is often the case where sites are provided by Tourism development bodies. Such sites are usually bland and neutral, lacking any imprint of the community as a unique experience. For a site to be effective and contribute to the long term well being of the community, it has to generate income. An essential part of the methodology is therefore to record the traffic on the web site, and assess its impact on the businesses. This is done by incorporating logs of responses and archives of visitor requests and feedback. However, these are only useful if there are past business records to compare against.

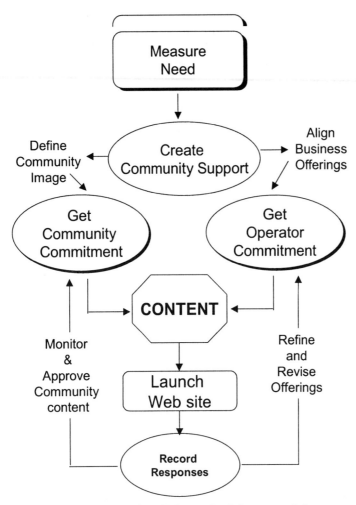

Figure 2: Web methodology model

One function of the operators' panel is to act as a clearing house for information, and to encourage small operators to keep better records so they can monitor their own performance over time. This monitoring process is essential because it forms the feedback mechanism by which the operators judge the payback from their investment in the site. It also provides the operators with an independent measure of the effects of changes recommended or insisted upon by the community panel. If the cultural requirements start impacting negatively on the site's success or it generates positive feedback from Internet visitors this can be discussed with the representatives on the community panel and the site can be amended accordingly.

The project is currently in its final stages and negations are taking place for a handover of the site to the local high school. Maintenance and development of the site will be passed to the students who will simultaneously learn about their own culture while acquiring IT skills for the future.

SUMMARY

The lesson of this research is that while implementing e-Commerce may be relatively easy technically, building it into a viable community tourism site is difficult. The skills of the average programmer can easily outpace the ability of the community to support the product (see Beale 2000). In order to be authentic, site content can only come from the subjects, and if they are not business oriented people, then some creative approach has to be devised in advance for guaranteeing a supply of reliable content. The support and interest of the general community is vital, but the site can only flourish if the business operators are not just involved, but harnessed as the driving force for the e-Commerce initiative. The experience of e-Commerce so far has been largely confined to standard western style business operations. But as the technology is extended into non-traditional applications, and as the technology itself changes, new methodologies will have to be constantly developed to implement new IT solutions.

Minicase – The Internet and Community Tourism in Nunavut

In November 1994 a symposium called 'Connecting the North' was organised to discuss the best options available for communities to link into the growing communication medium and since this time the presence of Canada's Arctic on this global communication medium has grown significantly (Perry 1996). While many of these sites exist predominantly for inter-community contact details on Inuit life and the local landscape provide valuable information through which to directly and indirectly shape tourist perceptions (Milne et al 1998). The key tourism related site is the NWT Virtual Explorers' Guide (http://www.edt.gov.nt.ca/guide/index.html) which offers a variety of information and tour options. This site offers access to information on the history of the land, vacation planning, different types of tours, parks, and contacts for Western and Eastern tourism operators.

Community visits are widely encouraged, 'traditional communities, steeped in history and Inuit culture ... many Inuit tour operators [are] willing to take you out to see their land and wildlife'. In fact the Guide provides an entire history of communities in Nunavut, from the 1950s to the present. This segment also prepares the tourist in terms of how to act and what to expect:

"You will find our people friendly, but sometimes shy. Ask permission before you take pictures.... Be careful not to be intrusive, and you'll find people quite willing to talk".

One marked difference between standard tour operator and government brochures and the Internet material is that the latter seems to place far more emphasis on 'our land', and stresses pride in way of life:

"We invite you to visit our land and share in our pride of culture and our love of the land. In the Eastern NWT, spend time with an Inuit elder as he frees the image of a polar bear from soapstone. Imagine the pull of a giant Arctic char on your line or gaze in awe at the great herds or caribou as you paddle a remote river."

Another common theme is the blend of modernity with tradition:

"It is a land where the people are still very much in touch with their past, but also caught up in the excitement of the birth of their own land, their beloved Nunavut" (NWT Virtual Explorers' Guide).

Thus the web appears to offer considerable potential for the Inuit of Baffin island to provide their interpretation of the Arctic landscape to potential tourists. The highly educated, high income profile of visitors to the region (see Milne et al 1998) makes it extremely likely that many visitors will have access to the Internet (something we are currently exploring in more detail). We should not pretend, however, that the Internet provides a total solution. Cost and technological barriers remain important impediments for peripheral regions that are attempting to reach and influence the market place through this new

---

Mini Case .... Continued.

distribution technology (see Milne et al 1998). At the same time it is important that communities and local have direct input into the web-site development process otherwise they run the risk of again placing the construction of 'place' in the hands of outsiders.

Useful URLS are at:

http://apa.nunanet.com/directory.html
http://www.napanet.net/~janetp/articles/inuit.html
http://www.arctic-travel.com/index.html
http://www.arctic-travel.com/territorypage.html

STUDY QUESTIONS

1. How will changes in the scope of e-Commerce applications affect the systems development life cycle model? What effect will religious, cultural and language differences have?

2. Can systems analysis techniques for standard computer systems development be transferred directly to an e-Commerce situation?

3. What methods are used in requirements analysis by e-Commerce software houses?

4. What is the best way to overcome the lack of technological awareness and skills among non business sectors of the population?

5. What should be the role of State, Local and National agencies in fostering e-Commerce for tourism?

6. Produce a classification of e-Commerce applications reflecting the specific needs of small, medium and large tourism operators.

7. A whale watching company takes tourists out to sea in inflatable boats to experience whales close up. They employ six boats and twenty staff. Specify a minimum hardware requirement for them to set up an e-Commerce marketing operation, and outline a plan for actually building the application.

8. Compare and contrast traditional tourism business and e-Commerce tourism business. How do you suggest one should transition from traditional to e-Commerce tourism?

9. How does a community control the nature, pace, and marketing of tourism development, so that local needs are met? How can tourism be more effectively linked to the surrounding economy?

REFERENCES

Avison, D.E. and A.T. Wood-Harper 1990. *Multiview: an exploration in information systems development.* McGraw-Hill, Maidenhead.

Beale, T. 2000. Requirements for a regional information infrastructure for sustainable communities: the case for community informatics, in M.Gurstein (ed) Community Informatics: Enabling Community Uses Of Information And Communications Technology, Hershey PA, Idea Group Publishing, pp 52-80.

Beirne, E and P. Curry 1999 The impact of the Internet on the information search process and tourism decision making, in Buhalis, D and Schertler, W (eds) Information and Communication Technologies in Tourism 1999, Springer Wien, New York, 88-97.

Britton, S. 1996. Tourism, Dependency and Development. In *The Sociology of Tourism: Theoretical and empirical investigations,* Y. Apostolopoulos, S. Leivadi, A. Yiannakis (eds), 155-172. London: Routledge.

Brohman, J. 1996 New directions in tourism for 3rd world development, *Annals of Tourism Research,* 23(1) 48-70.

Brown, F 1998 Tourism Reassessed: Blight or Blessing. Butterworth Heinemann, Oxford.

Bruce, D. 2000 Differential IT access and use patterns in rural and small-town Atlantic Canada, , in M.Gurstein (ed) Community Informatics: Enabling Community Uses Of Information And Communications Technology, Hershey PA, Idea Group Publishing, pp 136-150.

Buhalis, D. 1999. The costs and benefits of information technology and the Internet for small and medium-sized tourism enterprises, in Buhalis, D and Schertler, W (eds) Information and Communication Technologies in Tourism 1999, Springer Wien, New York, 218-227.

Buhalis, D. and Schertler, W (eds) 1999. Preface, in Buhalis, D and Schertler, W (eds) Information and Communication Technologies in Tourism 1999, Springer Wien, New York, v-vi.

Buhalis, D. 2000a, Marketing the competitive destination of the future, Tourism Management: Special Issue - the Competitive Destination, Vol.21(1), pp.97-116.

Buhalis, D. 2000b, Information Technology in Tourism: the state of the art, *Tourism Recreation Research*, Vol.25(1), p.41-58.

Chambers, R. 1993. Challenging the Professions: Frontiers for Rural Development. Intermediate Technology Publications: London.

Chambers, R. 1997. Whose Reality Counts? Putting the first last. Intermediate Technology Publications: London.

Checkland, P. and J. Scholes. 1990. *Soft systems methodology in action*. Wiley, Chichester.

Din, K. 1997. Tourism Development: Still in Search of a More Equitable Mode of Local Involvement. In *Tourism Development: Environment and Community Issues,* C. Cooper and S. Wanhill (eds), 153-162. New York: Wiley.

Drake, S. (Ed.), 1991. Local participation in ecotourism projects, in Whelan, T. (ed.), *Nature Tourism: managing for the environment,* Washington D.C: Island Press, 132-163.

Getz, D. and T.B. Jamal 1994. The Environment-Community Symbiosis: a case for collaborative community planning. *Journal of Sustainable Tourism* 2(3), 153-173.

Guler, S. and S. Klein, 1999. Hotel reservation systems on the Internet – custom design vs. standard software, in Buhalis, D and Schertler, W (eds) Information and Communication Technologies in Tourism 1999, Springer Wien, New York, 201-217.

Gunn, C. 1979. *Tourism Planning.* New York: Crane, Russak.

Gurstein, M. 2000 Introduction: Community informatics: enabling community uses of information and communications technology, in M.Gurstein (ed) Community Informatics: Enabling Community Uses Of Information And Communications Technology, Hershey PA, Idea Group Publishing, pp 1-31.

Harrison, D. and M. Price 1996. Fragile Environments, Fragile Communities? An Introduction. In *People and Tourism in Fragile Environments,* M. Price (ed), 1-18. New York: Wiley.

Henry, Ella and Kevin Pryor. 1998. *Sustainable Maori tourism in Tai Tokerau.* James Henare Maori Research Centre, University of Auckland, Auckland.

Jupiter Communications 1999. Travel suppliers missing online market potential, press release May 12. (www.jup.com/company/pressrelease)

LACN 1998. (see http://home.lacn.org/lacn/wr/default.html)

Loader, B.D., B. Hague and D. Eagle. 2000 Embedding the net: community empowerment in the age of information, in M.Gurstein (ed) Community Informatics: Enabling Community Uses Of Information And Communications Technology, Hershey PA, Idea Group Publishing, pp 81-103.

McNeill, L. 1997. *Travel in the Digital Age*, Bowerdean, London.

Mason, David. 1999. Are you really ready for the Internet? *Chartered Accountants Journal of NZ*. Volume 78 No.5 June 1999 pp32-35.

Midgley, J. et al., 1986. *Community Participation, Social Development and the State,* Methuen, London.

Milne, S. 1998. Tourism and Sustainable Development: The Global-Local Nexus. In: Hall, C.M. and Lew, A.A.(eds.): *Sustainable Tourism: A Geographical Perspective.* (pp.35-48) Longman: UK.

Milne, S. and Gill, K. 1998. Tourism and information technologies - theoretical debates and empirical realities, in Ioannides, D and Debbage, K (eds) The Economic Geography of Tourism: Theoretical Perspectives, Routledge, London, 123-138

Milne, S., Grekin, J., Woodley, S. and Wenzel G 1998. Tourism and the construction of place in Canadas Eastern Arctic, in G. Ringer (ed) Destinations: Tourism and the Construction of Place, Routledge, London, 101-120

Milne, S. and J. Ateljevic, 2001. Technology and service quality in the tourism and hospitality industry, in J. Kandampully et al (eds) Service Quality Management in Hospitality, Tourism and Leisure, Hawarth Press, New York. (in press)

Mitchell, Neil and Geoff Park. 1998. *Nga Pour Whakahii o te Tai Tokerau – Hokianga ki te Raki (The Identification of Sites of Special Environmental Interest – North Hokianga)* James Henare Maori Research Centre, University of Auckland, Auckland.

Mowforth M. and I. Munt 1998. *Tourism and Sustainability: New Tourism in the Third World.* London: Routledge.

Murphy, P. 1985. *Tourism: A Community Approach.* New York: Methuen.

Murphy, P.E. 1988. Community driven tourism planning. *Tourism Management,* 96-104.

Page, S.J., P. Forer and G.R. Lawton 1999 Small business development and tourism: terra ingognita? Tourism Management 20, 435-59.

Palvia Shailendra C. and Vemuri Vijay K., "Distribution Channels in Electronic Markets: A Functional Analysis of the "Disintermediation" Hypothesis," EM -- Electronic Markets: the International Journal of E-Commerce & Business Media, April, 1999.

Perry, Janet M. 1996. Inuit, Connecting the Far North in Quebec *OnTheInternet* 1996 available full text at http://www.napanet.net/~janetp/articles/inuit.html

Redclift, M. 1995. Sustainable Development and Popular Participation: a framework for analysis. In *Grassroots Environmental Action: Peoples Participation in Sustainable Development,* D. Ghai and J. Vivian (eds), 23-49. London: Routledge.

Schertler, W. and Berger-Koch, C 1999. Tourism as an information business: the strategic consequences of e-Commerce for business travel, in Buhalis, D and Schertler, W (eds) 1999 Information and Communication Technologies in Tourism 1999, Proceedings of the International Conference in Innsbruck, Austria. Springer Wien, New York, 25-35

Schon, D.A., B. Sanyal and W.J. Mitchel 1999 High Technology and Low Income Communities: Prospects for the Positive use of Advanced Information Technologies. Cambridge MA, MIT Press.

Singh, Debbie. 1997. *Statistical Socio-Economic Indicators for the North Hokianga Region.* James Henare Maori Research Centre, University of Auckland, Auckland.

Te Puni Kokiri, The Privacy Act 1993: Te Ture Matatuakiri, Matatapu 1993 (Wellington: Te Puni Kokiri, 1994), 7

Taylor, G. 1995. The Community Approach: does it really work? *Tourism Management* 16(7), 487-489.

Tosun, C. and C. Jenkins 1998. The Evolution of Tourism Planning in Third World Countries: A Critique. *Progress in Tourism and Hospitality Research* 4, 101-114.

Zazueta, A. 1995. *Policy Hits the Ground: Participation and Equity in Economic Policy-Making.* World Resources Institute, Washington.

SECTION - 4

Global System Development and Implementation

One of the greatest problems faced by the IT function in the multinational enterprise is development of systems. Throughout the entire development cycle - analysis, design, development, implementation, maintenance and operations - the scale and complexity of global information systems nags at the project teams, complicating their work. This section presents six chapters that uncover some of the best practices around systems development in the multinational enterprise.

The section starts with a case study from a large global transportation company and presents alternative IT development strategies that were tested. One of the key problems faced was aligning the tasks and mindsets of people that are so far apart in their working habits. A second chapter presents five operational tactics, accompanied by case examples, for implementing global IT systems. It explores the implications for companies going global and identifies what type of IT infrastructure is needed to support global operations. The third presents an analysis of how global software teams work together - across great geographical distances and across many time zones - to develop software and applications. The lessons from this chapter are designed to help the IT function better organize how it works. It discusses five centrifugal forces that work against a team including loss of control, coordination breakdown, communication poverty, federation of distributed units, and culture clashes.

A fourth chapter discusses the concept of the ``information system migration'' that tracks the business development of the multinational enterprise. We warns that unless the IT function adapts to the business evolution of the enterprise, support for its operations will dwindle. A fifth chapter discusses the extraordinarily important growth of enterprise resource planning (ERP) - SAP, Oracle, PeopleSoft - systems in the multinational enterprise. For years, multinationals have reported difficulties coming to grip with this problem. The chapter suggests that either a ``tightly or loosely coupled system'' is appropriate, and discusses why. The chapter reviews the concepts of control and coordination and the Bartlett & Ghoshal typology within this context. The section ends with a look at Executive Information Systems (EIS) in today's multinational enterprise. It argues that EIS needs to be an integral part of executive education within the multinational enterprise.

16

STRATEGIES FOR GLOBAL INFORMATION SYSTEMS DEVELOPMENT: A CRITICAL ANALYSIS

Murad Akmanligil
Fedex Corporation, USA

Prashant C. Palvia
The University of North Carolina at Greensboro, USA

ABSTRACT

Developing global information systems is a formidable task. Multinational companies operate in regions that are thousands of miles, many time zones, and many cultures away from the headquarters. Organizing the activities and aligning the tasks and mindsets of people that are so far apart and to actually change the way business is conducted through the use of new information systems is a major challenge. The global dimension presents even a bigger challenge. This chapter discusses alternative global IS development strategies that may be used and the factors that impact the selection of these strategies. Four systems from a large transportation company are presented as real life examples to demonstrate the viability of these strategies and the accompanying factors.

INTRODUCTION

Information technology (IT) is advancing constantly at exponential rates. Cheaper and faster computers and communication devices are introduced to the market every day. Nevertheless, the cost of building information systems (IS) still remains significantly high. Companies spend millions of dollars in IT to automate their processes, to improve decision making, and to gain strategic advantage. In spite of that, many systems are developed late and over-budget and unfortunately, many development efforts still fail. Ewusi-Mensah (1997) argues that the software industry is in the state of crisis and notes a study that was conducted by the Standish Group (reported in PC Week - Jan 1995). According to this study, 31% of new IS projects are canceled before completion at an estimated combined cost of $81 billion and 52.7% of the projects completed are 189% over budget at an additional cost of $59 billion. Management frustration with IT costs, backlog of new system requests, and establishing standards on infrastructure are forcing IT managers to seek alternative solutions to in-house development. Outsourcing and purchasing package software are frequently being selected as solutions to these problems.

A new and major factor complicating the issue of IS development and its success is the globalization of companies. Today, the trend towards globalization is phenomenal; it is to the extent that some industries such as electronics, computer, and pharmaceutical are considered predominantly global. In order to successfully compete in these industries, companies have to exploit the advantages of globalization. Globalization brings forth the necessity and challenge of coordinating the activities of the company on a worldwide basis, mostly accomplished through information technology. However, globalization drastically increases the complexity of the development process by introducing many new variables and unknowns. As Karimi and Konsynski (1991) note, variations in business environments, availability of resources, and technological and regulatory environments are faced by the IS organization as soon as a system crosses national boundaries.

There are various definitions of Global Information Systems (GIS) in the literature. Burn and Cheung (1996) define a GIS as an information system that is used across one or more national borders. This definition is simple and will be used in this chapter. The IS executive has many system development strategies to choose from in satisfying global system requirements. In addition to the known domestic challenge of choosing in-house development, outsourcing, or package software adoption, a global system presents additional challenges. Questions such as how to get support from subsidiaries for the system; how and who should go about gathering the information requirements from subsidiaries (or even whether to gather requirements from subsidiaries); who should build the system (if it is to be built in-house); how to exploit existing design and code from similar domestic applications; what code should be common and what should be local; how many versions of the code to support, etc., pose a wide variety of difficult choices. The choices are not clear-cut and require a careful consideration of a host of factors.

The next section identifies and discusses various global IS development (GISD) strategies. A model is then presented to capture the factors that need to be considered in the selection of a GISD strategy. An in-depth discussion of the model variables is provided. In the next section, four case studies are described that detail the various development strategies used in GIS projects. Finally, the last section provides a discussion of the findings and their implications.

GLOBAL INFORMATION SYSTEM DEVELOPMENT STRATEGIES

As information technology and software processes improve, firms find themselves faced with more options to solve their information requirement needs. Nelson, Richmond, and Seidmann (1996) state that a major problem facing the firm is to identify the acquisition option/development strategy that will maximize the net present value of software acquisition, subject to organizational considerations (e.g., corporate policy and resource availability)." While many system development strategies are available to choose from, it also makes the choice decision very difficult. We discuss alternatives available both in the domestic and global contexts.

In the domestic context, insourced development, package acquisition, and outsourcing are the primary development strategies available to companies. Additional alternatives are available to global companies. In the literature, eight GIS development strategies are identified:
1. Development with a multinational design team (MDT)
2. Parallel development (PD)
3. Central development (CD)
4. Core vs. local development (CL)
5. Best-in-firm software adoption (BIF)
6. Outsourced custom development (OC)
7. Unmodified package software acquisition (UP)
8. Modified package software acquisition (MP)

A framework is provided in Figure 1 that categorizes the development strategy by two dimensions: the development approach (custom or package) and number of countries involved in the development (domestic and international). The custom development approach is further divided into two classes to represent whether the customized system is built by developer internal or external to the firm. The above eight development strategies are then placed in appropriate cells (note that some strategies fall in multiple cells).

1) Development with a Multinational Design Team (MDT): With this strategy, a design team that is comprised of systems and user personnel from multiple sites of the company is formed. The team members gather at one location generally for months to work on the design of the system (Ives and Jarvenpaa 1991). It is argued that the participation of the involved parties not only allows the creation of a design that meets the requirements of all the regions of the company but also increases the likelihood of the acceptance of the software and the likelihood of adhering to international standards. However, the cost of this strategy is reported to be high (Ives and Jarvenpaa 1991). The right team leader (Vitalari and Wetherbe 1996) and the right team composition (Palvia and Lee 1996) are important for the success of the project completed with this strategy.

			DEVELOPED BY	
			DOMESTIC TEAM	INTERNATIONAL TEAM
Development Approach	Custom	Internal	CD	PD, CL, MDT
		External	OC	OC
	Package		MP, UP, CD	MP, UP, MDT

Figure 1 - GIS Development Strategy Framework

2) Parallel Development (PD): Vitalari and Wetherbe (1996) describe this strategy as one where the requirements gathering and the construction of the systems are done locally and where these systems are connected through bridges. Barker (1993) argues that in order to achieve timely IS development and to increase the chances of successful implementation, the systems must be developed locally (with some preplanning) and then integrated with other systems. Vitalari and Wetherbe (1996) observe that some companies use a variation of this strategy: representatives of teams at different locations, after gathering local requirements, come together at a central side and try to resolve the differences and determine a common structure. However, Ives and Jarvenpaa (1991) describe parallel development as one where the project is broken into multiple components and different components are designed and built at different locations. Coordination and consistency among these systems are provided through common development methodologies, shared software engineering tools, electronic mail, and consistent definitions of data.

3) Central Development (CD): With this approach the system is developed at one site (predominantly at the headquarters) and is installed at the subsidiaries. The advantages of this strategy is lower costs (compared to development with a Multinational Design Team and Parallel Development), the enforcement of standard operating procedures throughout the company, and better communications among the parties that are involved in the development of the system. The disadvantages are potential for resistance to the software at the subsidiaries, not satisfying some regions' major requirements, and diminishing buy-in from not-involved regions (Cash, McFarlan, and McKenney 1992).

4) Core vs. Local Development (CL): Collins and Kirsch (1999) in their study of five global IS projects observe that "project team structures were typically complex, reflecting the need for centralized effort to create a common global solution, while at the same time understanding and accommodating local needs." They, as well as Burn and Cheung (1996), point out the existence of a development approach where local IT departments tailor the components created by the headquarters (and/or some regions) to fit their needs. We call this development strategy "Core versus Local Development." While minimizing local conflicts, this strategy tends to increase coordination and control requirements.

5) Best-in-Firm Software Adoption (BIF): This strategy was observed to be the most common in software acquisition by Ives and Jarvenpaa (1991). With this approach, the best software that already exists anywhere in the company is selected to be implemented globally. The above authors state that generally, with this strategy, the roll-out of the software to the regions is gradual. More often than not, the software is not implemented as it is in all regions; some modifications are necessary due to differences in requirements and, sometimes, technological resources among regions. In some situations, it might be necessary to provide each region with their own versions of the software (Vitalari and Wetherbe 1996). This, however, will create duplication of effort and drastically increase the cost of maintenance in the long run. Vitalari and Wetherbe (1996) recommend changing the organization to fit the software rather than creating multiple versions of the same software.

6) Outsourced Custom Development (OC): Outsourcing is becoming a popular strategy in software development. Some companies are even experimenting with global outsourcing (McFarlan 1996, Meadows 1996). This strategy is chosen for various reasons: to implement and enforce global standards, to reduce cycle time in system development, to reduce costs, to gain access to state-of-the-art technological expertise, to shift focus to more strategic systems etc. (Apte 1994, Caldwell 1999, Kara 1999). Opponents of outsourcing argue that loss of control and flexibility, loss of qualified IS staff, and loss of competitive advantage in information management are major risks that outsourcing involves (Rao, Nam, and Chaudhury 1996). With this strategy, the system is developed or acquired by an external company (i.e., the service provider.) The service provider could choose to implement one or more of the other development strategies listed in this section.

7) Unmodified Package Software Acquisition (UP): More and more companies are purchasing package software rather than developing it themselves. Enterprise Resource Planning (ERP) systems are examples of package software which are gaining popularity among European and American companies (Haney 1998). This strategy provides a working system to the users right from the start. The global packages are generally parameter driven and can be configured extensively (Emmerson 1998). With unmodified package software, generally, vendors are able to provide better support and future modifications are guaranteed to be compatible with the application. Once again, the package may not fully meet the requirements and the firm may have to modify its processes to accommodate the software.

8) Modified Package Software Acquisition (MP): The "vanilla" (i.e., not modified) package does not always meet the requirements of all the regions of a company even if it is a parameter driven system. In these cases, the software might have to be modified to fit the needs of the company. Ragowsky and Stern (1995) suggest minimal modification of packages due to high development and maintenance costs accrued to maintain the integration of customizations with the upgrades of the package software.

A MODEL AND FACTORS FOR GIS DEVELOPMENT STRATEGIES

The model in figure 2 postulates the various factors that need examination in the selection of a GIS development strategy. Both the strategy and its success are dependent on these factors. Based on the review of IS development, IS outsourcing, and global IS literature, the following factors are identified as impacting the selection of a GIS development strategy: organizational characteristics, desired system characteristics, differences among subsidiaries, and IS department characteristics. These factors are discussed below.

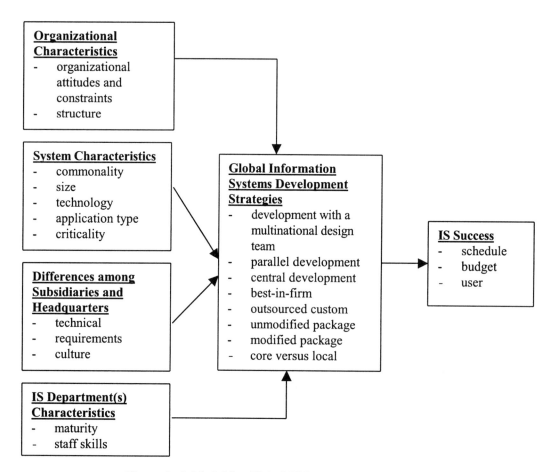

Figure 2: A Model for Global IS Development Strategies

Organizational Characteristics

Organizational characteristics deemed important in relation to the software development strategies are: organizational attitudes and constraints (Nelson, Richmond, and Seidmann 1996), and organization structure. A certain acquisition strategy may be preferred over others due to corporate policy or general organizational/management attitudes. For example, a corporation due to its polycentric disposition could choose to implement a policy that urges the subsidiaries or regions of the company to come up with their own solutions to their information requirements rather than depending on the headquarters. In another situation, management frustration over IT costs and response time or difficulties faced in installing global standards on infrastructure would be important factors that affect software acquisition decisions in favor of outsourcing (McFarlan 1996) or package software.

The organization structure of a corporation could also impact GIS development strategy selection. Following Karimi and Konsynski (1991, and Vitalari and Wetherbe (1996), the structure of a multinational organization can be classified based on the widely used framework of Ghoshal and Nohria (1993). According to this framework, there are four types of environments: (1) international environment where forces for both local responsiveness and global integration are weak, and the focus is on transferring and adapting parent company knowledge in foreign subsidiaries; (2) global environment where forces for global integration are strong but forces for local responsiveness are weak; and the structures are more centralized in strategic and operational decisions; (3) multinational environment where forces for local responsiveness are strong but forces for global integration are weak; and the organization is managed as a portfolio of decentralized multinational entities; and (4) transnational environment where forces for both global integration and local responsiveness are strong, and adaptation to all environmental situations utilizing knowledge and two way information flows is the key.

As an example, in a multinational company where the subsidiaries act mostly as domestic companies, the cost of systems development using multinational design teams will be considerably higher than in a transnational company. This is due to the limited means of and experience in coordination among subsidiaries and due to greater differences in business processes. Cash, McFarlan, and McKenney (1992) assert that as firms adopt different organization structures, they will need different levels of international IT support and coordination. The authors also argue that for the "central development" to be successful, the organization should have "established patterns of technology transfer, strong functional control over their subsidiaries, and some homogeneity in their manufacturing, accounting, and distribution practices." Therefore, centralized development is less likely to be used in corporations with a multinational structure compared to those with a global structure.

System Characteristics

The characteristics of the desired system play an important role in selection of the development strategy. Some key system characteristics are: commonality, size, technology, type, and criticality. Commonality is the extent to which a particular type of software is used by other companies. In the domestic context, Nelson, Richmond, and Seidmann (1996) found out through empirical evidence that common applications are more likely to be outsourced or bought as a package rather than being custom built. Relative size of the project (compared to other projects carried out by the company) is one of the factors that affect the risk of the project (McFarlan 1996). As the size of the project gets larger in terms of its cost, staffing levels, duration, or the number of departments that are affected by it, the coordination costs, and therefore the risk of the project, increases. Outsourcing the development of the system could reduce this risk (McFarlan 1996). Collaboration and exchange among subsidiaries and headquarters can be used to reduce the risk that arises from the size of the project. In developing a large system, subsidiaries could, depending on the organization structure, ask for help from other subsidiaries or headquarters (however on the negative side, the coordination and control costs would rise).

New technology, in general, increases the risk of the project and outsourcing projects that require new technology should be considered seriously since a technically skilled outsourcer can alleviate this risk (Nelson, Richmond, and Seidmann 1996). The risks of dealing with new technology can also be alleviated by collaboration among regions that do not have the expertise and those that have it. Application type is another system characteristic that affects development strategy selection. McFarlan (1996) argues that systems with low structure (such as decision support applications) are bad candidates for outsourcing. Since "highly structured" tasks have defined and fixed outputs, they are not subject to frequent change. Therefore, they are considerably easier to outsource. Finally, system criticality can also affect the choice of the development strategy. If a system directly helps the company build or maintain its core competencies or is central in implementing a key strategy of the firm, the system is deemed "critical". For the acquisition of critical systems, using multinational design team strategy might be more adequate than others since having a multinational team will help ensure the commitment of management in the involved countries; thereby increasing the likelihood of successful system (Vitalari and Wetherbe 1996). Furthermore, insourced development could be preferred over outsourced development to increase control over the system (Rao, Nam, and Chadhury 1996).

Differences Among Subsidiaries and Headquarters

Foreign subsidiaries and headquarters may have significant differences in technology, information requirements, and culture. Technology variations include stark differences in the availability and quality of both hardware and software. These in turn force a firm to use different vendor products in different subsidiaries. Such variations can force the implementation of multiple versions of the system that run on different platforms (Ives and Jarvenpaa 1991) or can necessitate the involvement of an external company with technical expertise in bridging such platforms. Thus differences across subsidiaries are major obstacles in integrating communication networks, hardware, and disparate systems software for global applications.

On the requirements, variations among subsidiaries can reach overwhelming levels. Even seemingly minor requirement differences among subsidiaries can necessitate major local tailoring (Keen, Bronsema, and Zuboff 1982). DiNardo (1996) points out that the parameter driven software they used in Asia was significantly challenged in terms of accommodating the national/regional differences. In order to prevent system development failures and to increase global ownership and smoother implementation of a GIS, Palvia and Lee (1996) recommend worldwide elicitation of requirements.

It is crucial that cultural differences among subsidiaries and headquarters be considered in making acquisition strategy decisions. Ambrosio (1993) contends that the biggest management challenges in implementing a successful global system involve cultural issues. Shore (1996) recommends the inclusion of national culture in any research that attempts to create linkages between headquarters and subsidiaries. Hofstede in his seminal book (1980) identified the four different dimensions of culture: power distance, uncertainty avoidance, masculinity, and individualism. As an example, organizations in less risk-taking cultures (i.e., high uncertainty avoidance) may find some of the development strategies more risk-prone than what they are accustomed to. As an aside, while acknowledging the connection between national and organization cultures, Robey and Rodriquez-Diaz (1989) argue that when dealing with information systems, organizational culture plays a more determining role than national culture. However, organizational culture may itself be influenced by national culture.

IS Department Characteristics

The maturity of the IS departments and the difference in skills of the staff in IS departments within the organization are considered to impact the selection of a development strategy. The ability (or the perception of ability) of the IS department to build the needed system will impact whether the system will be built internally or not (Nelson, Richmond, and Seidmann 1996). The maturity and experience of the IS department with developing global information systems also play an important role in acquisition decisions (Meadows 1996, Cash et al. 1992.) An IS department facing problems in establishing and enforcing global standards could choose to alleviate these problems by outsourcing (McFarlan 1996).

Skill set differences between headquarters' and subsidiaries' IS staff is another concern (Shore 1996). Lack of technical skills necessary for the development of the proposed system or lack of experience with large projects at the subsidiary or the region could influence the level of collaboration among regions and headquarters. Depending on the organizational policies and structure, lack of technical skills in regions could prevent the use of the parallel development approach and favor outsourcing or it could mandate extensive knowledge and resource sharing with the headquarters and other regions. On the other hand, headquarters' lack of knowledge of subsidiaries' business practices and cultures could mandate a cross-border solution (Palvia and Lee 1996).

System Success

The choice of an appropriate development strategy will determine its success. However, the choice is dependent on many factors as described above. Furthermore, the definition of success itself is a somewhat elusive concept which makes evaluation of the strategy difficult. Delone and McLean (1992) studied the concept of "information system success" and concluded that IS success is a multidimensional construct whose dimensions are system quality, information quality, use, user satisfaction, individual impact, and organizational impact. The authors argue that these dimensions are interrelated. For research and evaluation, they recommend, citing Markus and Robey (1988), that the choice of a success variable should be "a function of the objective of the study, the organizational context, the aspect of the information system which is addressed by the study, the independent variables under investigation, the research method, and the levels of analysis."

Not directly accounted for in the above IS success construct are two key aspects of development success: cost and project duration. The fact is that many projects today cost more than they were budgeted for and last longer than planned. Ewusi-Mensah (1997), as discussed earlier, argues that most information systems cannot be considered successful along these two dimensions.

CASES - GLOBAL INFORMATION SYSTEMS

Below four cases are discussed to illustrate some of the GIS development strategies described above. The cases also throw light on the factors influencing the choice of strategies and the success of the strategies. These cases are actual projects from a major transportation company (MTC) based in the U.S. However, the identity of the company and the people interviewed are concealed due to their request.

The Major Transportation Company (MTC) is a large company headquartered in the United States. This multinational company organized itself into five regions; each region being responsible for its own profits and losses. MTC, a highly customer oriented company, is trying to establish itself as a major player in the global network economy by leveraging information technology. The relatively large IT department of the company is largely centralized and the great majority of IT employees reside in the U.S. However, there are some additional IT personnel in other regions who are responsible for support, maintenance, and new development in their regions.

Recently, MTC started to implement an executive initiative to move its systems from mainframe platforms to client/server architecture. On the server side, Unix, C/C++, Sybase/Oracle and on the client side, Windows, Java, and Visual Basic are becoming company standards. The majority of MTC's applications are custom built in-house; however, the company has been experimenting with package software and domestic as well as global outsourcing.

Case 1: Global Clearance (GC) System

With growing international operations, MTC created several country-specific domestic systems to handle customs clearance operations. However, not all clearance-related processes were available from any single system. The clearance systems were not integrated with related functional systems such as International Credit/Collections, Duty/Tax charges, and Sort Operations. This situation, compounded with the fact that some processes were not automated and some were outsourced, made maintaining control of data very difficult at best. There was a need for a single system that enabled conducting all clearance related processes. Therefore, a project called Global Clearance was initiated. Global Clearance was to be one of the first custom built global systems in the company. The proposed system was expected to reduce costs by "eliminating manual processes and paperwork, managing dispute processing, increasing productivity, and reusing detailed customer information."

There was considerable commonality in the existing clearance systems. Eliminating this redundancy by creating a set of core components, which could be re-used in every country, was a major objective of the project. It was expected that this strategy would reduce the development, maintenance, and support costs in addition to reducing the cycle time for delivering new clearance systems. The objective was stated in the project plan as "to develop a new and improved industry standard for conducting global trade." Also, the system was planned to provide a single point of access to clearance related information and to automate Import Clearance in the major countries that the company operates. The project plan defined the scope as follows:

"The scope of Global Clearance system extends from the point at which information and/or goods enter the country of importation through to completion and archiving of the associated financial transaction and encompasses all systems and data required for clearance."

The system was to be implemented at every site that has more than 500 shipments per day; the estimated break-even-point. As of September 1996, 31 sites in 15 countries met this criterion. The project actually originated from another project which started in Europe and was called Europe Clearance. The requirements for Europe Clearance were gathered by a team that consisted of U.K. IS personnel and user representatives from several European countries. The user interface development for Europe Clearance was carried out in Brussels using a fourth generation language (4GL) tool called Uniface. U.K. was responsible for building the back end. After about a year, it was decided that the headquarters' IT department could help U.K. in developing the system and a project called "International Broker Clearance system" was merged with Europe Clearance to become the Global Clearance (GC) system.

During the mid-1990s, corporate headquarters, before the start of Europe Clearance, had mandated that new developed or bought systems would have multi-tiered software architectures. The application development manager of the project describes their efforts in identifying a development strategy that would alleviate the difficulties faced due to lack of expertise in this new technology as follows:

"I think we were looking at (outsourcing) to begin with to see how much of anything can be outsourced. And we always thought the broker piece was the central piece and the sooner we knew about it, (the sooner we could plan for it)... Before we really got going very far, we started looking at broker packages... It is hard to imagine today since things have changed so much but we didn't find any client server broker packages and we didn't find any

people that were interested in working with us to build one. I think we had one company that said in the future they might like to have one. It was pretty lean. "

Given this situation, the system had to be built in house. Since almost all of the clearance systems built before GC were not three tiered, the GC team could not use much code from these systems. Some faxing software from another system called Japan Broker was used with modifications and another system was studied to get business rules and ideas.

The decision to involve the headquarters in the development of Europe Clearance was made to expedite the development process since U.K. determined that the system could not be completed by the deadline. One explanation of U.K.'s delay was an unrealistic schedule given the resources that were available. The IT departments in the regions were much smaller than that of the headquarters. Unanticipated problems with new technology and "scope creeps" also seemed to have contributed to the delay. Headquarters could help as they had built at least functionally similar systems. Furthermore, some parts of a system called Japan Broker could be reused. One of the designers described how the joint development strategy would be implemented:

"Each site was going to take pieces of analysis and design and take it all the way through [the development life cycle]. The United Kingdom was going to do the user interface side since they recently had the necessary training. "

In the mean time, the headquarters asked an external company to do an audit of several existing systems, including the clearance operations. This audit included recommendations for changes to the existing clearance systems. These enhancement recommendations were incorporated into the requirements of the Global Clearance System.

Later into the project, the division of labor was changed. Headquarters IS department was asked to build *core and common* components and U.K. to build the *local* pieces. U.K. representative of the project defined core components as those that are "must have" and needed in almost all countries; common components are nice to have and shared by some countries; and local components as specific to a country. According to the project manager, 90% of the code was expected to be core and common and 10% to be local. A decision was made that regional IT groups will develop, install, and maintain the necessary local components and local connectivity. The core and common pieces built by headquarters would be scalable and reusable and the regions would be free to select the components they need and tailor them to their own needs.

A few months later, the development strategy was changed once again to give headquarters the responsibility of building the entire system. Analysis, design, and coding were carried out *centrally*, only at the Headquarters. The system was unit and assembly tested at the Headquarters, user acceptance and volume tested in the U.K. Training was conducted internally in the U.K.

During these strategy changes, the U.K. and headquarters' IT departments periodically communicated with each other and visited each other's sites in attempts to coordinate their efforts. The U.K. personnel were able to install the hardware for the system in the U.K. and do a "proof-of-concept" to determine whether the proposed technology would be able to support the business. However, U.K. concentrated most of their efforts on the hardware since they had a separate budget for it. The differences in priorities (e.g., hardware versus software), politics, limited resources available to U.K., and the different ways the two groups conducted analysis and design seem to have contributed to the shift of the development strategy from parallel development to core-local to central development.

Currently, the development of the system has stopped. Only the first phase of the development, out of the planned eleven, was finished. The partially finished system is being used at one location in the United Kingdom. That location uses Global Clearance in conjunction with their existing system to carry out clearance tasks. These two systems do not interface with each other.

There are multiple reasons for discontinuing Global Clearance System. The first phase of the system was internally funded and a proposal for the remaining ten phases was to be presented to the Board of Directors (BOD) after the first phase was complete. However, the delays in both Europe Clearance and GC and the increase in requested funding due to the broadened scope reduced the systems' chances of getting BOD approval. Furthermore, the development manager indicated that one of the reasons the GC project was discontinued is that IT executive management started saying that the regions know their needs better than the headquarters does and "are fully capable of writing their own local applications."

Case 2: Global Accounts Receivable (GAR)

One of the major reasons MTC started to look at the possibility of a new accounts receivable (AR) system was that the largest AR system seemed to be reaching its limits in terms of handling the company's transaction volumes. This system was handling the receivables by U.S. payors and was about 14 years old. As expected from a custom built in-house system, it was patched many times and was losing its flexibility to handle code changes.

Another reason MTC wanted a new AR system was to have the ability to have a global financial picture of the company as well as customers. There were many AR systems in the company (e.g., one for domestic, one for international, one for air freight, one for non-transportation, etc.) and these systems did not necessarily interface with each other. This situation made preparing financial documents and balancing different accounts very cumbersome if not impossible. It was hoped that an integrated and re-engineered system would help the company reduce revenue leakage, day's outstanding sales, and bad debt; increase controls on all revenue (such as from duty and taxes); and increase productivity.

During the summer of 1995, with re-engineering in mind, MTC asked a consulting company to conduct an analysis of the U.S. AR system. The consulting company determined that (1) MTC had high transaction processing costs due to high number of customers receiving EDI invoicing but not using EDI remittance; (2) inefficient and outdated procedures resulted in duplicate handling of customer inquiries, costly research, and low employee morale; and (3) the system that handles U.S. payors (which is the largest AR system) needed to be replaced due to its inability to support the growth rate of the transactions and inflexibility. Furthermore, two AR systems that handled about 90% of the transactions were more than 10 years old and were not Y2K compatible. A small system did not have source code available and was also not Y2K compatible. Thus, in general, it was a good time for a global AR system.

A decision was made to examine the accounts receivable software packages existing in the market to determine how much they meet the requirements of MTC. The strong emphasis on package solution was due to several reasons. First, it was determined that a new AR system was needed soon and extending the existing system would be very costly. Second, the existing systems were not Y2K compatible and there was not too much time before the year 2000 arrived. Third, there was an impression, at least outside of the accounting and revenue operations community, that accounts receivable is mostly the same from one company to the next. And finally, there was a directive from the upper management that package solutions should be considered before custom building systems.

Several Request For Proposals (RFP) were sent to vendors, three of which responded. Consistent with the new organizational guidelines, a client server based open system was being sought. A team was formed to evaluate the selected packages. Functional and architectural aspects, supported interfaces, global support by the vendor during and after installation were analyzed. On the architectural side, databases, client and server environments, development/reporting tools, deployment modularity, security, and fail-over capability of the packages were investigated. On the business side, cash applications, credit and collections, accounting, and global functionality were studied. Packages were graded by the team members along these dimensions and the results were submitted to the executive managers who also did their own grading. The tentatively selected package scored about 80 percent by the team members and 87 percent by the executive managers; whereas the company policy was that a package should satisfy 80 percent of the overall requirements to be acceptable. In addition to evaluation, the vendors were asked to make presentations of their software.

After a potential package was selected, a pilot implementation was conducted. The objective was to test the performance of the package, both online and batch. Due to the nature of the business at MTC (i.e., very high volume of transactions with small dollar amounts), performance was a critical issue. It was a requirement that the system have the capacity to handle the growing transaction volumes. Some team members also visited a company in the U.K. and in New York to observe real life implementations of the package. A high-level enhancement requirement document was prepared to bridge the gap between the capabilities of the package and the requirements of MTC. The vendor agreed to implement these enhancements as standard package upgrades.

After the selection was made, a project team that consisted of members from MTC, the vendor that built the package (ARC – AR Company), and another consulting company (CC – Consulting Company) was formed. The team's objective was to detail requirements for enhancements to the base product and to "build the business model" for first the U.S. and then the other regions. Building the business model consisted of determining the parameters of the system, the products/services to include in the system, etc.. It was a complicated process due to the highly parameterized nature of the package. A development team was also formed to help interface the package with existing systems and to help customize the package through report generation tools and hooks to external executables.

According to the U.S. Revenue Operations representative of the team, it was determined that the *core* functionality of the system would be modeled at the headquarters and the regions would be responsible for doing *local* tailoring. However, the company had problems "in pulling all the requirements and the organizations together in the international community." The representative of International Air Freight operations underlines some of the difficulties of global development:

"The main problem in working with the regions is (the decision of) when to bring them in. If it is too soon, they complain that we are wasting their time. If it is too late, they complain that we have already decided what we are going to do so why ask them now. (Due to their limited resources,) they have difficulty in providing dedicated support for the project."

Currently, GAR has been implemented in the U.S. and it is being used for air freight and special non-transportation receivables. The implementation in other regions was stopped and the package did not replace the two existing major receivable systems. One of the primary reasons for not being able to replace these two systems is that not all the enhancements to the package were developed. The most commonly voiced explanation for this discrepancy in the realization of the enhancements was that the required enhancements were relatively large and the vendor had limited resources, and the enhancements were not necessarily requested or wanted by other customers of the vendor. So the development and especially the maintenance of those enhancements would be very costly to them. In addition, the managing director of IT stressed another reason for the outcome:

"During the evaluation of packages we did not demand international representation. It was voluntary for regions to participate and we informed them about the progress but that is not enough."

Case 3: Logistics and Warehousing System (LWS)

Logistics and Warehousing System (LWS) is an information system to support the warehousing needs of the customers of MTC. MTC provides not only warehouses for its customers but also call centers to handle end customers' orders. End customers can choose carriers other than MTC. LWS supports the order entry and inventory accounting processes. The system also allows batch order entry through EDI. LWS runs on two Tandem machines in production and another Tandem machine is used for development; all machines are located in the U.S. The system is batch oriented; even the orders entered on-line are accumulated and processed as batches. The front-end of LWS is written in SCOBOL (screen COBOL) and the back end is written in COBOL85. A relational database, NSQL, is used.

The motivation for LWS was primarily strategic. It was expected that expansion into supply chain management would increase revenues due to the new line of business as well as increase the volume of existing transportation by attracting new customers with a "one-stop-shop" solution for their logistics needs. Thus, supporting electronic commerce was a key part of this initiative. According to the managing director of IT:

"(LWS is) the first attempt of MTC to expand beyond transportation to get into supply chain initiatives."

The origin of the need for a warehousing system goes back to mid 1980s. Then, a system was custom built internally to support warehousing of spare parts for a single customer. As more customers and more requirements were included in the system, it was decided that a package solution, called LWS, would better satisfy these requirements. In 1988, licenses to LWS were bought. Modifications were made to LWS by the vendor in order to satisfy MTC's requirements. In 1990, LWS went out of business; therefore, the source code of the system was acquired and was modified internally. In 1995, it became apparent that LWS could no longer support the business needs and thus, a major upgrade or a new system was needed.

In 1996, some maintenance activities were outsourced to an Offshore Outsoucing Company (OOC), based in Bangalore, India. The most important reason LWS was outsourced, according to the managing director of IT, was that "there was a certain amount of attempt to change what we are doing as a business." In order to enable the change, a new system to replace LWS was being sought. The people that needed to adapt to the change were going to be put to work on the new system. In order to free these resources, LWS was outsourced.

OOC was founded in 1992 and has offices in the U.S., Europe, South East Asia and Japan. The company offers solutions on a wide platform of technologies such as Tandem, mainframe, client server, Internet, object-oriented platforms, etc. OOC has a strong focus on quality; currently it is ISO 9001 and CMM level 4 certified. OOC keeps its costs down by employing a model called Coordinated Off-shore Onsite where majority of the work is carried out off-shore. This model is applied to the maintenance of LWS. A dedicated facility was created in India by OOC for MTC outsourcing tasks only. The network in India used by the OOC group is within the MTC firewall. Two communication lines between the two sites are established to facilitate data and voice transfer. Also, an Internet-based e-mail is used for communication among the project members.

Since the first outsourcing task in 1996, more and more maintenance gone to OOC. Currently, on site OOC and MTC employees conduct requirements gathering, analysis and design activities. Offshore OOC employees conduct detailed design, coding, and unit testing. Then, back in the U.S., assembly and user acceptance tests are conducted. Both on-site and off-shore facilities share the responsibility of production support; critical and time-sensitive problems are fixed on-site and others, including those that take longer, are fixed in India.

Currently, LWS is in maintenance mode. The changes to the system mostly stem from customer requests and are implemented using an approach similar to the waterfall model. Customers communicate their requests for system enhancements or problems by calling the Help Desk. Help Desk tries to resolve the customer's issues; however, if it cannot, it gets in touch with the BAA (Business Application Advisors) team. Each BAA member is assigned to work with a specific set of customers. Based on the analysis of customer's request, a work request is entered into a system. A board, called Change Management Board (CMB), comprised of managers and the IT managing director evaluates and prioritizes the work requests. Work requests are either rejected or approved for analysis. After approval, cost benefit analysis is conducted and results are presented to CMB. MTC could ask the customer to pay if the enhancement is costly or MTC could choose to finance the work itself. When a work request is authorized, a deadline is also determined.

After the Change Management Board's approval of the change, a request is sent to the software configuration group to check out the code. The work is coordinated with the offshore OOC site. Further analysis, design, assembly and user acceptance testing are done in the U.S.; detailed design, coding, and unit testing are done in India. Fixes and enhancements are loaded to production once a month.

The managing director of IT speaks highly of the outsourcing company. However, he says "there are some cultural differences that have to be kept in mind when dealing with (an offshore outsourcing company). If anything, they have a tendency not to question things." He recommends that staff which interacts with the offshore service provider needs to be educated on cultural differences. He also warns that if you have a weakness in your processes, offshore development magnifies it. However, offshore outsourcing, with a company like OOC, makes maintaining costs and quality achievable. It also provides easy access to skills that are very difficult to find in the U.S.

Case 4: Operations Service Level System (OSL)

Operations Service Level System (OSL) is a system that provides near real time information on the service performance (e.g., timely delivery) of each shipped package. This information enables the analysis of MTC's service to its customers. It also helps identify systematic problems in operations. The system not only provides drill-down capabilities from the corporate level to the individual scan of a package but also provides extensive Intranet based reporting capabilities, such as reporting by date, by product, by type of failure, by route, by customer account number, etc. The system is intended to replace its counterpart on the mainframe. The company has established a service quality index based on different types of service failures and all MTC employees' bonuses are affected by this index.

There were several motivations for the project. The leader of business team of the project summarizes the major motivations as follows:

"The idea with this project is that anyone who needs service level information should come to us now. Since the old system could not accommodate all requests from the different departments of the company, some had their own systems. The new system is supposed to be the single point of source for all service level information. Some departments needed

information, they needed a query based system and the old system did not have this capability. Using it was difficult too. They had to deal with Focus program tapes and not everybody could do that. Now, anybody can use this new system."

Some requests could not be satisfied by the old system, e.g., determining the source of service failure at locations that were not either the origin or the destination of shipment and the ability to analyze service levels by customer account. Existing mainframe system did not provide these capabilities due to the changes in the business and changes in the target users. Also the system being 15 years old was reaching its limit of growth and flexibility. The team leader stated that they wanted a system which made it easy to add new products and features as the company was adding and deleting products very frequently. Furthermore, there was a corporate initiative that required moving systems from the mainframe to a client server environment.

Purchasing package software for OSL was never seriously considered due to the unique nature of the company's business rules and data. The OSL itself was part of another project, called Service Squared which began in 1995. The main objective of Service Squared was to provide an enhanced version of the mainframe service-level program. Service Squared consisted of two parts: the scan processor and OSL. Scan processor was for gathering raw shipment data and contained the logic to determine the success or failure of a service. Both parts were completely outsourced to a single company. This decision to outsource was based on the fact that there were corporate guidelines for new systems to be client-server based and the company did not have enough experience in building a system with such high performance. However, the outsourcing effort was not very successful. The managing director explains:

"The system was developed in a remote location to MTC. We are in a dynamic environment and we need to develop them on site. Dynamics of MTC change rapidly. This group was detached from MTC and stayed isolated... If you cannot work with them face to face, the project can lose focus and not stay current with the business demand. I am not saying that you cannot develop systems offsite but you need to make sure that a lot of people are moving back and forth. We need MTC people "living" with the service provider company. In every outsourced project that I am aware of which is about half a dozen, the ones that were successful worked with MTC on-site."

The managing director added that the service provider had problems due to its rapid growth. One of the specific problems encountered was that the two components of the system (the scan processor and OSL) were designed and built to be highly integrated which reduced flexibility. Another reason for redesign was performance related technical problems due to the hardware platform. The project leader of OSL also argues that MTC was not ready to take over the system from the vendor since tremendous amount of training would be required. She added that technical requirements were not well defined due to MTC's inexperience with client server and object-oriented technology and due to inadequate requirements gathering on the vendor's side.

In December 1997, the systems were redesigned and the components decoupled from each other. Also, the project scope got bigger considerably to re-engineer the way the shipment information is processed. This new project, called Collection, is "a collection of infrastructure projects that support down-line shipment management applications." Collection is aimed to be the only source of shipment information for the entire corporation.

The redesign of the system and other phases of development were conducted centrally at one of the sites of MTC in the U.S. Some of the requirements were gathered from the existing mainframe system through code diving. In addition, a central committee, located at another site in the U.S., was formed to gather requirements as well. This committee consisted of representatives from many departments including operations, sales, legal, and international. The international business representative coordinated with the subject matter experts from the various regions. During the development process, this committee and the development team worked very closely. The designs of the screens were presented to users for their approval and user acceptance tests were conducted after development. A prototype of the system was built and benchmarked for performance since performance was a major concern and was one of the shortcomings of the outsourced system. Further, tests parallel to the existing mainframe system were conducted to ensure appropriate data handling.

The development of OSL is complete and it was in "soft-rollout" since June 1999. During soft-rollout, the system is to be used for training. It was expected to be fully rolled out and completely replace the existing mainframe system by September 1999.

DISCUSSION

Package Software

Purchasing a package software was one of the first development strategy examined in all of the projects. Cost effectiveness, as achieved through the economies of scale by the vendor, was probably the underlying reason. There seemed to be a consensus among the interviewees that package software acquisition is cheaper than all other alternatives. Similarly, maintenance costs are perceived to be less with package software. Another advantage of package software (especially unmodified package software) acquisition strategy is faster implementation. Faster system implementation allowed MTC to reap the benefits of the system sooner and helped maintain the involvement of departments outside IT. This opportunity, compounded with the possibility of eliminating the need to fix the existing accounts receivable system for Y2K compliance, influenced the development strategy decision of GAR.

Nevertheless, it is practically impossible to find a package that meets all of the requirements of a company. Package software acquisition strategy generally requires the company to change its business processes to accommodate the package. Therefore, with package software acquisition strategy, change and expectation management becomes crucial. If a package meeting the requirements of the company is not available or if the company is not willing to change its processes, one option is to ask the vendor to modify the software. However, this option is not available to most small to medium sized companies due to its associated high cost. The customer would not only have to pay for the customizations but also would have to incur other expenses such as cost of testing the modifications. If problems are found during these tests, the tests have to be reconducted after the problems are fixed. If the vendor does not incorporate the requested enhancements into its standard package, then further costs would be incurred in making sure that these enhancements work with future package upgrades. The existence of enhancements not incorporated in the standard product would also decrease the level of support provided by the vendor. In GAR's case, even though the vendor accepted to put the changes into the standard product, the modified package software strategy was one of the major reasons for the project's failure. Major modifications to the package software were requested from the vendor. The pace of the vendor's enhancement implementation was much slower than originally estimated which caused the project to lose momentum and then finally stopped it. A factor perhaps affecting the pace of the vendor is the realization that these enhancements may not be necessarily needed by other customers.

Custom Development - Outsourcing

When implementing package software is not desirable or not possible, custom building is the only other option. In custom development, a key decision is whether to involve vendors in the construction of the system, including different forms of outsourcing. and While package software solution is encouraged more than before at MTC, outsourcing is also steadily at rise. Increasing management frustration with the IT department provides one explanation, and there is evidence of such frustration at MTC with IT costs and delays in development. None of the MTC systems examined was developed on time and within budget. This frustration can be attributed to that MTC's IS department could not be considered mature by industry standards. Most of MTC's projects are at level 1 of the Capability and Maturity Model – CMM (Capability Maturity Model was developed by Carnegie Mellon University to measure the maturity of IS processes in an organization). CMM levels start from one (chaotic phase) and go to five (the most mature phase). Another explanation of the increase in outsourcing is the increasing popularity of outsourcing in the business world as well as in IT.

The maintenance of LWS was outsourced in order to free up resources to work on the new logistics project. It was decided that LWS would not be the logistics system of the future because it did not have an open architecture and was not client server based. Furthermore, LWS was batch oriented but an online system was desired. Once, it was decided that a new system was needed, management wanted to increase the predictability of maintaining LWS, which was another reason that they selected outsourced maintenance.

OSL management chose outsourcing over internal development because they did not have access to necessary levels of required skills in the new technologies with which MTC wanted its systems built. Even though OSL development was outsourced, OSL management was not planning to outsource its maintenance; they wanted it maintained internally. In cases where system development is outsourced but maintenance is not, it is crucial that the customer understands the design and code of the system developed by the vendor. The project manager of OSL argued that MTC was not ready to take over the system from the vendor because of the tremendous amount of training required to understand the details of the system.

Requirements gathering and preparing the outsourcing agreement are also important challenges of outsourcing. OSL suffered from MTC's inexperience with such tasks. The system developed by the vendor did not allow easy addition and deletion of new services and did not have the performance required to support the large transaction volumes of MTC. Since MTC frequently added, changed, and deleted services, both of these drawbacks were major problems for MTC.

Custom Development - Insourcing

When package development and outsourcing strategies are eliminated, the traditional insourced development strategy can be utilized. In global information systems development, insourcing has several alternatives: Central Development, Multinational Design Team, Parallel Development, Best in Firm, and Core versus Local Development.

Parallel development strategy, at least 'parallel code development', was not successfully implemented with GCS. The headquarters' IT personnel complained about having missed an opportunity to tap in to the talents that the company had in the U.K. One of the major reasons that this co-development attempt was fruitless was lack of accountability according to the technical lead of the project. He made the argument:

"I think it was more of a management issue than anything… You really need to have one person that would be the sponsor and the delegator… We had our own little teams and

there wasn't one person running both teams, saying "you guys are going to do this and you guys are going to do this and that is the way it is going to be."

Problems stemming from the lack of accountability were exacerbated by the fact that the U.K. project members felt betrayed when complete responsibility of developing the system was taken away from them and the reasons were not convincing to them. The headquarters' technical and design leads of the project argued that these feelings of resentment not only created a negative working environment between the U.S. and U.K. project members but also caused those in the U.K. to gradually shift their priority to other tasks. Further complicating the communications issue were cultural differences between countries, which were recognized by most of the interviewees. It was also suggested that the large time difference between the two sites and the fact that the two countries had different system development methodologies contributed to the frustration of both parties.

After the unsuccessful attempt in Parallel Development, GCS management decided to implement Core versus Local Development strategy. The manager of the development team argued that Core versus Local development more distinctly and clearly separates the responsibilities of the involved regions. This separation of responsibilities was expected to promote accountability of the involved parties. Also, with this development strategy, the dependencies of the sites on each other were expected to decrease. Less coupling among sites was expected to expedite the development of the system since there would be less need for communication. Such allocation of responsibilities, which allowed most communication among project members by face to face, was expected to decrease cost of coordination. The differences in the system development methodologies of the various sites was another reason that loose coupling was welcomed. However, the expectations still did not come true largely due to the fact that U.K.'s priorities were increasingly shifting to local tasks, and finally Central Development had to be adopted by the headquarters.

Insourced Central Development was also used in the OSL project. Here, the primary reason was that the regions did not have enough resources to help build the system. As suggested in the literature, it was expected that central development would lead to more economies of scale and greater efficiencies.

CONCLUSIONS

This chapter has described various strategies for the development of global information systems. Based on the model and discussion of the cases, several major findings stand out. First, several strategies exist for GIS development. We described eight such strategies. These represent major ways of conducting development and distributing work between internal and external organizational entities. We are certain that variations and extensions to these strategies are possible and practiced in global firms. Second, no single strategy stands out. A model was presented which underlined the factors that need to be considered in strategy selection. The cases illustrated how these factors manifest themselves in actual practice.

Two other findings, not anticipated but evinced by the cases, are significant. First, depending on the complexity, global organizations may need multiple strategies for system development. Different strategies may be suitable for different phases of the life cycle of the same project. For example, while analysis and design may be conducted at the headquarters, coding may actually be outsourced to a foreign vendor. Second, strategy selection is not necessarily a single static decision made at a single point in time. During the development life cycle, organizations may need to continually reevaluate their resources and problems, and may have to dynamically readjust development strategy. Given the complexity and long durations of the projects discussed in this chapter, major realignments in strategy were undertaken in many cases.

STUDY QUESTIONS

1. What are the major GIS development strategies? Briefly describe three of them.

2. Why is GIS development strategy important to the corporation?

3. What are the different factors that impact the selection of a development strategy?

4. Discuss the impact of project size to the development strategy.

5. What is the impact of GIS development strategy on system development success?

6. What are the factors that influenced the success of the GAR system? Discuss what you would do differently to increase the success of the system.

REFERENCES

Apte, Uday. 1994. "Globalization of information systems outsourcing; Opportunities and managerial challenges." Edwin L. Cox School of Business, Southern Methodist University, Sept. Candace Deans, and Jaak Jurison, eds. In *Information Technology in a Global Business Environment* 1996. Danvers: Boyd and Fraser Publishing.

Barker, Robert. 1993. "Information systems development in a global environment." *Business Forum*, vol. 18, no 1,2, pp. 57-59.

Burn, Janice M. And H. K. Cheung. 1996. "Information Systems Resources Structure and Management in Multinational Organizations." In Prashant Palvia, Shailendra Palvia, and Edward Roche, eds, *Global Information Technology and Systems Management: Key Issues and* Trends. Nashua: Ivy League Publishing. Pp239-322.

Caldwell, Bruce. 1999. "Ford revs up app dev." *Informationweek*, issue 717 (Jan 18), p30.

Cash, James, F. Warren McFarlan, and James McKenney. 1992. *Corporate Information Systems Management: The issues facing senior executives.* 3rd ed. Homewood, IL: Irwin.

Cash, James, F. Warren McFarlan, James McKenney, and Lynda Applegate. 1992. *Corporate Information Systems Management: text and cases.* 3rd ed. Homewood, IL: Irwin.

Chandler, Alfred. 1962. *Strategy and structure: Chapters in the history of American industrial enterprise.* Cambridge, Massachusetts: MIT Press.

Collins, Rosann Webb and Laurie Kirsch 1999. *Crossing Boundaries: The deployment of Global IT Solutions.* Pinnaflex Educational Resources, Inc.

Delone, William. 1988. "Determinants of success for computer usage in small business." *MISQ*, March, 51-61.

Delone, William and Ephraim McLean. 1992. "Information system success: The quest for dependent variable." *Information Systems Research*, 3, 1, 60-95.

DiNardo, George. 1996. "Regional banking and credit card processing at Citibank Consumer Banking and its global implications." In Prashant Palvia, Shailendra Palvia, and Edward Roche, eds, *Global Information Technology and Systems Management: Key Issues and Trends.* Nashua: Ivy League Publishing. Pp. 577-591.

Emmerson, Andrew. 1998. "BT and Pinacl start stacking the odds." *Communications International*, 25, 1, 22-23.

Ewusi-Mensah, Kweku. "Critical issues in abandoned IS development Projects". *Communications of the ACM*, 40, 9, 74-80. September 1997.

Ghoshal, Sumantra and Nitin Nohria. 1993. "Horses for courses: Organizational forms for multinational corporations." *Sloan Management Review*, 34, 2, 23-35.

Haney, Clare. "Shipper changes course for SAP R/3." Computerworld, 32, 11, 58.

Hofstede, G. (1980). *Culture's consequences: International differences in work-related values*. CA: Sage.

Ives, Blake and Sirkka Jarvenpaa. 1991. "Applications of global information technology: Key issues for management." *MIS Quarterly*, 15, 1, 33-49.

Kara, Dan. 1999. "Sourcing solutions for wired world emerging." *Software Magazine*, 19, 1, 60-71.

Karimi, Jahangir and Benn Konsynski. Spring 1991. "Globalization and information management strategies." *Journal of MIS*, 7, 4, 7-26.

Keen, P. G. W., G. S. Bronsema, and S. Zuboff. 1982. "Implementing common systems: One organization's experience." *Systems, Objectives, and Solutions*, 2, 125-142.

Keen, P. G. W. And M. S. Scott-Morton. 1978. *Decision support systems: An organizational perspective*. Reading: Massachusetts: Addison-Wesley.

Markus, Lynne and Daniel Robey. 1988. "Information technology and organization change: Causal structure in theory and research." *Management Science*, 34, 5, 583-598.

McFarlan, Warren. 1996. "Issues in global outsourcing." In Prashant Palvia, Shailendra Palvia, and Edward Roche, eds, *Global Information Technology and Systems Management: Key Issues and Trends*. Nashua: Ivy League Publishing. pp. 352-364.

Meadows, C. J. 1996. "Globalizing software development." *Journal of Global Information Management*, 4, 1.

Nelson, Paul, William Richmond, and Abraham Seidmann. 1996. "Two dimensions of software acquisition." *Communications of the ACM*, 39, 7, 29-35.

Palvia, Prashant and Shailendra Palvia. 1996. "Understanding the global IT environment: Representative world issues." In Prashant Palvia, Shailendra Palvia, and Edward Roche, eds, *Global Information Technology and Systems Management: Key Issues and Trends*. Nashua: Ivy League Publishing.

Palvia, Shailendra, and Kenny Lee. 1996. "Developing and implementing global IS: Lessons from Seagate Technology." In Prashant Palvia, Shailendra Palvia, and Edward Roche, eds, *Global Information Technology and Systems Management: Key Issues and Trends*. Nashua: Ivy League Publishing.

Rao, H. Raghav, Kichan Nam, and A. Chaudhury. 1996. "Information systems outsourcing." *Communications of the ACM*, 39, 7, 27-28. July.

Robey, Daniel, and Andes Rodriquez-Diaz. 1989. "The organizational and cultural context of systems implementation: Case experience from Latin America." *Information and Management*, 17, 229-239.

Shore, Barry. 1996. "A conceptual framework to assess gaps in IS cultures between headquarters and foreign subsidiaries." In Prashant Palvia, Shailendra Palvia, and Edward Roche, eds, *Global Information Technology and Systems Management: Key Issues and Trends*. Nashua: Ivy League Publishing. Pp. 191-208.

Vitalari, Nicolas and James C. Wetherbe. 1996. "Emerging best practices in global systems development." In Prashant Palvia, Shailendra Palvia, and Edward Roche, eds, *Global Information Technology and Systems Management: Key Issues and Trends*. Nashua: Ivy League Publishing. Pp. 325-351.

Zmud, Robert. 1980. "Management of large software development efforts." *MIS Quarterly*, 4, 2, 45-55.

17

Emerging Best Practices in Global Systems Development

Brian D. Janz
The University of Memphis, USA

Nicholas P. Vitalari
The Concours Group, USA

James C. Wetherbe
Texas Tech University and
University of Minnesota, USA

ABSTRACT

With companies employing global structures to gain competitive advantages and ensure profitability, globalization of business is accelerating at a phenomenal rate. The primary objectives of this chapter are to explore the implications for companies going global and to identify the information technology (IT) infrastructure required to support global operations. The chapter draws upon previous work on global management and the role of IT in global enterprise. Five operational tactics, accompanied by case examples, for implementing the predominant IT strategy are also presented. The chapter concludes with an extensive look at five strategies for successful global applications development, and the changing role of information systems (IS).

INTRODUCTION

Global business is accelerating at a phenomenal rate. Since 1950, world trade has proliferated over 700%, while world GDP has grown 400%. Rarely a week goes by where the balance of trade between the major countries of the world (frequently, the U.S.A. and Japan) is not a news item. Exports are key to that growth, with most countries emphasizing exports and the balance of trade as a means and measure of economic growth and national vitality. In fact, one of the primary reasons for the imbalance of trade between the U.S.A. and Japan was Japan's concentration on exports (automobiles, electronics, etc.) for fueling internal growth, while the U.S.A. looked inward at its domestic markets. Whereas domestic markets may be saturated or limited, global markets often offer opportunities for profits and competitive advantage.

Companies are employing global structures to gain competitive advantages and ensure profitability. Some of the realized or expected economic benefits of globalization include:

- Economies of scale due to expanded markets for standardized products;

- Ability to locate value chain activities in locations offering strategic advantages, e.g., low cost labor, skilled workers, financial markets, physical infrastructure, customer proximity; and
- Diversification of demand in multiple markets stabilizes overall firm performance in the face of economic fluctuations in individual markets.

In this chapter, we explore the implications of companies "going global" and particularly the implications of accelerating improvements in information technology (IT), including the IT infrastructure required to support global operations. Using Bartlett and Ghoshal's model (1989) as the foundation, we examine four globalization structures employed by companies and Konsynski and Karimi's (1993) four approaches for aligning global structures with information management strategies. A discussion of the impact of companies' globalization on their industries and the ramifications for IT follows. The focus of the next section is the evolving IT strategy, examining five tactics for implementing the transnational strategy supported by case examples. Five strategies for success in global applications development follow. The chapter concludes with a look at the changing role of IT in future globalization efforts.

GOING GLOBAL: COMPETING IN
THE INTERNATIONAL MARKETPLACE

What does the often-used phrase *going global* really mean and why is it of interest from an information technology perspective? From a company perspective, going global means operating as a single, unified company worldwide, balancing resources across the entire organization to implement a structure to compete with other firms and maximize total customer value. Operating as a global company entails different structures due to local, regional, national and worldwide economic, political, and social conditions. These structures in turn determine a firm's management control systems, operations, and sales. Ultimately they affect the development, deployment, and maintenance of information systems and the related IT infrastructure.

The role of IT in a globally operating company is a force for dissolving boundaries-- time distance, cultural, language, governmental, regulatory, organizational, customer, functional, and competitor, to name a few. IT enables an organization to operate as if time and distance did not exist. The Internet for example, blurs the boundaries of time and space and is an example of an emerging global infrastructure for the transport, storage, and retrieval of information and ultimately the conduit of electronic commerce. In reality, IT is an essential component for enabling firms to globalize and is critical to their success. Furthermore, IT is pivotal to the operation of the global marketplace itself. For example, shipping ports such as Singapore's TradeNet can now provide in-bound ships with customs clearances and other services based on digital manifestos that are accessible online. Future technologies will continue to evolve and further support new and more streamlined forms of global trading and transaction processing.

The rivalry between tire manufacturers Firestone and Bridgestone demonstrates the competitive dynamics of going global. At one point, Firestone had 60% of the U.S. tire market along with a great reputation and strong brand identity. Bridgestone, on the other hand, was located in Japan with about 20% of the Japanese tire market. Bridgestone sold tires in Europe (with market shares of 9% in Germany and 11% in England), Korea, Indonesia, and a variety of other places. Thus, while Bridgestone had a presence in many countries, they did not hold the predominant market share in any country. Then Bridgestone became interested in entering the U. S. market. Advisors suggested that this plan was not feasible, that there was no way to do it successfully. But Bridgestone decided to enter the U.S. market and its first move was to undercut Firestone prices by 20%. Firestone's response was to drop its prices. What did Bridgestone do? They cut its prices another 5%.

Firestone spent more money on advertising, to no avail. Firestone cut prices; Bridgestone cut prices another 5%. Firestone cut its prices again; Bridgestone cut prices another 5%. Firestone complained to the U.S. government; Bridgestone cut prices another 5%. Of course, the outcome was that Firestone's market presence was dramatically reduced.

Bridgestone accomplished this remarkable feat by raising their prices in other markets around the world using that as leverage to supplant Firestone in the U.S. In addition, by expanding their global presence, Bridgestone was able to take advantage of improved cost structures as a result of increased economies of scale. Consequently, Bridgestone/Japan became one of the big three tire manufacturers, competing with Goodyear/U.S. and Michelin/Europe.

Pressures Driving Localization

The global competitive landscape is also defined by many local factors. While many managers realize that local cultures and circumstances play a role in global competition, few realize the subtleties. For example, many managers realize the difference between doing business in Singapore versus France, but fail to recognize the importance from a global standpoint of conducting business in Midwest region versus the Southwest region of the United States. Cultural and local subtleties exist within presumably homogeneous cultures. The astute global firm incorporates such features into their strategies. The following factors are some of the reasons for acting local, i.e. the pressures driving localization:

- Local languages
- Local cultures
- Local business practices
- Local taste
- Local competitors
- Proximity to local customer
- National and regional protectionism
- Regulations, tariffs
- Communications weaknesses
- Labor unions
- Transportation
- Quality of local labor

Evaluating these pressures is most useful from the perspective of a particular industry by creating an industry overlay for the above list. For example, create an overlay using the consumer products industry, and more specifically the classic soap consumer industry. Which localization pressures from the list above would be pertinent? The first might be local competitors; with transportation second; then local taste. If a company is going to manufacture soap, local labor, proximity to the customer, labor unions, local business practices, cultures, and language all become important. The machine tools industry is another interesting example. Both Japan and Taiwan have been very successful bringing machine tools into North America. Regulations and tariffs on machine tools, for instance, are much less critical than they would be for the insurance or consumer products industries. The same is true for local taste, e.g. a mill is a mill, a bulldozer is a bulldozer, etc. Thus, acting local is different depending on the industry and there are important ramifications from an information technology standpoint.

Status of Globalization

The status of globalization in different parts of the world varies based on the indigenous situation in each of the areas. e.g., the general business climate, IT infrastructure, market characteristics, boundaries, or obstacles. In North America for example, micro-economies (i.e., the economic conditions and factors of a particular region such as the Midwest, the Research Triangle of North Carolina, Southern California) are dominating the landscape of economic activity. In Europe, strong ethnic identities are a major factor requiring consideration during globalization. The evolving infrastructures in Latin America and Southeast Asia impact companies' globalization efforts in those two regions. In Southeast Asia, *leapfrog computing* (rejecting the conservative, proven, evolutionary approaches and employing state-of-the art computing platforms and practices (e.g., web-based computing, client/server technology, multimedia, etc.) provides its own set of challenges to companies with more traditional approaches. These factors are all pertinent to determining the best global structure to use when entering a new region or market, or when evaluating whether a certain approach is working or not working effectively.

GLOBAL STRUCTURES MODEL

In 1989, Professors Bartlett and Ghoshal formulated a powerful framework to view global organizational structures based on observations in the marketplace. The model postulates that global firms move from a traditional, divisional organization based on a domestic model of business, to a more elaborate and globally compatible organizational structure as they gain experience and success in global markets. They argue that, in general, a global firm can be characterized into four strategic structures: 1) multinational, 2) global, 3) international, and 4) transnational (see Figure 1).

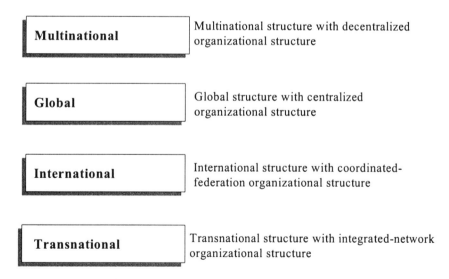

Figure 1: Global Business Structures Model

Multinational Structure with Decentralized Organizational Structure: In the globalization process, Companies employing this structure have a headquarters base and operating units in various countries or markets. This structure might also be described as the classic, domestically controlled model that is really just an extension of a divisionalized organization. There is little difference whether the company is headquartered in France, the U.K., the U.S., or Germany--the respective domestic business units tend to control their portion of the global operation. Organizationally, there are fairly loose controls with strategic decisions made remotely. Inward flowing arrows could represent the lines of communication from the remote business units to headquarters indicating that the remote sites funnel large quantities of information into headquarters. Strong financial reporting flow is a primary characteristic of the multinational structure. In fact, that is how control is exercised. Redundancy is a primary disadvantage because each site is performing its own activities. From an IT perspective, site autonomy creates difficulty for dissolving cross-functional boundaries, or developing compatible technology platforms.

Global structure with Centralized Organizational Structure: Used frequently by those firms that ventured early into going global, this structure involves a centralized organization with a global management perspective. The global structure involves a strong headquarters base and operating units in various countries or markets. The global structure presumes that headquarters knows best what is useful and valuable at distributed sites and that headquarters knows what is happening remotely across many boundaries, e.g., different cultures or methods of operating, since all communication is outward from headquarters where all strategic decisions are made. This structure is difficult to maintain and keep stable. Unilateral information flow (from the headquarters location to the remote sites) allows little room for remote input. Thus site differences and local advantages are ignored operationally and, as a result, the information systems that are developed and used often do not incorporate the business requirements of the remote locations.

International Structure with Coordinated-Federation Organizational Structure: The international structure, is a more contemporary approach that marries an international management perspective with an organization of coordinated federations, i.e., local units that have a federated relationship with each other. Assets and responsibilities are decentralized to the federations. Formal control systems exist, but the federations are more likely to work together for the good of their common customers with headquarters supporting and encouraging such an approach. However, with assets and responsibilities decentralized, coordination, sharing, and balancing of information or information systems between units is difficult, although the possibility for some coordination between the two does exist.

Transnational Structure with Coordinated-Federation Organizational Structure: The transnational structure is the most contemporary approach and has the most promise for the future. With this structure, management has an international perspective in which the organization structure is a web-like, integrated network. Headquarters is highly involved in the complexities of both coordination activities across locations and the overall strategic decision processes. Capabilities, resources, and decision making are distributed to the remote sites where the resources are needed and the decisions are made. There are heavy flows of materials, people, information, and technology. Consequently, internal labor and resource markets develop, high coordination costs are incurred, and an absolute dependence on information systems and technology is created.

Bartlett and Ghoshal's framework is germane to our analysis for several reasons. First, the framework illustrates that as firms become more sophisticated, the organizational model moves to a more loosely coupled, market-coordinated structure. The move to structures that are more responsive to global markets reflects the need for more diversity in global operations and more flexible responsiveness to local market demands. Fortunately, advances in information technologies like network and communications technology provide the capacity to handle greater diversity in operations through integrated systems, E-mail, groupware (e.g., Lotus Notes), intranets, and Internet compliant web servers. Given these technology developments, a growing number of researchers on organization theory and the global structure of firms have argued that information technology affects the structure of the firm (see Miles and Snow, 1994; Venkatesh and Vitalari, 1992; and Ives and Jarvenpaa, 1991) and that ultimately firms will move to a more networked, loosely-coupled structure similar to the transnational structure (see also Jarvenpaa and Ives, 1994; and Vitalari, 1990).

Second, as firms move to the international and transnational models, the control model changes by becoming more decentralized, permitting more local autonomy and local decision rights, but with the cost of more complex control and coordination systems. Often, these increases in autonomy and decentralization result from reengineering efforts.

Third, although the ultimate transnational form is the most globally sophisticated, all forms are found at work today and have varying levels of success. Furthermore, since the firm structure varies, particularly around control and coordination, it is likely that the underlying information systems strategies and infrastructure will vary according to each of the four structures.

Jarvenpaa and Ives (1993) examined empirically whether or not information technology structures varied according to Bartlett and Ghoshal's categories and found some support. Alavi and Young (1992) have also postulated similar relationships between firm structure and information technology use. We would argue that, although the empirical data may be only suggestive at this point, as networks and information technology become pervasive, the infrastructure to allow firms to operate in a more distributed but coordinated fashion will increase. It is further expected that global firms will be among the first to attempt to exploit these technological capabilities fully and thereby move them closer to the transnational model.

ALIGNING GLOBAL STRUCTURES AND INFORMATION STRATEGIES

In 1993, Konsynski and Karimi (1993) took Bartlett and Ghoshal's framework and explored its implications for information systems. Konsynski and Karimi analyzed each of the four structures and proposed four different coordination strategies and the likely IS structure (see Table 1).

Table 1: Alignment of Global and Information Management Strategies

Business Structure	Coordination/ Control strategy	IS structure
Multinational/ decentralized federation	Socialization	Decentralization: Stand-alone Databases and processes
Global centralized federation	Centralization	Centralization: centralized databases and processes
International and interorganizational / coordinated federation	Formalization	IOS: linked databases and processes
Transnational/ integrated network	Co-opting	Integrated architecture: shared databases and processes

Source: Adapted from Konsynski and Karimi (1993)

In the first example, the multinational strategy, Konsynski and Karimi contend that socialization is the key coordination control strategy to making this global structure work, i.e., people in the organization must believe this will work to overcome all the other issues working against it. And the correct IS structure is one of decentralization: stand-alone databases and processes, with information funneled back to the headquarters.

In the second example, centralization is the key coordination control strategy and IS structure, including centralized databases and processes. This translates to strong central control, and having the authority to mandate common systems. In fact, some research supports this approach as the best way to start going global, and then move into the other dimensions gradually.

Linking the databases and processes of interorganizational systems (IOS) is the third IS structure, facilitated through formalizing the interaction between organizational units, the federations. Coordination and control is done primarily through formal means, usually from headquarters. Since this is a very mixed model, linking together independent systems is probably the best approach from an IS development standpoint.

Finally, an integrated IS architecture with shared databases and processes is essential to aligning the global structures and informational strategies in the transnational model. The approach for accomplishing it is through co-opting and forming alliances.

From an information systems developer perspective, the coordination control strategy is critical to success. For an IS developer in a multinational, decentralized federation, for example, the only way coordination can occur is through socialization of management. That is, individual managers in the various countries or units have to have some sort of common, global vision. Otherwise, for example, if the developer goes to France to create a global system, the people there may be totally uncooperative because they see no need for what is being developed.

To facilitate globalization efforts, IS personnel must identify the coordination control approaches in their organizations, and then determine how best to leverage them to accomplish having the various organization units share data and information, build common systems, etc. Often, there may be multiple approaches, e.g., some parts of the firm may be highly socialized and believe in the global process, others may be using the formal strategy, while still others are co-opting. The challenge is to find common concerns, common interests, or common values and form alliances accordingly.

For the purpose of this chapter, Konsynski and Karimi's analysis suggests that we should observe different IS strategies and systems in the global marketplace across firms. Both Bartlett and Ghoshal's framework and Konsynski and Karimi's analyses suggest that in the long run, most firms will progress to the transnational model. The move to the transnational model is consistent with broader trends in organization structure and design discussed by Miles and Snow (1994), Drucker (1988), Vitalari (1992), and Lipnak and Stamps (1994), which emphasize the emerging network-orientation of organizational structures.

In the next section we examine five tactics that characterize the move to the transnational organizational model among global corporations. The five tactics represent the linking of information technology capabilities with business process innovations that enable the more loosely coupled organizational structure indicative of the transnational structure.

IMPLEMENTING THE TRANSNATIONAL MODEL

Figure 2 combines the pressures for localization, the pressures for globalization, and the four structure models, and illustrates the move to the transnational model. The transnational structure is effective when the pressures to globalize and localize are high because a company can maintain global economies and be locally responsive at the same time. Yet, it is also important to note that despite the movement toward the transnational model, some firms may find it useful to operate under other structures.

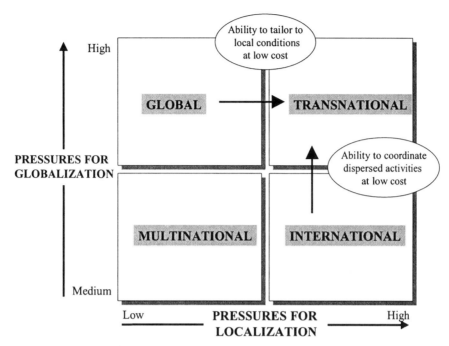

Figure 2: Global and Local Pressures vs. Structure Models

For example, if the pressures for globalization are medium (low was not used on the global scale because our research revealed there were no industries with a low need to globalize) and pressures for localization are low the multinational structure applies. The global structure works best where there is high pressure for globalization and low pressure for localization (homogeneous products). Where localization is high and the pressures for globalization are medium, the international model seems to fit best. Given the increasing pressures to globalize and localize simultaneously, the transnational model is evolving as the desired structure for companies and IT.

FIVE TACTICS FOR IMPLEMENTING THE TRANSNATIONAL MODEL

Companies have used the five tactics presented in Table 2 to facilitate the implementation of the transnational model. Since these five tactics are most easily understood in the context of the experience of actual companies, the following applicable examples are offered.

Mass Customization

In the book Future Perfect (1987), Stan Davis proposes the idea of product and service customization for an individual on a mass basis as being the ultimate end point of the information age. Currently, the most common examples of mass customization are found on the Internet and in the telecommunications, mass media, and consumer products industries, where some products and services are tailored for each consumer on the basis of unique needs (see Figure 3). When the concept of mass customization is applied in the global context, the firm looks at local requirements and attempts to customize products to meet those needs.

For example, Amazon.com, the pioneer in Internet-based book selling, recommends individually customized reading recommendations to their customers based on past purchase histories. The apparel industry is now finding companies enter the electronic commerce marketplace offering clothes with "the perfect fit" and virtual runway models when online customers enter their body measurements. In the publishing industry, selective binding, wherein specialized advertising inserts or regional stories are inserted into the mass publication, is commonplace. Selective binding allows almost all national and international media firms to combine unique content of interest to local settings with common or reusable content that has mass appeal. Publications such as Time, USA Today, the Wall Street Journal, and U.S. News and World Report, selectively bind inserts, advertisements, and stories to fit regional needs. USA Today, for instance, performs selective binding on a centralized basis for the most part. Then, using satellite-broadcasting technology sends different versions of the newspaper all over the U.S.A., appealing to local readership, cultural tastes, micro-economies, and other regional factors. Selective binding technology is

Table 2: Five Transnational Implementation Tactics

1	Mass Customization (synergies through global research and development)
2	Global Supply Chain Management
3	Global Intelligence and Information Resources
4	Global Customer Service
5	Global Alliances

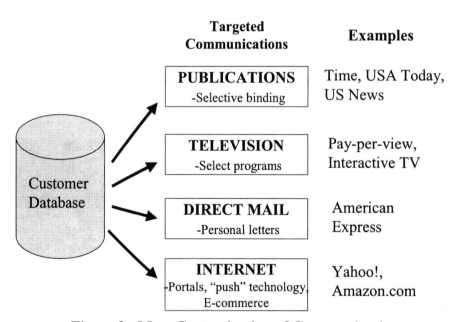

Figure 3: Mass Customization of Communications

also seen in the creation of mail order catalogs based on the examination of regional and individual consumer regional conditions. Similarly, AT&T, MCI WorldCom, Time-Warner, and Sprint provide different telecommunications services based on regional preferences. For example, both AT&T and Time-Warner envision using customer profiles, proprietary customer data warehouses, and regional information to develop customized television programming to the individual cable television consumer. With the advent of telephone caller-ID technologies, the capability to further refine the service that accompanies these products is expected to progress rapidly. For example, by knowing the origin of the phone call through caller-ID, region-specific pay-per-view programming can be ordered over the telephone and can then be delivered directly to the television without the need for human intervention.

The common denominator in the mass communication strategy is the use of market information drawn from multiple sources on mass, regional and individual trends, preferences, and buying behavior. This information is collected by global firms in massive data warehouses, is analyzed, and is then employed to form custom responses to individual and regional market needs around the world.

Table 3: Mass Customization. Global Research & Development Case Example

TACTIC:	MASS CUSTOMIZATION / GLOBAL RESEARCH & DEVELOPMENT
CASE EXAMPLE:	Pharmaceutical
IT: ENVIRONMENT	Global database, global network (electronic conferencing, electronic mail)
OBJECTIVES:	➤ Scale economies in R&D, leveraging distinctive competencies ➤ Local product externals with standard internals for scale economies in manufacturing
COMMENTS:	The IT environment and the first objective are particularly pertinent to the pharmaceutical industry, where R&D is going on all over the world and scientists need to keep in constant contact. Genetics research is another area information is shared via global networks, e.g., over the Internet.

Table 3 provides an example of mass customization thinking employed in the specialty chemical and pharmaceutical industries where firms have leveraged global research and development (R&D) activities occurring in regional locations, as well as regional best-practice marketing and promotional activities. These activities are leveraged via interchange of information throughout the firm's wide-area network, email, and group support software to optimize local product information with global manufacturing scale objectives.

Global Supply Chain Management

While mass communication seeks to meet customer requirements on a global basis, the global supply chain management strategy seeks to optimize manufacturing cycle times and costs across an organization's supply chain of suppliers and customers. Global sourcing and logistics attempts to obtain materials from vendors as close to the production site as possible and to establish global sourcing agreements with materials vendors who will guarantee material consistency and delivery schedules on a global basis. One growing addition to the global sourcing and logistics strategy is to create joint agreements to co-locate warehouse, manufacturing, and logistics facilities at optimized regional locations. Such ventures, which combine multiple companies, are feasible due to electronic data interchange (EDI), Internet-EDI, as well as other computer-based interorganizational systems. In fact, with the emergence of secure "tunneling protocols" and the cost-effectiveness of the Internet, the growth rate of Internet-based EDI is expected to far outstrip traditional EDI.

Two firms exemplify the global supply chain management strategy: Federal Express (FedEx) and Benetton. FedEx has found success by: 1) understanding the importance of information technology in connecting suppliers and customers, 2) appreciating the subtleties of supply chain characteristics in their customers' industries, and 3) serving as a supply chain management consultant to their customers. Benetton has found success by: 1) simplifying their products, and 2) simplifying production to enable optimized global sourcing and logistics solutions. In both examples, the solutions depend heavily on the use of information technology. As seen in Table 4, Benetton has created a global telecommunications network which links point-of-sale information to manufacturing technologies through to the warehouse to create a global sourcing and logistics solution. Suppliers are expected to meet demand and delivery schedules and are provided information to meet logistics objectives.

Table 4: Global Outsourcing & Logistics Case Example

TACTIC:	GLOBAL OUTSOURCING & LOGISTICS
CASE EXAMPLE:	Benetton
IT: ENVIRONMENT	Global network, electronic point-of-sale (EPOS) terminals in 4000 stores, CAD/CAM in central manufacturing, robots and laser scanner in their automated warehouse
RESULTS:	➢ Produce 2000 sweaters per hour using CAD/CAM ➢ Quick response (in stores in ten days) ➢ Reduced inventories (just-in-time)
COMMENTS:	Captures information over global network from EPOS terminals. Automated control entire assembly process (e.g., fabric cutting, dyeing, assembly), sending finished goods to the automated warehouse (JIT inventory). Fast response--10 days start to finish. By reducing the number of designs, they premanufacture most items, dyeing products *after customer order*. Consequently, they are able to deliver on a global basis and customize to local preferences.

Recently, global logistics organizations such as FedEx, Manugistics, i2, United Parcel Service, and others have begun offering outsourcing solutions that essentially take over the sourcing and logistics operation of major companies and assure that global operations can be optimized. Such shippers even implement a shipper terminated policy wherein suppliers' products are rejected if not received in time to meet agreed-to, just-in-time scheduling windows set by their customers.

Supply chain management is also seen in the global banking industry. The importance of financial information systems, which are globally and regionally structured, is paramount to a global financial institution's survival. Regional conditions abound and the condition affects the types of financial instruments and characteristics of financial services that are offered. Similarly, in the apparel industry, the supply chain has long been global in scope. An understanding of customer demand for finished goods, and the impact such demand has on upstream suppliers of raw materials, is important. Armed with this real-time knowledge from supply chain networks, suppliers can be more responsive to downstream customers and eliminate waste, excess inventory, and ultimately costs for all parties involved. As can be seen from Table 5, Reebok has been a pioneer in applying technology throughout its supply chain.

For all supply chain initiatives, it is an awareness of one's place in the supply chain that is critical to success as well as having end-to-end networking and application solutions (e.g., procurement systems, inventory systems, manufacturing systems, materials forecasting systems, etc.) that permit an instantaneous "push" of information to suppliers and customers upstream and downstream whenever supply chain transactions occur anywhere in the chain.

Table 5: Global Supply Chain Management Case Example

TACTIC:	GLOBAL SUPPLY CHAIN MANAGEMENT
CASE EXAMPLE:	Reebok and global supply chain partners
IT: ENVIRONMENT	Global network with contract manufacturers and distributors utilizing an Enterprise Resource Planning (ERP) System
RESULTS:	An interorganizational and global ERP system that can track information up and down the supply chain including: ➢ Customer and product forecast data ➢ Order and payment data ➢ Inventory and warehouse status
COMMENTS:	Reebok found it necessary to build a consortium of other apparel manufacturers in order to create the critical mass necessary for the ERP vendor to justify and consequently develop the supply chain software tailored for the apparel industry.

Global Intelligence and Information Resources

Maintaining the appropriate level of understanding of local and global conditions of the business prior to the advent of computer and communication technology was a daunting, almost impossible task. However, the ability to mount an effective campaign for global intelligence is now within the reach of most companies. The proliferation of Internet service providers (ISPs) and other information network providers (e.g., America Online (AOL), AT&T, etc.), the related growth in the off-the-shelf software (e.g., Netscape, Microsoft Windows, Lotus Notes, etc.), and de facto industry standards (e.g., the World Wide Web, HTML, TCP/IP, etc.) enables firms to establish, with relative ease, global intelligence networks with facilities for information collection, interchange, storage, and distribution inside their own company (e.g., intranets) and outside the companies (e.g., extranets).

Along with the proliferation of network capabilities has been the concomitant rise in information resources available in local markets throughout the world. With the force of network externalities, the more sites created leads to more users and this in turn leads to more information resources at lower cost. Thus, as the worldwide digital infrastructure develops, the ability to conduct global intelligence cost-effectively and efficiently increases rapidly. For example, most global firms today maintain a collection of local databases assembled from internal and external sources. Many external providers offer customized data and actually develop specialized filters and transmit or "push" the information into a firm's information systems. Often, firms attempt to gather local intelligence on economic indicators, customers, business performance, competitors, and market conditions to make appropriate modifications to business strategies. From an information technology standpoint, the real differentiation among global firms is seen in the degree of seamless integration between the global intelligence activity and internal information sources and decision processes supporting company operations.

Global Customer Service

Major advances in global customer service depend on effective use of information technology. Many global industrial manufacturers depend heavily on suppliers, which can provide a single global view of the customer. Global customer service is now a highly sought after competitive advantage. For example, a global manufacturer expects to know order status, delivery schedules, invoices, outstanding balances, and quantity of business on a global basis. The global manufacturer also expects consistent prices, consistent performance, and consistent quality. The service layer supporting global operations increasingly determines which suppliers are selected and which are avoided. At the basis of global customer operations are global databases, common customer codes, sales force automation, interorganizational systems and interconnected supplier systems with manufacturer's systems.

The same trends and conditions apply to other sectors. For example, investment banking and global retail banking success depend on global customer service operations. Customers of all types depend on access to financial markets and resources anywhere, anytime. Similarly, the airline, hospitality, and telecommunications industries require global customer service operations. American Express Corporation, perhaps the preeminent global player in customer service, has offices with a full spectrum of financial and travel services all over the world. Table 6 illustrates some of the services offered by American Express. Although many travel companies and credit card consortia have copied American Express, it still stands out as best practice in global customer service.

Table 6: Global Customer Service Case Example

TACTIC:	GLOBAL CUSTOMER SERVICE
CASE EXAMPLE:	American Express
IT: ENVIRONMENT	Global network linked from local branches and local merchants to the customer database and medical or legal referrals database
RESULTS:	Offers companies faced with the common needs of traveling consumers (e.g., airlines, hotels, car rental, credit card usage, etc.), these customer service solutions: ➢ World-wide access to funds ➢ "Global assist" Hotline ➢ Emergency credit card replacement ➢ 24-hour customer service
COMMENTS:	At the height of their operations, American Express was spending about one billion dollars a year on computing because their entire business is the information business. They had an early vision of what travelers would need, implemented it, and deliver it via a global network to airport kiosks and local branches. If someone loses a card, they send the information over the network and reproduce it locally. For cash advances, they comply with the local requirements on branch or non-branch banking. Regardless of the local requirements, they honor every request made of them. That's global customer service!

Global Alliances

Being able to develop global alliances is perhaps the most important tactic to achieving a transnational structure in that the previous four tactics often depend on the existence of a healthy network of allied organizations. As such, global alliances have become much more common in all industries, with industry participants looking for increased influence and economies of scale. By aligning and sharing key resources and assets, each company benefits in gaining access to new markets or by gaining new skills and competencies.

The airline industry offers several examples of global alliances and illustrates the necessity of information technology to deliver global business objectives. Almost all airlines have formed alliances to gain access to markets, provide new service levels to local customers, and encourage customer loyalty (examples include British Airways and U.S. Air, KLM and Northwest, Delta and Virgin, and American Airlines and Quantas). As mentioned in the discussion on global sourcing, alliances provide an effective way to make use of resources without major investment and ownership. Table 7 illustrates perhaps one of the most unique alliance partnerships in that it is composed entirely of organizations that compete with each other. The International Airlines Technical Pool, or IATP, is an association of airlines from around the world that work together to share expensive aircraft parts, putting these expensive parts around the world to assist associate members wherever they might be and whenever they might need emergency aircraft maintenance (IATP Pionairs, 1995). The IATP story shows that significant benefits can accrue to organizations if they are willing to overcome market challenges as well as differences of company politics and culture and nature of origin. Most importantly, such alliances are only feasible due to information technology that can track collections of data about travel routes, fleet distribution, and the location of key aircraft parts.

Table 7: Global Alliances Case Example

TACTIC:	GLOBAL ALLIANCES
CASE EXAMPLE:	The International Airlines Technical Pool (IATP)
IT: ENVIRONMENT	Global network connecting a world-wide association of airline companies
RESULTS:	➤ Coordination of maintenance schedules ➤ Sharing of technical expertise ➤ Pooling and distribution of high-cost aircraft replacement parts
COMMENTS:	In existence for over 50 years, the sheer magnitude of information related to aircraft parts, maintenance, and transfer pricing made IT a critical necessity since the 1960's. A classic, yet very uncommon example of otherwise ruthless competitors joining together for mutual benefit.

Global Tactics Evolution

In the prior paragraphs, we reviewed five implementation tactics as separate approaches. In reality, each of the tactics is utilized in combination. For example, a firm may use global information sources to customer understanding and then, in turn, use that information to establish and monitor a global customer services strategy. A global alliance may be used to take advantage of global sourcing abilities in the alliance. As firm sophistication rises with regard to global operations, one can expect the transnational firm to employ many of the tactics discussed, adding new ones as the global information technology infrastructure progresses.

**CRITICAL SUCCESS FACTORS
FOR GLOBAL INFORMATION SYSTEMS**

From our research on several case studies, we have investigated a wide range of industries, observed both successes and failures, noted the resulting systems that were implemented, and the key factors attributing to success or failure of these globally operating companies.

Some common denominators appear to be evident upon closer examination of the system implementation failures and of the successes. For example, a lack of standards and regional differences are two key reasons why implementation was unsuccessful. On the other hand, the companies tallied successes where standards were in place and adhered to, where regional differences were identified and incorporated, or where there was a high need for the system across business units.

In assessing the successes and failures of these case studies, technology issues are often not the overriding factor tipping the scale either way. Rather, it is the *soft side* -- the management structure, the strategy of the organization, and the cultural climate, the ability to build healthy alliances -- that dictates success or failure. Some of these equally important issues are presented in Table 8.

Table 8: Other Global Issues

Issue	Facets	Discussion
Sorting It Out	Cultural vs. Organizational vs. Personal boundaries	Companies had difficulty distinguishing between cultural, organizational and personal issues. Often, organizational issues were more divisive than cultural issues. In fact, one company said they had greater difficulty building applications across domestic operations than in subsidiaries in other countries, i. e., the organizational boundary factor. Others indicated that personal barriers or personal problems created obstacles to building global systems.
Rates of Growth and Change in Markets and Regions	Status Market Position Capability	The different rates of growth and change in different markets and regions are another issues. The different statuses of the various globalization environments (e. g., North America, Europe,...) affect globalization strategies. And a company may have different market positions in different regions with differing capabilities it can mobilize. Depending on what is happening in the markets, a company may be forced to operate in ways which it had not predicted.
Mandates and Leadership	Common communication, common frameworks, common goals, common practices.	This issue has to do with the extent to which solutions can be forced or mandated versus getting consensus. Contrary to the way we personally might like to believe this could be done, the research supports that the greatest successes occurred in organizations where strategies were mandated or implemented by a very strong leader and team. In the international trading system that was so successful, the need (information deficit) was so great that people just bought into it. So the issue is to what extent can a company establish common frameworks for communication, goals, and practices as a means to going global. Trying to get everyone to agree is not very expedient when a company is faced with extensive diversity, differences, and boundaries. Sometimes mandating a solution, while it does not ensure success, is the only feasible approach.

STRATEGIES FOR GLOBAL APPLICATIONS DEVELOPMENT

Given the critical success and failure factors previously discussed, one of the most important factors associated with success is following the right systems development strategy. Based on the cited case studies, research, consulting experience, and pertinent literature, the five strategies appearing in Table 9 offer suggestions for developing global applications. Note that there is no one best strategy. Rather, there are strategies that can be adopted in a mix and match manner.

Table 9: Five Strategies for Global Applications Development

1	Mandate use of best-in-firm application system
2	Use commercial off-the-shelf software packages
3	Cross-boundary development teams
4	Parallel development
5	Utilizing Software Components for Systems Development

Mandate Use of Best-in-Firm Application Systems

The basic philosophy behind this strategy is to search throughout the organization for the global application which best fits the business experience of every unit, i.e., the proven one, and then determine whether the common system can be modified into a single, common system that will be acceptable to all global units. The following questions must be asked:

- Can it be globally deployed?
- Does the current IT architecture support it?
- Is the right equipment available to support it (i.e., hardware, networks, etc.)?
- To what extent is the application consistent with best practice?
- What is available in the marketplace?
- Is it feasible to mandate common use as the deployment option?

In addition to the above criteria, it is important to note that the best-in-firm strategy is based on several important assumptions: 1) The software provides the best match to the business process it supports; 2) It is better to modify the business organizations or processes to conform to the best-in-firm model; and 3) The firm can overcome local cultural and behavioral barriers to garner the appropriate level of acceptance.

A variation on mandating the best-in-firm system is to transform the best-in-firm system with local modifications on an as needed basis. The same evaluation process identified above is used. Essentially, the common system is cloned, and limited, but agreed upon changes are made to the system according to local demands, and then a separate modified version is deployed locally. However, even if this strategy is managed correctly, the change and configuration management issues proliferate. In essence, the global firm ends up with a portfolio of many individual systems doing largely the same tasks, duplicating effort, and increasing the cost of maintenance in the long run. Thus, experience in the vast majority of successful cases has shown (and this is an important point) that if the best-in-firm strategy is chosen: *it is far better to alter the organization to fit the system rather than modifying the system for local conditions.*

Use of Commercial Off-the-Shelf Packages

Conceptually, this strategy is similar to the first strategy in that it starts with something rather than nothing – in this case using a commercially available software package -- for ultimate global deployment and use. This approach has been popular in Europe and is gaining in popularity in North America and elsewhere with packages offered by SAP, Baan, Oracle, PeopleSoft, J.D. Edwards, and others. Many of these packages are referred to as enterprise resource planning (ERP) systems and provide integrated software solutions across the enterprise (e.g., general ledger, human resources, manufacturing, sales, etc.). Although these ERP systems can be extensively modified, best practice in package implementation recommends minimal modification to the package and that additionally required functionality not found in the package should be built independently and interfaced with the package. Often, this independent functionality "wraps" around or "cocoons" the commercial package, with application programming interfaces (APIs) to facilitate interaction with other packages and systems. Cocooning has the added benefit or preserving package integrity for future enhancements.

The commercial software package strategy includes the following steps:

- Use JAD (joint application development) methods to determine requirements and prototypes to validate requirements;
- Incorporate an overall problem-solving focus with the JAD methodology rather than just a "build the system" mentality;
- Limit the number of vendors to be examined;
- Do not attempt to achieve a perfect fit between software product and requirements;
- Test candidate packages and negotiate with vendor;
- Adopt a time box approach for project management (see Wetherbe and Vitalari, 1994, for a description of the time box approach) where actual business results are tracked rather than just project milestones;
- Cocoon any changes in other systems to preserve package functionality, integrity, and future vendor-supported upgrades and modifications;
- Change the business process and organization to conform to the package; and
- Adopt and enforce architectural assumptions and standards implied in the package.

The package approach has been successfully applied in a number of industries. A large global consumer products firm, a large global manufacturer, and a global petroleum products firm have used this strategy to completely redefine their operations and support global operations.

The consumer products company used an IBM AS/400 hardware platform, and rolled their application out in Southeast Asia, the U.S.A, Europe, and Latin America. The manufacturing company operates in Singapore, Japan, Korea, U.S.A., and three European areas. The petroleum firm was able to completely integrate European operations and establish standard operating procedures across locations.

Cross-Boundary/Cross-Functional Development Teams

Today's integrated systems span organizational boundaries as well as national cultures. Consequently, the philosophy behind this strategy is to obtain support for global applications through the appropriate leadership and the appropriate multi-cultural, multi-disciplinary team. The team leader is a key position. The leader should be multi-culturally aware, and serve at least as a benevolent dictator (dictator in the worst case). This strategy employs the following steps:

a) Identify and assemble the multicultural and multidisciplinary team;
b) Assure the team is composed of opinion leaders and has strong leadership;
c) Identify specific business problems the new system should address;
d) Use JAD + Prototype + Time box to develop the application;
e) Track the resolution of identified business problems in the project plan rather than simply tracking application-specific milestones;
f) Adopt a progressive rollout strategy and clone rollout teams;
g) Incorporate local talent to build the application.

Generally the core team is fairly small--eight to ten people. When the application building process commences, the team size increases and incorporates local talent as needed. In this way, the cross-boundary/cross-functional takes on a "virtual" flavor.

Research in this area included banks, a worldwide manufacturing company, headquartered in Sweden with divisions in the U.S.A. and the Far East, and a medical products firm headquartered in the U.S.A. with product development and manufacturing divisions in the U.S.A. and Europe. The manufacturing company, in particular, contended that once it moved to cross-boundary development teams, the application development process worked much more effectively. In fact, the company now uses cross-boundary development teams everywhere in the world. Recently, the manufacturer deployed a system in Louisiana/Alabama/Florida using a cross-cultural team for building the system. Medtronic, a world leader in cardiac pacing products, has used this strong leader, multi-cultural team approach very effectively.

Parallel Development Teams

This strategy differs from the previous three because the underlying philosophy emphasizes regional differences right from the beginning with steps established later to create a global system. Using parallel development teams for systems development is approached in this way:

a) Local or regional teams are formed;
b) Local teams examine local requirements for application and infrastructure requirements;
c) Separate systems are constructed for each location or region;
d) Applications interconnections are established via bridges (e.g., internal EDI, intranets, etc.);
e) Strong decoupling maintained.

This strategy relies on cooperation at the end to create the global system. Eventually, a multi-cultural, cross-boundary team develops from this approach. One variation observed had the local teams come together at a central site after developing their local requirements. At the central site they resolved differences building the system with a certain percentage of regional differences, but with a common structure. Care must be exercised with this approach since despite obtaining local input and having representation, the local representatives may encounter problems upon returning to their local units, perhaps being accused of selling out, omitting strong regional preferences, and not bringing back the system the region wants.

Utilizing Software Components for Systems Development

The final strategy is more of a systems development philosophy and as such, is a strategy that can be employed in any of the previous four systems development strategies. In essence it entails utilizing object-oriented class libraries for a component-based "plug and play" systems development strategy. This approach makes heavy use of object-oriented technology, and approaches development following this methodology:

a) Cross-boundary development teams work to develop local and global requirements;
b) A version 1 object class architecture established;
c) The need for high-level, reusable object-based components are assessed;
d) A search for pre-existing relevant commercial class libraries is conducted;
e) A fast-cycle development approach is used to develop class libraries;
f) The object class architecture refined and local and global class variation and standards established;
g) Integration and rollout in concert with existing legacy architectures.

This development philosophy takes advantage of the fact that different object class libraries reflect the different local and global requirements and that there can be inheritance within the object structure. Once the common objects are identified, they can be combined into higher-level "components" and variations can be incorporated to reflect local requirements. The end result is a system that operates locally with global commonality. This philosophy can be used by either cross-functional development teams or parallel development teams, and the component-based nature of the philosophy lends itself to either maintaining and enhancing best-in-firm systems or customizing off-the-shelf applications.

Two very different examples of this strategy have been observed. The first example, a small, trading system using the NEXTStep development environment was very successful. The second example was a much more ambitious effort for a global order entry and order fulfillment system. With C++ being used in a client-server environment, the object class architecture was much more complex for the second project, but advantageous at the same time in that the needs of both the order entry and order fulfillment systems were balanced.

CREATING A TRANSNATIONAL IT DEPARTMENT

The extensive consolidation around going global requires that both companies, and IT personnel re-think their role in the organization. The global movement demands a shift from passive (order takers) to active problem solvers (information sharers); from cost driven to business or customer value driven; from independent support to intimate partner. In the absence of a company-wide global business structure, research suggests that IT managers should create a prototype transnational IT department to effectively deliver and support IS in their organizations. The following four-step approach provides one proven method for success:

1. Conduct a skills inventory, identifying within organization "centers of competence";
2. Define technology management principles, models, and standards (seeking senior management endorsement when the timing is right);
3. Link up--expand the global network for information systems professionals and provide other mechanisms (e.g., meetings, electronic mailing lists, bulletin board systems, group support systems) for sharing and learning; and
4. Look for opportunities for rationalizing systems and data center operations regionally and globally.

CONCLUSIONS

In this chapter, we have examined a range of contemporary strategies employed by global corporations in the use of information technology. We have argued that the structure of the global firm differs substantially from strictly domestic firms and that this structure has an impact on the information technology strategies deployed. In addition our observations of the global setting suggest that most firms with global objectives and operating models are moving over time to the transnational model. Interestingly, the transnational model more closely resembles some of the recent network-style organizational structures that are more team-based and flat in comparison to the classic, divisionalized structure.

We have noted that many of the firms observed in our work utilize at least five major tactics to leverage information technology for global purposes. In many cases, these tactics are also consistent with recent reengineering plays to take advantage of process simplification and the power of shared databases. We argued that the actual process of systems delivery and implementation plays a significant role in the use of technology in global operations. "Soft" issues like teamwork, alliance building, and change management, traditionally an important issue in systems implementation, seem to play an even more important role in the successful implementation of global systems.

Finally, we have suggested that senior information executives in global firms begin to model their own IT organizations on the transnational model. By moving to the transnational model within the IT organization, IT managers and professionals will become familiar with the issues of network organizational design and operating in a highly distributed fashion.

As firms enter the 21st century, it is becoming increasingly clear that technology is further blurring traditional boundaries and our sense of time and space. Perhaps in the long run, we will look back and consider the global firm an interesting anachronism for a point in time when human collaboration and organizational structures were limited more by local traditions than by technological capabilities.

Minicase - Information Technology, Culture, and Learning at Fedex[1]

By all accounts, the Federal Express Corporation, or "FedEx," is a global success story. In 28 years the company has grown from a start-up to an industry leader in the overnight package-delivery business. A case in point: for four hours every evening, the Memphis International Airport becomes the busiest airport in the world as FedEx airplanes land and take off every 45 seconds in an effort to successfully haul over 2.5 million packages -- in excess of two million pounds of air freight -- every 24 hours. Today, FedEx employs more than 110,000 people, flies over 500 airplanes, and drives almost 36,000 vehicles around the world. In addition to continuously seeking out innovative uses for IT, FedEx is finding that long-term global success depends on placing a high priority on cultural issues.

Information Technology: A Corporate Priority
One way to judge the priority that an organization places on IT is to examine the IT budget. Now a $10-billion company, FedEx spends $500 million annually on information technology development. Investing in IT appears to be money well spent. FedEx counts on information technology to boost growth and flatten costs. According to Fred Smith, the chairman, CEO, and founder of FedEx, "We're getting a higher payoff from information systems than from adding aircraft. It lets us save potentially hundreds of millions of dollars."

COSMOS: A Platform for IT Synergy
As FedEx's business volumes accelerated over time, the management and information systems the company had been using to control operations were becoming obsolete and unable to support

Minicase .... Continued.

the requirements of the company. FedEx realized that it needed to upgrade those systems or risk the possibility of compromising customer service. Using a "best practice" approach, FedEx executives looked outside the company to the computerized reservation systems the commercial airlines had developed to develop FedEx's automated transaction processing systems. That development group gave birth to COSMOS—Customer Oriented Services and Management Operating System.

COSMOS connects the physical handling of packages with information concerning each shipment -- from the time the customer requests service to the package's delivery. FedEx employees often offer the following analogy that reflects the significance of the impact:

If passenger airlines had systems comparable to FedEx's, whenever you were traveling, your family, friends, or business associates would be able to sign onto the Internet and in real-time learn your exact location, as well as every step of your trip history. They would know whether you were in the air or on the ground, and how close you were to your destination. If you happened to be in a cab, they'd know its number as well as the cab's destination. And, with that information, they would be able to phone the taxi and speak with you directly.

Another benefit FedEx experienced from the COSMOS development effort had to do with second-order innovations -- that is, COSMOS as an innovation in turn served as a catalyst for other innovations. For example, the following IT applications are just a few that can be traced back to COSMOS:

• SuperTracker, a computerized tracking system that customers can use to determine where any package or document is at any moment -- from pickup through delivery.

• DADS, a digitally assisted dispatch system that communicates to couriers through computers in their vans. DADS provides quick courier response to dispatches and allows them to manage their time and routes efficiently and accurately.

• POWERSHIP, the software for customers' on-premise computers, which now process about one-third of all FedEx shipments. The POWERSHIP systems provide automated billing, allow customers direct access to their package information, and supply detailed information and shipping instructions for international shippers.

The POWERSHIP application represents one of the industry's most effective uses of customer on-premise technology. As an inter-organizational information system, POWERSHIP allows FedEx to enhance the customer relationship through computer networking. The vast majority of the company's shipments today are made via POWERSHIP or via FedExShip electronic shipping systems. In addition, FedEx has capitalized on electronic commerce (EC) over the Internet's world-wide Web (WWW). The company introduced its first Web site in the fall of 1994. Its home page gives FedEx customers access to a great deal of useful information, including its POWER SHIP database. Every day, thousands of customers with service-related questions or issues find answers on FedEx's Web site rather than relying on customer service representatives. This "self-service" saves the company millions of dollars a year.

EC over the Internet has an additional benefit for MNCs with a global customer set. The regulation and politics of foreign countries can at times impede the flow of information and penetration of IT solutions in the form of dictating hardware and software vendors to use, protocols to follow, etc. Internet-based EC provides a universally-accessible network that places the burden associated with unique requirements endemic to a particular country on the organizations located in that country.

A strategy completely focused on IT may not be the best strategy for MNCs participating in the global marketplace however. FedEx also places a high priority on other important dimensions that serve as critical components to the success of their overall business strategy.

Minicase .... Continued.

Understanding Culture
Unfortunately, having a world-class IT infrastructure that spans the globe does not insure global success. For example, most organizations understand that the cultural environment profoundly affects global business. However, there is a potential chasm between *understanding* these implications and effectively *implementing* a strategy given the political and cultural implications. Over time, FedEx has found ways to conduct business effectively around the world.

One of the most important things an organization can do to effectively deal with foreign national cultures is to first have a good understanding of their own organizational culture. At FedEx, delivering every package "absolutely, positively" on time is the essence of their organizational culture. In addition to a macroculture, FedEx also has several "microcultures" that co-exist along with the macroculture. For example, the sense that FedEx is an industry-leading innovator in the use of IT is a microculture that permeates FedEx's IT organization. The couriers that drive FedEx trucks and deliver packages to customers have their own microculture that suggests that all packages will be delivered on time regardless of the situation.

FedEx not only tolerates these microcultures, but also encourages them as long as they are consistent with the overall quality and service maxims, which exist in the macroculture. This attention to culture as well as a strong, succinctly stated macroculture is essential to a company when it expands into overseas markets. FedEx learned that when it moved into Asia in 1991.

Bridging the International Culture Gap
FedEx has always recognized that their couriers are the people who have the most direct contact with FedEx customers. In Asia, however, people regard delivery personnel at a low level in the occupation hierarchy. As a result, human resources consultants back in the United States had set wage scales and job descriptions based on the earnings of Asian messengers. Consequently, FedEx found itself hiring unskilled and untrained workers -- people at the lowest pay scale -- to fill its courier slots. To an executive sitting in Memphis, this seemed a perfectly acceptable recruiting policy. To a customer in Hong Kong, it meant disaster. A courier dispatched to pick up three boxes, for example, would absolutely refuse to accept any more than three. In the United States, the FedEx courier was committed to 100 percent customer satisfaction. It looked like 100 percent customer satisfaction would be unattainable in Asia. FedEx had no choice but to fully understand the Asian culture and try to find areas where it and FedEx's corporate culture could be adapted to be consistent with the FedEx culture as well as world-wide customer expectations. As FedEx's senior vice president for Asia and Pacific Operations said, "It took us four years, and a lot of effort. We didn't want to impose American values in Asia, but we felt we had to keep to our core corporate philosophy. We tried to train the Hong Kong couriers to understand that service comes first, and we tried to train them to understand what FedEx means by service." Today, when Hong Kong couriers arrive at pickups, they courteously accept customer orders and react competently and intelligently to the unexpected. FedEx devoted a lot of time and attention -- not to mention money -- to hiring and training the couriers who would ultimately become assets to the company.

FedEx has spent time and effort in an attempt to find the balance between offending people (i.e., "You are trying to Americanize us") while helping them to understand that FedEx is a global company. FedEx has had countless group meetings with employees, and has sponsored many cultural training programs. FedEx has provided English language training at its expense and has given employees who complete the course a pay premium. FedEx's management development courses stress the cultures of the countries where their people work, and help managers understand that cultural differences matter from everyone's point of view. Overall, FedEx's strength has been its ability to learn and benefit from the challenging lessons of its early forays into foreign markets. The company redesigned its strategies in ways that complement each culture's preferences, and now it is enjoying successful growth in both Europe and Asia.

Minicase .... Continued.

Conclusions

FedEx's use of IT is often mentioned as the dominant characteristic explaining their long-term business success. In actuality, the environment at FedEx is more complex than that. To be sure, IT is a top priority at FedEx and it has staked its future success on the ability of it to capitalize on innovative ways to use IT for competitive advantage. However, this point focuses on only one of FedEx's priorities. In addition to IT, FedEx has been and continues to be ever mindful of the confluence of organizational culture, the prevailing national cultures of its customers and worldwide locations, and the impact that this cultural amalgam has on global operations.

IT and culture are not mutually exclusive but rather tightly coupled. It is perhaps useful to think of IT and culture in the following terms:

- Culture is pervasive and constantly changing (albeit relatively slowly). Everything an organization does is affected by it. Ignoring it in business or academia constitutes ignoring a defining boundary condition or potentially confounding force. Learning how to lever culture can and should be a core competency worth striving for.

- IT should be viewed as the facilitator for culture, learning, and ultimately organizational performance. For example, IT can serve to define culture (e.g., "we are a technology leader"), and can also serve as the common thread which binds otherwise disparate cultures together (e.g., "things are done differently in Asia, but they recognize the importance of IT just like we do here."). In terms of organizational learning, IT is critical in measuring and gathering performance information, assisting in the evaluation of the information, and ultimately disseminating findings (i.e., learning) throughout the organization.

1. This minicase was excerpted from an article in the *Journal of Global Information Technology Management*, volume 1, issue 1, pp. 17-26.

STUDY QUESTIONS

1. Discuss the challenges and issues that systems developers must contend with in each of the strategies outlined in Konsynski and Karimi's alignment of global and information framework presented in the chapter. From a purely technological perspective, is there a strategy that is most desirable?

2. Mass customization was identified as one tactic that could help in implementing the Transnational Model. Identify an additional example of an organization that is capitalizing on mass customization and explain how they are achieving mass customization.

3. Global supply chain management was identified as one tactic that could help in implementing the Transnational Model. Identify an additional example of an organization that is capitalizing on supply chain management and explain how they are achieving benefits.

4. Customer service was identified as one tactic that could help in implementing the Transnational Model. Identify an additional example of an organization that is capitalizing on superior customer service and explain how they are achieving success with this tactic.

5. Developing global alliances was identified as one tactic that could help in implementing the Transnational Model. Identify an additional example of an organization that is capitalizing on their global alliances and explain how they are achieving mass success with this tactic.

6. The five strategies for global applications development have a lot in common. After reviewing these strategies, put yourself in the role of a global applications development manager and discuss the top three goals that you would concentrate on in developing global applications. In addition, justify why you chose these particular goals.

REFERENCES

Alavi, M. and Young, G. *Information Technology In an International Enterprise An Organizing Framework*, *Global Issues of Information Technology Management*, P. Salvia, S. Salvia, and R. Zigli, (eds.), Idea Group Publishing, 1992, pp. 495-56.

Bartlett, C.A. and Ghoshal, S. *Managing Across Borders: The Transnational Solution*, Harvard Business School Press, 1989.

Davis, S. *Future Perfect*, Addison-Wesley Publishing Company, 1987.

Drucker, P. The Information-Based Organization, *The Harvard Business Review*, January-February, 1988, pp. 45-53.

IATP Pionairs Association. *The IATP Story : The International Airlines Technical Pool and How It Came to Be.* Published by the IATP Pionairs Association, 1995.

Ives, B. and Jarvenpaa, S. Applications of Global Information Technology Issues for Management, *MIS Quarterly*, March 1991, pp. 33-49.

Jarvenpaa, S. and Ives, B. The Global Network Organization of the Future Information Management Opportunities and Challenges, *Journal of Management Information Systems*, Vol. 10, No 4, Spring 1994, pp. 25-27.

Jarvenpaa, S. and Ives, B. Organizing for Global Competition. The Fit of Information Technology, *Decision Sciences*, Vol. 24, No. 3, 1993, pp. 547-580.

Konsynski, B.R. and Karimi, J. *On the Design of Global Information Systems.* In S. P. Bradley, J.A. Hausman, and R. L. Nolan (eds.) *Globalization, Technology, and Competition: The Fusion of Computers and Telecommunications in the 1990s*, Harvard Business School Press, 1993.

Lipnak, J. and Stamps, J. *The Age of the Network Organizing Principles for the 21st Century*, Oliver Wright Publications, Inc., 1994.

Miles, R. and Snow, C. *Fit Failure and the Hall of Fame*, Simon and Schuster Inc., 1994.

Venkatesh, A. and Vitalari, N. An Emerging Distributed Work Arrangement: An Investigation of Computer-based Supplemental Work at Home, *Management Science*, Vol. 38, No 12, December, 1992.

Vitalari, N. *Exploring the Type-D Organization. Distributed Work Arrangement, Information Technology and Organizational Design*, *Research Issues in Information Systems: An Agenda for the 1990's*, A. M. Jenkins et. al. (Eds.), Wm. C. Brown Publishers, 1990.

Wetherbe, J. and Vitalari, N. *Systems Analysis and Design Best Practices*, West Publishing, 1994.

18

Global Software Teams:
A Framework for Managerial Problems and Solutions

Erran Carmel
American University, Washington, D.C., USA

ABSTRACT

With the rapid globalization of software development, many software projects are now dispersed in multiple sites-- in many countries. A globally dispersed software development team presents some unique management problems that did not exist for the classic, traditional, co-located team. The global software team framework assists us in understanding the problems and appropriate managerial solutions. The global software team framework makes use of a physical metaphor -- of forces that pull outward and pull inward. The five centrifugal forces that exert outward pressure on the global software team's performance are: loss of control, coordination breakdown, communication poverty, federation of distributed units, and culture clashes. The six centripetal forces that exert inward pressure on the team for more effective performance are: collaborative technology, team building, leadership, product architecture and task allocation, software development methodology, and telecommunications infrastructure.

INTRODUCTION

With the rapid globalization of software development, many software projects are now dispersed-- in many countries. In fact, among multinationals and leading software companies, it is common to find projects collaborating across three, or four, or five different national sites. A globally dispersed software development team presents unique management problems that did not exist for the classic, traditional, co-located team. This set of (relatively) new problems is the subject of this chapter.

The chapter is based primarily on this author's recent book: *Global Software Teams: Collaborating Across Borders And Time Zones* (Carmel, 1999). Additional material has been added and some concepts have been refined further. As a style convention no further citations of the book will appear in the chapter.

A *global software team* is defined as separated by a national boundary while actively collaborating on a *common* software/systems project. Typically, a project manager heads the team. Each of the dispersed sites has a local manager and perhaps one or more team leaders who supervise and coordinate the activities of the designers and other professionals. Note that the convention used here is that a (global software) *team* consists of two or more (internationally distributed) *sites*.

This chapter is structured as follows. The next section discusses the background for the emergence of global software teams. These are the macro-economic, strategic, and managerial factors driving globalization of software development. This is followed by an introduction to the practical framework for global software teams -- the centrifugal and centripetal forces that (respectively) pull a team outward and pull it back inward. The subsequent section lays out the centrifugal forces -- the five basic problem areas in a global software team. This is followed by a lengthier section describing the six centripetal forces -- the set of managerial, methodological, and communication solutions that bring the team together for more effective work. The final section presents the guiding principles that underlie the six centripetal forces.

A global software team is separated by a national boundary while actively collaborating on a *common* software/systems project.

GLOBALIZATION OF SOFTWARE DEVELOPMENT AND REASONS FOR EMERGENCE OF GLOBAL SOFTWARE TEAMS

Globalization of the world economy has moved hand-in-hand with the growing size of the information technology sector. Spending on all information and computer communications technology exceeds $1.8 trillion, representing 6% of the aggregate global Gross Domestic Product; of this amount, spending on internal systems development, IT services, and software, combined, exceeds $650 billion (WITSA 1998; all figures are for 1997). The latter figure represents a good approximation for the total global spending on software development -- the aggregation of several million software professionals developing software for a variety of applications all around the world. The globalization of software development began receiving attention by scholars in the 1990s (Heeks, 1999; Mowery, 1996; Jones 1994).

The emergence of global software teams is perhaps best explained by the emergence of pockets of software developers in many "new" countries-- literally all over the globe. Nations such as Chile, Brazil, Ireland, Finland, Russia, Australia, China, and Philippines are all actively participating in the global software market. Of particular note here are two software stars: India (exporting upwards of $2.5 billion in software services in 1999 and producing roughly 50,000 new software professionals per year) and Israel (with approximately 2000 high-tech firms many of which are producing software products for the Internet, networks, and information security markets). Nearly every nation with pockets of educated workforce is studying or beginning to participate in the global software market. The globalization of software means that there are pockets of expertise that can be tapped virtually anywhere in the world.

While supply of software professionals is emerging in "new" locations, there is a shortage of software professionals in the advanced nations of North America, Europe, and several other nations (Rubin, 1997; Barr and Tessler, 1997; ITAA, 1998). The large labor resources of software professionals in other nations are, by and large, not mobile. The three largest pools of software labor -- in Russia, China, and India -- cannot board airplanes tomorrow and move to London and Los Angeles to satisfy demand.

Another factor, quite obvious to any reader of this chapter, is that technology has finally enabled global teams. The Internet has technologically facilitated collaboration across geographic distance. Recall that as recently as the early 1990s, sending files across networks, or as attachments in electronic mail messages, was extremely difficult. Today, this technological obstacle has been ameliorated, though not entirely eliminated.

Another set of factors driving the emergence of global software teams is at the industry, at the firm, and at the project level. The first of these factors is the paradigm of outsourcing, a corollary of the emerging virtual organization. Firms are increasingly comfortable with the notion of outsourcing key services that once were done in-house. In recent years we have heard more and more about global outsourcing and offshore programming. In parallel, the 1990s have seen massive globalization of product and service firms (often through global mergers and acquisitions) who then must manage massive, often distributed, global systems projects.

Time and money also drive the individual firm decisions. The cost savings of employing programming talent in developing nations such as India or China are often significant, if properly managed. Loaded costs for software professionals from emerging nations are often only 10% to 30% of those in advanced industrialized countries. Globalization is also driven by time-to-market. A well-managed global team has the potential of collapsing time-to-market, by taking advantage of time zone differences using an approach called follow-the-sun. Follow-the-sun takes advantage of time zone differences by setting up sites in three dispersed global sites to create a nonstop work environment where work is passed from one site to another via computer networks. Thus, follow-the-sun emulates the traditional three shift (nonstop) factory.

A host of other lesser factors exist. For example, for political-strategic reasons, many large global firms must set up development sites in nations with which they do business. Separately, many firms need to set-up development centers near their best and most important customers. For example, Dutch-based Baan set up a software development center next to its important US customer, Boeing.

Primarily due to the impact of distance, five centrifugal forces exert pressure outward on a global software team. Outward pressure is a metaphor for team dynamics that make it less effective in its collaborative work and hence produces a poor product as measured by time-to-completion, budget, and quality measures. The five centrifugal forces (figure 1) are:

Loss of Control: Control is the process of adhering to goals, policies or standards (implicit in these are levels of quality). In a co-located project team, managers often rely on the tried-and-true control method of MBWA (Management By Walking Around) and face-to-face meetings. However, in a global software team managers are reduced to assessing task completion and quality with less than an ideal picture of what is really happening. Decision-making is dispersed and the influence of the central person or central body is reduced.

Coordination Breakdown: Coordination is the act of integrating each task and organizational unit so that it contributes to the overall objective. Software development is an activity that is highly complex and requires many small acts of coordination and problem solving -- many small adjustments and frequent problem solving between people working on various software artifacts, e.g., a design document, a computer program, or an online screen (Hersleb and Grinter, 1999). When everyone is located along the same corridor, these adjustments are made by team members themselves quickly and informally. When members are far, these adjustments are often not made until it is too late and hence add to project cost or cycle time.

Communication Poverty: Communication richness is defined as two-way interaction of more than one sensory channel (Trevino, et al, 1987). Face-to-face communication is the richest form of communication, while snail-mail is poorest. Asynchronous forms of communications such as e-mail and voicemail are not considered "communication rich." It is precisely these "non-rich" (or poor) communications that are most commonly used by members of global software teams. When we communicate face-to-face we transmit much more than the objective text of our message. Much of the message is in body language and context. Nonverbal communication is particularly important to "high context" cultures outside the North American /North European axis. In contrast, e-mail messages are often obtuse, and we do not have the luxury of receiving instant clarification.

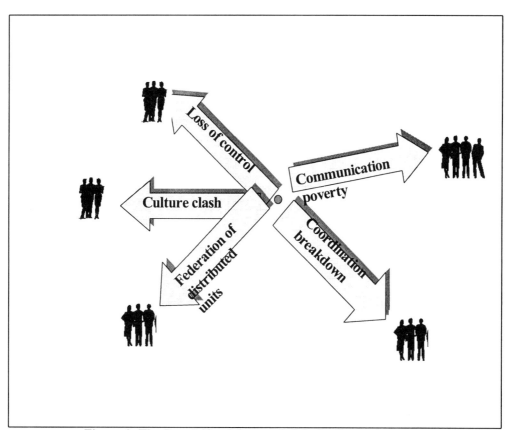

Figure 1: The 5 centrifugal forces of global software teams

Federation of Distributed Units: A loose federation of development units thousands of kilometers from each other does not necessarily make a "real team" (cf. Hackman 1990). A real team is perceived to be a team by all its members, has a common set of goals and tasks, shares its rewards, and has collective responsibility for its products. Few of the global software teams studied by this author satisfied even some of the characteristics of a "real team."

Global software teams are rarely cohesive. Cohesive teams function more effectively since cohesion leads to enhanced motivation and harder work relative to non-cohesive teams.

Adler (1997) writes that cohesion is more difficult in cross-cultural teams due to mistrust, in-group conversations, low interpersonal attractiveness, incidents of miscommunication due to language, and other reasons.

Trust between team members is important for effective team functioning. When one receives an e-mail message from a distant team member 10,000 kilometers away, one inevitably asks himself: Do I trust this message? Do I trust the person who sent it? Teams need to go through a maturation process in order to reach trusting and effective shared work. This maturation is lengthy for any team, particularly a dispersed team.

Culture clashes: Global software teams are culturally diverse across sites. This leaves plenty of room for misunderstandings, miscommunication, frustration, and even animosity. Each one of us is a member of a (national/ethnic) culture that influences how we behave and how we perceive others: from the notions of good and evil to the etiquette of proper dialogue (Schneider and Barsoux, 1997). Some argue that globalization has eliminated these differences: the global computer culture (the common professional culture that binds computer workers) and the global business culture (the common values of competitiveness, free-trade, and efficiency). Furthermore, both the global computer culture and global business culture are heavily influenced by US cultural norms and use English as the lingua franca. In spite of homogenization, cultural differences do exist and do lead to problems.

THE SOLUTIONS: THE SIX CENTRIPETAL FORCES FOR SUCCESSFUL GLOBAL SOFTWARE TEAMS

The six centripetal forces – the solutions –exert force inward within the global software team making it more effective (figure 2). Global software teams need to create centripetal forces in order to counter the centrifugal forces (the unique problems) that propel the team outward from its center.

Centripetal Force 1: Collaborative Technology

For our purposes collaborative technology includes two broad categories of software support: generic collaborative technology and task-specific collaborative technology, namely collaborative technology to support software engineering. The first category includes the familiar technologies of e-mail, groupware, discussion groups, chat, video-conferencing, audio-conferencing, instant messaging, shared whiteboard, etc. The second category includes Software Configuration Management (SCM), project management, CASE, defect tracking systems, etc.

Global software teams need to standardize their tools across sites, usually by buying packaged tools and utilities. A new class of web-based software addresses the need to support distributed teams, e.g., TeamCenter from Inovie Software and eRoom. While most collaborative technology can be purchased, teams will need to spend some time integrating software tools and building web pages, workflow, and template layers to integrate the off-the-shelf software. Most teams will end up using only a subset of the tools available to them in the marketplace, so they must balance the various tools along two key dimensions: (1) synchronous/asynchronous, (2) generic/task specific to software engineering. That is, the team should use several asynchronous and several synchronous tools, and use several generic tools alongside several software engineering collaborative technology tools.

Management must invest in two dimensions of human resources that relate to collaborative technology: training and support. Given that some of these technologies are complex (e.g., SCM) they require training. Furthermore, given that the various collaborative technology platforms are mission-critical, it is wise to assign a full-time collaborative technology specialist to support the team.

Unfortunately, rejection of some collaborative tools is common. Programmers love e-mail, but dislike other structured features of groupware platforms. Collaborative technology to support software engineering also generates resistance within development units (for example, the distaste created by CASE tools-- Computer Assisted Software Engineering-- is such that the term is no longer used in any marketing brochures). Thus collaborative technology requires time and attention by the team's managerial layer: from the project manager, through the team leaders, and often the senior management and executive layer. These individuals must lead the team members to intensive and effective use of collaborative technology through persuasion, leadership, by example, and via rewards.

Centripetal Force 2: Team building

The effective software organization needs to build a *real* team from the dispersed sites. Cynics refer to "virtual team" as an oxymoron. A real team (cf. Hackman, 1990) is perceived to be a team by its members and by those outside it. It has collective responsibility for its product and works on interdependent tasks. It shares rewards. Collaborative technology alone cannot bring about a "real team." Generally, technology can enhance team effectiveness when team members already have established relationships and a sense of affinity.

In spite of the difficulties, the successful global software can bring about some sense of "teamness" that makes the federation of distributed units more effective.

The first step is to improve communication. Communication within dispersed teams suffers because of distance, technologies, as well as cultural and language difficulties. The lingua franca of software is English. So all participants need to improve their speaking and listening abilities in English. Management needs to invest in English-as-a Foreign-Language courses for non-native speakers. All team members, both native English speakers and those who are not, need to become aware of *active* listening techniques (Phillips, 1994): how to ask many polite questions, how to ask for rephrasing, how to check for understanding how to ask the other "did you mean that?" One such technique is the funnel approach (Phillips, 1994) in which one begins with broad questions, follows up with factual questions, and moves towards feelings and then motives (e.g., what did you like about designing that screen widget?")

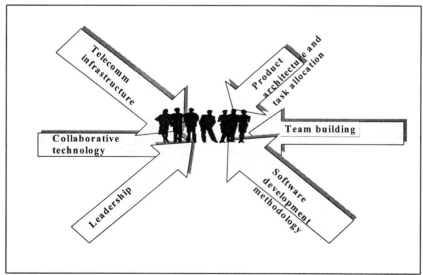

Figure 2: The six centripetal forces of global software teams

Communication is greatly enhanced by establishing communication protocols. A protocol is a set of codes prescribing adherence to certain behaviors and responses. Examples are protocols for responsiveness (e.g., how quickly to respond to a voicemail), for frequency of communication, and for handling trouble/conflict (O'Hara-Devereaux and Johansen, 1994). Yet another protocol is for e-mail usage (e.g., acknowledge every e-mail within one working day; create and use templates for administrative messages such as meeting announcements)(O'Hara-Devereaux and Johansen 1994; Grenier and Metes, 1995). Finally, meeting protocols -- face-to-face, video, and audio-- make the meetings more effective and shorter.

Effective communication and high levels of trust typically follow *face-to-face* interactions between people. In spite of the technology, global software teams need to create many opportunities for team members to meet face-to-face. In the better teams the author noted another kind of technology-- the airplane. In order to bring about face-to-face interactions, the best excuse for travel is the project kick-off meeting.

The kick off meeting (of several days in duration) needs to include several process topics which will make the team function better once everyone returns to their respective offices. These include: communication protocols and e-mail protocols mentioned above; customized cultural awareness workshops for each of the national groups represented; and presentation of the software development methodology. Organizers need to augment these topics and create social situations in which the various site members interact in order to build trust.

In addition to the kick-off and other milestone meetings, the project manager should be engaged in frequent traveling, as should the team leaders. Other team members should be encouraged to travel for longer periods, in what many call "rotations." A rotation is travel by an individual to another site for a period of one to four months -- long enough to form a bond with other team members, but not long enough to necessitate a full move of one's life to another country.

Bridging cultural differences comes about by building awareness of other cultures. Unless one spends time in another culture (via extended travel), the best way to achieve this is through customized cultural workshops for each national site (e.g, one needs to explain the Danish culture to the Americans and the American culture to the Danes). These workshops should be scheduled early in the development cycle.

Besides the handshakes that take place in face-to-face meetings, team cohesion has to be fostered through collaborative technology. Today, the team web site is the central element in bringing the team together (cf. McConnell, 1998, page 93). The team web page needs to have full informational displays for each of the following high level menu items: project tracking (e.g., task list); project planning (e.g., QA plan; or the glossary of process model components), work products (e.g., the user interface prototype), project deliverables (e.g., the current software version), announcements and news (e.g., the upcoming visit by the Chief Technology Officer of Sun); personal information (e.g, personal biographies, photos from recent vacations); team (e.g, organization chart); time (e.g., time difference between each site, holiday calendar).

Time zone differences are also addressed through awareness. In fact, many global team members have surprisingly little personal experience with time zone differences and are confused by the different workday norms and holiday schedules in other countries. These two should be explained and listed prominently on the common web site. Some global teams also set up an "overlap window" -- a period of time in which all members are at the office to exchange synchronous messages -- telephone, audio-conference, and video-conference.

Centripetal Force 3: Leadership

The dispersed global team needs a special kind of leadership. The project team manager (or other key person) acts as the glue that binds the units together.

In this author's study, global software managers were asked to self-rate themselves as managers. Each manager was asked to allocate ten points among three dimensions: technical, managerial, and global orientation, according to his/her assessment of relative strengths (Jarvenpaa and Tractinsky, 1995) Separately, the author classified these managers as either *effective* or *accidental* global software managers after an interview. The results were instructive: those that were classified as "accidental managers" rated themselves highly on technical skills. Those classified as "effective managers" rated themselves highly on managerial and global skills.

Five unique leadership qualities allow the global software manager to handle the multi-cultural and dispersed components of her role. These five unique qualities are summarized in the acronym MERIT: Multi-culturalist, E-facilitator, Recognition promoter, Internationalist, Traveler.

> *Multi-culturalist.* The global software manager gracefully switches from culture to culture and from style to style. While American managers like egalitarian relationships and participatory decision making (consensus-style supervision), Asian and other cultures that revere hierarchy (high power distance) expect leaders to be strong, decisive, and not expect much feedback (authoritarian-style supervision).

> *Electronic Facilitator.* The global software manager is a superb e-facilitator and e-communicator. The global software manager succeeds (in part) due to effective e-presence (similar to tele-presence for politicians). He can communicate a vision from a distance to all sites, and then link actions to that vision (Phillips, 1994). She is a natural facilitator of all types of electronic conversations: conferences, e-mail, and issue lists. And she makes sure that everyone is participating and contributing.

> *Recognition Promoter.* The global software manager is a master at promoting the virtues of global software teams at headquarters and is constantly receiving recognition and resources at headquarters.

> *Internationalist.* The global software manager has an intellectual appetite for all that is international. He follows world events, political developments, national histories, different telecommunications regulatory issues, sports, and the arts.

> *Traveler.* Rather than the traditional form of MBWA (Management By Walking Around), global software team leaders need to practice MBFA (Management By Flying Around) (Leonard, et al, 1997). He makes sure to have face-to-face time with team members at all sites in formal and informal meetings. She is effective at face-to-face communication in spite of not speaking the native languages of all team members.

Centripetal Force 4: Product Architecture and Task Allocation

It is management's responsibility to recognize that product architecture and task allocation need heightened attention when teams are distributed.

Figure 3 shows three types of task allocation strategy for the global software team. In *module-based* allocation each site is assigned one of two modules to develop. Each site works separately and independently (as much as possible) and integrates their respective work products toward the end of the cycle. In *phased-based* allocation site B performs the first phase (e.g., design), and hands off the design to site A which performs the next phase of the cycle, e.g., programming, and so on. The third case is *integrated allocation*, (at the extreme it can be *follow-the-sun*). This form of task allocation takes place when the dispersed sites work closely together across modules and across the entire development cycle.

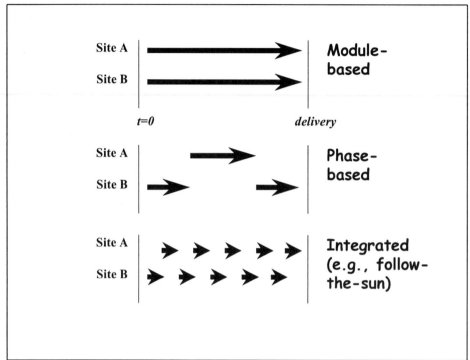

Figure 3: Task allocation strategies for global software teams

Software architecture is particularly important for module-based task allocation. Software architecture is a distinct part of the design process. Architecture, among other objectives, defines the components or modules. The architecture embodies information about the ways in which components interact with each other and hides other information. Product architecture is based on the principle of modularity which makes tasks intellectually manageable.

Global managers must architect or re-architect before dispersion of the team (cf. Hersleb and Grinter, 1999). Projects that do not invest in this early stage of the life-cycle will run into severe coordination problems later. Once the product itself is architecturally stable, the team structure itself should be designed. That is, design the product before the team. Strong architecture must be preserved and continuously revisited throughout the development cycle. Hence, the team needs an architect -- in the form of one person or an architecture committee.

Managing the hand-off (transition from one site to another) is particularly important for phase-based task allocation. In this form of collaboration, management must carefully design and facilitate the hand-off from one global site to another. It is in the hand-off that problems arise because of communication, poor documentation, different expectations, and weak problem resolution processes.

Much more attention, still, is needed for teams that practice round- the-clock/ follow-the-sun development. The concept of follow-the-sun works as follows. When the California site finishes its work for the day, it sends its work, such as design modules or source code, to its sister team in Bangalore, India (10 1/2 time zones away). As members of this site finish their morning coffee, they read through the questions, summaries and instructions written by their American colleagues and proceed to continue their work. As the sun sets in Bangalore, the local site finishes its day's tasks, reversing the information flow, albeit with its day's worth of added value. The (theoretical) result is a 50% reduction in time-to-market.

Task allocation in global software teams tends to mature over time as depicted by Figure 4 and Figure 5. Figure 4 depicts an evolutionary process, labeled a "stage model." In Stage 1 all development activities are co-located at headquarters. In Stage 2 distant development sites are added, but coordination is still centralized. And in Stage 3 the various remote development sites begin to assume greater responsibility for tasks. Figure 5 (derived in part from Apte and Mason, 1995), depicts the enhanced responsibility over time. At first, highly structured, easily manageable, low-risk tasks are assigned to the remote sites, such as porting software from one platform to another. Over time, tasks become less structured and greater responsibility is assigned to the remote team.

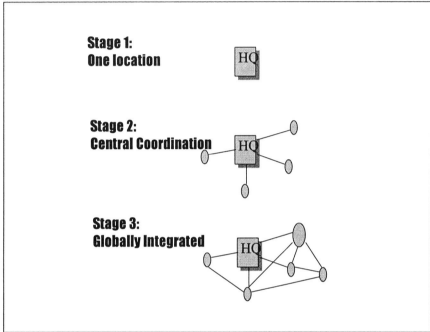

Figure 4: The stage model of global software teams

Centripetal Force 5: Software Development Methodology

The software development methodology is the common language of tasks and quality that defines collaboration. The methodology defines day-to-day norms, such as "what is the meaning of a bug?" or "how does one define a completed milestone?" These items are frequently the source of disagreements and misunderstandings between development units. Literally thousands of acceptable process components (a.k.a. methodologies) exist. Every organization comes to a collaboration with its own methodology and thus the methodology is part of the work unit's organizational culture. And these cultural differences can be more severe than differences in national culture.

The two key management imperatives in this regard are: (1) impose a common methodology. If a mandated standard is unpalatable, than a blend of the two units' respective methodologies is needed, or at the very least an agreement on high level process components such as stages and their respective entry and exit conditions --all in writing. (2) Continue to define key process terminology daily in writing and publish these on the team web site (Rothman, 1998).

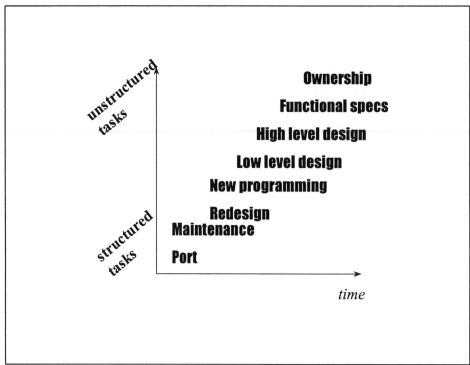

Figure 5: Interaction of time (surrogate for maturity) and degree of task structure on task type of new software development sites

Centripetal Force 6: Telecommunications Infrastructure

Given the very high coordination need *no* serious collaborative global software effort should be undertaken unless the team is using reliable, high-speed connections for all forms of data communications. For sites in emerging nations, the same maxim holds true for Plain Old Telephone Service (POTS). Reliable POTS is needed for voice, fax, and perhaps some data. Until just a few years ago voice and data connections to India were very expensive, unreliable, and lengthy to set up. Telecommunications hurdles are diminishing at a fairly rapid pace. POTS and Internet services are rapidly improving in China, Russia, and India and other developing / emerging nations.

Note that even when all sites are connected via tera-bit connections, some communication needs will not be satisfied. Electronics are only a partial substitute for human interaction. Travel is still needed between sites. Amongst those projects studied there was no correlation between the sophistication of the telecommunication infrastructure and the amount of travel by team members. In some of the better endowed projects, with excellent communication infrastructure, members traveled *more* than those projects with less infrastructure.

SUMMARY: THE GUIDING PRINCIPLES FOR GLOBAL SOFTWARE TEAMS

Many of the effective practices-- particularly for centripetal forces No. 1,2,3 (collaborative technology, team building, leadership)-- stem from the following six guiding principles:

1. ***Encourage lateral communication and coordination.*** A technology team cannot coordinate effectively if every small adjustment and problem is "pushed" for resolution up the hierarchy to supervisory and managerial levels. Hence, management must encourage

lateral communication and coordination between members in distant sites. This can be fostered via face-to-face meetings, personnel rotations, mirror organizations (a symmetric organization at each site with identical organizational structures and formal roles), and of course, by encouraging direct e-mails across sites (Galbraith, 1995).

Figure 6 presents a team structure that facilitates lateral communication. The team structure is built around a core rather than as a typical hierarchical pyramid organization. It is agnostic as to geographic location. Small units, headed by team leaders, appear at the bottom and the left of the chart. The center is occupied by individuals and/or committees that play the key unifying roles of project management, architecture, process management, etc. Two key support roles appear at the top right -- collaborative technology and methodology. A full-time person should be responsible for each of these roles since these are key process and technology elements within the global software team.

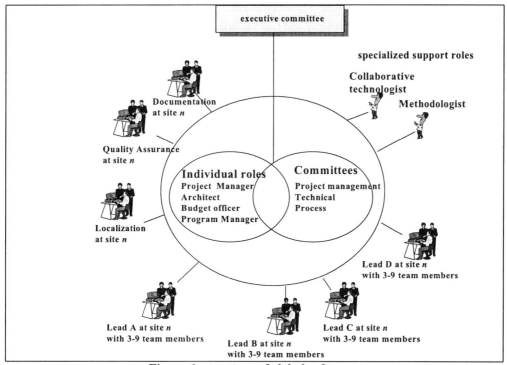

Figure 6: structure of global software team

2. ***Be more formal and more informal.*** This sounds like a contradiction at first, but in fact it is complementary. A dispersed team has to formalize some communications that otherwise would be informal if the team were co-located. Formalization leads to more effective communication—that which is understood by the receiver. Examples of formalisms that are needed are: templates in groupware that track issues or bugs; introduction of elements of process improvement (e.g., moving up the CMM); broad use of a SCM; structured weekly video-meetings, better planning norms (which improve transparency, in turn leading to trust). At the same time the team management has to foster informal communication within the dispersed team, where little communication would exist otherwise (see principle no. 1).

3. ***Give everyone a 360° view.*** In absence of buildings and people, dispersed team members need to be given a sense of where each member is relative to each other member --- above him, below him, and laterally from him in the team hierarchy. This idea is similar to the

notion of organizational transparency, which calls for clear individual roles/tasks and group roles/tasks. This principle is achieved, in part, through the team web page mentioned earlier. Team members in sites distant from headquarters will benefit most from implementing this principle.

4. ***Establish trust early in the project and foster it throughout.*** "Trust," is a fuzzy notion, that is receiving greater attention now due to the advent of virtual teams and the anonymity of electronic commerce (Jarvenpaa and Leidner, 1998). Team members that collaborate need to trust each other to bring about effective teamwork. They must trust that the messages relayed to them from peers and supervisors serve a common goal. In the absence of trust, individuals will engage in unproductive behavior such as competing and redundant work. Trust is best established through face-to-face encounters, preferably beginning with the kick-off meeting. In the absence of the face-to-face meetings, trust is conveyed via telephone and e-mail by respect, professionalism, and dependability.

5. ***Establish team memory.*** The team memory facilitates sharing of information and knowledge across the team sites. Groupware and web technologies support this principle quite well. The team memory is a repository of all documents and objects related to development -- from meeting summaries, through design iterations, through program reviews. Because team members can find information by themselves, a team memory/repository also offloads some of the burden from project managers, team leaders, and subject matter experts within the team.

6. ***Be aware of culture and be aware of language.*** Cultural differences can lead to mistrust between team members. Different English language abilities lead to miscommunication. Issues of language sensitivity and culture need to be addressed by building awareness (orchestrated by management) through culture workshops, communication protocols, and by example. Awareness means recognizing strengths and weaknesses of different collaborative technologies-- which are never culturally neutral. For example, e-mail is an important communication tool for team members who are weak in English because e-mail communication allows people to read and write at their own pace rather than in real-time.

STUDY QUESTIONS

1. Survey the global economic forces of supply and demand for software professionals that spur/drive global software teams.

2. Why is it more difficult to manage a team that is 10000 kilometers away?

3. Why is it more difficult to work with a peer that is 10000 kilometers away?

4. Survey the team-building techniques for overcoming the difficulties inherent in global software teams

REFERENCES

Adler, N.J., *International Dimensions of Organizational Behavior,* Southwestern College Publishing, 1997.

Apte, U. M. and Mason, R.M. "Global Disaggregation of Information-intensive Services," *Management Science,* (41:7), July 1995, pp. 1250-1262.

Barr, A. and Tessler, S. "How Will the Software Talent Shortage End?" *Stanford Computer Industry Project,* November 1997, http://www.stanford.edu/group/scip/avsgt/

Carmel, E. *Global Software Teams: Collaborating Aacross Borders and Time Zones*. Upper Saddle River, N.J.: Prentice Hall PTR, 1999.

Galbraith, J.R., *Designing Organizations*, San Francisco: Jossey-Bass Publishers, 1995.

Gerry, G.C. "Off-shore Programming: the Wave of the Future?" *Performance Computing*, May 1999.

Grenier, R. and Metes, G., *Going Virtual: Moving your Organization into the 21st century*, Upper Saddle River, N.J.: Prentice Hall, 1995.

Hackman, J.R., *Groups that work and those that don't*, San Francisco: Jossey-Bass, 1990.

Heeks, R. B, "Software Strategies in Developing Countries," *Communications of the ACM*, (42:6), June 1999, pp.15-20.

Hersleb, J.D. and Grinter, R.E. "Splitting the Organization and Integrating the Code: Conway's Law Revisited," *Proceedings of the International Conference on Software Engineering*, 1999.

ITAA, *Help Wanted 2: A Call for Collaborative Action for the New Millenium*, available from the Information Technology Association of America, www.itaa.org, January, 1998.

Jarvenpaa, S. and Tractinsky, N. "Information Systems Design Decisions in a Global Versus Domestic Context," *Management Information Systems Quarterly* (19:4), pp.507-534, December, 1995.

Jarvenpaa, S., L. and Leidner, D.E., "Communication and Trust in Global Virtual Teams," *Journal of Computer-Mediated Communication*, (3:4) June 1998. This is an electronic journal available at http://jcmc.huji.ac.il/

Jones, C. "Globalization of Software Supply and Demand," *IEEE Software*, (11:6), November 1994, pp. 17-24.

Leonard, D.A. Brands, P., Edmondson, A. Fenwick, J. "Virtual teams: Using Communication Technology to Manage Geographically Gispersed Development Groups." in *Sense and Respond: Capturing Value in the Network Era*, edited by S. P. Bradley and R.L. Nolan. Cambridge: Harvard Business School Press, 1997.

McConnell, S. *Software Project survival guide*. Redmond, Washington: Microsoft Press, 1998.

Mowery, D.C., *The International Computer Software Industry: A Comparative Study of Industry Evolution and Structure*, Oxford University Press, 1996.

O'Hara-Devereaux, M and Johansen, R., *Globalwork: Bridging Distance, Culture and Time*, San Francisco: Jossey-Bass, 1994.

Phillips, N. *Managing International Teams*. Bur Ridge, Illinois: Irwin Professional Publishing, 1994.

Rothman, J., "Managing Global Teams," *Software Development*, August 1998, pp. 36-40.

Rubin, H.A., *Critical Issues: the Global Software Engineering and Information Technology Competitiveness of the United States*, report presented to the US Department of Commerce, March 1997, available from Rubin Systems in Pound Ridge, New York; www.hrubin.com.

Schneider, S.C. and J. Barsoux, *Managing Across Cultures*, London: Prentice Hall, 1997.

Trevino, L.K., R.H. Daft and R.L. Lengel, "Media Symbolism, Media Richness, and Media Choice in Organizations," *Communication Research*, (14:5), October, 1987.

WITSA (World Information Technology and Services Alliance), *Digital Planet: The Global Information Economy*, Vienna, Virginia: WITSA, October, 1998.

19

The Design of Information Systems for the International Firm: A Grounded Theory of Some Critical Issues

Hans Lehmann
University of Auckland, New Zealand

ABSTRACT

International Information Systems have taken on increased importance as organisations develop and refine their global operations. A number of researchers have proposed frameworks for categorising and analysing these systems. Little research has been done to test these frameworks or to assess their relevance over time. This chapter summarises the evolution of an IIS as it follows its organisation's global business development. Using a Case History method in the Grounded Theory tradition the chapter supports the notion of an "information system migration" following the development of the Global Business Strategy of the Multi-National enterprise through various stages. Failure of the IIS to adapt to the organisation's strategy changes sets up a field of antagonistic forces, in which business resistance eventually defeated all attempts by the information technology people to install a standard global information system. Although the case yielded data rich enough to establish some conceptual foundations, further research will be necessary to progress towards a possible substantive theory of international information systems development..

INTRODUCTION

Until recently, international information systems (IIS), i.e. information systems for use in multinational enterprises have been "...sometimes ignored altogether" (King & Sethi, 1993) and academic research is sparse (Cash, McFarlan & McKenney, 1992). However, little of even the current research is of direct help to systems building practitioners, who have come to regard IIS as difficult and risky. This is illustrated in a survey (KPMG, 1993) where only 8% of some 80 European firms had completed IIS development satisfactorily. This chapter investigates the driving forces for an IIS architecture. Architecture throughout this chapter includes the ordered structure of both information technology and information systems applications.

The architecture of an information system is considered an important building block for the successful development of any complex system (Earl, 1989). Any such theory can thus contribute to a framework for the development of IIS, which, in turn, would significantly assist in reducing their complexity and the risk inherent in building them. To distinguish IIS from other distributed systems, in this chapter IIS are defined as distributed information systems that support similar business activities in highly diverse environments, commonly found across country boundaries.

Following a literature review and a brief discussion of the research method employed, the main part of the chapter is the description and discussion of the findings from the case history. Finally, conclusions are drawn and an outline of the further research is presented.

INTERNATIONAL INFORMATION SYSTEMS IN THE LITERATURE

Past research into IIS is sporadic (Lehmann, 1996a) and spread over a wide array of topics. Only in the last few years have researchers begun to direct their attention onto some aspects of the design and development of IIS. Some of this recent research focuses on the structure and architecture of IIS.

The Architecture of International Information Systems

A number of researchers of IIS architectures use a framework for the classification of enterprises operating in more than one country which was developed by Bartlett and Ghoshal in 1989.

Their model is centred on the level and intensity of global control versus local autonomy:

- 'Global' means high global control while 'Multinationals' have high local control;
- 'Internationals' are an interim state, transiting towards a balance of local and global;
- 'Transnational' organisations balance tight global control whilst vigorously fostering local autonomy. This strategy of "think global and act local" is considered optimal for many international operations.

Butler Cox (1991) also put a developmental perspective on the Bartlett-Goshal framework. In their terminology, companies seem to become active internationally first as 'Exporter' of their goods or services - usually applying a *'Global'* business strategy (Italics denote the Bartlett & Goshal classification). Increased activity in any one location encourages autonomy for local operations, taking on the role of 'National Adapter', similar to the *'Multinational'* classification. In the next phase this degree of autonomy is counterbalanced by some global control as ' Central Co-ordinator', i.e. an *'International'* firm. Finally, as global operations mature, firms move towards a status of 'Global Co-ordinator' (equivalent to the *'Transnational'*). Figure 1 below demonstrates the Bartlett and Ghoshal (1991) classification and shows the 'migration paths' suggested by Butler Cox (1991).

A number of researchers developed models of IIS with a direct, one-to-one relationship between Bartlett and Ghoshal's global business strategies and these systems architectures. Table 1 below contains an overview of the main architecture frameworks.

It seems that just as the *'international'* business strategy is an intermediary stage, so are the corresponding global information technology configurations. If these 'replicated', or 'inter-organisational', or even 'intellectually-synergised' structures are regarded as embryonic versions of 'integrated' architectures, then just three generic architectures would need to be defined, namely:

- Centralised;
- Decentralised (including autonomous and independent); and
- Integrated.

Whilst the centralised and decentralised structures have been researched over a number of years and are by now well understood, the nature of the 'integrated' structure/architecture has rarely been an object of empirical study. However, the very nature of the systems under investigation makes it possible to establish some common sense, *a-priori* postulates as to the shape of their architecture.

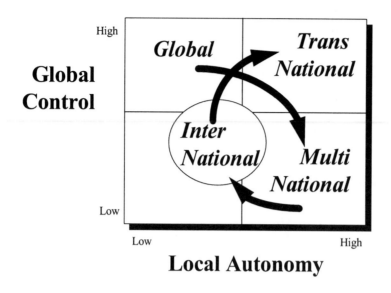

Figure 1. Classification and Migration through Global Business Strategies

Table 1. Architecture configurations in the literature

Bartlett & Ghoshal	Butler Cox (1991)	Kosynski & Karimi (1993)	Sankar et al (1993)	Jarvenpaa & Ives (1994)
Global	Centralised	Centralisation	Centralised	Headquarters-driven
Multinational	Autonomous	Decentralisation	Decentralised	Independent
International	Replicated	Inter-organisational	*(undefined)*	Intellectual Synergy
Transnational	Integrated	Integrated	Integrated	Integrated

International information systems support common functions across a number of local sites. The common sense deduction from this is the obvious requirement that such systems would have parts that are common to all sites and other parts, which are specific to individual localities. The basis of this concept, ie the need for variation in international systems to accommodate differing local circumstances has been established by Keen et al. as early as 1982, when a paradigm of a 'common core' of information systems applications with 'local' alterations was first articulated. There has been little further development of this model as far as the functionality of application systems is concerned and researchers conclude that "the literature offers little guidance for...local versus common applications"(Ives et al, 1991).

Building on 'lived' experience in the development and implementation of IIS, a two-dimensional topology systems has therefore been postulated (Lehmann, 1996b) as an architecture model for international information systems. The topology would thus consist of a 'common core' and 'local variations' of the system, linked together by a 'core/local interface', as shown in Figure 2 below.

RESEARCH METHODOLOGY

The dearth of IIS research makes qualitative, theory building methods an appropriate choice. Such methods are well established in organisational research and are becoming accepted in information systems research too. In Sociology, Glaser and Strauss (1967) had already developed a specific inductive method which they termed the 'Grounded Theory' approach, where theory is left to 'emerge' from the data - in which it is 'grounded'. Since the early

1980s, grounded theory research had been used in a number of business studies and is becoming also popular Information Systems researchers.

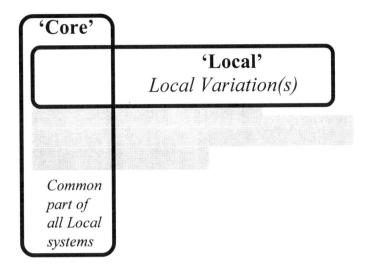

Figure 2: Conceptual architecture model for international information systems

The following section gives a - highly abridged - case history of an attempt to develop an international information system for a large enterprise in the food industry, headquartered in Australasia. The case analysis is based on some 60 hours of interviews with key executive and management staff, about half of which were information technology people. A substantial reference collection of supporting documentation supported the oral record.

CASE HISTORY: AUSTRALASIAN FOOD PRODUCERS' CO-OP

Background

The marketing authorities for land-based industries (such as fruit growers, meat producers, dairy farmers, forestry, etc.) are often large companies with strong international presence. The Australasian Food Producers' Co-op (the 'Co-op') with some $4.5bn revenue is one of the largest of those (All names within the enterprise have been changed and all money figures are in US Dollars).. Like the others, the Co-op is a 'statutory monopoly', as there is legislation which prohibits any other organisation from trading their produce in international markets. With about a quarter from raw materials and manufacturing outside Australasia, the Co-op is a mature transnational operator. Structured into nine regional holding companies, in 1997 it has a presence in 135 offices in 40 countries.

The 15,000 primary producers are organised into 18 co-operative 'Production Companies' (ProdCos), in which the farmers own in shares proportional to their production. The ProdCos collectively own the Co-op. This tight vertical integration is seen as a big advantage. It allows the Co-op to act as one cohesive enterprise and to develop a critical mass needed in most of its major markets. Figure 3 shows this structure and the product flow.

Business background

Prior to the mid 1970s Australasia exported the vast majority of its produce to the United Kingdom, who, under Commonwealth rules, used to accept it all. Once the UK had joined the

European Union, however, they had to give free access to all other EU members, and cut the Co-op's quota severely. Australasia had to develop new markets. A number of subsidiary offices was set up rapidly and agencies were nominated in the US and Canada.

This policy of local autonomy was successful. Within a decade the Co-op had built a presence in more than thirty countries and had managed, throughout, to secure a satisfactory return for all their primary producers.

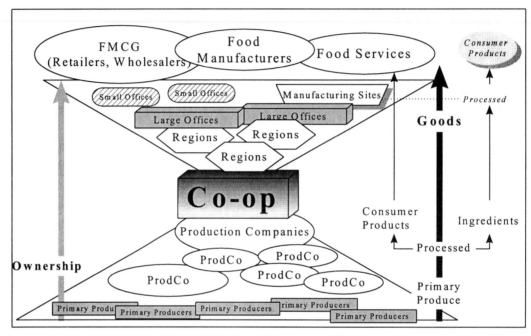

Figure 3. Business Structure of the Co-o

At the onset of the 90s, however, competition for the Cop-op had become increasingly global. With the emergence of global brands (such as Coca Cola, McDonalds, etc.); the Co-op needed to develop global brands themselves and had to have sufficient command (and control) to mount synchronised international marketing and logistics operations. With the arrival of a new Chief Executive Officer in 1992, the Co-op began a concerted campaign to shift authority and control back to head-office, within a vision of balanced central control and local flexibility. Figure 4 below shows this development in terms of the Bartlett and Ghoshal classification.

Part of this new policy was a critical look at the role of information systems throughout the Co-op's operations.

The IS Landscape in 1992

During the 'global' phase, the Co-op had built up a sizeable IS department with a mainframe operation at the head-office, linking up with all the main subsidiary offices and ProdCos throughout the 'home' country. Information systems applications were firmly concentrated on the needs of producers and local production –co-operatives and were of the nature of traditional transaction processing systems, housed on the large central mainframe. Foreign activities were few and hardly needed computer support. The forced expansion drive in the 80's, however, lead to an increased need by local operations to be supported with information systems. By 1992, a number of regional offices had bought computers and software to suit their own, individual requirements. Figure 5 below shows the distribution of computer equipment in 1992.

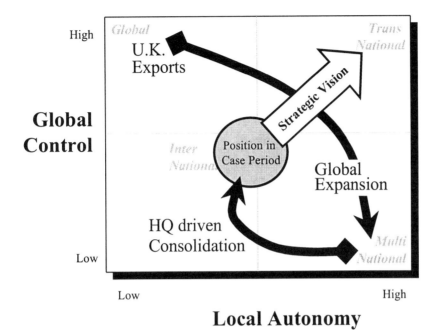

Figure 4: The Co-op's migration of global business strategy

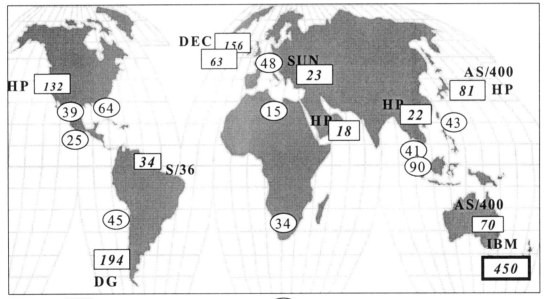

Legend: $\boxed{123}$ Mainframes or Minis of **MAKE**; or $\textcircled{123}$ WINTEL LANs; with *123 Terminals* or 123 PCs

Figure 5: Configuration of Information Technology across the globe in 1992

The Global Information Systems Project

Against this background of a proliferation of uncoordinated local systems on the one hand and a declared policy of more control from the Co-op's centre on the other, the Co-op's IS Department, in April 1992 took the initiative to establish a "Framework for Information

Systems". The IS Department's initiative was welcomed by the Co-op's executive board, who were not all too comfortable with information technology and described themselves often as "benign illiterates" when "it comes to computers".

This 'framework' was going to be the basis for globally common technology, communications, data/information and application software standards, effective for all of the Co-op's 135 offices in 35 countries. Subsequently, late in 1992, the 'Food Information Systems Technology' (FIST) project was created by the IS Department to implement the 'Framework's' in three stages:

1. Development of a 'prototype' system with a representative site;
2. Implementation of the prototype in a small number of 'pilot' sites;
3. Synchronised 'roll-out' of the 'global system' into all the regions and offices.

Estimated completion dates were late 1993, early 1995 and mid 1996 respectively. In 1992 the North America region (NA) had started to embark on a review of its ageing IBM S/34. At the same time, Singapore was also looking to upgrade their fragmented PC-based installation to cope with the rapid growth in the region. Both sites thus became candidates for the development of the prototype and also as pilot sites for further implementation.

The Pilot Project(s)

The FIST team agreed to a first project milestone of June 1994 - nine months hence - by which time it would have:

- selected technology;
- completed the prototype;
- tested and modified it as a pilot; and
- gone live with the new system in North America and Singapore, as the first global standard systems.

The requirements for NA were set out as a 'benchmark' for all other sites. However, Singapore were quite concerned when the FIST team restricted itself to developing a data model for North America as a global 'benchmark model' – and comparing it with the South East Asia region, instead of investigating their needs *in loco*. When the FIST team subsequently found a "90 - 95% match" between the two regions, the head of the Singapore office opted out of the Pilot. He felt strongly that, as North America's predominant business is in the industrial produce market, any model based on their requirements would not at all fit South East Asia ("nor Europe, for that matter"), as their scope of business mainly covers the consumer and food manufacturing markets. He was also very critical of what he called the "top-down-approach" taken by FIST. With very little participation by the regions, he feared the systems would be missing most significant, actual requirements of the local business - "just like the other past failures of the Computer Centre". By the end of 1993, North America was therefore the only pilot site.

As the North America pilot missed the June 1994 deadline, a Request for Proposal (RFP), asking for firm quotes for software, hardware and communications technology to be used internationally in the Co-op's 130 offices in 35 countries, was issued to ORACLE, IBM and UNISYS. The RFP was based on the "benchmark" model, which was by now also criticised by the North America management as at "too high a level" to be useful for requirements specification.

In view of this spreading resistance, the FIST team enlisted the help of the CEO, who issues a sharply worded edict to the regional management teams, ordering them to give FIST all necessary help. This silenced the North America executive and brought the project back into life.

After a rapid evaluation by the FIST team with some North America input, ORACLE was chosen as the main provider for data base middleware and, together with DATALOGIX (then a medium sized New Jersey based software house) for applications software. Hardware and communications technology was not selected.

At the same time, the 'benchmark model' was now compared with Europe and another "90% to 95%" match was declared by the FIST team. However, the regional manager for Europe echoed the sentiments of his North American counterpart when he remarked that "These models are so general, they'd make Disney look like us." The European region, wary of the CEO support the FIST team could enlist, used this 'difference' in the models to distance itself from the project and subsequently opted out of the FIST programme, indicating to the Co-op HQ that it would much prefer to pursue its own regional information technology strategy.

At this stage, to counter the renewed, strongly mounting resistance to their vision of one global, standard system for every subsidiary office, the FIST team embarked on a design review to modify the global standard design such that it would become easier for regional and local business management to accept their information system proposals. They began to look at what applications should be the same throughout the Group and where the global standard could be loosened, and which application areas could be different for local subsidiaries.

The outcome of these definitions was a re-formulation of the 'standard' global system, which has the main business operation ETC (the stream-lined "Enquiry-To-Cash" process), as the framework for the 'Core' information systems. This then leaves a residue of loosely defined "manufacturing and marketing operations "as the 'Local' applications to be selected by each office individually.

Having published these new 'Framework' details, and announced the ETC framework as the new 'global operations paradigm', the FIST team began with the implementation and modifications of the software in North America in September 1994.

Nearly immediately they encountered serious problems: The manufacturing and distribution modules – selected from the 'benchmark models' - would not conform with the real business processes in the regional operations they were expected to support. The changes to the software chosen in the RFP exercise were estimated to cost $1,8m. Moreover, at this time, Oracle were negotiating with Datalogix about absorbing the Datalogix Distribution modules into their own ones. For the duration of these negotiations no work on the software was done.

In response, FIST decreed that the North America region must adapt its operating procedures and processes to conform to the new operations paradigm. In order to achieve this, a 'Business-Process-Reengineering' sub-project was embarked on in the North America region. Regional management, however, maintained that there was very little to be gained from such a major upheaval and resisted the implementation of the re-engineering project. By mid 1995 North America reached an agreement to abandon the pilot efforts and to alter its software so that it reflected their local requirements.

In early 1995, the Co-op decided to open a new office in the Middle East region, in Dubai and by mid 1995, there were 12 people in the office. To replace North America, the FIST team selected Dubai as the new pilot site to test out the common global system for the Co-op. The first installation was going to be the 'standard' Oracle Financials together with business procedures defined around the system. The first target date for completion was September 1995. However, for want of adequate local support, the systems could not be developed on site - it was therefore decided to develop the first prototype at head office. In

November 1996 the standard Oracle Financials were handed over to Dubai as a working system.

FIST now presented the Dubai system as the successful global pilot, demonstrating a set of economics to show the benefits of the global information system. Based on this justification, they announced a Global Roll-Out programme, starting from early 1997, to implement FIST throughout the world. However, many of the regional executive members doubted first of all the relevance of the Dubai economic justification case and secondly questioned how representative a tiny office in a fringe market could be as a model for a global system. No agreement was reached as to how FIST would proceed.

Developments concerning FIST at the head office

The major difficulties with the FIST project, especially the missed deadlines, the significant costs (by 1995 approx. $ 8m) without any noticeable results and the refusal by major regions to accept the FIST system began to raise doubts in the mind of the CEO. In mid 1996 he commissioned Ernst & Young to evaluate the FIST projects. Their report was critical of FIST as being overly ambitious and not achievable within the time frame or the existing project set-up. This proved to be a turning point: The CEO re-aligned the IT portfolio - and with it FIST - into the Finance department, whose General Manager had been an open critic of the project for a long time. As early as March 1995 he had called for a critical review of the "real" reasons for wanting to spend $21m and had advocated that business reasons should drive the project, not technology. In his first meeting with the FIST team (in September 1997) he terminated the project and called for a broadly based study of global versus local information technology strategy.

FINDINGS AND INTERPRETATION OF THE CASE

There are three fundamental building blocks in Grounded Theory research tradition: the 'seed concepts', which determine the field of research; the 'categories' and their 'properties', i.e. the various facts in the case and their aspects and manifestations; a system of 'relations' binds the categories together into an emerging theory. Glaser & Strauss, (1967) see theory as a process, in which 'categories' are directly grounded in observed fact, whereas 'relations' are conceptualised by inference from the unfolding story in order to bring to it a temporal, correlational; or causal order.

The analysis of the case is based on interviews with key management and staff of the Co-op in Australasia, North America and Europe. Furthermore, a selection of internal documents (memos, minutes and reports) was used to underpin and extend the information gathered in the interviews.

The core categories found in the Co-op case fell into two domains, depending on whether the category stems from the business or information technology arena. In both domains the factors contributed to considerable dynamics in the interplay between categories.

The six core categories in the business dynamics domain can be summarised as follows:

1. Nature of the Business; the aspects of the Co-op's business specifically relevant for the global IS project
2. Global Business Strategy; the relevant aspects of the Co-op's current global business strategy
3. Lack of IT Experience; the Co-op's inexperience and lack of "IT awareness" culture
4. Migration of Global Strategy; the changes (and their history) of the Co-op's global business strategy

5. Tradition of Local Autonomy; the degree of freedom enjoyed and defended by regional and local management
6. Rejection of Global IS; actions and manoeuvres to avoid the acceptance of a global standard system

The business dynamics categories are the main originators of influence over the Co-op's position vis-à-vis information technology and the international information system. The Nature of the Business, is the most fundamental influence. Its structural uniqueness determines the essential characteristics of the Global Business Strategy. Similarly, the particulars of its external - market and industry - evolution have caused this strategy to change in a distinct Migration of Global Strategy. All three of these factors combine to form a Tradition of Autonomy among the Co-op's local offices and regions.

Although assisted by other influences, this tradition of autonomy is the main shaper of an attitude of Rejection of the Global Information System, which in itself is then a major influence in the development of the global system. The other information technology related category is a Lack of IT Experience in information technology matters at the Co-op's headquarters. The political element of the Co-op's nature of business is a partial reason for this. In turn, the Co-op's naivety in information technology at the centre reinforces the Tradition of Local Autonomy, this time with respect to information systems. Figure 6 below shows the interplay of the major categories and relations within the business dynamics domain.

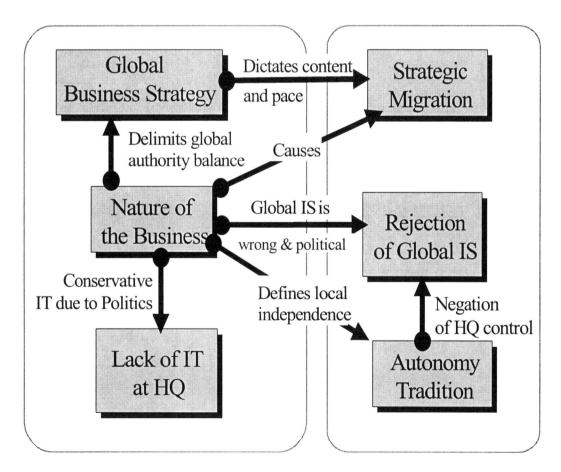

Figure 6: Business Dynamics: Main Categories and Major Relations

There are seven core category families in the information technology field:

1. Analysis (methods and paradigms); the main assumptions and paradigms governing the analysis of the business requirements for the global IS
2. Capacity, the level of conceptual capability; i.e. the ability to conceptualise and think through complex issues
3. IS Professional Skills; quality of the professional skills brought to bear on the systems development process
4. IS Initiative; the global IS project was initiated by IS, and not from the business
5. Domestic Mindset; inadequacy in the understanding of international issues and situations
6. IS by Force; using political power play to force the business to accept the global IS
7. Global Standard IS Design; the standardised, centrist nature of the global IS design ("One system fits all")

Four 'conditioning' factors (as the 'independent variables') shape the character of the three 'effector' categories (as the 'dependent variables') in this group. 'Effector' categories are the ones engaged in the major interaction between the IT ad Business domains.

The most fundamental conditioner category – termed 'Capacity' - is the level and degree of of conceptual capability brought to bear on the design of the system, i.e. the ability to conceptualise and think through thorny issues. The lack (or low level) of it has had a dampening effect on the other conditioning categories, but most of all on Analysis, the repository of the (mostly erroneous) paradigms used in the system building activity. These were complemented by the (often low) quality of the Information Systems Professional Skills brought to bear and the evidence of a pronounced inadequacy to comprehend international issues, summarised in the Domestic Mindset category.

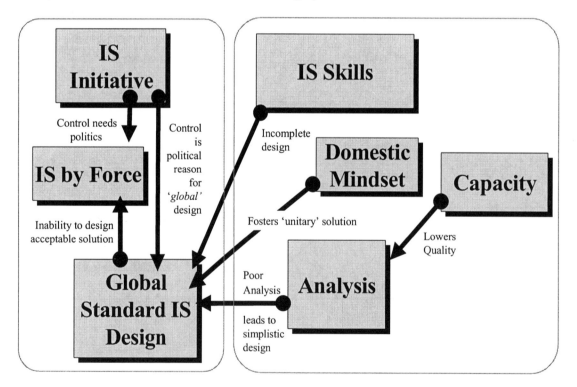

Figure 7: Categories and Relations in the Information Technology domain

In concert they affect most of all the standardised, centrist nature of the international system, brought together in the Global Standard IS Design category. This is the main interface with the business domain. The two other effectors are:

- the fact that the whole project is an IS Initiative, in response to perceived inefficiencies in the international operations of the Co-op, and with a strong element of using information systems as instruments of central control;
- a consequence of the inability to deal in a rational way with the business people's rejection of the global system and therefore resorting to political power-play. This was termed IS by Force. Figure 7 shows the interplay between the major categories within the Information Technology domain.

'Capacity', the (in)ability to conceptualise and think through thorny issues, has the most detailed influences on the other categories – because of its nature as a fundamental category and a basic requirement for information systems design and development. The greater complexity of an international information systems environment places greater significance on this factor. Similarly, the 'Analysis' category (the repository for the major methods and paradigms applied in the systems design process) exerts a broad influence across most other factors in the information technology domain. The fallacy of several of the underlying paradigms acts as a direct influence on the character of the Global IS Design:

- Globally standardised nature of the application systems) reflects the belief that they are all serving identical, merely geographically separate, businesses; consequently;
- Globally standardised technology (again, 'one fits all') is stipulated because of the erroneous assumption that identical applications require identical hardware to run on.

The summarisation level displayed in Figure 7 (and Figure 6) masks the fact that the interaction between the categories is multidimensional and very richly interwoven.

Figure **8** below gives an outline demonstration of the complexity and intricacy of the inter-relationships between the core categories in the Information Technology Domain.

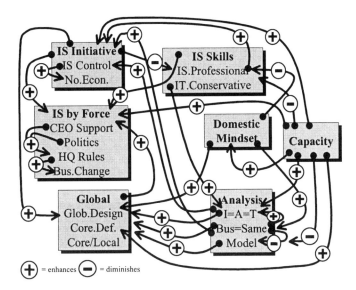

Figure 8: Overview of all Interaction between Categories in the IT Domain

The following paragraphs set out and discuss in more detail the interaction between categories and their sub-categories within the information technology domain.

CATEGORY DYNAMICS IN THE INFORMATION TECHNOLOGY DOMAIN

Each category, and where appropriate the sub-category which constitute it, are described in turn in the following paragraphs and their inter-relationships are set out. The independent variables, i.e. the 'conditioning' categories are covered first, followed by the three 'effectors' or dependent variables.

Analysis

This category encompasses the various processes of assimilating and understanding the realities of the Co-op's international business in preparation for designing an information system for its use. This core category, which is the consolidation of the process's quality aspects, comprises three categories, namely

1. Equating Information with Application and Technology Infrastructure ("*I=A=T*" for short) is the fallacy that a global, standard system on standard hardware is the only solution to common information requirements. This uncritical belief has the nature of a 'paradigm', i.e. a largely unquestioned framework;
2. Business Sameness, i.e. the – superficial – notion that all the businesses in the Group are essentially the same and can therefore be supported by the same information system, irrespective of location size or nature of the business. This simplistic view resulted from the application of too high a level of abstraction in the conceptualisation of business goals and processes.
3. Data/Business Modelling turned out to be an altogether insufficient tool for the specification of functional requirements of business processes and operations; furthermore, it proved inadequate for comparisons between different local/regional offices. The modelling techniques were carried out at too high a level of abstraction, so *eo ipso* returned very general models with a high degree of similarity, although the underlying businesses were significantly and substantially different from each other in several of dimensions. In this way, they were significantly deepening the Business Sameness fallacy described above;

The Analysis category has a major influence on the Global Design (which is detailed under that heading). It furthermore influences the IS Initiation category, where the Business Sameness assumption was instrumental in initiating the project of standardising the international information technology infrastructure throughout the Group – which in turn lead to FIST.

The I=A=T sub-category had an influence on the IS Department's interpretation of the change in international business strategy the Co-op undertook from 1992 onwards (i.e. the *Business Strategy Migration* to introduce a *transnational* strategy). The increased need for centrally defined, standard, information throughout the group was – mistakenly - interpreted by the IS people as a turn to a *global* strategy(i.e. towards strong central domination) for which a standard, global system would be a suitably stringent control mechanism. Thus I=A=T is also influential for introducing the IS Control component of IS Initiation.

Information Systems Skills

The quality of the 'trade-craft', the professional skills applied to the information systems project received a strong emphasis throughout the case history. This has two aspects:

1. the degree of professionalism, i.e. the adherence – or not - to what is considered good practice in information systems work;
2. the level of 'state-of –the-art' inherent in the design and technology architecture of the international information system.

The degree of "IS Professionalism" expressed throughout the case is low and is reflected in many incidents of significant deviation from 'good practice'. Examples are:

- Analysis and subsequent specifications of requirements happened at a very high level (because of *Data/Business Modelling*); as the basis for a global request for proposal (RFP) and subsequently as the foundation for a worldwide system, the this was not useful and often wrong;
- Mis-management of the RFP process:
    o   not giving vendors enough time to prepare a global proposal; and subsequently
    o   eliminating two serious contenders by applying mechanical (point-scoring) evaluation methods to their proposal document;
- Poor estimating resulting in seriously unrealistic timeframes for developing an international information system and implementing it around the world;
- Confusion about the implementation steps, especially the role of business process paradigms, prototypes and pilots;
- Sparse project management and project planning for the development and implementation phases;
- Refusal to involve users in the development had two detrimental consequences:
    o   it lead to incomplete and wrong requirements specifications in the first instance;
    o   users did not accept the resulting system as it was not 'their own' – and it had the wrong functionality;

The notion that the information systems strategy and architecture is below 'state-of-the-art' forms the "IS Conservatism" sub-category. It is to a significant part anchored in the Co-op's *Lack of Information Technology Sophistication* and their conservatism in all things computers. Subsequently, the global systems project started out in the mid-1990s with an early 1980s technology architecture, i.e. minicomputers, relational databases and private communication networks. It was not making allowance for the – by then established - client/server concepts and the architectural implications of the – already firmly emergent - Internet.

This (lack of) "State-of-the-Art", i.e. the outdated information technology architecture, serves to reinforce the "$I=A=T$" category. With 1980s technology, equating *Information* with *Application* with *Technology Infrastructure* was often the only technical option to achieve accurate, and congruous, information across diverse locations.

Domestic Mindset

This core category is about applying a set of predominantly domestic experiences, parameters and knowledge to the task of developing and implementing an international information system. The major characteristics of this category are:

1. Ignorance of the individually different business conditions and cultural environments in the countries where regional and local offices are situated;

2. Neglect to find out about business differences with a significant impact on the global systems design;
   Example: the "standard account structure" of the global system (and its 56 digit code) is illegal in most of Europe – where account structures are prescribed in tax statutes;

3. Failure to understand the intricacies of the organisational (and political) considerations which govern vendor support for international locations;
   Example: the North America office, 30kms north of ORACLE's HQ and World Centre of Excellence for financial software, was supported – for internal commission reasons - by ORACLE in Australasia;

4. Underestimating the time and effort required for managing and progressing international projects;
   Example: The initial estimate for developing the global system and then implementing it in 130 offices in 35 countries was for 18 months to 2 years;

5. Failure to find a method for specifying requirements for all local offices before most of them are invalidated and superseded by changes in business processes and operation.
   Example: Whilst the IS people at HQ were specifying the North America requirements the business changed – long before the system was written.

The parochial concentration on the narrow environment has a direct influence on (the quality of) Analysis, where an inability to see beyond local boundaries strengthens the *Business Sameness* category. The uncritical application of domestic parameters, especially when estimating project effort or assessing vendor capabilities, has a negative effect on the Information Systems Skills category, where it further lowers the *low professionalism* aspect. Ignorance, and neglecting to combat it, worsens the difficulties with identifying the appropriate *Core/Local* balance in the Global Design category.

Capacity

Referred to by one of the Co-op's executives as *"the...general measure of intellectual horsepower"*, this core category assimilates the qualities of being able to (a) conceptualise and abstract from (usually complex and convoluted) real-life situations, (b) understand and internalise intricate business process and operations settings; and to (c) develop from this base a set of solutions which are logically sound and can be implemented.

This capacity to work through problems manifested itself predominantly in its negative form, i.e. by a low level of problem dissection and solving capability. Examples are:

- Confused and woolly concepts (such as the A and B Product classification) could not be resolved and straightened into workable information systems concepts;
- A 60-digit concatenated "standard product identifier" in response to the requirements of unified production planning and allocation is a demonstration of the inability to go beyond simplistic, trivial 'solutions' which are practically inoperable;

The general nature of this category means that it has an influence on most of the other conditioners. It diminishes the quality of Analysis overall, but more specifically

1. it seems to be a cause for the incapacity to pitch the *Data/Business Modelling* at the right level;

2. in the *Business Sameness* category it enhances the tendency to ignore legitimate differences in regional/local businesses;
3. the inadequacy of conceptual reasoning is (together with the lack of *State-of-the-Art* thinking) responsible for the *I=A=T* fallacy.

Within the Information Systems Skills category, it tends to decrease the *low professionalism* further and it also reinforces the tendency to conservatism in the *State-of-the-Art* category.

The propensity to judge international environments through the eyes of domestic experience in the Domestic Mindset is strengthened by the ineptitude for penetrating environmental, cultural and business process differences.

Not being very good at analysing and solving problems also influences the 'effector' categories. The inability to work through the arguments and issues unearthed in the *Rejection of the Global Information Systems* category in a rational, logical and practical way is an indirect influence – and cause – of the IS by Force category in which politicising the argument is used as an escape from providing solutions.

IS Initiative is influenced in the same indirect way. Lack of understanding lead to a misinterpretation of the *Business Strategy Migration* where the re-establishing of control in a *Transnational* sense is interpreted by the IS people as a return to centrist power in the sense of the historical *Global* strategy. A standard, global, information system was seen as the control mechanism best suited for this, thereby creating the seeds for IS Control. Figure 9 below shows this.

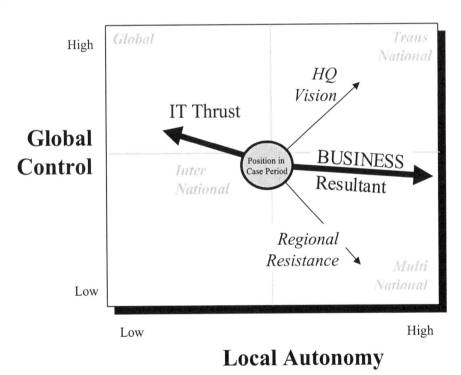

Figure 9: Vectors of Strategic Thrust in the Co-op

Regional management puts in a show of resistance against the – suspected – increase in central control and makes its own case of increased regional and local independence from head office. Depicted as vectors, they go for minimal control and maximum autonomy, whereas the CEO's strategic vision balances more regional autonomy with an equal amount of central control over global concerns (e.g. branding, global product strategies, etc). The Information Technology people misunderstand both and push strongly for a policy of full central control exerted by a globally standardised information systems. In the end, the Information Technology strategic thrust is nearly diametrically opposed to the – resultant – direction of where the business wants to go.

IS Initiative

The information systems department in the early 1990s initiated the Global Information Systems Project, i.e. it did not stem from the Business side of the Co-op. The IS people did so mainly because the international information systems architecture as it was then was an untidy conglomerate of hardware and software, with no common standards, and very few shared applications. This had lead to a high level of duplication of effort, processes and inventories in the individual offices and regions. IS subsequently presumed that a common information systems and technology platform would be more efficient. However, the business side had difficulties understanding why they should undergo a series of fundamental upheavals in their business processes , which, as far as they could see, had not found wanting for business reasons. To them the Global IS Project was a 'solution without a problem' – a significant contributor to the *Rejection of the Global Information Systems* category.

The corollary of this initiative and its consequences for the history of the project are found in two other main components that make up this core category. They are:

1. The business side always maintained that there was No Economic Justification for the global system, pointing to the efficacy of their - functioning – local systems. The cost justifications (in terms of people savings, etc) brought forward by the IS people lacked credibility with the business who thought them to be political window-dressing;
2. The interpretation of the central IS as central Control in disguise;

The political nature of the IS Control category also produces a disincentive for the business side to get 'involved' in the global information systems project, thus perpetuating the lack of Economic Justification for the system.

The IS Initiative has major influences on the other two 'effector' categories. The IS as Control element is the main political reason for the centrist, standardised character of the *Global Design* category. Similarly, the factual core of IS Initiative, and especially, again, the IS as Control element are the root causes of the *IS by Force* factor.

IS Initiative itself is influenced and shaped by a number of categories. Outside the Information Technology Dynamics, two Business Dynamics categories affect it, namely

1. *Nature of the Business,* which heightens the necessity to receive accurate, timely information in great detail and very fast; this, in turn, was used to legitimise the political motives which created IS as Control; and
2. *Business Strategy Migration,* where the transformation to a *transnational* strategy was misread as a return to full, centrist direction and control.

The IS Initiative is part of a cause –effect chain, which is a major part of the *Force Field* interaction between the two domains. It interacts with the *Rejection of the Global Information Systems* on the business side and with *IS by Force* in the information technology domain. This is detailed below.

Global Design

This is the largest category in terms of attributable occurrences, of which it attracted 82. The core is made up of three main categories. The major one refers to the centrist, globally standardised, design of the system. The other two focus on the definition of what should be the scope of this common information system on the one hand, and on the difficulties of establishing such a definition on the other hand.

The Global Nature of the system is the collation of all the standardised, globally equal elements of the information systems and technology architecture. The business people generally comment on it negatively, reflecting how much this category is a causal factor for the *Rejection of the Global Information Systems*. The focal point of the negative comments is the impossibility to implement such a rigidly standard system over the widely differing regional and local offices. Specific points raised were:

- It would be wasteful to implement a large system in small offices;
- It would not be possible to implement in a reasonable timeframe;
- It had not and cannot be specified in sufficient detail;
- It will not achieve the cost savings;
- Management and support of the global system are not happening;
- Production planning and product allocation need to be centrally managed; everything else is too difficult to run from HQ.

Positive arguments – from IS people – are strongly influenced by the *Business Sameness* argument, which itself is reinforced through the other *Analysis* components (i.e. *Data/Business Modelling* and *I=A=T*). Also visible is the influence of the political thinking inherent in *IS as Control,* which shaped the global design principles.

The Common Core category contains all the arguments concerning the definition of the scope of the common, global system. Initially (showing the influence of *IS as Control*) this was to be mainly the financial systems, but was then enhanced by sales order and inventory applications. However, this definition changed considerably over time and had three phases:

1. Initially there was going to be a local content, but in the end all systems were going to be 'global';
2. The common system would reflect the streamlined, standardised 'core processes' (the result of a planned, global BPR exercise);
3. Lastly (after all of the above had failed to materialise, and the project had changed management) the notion of a 'thin' core, containing the technology infrastructure, was given. In this phase, common applications would be 'offered' but nobody would have to accept them.

In practical terms, only a standard financial system for a small subsidiary was ever implemented.

The Core/Local Split is the distillation of the difficulties, and ultimately the inability, in coming to a definition of what should be core and what should be local – in terms of information systems, technology and 'streamlined' business processes. Again, the effort to resolve this problem went through a number of stages:

1. All information systems would be global and standard;
2. Only the 'administrative' systems would be global and standard;

3. Only the 'strategic' systems would be global and standard;
4. What is 'important to the Co-op's business' would be supported by a global and standard information system;

After all had failed to work, the new definition was 'to be linked to the Co-op's and the regional strategies' and would be decided in conjunction with the local management. All the 'conditioners' influence Global Design:

*   *Analysis/I=A=T* makes it difficult to see beyond a standardised technology and applications platform, i.e. the Global Nature of the international system. This is further reinforced by *Capability*: the simplest form of an international system is a globally standardised one – a low level of analytical capability makes this the simplistic, trivial, default solution;
*   *Analysis/Business Sameness* leads to the adoption of unsuitable and unaccepted Common Core definitions;
*   The use of unsuitable business process specification tools in *Analysis/Model* result in overly simple models of very little use for defining the Core/Local Split. This is further aggravated by the lack of understanding for regional/local issues inherent in the *Domestic Mindset* category;
*   All the conceptual difficulties with seeing beyond rigid standardisation are further enhanced by the shortcomings of *Information Systems Skills*, especially the inability to arrive at requirements specifications at a level appropriate for systems design and development.

The *IS as Control* element of *IS Initiative* is the political cause for the Global Nature of the system. This is especially highlighted by the fact that a unified financial system is at the heart of the global systems concept: Financials are the first global software included in the global design, followed by distribution software (which, however, was never implemented anywhere).

IS by Force

This core category comprises the activities to do with the attempt to implement the information system by dictating the regions' and local offices' business operations from the centre, using political power. The category is made up of four sub-categories:

1. When the resistance to the global system threatened to stop the project, the project team enlisted CEO Support in an effort to overcome the regions' rational arguments with political clout;
2. Using Political Arguments to disarm users' reasons for withholding acceptance of the system. This is in part a consequence of *Capability,* specifically the inability to resolve those objections in a rational way. In part, too, the political *Nature of the* Co-op's *Business* is an influence here;
3. Both 1. and 2. then contribute to HQ Rules, which is the attitude that the global system will be implemented by central fiat and that the regions and local offices will accept the system and implement it as, when and how they are told;
4. The application of 3. subsequently created a policy and principle, that, if there are discrepancies between the business operations and the system, the Business will Change, not the system.

Of the 'conditioners', the lack of *Capability* to conceptualise and resolve the reasons why the business people were rejecting the global system is a main influence. This is further enhanced by the lack of user involvement, to the point of ruling it out altogether, which is part of the *Information Systems Skills* category.

Linked to the whole syndrome of failure to deal with the users' reactions to the global system, is the influence of the effector *IS Initiative,* which excludes the regions and local offices from the start. Furthermore, the *IS as Control* element of that category, with its inherently political character, is closely related to the manipulative motivation which powers IS by Force. The main influence, however, is indirect and stems from *Global Design*, the root cause of *Rejection of the Global System*, which, in turn, evokes IS by Force.

THE FORCE FIELD

Whilst most of the categories affect each other in a number of ways, the two dynamics domains seem to set up a force field (in the sense of Lewin, 1952), as an arena for the interactions between the business and information technology interests. The force field is dominated by the interplay of two key categories. The major interplay is between the Global Design category, which is a causal factor in the business Rejection of the Global System. Figure 10 below illustrates this.

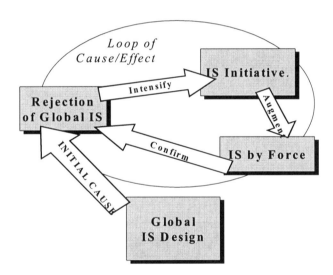

**Figure 10. Interaction Cycle: Rejection of the International Information System –
Reaction by the Information Technology function**

The interactions between the opposing sides of the force field were driven by the confrontational stances of the business and IT 'factions' across a range of issues. The international information systems project provided a – convenient - focal point of the clash between the antagonistic self-interest of both central and regional business entities versus the information technology faction.

The forces acting in that field are of considerable magnitude. Initially, the conflict was a clash of divergent interests and goals – regional management wanting to preserve their Tradition of Autonomy and the IT people bent on using their international information systems as a means of stringent head-office control. Rejection was made easy because the design of the system was so obviously not appropriate for the business.

However, after the initial Rejection of the Global Information System category, a series of interactions developed which eventually engaged the opposing sides in a cycle of rejection and reaction which in the end proved strong enough to stop the information systems project altogether.

The cycle starts with the Rejection of the Global Information System in response to the IS Initiative which proposed a globally identical system and technology with uniform functionality. This in turn lead to an intensification of the IS Initiative category as the IT people now reacted to this. After initial attempts to incorporate business objections into the Global IS Design floundered for reasons of deficient Systems Building Capacity, the IS people resorted to political means, IS by Force and the business reacted in kind. Table 2 below shows the case's iterations through this circle of adversarial altercations.

Table 2. Iteration through the Rejection/Reaction Cycle

Cycle	Rejection	Reaction
1	The initial FIST proposal is rejected for it's misalignment with Global Business Strategy	IT tries to prove that all business are the same; ergo, the global standard will work
2	As this is obviously incorrect, the business suspects central control as FIST's motive	IT enlists the CEO to order the Regions to implement the standard FIST
3	Regions demonstrate their different products, markets and business processes	IT propose Business Process Re-Engineering to align business operations with FIST
4	Regions and Ernst & Young reject BPR as unwarranted, overly ambitious and costly	IT shows vastly favourable global benefit projections (based on Dubai's experience)
5	CEO stops FIST and re-aligns the IT Dept.	

CONCLUSION AND FUTURE RESEARCH

The Co-op's case yielded a rich set of categories and relations, of a relevant and detailed nature so as to encourage the beginnings of the formulation of a substantive theory of the factors that affect and the shape and the process of building an international information systems. This vindicates the use of cases and the grounded theory method as a vehicle to elicit insights into this complex field.

The case of the Co-op's attempt to generate an international information system indicates the importance of strategy alignment between the multi-national firm and its information technology function in terms of the Global Business Strategy followed by the enterprise. The case further showed that the requirements for professionalism and in-depth understanding of international issues are essential for even starting an international information systems project. Absence of any of these ingredients seems conducive to establishing an environment for political interaction, which is unproductive and does not further the implementation and acceptance of the international information systems. Engaging in political battles, especially, detracts from the objectives of the exercise and ultimately results in the demise of the project altogether.

The case has uncovered two main principles of factor interaction in international information systems: Firstly, there is a natural force field between the business and the IT people in the design and implementation processes for an international information system;

Secondly, the notion that there is a force field in which the dynamics between central and local business people are played out; Thirdly, that the interaction between business and IT people take the form of a cause-and-effect loop, where any action by one of the actors initiates a response by the other; These interactions are either rational or political, depending on two conditions:

1. If the international information systems fits the Global Business Strategy of the business, then the chances of its acceptance by the business people are enhanced and interactions will be predominantly rational;
2. Limited capacity on the side of the IT people to analyse the complexities of an international information systems and to understand that it is different from a domestic information system can lead to irrational interchanges and antagonistic politics – and eventually the termination of the international information systems project..

The case produced a comprehensive set of basic, core-type, categories and a number of convincing relationships between them, which are very plausible candidates for establishing a first set of theoretical concepts. However, in order to start formulating a more detailed – and verifiable – substantive theory a number of the categories need more detail before they are 'saturated' in terms of the grounded theory methodology. 'Theoretical sampling' for similar or contrasting cases needs now to occur to make this possible.

STUDY QUESTIONS

1. Describe the Bartlett & Ghoshal framework of the global business strategies a multi-national company might adopt.

2. Explain how the Co-op's global business strategies changed during the firm's history.

3. What is the relevance of global business strategies to the way in which an MNC organises its international information technology? Discuss.

4. Altogether 12 main factors were found in the case, which influence the acceptance of an international information system by its users. How were they grouped and what were their main interactions with one another?

5. Define and discuss 4 main factors for IIS acceptance emerging from the Co-op case and describe how they interact.

6. Describe and discuss the generic architecture that sets out the 'topology' of an international information system.

7. What were the main factors in the rejection of FIST by its users?

8. Describe the cycle of user rejection and the IT people's reaction

REFERENCES

Bartlett, C.A., Ghoshal, S. (1989). *Managing Across Borders: The Transnational Solution*. Boston. Harvard Business School Press

Butler Cox plc. (1991). *Globalisation: The Information Technology Challenge.* Amdahl Executive Institute Research Report. London.

Cash, J.I. Jr., McFarlan, W.F. and McKenney, J.L. (1992*). Corporate Information Systems - The Issues Facing Senior Executives.* Homewood. Irwin.

Earl, M. J. (1989). *Management Strategies for Information Technology.* Prentice-Hall, London.

Glaser, B.G., and Strauss, A.L., (1967). *The discovery of grounded theory.* Aldine Publishing Company, Hawthorne, New York.

Ives, B., Jarvenpaa, S.L. (1991). Applications of Global Information Technology : Key Issues for Management. *MIS Quarterly.*

Jarvenpaa, S.L., Ives, B. 1994. Organisational Fit and Flexibility: IT Design Principles for a Globally Competing Firm. *Research in Strategic Management and Information Technology,* Vol 1, pp1-39

Keen, P. G. W., Bronsema, G. S. and Auboff, S. (1982). Implementing Common Systems: One Organisation's Experience. *Systems, Objectives and Solutions.* 2.

King, W. R. and Sethi, V. (1993). Developing Transnational Information Systems: A Case Study. *OMEGA International Journal of Management Science,* 21, 1, 53-59.

Konsynski, B. R. and Karimi, J. (1993). On the Design of Global Information Systems. *Globalization, Technology and Competition.* Bradley, S.P., Hausman, J.A. and Nolan, R.L. (Ed's). Boston. Harvard Business Press.

Lehmann, H.P. 1996a A Research Note on the methodology and domain of international information systems research. *Working Paper of the Department of Management Science and Information Systems, University of Auckland,* May 1996

Lehmann, H.P. 1996b Towards a common architecture paradigm for the global application of information systems. *Proceedings Of The IFIP WG 8.4 Working Conference On The International Office Of The Future,* Tucson, Arizona, April 1996.

Lewin, K., 1952: Field theory in social science : selected theoretical papers. (D Cartwright, Ed.) Tavistock, London, United Kingdom.

Miles, M. B., Huberman, A. M. (1994) *Qualitative Data Analysis.* Sage Publications, Thousand Oaks.

Sankar, C., Apte, U. and Palvia, P.(1993). Global Information Architectures: Alternatives and Trade-offs. *International Journal of Information Management,* (1993), 13, 84-93.

20

Successful Implementation of ERP Systems for Multinationals: Using Control and Coordination Artifacts

Steven John Simon
Mercer University, USA

ABSTRACT

The dominant market for Enterprise Resource Planning (ERP) vendors has traditionally been the largest of multinational corporations (MNCs). Until recently, most vendors (SAP, PeopleSoft, Oracle, etc) have promoted a "one size fits all" solution built upon "industry best practices." This approach forced organizations to either conform to the "industry best practices" and configuration suggested by vendors and implementation consultants or embark upon extremely costly reconfiguration of their ERP package. This chapter explores an innovation in SAP's R/3 package - Application Link Embedding (ALE) - which allows the organization to disperse the package throughout its globally distribute units. The chapter reviews the concepts of control, coordination, their trade-offs, and Bartlett and Ghoshal's topology of MNC strategy. ERP systems are introduced along with the discussion of their strengths. Two architectures are suggested as a basis for system configuration - tightly and loosely coupled systems. Next, the concepts of control and coordination and Bartlett and Ghoshal's topology are combined to create a strategic orientation for the MNC. Finally, this strategic orientation is compared against an ideal ERP configuration or enterprise information architecture.

INTRODUCTION

Fast changing market requirements and fiercer competition mean that corporate business processes are subject to unrelenting pressure to adapt and be modified. The key factors driving these changes are global competition, ever-shorter production and product cycles, and shrinking profit margins. Speed, flexibility, and simplicity are the crucial ingredients for the success of business process reengineering. But the individual processes involved are not getting simpler. Increasingly, they are being extended to embrace multiple companies, customers, suppliers, and autonomous business units within the enterprise. In this scenario, users are calling for economical and easy-to-use distributed applications. This goal requires a delicate balance between highly integrated business application systems on one side and enough decoupling to permit temporary stand-alone operation at the same time.

Boar (1999) classifies the current global environment as that of hypercompetition. Hypercompetition is a state of intense and often lethal competition caused by the concurrence of market factors including power shift to customers, rapid decline of entry barriers, accelerating technology, and deregulation. These forces have led to an evolution in MNC strategies which yield strategic orientation and structures ranging from the highly centralized *global* enterprise to the dispersed *transnational* organization. Reliance on information technology is common across all organization structures. The control/coordination orientation of an MNC can help in determining the most suitable information architecture. An examination of large and medium sized (Fortune 5000) MNCs finds that the majority of these firms are turning to ERP systems to assist them in leveraging environmental forces in their favor and against their competition. For a firm, ERP packages provide a single system solution leading to a tightly coupled (a single highly integrated system) information architecture. This tightly coupled system - while providing advantages of a standardized and highly controlled environment - is often not the optimum architecture for a widely dispersed MNC, especially if that firm has subsidiaries that operate in a semi-autonomous manner. As a result, MNCs are posed with the problem of how to distribute their information assets without sacrificing the desired high degree of integration.

This chapter examines the appropriateness and effectiveness of the distributed information architecture in the context of global enterprise resource planning (ERP) implementation. Specifically, the chapter 1) investigates the relationship between such appropriateness and effectiveness and two key processes of integration - coordination and control, 2) reviews a framework to provide an organization with help in selecting the optimum information architecture, and 3) identifies an optimum ERP environment for organization structures.

Tutorial:

Control/coordination Artifacts

Control and coordination are integral elements of all organizations. Control is used to maintain governance over people or organizational elements. Within an IS context, control is used by imposing rules and regulations on the utilization of equipment or the access to and storage of information. Coordination, which seeks the achieve the same goals, is considered to be implemented by connecting varius people or parts of the organization through the information systems. They are generally used in conjunction with each other and not mutually exclusive.

Information Architecture

Information architecture is a high-level map of information requirements of an organization. It is a personnel, organization, and technology independent profile of the major information categories used within an enterprise. It is also viewed as a set of policies and rules that govern an organization's actual and planned arrangements of computers, data, human resources, communications, software, hardware, and management responsibilities. IA structures are varied and include tightly couples system models where applications and data reside on a single centralized machine for the entire organization to loosely couple system models which disperse applications and data throughout the enterprise. IA also extends to the locus of decision making within an organization.

CONTROL, COORDINATION, AND THEIR TRADEOFFS

Control can be defined as a process which brings about adherence to a goal or target through the exercise of power or authority. Control is also used to manage the integration of activities within an MNC. The importance of control as an integrating mechanism within organizations stems from the fact that it reduces uncertainty, increases predictability and ensures that behaviors originating in separate parts of the organization are compatible and support common organizational goals (Egelhoff 1984). A wide range of organizational mechanisms exist to manage activities. These mechanisms are usually manifested as constraints or parameters imposed on subsidiaries by headquarters for the purpose of managing or tracking subsidiary performance, usually in the form of standardized reporting procedures. Control mechanisms can be expected to vary with the structure of firms operating in the global environment. These mechanisms include efforts at centralization and formalization of departments and in the context of this chapter, take the form of highly centralized information and communication systems which are operated using rigid rules and regulations. Firms will seek to align their control mechanisms with their strategies and structures in hopes of attaining competitive advantage. To achieve advantages, the configuration of the firm's information architecture must reflect the firm's strategic objectives.

Coordination is a part of all organizations that have a certain degree of specialization or differentiation among their parts, mandating some sort of coordinated effort across them. A mechanism of coordination can be considered any administrative tool used for achieving integration among different units within an organization. Coordination as compared with control should be less direct and less costly (Cray 1984). In an MNC, coordination involves sharing and use of information about activities within the firm's value chain by different facilities. The greater the level of interdependence within the organization, the greater the need for integration. This is true especially in cases of manufacturing MNCs whose subsidiaries perform sequential tasks in manufacturing operations. Kogut (1985) suggests that the coordination of value chain activities provides critical competitive advantage for a multinational corporation. An MNC's distinctive competency is based on its 1) capabilities to perform value chain activities and 2) ability to capture competitive advantages through superior coordination of activities between different country locations. The essence of coordination is the communication and processing of information (Malone et al 1987). Therefore, a firm's ability to coordinate a worldwide business successfully is contingent upon the creation of appropriate organizational structures and relationships within which flows of information can take place efficiently and effectively (Galbraith 1977). The effectiveness and efficiency of these information flows should be directly related to the alignment of the firm's information architecture with corporation's strategy and structure.

Uses of information technology for coordination of strategic advantage are seen in interorganizational systems which electronically link activities of firms at different stages of the value chain. MNCs with high levels of coordination can be characterized by mutual dependence between headquarters and subsidiaries with high degrees of cooperation and joint problem-solving. Innovations in information technology in the past two decades have greatly reduced coordination costs by reducing both the time and cost of communicating information and knowledge (Karmi and Konsynski 1991). The reduction in coordination costs have in turn accelerated changes in the global market place and encouraged MNCs to modify their organizational and information structures to take advantage of market opportunities.

The preceding discussion assumes that control and coordination are distinct and separate, yet both attempt to accomplish the integration of a firm's multifarious business processes. In reality the applications of control and coordination are performed in concert with one another. What is the relationship between them and how is it associated with the strategic aspects of information architecture? The concept of the trade-off between control and coordination form the basis for exploration of an MNC strategy. Consider how a firm whose headquarters wishes to exert a high degree of control over its subsidiaries might structure its information architecture with one way information flows. These information flows allow data in the form of reports to flow from the subsidiary to the headquarters, but knowledge in the form of decisions flows from headquarters to the subsidiaries[1]. In this type of information architecture one would expect to find little if any information flow between subsidiaries. On the other hand, a firm's strategy based on low levels of control might seek an information architecture designed to provide dense two-way communication. A system of this

---

[1]   In the context of this discussion, information flows might also be considered data flows, which take the form of standardized or routine reports. Knowledge flows, on the other hand, take the form of decisions and value-added information.

nature could promote closeness of contact between headquarters and subsidiary and perhaps enhance information and knowledge flow between subsidiaries.

To some extent control and coordination work as substitutes for one another in that each can integrate the subsidiary into the firm. The use of varying degrees of either control or coordination and more especially their use together will help determine the firm's strategic orientation. For instance, there are cases when the subsidiary is not likely to deviate from overall organizational policy, when predictability is high, or if the organization views the world as a single market. Under these circumstances, the information architecture of the MNC could be designed to help channel the downward direction of information and knowledge flows, centralize decision making authority and minimize costs. In other situations, the firm might provide a product adapted to each individual market or operate in an environment requiring substantial local involvement. Additionally, environmental influences in the form of market or governmental pressures for local responsiveness could affect firm strategy. As external or environmental conditions increase in number or degree, the headquarters unit becomes more flexible with subsidiaries as the cost of applying control increases. To counteract increasing costs, MNCs employ more coordination throughout their organization, which in turn affects the development of the information architecture. The next section briefly reviews Bartlett and Ghoshal's topology of firm strategic disposition.

STRATEGIC DISPOSITION OF MULTINATIONAL CORPORATIONS

The decision to distribute an organization's information resources should be made on business and not technical factors. A widely used framework to describe the strategic disposition of MNCs is based on the global/transnational continuum developed by Bartlett and Ghoshal (1989). Their topology of firm type was used by Jarvenpaa and Ives (1991) to classify decision-making structures in their investigation of global information technology "fit." This chapter also adopts the Bartlett and Ghoshal topology to explain strategic positions of MNCs with regard to application of control and coordination concepts for choosing an appropriate information architecture. A brief description of each classification is summarized below.

Global: This organization is driven by the need for global efficiency, while having structures that are more centralized in their strategic and operational decisions. Their unit of analysis is the world and their products and strategies are developed to exploit and integrate a unitary world market (Bartlett and Ghoshal 1989, p. 14). As a result of this centralized structure the majority of decisions are made at the headquarters level and propagated to the subsidiaries. A structure of this nature suggests a strategy based on high levels of control and low levels of coordination.

International: Transferring and adapting the parent company's knowledge or expertise to foreign subsidiaries is the hallmark of this MNC structure. The parent retains influence and control, but less than in a classic global structure; national units can adapt products and ideas (Bartlett and Ghoshal 1989, p. 14). This structure continues to exploit knowledge on a worldwide basis, using high levels of control coupled with high levels of coordination.

Multinational: A developed structure which allows the company to be sensitive and responsive to the different national environments is the characteristic of the multinational firm. This organization manages its subsidiaries as though they were components of a portfolio of multinational entities (Bartlett and Ghoshal 1989). Given the independence of the subsidiaries operating in this organization the headquarters exercises low control and low coordination.

Transnational: This organization seeks a balance between the pressures for global integration and the pressures for local responsiveness. Adaptation to all environmental situations is key to the philosophy of this firm, utilizing knowledge and two way information flows throughout the organization. Its strategies force the firm to have structures considered both centralized and decentralized simultaneously. Transnational firms have higher degrees of coordination with control (low) dispersed throughout the organization.

The next section provides an introduction to ERP software and explains the impact of control and coordination issues when implementing these packages.

ERP SYSTEMS[2]

This section explores Enterprise Resource Planning (ERP) systems, types of information architectures or configurations for these systems while providing advantages and disadvantages for each configuration, and introduces Application Link Embedding as tool to enhance system configuration. Enterprise Resource Planning is a term used to describe business software that is 1) multifunctional in scope, 2) integrated in nature, and 3) modular in structure. An ERP software solution is appropriate when an organization is seeking the benefits of integration and contemporary best practices in its information system, looking for a full range of functionality throughout its organization, and seeking to limit its implementation and ongoing support costs (Norris et al 1998). Historically, the market for ERP solutions has been large multinational manufacturing companies (revenues over $1 billion) which operate in a discreet manufacturing environment. Today, however, the market is expanding to mid- ($250 million to $1 billion) and small- (under $250 million) companies across a wide range of industry sectors. The market is dominated by SAP-AG of Germany which holds over 70% of the ERP software market with their R/3 system.

ERP systems have their origins in Manufacturing Resource Planning (MRP) software with installations traditionally in large scale manufacturing facilities, although recently the trend is to extend installations to industry sectors including telecommunications, public sector (local, state, & federal governments including educational institutions), insurance, gas & oil, and high tech manufacturing. Firms using the software generally seek process-oriented increases in productivity, up-to-the-minute access to timely and current information, and of course cost savings. The systems are known for their process orientation to enhance an organization's move to team orientation, breaking down former departmental boundaries and thinking, and to strengthen initiative and motivation. The ultimate goal of organizations implementing ERP systems is to optimize the organization and its processes, with the ultimate goal of maximizing their profits. Most packages are customizable and provide flexibility to the organization depending on which components they choose to use and how they implement them. Since the system is fully configurable (organizations have the flexibility to change the package to meet their unique requirements), the organization "turns on" only those portions of the package it requires. The systems are designed with an open architecture facilitating expansion for future modules and allowing "bolt-on" applications from approved vendors. As of the end of 1999, the packages are being enhanced with tools such as data warehousing, planning optimizers and decision support tools, and electronic commerce tools.

The issues of control and coordination change slightly with regard to ERP systems. To achieve the benefits from an ERP implementation, organizations usually standardize their business processes. To what extent should business processes be standardized across globally dispersed operations of an MNC – is an ongoing debate. One issue regarding ERP systems is clear; to achieve any of the benefits, an organization must establish process and data standards

---

[2]   Additional information on ERP and SAP's R/3 can be found at www.peoplesoft.com, www.sap.com,www.oracle.com, or in one of many current business publications.

- including nomenclature, file & field sizes, and common part numbering where applicable. This in itself is a base level of control which MUST be established. Accompanying these standards are usually a series of procedural standards as well as those which govern how the system is used and what processes are integrated.

The R/3 package, like many ERP systems, is built around a central database (see Figure 1). The database is generally recommended by the ERP vendor and is developed by an outside vendor selected by the implementing organization. For instance, the vast majority of SAP implementations are powered by an Oracle database. The ERP system has the functionality to drill into the database to create tables and manage information. The ERP package's modules utilize information required to perform certain functions and then updates the database accordingly. Based on specified business processes, the system is designed so that events in one module trigger other modules into action. Since the modules share information and are linked via the organization's process model, the organization gains efficiencies unobtainable under legacy systems whose data sharing abilities were limited. The system also provides the organization with a second-by-second snapshot of financial, personnel, and other activities.

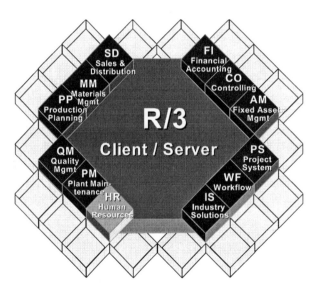

Figure 1: Model of SAP's R/3 System
(Source: www.sap.com)

The ultimate aim of a global ERP system and its supporting architecture is to identify a company's long_term IT goals and translate them into a global IT infrastructure that will assure the company's future success in the market. In the past, IT infrastructures were mostly designed from the purely technical perspective of information processing. But the emergence of new electronic markets and sales channels means that a company's IT infrastructure is rapidly evolving as an integral part of its overall business strategy. Given this context, companies are taking a new approach to designing their enterprisewide infrastructures, and project teams and consultants are acquiring a whole range of new skills. It is also becoming more and more important to involve top management in the information architecture process and to analyze critical success factors in a company's core markets.

Past studies reveal that a typical multinational company has five main objectives when it sets up a global ERP infrastructure:

1. To harmonize the business processes across departmental and national boundaries
2. To harmonize the group reporting structure

3. To develop a global, distributed system topology
4. To choose an implementation and rollout strategy for all departments and all countries
5. To develop a binding global concept for all subprojects and implementation partners

To accomplish organizational goals and insure successful implementation of the ERP systems, an MNC must develop an enterprise resource infrastructure plan which examines the organization in a top-down process. This plan begins with the analysis of the entire enterprise and establishes the overall objectives for the ERP project while creating "views" of the current structure of the MNC including legal, market, human resources, technology, and others. Next the organization and its processes are modeled and mapped to assist in the determination of the ERP system's structure. The third step begins to examine how the ERP's technological infrastructure will be mapped on to the organization model. Ultimately, as this step progresses, the ERP organization model and the ERP system structural landscape are brought together leading to technology issues such as data integration, design of cross-functional information flows, modifications in process design, and eventually modification of daily operations. A key deliverable of this enterprise resource infrastructure plan is the development of the ERP information architecture. Discussed in the next section, this information architecture assists in the optimal configuration of the MNC's hardware architecture and the ERP software package.

TWO MODELS FOR ERP INFORMATION ARCHITECTURE

Two models of ERP architecture are shown in Figure 2. The traditional model of an ERP architecture is built around a single installation of an ERP software. For the SAP R/3 package, the system is driven by a single system identification (SID) with each SID wholly owning its database - logically and physically. This *tightly coupled system* - used primarily to enhance the performance - relies on a single data center with PCs acting as the system's user interface, the only distributed part of the system. In some cases, the system could create instances - technical subsets of the entire package tailored for specific tasks or users - which distribute some processes. Advantages of a tightly coupled centralized system include lower costs, higher levels of control, and ease of upgrades.

On the other hand, *loosely coupled* or distributed applications are based on replicated and consequently redundant data instances driven by detailed and specific synchronization rules. In these systems, changes in distributed data simultaneously trigger communications for asynchronous copying of these changes to the data records. This system, using the most current IT, maintains the data in its most current state providing the distributed system with the same advantages formerly available only to tightly coupled systems. MNCs have moved to distributed systems to achieve greater flexibility for all their organization units so they can holistically adjust their global business processes while tuning local processes to the rapidly changing conditions in the global marketplace. Advantages of the loosely coupled system include

1. The ability to provide managers with prompt and accurate information.
2. The ability to maintain high levels of customer satisfaction.
3. The optimization of the flow of data between the ERP system and other systems - internal and external.
4. The ability to insure that business processes were executed efficiently across a globally dispersed enterprise and optimize for each organizational unit.
5. Improved efficiency of system maintenance -dispersed components can operate independently when required, e.g. elements of the system can be taken down at appropriate times at individual locations (e.g. regional holidays) and component failures do not significantly impact the entire system.

6.   Simplify the move to decentralized management structures for MNCs whose units operate in disparate environmental conditions

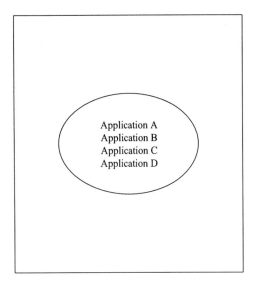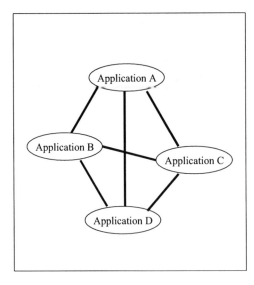

Tightly Couple Model   **Loosely Couple Model**

Figure 2: Tightly vs. Loosely Coupled Models

Systems architectures of this type also assist in the development of virtual organizations and can easily assist in reconfiguration of system applications during mergers and joint ventures.

To facilitate a loosely coupled architecture, the R/3 system relies on Applications Link Embedding (ALE) - an open communications system. ALE permits the seamless incorporation of autonomous application systems and components in the business communications model and provides the basis for supply chain management. It provides the loosely coupled environment with hardware/software independent communication, tighter security, decreased response times, cross release communications, the ability to easily communicate outside the R/3 system, and an extension of EDI. It is based on open communications protocols and is fully EDI compliant.

Within the SAP system, using ALE to create a loosely coupled environment allows different versions of the R/3 system to fluidly communicate with each other. This facilitates the scheduling of system upgrades at the convenience of the business model and not the demands of technology. The movement to loosely coupled or distributed systems should be made based on strategic factors and the firm's business model and not based on technical factors. Other factors to consider when making this decision include organization culture, management style and organizational structure at headquarters and local units, and the vision and desires of top management.

The next section integrates the concepts of control and coordination, Bartlett and Ghoshal's topology, and the enterprise information architecture models described above. Once elements listed above are integrated several information architectures are presented for each of the strategic types in the B&G topology with industry examples provided.

A FRAMEWORK FOR ENTERPRISE INFORMATION ARCHITECTURE FIT

This section plots the MNC on the control/coordination matrix by strategic type as indicated by the Bartlett and Ghoshal topology, provides a suggested ERP configuration, and illustrates that configuration with a corporate example. As illustrated in Figure 3, firms that are lower in coordination tend to be to the left side of the graph and have tightly coupled architectures. Firms exhibiting a preference for higher levels of coordination are located on the right side of the matrix and have a loosely coupled architecture.[3]

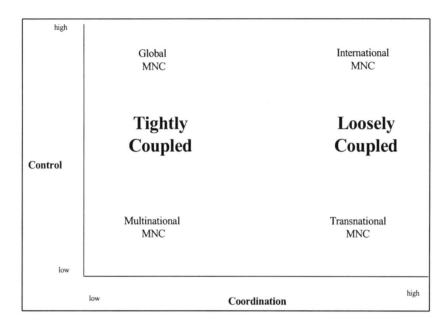

Figure 3: Enterprise Information Architecture Framework

Starting with the lower left quadrant, MNCs of this type require low levels of both control and coordination. This MNC is classified by the Bartlett and Ghoshal topology as *Multinational*. This firm type operates its units as if they were semi-autonomous, functioning in an independent fashion. These firms have unique operating environments in each market with units sharing a minimal amount of information with each other or the headquarters. This strategic type is prone to implement an enterprise information architecture based on the tightly coupled model. One would expect to find that under these operating conditions, ERP systems would be independently operated at each sub-unit level with minimal integration. Despite their adherence to the traditional model of a tightly coupled ERP system - individually situated at each location - there is still integration at a global level. As seen in Figure 4, the organization is connected to the top levels via the CO or controlling module. The use of this module is to provide a link for financial and production reporting. The IBM Personal Systems Group (PSG)[4] – is a example of this configuration. IBM's globally dispersed plants and distribution centers each have a separate R/3 installation which manages their operations.

The systems are interconnected via the PSG headquarters, for financial and production reporting. In this case the system also allows individual plants to coordinate shared sourcing

---

[3]   This model does not suggest that one architecture is better than another.

[4]   The PSG division manufactures and sells PCs, notebooks, and NetFinity Servers mainly
         to retail outlets and increasingly direct to consumers.

and distribution services, where applicable. One might argue that PSG is not a valid example if the traditional model of global sourcing is applied - one plant makes a single product for the whole world market (economies of scale). PSG currently manufactures and distributes machines in the same market with customized configurations to meet the specifications and desires of those customers. Systems are currently installed in two plants (Mexico and North Carolina) and two centers in North America, one in Scotland, and installations are scheduled for South America and the Asia/Pacific area.

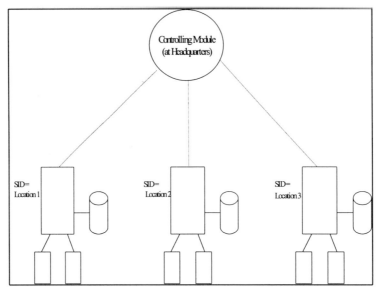

Figure 4: Multinational Enterprise IA Configuration
(Each locale system is independent and linked only to HQ for financial and production reporting)

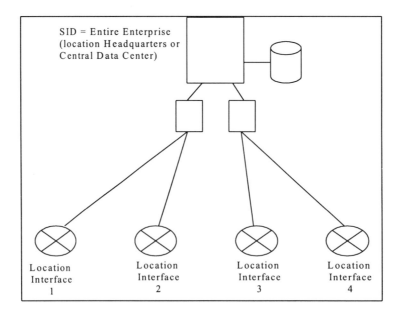

Figure 5: Global Enterprise IA Configuration
(All functions are housed in the HQ system with interfaces at local operating unit.)

The upper left quadrant of the matrix in Figure-3 represents the *Global* firm type which seeks high levels of control throughout the organization but uses minimal levels of coordination to achieve those objectives. This firm type has historically sought to administer its organization from corporate headquarters and has centralized functions such as decision making, information systems, and research & development. The global firm's strategic fit also indicates a tightly coupled enterprise information architecture. The optimum configuration, however, is different from that of the Multinational. While the Multinational would be expected to operate independent systems, the Global firm centralizes operations - usually at headquarters - and disperses the user interface to their operating units. This method allows the Global firm to exercise complete control over it units and over the actual systems, as well as ownership of the data. An example of this ERP configuration is the Storage Division of IBM. This operating unit of IBM runs its world wide operations using an installation of SAP's R/3 product from its main plant located on the west coast of the United States. Its plants and sales offices around the world are connected to the R/3 system through their PC interfaces. As seen in Figure 5, the entire operation is a classically designed tightly coupled system, with a single instance of the package owning one database.

The next strategic type is located in the upper right quadrant of the matrix and illustrates high coordination/high control. The *International* type MNC is built on a geographic model which attempts to capitalize on regional markets composed of consumers with similar traits. These firms seek to benefit from a hybrid model with control of the organization located in a number of geographically dispersed regional headquarters. Like the Global strategic type, the International MNC places system functionality in its headquarters unit with operating units accessing via the user interface (see Figure 6). Since the organization is globally dispersed yet regionally controlled, the headquarters still maintains a "link" into the ERP system through the Controlling (CO) module. Therefore the CO module is dispersed throughout the headquarters organization (both the main HQ and the Regional HQs). The balance of the system is dispersed in each regional area, with each installation in a Region owning its own database. If properly configured, this derivative of the loosely coupled system will retain the ability to pass information from the Regional systems to the main HQ system and vice versa.

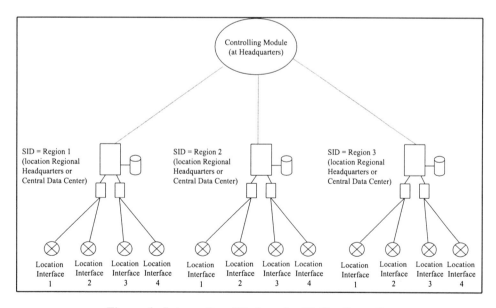

Figure 6: International Enterprise IA Configuration
(All functions are housed in the Regional Headquarter system with interfaces at local operating unit.)

The automobile manufacturers - Ford, GM, Daimlier-Chrysler, BMW, etc - use this model of configuration. The regional headquarters location for systems and system functionality provide these firms with the ability to manage their global supply chains while still localizing their products and operations to a specific geographical area. It is not surprising that the structure of their organization and their operational practices match this type of configuration. Another reason that these firms have adopted this strategy of configuration is their size and scope. Their size suggests that a single installation in a centralized location would present problems and increase the costs of global communication.

The advantage of this configuration is the segmentation of data and processes for each region. If the regions are uniquely different, then one must consider optimizing the processes that drive the business for each region. Therefore, the arrangement and configuration of each installation would vary. Under these circumstances, it is critical that the overall organization establish a priori standards for data, data sharing (when required), reporting standards, and system procedures. Without these standards the distributed system will not be able to effectively exchange information at any level.

The final strategic type is the *transnational* MNC. This firm, also called the networked organization, occupies the high coordination/medium control area of the matrix and seeks to capitalize on the best available alternatives. Using the loosely coupled template, this firm disperses the appropriate modules of its ERP system to the most applicable location within its organization. For instance, manufacturing modules might be dispersed throughout the firm's global manufacturing facilities, sales modules would be located in each sales office, distribution components in distribution centers, human resources modules in each location, and finance and controlling functions located in headquarters. Interestingly, with this type of configuration (see Figure 7), each location would have its own SID - owning its own database - but those installations would be linked to all other installations providing real-time information exchange when required.

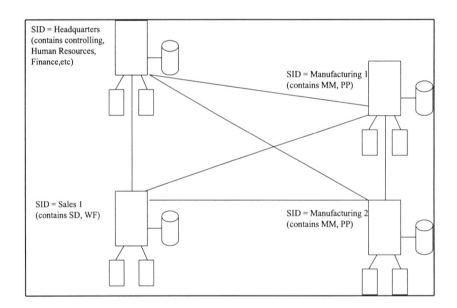

Figure 7: Transnational Enterprise IA Configuration
(Distributed yet fully integrated system with modules dispersed to functional location.)
(Module legend: SD=Sales & Distribution; WF =Work Flow;
MM = Materials Management; PP =Production Planning)

Proctor and Gamble (P&G) illustrates the dispersed and loosely coupled configuration of the transnational MNC. It is an example of the network company whose operations thrive on shared information from every market. Management of this organization feels that they are able to gather unique synergies from the dispersed yet shared systems allowing them to quickly adapt products and modify marketing based on "lessons learned."   Their organizational culture also supports the idea of dispersing systems - providing local ownership - yet openly connecting those systems to a holistic organization.

The main advantage of this configuration is the ability to decentralize decision making while still maintaining a high level of integration throughout the entire system. This allows managers to "think globally and act locally," letting the company to be more responsive to rapidly changing environments. Additionally, as stated earlier, a widely dispersed system is more robust. If one part of the system fails or requires extensive maintenance, the system can be configured to by-pass that component while directing operations to other areas.

To summarize, given the factors discussed in this chapter, MNCs electing to use ERP systems have the ability to optimize their organization strategy and their system configuration. This optimization should allow the MNC to better compete in the dynamic global environment in which they operate.

CONCLUSION

The ERP market as of November, 2000 is expected to exceed $10 billion per year. With the Y2K problem behind us now and the progressive expansion of ERP systems into medium and smaller sized firms, the hidden demand is likely to unleash, driving the number of installations and market revenues even higher. The continued movement of firms to global markets and global sources of supply on top of the hyper-competitive business climate will make ERP systems more critical to MNCs. A proper fit between the firm's strategy and Enterprise Information Architecture and consequently the actual configuration of the ERP package will provide the opportunity for MNCs to garner greater efficiencies and potentially more competitive advantage. This chapter presented one model for analyzing and configuring the firm's architecture and system. While no single configuration can be prescribed for each organization, each strategic type, or each component of an organization. The optimization of the entire MNC's business processes is critical to leverage the major expense undertaken during the ERP implementation.

The study of global information systems is an academic discipline still in its very early stages. The rapid movement of organizations into the world of electronic commerce has also place then in the global IS realm. As a result, academics are struggling to understand how new economic models driven by global e-commerce are impacting organizations and consumers. This chapter proposes a framework that academics can use to explain the design of organizations, their strategies, and enterprise information architectures . While exploratory and designed with ERP systems in mind, the framework is generalizable to the International Business discipline and can be used for most types of large scale information systems. This could provide the basis for a range of new instruments used to understand the interaction among organizations - internally and externally, their customers and suppliers, and the ultimate consumers.

The results and conclusions of this work should provide practitioners with a guide to design their overall information architectures and assist organizations that are considering the implementation of large scale information systems. As discussed in the chapter, the ability to achieve competitive advantage in today's hypercompetitve environment is contingent on the ability to achieve the optimum fit between the firm's desired structure and it's information resources. This can also be measured as the balance of control and coordination. This chapter provides a framework through which managers can examine their firm's overall strategy and information architecture to determine relative fit. Practitioners whose firm's are considering or implementing large scale systems will benefit since the chapter provides them with additional items that will assist them in achieving success. The cost of implementation failure is so great (one well publicized case resulted in bankruptcy) that all contingencies must be considered prior to undertaking the project. One of the most difficult aspects of an implementation project is the configuration of the system, which once completed is the blueprint from which the company is operated. Proper alignment of the enterprise information architecture and the overall strategy of the organization will provide an excellent guide to begin a logical ERP configuration.

Given that global markets and their environments are turbulent and subject to rapid change; vendors, consultants, and customers are seeking solutions allowing them to react and anticipant changes. As a result, recommendations have been made suggesting that the optimal model for some firms is a hybrid between the transnational and international enterprise information architecture. This hybrid model would place the majority of functionality in regional data centers with the balance of functionality located closest to its application - sales, manufacturing, or decision making. The idea behind this new hybrid model is to accommodate the move to global electronic commerce. Assuming under this new model that orders, customer interaction, and supplier interaction (for the most part) will be conducted via electronic means, a regional data center would house the ERP systems for those applications as well as the applications that schedule and monitor production - including key links to suppliers and vendors. This hybrid system improves both control and coordination and, in theory, at a much lower cost. Additionally, this model would allow the MNCs to centralize their staff and facilities in that regional location, again creating synergies and cost savings. This model does have some negatives, in particular maintenance and problems associated with disaster recovery. Despite the chosen model, ERP systems are becoming a critical element of an MNC's strategic framework and information architecture.

Mini Case - Dow Corning: A World Leader

Dow Corning Corp. is a world leader in the manufacture of silicon-based materials. Operating in Europe, Asia and the US, the enterprise has approximately nine thousand employees in 25 countries around the globe. Annual sales are US$ 2.6 billion. In order to maintain and strengthen their market position, Dow Corning has embarked on introducing a state-of-the-art IT infrastructure that would give them greater control over their supply chain and improve customer satisfaction.

Dow Corning's legacy IT systems, primarily mainframe-based, were hitting hard against the limits of their capabilities, especially in an area vital to the competitiveness of a manufacturer: supply chain management. A major obstacle was lack of integration, coupled with system redundancy. In many instances, it was simply not possible to access and analyze much of the data needed for effective planning. This hampered decision-making across the entire extended enterprise. It became clear that more powerful client/server hardware and cutting edge software were needed if Dow Corning was going to improve data transparency and, ultimately, responsiveness.

ERP software offered Dow Corning the functionality, flexibility and tight integration it sought. The first step was to create a state-of-the-art ERP backbone, based on SAP R/3. This created an end-to-end environment, seamlessly linking all key processes from order generation, to production planning, to ware- house procedures, to transportation moves through to delivery and billing. The ERP solution provides manufacturers such as Dow Corning with analysis, planning and simulation tools that can draw on up-to-the-minute data from diverse internal and external sources, increasing transparency while decreasing errors and costs. What's more, the ERP environment allows those plans to be put into action. Implementation targeted the main supply chain and took just nine months from design to deliver. In a collaborative effort by a team of SAP consultants and Dow Corning employees, business requirements were transformed into system requirements and design. The primary focus of both teams was configuration of the ERP solution to fit Dow's business strategy.

Dow Corning has been able to establish an information architecture that meshes with its business structure that enables supply and demand to be balanced around the world. Dow chose a loosely couple architecture which matched its strategic disposition and allowed employees open access to information in a highly coordinated structure. With access to global, real-time facts and figures, decision-makers can now coordinate people, plants and processes with far greater ease, matching production to market requirements on a global scale. The company expects to realize major savings, particularly in the area of materials management costs, when all supply chains are enabled. One of Dow Corning's major objectives was to raise the quality of customer service. Customers are provided with reliable delivery commitments, evaluating new market share with confidence, and supplying on-

Mini Case .... Continued.

time all contribute to overall customer satisfaction. The global implementation of SAP matched to its strategic objectives enabled the corporation to rebalance and optimize demand forecasts according to various criteria, including transportation costs, order destination, etc. Dow Corning can now delivery more precisely what their customers need, when they need it.

STUDY QUESTIONS

1. Explain the terms control and coordination and how they fit into information technology. Provide a examples of how organizations use information systems to support both mechanisms.

2. Discuss why multinational corporations would choose one strategic disposition over another. Provide examples of firms which fit a particular type and explain why.

3. What are ERP systems and why to firms implement them?

4. Explain the difference between tightly and loosely coupled information architectures.

5. Describe the transnational MNC type and explain why this organization has unique information resource requirements.

REFERENCES

Bartlett, C.A. and Ghoshal, S. *Managing Across Borders. The Transnational Solution.* Boston: Harvard Business School Press, 1989.

Cray, D. "Control and Coordination in Mutlinational Corporations," *Journal of International Business Studies*, Fall 1984, pp. 85-98.

Egelhoff, W.G. "Patterns of Control in U.S., UK, and European Multinational Corporations," *Journal of International Business Studies*, Fall 1984, pp. 73-83.

Galbraith, J.R.*Organizational Design.* Boston: Addison-Wesley Publishing Co., 1977.

Jarvenpaa, S.L. and Ives, B. "Organizing for Global Competition: The Fit of Information Technology," *Decision Sciences*, 24(3), 1991, pp. 547-574.

Kogut, B. "Designing Global Strategies: Profiting From Operational Flexibility," *Sloan Management Review*, Fall 1985, pp. 27-38.

Malone, T.W., Yates, J., and Benjamin, R.I. "Electronic Markets and Electronic Hierarchies," *Communications of the ACM*, June 1987, pp. 484-497.

Norris G., Wright, I., Hurley, J.R., Dunleavy, J., and Gibson, A. *SAP An Executives Comprehensive Guide.* New York: John Wiley, 1998.

Prahalad, C.K. and Doz, Y.L. *The Mulitnational Mission: Balancing Local Demands and Global Vision.* New York: The Free Press, 1987.

Simon, S. J. "An Information Perspective on the Effectiveness of Headquarters-Subsidiary Relations: Issues of Control and Coordination," in Palvia, P., Palvia, S., Roche, E. Eds. *Global Information Technology and Systems Management: Key Issues and Trends,* 1996.

21

Developing Global Executive Information Systems

Anil Kumar
The University of Wisconsin-Whitewater, USA

Prashant C. Palvia
The University of North Carolina at Greensboro, USA

ABSTRACT

The globalization of businesses, facilitated to a large extent by advances in computers and communications technology, creates tremendous demands for information. This information originates worldwide and is needed for decision-making by senior executives in global corporations. Executive information systems developed to provide information for senior executives fail to incorporate the global dimension. In this chapter we discuss the issues for designing, developing, using, and managing a global executive information system (global EIS). The issues discussed are based on the results of a study that was conducted to explore the need for global EIS for executives working in global corporations. These results are discussed in the context of a framework developed specifically for a global EIS.

INTRODUCTION

As a result of globalization there is a tremendous demand for information that is needed for executive decision-making. Senior executives in global corporations need information about worldwide customers, competitors and suppliers, organizational performance in worldwide subsidiaries, and different national environments where a company has operations, such as the recent (1999) political turmoil in Indonesia. This information is crucial for decision-making as the global business environment is unpredictable and very dynamic. The only constant in this environment is the rapid change that is taking place worldwide.

The need for information necessitates that executives use an information system that is designed and developed to provide the relevant information to executives in a timely manner. This system focuses on the specific information needs of senior executives in an organization. Executive information systems (Houdeshel & Watson, 1987; Leidner & Elam, 1994; Matthews & Shoebridge, 1992; Meall, 1990; Moynihan, 1993; Rockart and Treacy, 1982; Turban, 1995; Watson et al. 1991) that provide this information for decision-making do not incorporate the international dimension. There is clearly a need by global organizations to develop an information system that incorporates the international dimension. We call such a system a global EIS. A global EIS is defined as a computer-based information system that provides easy access to internal and external information (both domestic and international). This system is used to support the analysis and decision-making functions of senior executives working at headquarters and worldwide subsidiaries of a global organization. This chapter focuses on discussing the issues that pertain to developing a global EIS. The specific research question that is addressed is the following.

What are the key issues in the design, development, structure, use, and management of global executive information systems?

As executive decision-making deals primarily with strategic information that is nonroutine in nature, it is important that executives have access to this information. Global corporations that do not develop global executive information systems for senior executives, necessary to address the information needs of executives, would fail to keep up with changes that are taking place worldwide. This leads to ineffective decision-making by senior executives, as they will be ill informed about events that take place in the international arena.

RESEARCH FOUNDATION

In 1982 Rockart and Treacy pointed out a trend of increased computer usage by CEOs in corporations. These computer-based information systems that were designed to support executives in an organization were called executive information systems. These systems were designed with the objective of overcoming the limitations provided by other computer-based information systems, i.e., management information systems in the 1960s (Gorry & Morton 1971) and decision support systems in the 1970s (Sprague 1980). The advent of executive information systems in the late 1970s and early 1980s promised to provide support for executives, with little computing skills required of users. Today, executive information systems are one of the fastest growing applications in U.S. organizations. Turban (1995) highlights the growth of EISs in the 1980s. He points out that by 1986 one-third of the large U.S. corporations were using EISs and the figure had risen to 50% in 1989. Stedman (1998) points out that executive information systems developed for CEOs are "seeing a renaissance". Various scholars (Houdeshel & Watson, 1987; Leidner & Elam, 1994; Matthews & Shoebridge, 1992; Meall, 1990; Moynihan, 1993; Turban, 1995; Watson et al. 1991) published scholarly works on the characteristics and benefits of using an EIS. Vandenbosch & Huff (1997) examine the different ways in which executives use EIS to retrieve information. None of the above-mentioned studies though addresses the global dimension.

Palvia et al. (1996) raised the issue that executive information systems used by executives in global organizations need to be global in scope. They call a system developed specifically for this purpose a global EIS. In their paper, they conducted an exploratory study to identify in macro categories, the types of information required by executives in a global EIS, the current level of use of such information, and the sources of such information.

Watson (1995) pointed out that EIS development in other nations should be interesting to study. Comparisons of EISs developed in different parts of the world would provide useful insights that would help in the development of global executive information systems. Eom (1994) discussed the emergence of "transnational management support systems" (TMSS) for organizations operating in the changing global environment. He highlighted the significance of the EIS component in TMSS, by stating that one of the functional requirements for such a system would be global data access. Min and Eom (1994) talked about developing an integrated decision support system- (IDSS) for handling the complexities and the uncertainties of global logistics operations. They defined such a system as: "A world-wide network of multi-user decision support systems that integrates the MNF's (multinational firm) various logistics operations and standardizes databases across national, cultural, and market boundaries... (p. 31)"

Violano (1988) described Citicorp's Global Report System as one that provides executives with real time information on international banking. The system filters, integrates, and organizes financial information (e.g., international currency trading, foreign exchange, geographic countries and regions) for senior executives. Not only does the system provide information for executives, it also allows the user to search desired topics. This puts the "world at your hands" according to Violano.

Iyer and Schkade (1987) discussed different characteristics of multinational management support systems. They point out that managers of multinational corporations are often "inundated with unsolicited information from several sources." It becomes important not only to retain such information, but also to organize it for future use. They proposed the use of an ESS, which will not only allows executives to scan the information, but also performs ad-hoc analysis for evaluating decision tasks.

The systems described above allow global organizations to integrate information from the disparate information systems that are used worldwide. In recent times organizations have increasingly used enterprise resource planning (ERP) systems such as SAP, BAAN, PeopleSoft, Oracle and J.D. Edwards, to integrate disparate sources of information that resides in worldwide subsidiaries. While ERP systems allow organizations to integrate functional information systems (human resources, finance, production, etc.) in an organization, they are not developed to support semi-structured and unstructured decision-making functions in an organization. Further the need for control and coordination in global organizations places a heavy reliance on underlying telecommunications networks that are used to support such information systems in organizations. The explosion of the Internet in recent years enables an organization to exploit this technology in supporting such systems. Top management in global organizations need to address and support the design and development of a global executive information system.

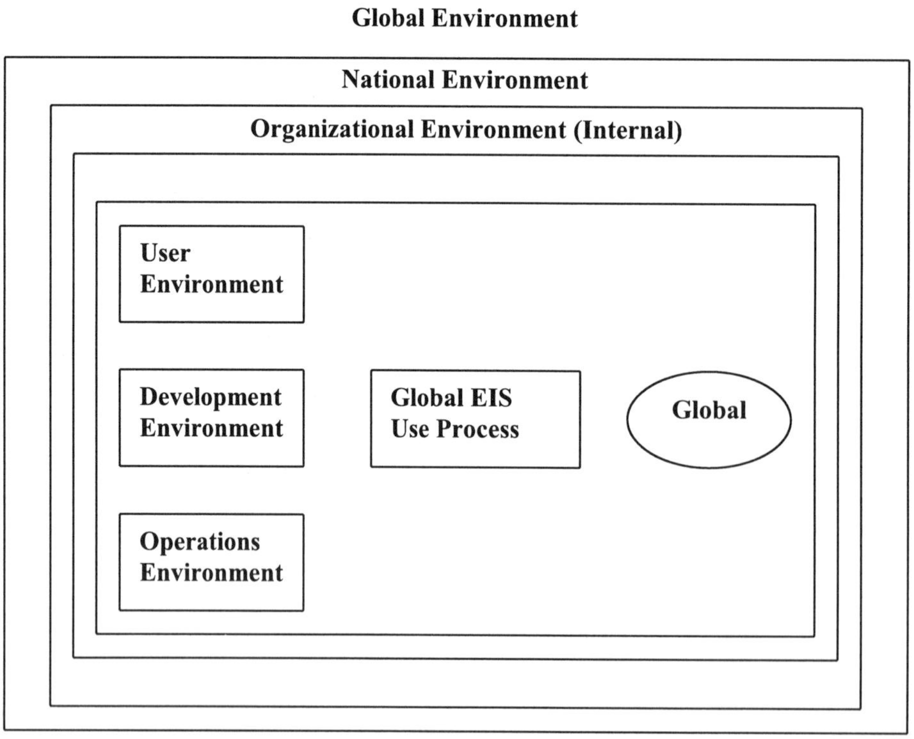

Global Environment

Figure 1: Global EIS Research Framework

RESEARCH FRAMEWORK

In this chapter the research framework proposed by Ives, Hamilton and Davis (1980) is modified and extended to incorporate the issues pertaining to international information systems and executive information systems. The proposed framework provides a meaningful foundation of the issues that are of importance for the study of global executive information systems. The framework we use to address the research question listed in an earlier section is shown in Figure 1.

The global environment of the organization represents those variables that are unique in different countries, for example host countries where an organization operates. The impact of these variables on a global EIS is examined in this environment. The national environment depicts the home country, of an organization. It interacts both with the global environment and the organizational environment. The organizational environment in the framework helps an analyst to examine the dynamic relationship between the environment and the organization, such as the impact that the usage of a global EIS has on an organization or the impact of the organization on the global EIS. The other variables used in the framework are for identifying global EIS users, developers, resources required, and the attributes of the global EIS system.

RESULTS AND DISCUSSION

In this section we report the results of the study followed by a discussion of the results. The different components of the research framework are discussed and the results are compared to existing literature. Differences where significant are also explored with respect to companies that use a global executive information system or EIS, and companies that do not use any system.

The Study

The survey population for the questionnaire was chosen from the *Information Week* list of the 500 biggest and best corporate users of information technology. This list was matched with databases like the *World Directory of Multinational Enterprises* and the *Fortune Industrial and Service 500's* to develop a list of global organizations. It was assumed that as leaders of information technology usage, these companies would be potential candidates to have a global EIS or an EIS.

The respondents (48 organizations) for the study included global companies headquartered in different parts of the United States and the world. Of the total respondents, 86% of the companies had their headquarters in the United States and the remaining 14% had their headquarters in other countries of the world. The number of manufacturing sector companies was 23 and the number of service sector companies was 25. In the manufacturing sector companies, respondents included chemicals/health care, industrial, commercial electronics/computers, and consumer goods. The service sector category included companies from the following industries: transport, financial institutions, software development/consulting, telecommunications services, media, retail, pest control, and entertainment.

Fifty percent of the responding companies (N=34) have assets over $10 billion and the remaining companies had assets of less than $10 billion. Forty percent of the responding (N = 39) companies had revenues over $10 billion and the remaining 60% had revenues of less than $10 billion a year. The IS budget for the responding companies (N = 26) used in the study was between $100 million and $5 billion. Twenty-seven percent of the companies had an IS budget of over $1 billion, whereas the remaining 73% of the companies had an IS budget of less than $1 billion. All the 26 companies for which IS budgets are reported were included in the *Information Week* list of the biggest and best users of information technology.

The majority of the respondents (N = 45) for the study were Vice Presidents and/or Directors of the IS function in their respective organizations, followed by IS managers, CIO, Project leaders and consultants, etc. The average total work experience of the respondents is 23 years, and the average IS experience of the respondents is 18 years (N = 43). Of the total companies that responded (N = 35), the average foreign involvement is 38% approximately. Foreign involvement is measured by dividing revenues from international operations by total revenue.

Fifty-seven percent of the companies (N = 48) responded in the positive when asked if they had an EIS being used in their companies. Twenty-eight percent of the companies (N = 48) responded that they use a global EIS for their senior executives. Only six of these companies answered about the scope of the system that was being used in these companies. In all six cases the global EIS was being used enterprise wide or all executives in the global organization were using the system.

Reasons for Developing a Global EIS and Potential Problems

The study identified several reasons why global organizations should develop a global EIS and the potential problems that can be faced during the development of the system. Table 1 shows the results for the reasons for developing a global EIS.

Increase in the quality of decision-making, the usefulness of a global EIS for making strategic decisions, and providing organizations with competitive advantages are perceived to be important factors for developing a global EIS. Surprisingly, access to unavailable information is not considered to be a very important reason for developing a global EIS. It is possible that respondents feel that information can be made accessible for executives, but the problem lies in putting it together and providing it in a system that can be used easily by executives.

Table 1: Reasons for developing a Global EIS

Reasons	Yes	No
Increases quality of decision-making	97.9	2.1
Useful for making strategic decisions	85.4	14.6
Provides organization with competitive advantage	77.1	22.9
Access to unavailable information	60.4	39.6

Table 2: Problems in developing a Global EIS

Problems	Yes	No
Defining the objectives of the system	81.3	18.2
Determining the information requirements of the system	79.2	20.8
Getting executives to use the system	58.3	41.7
Determining hardware and software required for system	25.0	75.0
Regional IT support in subsidiaries	20.8	79.2

Table 2 highlights some potential problems for developing a global EIS. Defining the objectives of the global EIS and determining the information requirements of the system are the two main problems in the opinion of the respondents. This is consistent with the EIS literature findings (Young & Watson, 1995). It is important for developers to understand what is 'needed' by an executive and then develop a system that supports that need. An executives work environment encompasses a wide range of activities, which makes it difficult to develop a system that can adequately assist an executive. The fact that the users of the system include executives from different parts of the world makes the task of defining needs even more difficult. Getting executives to use the system was not considered to be a major problem. With the rapid advances in technology, executives will find it difficult to perform their jobs if they do not use technology. This might be a problem in subsidiaries located in certain parts of the world, as discussed earlier in the chapter. Determining the hardware and software required for the system and providing regional IT support in subsidiaries is not considered to be a problem in developing a global EIS.

Global Environment

The global environment of an organization is characterized by factors that are unique and vary with countries where an organization operates. Some factors such as the national government, local culture, and economy etc. are fixed. Incorporating the influence of these factors in a global EIS is not practical. Factors such as currencies, languages, and measurement units are changeable and can easily be incorporated in a global EIS. These features, when incorporated into such a system, may potentially impact the usage/diffusion of a global EIS.

Q. What are the features that are desirable in a global executive information system (reflecting differences in languages, currencies, measurement unit's etc.)?

As per Table 3, inclusion of different currencies (87.5%) in a global EIS is considered to be an important feature by a majority of the respondents. Since most of the time senior executives examine and evaluate financial data in an organization it becomes important to include different currencies. The ability to convert from different currencies to dollars and make comparisons of sales worldwide will assist executives in making better decisions.

Table 3: Features of a Global EIS desired by executives worldwide

Features desired	Important/very important (percent)	Somewhat important (percent)	Not important/of little importance (percent)
Inclusion of different currencies	56.2	31.3	12.5
Multi-lingual capabilities	33.3	41.7	25.0
Inclusion of different measurement units (e.g. metric system)	33.3	35.4	31.3

A system that is developed for executives working in a global organization must include multi-lingual capabilities for greater acceptance. The results show that three-fourths of the respondents (75.0%) are of the opinion that a global EIS should incorporate multi-lingual capabilities. Not only does it become easier for executives worldwide to use a system with multi-lingual capabilities, it also would encourage executives to use it more frequently. Care must be taken during global EIS implementation to ensure that for implementing such a system the users are provided with multi-lingual email facility to enable communication across borders.

Senior executives are primarily concerned with financial data, rather than quantities of units sold in different measurement units. This explains the fact that not too many respondents consider inclusion of different measurement units (68.7%) to be equally important. The fact that there are only two main measurement systems used in most parts of the world might also explain the opinions of the respondents.

National Environment

The national environment of a company represents the home country of an organization. The environmental forces in the national environment of an organization create the need for information for a global organization. Collecting and analyzing information from different sources that are available to an organization in its national environment fulfill this organizational need. Egelhoff (1991) points out that "currently there is a danger that new international business strategies are being created with too little consideration for the high information-processing requirements that accompany them."

Q. What are the different external sources of information that can be used for a global executive information system?

The highest recommended source of external information is on-line databases (Table 4). A likely explanation for the popularity and preference for on-line databases is the explosive growth of the Internet and the easy availability of data on the World Wide Web in recent years. Not only are the data more readily available, it is also easy to access and is becoming increasingly accurate and reliable (especially when obtained from multiple sources). Other sources considered important are suppliers/customers/trade associations, trade/general/government publications, academic institutions/private research labs, and information brokers/consultants. It is clear that most of the widely preferred sources of external data are hard sources. This result is in contrast from an earlier study (Palvia et al. 1996), which identified non-computer based resources as the most-cited sources of international business information. As stated earlier in this paragraph the recent explosion of the Internet and easy availability of data possibly explains the respondents' preference for computer-based sources of information. Further Egelhoff (1991) points out that the "subject or content is an important structural dimension of information-processing" in multinational corporations. For example information on different country matters such as the financial laws, taxation structure, market information, legal restrictions, etc. are increasingly being made available on the Internet by nations worldwide. This makes it easier for global companies to search for such information on-line and hence explains the popularity of this resource.

Sources of external data not used as frequently as in the past include: chambers of commerce, conferences/trade shows, business travels, and personal contacts. A possible reason for the low use of chambers of commerce and conferences/trade shows is the fact that some of these sources are confined to the gathering and collecting of data pertaining to the local environment rather than international data. International conferences, conventions and trade shows, which were not included in the list of options for the respondents, are potential sources for gathering and collecting international data. While personal contacts and travels do provide invaluable insights, a high reliance on these sources is not warranted any more as is borne out by the results. These results imply that easy and free access to data on the Internet is welcome by organizations as a source of external data.

Table 4: Sources of information and their percent frequency use

Source of information	All Companies (N=48)	Companies without EIS/global EIS (N=21)	Companies with EIS (N=27)	
			Global EIS (N=13)	**EIS (N=14)**
On-line databases	40	17	11	12
Suppliers/customers/trade associations	32	13	8	11
Published (trade/general/government publications)	31	12	9	10
Academic institutions/private research labs.	28	11	11	6
Information brokers/consultants	26	10	7	9
Chambers of commerce	17	7	6	4
Conferences/trade shows	17	7	6	4
Business Travels	15	5	5	5
Personal contacts	15	7	3	5

Organizational Environment

Daft (1992) defines an organization as "social entities that are goal-directed, deliberately structured activity system with an identifiable boundary." The boundary identifies the elements, which are within the organization (internal), and those elements that are a part of its external environment. The absorption of information technology (such as global EIS) in a global organization changes the "anatomy of the corporation and the mindset of its people" (Passino & Severance, 1990, p. 76). It becomes important to identify and understand the potential impact that the usage of a global EIS has on the organization, for example organizational strategy, structure, learning, and design, etc. Not only do we need to identify and understand the impact of the usage of a global EIS, it is important to prepare the people who will be impacted by the change. If the people (executives) are not prepared and willing to accept this change, the introduction of a global EIS will not be successful. The issues that are of importance and need to be explored are:

Q. How does the usage of a global executive information system impact the organization?

Table 5 shows the percent frequency of each of the impact factors. A vast majority of the respondents agree that the usage of a global EIS in an organization leads to an increase in the confidence of decision-making. This indicates that with access to greater amounts of relevant information, executives feel more confidence in their decision-making. It also explains why approximately two-thirds of the respondents agree that use of a global EIS will lead to an increase in organizational scanning of internal and external environments of a company. For example: Do we enter a new market? Do we introduce a new product? What is the IT infrastructure in a country where a new technology is planned to be implemented? Is there adequate service available in a country to support hardware and software that is planned to be implemented? To satisfy the need of executives for more international information to be used in a global EIS, an organization will have to scan more sources of internal and external information. More than three-fourths of the respondents also agree that with greater information available to executives in a global organization, individual and organizational learning will increase. It is evident that this increase in learning is a consequence of the availability of more information in an organization that can be used by executives in their decision-making process. Availability of more information that is organized and managed using a global EIS would allow executives in an organization to take advantage of the extra information.

Table 5: Impact of usage of a Global EIS in an organization

Impact	Agree/strongly agree (percent)	Neither agree or disagree (percent)	Disagree/strongly disagree (percent)
Increases confidence in decision-making	87.6	10.4	2.0
Increases individual and organizational learning	81.2	10.4	8.4
Leads to increase in organizational scanning of internal and external environments	68.8	29.2	2.0
Decreases the number of organizational levels involved in decision-making	31.3	33.3	35.4
Decreases involvement of subordinates in analysis	23.0	22.9	54.1
Decreases frequency and duration of executive meetings	18.8	43.8	37.4

The results show that slightly less than one-thirds of the respondents agree that the use of a global EIS will lead to a decrease in the organizational levels involved in decision-making. Further, less than one-fourth of the respondents agree that the use of a global EIS will lead to a decrease in the involvement of subordinates in analysis, or a decrease in the frequency and duration of executive meetings. These results point out that even though the confidence of executives in decision-making is higher with the use of a global EIS, it does not necessarily impact the organizational structure and processes used for decision-making. Levels of organizational hierarchy that are involved in the decision-making process can impact the speed of the decision-making process. Speed of executive decision-making in the international environment is crucial at times due to the level of competition that an organization faces. A failure to make decisions fast enough can result in lost revenues for a global organization as other international players in the market can move in and benefit from such situations. A possible explanation could be the fact that it would take more time before executives feel comfortable with relying primarily on a global EIS for decision-making. A change in their work style, for example less reliance on subordinates for analysis etc., would take time. Also meetings for executives are a source of both information gathering and a social process. A decrease in the number of meetings impacts the social aspect of the work of an executive and may not be welcomed by executives. This explains the fact that respondents do not agree that the use of a global EIS will lead to a decrease in the frequency and duration of executive meetings.

Global EIS User Environment

The user environment identifies the scope of the global EIS that is developed for the users, and the primary users of the global EIS. It becomes important to determine the scope of the global EIS project at the beginning of the development process. Wetherbe (1991) points out those revisions that are required to be made to an EIS are very expensive. This necessitates that an organization should decide up-front whether a global EIS should be developed for the global organization or should a global EIS be developed for regional areas in a global organization, for example Asia-Pacific, Europe etc. Other possibilities that can be explored by organizations are to develop a global EIS for a specific product division and/or a department/functional unit for the entire organization. Watson et al. (1991) point out the existence of EIS that are developed for functional areas rather than for an organization.

Q. What should be the scope of the global executive information system?

Table 6 shows the frequency percentage for the different categories pertaining to the scope of a global EIS. More than three-fourths of the respondents were of the opinion that the scope of the global EIS should be enterprise-wide, i.e., the global organization. Users of a global EIS and/or EIS were more favorable in selecting the global organization for the scope of the system. This signifies that based on experience and actual usage of these organizations it is important to develop the system for the entire organization. Very few respondents recommended the regional organization (12.5%), product division (6.3%) or the department/function (2.0%) as the scope for a global EIS. Watson et al. (1991) talk about the existence of some EIS that are developed for functional areas in a business. We can make the conclusion that the majority of the EIS are developed for the entire organization, which is consistent with the results of this study.

Table 6: Scope of the Global EIS

Scope of global EIS	All Companies (N=48)	Companies without EIS or global EIS (N=21)	Companies with EIS (N=27)	
			Global EIS (N=13)	EIS (N=14)
Global organization	38 (79.2%)	15 (71.4%)	11 (84.6%)	12 (85.7%)
Regional organization	6 (12.5%)	5 (23.8%)	1 (7.7%)	-
Product division	3 (6.3%)	-	1 (7.7%)	2 (14.3%)
Department/function	1 (2%)	1 (4.76%)	-	-

The scope of the system that is developed will determine to a large extent the primary users of the system, executive decision-makers (senior and/or middle management) at headquarters and subsidiaries. If middle management at headquarters and subsidiaries are to be included as primary users of the system, then job functions, work styles, and support needs of these users will have to be taken into account (DeLong & Rockart, 1992) for developing the system. Egelhoff (1991) states that it is important to differentiate between the "purpose and perspective of information processing." As information needs are different at different levels in an organization it is important to identify the users of an information system to ensure success.

Q. Who are the primary users of the global executive information system?

Table 7: Primary users of a Global EIS

Primary users	Percent Frequency
Top management (headquarters only)	97.9
Top management (subsidiaries only)	89.6
CEO (headquarters)	81.3
Middle management (headquarters only)	64.6
Middle management (subsidiaries only)	60.4

As Table 7 indicates, a majority of the respondents recommended the CEO and top management at headquarters and subsidiaries of a global organization as primary users of a global EIS. There is not overwhelming support for including middle management at headquarters or in subsidiaries as primary users of a global EIS compared to support for including senior management. As a global EIS is designed specifically for senior executives working in a global organization, the results are reinforcing. Middle management if included as primary users of the system would create the need for additional capabilities (DeLong & Rockart, 1992) to be provided in a global EIS. These capabilities are based on specific job functions, work styles, and support needs of middle management in an organization.

It is interesting to note that respondents feel that senior management in subsidiaries should be included as primary users of the system. This will benefit the entire organization as decision-making will be facilitated across the organization. Some of the respondents who included "others" in their choice offered the following comments: 'external customers (business partners) may also want/need access'; 'professionals, e.g., engineers, research scientists etc.'; and 'strategic planners, financial analysts, etc.' Including external customers, though highly desirable, can create security problems for an organizational information system.

Global EIS Development Environment

This environment identifies the assigning of responsibilities for planning the development of the global EIS, the methodologies and techniques for determining information requirements and the development of a global EIS, in-house versus customized development of the global EIS, and the characteristics of the development team and its members. It is important to identify at the beginning of any project the people who should be responsible for planning the development of the system. As a global EIS is intended for use by senior executives, working worldwide in a global organization, the process of planning the project and assigning responsibilities becomes even more complex and significant. The person(s) who are assigned this responsibility should ensure that the global EIS is developed within the context of the overall objectives of the global organization. Buss (1982) points out that an "international computer council" should be created to develop plans for international information systems and to ensure that they are compatible with corporate objectives.

Q. Who is responsible for planning the development of the global executive information system?

One-thirds of the respondents felt that a steering committee should be made responsible for planning the global EIS project (Table 8). This result indicates that respondents do not want any one person to be made responsible for planning the project. It also agrees with Buss's (1982) recommendation that an "international computer council" be created to develop plans for global information systems and to ensure that they are compatible with corporate plans. This group of people, drawn from different parts of the world, would be able to provide better direction for the project. It would also provide a sense of ownership for people working in subsidiaries.

Table 8: Person(s) responsible for planning the Global EIS

Person(s)	Percent frequency
Steering committee	33.3
CIO (chief information officer)	27.1
Executive sponsor	16.7
Operating sponsor	14.5
Initiator of the Global EIS project	6.3
Others	2.1

A key issue in developing information systems for executives is making sure that their requirements are fulfilled by the system. Wetherbe (1991) points out that a lot of the systems (EIS) fail because the requirements of executives are not adequately met. He talks about the different approaches that can be used for eliciting executive information requirements correctly. Watson and Frolick (1992) state that determining an executive's information requirements can be a difficult task. The authors discuss several strategies for overcoming this obstacle and correctly determining information requirements. In addition identifying information requirements for an EIS has been ranked as the number one concern in several studies (Paller, 1990; Stecklow, 1989; Watson & Frolick, 1992). It is critical to identify the methodologies that can be used for determining and validating information requirements for a global EIS.

Q. What methodology should be used to determine and validate information requirements for a global executive information system?

It should be pointed out here that a working definition of critical success factors, prototyping, and ends-means analysis was provided for the respondents. The three methodologies perceived to be important by respondents are asking executives, critical success factors, and prototyping (Table 9). Asking executives directly for the information they need or the use of critical success factors for an executives work environment can be used to come up with a conceptual understanding or framework of information required by executives. Care must be taken to see how executives are asked for their information requirements.

Prototyping can then be used for determining the detailed requirements of the system. This explains the respondents' choice of selecting these three methodologies. The methodologies selected by respondents agree with the literature (Watson & Frolick, 1992; Wetherbe, 1991). It is interesting to note that respondents selected methodologies which not only assist developers to draw a conceptual framework, but also to determine details required for a global EIS. Some of the respondents who chose "others" as one of their choices mentioned the following methodologies: 'bench marking, brainstorming, joint requirements determination, information analysis, and work process'. However no explanations were provided for including these methodologies.

Table 9: Methodologies for determining and validating information requirements of a Global EIS

Methodologies	Percent frequency
Asking executives	81.3
Critical success factors	79.2
Prototyping	77.1
Deriving from an existing application	41.7
Ends-means analysis	33.3

The methodology used to develop a global EIS is important because of the specific requirements/needs of executives. The choices can vary from using the traditional long-term approach (SDLC) to an iterative approach, i.e., prototyping. The time taken to develop the first version of the system is the major factor. The literature (Moad, 1988; Rainer & Watson, 1995; Runge, 1988) points out the importance of delivering the first EIS application quickly so that executives are interested in the project. This implies that using a development methodology which helps developing the first application in a rather short time period may be more desirable for developing a global EIS.

Q. What methodology should be used to develop a global executive information system?

Table 10: Development methodologies for a Global EIS

Development methodologies	Percent frequency
Prototyping	66.7
Joint application development	62.5
Data modeling	58.3
Information engineering	45.8
SDLC	41.7
Structured methodologies	41.7

As per Table 10, prototyping is the most popular methodology and highlights the fact that development time is an important factor in global EIS implementation. Other reasons that can possibly explain the respondents' choice, may include the unstructured nature of information required for decision-making in an executive's work environment and the difficulty of determining information requirements. Prototyping provides executives a chance to preview the results of the system from time-to-time and recommend any changes that they feel should be incorporated. This result also agrees with the literature (Moad, 1988; Rainer & Watson, 1995; Runge, 1988). Joint application development (62.5%) provides an opportunity for developers and users to work together during the development process. This ensures to a great extent that the system that is finally developed meets the users requirements (Wetherbe, 1991). It explains the respondent' preference for this methodology. Other methodologies selected by respondents were not considered very important for developing a global EIS.

A global EIS can be developed in-house, customization of off-the-shelf software, a combination of the two, or by using off-the-shelf software (Paller & Laska, 1990 as cited in Watson et al. 1991; Rockart & DeLong, 1988). The availability of several EIS products in the market (Comshare EIS, IBM Office Vision, Pilot Command Center, Digital DEC Decisions in Nord & Nord, 1995; and EXECUCOM-Executive Edge and IBM-Executive Decisions in Watson et al., 1991) may make it attractive to customize these products to incorporate the international dimensions for a global EIS.

Q. How should the global executive information system be developed (in-house vs. customization of off-the-shelf software product)?

According to Table 11, three-fourths of the respondents thought that a combination of in-house development and customization of off-the-shelf software is the most appropriate approach for developing a global EIS (Rockart & Delong, 1988; Watson et al., 1991). The result is not surprising, as there are several vendors in the market who provide an EIS solution for organizations. Customization of the EIS product to include the international dimension would enable an organization to have a system in place in a short time frame. Executives would support this, as they are able to use the system early on. Changes, if required, can then be incorporated as desired by the executives.

Table 11: Approaches for developing a Global EIS

Approaches	Percent Frequency
Combination of in-house development and off-the-shelf software customization	75.0
In-house development	10.4
Off-the-shelf software	8.3
Other	6.3

Whether it is an in-house effort or a customization of an EIS product, it is important to identify the people who should be involved with the development of a global EIS, the skills that they should have, and the number of people that should be on the development team. It becomes even more important in the context of a global organization because team members can be from different parts of the world. A system that is developed by headquarters staff may not be acceptable in subsidiaries. Buss (1982) points out that it is crucial for organizations to overcome the '*not invented here*' syndrome and convince country managers that it makes business sense to use application programs developed elsewhere. Organizations forming global software teams comprised of members from different parts of the world may face problems associated with "*out of sight out of mind*" (Carmel, 1999) mentality that negatively impacts the working of such teams. Control and coordination issues need to be resolved and the cost incurred for this may be huge.

Q. Who should develop the global executive information system?

A majority of the respondents (83.3%) felt that cross-national teams (i.e., combination of headquarters and subsidiary employees) would be the best combination of people for developing the system. This is important in view of the fact that users in subsidiaries will feel an ownership of the system if they are involved in its development (Buss, 1982, Roche 1992). Subsidiary use of the system would increase through this involvement in the development process. However it must be mentioned here that cross-national teams place a tremendous burden on organizational resources due to the level of control and coordination that is required. Also a prerequisite for using such teams for developing systems is the availability of an excellent communications infrastructure.

Q. What are the skills required of members on the Global EIS development team?

The following six skills were identified as vital for potential members of the development team: business area knowledge, interpersonal skills, IS (technical skills), cultural (language skills), data knowledge and an executive perspective. An "others" category was also included for respondents to identify a new skill. The results are presented in Table 12.

Table 12: Global EIS development team skills required

Skills	Percent frequency
Business area knowledge	95.8
IS (technical skills)	75.0
Interpersonal skills	70.8
Executive perspective	68.8
Data knowledge	68.8
Cultural (language) skills	45.8

It is interesting to observe that business area knowledge was rated higher than IS technical skills. This highlights the fact that it is important for global EIS developers to have an excellent understanding of the functional areas of the business and also the job environment of an executive (Watson et al., 1991). Respondents also considered interpersonal skills, an executive perspective, and data knowledge as important desirable skills. Surprisingly, familiarity with a foreign language was not considered important in view of the fact that a majority of the respondents favored a cross-national team of developers. A possible explanation can be the fact that most IS trained people or other members of the team would have an understanding and working knowledge of the English language.

Global EIS Operations Environment

The global EIS environment is used for identifying the hardware resources and the processing centers required to operate the global EIS. Respondents were asked to choose the most effective hardware configuration from the following: centralized (mainframe/minicomputer-based); decentralized (minicomputer/PCS/LANs) or distributed (enterprise wide networks/WANs using workstations). Table 13 shows the preferences of respondents for the most effective hardware configuration for a global EIS.

Table 13 shows that two-thirds of the respondents feel that a distributed hardware configuration would be the most effective for a global EIS. This is a fitting response as it highlights the fact that respondents want executives in subsidiaries to be using the global EIS. In the Watson et al. (1991) study the hardware configuration that was most desirable for an EIS was the mainframe approach (shared mainframe and a PC network connected to a mainframe). Volonino, Watson, and Robinson (1995) recommend using networked workstations for an EIS. The results of this study are consistent with the literature keeping in mind the fact that the recommended hardware configuration would support a system that would be used worldwide.

Table 13: Hardware configuration for a Global EIS

Configuration	Percent frequency
Distributed	67
Decentralized	15
Centralized	12
Others	6

When asked where to locate the processing center(s) for global executive information, respondents were provided with three choices: headquarters only, regional (e.g., European) processing centers, and/or country (subsidiaries) processing centers. The results are provided in Table 14. More than half the respondents prefer global executive information to be processed at headquarters. The need to have a central point of control in an organization, a place where key decisions are made, is a possible explanation for the fact that respondents want data to be collected from different offices worldwide using an enterprise wide system, but processed and analyzed at the headquarters. The information can then be distributed over the different regional and country centers in a global organization.

Table 14: Global EIS processing center(s)

Location	Percent frequency
Headquarters only	52.1
Regional centers	43.8
Country processing centers	22.9

Global EIS Use Process

Q. How does the use of a GEIS impact the work of an executive?

The global EIS use process measures the impact of using a global EIS, on the work of an executive and satisfaction resulting from the usage of the system. The study identified three major impacts as a result of using a global EIS: improved quality of decision-making, improved productivity in decision-making and faster task completion. Table 15 presents the results of the impact of using a global EIS on the work of an executive.

As Table 15 indicates, an overwhelming majority of the respondents believe that the use of a global EIS results in an improvement in the quality of decision-making. More than two-thirds of respondents also believe that the usage of a global EIS results in improved productivity in the decision-making process. The results clearly show that access to timely information (external and internal) leads to an improvement in the decision-making process and the quality of decisions made.

Table 15: Impact of using a Global EIS on Executive work

Impact	Yes	No
Improved quality of decision-making	95.8%	4.2%
Improved productivity in decision-making	70.8%	29.2%
Faster task completion (i.e., faster implementation)	27.1%	72.9%

Respondents (72.9%) do not believe that the usage of a global EIS results in faster task completion for executives. The result is different from what the literature indicates (Elam & Leidner, 1995; Rainer & Watson, 1995; Watson et al., 1993). In an earlier section it was shown that the use of a global EIS by executives does not lead to a decrease in the involvement of subordinates for analysis of information. The need for detailed analysis of information by executives may lead to more time being spent before the final decision is made. Also the fact that international information is being analyzed can impact the time that is taken for analysis. Although an executive can make a faster decision from the data that is available, it is more difficult to actually carry out decisions (e.g. task completion), since international coordination is more time consuming and difficult. This could be a possible explanation for the respondents' viewpoint.

Global EIS Architecture

The literature (Houdeshel & Watson, 1987; Rockart & DeLong, 1988; Watson et al.,1991) points out that data are a very important part of an EIS, as it forms the basis of the information that is provided to executives by the EIS. The question that arises in the case of a global EIS is the scope of the data that should be included in a global EIS and the potential problems with respect to managing this data. In an earlier section it was reported that 79.2% of the respondents were of the opinion that the scope of the global EIS should be the global organization. The majority of the respondents (91.6%) felt that the scope of the data that is included in a global EIS should be the global organization. This data is internal to the organization and would be extracted from operational databases that exist in the organization, e.g., transaction processing systems and functional areas (Watson et al., 1991). All respondents agree that data integrity (100%), data security (100%), and data standards (100%)

are important issues for the management of data that is used for generating information for a global EIS.

Mintzberg (1975) and Zmud (1986) point out the significance of internal data that is captured from human sources and that it is very important to understand complex problems. Watson et al. (1991) define this as "soft-data" and include news, rumors, opinions, ideas, predictions, explanations, and plans in this category of data. In their opinion, capturing these data as a part of an EIS can be a difficult process but that it will add to the "richness" of the information that is provided by an EIS. Respondents (73.0%) agree that it is important to include soft data in a global EIS and that the inclusion of such data in the global EIS will lead to a better quality system being developed.

Watson et al. (1991) point out that the ease with which the executives can use a system developed for them is very important. All the respondents (100%) in this study were of the opinion that the ease of use of a global EIS is an important issue. If executives have to be trained for more than a few minutes to use the system then it will not satisfy the executives.

Information that is generated by an EIS should be presented to executives in different formats, for example tables, graphs, text, etc. (Friend, 1988; Houdshel & Watson, 1987; Rockart & DeLong, 1988; Watson et al., 1991). All the respondents (100%) were of the opinion that the information should be presented to the executives in a desired format, 95.8% of the respondents recommended the use of graphics for presenting information, and 93.7% of the respondents recommended using color for presenting information to the executives. These results point out that executives should be provided information by a global EIS in different formats and the use of graphs and color is highly desirable.

Providing electronic mail as a capability for information presentation in an EIS is mentioned in the literature (Jordan, 1993; Watson et al., 1991). In this study, 79.2% of the respondents were of the opinion that incorporating electronic mail capabilities in a global EIS is important. The electronic mail capability would allow executives to communicate with other people from anywhere at any time. This is very important in a global organization as it reduces the need to meet people from different subsidiaries from time-to-time.

Rockart and DeLong (1988) indicate using electronic calendars in an EIS as an organizing tool for executives. 60.4% of the respondents in this study were of the opinion that a "scheduler" for appointments was of importance to them. This would allow executives to keep track of their appointments, especially when they are traveling.

CONCLUSION

This chapter reports the findings of a study from 48 global organizations. These findings discuss the issues involved in developing, using, and managing a global EIS. Some of the results that are reported in this chapter are consistent with the EIS literature. Additional insights of respondents with respect to a global system being developed for senior executives are presented for the first time. A few of the key findings are as follows:

- The scope of the system i.e. global EIS, should be the global organization rather than regional, product division, and/or departmental/functional.
- A global EIS should have the capability of presenting information in multiple currencies and languages.
- Hard-sources of information such as on-line databases, published information and academic institutions, are preferred sources for deriving international business for a global EIS. This information can be combined with internal organizational data in a meaningful context to provide useful information for executives.
- Using a global EIS leads to increased confidence in decision-making and increased organizational and individual learning.

- There is strong support to include the CEO and top management at headquarters and subsidiaries as primary users of a global EIS.
- Steering committees should be made responsible for planning the global EIS development project.
- Asking executives directly is the recommended methodology for eliciting information requirements of executives.
- A cross-cultural team comprised of 6-10 people should develop the global EIS. Business skills are considered the most important skills required of these people.
- A distributed configuration using an enterprise-wide network (WANs with workstations for interface) is the preferred hardware configuration for using a global EIS.
- Data integrity, security, and standards are considered to be important issues with respect to data management.

A few surprises include:

- Respondents indicated that the use of a global EIS will not lead to a decrease in the number of organizational levels involved in decision-making, a decrease in the involvement of subordinates required for analysis, or a decrease in the frequency and duration of executive meetings. This impacts the time taken for executive decision-making in global corporations, which in turn can result in lost revenues as local companies or other international competitors in the region may make decisions faster based on their knowledge of the environment.
- The use of a global EIS does not lead to faster task completion for an executive.
- Respondents want data to be processed at headquarters, rather than at regional or country processing centers.

Mini Case - Using the Internet for Executive Information Systems

As the world continues its progress towards becoming a truly interrelated global economy senior executives in global organizations need access to information that can be provided using a Global Executive Information System (Global EIS). This information pertains to internal operations of an organization as well as external information that relates to the global environment that an organization competes in. For example the recent economic turmoil in several parts of the world, especially Asian countries, created a need for an increased flow of information related to national markets and local economic conditions. A significant part of this environmental information required by senior executives is available using the Internet. With Internet diffusion continuing to explode worldwide there is an opportunity to integrate existing systems, such as a Global EIS, with information available using the Internet. The ease of availability and use of information using the Internet makes it pertinent that a Global EIS developed for executive use incorporates this information. Information on global competitors, national markets, local laws, global supply chains etc. can easily be integrated to an existing Global EIS to enhance the value of these systems. Greater and timely access to information will enable senior executives to make more-informed business decisions and react more quickly in an often unpredictable and dynamic environment. Ken Harris[1], CIO of Nike Inc. points out that "being able to have a global view of our supply chain electronically, end to end, and to better share information with all our partners, would make us better decision makers."

Geomarkets.com focuses on providing global e-business intelligence and a network of contacts to help a company shape its international e-business plan. This information is invaluable and includes "big picture" data on overseas companies. Environmental data that includes information on unstable markets worldwide can easily be integrated with an existing EIS to add more value for executives. This integrated data enables executives to make decisions on entering new markets worldwide as they develop a better understanding of local needs. Assumptions and experiences about worldwide customers, supply-chain management, international markets, technology infrastructures etc. are truly globalized.

Mini Case .... Continued.

VF Corp., a $5 billion manufacturer of apparel such as Lee and Wrangler jeans and Vanity Fair lingerie, plans to install wireless LANs in the 200 manufacturing plants to tie automated manufacturing systems into an enterprise information system. This system will feed information directly into an ERP system (SAP AG) that is to be installed worldwide. Information from this system will be available real-time to executives enabling them to make better decisions on raw material costs and garment output. Manufacturing efforts by the company will be quickly able to meet the changing demands of worldwide consumers as a result of using this system. The process of changing styles in manufacturing plants will be reduced by 15 to 20% from the existing five days resulting in significant cost savings for the company.

Discussion Questions
1. What are the challenges that the diffusion of the Internet worldwide will create for developers of a Global EIS?
2. Discuss the issues involved with providing access to corporate data in a Global EIS to senior executives using wireless devices?
3. Identify and discuss the impact of new technologies, such as XML, on developing a Global EIS?

STUDY QUESTIONS

1. Discuss the role of the Internet in developing a better quality global EIS?
2. How should a global EIS be integrated with other information systems that a global organization uses?
3. What are the trade-offs associated with processing data at regional and/or country centers? How can these problems be overcome?

REFERENCES

Buss, M.D.J. (1982, September-October). Managing international information systems. *Harvard Business Review*, 153-162.

Carmel, E. (1999). *Global Software Teams: Collaborating Across Borders and Time Zones*. (p. 42) Prentice Hall PTR, Upper saddle River, NJ 07458.

Daft, R.L. (1992). *Organizational theory and design*. (p. 71). New York: West Publishing Company.

DeLong, D.W., & Rockart, J.F. (1992). Identifying the attributes of successful executive support system implementation. In H.J. Watson, R. K. Rainer, & G. Houdeshel (Eds.), *Executive information systems: Emergence, development, impact* (pp. 257-277). New York: John Wiley & Sons, Inc.

Egelhoff, W.G. (1991). Information-Processing theory and the Multinational Enterprise. *Journal of International Business Studies*, 22(3), p. 341.

Eom, S.B. (1994, Spring). Transnational management strategies: An emerging tool for global strategic management. *SAM Advanced Management Journal*, 59(2), 22-27.

Elam, J.J., & Leidner, D.G. (1995). EIS adoption, use, and impact: The executive perspective. *Decision Support Systems*, 14, 89-103.

Friend, D. (1990, March). EIS and the collapse of the information pyramid. *Information Center*, 6(3), 22-28.

Gorry, G.A., & Morton, M.S. (Fall 1971). A Framework for Management Information Systems. *Sloan Management Review*, 13, 55-70.

Houdeshel, G., & Watson, H.J. (1987, March). The management information and decision support (MIDS) system at Lockheed-Georgia. *MIS Quarterly*, 11(1), 127-140.

Ives, B., Hamilton, S., & Davis, G.B. (1980, September). A framework for research in computer-based management information systems. *Management Science*, 26(9), 910-934.

Iyer, R.K. & Schkade, L.L. (1987). Management support systems for multinational business. *Information and Management*, 12, 59-64.

Jordan, E. (1993, August). Executive information systems for the chief information officer. *International Journal of Information Management*, 13(4), 249-259.

Leidner, D.E., & Elam, J.J. (1994). Senior and middle management use of EIS: A descriptive study. *Proceedings of the Twenty-Seventh Annual Hawaii International Conference on Systems Sciences.*

Matthews, R., & Shoebridge, A. (1992, December). EIS-A guide for executives. *Long Range Planning*, 25(6), 94-101.

Meall, L. (1990, September). EIS: Sharpening the executive's competitive edge. *Accountancy*, 106(1165), 125-128.

Min, H., & Eom, S.B. (1994). An integrated decision support system for global logistics. *International Journal of Physical Distribution and Logistics Management,* 24(1), 29-39.

Mintzberg, H. (1975, August). The manager's job: Folklore and fact. *Harvard Business Review*, 53(4), 49-61.

Moad, J. (1988, May 15). The latest challenge for IS is in the executive suite. *Datamation*, 43.

Moynihan, G.P. (1993, July). An executive information system: Planning for post-implementation at NASA. *Journal of Systems Management,* 44(7), 8-14.

Paller, A. (1990, January). *EIS conference report*, p. 4.

Palvia, P., Kumar, A., Kumar, N., & Hendon, R. (1996). Information requirements of a global EIS: An exploratory macro assessment. *Decision Support Systems*, 16, 169-179.

Passino, Jr., J.H., & Severance, D.G. (1990, Spring). Harnessing the potential of information technology for support of the new global organization. *Human Resource Management*, 29(1), 69-76.

Rainer, Jr., R.K., & Watson, H.J. (1995). What does it take for successful executive information systems? *Decision Support Systems*, 14, 147-156.

Roche, E. M. (1992). *Managing Information Technology in Multinational Corporations*. Macmillan Publishing Company, New York, New York 10022.

Rockart, J.F., & DeLong, D.W. (1988). *Executive support systems: The emergence of top management computer use*. Homewood, IL: Dow Jones-Irwin.

Rockart, J.F., & Treacy, M.E. (1982, January-February). The CEO goes on-line. *Harvard Business Review, 60*(1), 81-93.

Runge, L. (1988, June). On the executive's desk. *Information Center, 4*(6), 34-38.

Sprague, R. H. (December 1980). A Framework for the Development of Decision Support Systems. *Management Information Systems Quarterly*, 4(4), 1-26.

Stecklow, S. (1989, April). The new executive information systems. *Lotus*, 51-53.

Stedman, C. (July 06, 1998). Information tools for the CEO see renaissance. *Computerworld.*

Turban, E. (1995*). Decision support and expert systems: Management support systems* (Rev. ed., pp. 400-440). Englewood Cliffs, NJ: Prentice Hall.

Vandenbosch, B., & Huff, S.L. (March 1997). Searching and scanning: How executives obtain information from executive information systems. *MIS Quarterly*, 21(1), p.81.

Violano, M. (1988, May). Friendly software for the bank CEO. *Bankers Monthly,* 105(5), 44-48.

Volonino, L., Watson, H.J., & Robinson, S. (1995). Using EIS to respond to dynamic business conditions. *Decision Support Systems, 14,* 105-116.

Watson, H.J. (1995, Spring). International aspects of executive information systems. *Journal of Global Information Management, 3*(2), 3.

Watson, H.J., Elam, J., Harris. J., Hertz, E., Rainer, R.K., Swift, R.S., Vogel, D.R. (1993). Panel: A research agenda for executive information systems. *Proceedings of the IEEE*, USA, 233-237.

Watson, H.J., & Frolick, M.N. (1992). Determining information requirements for an executive information system. In H.J. Watson, R. K. Rainer, & G. Houdeshel (Eds.), *Executive information systems: Emergence, development, impact* (pp. 161-175). New York: John Wiley & Sons, Inc.

Watson, H.J., Rainer Jr., R. K., & Koh, C.E. (1991, March). Executive information systems: A framework for development and a survey of current practices. *MIS Quarterly*, 13-30.

Wetherbe, J.C. (1991). Executive information requirements: Getting it right. *MIS Quarterly*, 51-65.

Young, D., & Watson, H.J. (1995). Determinates of EIS acceptance. *Information and Management, 29*, 153-164.

Zmud, R.W. (1986). Supporting senior executives through decision support technologies: A review and directions for future research. In E.R. McLean & H.G. Sol (Eds.), *Decision support systems: A decade in perspective* (pp. 87-101). North-Holland, Amsterdam: Elsevier Science Publishers.

SECTION - 5

GLOBAL SOFTWARE OUTSOURCING

The rapid development of international networking has indirectly spawned a new industry - global software outsourcing. Outsourcing is the act of paying external organizations to develop software and applications or in some cases to take over the IT function of the enterprise. In some cases, the IT employees are transferred to the company providing the outsourcing services.

Originally, outsourcing grew quickly as companies learned how to process specific types of information, e.g. medical claims, and then marketed the service to many different companies that had the same problem, like insurance companies. For a while, some companies adopted the "core capabilities" argument in which they considered IT to not be "core" to their company, thus turning it over to be outsourced. In some cases, the pendulum has come back, leading to a realization that many IT functions are too important to be given to outsiders. The debate continues in an endless circle.

In the multinational enterprise, it has long been recognized that the very high distribution of data centers, some in developing countries, has opened up possibilities for ``harvesting'' of less expensive labor around the world. In the past decade, however, we have seen the very dramatic growth of outsourcing, and the widespread use of international outsourcing arrangements.

This section presents two chapters on global software outsourcing. The first chapter investigates some of the basic drivers in favor of outsourcing, and then discusses some of the specific challenges of outsourcing in the international environment. The second shows how use of location economics can be used to facilitate optimal arrangement of the global software outsourcing decision.

22

Key Influence Factors and Issues in Global IT Outsourcing Management

Ned Kumar
Federal Express Corporation, USA

Prashant C. Palvia
The University of North Carolina at Greensboro, USA

ABSTRACT

This chapter provides an understanding about the complexities involved in global IT outsourcing and the management initiatives needed for the successful implementation of a global IT outsourcing partnership. Technological advances combined with increased globalization and competitive pressures have forced many firms to consider alternatives that will reduce organizational cost, and at the same time create and/or maintain their competitive advantage in the global market. Increasingly, the phenomenon of outsourcing is being considered by many firms as a solution to their IT needs and problems. Outsourcing provides them with a way out of skyrocketing IT expenditures at the same time allowing them to use some of the state-of-the art technologies and facilities. Even though there has been a plethora of studies done on domestic outsourcing of information systems, the research on outsourcing outside national borders, called global outsourcing, has been scarce. One of the areas which has been especially neglected in the literature is the area of outsourcing management. Anecdotal evidence points to the fact that even the best outsourcing deals can go sour if not managed properly. In the context of global IT outsourcing, the management of the outsourcing relationship becomes even more complex because of the geographical distance and the difference in the national and organizational cultures of the client and vendor firms. This chapter identifies the key elements that should be considered while managing an outsourcing relationship with a 'foreign' vendor and the role the manager should play in a given global outsourcing context.

INTRODUCTION

Most of the extant literature on information technology outsourcing deals with outsourcing within national boundaries (domestic outsourcing). It is only recently that many firms have begun to look at global IT outsourcing as a more profitable venture than domestic outsourcing. We define global IT outsourcing as *any contribution to a client organization by one or more external vendors with a different country of origin in tangible, intangible, human, and/or nonhuman resources related to the IT infrastructure.* Like domestic outsourcing, global IT outsourcing is also driven by transaction cost economies in terms of personnel (there is a significant disparity in cost of labor among developing and underdeveloped countries), skill (more efficient programmers at a cheaper cost), and productivity (more productive as compared to internal development). But unlike domestic outsourcing, a firm may decide to globally outsource part or all of its IT infrastructure for reasons other than that of cost. For example, a firm in a one country may decide to tie in with a vendor in another country so as to facilitate its product entry into that country. Or, it may opt to globally outsource some of its IT so as to gain access to new market opportunities (Heeks, 1996) and/or as an option for developing a global information system (Apte & Winniford, 1991).

One of the reasons for the phenomenal increase in global information systems outsourcing is the tremendous advances in telecommunications technology. This has allowed geographic boundaries to become blurred and has encouraged firms to seek resources from locations that provide the best competitive advantage. Some of the key factors influencing the choice of global information systems outsourcing have been lower cost, inability to hire and retain qualified personnel in the home country, and the increased emphasis on speed, vis-a-vis the time from project initiation to system installation (Patane and Jurison, 1994). In case of software development, an additional incentive for firms to globally outsource [to developing countries like India] is the high salaries and overhead cost in the industrialized nations.

The topic of IT outsourcing management is a relatively unexplored area within both domestic and global outsourcing research communities. Nevertheless, both researchers as well as practitioners agree that outsourcing management is one of the most critical factors contributing to the success of an outsourcing deal. This chapter puts in perspective the key areas to be considered in global IT outsourcing management and describes some of the better strategies for a given set of contingent influence factors.

We first take a look at some of the key past research done in the outsourcing area, both on the domestic and the international front. Then we look at some of the major dimensions to be considered while managing a global IT outsourcing relationship, followed by factors which makes global IT outsourcing management a difficult task. This chapter concludes with a discussion of some key results and implications with some directions for future research.

A REVIEW OF IT OUTSOURCING

As mentioned earlier, the literature related to global IT outsourcing management (GITOM) is not very extensive. Nevertheless, a study of past research in domestic and global IT outsourcing in general can serve as a point of reference and give us a better perspective in understanding the issues related to managing an outsourcing relationship with a foreign vendor. The following highlights some of the key research and studies undertaken in the area of domestic and global IT outsourcing.

General Issues

Before we look at some of the studies in the area of IT outsourcing, it should be noted that the term outsourcing has various connotations and that it falls into many categories. One of the basic definitions on outsourcing was given by Due (1992; 78) as, "the transfer of part or all of an organization's existing data processing hardware, software, communications network, and systems personnel to a third party." An alternative view (as opposed to transfer of assets) of outsourcing was offered by Takac (1994, 140) as "the process of retaining ownership of assets but relinquishing day-to-day operation of facilities to an outside organization which provides a contracted service at an agreed cost." One of the most complete definitions for IT outsourcing was offered by Loh and Venkatraman (1992a); they define outsourcing as *"the significant contribution by external vendors in the physical and/or human resources associated with the entire or specific components of the IT infrastructure in the user organization* (p.9)." This definition addresses the issue of ownership for both the physical resources and human resources.

Anecdotal evidence also suggests that IS managers turn to outsourcing for different reasons and as such they perceive the role of outsourcing in different ways (Nam el al., 1995). Also, the role of information systems varies across firms (Palvia & Parzinger, 1995), which in turn results in different IS policies (Nam et al., 1995). Therefore the scale and type of IT outsourcing is contingent on the firm's perceived role of its information systems.

IT Outsourcing

In recent times, IT outsourcing has gained increased prominence, both among academics and practitioners, due to the many high profile multi-million dollar cases involving "respectable" firms. There is a vast amount of research on domestic IT outsourcing dealing with a host of issues like reasons for outsourcing, selection of an outsourcing vendor, consequences of outsourcing, risks involved in information systems outsourcing, and the importance of a good contract. Since the focus of this chapter is on global IT outsourcing relationships, only some of the recent key studies in domestic IT outsourcing are summarized below.

General Issues/ Risk in outsourcing	Outsourcing policies /Performance impact	Outsourcing Relationships
Nelson et.al. (1996) Cash et.al. (1992) Benko (1993) Palvia (1995) Gurbaxani (1996) Loh & Venkatraman (1992a,b)	Malhotra (1995) Lacity et al. (1995) Gupta & Govindarajan (1986)	Nam et. Al (1996) Guterl (1996) McFarlan & Nolan (1995)

The conclusions from these studies emphasizes the need for careful planning and implementation of the outsourcing arrangement in order to reap significant benefits. When the firm is involved with outsourcing vendors based outside of the United States, they have to develop a very different strategic and organizational outlook than firms involved only in domestic sourcing. Since different cultures communicate distinctively with respect to IT management (Sauter, 1992; Ein-dor et al. 1993), it is imperative that one look at these differences when considering a global outsourcing arrangement (in addition to the traditional issues like cost, vendor competency, technology etc.). From a reference point of view, some key studies in the area of global IT outsourcing are enumerated below.

General Issues /Risks	Managerial Considerations	Contracts /Relationships
Patane and Jurison (1994) Willcocks et.al (1995) Heywood (1994)	Apte and Winniford (1991) McFarlan (1995)	Sharland (1993) Heeks (1996) Davis (1992) Pastore (1996) Klepper (1995)

Further reading in the area of global IT outsourcing suggests that there is a scarcity of information and studies in the area of global IT outsourcing management. This chapters addresses this issue and gives a better understanding of the different management styles that could be used by executives in managing a global IT outsourcing relationship. In order to achieve this, the remainder of this chapter focuses on the key elements in managing a global

IT outsourcing relationship successfully, the issues and problems facing firms involved in global IT outsourcing and the best management strategies under different outsourcing scenarios.

A RESEARCH FRAMEWORK

The following research model is presented so as to gain a better understanding of the outsourcing management process and to put a perspective on the different components involved while managing an outsourcing relationship.

The GITOM (Global Information Technology Outsourcing Management) model has four major components: influence factors which represents the various issues and problems that affect the relationship management in an outsourcing arrangement; management strategies, which includes the combination of one or more management elements (discussed in detail in the next section); moderating factors, conditions or characteristics in a relationship that changes the 'normal' management style (e.g age of the partnership, client attributes, vendor attributes), and is highly contextual; and lastly performance implications (e.g effectiveness, efficiency, commitment), which are nothing but the dimensions by which the client management and the vendor firm agrees on judge the success of their relationship. This chapter focuses primarily on the issues pertaining to or affecting global IT outsourcing management strategy and the primary elements which composes that strategy.

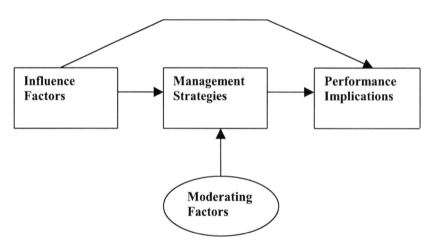

Figure 1: Issues Pertinent to GITOM

ELEMENTS OF MANAGEMENT STRATEGY

Relationship management is a complex task. And when the players involved are from different cultures, as is in the case of a global IT outsourcing arrangement, the task of managing the relationship becomes even more difficult. To get a fundamental understanding of this process, and to do a better job of management, it is imperative that one understands the underlying dimensions and elements that make up the overall management strategy. This section provides a review of the elements relevant to the domain of global IT outsourcing management. Based on the broader literature on firm-subunit relationships (Doz et al. 1990, Gupta & Govindarajan, 1991), the managerial elements for global IT outsourcing incorporates *structural variables* (Control Mechanisms, Integrative Mechanisms, and Contract Mechanisms), *compensation variables* (Incentive mechanisms), and *process variables* (Communication Mechanisms, Conflict Resolution Mechanisms).

Control Mechanisms

"The purpose of control is to minimize idiosyncratic behavior and to hold individuals or groups to enunciated policy, thus making performance predictable " (Tannenbaum 1968, p 3). Broadly speaking, two categories of control mechanisms can be identified in the literature -- formal and informal (Jaworski, 1988). In formal control, written, management established mechanisms are set down to influence the desired party so as to achieve a desired outcome, where as in informal control, the mechanisms are less rigid, unwritten, and typically worker-established (Jaworski, 1988). Formal control can further be classified into two groups - outcome control and behavior (process) control. Gupta and Govindarajan (1991, pp782) expressed these terms as follows: "Outcome control can be defined as reliance only on the end results for assessing a subsidiary manager's performance, whereas behavior (process) control can be defined as reliance on surveillance over the manager's decisions and actions that are expected to produce the hoped-for end results." Output control gives the organizational members the flexibility to choose any means to achieve a desired outcome. Behavior control, on the other hand, is more restrictive than output control and imposes on the members specific constraints with regards to the task at hand.

An example of formal control is the bureaucratic control system. In a bureaucratic system, control is established with the help of explicit rules and regulations which specify the desired performance in terms of output and/or behavior (Baliga and Jaeger, 1984). As a result, performance evaluation in this type of control involves comparing the member's behavior and output to a pre-established standard. Training and socialization in this type of control is fairly straightforward and simple. New members are indoctrinated about the rules and regulations in the organization.

An alternative to bureaucratic control is a cultural control system wherein control is established through informal and implicit mechanisms (Baliga and Jaeger, 1984). In a cultural control system, the shared values and beliefs within an organization guide the norms and behavior of the personnel in that organization. This type of control can be found in organizations with low turnover and a strong 'organizational culture' where the employees have accepted the 'company way' of doing things. Practices like long-term employment guarantees and consensual decision making aid the implementation of a cultural control system by providing the members with stability in a cultural group and interaction to assimilate and share the cultural values. Training and socialization in a cultural control setting is more critical and extensive than in the bureaucratic control system. In addition to the rules and regulations, a member must also absorb and accept the 'subtle' and complex control system which is based on a range of 'essential' values (Baliga and Jaeger, 1984). Performance evaluation in a cultural control system is done through interpersonal interactions.

Within the context of global IT outsourcing, control mechanisms are needed so as to monitor the performance of the vendor and to achieve a successful outsourcing partnership with the vendor. In short, these strategies refer to the amount and type of "power" the client can execute on the vendor. The type of control mechanisms which need to be established will vary from client to client depending on the environmental and contextual factors specific to the firm-dyad relationship. Vendors from certain nationalities would react to certain control mechanisms more favorably than others. The type of control mechanisms suited for a particular global IT outsourcing partnership is also dependent on the attributes of the outsourced IT and the cultural differences between the client and the vendor organizations.

Interorganizational Coordination

When two firms enter into a cooperative relationship, the issue of coordination plays an important role in the performance of that venture. In any outsourcing relationship, coordination between the client and the vendor is a must for the success of that relationship. The emphasis here is more on the degree of coordination rather than the actual mechanism of coordination itself. Coordination between any two parties can be conceptualized in terms of two dimensions-- the breadth of coordination (number of parties involved in the coordination network), and the diversity of coordination (the number of functions coordinated). Extending these results to the global IT outsourcing scenario, the amount of coordination required between the client firm and the outsourcing vendor will depend on the "volume" of IT outsourced and the extent of vendor involvement (Nam et al., 1996).

Past research (Galbraith, 1977) has identified several key formal structural mechanisms for coordination between subunits in an organization. The least complex of these integrative mechanisms are liaison positions, and the most complex type is matrix structure. Between these two extremes we have two other type of integrative mechanisms, namely cross-unit committees and integrator roles. The more complex the integrative mechanism, the more effective the firm-dyad will be in processing information and in coordinating the activities between interdependent units. On the other hand, the more complex the mechanism is, the more costly it is to implement such a mechanism.

To summarize, the 'coordination' element of management strategy refers to the degree of integration between the client firm and a vendor firm in a global IT outsourcing context. The more sophisticated the coordination mechanism between the vendor and the client, the more efficient the ability to process and exchange information. The degree of coordination will also be affected by the attributes of transaction in the outsourcing relationship.

For the successful management of any outsourcing relationship, the client firm should first look at what is being outsourced, how critical is the outsourced IT to the rest of the firm's operations, and what impact does the outsourced IT have on the success of the firm in the market place before it decides on a coordinating mechanism.

Contract Specificity

One of the basic requirements of a good outsourcing partnership is a good contract. The "science of the contract" plays an important role in determining the success of an outsourcing deal (Pastore, 1996). As one of the trade journals put it, "The key to managing the outsourcing vendor is the contract. The contract establishes, among other things, the cost for processing at various levels of use, specifies the acceptable performance parameters, provides penalties for substandard performance and details the terms under which the relationship can be terminated" (Computerworld, January 8, 1990: p72). When the outsourcing deal involves a vendor from another country, it becomes even more imperative that certain amount of flexibility be build into the contract to handle future contingencies. Contingent clauses built into the contract would come into effect under certain mutually agreed upon 'parameter changes'. Even under relatively 'stable' conditions, incomplete contracts are a useful tool for the management of a global IT outsourcing relationship. As Doz, Prahalad, and Hamel (1990, pp143) puts it, "... over time partners are likely to develop a better mutual understanding, a more realistic assessment of the potential value of their contribution, of the conditions needed for value creation, a greater appreciation of each other's *modus operandi* and cultures, as well as (hopefully) more trust. This may usefully lead them to renegotiate their agreements to improve effectiveness over time." In short, the degree of contract specificity could affect the outcome and success of a global outsourcing deal over time

The 'contract specificity' element of the global IT outsourcing management strategy helps the client in deciding when to have a highly specific contract and when the contract can be less comprehensive without undue risk or loss to the firm. In other words, it aids the client firm in making a decision on the amount of flexibility that should be built into the contract during renegotiation or modification of the original contract.

Collaborative Communication

The intensity of communication between any two organizations can be conceptualized in terms of four dimensions: frequency, informality, openness, and the density (bidirectionality) of communication. The density of communication was defined by Gupta & Govindarajan (1991) as "the number of people in the two units who interact with each other across organizational boundaries." It has been found that increased levels of these dimensions is associated with increased commitment, satisfaction, and coordination. Also establishing good collaborative communication channels creates an atmosphere of mutual support and respect, which in turn impact the success of the partnership.

On another level, the choice of a particular communication channel in a global IT outsourcing relationship would depend on the nature of the outsourced IT and the environmental contexts surrounding that partnership (Spee, 1994). In their study, Daft and Lengel (1986) clarified the difference between the amount of information transmitted through a medium and the medium's richness. They also argued that the under conditions of high uncertainty, the amount of information transmitted would be high; and under conditions of high equivocality, the media should be rich enough to facilitate debate and clarification (Daft and Lengel, 1986). It has also been suggested that situational factors, symbolic considerations and social influence play a role in the selection of a particular medium for communication (Markus 1992, cited in Spee 1994).

Essentially, the 'communication' element of the global IT outsourcing management strategy represents the type and quality of communication channels which needs to be established between the vendor and the client. Certain outsourcing contexts calls for establishing a very informal and open communication channels between many people from both the client and the vendor firms. On the other hand, for certain outsourcing scenarios, a one person formal link between the client and the vendor is enough. Proper management of communication between the client and the vendor would enhance the performance of the outsourcing relationship.

Conflict Management

Since global IT outsourcing involves players from different organizations and nationality, it is almost inevitable that conflicts would arise during the course of the relationship. It has been stipulated that when decisions are made by a 'coalition', the coalition members may differ in the interpretation of a given situation, and may pursue different priorities, which in turn results in conflicts regarding the importance of various factors (Ungson et al. 1981). The nature and structure of conflicts (negotiation problem) and its resolution would very much depend on the specific outsourcing context in terms of the level of interdependency and the environmental attributes. In many instances, negotiations during conflict resolution often end in 'suboptimal' agreements (Mumpower 1991). As Raiffa (1982) puts it, "Often, disputants fail to reach an agreement when, in fact, a compromise does exist that could be to the advantage of all concerned. And the agreements they do make are frequently inefficient: they could have made others that they all would have preferred" (p.358).

With regards to global IT outsourcing relationships, conflict management strategies are devised for those cases where the "...individuals are in conflict because they want different things, but must settle for the same thing" (Mumpower 1991, p.1305). Within the context of a global IT outsourcing partnership, the problem of conflict management is compounded because the level of 'importance' placed by the client and the vendor on a particular issue may differ considerably (Clark, 1993). It is also contended in this thesis that because of the 'global' nature of the client-vendor relationship, optimal conflict management strategies would vary from vendor to vendor. For example, it has been suggested that for transactions which are low on asset-specificity, *non-relational conflict resolution modes*, such as switching and litigation, would be more efficient than other conflict resolution modes (Spee, 1994). This is because, under conditions of low asset-specificity, neither parties are inclined to be committed to each other. On the other hand, when asset specificity is high, the service provider (vendor) has a vested interest in the transaction and conflict resolution is better achieved by *relational conflict resolution modes*, such as appeals to shared values and internal hierarchy (Speer 1994).

On another dimension, two general strategies of concession can be identified to solve conflicts arising from an outsourcing relationship. The first strategy, *compromise*, involves both the parties agreeing to position intermediate between each other's initial bargaining positions for a particular issue under consideration. The second strategy, *horse trading or logrolling*, consists of each party agreeing to trade-offs such that each party gets what they want on certain issues (Mumpower, 1991; Forman and Cohen, 1970).

To summarize, since global IT outsourcing arrangement calls for a 'coalition' between two parties with different nationalities, it is inevitable that certain conflicts may arise during the course of the partnership. These disagreements may manifest themselves in the form of 'conflict of interest' (the client and the vendor do not agree on the preferred outcome from doing a particular task), 'conflict of understanding' (where in the client and the vendor disagree over the optimal way to approach a problem or to attain a shared goal), and/or 'conflicting ideologies' (the client and the vendor have a clash of ideologies resulting from national and organizational differences) (Druckman, 1993). Conflict management strategies are needed to facilitate the resolution of these conflicts if sustainable benefits are to be obtained from the outsourcing relationship. The type of conflict resolution strategies employed would depend on situational factors like the nature of the conflict, cultural background of the conflicting parties and the level of conflict.

ISSUES IN MANAGING GLOBAL IT OUTSOURCING RELATIONSHIPS

There are a variety of issues and factors that has a direct impact on how the aforesaid management elements are combined to makeup a global IT outsourcing management strategy. These issues are highly contextual both from a intra and inter firm point of view, and any client firm would do well to study them carefully before deciding on how to manage their global IT vendor.

1. A key issue which has to be determined is whether the IT being outsourced plays a central role in the core strategy of the firm. The strategic impact of the outsourced IT to the client firm's operation and success would shape it's managerial response in terms of the nature of interorganizational relationship with the vendor firm. Another issue the client firm should determine is the degree of criticality of the outsourced IT vis-a-vis the operation and success of the organization. The criticality of the outsourced IT would determine the degree of control and delegation to be exercised in an outsourcing relationship (Ang, 1993).

2. Technological uncertainty is another key problem facing the managers in a global IT outsourcing relationship (Ang, 1993). In an IT outsourcing arrangement, uncertainty

could result from human actions such as strategic nondisclosure, disguise, or distortion of information (Loh, 1993; Williamson, 1986). As a result of such uncertainty, one of the parties in the exchange would be tempted to act in an opportunistic manner. Another form of uncertainty pertains to the technology being outsourced. First, there is the issue dealing with the kind of technology being used to fulfill the contract - is it state of the art, is it going to become obsolete in the next couple of years, is it difficult to maintain and troubleshoot etc. Also, specification adjustments are needed as new technological developments take place. Technological uncertainty becomes especially acute in the case of emerging technologies.

3. Another factor affecting the choice of a particular management strategy is the degree of functional complexity in the outsourced IT. Ang (1993, pp40) refers to functional complexity as "the difficulty of coordinating an increasing number of differentiated yet interrelated activities in IS services." The major activities associated with IS services include: developing an IS strategy, IT planning, capacity management, production management, human resource management, security management, PC management, and network management (Cash et al. 1988; Ang 1993). Sometimes, the clients run a variety of software applications on geographically dispersed platforms using different computer configurations. The complexity of the outsourced IT brings in additional issues to be considered while devising a successful global IT management strategy.

4. One issue which has a direct impact on the 'control' and 'coordination' element of the global IT outsourcing management strategy is the procedural knowledge, which refers to "the degree to which the task activities can be defined or to which cause-effect knowledge is clear" (Ramaswami 1996). Procedural knowledge is high for those IT applications that are routine, clear, and where the information requirements are unambiguous (Leifer and Mills 1996). The level of procedural knowledge in an outsourcing relationship can also be viewed in terms of the uncertainty and equivocality present in the 'task' performed by the vendor. Uncertainty has been defined as "the difference between the amount of information required to perform the task and the amount of information already possessed by the organization" (Galbraith 1977). Equivocality, on the other hand, implies the presence of multiple and conflicting interpretations. Outsourcing contexts with a high level of procedural knowledge can be said to have high information certainty and low equivocality (Leifer and Mills 1996).

5. In a global IT outsourcing scenario, asset specificity becomes a major cause of concern when managing the outsourcing relationship. Whether it is technological resource specificity (explicit usage of hardware, software, communication architechtures etc) or human resource specificity (unique experience, knowledge, and skills the vendor has), the client firm has to incorporate certain elements into their management strategy so that the vendor does not take undue advantage of the situation and also so that they don't have to be exclusively be dependent on the 'good-faith behavior' of the vendor.

6. One of the major issues faced by the client firm in managing a global IT outsourcing relationship is the difference in culture between their firm and the vendor firm. Since the outsourcing arrangement involves a difference in the country of origin of the vendor and the client, cultural differences assume a very crucial role in the management of the outsourcing relationship. A very good grasp of the cultural differences between different countries can be learnt by looking at the dimensions put forth by Hofstede (1980). In his study, Hofstede delineated the cultural variations between nations along four dimensions: individualism, power distance, uncertainty avoidance, and masculinity.

7. And lastly, the degree of interdependency between the client and the vendor firm could pose a problem for the client firm if not managed properly. Depending on whether the interdependency (Thompson, 1967) is pooled (the client and the vendor firms share common resources but are otherwise autonomous), sequential (the 'output' of the vendor firm is used as an input by the client organization), or reciprocal (both the client and the vendor organizations use each other's 'output' for their operation), the management of the global IT outsourcing relationship becomes more involved and complicated.

RESULTS AND IMPLICATIONS

To determine some of the issues in global IT outsourcing, and to learn about the different management strategies used by managers in successfully manage their outsourcing relationships, a survey questionnaire was administered to the IS managers in a select group of sample firms involved in global IT outsourcing. The results and implications from this study is summarized below.

1. There was a direct relationship between the age of the partnership and the scope of the outsourcing contract. This suggests that the longer a client firm has been dealing with a particular global vendor, the more the degree of mutual trust they developed in each other. This in turn motivated the client firm to outsource more of their IT activities to that particular vendor. Also, the longer the working relationship between the client and the vendor firms, the more stable the 'understanding' they have in terms of management expectations and performance.

2. Among a variety of attributes and factors offered as the reason for choosing a particular global IT outsourcing vendor, most firms picked 'competitive pricing' and 'Similarities in corporate culture' as the two most important factors. This should not come as a surprise as the closer the global vendor is to the client firm in terms of culture, the more easily can the client firm identify with and manage the outsourcing relationship.

3. Contrary to what was expected, many firms with a sophisticated software portfolio and different hardware platforms had insignificant monitoring systems in place to monitor their vendor's performance. At first this came as a surprise, but then it was attributed to the fact that the global IT vendor had much more expertise in these 'state-of-the-art' technologies than the client firm, and the client firms were happy to just concentrate on their core businesses and give the vendor the flexibility to do as they see fit (with respect to the outsourced activity). This was further confirmed by the fact that many clients let their vendors do the forecasting when it came to 'technological trends' vis-à-vis the outsourced funtion. It is also interesting to note here that some firms decision to 'stay way' was partly because of the differences in culture between their firm and their global vendor.

4. Firms outsourcing strategic applications had very formal communication channels and explicit control mechanisms established with their global vendors. This in line with the fact that strategic applications drive the core business of the client firm and thus the client firms were less willing to give the vendor complete autonomy in their activities. Also, formal communication channels and explicit contracts reduced the chances of any misunderstanding later on in the relationship.

5. Firms who successfully managed their relationship with global vendors from "collectivistic" culture countries (e.g., India) had a lot of flexibility built into their control and monitoring mechanisms. Global vendors from these countries were more accepting of the client firm's values and philosophies and were more willing to accept changes. In turn the client firms were more flexible in how these firms were monitored in terms of their tasks and performance.

6. It came as no big surprise that many client firms who had outsourced their IT applications to vendor from countries with a culture distinctly different from theirs had an outcome based control mechanism in place to manage the relationship. This is understandable since an outcome based control eliminated the need for extensive interaction with the vendor firm and thus reduced the chances of any misunderstandings.

7. In cases where the outcomes were not readily measurable (low performance documentation), client firms used a process control approach to measure the vendor performance and maintain a successful outsourcing relationship. By constraining and 'measuring' the subtasks involved in the outsourcing application, the client firm eliminated the trouble of keeping up with rapidly changing technology or changing standards.

CURRENT TRENDS IN OUTSOURCING

With the burgeoning growth of the E-commerce Market, new outsourcing models have come into play that better utilize the efficiencies of the internet. One of the most successful of these models is the ASP (Application Service Provider) model, which meshes very well with E-commerce and allows for companies to scale their expenditures based on their projected growth. Another model that owes its existence to the Internet age is the Netsourcing model wherein an organization outsources its IT and networking infrastructures for e-business applications. Finally, there has been a tremendous growth of Business Service Providers (BSP), where you contract out an entire service unit of the company to save cost and maximize efficiency. The following paragraphs briefly analyzes the ASP and Netsourcing trends in the outsourcing industry.

The ASP Model

The ASP model advocates handing over of key business functions to a third party Application Service Provider. This model has gained popularity in today's internet world precisely because it allows start-ups and E-commerce neophytes to gradually scale their expenditures in step with their business expansion and the fact that it is an 'internet' solution. As with outsourcing in general, the ASP solution also frees up the company's commitment to keep up with the technology and retaining skilled employees.

As always, these benefits from ASP outsourcing also comes with certain caution. First and foremost, companies should be very careful in how they select an ASP and who they select. Being a relatively new field, many ASPs are new companies that still do not have a well-developed process that account for all contingencies. In other words, it is to the client's benefit to make sure that their ASP has a good disaster recovery system and have clearly spelt out Service Level Agreements (SLA). In summary, it is caveat emptor when a firm outsources to an ASP. They should select an ASP with not only staying power, but one with a well-though out process for accountability.

The NetSourcing Model

In the NetSourcing model, entire networking infrastructures are outsourced to a third-party to benefit from their expertise and efficiencies. For example, MiracleNet.com, an Internet Service Provider, uses a firm called Intira as their Netsourcer to run a smooth customer support operation. For an ISO, problems with getting online and customer service directly translates to lost revenue. In this example, what Intira offers is a single point of accountability for customer service and support, and the ability for MiracleNet to expand and grow.

From a general perspective, the Netsourcing model allows a company to leverage benefits from a whole suite of expertise. Netsourcing allows an ISO to not only have a smooth operation, but also benefit from the expertise provided by the security experts, database architects, database administrators, performance management specialist, networking engineers and maintenance support professionals.

In short, companies with high-tech needs, for example Internet Service Providers can benefit from Netsourcing, whereby they can meet their growing needs without having to maintain in-house staff and infrastruture.

CONCLUSION

In conclusion, outsourcing is a great strategy for many number of reasons, provided the decision is arrived through a well-thought out process. Whether it is traditional outsourcing of simple IT processes, or the outsourcing of entire infrastructures through Netsourcing, a client can benefit from following a certain set of guidelines. Listed below are a few key areas which should be considered by an organization before they delve into any form of outsourcing.

(i)   Define precisely what you want to outsource. Are you planning to outsource IT staffing, or the entire IT and network infrastructure. Or maybe you only want to outsoure the database maintenance part of your business. This step is critical as your needs and goals as to what you want outsourced has a direct bearing on who and what kind of outsourcing provider you will be looking for.

(ii)   Do your homework when selecting an outsourcer. This is specially true in areas like ASP outsourcing as the entire ASP market is relatively new and unstable. Check on attributes like: are they publicly traded; are they listed on any exchanges; do they have staying power etc.

(iii)   Select an outsourcing provider that can grow with you and can scale their services easily as your business flourishes.

(iv)   Have clear metrics or Service Level Agreements (SLA) and process boundaries that would define a successful relationship with your Outsourcing provider.

(v)   Study the provider's business model and have contracts that would contribute to mutual profitability.

(vi)   If possible, have the outsourcing provider assign one empowered 'Project Manager' responsible for all activities vis-à-vis the outsourced area. This ensures responsibility on the part of the provider and also establishes a feedback path between the company and the outsourcing provider.

Minicase - Netsourcing: the Life Blood of an ISO
By Steve Gust: (Source: http://www.outsourcing-journal.com/issues/nov2000/html/cust_cl.html)

Entering the dot-com world is a real adventure for many businesses. A company needs to be prepared for the stiff market presence and competition from the AOLs of the world. Intira is the tool that MiracleNet.com, an Internet Access Provider, uses as it slices up its share of the market.

Larry Marcus, president and chief executive officer, of NY based MiracleNet.com knows that his service needs to be up to par when it comes to being an ISO. There are simply too many others out there. AOL, EarthLink and MSN are always looking for information Superhighway travelers. MiracleNet.com offers subscribers a chance to make money with memberships. If there are hiccups getting online, revenue can be lost. That's where Intira comes in, Marcus said. "They've standardized everything, and have cared about applications," he said. Last year MiracleNet.com needed a way to enter e-business and got it with Intira, a business that keeps MiracleNet.com open 24-7. The company entered into a three-year, $2.2 million contract. The challenge is providing the predictable service and performance required to ensure a successful foray into e-business. A continent away, Intira, near Silicon Valley in Pleasanton, Calif., has the resources to keep an ISO like MiracleNet.com up and running. Not only do they keep it in operation, but they also offer the ability to expand and grow.

Marcus wants to take MiracleNet.com to even higher levels. When the application goes down, an ISO is essentially out of business. Originally a free service, slumping Internet ad rates, sent MiracleNet.com into the paid subscriber field. Currently with 20,000 customers, the CEO has a goal of 100,000 in the near future. For $21.95 a month, it pays members monthly for referrals and offers half price motion picture tickets. It also offers personal web sites, chances at free trips and revenue sharing for additional products and services. There are also e-mail reminders for important dates. Without the proper netsourcer, such as Intira, it can all fall apart and fracture a company's bottom line.

Giving topnotch technical expertise Intira calls itself a netsourcer, an outsourcer of IT and networking infrastructures for e-business applications. Intira accomplishes most of its mission with a single point of accountability for customer service and support. This aspect of service is called the OneSource-One Call Customer Support program, and is available for Fortune 1000 organizations, dot-coms such as MiracleNet.com, application service providers and independent software vendors. With offices throughout the United States and Canada, Intira is said to have been the only vendor to demonstrate technical expertise in the pre-sale effort.

Marcus was most impressed with the service level agreement Intira offers. Its SLAs guarantee 99.95 percent availability. "It's obvious they do a good job and are serious about it judging on the SLA," Marcus said. The speed of the data provided by Intira has also impressed him. The communications he shares with them is another positive. "We've outsourced with different companies and it's not always been pleasant," he said. The implementation of the Intira system was a challenge but the outsourcer was determined to "make it right."

With engineering expertise available, Intira has also helped MiracleNet.com streamline data. MiracleNet.com's praise of its outsourcer is especially impressive given its association with other technology leaders including Microsoft, IBM, and e-Quest Technologies, Inc. For Intira, the goal is simple. It wants to be a seamless extension of the company's IT organization.

The service management centers of the Netsourcer have several technical advantages that an ISO requires including networking engineers, security experts, database architects and administrators, data storage professionals, performance management specialists, server and operating systems engineers and operations and maintenance support professionals. For Marcus they're all just a cell phone call away. The SMC engineers are able to identify, isolate and resolve potential service interruptions before they can even affect an application's availability.

Some other major Intira customers include Armstrong World Industries, a building materials company; EMC Corp., world leader in information storage; and Military.com, a military Internet site serving 80 million-member American military community. As with most agreements, the goal for Intira is to provide cutting edge technology and reduce total cost of ownership so that companies such as MiracleNet can focus on building the core business, which Marcus hopes will mean more and more subscribers taking advantage of an ISO to promote growth. All of this comes at what Intira calls "a controlled, predictable fee." In MiracleNet.com's case, where a few days business can affect profit ratios, Intira was also able to set up shop in somewhat quick order. Other benefits? A company with Intira can cut back on its technology and staffing investments. For Marcus, he has the peace of mind knowing that a vital portion of his business is done right.

Mini Case .... Continued.

That, too, is part of Intira's goal, as the outsourcer wants to be a full-fledged partner in success. Intira has also given MiracleNet.com other business contacts. As a dot-com player, Marcus is careful about whom he does business with and who has experience. One of the retail sites on MiracleNet.com went into bankruptcy, causing some customer discontent. There is no such discontent with Intira and its e-business connection. Still, the CEO fully urges any company to study outsourcers before an agreement is reached. "Make sure you check references and look at financial records," he said. "Look at their Dunn and Bradstreet rating also."

In summary, High-tech needs, such as Internet service access, can easily outstrip the abilities of an in-house staff. Others in the market may have the answers with technology that delivers at a lower price. Netsourcing is the outsourcing response for Internet access, a leading market in the global economy.

STUDY QUESTIONS

1. What is the difference between domestic IT outsourcing and global IT outsourcing ? Discuss some of the underlying reasons why a firm might opt for outsourcing its systems and technologies globally?

2. *"The Age of the outsourcing partnership between the client and the vendor can change (moderate) the management style used to manage the outsourcing relationship"*. Briefly postulate why this might be so.

3. What are the different types of control mechanisms that can be used by the client firm to manage their global IT outsourcing relationship?

4. What are some of the situations under which a client firm might want to sign an "incomplete" contract?

5. Discuss the various conflict resolution modes for varying degree of asset specificity in a global IT outsourcing relationship.

REFERENCES

Ang, Soon. (1993). *The Etiology of Information Systems Outsourcing*. Doctoral Dissertation. University of Minnesota, Minnesota.

Apte, U., & Winniford, M. (1991). Global Outsourcing of Information Systems Functions: Opportunities and Challenges," *Proceedings of the Information Resource Management Association International Conference 1991*, Memphis, 58-67.

Baliga, B.R., & Jaeger, A.M. (Fall 1984). Multinational Corporations: Control Systems and Delegation Issues. *Journal of International Business Studies*, 25-40.

Benko, Cathleen. (Spring 1993). Outsourcing Evaluation: A Profitable Process. *Information Systems Management*.

Caldwell, Bruce. (1995a, November 6). Outsourcing Megatrends. *Informationweek*, pp. 34- 56.

Cash, J.I., Jr., McFarlan, F.W., & McKenney, J.L.(1992). *Corporate Information Systems* (3rd ed.) , Business One Irwin, Homewood, Illinois.

Cash, J.I., F.W.McFarlan, J.L.McKenney, & M.R.Vitale. (1988). *Corporate Information Systems Management: Text and Cases* (2nd ed.), Homewood, IL:Irwin Publishing.

Clark, Mary E. (1993). Symptoms of Cultural Pathologies: A Hypothesis, in D.J.D. Sandole and H.V.Merwe (Eds*.), Conflict Resolution Theory and Practice: Integration and Application.* (Pp. 43-54). Manchester University Press, Manchester

Daft, R.L. & Lengel, R.H. (1986). Organizational Information Requirements, Media Richness and Structural Design. *Management Science*, 32, 554-571.

Davis, E.W. (1992, July-Aug). Global Outsourcing: Have U.S. Managers Thrown the Baby Out with the Bath Water?, *Business Horizons*, 58-65

Davis, K. (1996). *IT Outsourcing Relationships: An Exploratory Study of Interorganizational Control Mechanisms*, Unpublished doctoral dissertation, Harvard University.

Doz, Yves, Prahalad, C.K., and Hamel, Gary. (1990). Control, Change, and Flexibility: The Dilemma of Transnational Collaboration in Bartlett, C., Doz, Y., and Hedlund, G. (eds) *Managing the Global Firm.* London: Routledge: 117-143.

Druckman, D. (1993). An Analytical Research Agenda for Conflict and Conflict Resolution. In D.J.D. Sandole and H.V.Merwe (Eds*.), Conflict Resolution Theory and Practice: Integration and Application.* (Pp. 25-42). Manchester University Press, Manchester.

Ein-Dor, P., Segev, E. And Orgad, M. (Winter 1993). The Effect of National Culture on IS: Implications for International Information Systems. *Journal of Global Information Management*, 1(1), 33-44.

Forman, L.A. and Cohen, M.D. (1970). Compromise and Logroll: Comparing the Efficiency of Two Bargaining Processes, *Behavioral Science*, 15, 180-183.

Galbraith, J. (!977). *Designing Complex Organizations.* Addison-Wesley, Reading, Massachussets.

Govindarajan, V. & Fisher, J. (1990). Strategy, Control Systems, and Resource Sharing: Effects on Business-Unit Performance*. Academy of Management Journal*, 33, 259-285.

Grossman, S.J. and Hart, O.D. (1983). An Analysis of the Principal-Agent Problem, *Econometrica,* 51, 7-45.

Gupta, A.K. & Govindarajan, V. (1986). Resource Sharing among SBUs: Strategic Antecedents and Administrative Implications. *Academy of Mangement Journal*, 29, 695-714.

Gurbaxani, V. (1996, July).The New World of Information Technology Outsourcing. *Communications of the ACM,* 39 (7), 45-46.

Guterl, F. (1996). How to Manage Your Outsourcer. *Datamation*, March 1, 1996, 79-83.

Heeks, R. (1996). Global Software Outsourcing to India by Multinational Clients, in P. Palvia, S., Palvia, & E. Roche, *Global Information Technology and Systems Management: Key Issues and Trends* (pp.), Ivy League Publishing, Nashua, NH.

Heywood, P. (1994, Nov. 21). Global Outsourcing: What Works, What Doesn't. *Data Communications*, 75-80.

Klepper, R. (1995). Outsourcing Relationships. In M. Khosrowput (Ed.), *Managing Information Technology Investments with Outsourcing* (pp. 219-243), Idea Group Publishing, Harrisburg, USA.

Lacity, M.C., Willcocks, L.P., & Feeny, D.F. (1995, May-June). IT Outsourcing: Maximize flexibility and Control. *Harvard Business Review*, 84-93.

Lacity, M.C. and Hirschheim, R. (1993). *Information Systems Outsourcing: Myths,Metaphors, and Realities*, New York, John Wiley & Sons.

Leifer, Richard and Mills, P.K. (1996). An Information Processing Approach for Deciding Upon Control Strategies and Reducing Control Loss in Emerging Organizations *Journal of Management*, 22 (1), 113-137.

Loh, L.Y.. (1993). *The Economics and Organization of Information Technology Governance: Sourcing Strategies for Corporate Information Infrastructure.* Doctoral Dissertation. MIT, Massachusetts.

Loh, L. & Venkatraman, N. (1992a, December). Diffusion of Information Technology Outsourcing: Influence Sources and the Kodak Effect. *Information Systems Research*, 334-358.

Loh, L. & Venkatraman, N. (1992b, Summer). Determinants of Information Technology Outsourcing: A Cross-Sectional Analysis. *Journal of Management Information Systems*, 9 (1), 7-24.

Malhotra, Y. (1995). IS Productivity And Outsourcing Policy: A Conceptual Framework and Empirical Analysis, in *the Proceedings of the First America's Conference of Information Systems*, Pittsburg, USA, 142-144.

McFarlan, F.W. and Nolan, R.L. (1995, Winter). How to Manage an IT Outsourcing Alliance, *Sloan Management Review*, 9-23.

Mumpower, Jerly L. (1991, October). The Judgement Policies Of Negotiators And The Structure Of Negotiation Problems, *Management Science.*, 37 (10), 1304-1324.

Nam, K., Rajagopalan, S., Rao, H.R. & Chaudury, A. (1996, July). A Two-Level Investigation of Information Systems Outsourcing. *Communications of the ACM*, 39 (7), 36-44.

Nam, K., Chaudhury, A., and Raghav Rao, H. A mixed interger model of bidding strategies for outsourcing. *European Journal Of Operational Research*, 87 (1995) 257-273

Nelson, P., Richmond, W. and Seidmann, A. (1996, July). Two Dimensions of Software Acquisition. *Communications of the ACM*, 39 (7), 29-35.

Palvia, P. (1995). A Dialectic View of Information Systems Outsourcing. *Information & Management*, 29, 265-275.

Pastore, Richard. (1996, May 15). The Art of the Deal. *CIO Magazine*. http://www.cio.com/. [June 1 1996]

Patane, J.R. & Jurison, J. (1994, June). Is Global Outsourcing Diminishing the Prospects for American Programmers?. *Journal of Systems Management*, 6-10.

Raiffa, H. *The Art and Science of Negotiation*, Belknap/Harvard University Press, Cambridge, MA,1982.

Sauter, V. (1992). Cross Cultural Aspects of Model Management Needs in a Transnational Decision Support System. In *The Global Issues of Information Technology Management*, edited by Palvia, Palvia, and Zigli, Idea Group Publishing.

Sharland, A.P., *International Outsourcing: An Empirical Study of the Role of Transactions Costs and Competitive Advantage in the International Buyer/Supplier Relationships*, Unpublished Doctoral Dissertation, The Florida State University, 1993.

Spee, J.C. (1994). *Restructuring Corporate Staff Functions Through Outsourcing.*. Unpublished Doctoral Dissertation. The Claremont Graduate School, California.

Takac, P.F. (1994). Outsourcing: a key to controlling escalating IT costs?. *International Journal of Technology Management*, 9 (2), 139-155.

Tannenbaum, (1968*). Control in Organizations*, McGraw Hill.

Thompson,. J.D (1967). *Organizations in Action*, McGraw Hill.

Ungson, G.R., Braunstein, D.N., and Hall, P.D. 1981. Managerial Information Processing: A Research Review. *Administrative Science Quarterly*, 26, 116-134.

Willcocks, L., Lacity, M. And Fitzgerald, G., (1995). Information Technology Outsourcing in Europe and the USA: Assessment Issues. *International Journal of Information Management.*, vol. 15, no. 5, pp. 333-351.

23

Location Economics and
Global Software Development Centers

Hemant K Jain
University of Wisconsin- Milwaukee, USA

Jaeki Song
University of Wisconsin- Milwaukee, USA

ABSTRACT

A severe shortage and increasing costs of Information Technology professionals are forcing software development companies to explore global system development strategies. The main objective of this chapter is to present a conceptual model for global software development that considers economic, political, managerial, and technical environments. A review of relevant literature from economics, global manufacturing and global R & D is presented and factors affecting the global software development decision are identified. The conceptual framework addresses the global software development decision and the selection of development center locations. The model provides insight into the reasons for choosing a particular country among possible locations.

INTRODUCTION

In the last thirty years, multinational corporations have significantly expanded their strategy of manufacturing products globally. The motivations for this trend have been lower labor cost and access to large consumer markets. Recently, many corporations have embarked on a strategy of global Research & Development to take advantage of the highly skilled human resources available all over the world.

The globalization provides business value by increasing (globalizing) the markets for a certain specialized product/service as well as intangible assets, such as technological know-how, marketing ability, and effective management [Helpman, E., 1984, Morck, R., and Yeung B., 1992]. Rapidly developing information and communication technology enhances globalization by creating location independence. Geographical distance is losing significance for business. Teams working at different locations in different time zones can be brought together through technology to address problems [Jarvenpaa, S. L. and B. Ives, 1994, McFarlan, F. W. 1996]. Various globalization models such as wholly owned subsidiaries, joint ventures, or outsourcing have been used.

The growing cost of software development and the severe shortage of skilled professionals are stimulating a significant change in the software development strategy of many companies. They are adopting new technologies to develop applications more efficiently. Some companies are locating their development facilities in various parts of the world. The motivations for such a move are similar to those for global research and development, i.e. availability of highly skilled human resources. Additionally, there is significant wage differential. For example, wages of highly skilled software engineers in India are lower than in the United States [Natarjan, A , 1999]. Furthermore, in India software professionals are the highest paid professionals, thus attracting the best talent of the country to this profession.

This is a major impetus to software companies moving towards overseas development centers. Some developing countries in Asia and South America have been making significant efforts to attract companies from the USA and Europe to establish software development centers in their areas. For instance, India has the second largest number of software professionals after the USA [Heeks, R , 1996]. Currently, many multinational companies, like Microsoft, Oracle, Novell, Hewlett-Packard, Texas Instrument, and Adobe, have software development centers setup in India. Similarly, many global corporations have set up software centers in Ireland, Brazil and Philippines.

This trend towards global software development has been facilitated by developments in information and networking technologies. Explosive growth of the Internet has played a significant role in facilitating communication. The global network enables companies to exchange information more efficiently, eliminating time and place constraints. However, other significant factors such as economic, technical, and political, need to be considered in making a decision to develop software globally and in selecting a development center location. This chapter presents a conceptual model to help support a global software development decision and to select a location for a development center.

GLOBAL SOFTWARE DEVELOPMENT MODEL

The decision to develop software globally is a complex one. Many factors of a home country that motivates the establishment of global development centers need to be considered. Similarly, in deciding a location for the development center many factors related to the host country need to be considered. This chapter explores the home and host country factors associated with selecting a location among the possible countries. Figure 1 summarizes the global software development model with respect to home and host country factors.

The motivation for an organization to consider global software development (GSD) is generally driven by three major factors that depend on the characteristics of the organization and the environment in the home country, termed as home county factors. One of the major motivating factors may be the availability or lack of availability of skilled Information Technology professionals in the home country, accompanied by their high cost. The efforts and skills required in setting up overseas development centers are significant, making it difficult for small companies and companies which lack management expertise to embark on this strategy. Thus, the size of the organization and IT management expertise are important home country factors that need to be considered in a GSD decision. Particularly, global software development companies need to seek the availability of IT manager who is familiar with working environments of the host country. Thus, the availability of IT manager may affect selection of GSD location (dotted line in figure 1).

Closely related to the GSD decision is the selection of a county(s) as a location for the development center. Many important factors (termed as host country factors) need to be considered in selecting a location. First, the supply and cost of highly skilled Information Technology professionals must be taken into account. This supply depends on the education and training infrastructure of the country. Other essential factors that need to be considered are the basic infrastructure, including the cost of acquiring reliable communication and physical infrastructure. The expected cost advantage may depend on the cost of living in the country. The risks related to the location decision can be in two major areas, the risk related to fluctuations in the exchange rate and political risk. Obviously, there are many other factors that may influence the success of a GSD effort, but the proposed model incorporates the most important and directly relevant factors. Each of the home country and host county factors represented in the model are discussed in details here along with their theoretical basis.

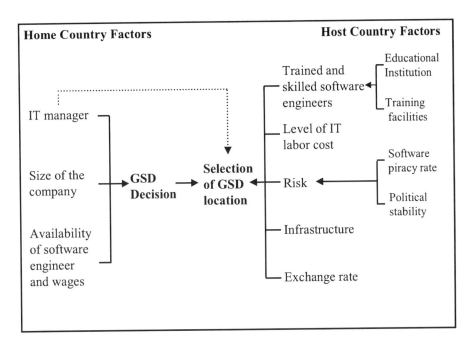

Figure 1: Global Software Development Model

HOME COUNTRY FACTORS

A decision to embark on global software development is influenced by economic, political, managerial and technical factors that may motivate the Global Software Development. Based on our survey of literature, we identified home country factors as the capacity of the organization, its capability to manage global technology projects and the availability and cost of skilled IT workforce in the home country.

Information Technology (IT) Manager

Globalization requires special skills of IT managers since it reveals cultural differences including language, educational background, and relationships between managers and workers [Ives, B. and S. L. Jarvenpaa, 1991]. The manager responsible for global software development needs to be skilled in distributed development techniques and should be familiar with the host country's culture, such as the political and social environments. In software development, knowledge plays an important role and it needs to be effectively transferred across geographically distanced locations [Barlett, C.A. and S. Ghoshal, 1987, Kleinknecht, A. and J. Wenger, 1998]. We, therefore, posit that managers should be able to communicate across international cultures, to deliver technology, to integrate knowledge, and to educate human resources of host country.

Size of the Company

The size of the company has been considered an important factor in organizational studies [Kimberly, 1976]. In this chapter, size refers to the capability of a company to create and to maintain scale economies that can work on a national and regional basis [Ang, S. and D.W. Straub, 1998, Kettinger, W. J. 1994]. Palvia and Hunter [Palvia S. and M.G. Hunter, 1996] identify organizational size as a critical factor in software development projects conducted across different countries. Global software development projects require companies with sizable technical staffs and financial capacity.

Shortage of skilled IT professional and High Level of Wage

The tremendous growth of the software industry and the increased complexity of modern software have created an unprecedented demand for highly skilled software developers. Additionally, the competitive nature of the industry has placed a heavy demand to reduce the time to market. This has created a severe shortage of IT professionals especially in developed countries like the United States and Western Europe, and has significantly increased wages [Dept of Commerce, 1998] resulting in increased software development costs [Kemerer, C.F., 1998]. Figure 2 shows the average annual wage of core software industry employees from 1990 to 1998 in USA. As can be seen from figure 2, the average wage was $66,500 and $68,900 in 1997 and 1998 respectively. This is significantly higher than the average wage of $29,800 in 1997 for all professions in private industry excluding the core software industry [Business Software Alliance, 1998 and 1999].

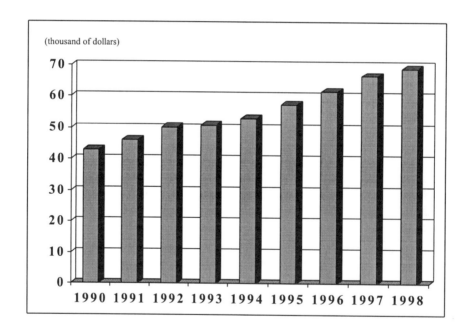

Figure 2: Annual Wages per Employee in the Core Software Industry
(Source: Nathan Associate Inc. in Business Software Alliance Report (1999))

Moreover, in the software industry, the economic equilibrium has moved because demand exceeds supply, which leads to increasing annual wage rates. Table 1 shows the comparison of US wages in the core software industry with high tech manufacturing and all private industry excluding core software industry. As can be seen, the percentage increase in core software industry has been significantly higher than in any other industry.

Table 1. Average Annual Wage of Employee in Industry (thousand of dollars)

Industry	1994	1995	1996	1997	Growth
High –Tech Manufacturing					
Consumer Electronic	37.1	36.7	39.2	41.8	4.1%
Communications Equipment	43.8	46.0	48.4	52.3	6.0%
Electronic Components and Accessories	30.1	31.0	32.1	34.0	4.1%
Defense Electronics	49.1	52.1	56.7	57.8	5.6%
Industrial Electronics	39.1	41.6	44.1	47.1	6.4%
Electromedical Equipment	43.7	46.8	49.8	51.9	5.9%
Photonics	46.7	50.3	52.2	54.0	4.9%
Core Software Industry	53.4	57.3	61.5	66.5	7.6%
All Private Industry but Core Software	26.4	27.3	28.4	29.8	4.2%

Source: Nathan Associates Inc. in Business Software Alliance Report (1999)

These increased wages and the shortage of IT professionals have motivated corporations to adopt various strategies such as temporary workers on H1-B visa, outsourcing and overseas software development centers. The first option generally does not result in any cost saving to the corporation, as H1-B visa worker needs to be paid competitive salaries. Global outsourcing results in some cost savings [McFarlan, F. W., 1996]. McFarlan [McFarlan, F. W., 1996] suggests following practices that can reduce cost of global outsourcing and increase likelihood of success:

- Visit the country to identify companies with strong technical capabilities but weak marketing presence in USA/Europe. This is expected to result in lower cost
- Start with modest projects
- Plan for managing internal hostility

A significant potential concern and risk of global outsourcing identified by McFarlan [McFarlan, F. W., 1996] is losing control over an important corporate resource. In addition, package software developers and large technology-intensive corporations may not want to depend on an outsourcer for critical strategic work. Overseas software development centers are considered a viable option in these situations.

HOST COUNTRY FACTORS

Successful global software development requires significant investment in setting up operations and hiring skilled IT professionals in the host country. The most effective way to serve a global market is with a location-based approach with a macro level analysis that considers not only traditional economic factors such as natural resources and labor costs, but also available human resources with specialized skills [Authur, W. B., 1996, MacCormack, A.D., et al.,1994]. Major host country factors that need to be considered in selecting the locations for global software development are the availability of trained or potentially trainable IT professionals, political stability, the macroeconomic environment and the technical and/or basic infrastructure.

Trained and Skilled Software Engineers

Software development heavily depends on the skills and knowledge of the developers. This skill and knowledge can be built through education, training and experience. The final quality of software depends upon the engineer's knowledge [Robilland, P. N., 1999]. The complex nature of most software development projects requires skilled and experienced software engineers who are familiar with different types of technologies such as hardware, operating systems, and software development languages [Meyer, A.D., 1991]. Such engineers can mitigate many of the risks including the lack of required knowledge in a project that may occur during the development process [Keil, M.,et al., 1998]. Moitra [Moitra, D. 2000] identifies factors that contribute to the growth of a countries' software industry as:

- availability of a highly competent and large latent pool
- world-class quality and high process maturity
- competitive cost structures
- rapid delivery capability
- language

The availability of skilled IT professionals varies between different countries. India has established itself as a top source of high quality skilled IT professionals. India has the world's second largest pool of English speaking scientific and technical professionals [Moitra, D. 2000]. The Indian software industry employs approximately 300,000 people. India has set a goal of $50 billion dollars software industry by year 2008. To reach this goal India, must add approximately 200,000 developers a year [Moitra, D. 2000]. Other countries with significant numbers of skilled professionals are Brazil, Ireland and Russia. Table 2 represents the number software companies, the number of software engineers and number of graduates each year for these countries for which 1996 data were available.

Table 2. Information related to IT professionals

Country	Number of software development company	Number of software engineers	Number of new software graduates every year
BRAZIL	About 8,000	64,000	7,500
INDIA	About 300	130,000	20,000
IRELAND	About 500	13,000	12,000
RUSSIA	100-120	55,000	4,500

Source: Computerworld (1996)

Educational Institution and Training Facilities

Education and training are generally used to support the knowledge accumulation process of software professionals. The level at which these processes are prevalent and well established in the host country determine the level and quality of the IT work force available [Banker, R. D., et al., 1998]. Substantial differences between various countries exist in this dimension. For instance, based on the most recent reports, India has about 500 computer educational centers, 1,000 technical institutes, and 500 universities. According to a recent report by NASSCOM, the IT training segment grew at over 32.7% during 1998-99. Indian universities annually churn out nearly 90,000 engineering graduates with many private training houses producing similar numbers (with varying degree of skill and quality) [Moitra, D. 2000]. A new generation of institutes, called Indian Institutes of Information Technology, has been set up. In Philippines, there were 12,000 computer science and computer engineering students in 1989. In 1993, there were 60,000 students and 5,000 graduates per year entering IT professions [Meadows, C. J. 1996].

Wages of IT Professionals

Labor cost is a significant factor in the location decision particularly for companies operating in labor-intensive industries such as software development. The wage rates of IT professionals in under-developed and developing countries are significantly lower than developed countries. The relatively successful industrialization of several low-wage Asian countries has given rise to concern about an increasing challenge from international competition [Kleinknecht, A. and J. Wenger, 1998]. For example, the average salary for engineers who have at least 5 years experiences in India is about $10,000 U.S. dollars. However, increased demand from many developed countries is putting significant pressure on wages in India. With increasing competition for resources, the ability to attract, develop, and retain high quality employees is indeed the name of the game. A variety of approaches such as hiring experienced people from other companies, advertisements, job portals, campus recruitment, head hunters, joint industry-academic programs, employee referrals are used for attracting qualified employees [Moitra, D. 2000]. The strategies for retaining employees used by many companies are [Moitra, D. 2000]:

- continuous learning opportunities
- high quality work
- competitive compensation
- career progression
- stock option

Russia has almost the same level of salary. However, the salaries of engineers in Brazil and Ireland are about $ 22,000 and $45,000, respectively.

Another factor indicative of the health of the IT labor market is a strong domestic IT market and the penetration of technology, indicated by the use of PCs, internet users etc. Table 3 presents the current standings and targets for the IT industry in India. Unfortunately, similar data for other countries are not available.

Table 3. Status of IT Industry in India (Millions)

	Present Level on 31 March 2000	**Target 2008**
Total Number of PCs	4.3	20
Internet Subscribers	0.77	35
Internet Users	3.2	100
Cable TV Subscribers	37	70
Fixed Phones	26	125
Television Sets	75	225
Software Industry in India	5,700	87,000
Software exports from India	3,900	50,000
IT industry in India	8,600	140,000

Source: NASSCOM

Level of Risk

Since Global Software Development involves significant investment, the level of risk in GSD needs to be considered. The definition of risks in GSD can be quite broad; they include protection of intellectual property rights, political stability, and economic stability. Cultural differences and the quality of the legal system also contribute to the risk. In GSD projects, the most important risk factors are the intellectual property rights and political stability.

The pervasiveness of software piracy throughout the world is having a profound effect on the software industry and the development of intellectual properties and technologies. The software piracy rate can indicate the level of protection of intellectual properties in a country. A recent report shows that the rate of software piracy in some developing countries is extremely high compared to United States (See table 4). For example, the piracy rates of Russia were 89%. This rate indicates that 89% of software available in Russia was illegally pirated. This risk reflects that there exists uncertainty in Russia, and in turn companies may hesitate to develop software in that country.

Table 4. Software piracy rate and economic indicators

Country	Piracy Rate (%)		Software Retail Revenue*		Per Capital GDP**	
	1996	1997	1996	1997	1996	1997
India	79	69	255.3	184.7	1500	1600
Brazil	68	62	356.4	395	6100	6300
Ireland	70	65	45.7	46.8	15400	16800
Russia	91	89	383.3	251.8	5300	5200
Switzerland	43	39	99.5	92.9	22400	22600
U.S.	27	27	2360.9	2779.7	27500	28600

Source: Business Software Alliance and World Bank (1999)
* Million of dollars, ** dollars

However, the piracy rates in developed countries, Switzerland and U.S., are relatively low 39% and 27%, respectively. As indicated by table 4, the piracy rate is significantly related to retail sales. Developed countries with relatively high per capita GDP exhibit relatively low piracy rate and relatively high software retail revenue.

The global environment may pose threats and obstacles to IT development projects not generally encountered in the United States or other developed countries. Factors, such as regulations, legal protections, work-rule, protection tariffs, and political stability need to be considered in selecting the development location. Political instability increases the uncertainty and risk of the investment [Kogut B., and N. Kulatilaka, 1994, Loree, D.W., and S.E. Guisinger, 1995, tranctinsky, N. abd S.L. Jarvenpaa, 1995, Wheeler, D. and A. Mody, 1992]. Table 5 presents the level of political stability index (0 to 100) for six countries. In the table, a high index represents stable political environments.

Table 5. Political Stability

Country	1996	1997	1998
India	69	68.8	63.8
Brazil	67	71.3	67.8
Ireland	88.5	88	86.8
Russia	62.5	66	63.8
Switzerland	89.5	86.3	88.3
U.S.	86	80.8	81.8

Source: World Bank (1999)

Infrastructure

Communication infrastructure has played a crucial role in economic globalization. To exchange information in GSD, engineers or managers in the home and host countries need to effectively communicate. Meyer [Meyer, A.D. 1991] points out that the productivity of engineers in a global firm depends on the extent of his or her ability to tap into an appropriate network of information flow because face-to-face communication is not suitable for a geographically dispersed organization. Recent studies show that global communication infrastructure enhances productivity, efficiency, and relationships among companies and is significantly related to globalization [Mariotti, S. and L. Piscitello, 1995, Streeter, L.A., at el., 1996]. Chen and Chen [Chen, H. and Tain-Jy Chen, 1998] point out that global communication infrastructure is particularly useful for entering an immature market in which institutions that facilitate internationalization are still lacking. In other words, it is possible in some cases to have relatively less developed communication infrastructure within the country but an acceptable international communication infrastructure. More importantly, the technology infrastructure not only affects information exchange, but also impacts production, distribution and technology transfer. Communication infrastructure that makes an effective and efficient information exchange between the home and host country locations possible is a profound requirement for supporting global operation and is indeed an important determinant in location choice [Vitalari, N.P., and J.C. Wetherbe, 1995]. Poor host country connectivity requires additional costs, for example, communication cost in India is relatively high (see table 6), however, India's communication infrastructure is undergoing some deregulation and it is hoped that the private sector will play a major role in improving the infrastructure [NASSCOM, 2001].

Rapid progress in technology is reshaping the global economy and increasing the importance of knowledge and knowledgeable workers in the economy. Countries can derive a significant competitive advantage from their knowledgeable workers. A highly developed technical infrastructure enables development and the transfer of new technology to businesses. The availability of skilled human resources can provide only a partial picture of the technical infrastructure of the country.

The term information infrastructure includes the penetration of the information economy represented by newspapers, radios, television sets, personal computers, and Internet hosts.

Table 6. Infrastructure

Country	Communication Infrastructure	Technical Infrastructure	Information infrastructure	
	Telephone Line per 1000 peoples	Technician and scientist in R&D	PC per 1000 peoples	Internet Host per 1000 peoples
India	15	151	1.5	0.05
Brazil	96	165	18.21	4.2
Ireland	395	1971	145	90.89
Russia	175	4358	23.7	5.51
Switzerland	640	2409	408.5	207.8
U.S.	640	3732	362.4	442.11

Source: World Bank (1999)

According to NASSCOM report [NASSCOM 2001], India has dominated other Asian countries in infrastructure based on a variety of criteria, such as the generation of foreign direct investment, the introduction of new technology, the transfer of skills and an increase in competitiveness. Table 6 summarizes the results of a World Bank study on infrastructure provided by various countries as measured by communication, technical and information infrastructure.

Exchange Rate

Exchange rates are another important factor that needs to be considered when companies do business globally. For example, issues and risks related to the devaluation of local currencies and evolving new payment systems need to be considered [Woodward, D.P., and R. J. Rolfe, 1993]. The economic and financial crises in Asia in 1999 provided opportunities to reduce the cost of setting up GSD operations and reduced the labor cost for a short period. However, this exchange rate fluctuation has a negative impact on the market entry decision because of the increased uncertainty that results in the hesitation and postponement of an investment decision [Wallace, C. D. 1990]. Therefore, exchange rate volatility can be one of the major indicators used to gauge the economic stability of a country and one of the important factors affecting the decision regarding a development location [Kogut, B. and N. Kulatilaka, 1994].

OTHER MACRO AND MICRO LEVEL FACTORS

The model presented above identifies major factors affecting the Global Software Development decision and the selection of the development location. Additionally, a number of other macro and micro level factors need to be considered.

Macro-Level Considerations: Language, Tax, and Quality

An English-speaking population may be one of the most important factors to decide the best location for setting up a software development center. An English-speaking population may reduce the cost of educating the staff and transferring knowledge and technology. It would also help reduce the ongoing communication cost.

Another macro level consideration is tax incentives. Some host countries may provide tax incentives to global corporations to make it attractive for them to setup a development center. Inducing global companies to set up development centers can stimulate a host country's economic activity, reduce unemployment and produce demand in domestic markets.

To succeed in the market place a software development company needs to deliver quality products and/or services that meet user requirements. The quality of software can be defined as "the extent to which the product satisfies its specifications" [Schach, S. R., 1997, p. 111]. Singapore, one of the leading countries in IT, produces high quality software in terms of International Standards such as ISO 9000, SEI CMM, SPICE etc. However, the cost for developing software in Singapore is relatively high compared to other Asian countries. The Philippines produces software of relatively low quality with low cost. India takes a leadership position concerning quality and cost. The Software Engineering Institute at Carnegie-Melon University (CMU) classifies software development companies based on their quality practices. They certify the companies at various levels starting from level 1 (lowest) to level 5 representing the best software development practices. More than 55 percent of the CMU level 5 companies in the world are in India [Moitra, D. 2000]. Table 7 represents the results of a survey of 300 companies conducted by NASSCOM in May 2000 to ascertain the adoption of International quality standards by Indian software companies.

Table 7. International Quality Certification of Indian software companies

Quality Certification	Number of Companies
Already acquired ISO 9000 or SEI Level 2 other equivalent certification	148
In the process of acquiring certification (will acquire by December 2000)	85
Plan to acquire between January 2001 and December 2001	51
No plans at present	16

SEI Quality Certification	Number of Companies as on 31 May 2000	Number of Companies expected by March 2001
Acquired Level 5	15	25
Acquired Level 4	14	20
Acquired Level 3	07	40

Source: NASSCOM

Figure 3 provides a cost quality comparison of a number of countries provided by NASSCOM. Therefore, when software development companies determine the location of offshore software development centers, they need to seriously analyze cost as well as quality.

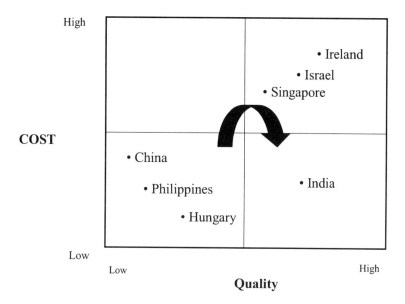

Figure 3.: Cost Vs. Quality
Source: NASSCOM (http://www.nasscom.org)

Micro-Level Considerations

Once a global software development company decides on a specific country, the company needs to consider micro-level factors such as project size, project structure, the technology used by the project, the staff's experience with the technology and the development processes used by the project [McFarlan, F. W., 1996]. The larger projects in terms of dollar expense, staffing levels, and elapsed time are more appealing for global development as the larger base can more easily cover the inevitable coordination costs. However, very large projects compared to companies experience may increase the risk. Experience of the development team with the technology used by the project needs to be considered for some projects, the nature of the task defines the processing, file/database structures and output completely from the moment of project conceptualization. Such projects can be classified as "highly structured". Highly structured projects are easiest for global development [McFarlan, F. W., 1996]. They also carry lower risk than projects whose outputs are more subject to the user manager's changing judgment on desirable features. According to MacFarlan [McFarlan, F. W., 1996] large highly structured projects almost irrespective of the technology can be safely developed globally. Conversely, projects which have elements of low structure and whose specifications are likely to evolve over time, the geographic distance may turn out to be a real problem. Table 8 adopted from McFlaran [McFarlan, F. W., 1996] summarizes the effect of technology and project structure on global development.

Another consideration may be the total elapsed time for the project. In this competitive business environment, the time to market is becoming increasingly important. The proper selection of development locations may enable the sequential development of projects in different countries. For example Lines 1 to 100 of the code is developed in country A, at the end of the working day for country A the work is transferred to country B producing line 101 to 200, and so on. Figure 4 represents the sequential development concept. In this case, countries are located in different time zones. This strategy allows for a reduction in the project schedule, however the management of the project could be a difficulty. In both cases, communication among managers and workers is one of the critical success factors for transferring and sharing knowledge and procedures.

Table 8: Effect of Degree of Structure, Company-Relative Technology, and Project Size on Project Implementation Risk

Low Technology	**Large project**	Poor global outsourcing candidate	Good global outsourcing candidate
	Small project	Poor global outsourcing candidate	Poor global outsourcing candidate unless part of a portfolio
High Technology	**Large project**	Poor global outsourcing candidate	Good global outsourcing candidate if partner has technology skills
	Small project	Poor global outsourcing candidate	Poor global outsourcing candidate unless part of portfolio and partner has technology skills

[Source: McFalran (1996) p. 356]

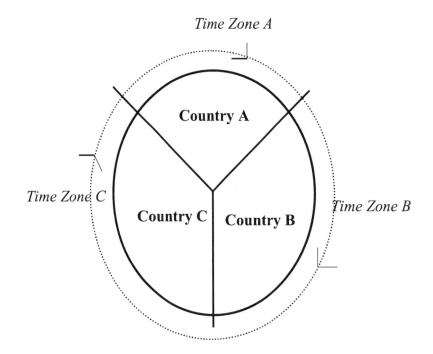

Figure 4: Sequential Software Development

MANAGERIAL IMPLICATIONS

Globalization is affecting almost every business and industry in the world. Globalization of manufacturing has become very well established in last thirty years. Various theories and models exist to help managers decide on whether to globalize the manufacturing operations and choose locations. More recently shortage of skilled personal in developed countries and abundant supply of well-qualified scientists and engineers in developing countries, Eastern Europe and former Soviet Union has started a trend towards global Research & Development.

Increased use of Information Technology (IT) and severe shortage of skilled IT professionals accompanied by higher cost are forcing the managers of IT organizations to explore various alternatives to meet user requirements, reduce cost and improve quality. Many managers are considering the global software development option, which allow them to take advantage of skilled IT professionals available at a lower cost in developing countries.

Little theory, frameworks or conceptual models are available in the literature to help managers decide whether to embark on global software development by setting up software/system development centers in various parts of the world, help justify such decision and decide on location(s) for the development center. This chapter presents a conceptual model for global software development decision. The model is based on experiences in global manufacturing and global Research & Development but considers the unique nature of software/system development.

As described in the model, before embarking on global software development, managers need to critically evaluate their home country environment consisting of availability and cost of software professionals. Tracking and analyzing cost of previous and ongoing development projects and looking at industry forecasts can accomplish this. Next the capability of IT managers to manage a global team of developers located in various parts of the world needs to be critically evaluated. This capability may depend on the global exposure of the managers, their sensitivity to cultural and language issues and experience in managing remote operations. The size of the organization especially the size of IT development operation also needs to be considered. Small development operation makes it difficulty to justify investment in setting up infrastructure for global development.

Once a global software development decision is made, it is necessary to understand the differences among the countries as a possible location for development center. The management can use various host country factors identified in the model to objectively and systematically evaluate each alternative. Publicly available data on various countries can be used for this purpose. The commerce department of the country can also provide data not available in the public domain.

Finally, the most frequently discussed issue in MIS is the alignment between business strategy and information system management. Previous research has emphasized the benefits of establishing a link between business-strategic planning and technology-strategic planning. In this sense, a global software development issue also needs to significantly consider establishing an alignment that requires cooperation between the senior business managers and the senior IS technology managers.

SUMMARY

Increasing numbers of companies are relying on Information Technology to gain a competitive advantage and support globalization. To support this trend, a software development strategy must deliver high quality solutions in shorter times and at lower costs [Kemerer 1998, Slaughter 1998]. The potential of significant cost savings and the availability of highly skilled IT professionals in developing countries are fueling the growth of Global Software Development. Some countries have a relatively abundant supply of skilled IT workforce, training facilities and are rapidly improving the technical infrastructure, such as the communication network. Also, the political stability and security of intellectual property are improving in many of these countries. Maturing project management knowledge and skills in these countries are also making them attractive locations for software development centers. Furthermore, exchange rates play an important role in selecting software development centers.

Organizations can avoid failure of global software development effort by systematically and objectively analyzing the development decision and selecting appropriate locations. The conceptual model presented in this chapter, which incorporates various political, economic, technical and managerial factors, can provide a basis for such an analysis.

Once a company selects the best location using macro-level analyses, the company needs to analyze micro-level factors, such as the availability of technology, detailed human resource, communication for sharing knowledge, and an alignment between business strategy and IT strategy. Future study requires more detailed analysis of these micro level factors and a comparison of global software development strategy with the outsourcing strategy.

Mini Case

Component Development, Inc. is a large company that develops and market software. The company is located in Milwaukee, Wisconsin. The company is a global enterprise headquartered in Milwaukee ,Wisconsin. It develops software components for electronics systems. The company employees more than 500 software engineers and had sales of $50 million in 2000.

From 1988 to 2000, the company's market share dropped from an estimated 20 percent to 7 percent due to competition provided by other companies and dramatically increased costs of developing software. Also, they had trouble recruiting qualified software engineers in the U.S. To solve this problem, the company has struggled to develop a strategy for obtaining new competitive advantages. Finally, the company decided to develop software globally. At first, many IT managers in the company felt that there are many obstacles to global development, expertise in various countries and communication were the two major ones. The company recently recruited a new CIO, Richard Freeman, and a IT managers who are very familiar with foreign countries in terms of culture and environments. A global software development (GSD) team was created to formally examine benefits and feasible location centers. The GSD team needs to find the best location for developing software that will generate competitive advantages.

Your boss, Richard Freeman, has given you the task to identify a county for developing software. You must visit three countries, India, Russia, and Ireland, and report back to Richard identifying and discussing each factor that plays an important role to select an appropriate location. Generate a report, which compares and contrasts factors for selecting the most appropriate location to globally develop software.

STUDY QUESTIONS

1. What is the role of the IT manager in developing software globally?
2. Discuss the most important home country factors in global software development.
3. What are the major factors in select a host country for developing software?
4. What advantages and disadvantages are there to develop software globally?

REFERENCES

Ang, S. and D. W. Straub, "Production and transaction economies and IS outsourcing A study in the US banking industry," *MIS Quarterly* (22:4), 1998, pp. 535-552.

Authur, W. B. "Increasing returns and the new world of business," *Harvard Business Review*, (July-August), 1996, pp. 100-109.

Banker, R. D. and Davis, G. B. and S. A. Slaughter, "Software Development Practices, Software Complexity, and Software Maintenance Performance: A Field Study," *Management Science* (44:4), 1998, pp. 433-450

Barlett, C. A., and S. Ghoshal, "Managing across boarders: New strategic requirements," *Sloan Management Review*, Summer, 1987, pp. 7-17.

Business Software Alliance, *Global Software Piracy Report*, Washington DC, Business, 1998.

Business Software Alliance, *Forecasting a Robust Future: An Economic Study of the U.S. Software Industry*, Washington DC, Business, June, 1999.

Chen, H. and Tain-Jy Chen, "Network linkages and location choice in foreign direct investment," *Journal of International Business Studies* (29:3), 1998, pp. 445-467.

ComputerWorld, "*In Depth: Look out, Here comes India*," February, 26, 1996.

Cyranek, G. and S. C. Bhatnagar, *Technology Transfer for Development*, Tata, McGraw-Hill, New Delhi, 1992.
Department of Commerce, *America's New Deficit: The shortage of Information Technology Workers*, 1998.
Heeks, R., "Global Software Outsourcing to India by Multinational Corporations," in Palvia, P. C., Palvia, S. C., and E. M. Roche, eds., *Global Information Technology and Systems Management: Key Issues and Trends*, Nashua, NH, IVY League Publishing, 1996, 365-392

Helpman, E., "A simple theory of international trade with multinational corporations," *Journal of Political Economics* (92), 1984, pp. 451-471.

Jarvenpaa, S. L. and B. Ives, "Organizing for global competition: The fit of information technology," *Decision Sciences* (24:3), 1994, pp.547-580.

Ives, B. and S. L. Jarvenpaa, "Application of global information technology," *MIS Quarterly*, (15:1), 1991, pp. 33-49.

Keil, M., Cule, P. E., Lyytinen, K. and R. C. Schmidt, "A framework for identifying software project risks," *Communications of the ACM* (41:11), 1998, pp. 76-83.

Kemerer, C. F., "Progress, Obstacles, and Opportunities in Software Engineering Economics", *Communications of the ACM* (41:8), 1998, pp. 63-66.

Kettinger, W. J., Grover, V., Guha, S., and A. H. Segars, "Strategic information system revisited: A study in sustainability and performance," *MIS Quarterly* (18:1), 1994, pp. 31-54.

Kimberly, J. R., "Organizational size and the structualist perspective: A rive, critique, and proposal," *Administrative Science Quarterly*, (21), 1976, pp. 571-597.

Kleinknecht, A. and J. Wenger, "The myth of economic globalization," *Cambridge Journal of Economics* (22:5), 1998. pp. 637-647.

Kogut, B., and N. Kulatilaka "Operating flexibility, global manufacturing, and the option value of a multinational network, *Management Science* (40:1), 1994, pp.123-139

Loree, D. W., and S. E. Guisinger, "Policy and non-policy determinants of U.S. equity foreign direct investment," *Journal of International Business Studies* (26:2), 1995, pp. 281-299.

MacCormack, A. D., Newman, L. J., III, and D. B. Rosenfield, "The new dynamics of global manufacturing site location," *Sloan Management Review*, Summer, 1994, pp. 69-80.

Mariotti, S. and L. Piscitello, "Information costs and location of FDIs within the host country: Empirical evidence from Italy," *Journal of International Business Studies* (26:4), 1995, pp. 815-841.

McFarlan, F. W. "Issues In Global Outsourcing," in Palvia, P. C., Palvia, S. C., and E. M. Roche, eds., *Global Information Technology and Systems Management: Key Issues and Trends*, Nashua, NH, IVY League Publishing, 1996, pp. 352-364.

Meadows, C. J., "Software development capabilities- A comparative analysis: India vs. Philippines," in Odedra-Straub eds., *Global IT and Socio-Economic Development*, Ivy League Publishing, 1996, pp.

Meyer, A. D. "Tech talk: How managers are stimulating global R&D communication," *Sloan Management Review*, 1991, pp. 49-58.

Moitra, D., "India's software industry," *IEEE Software*, Jan/Feb, 2000, pp. 77-80.

Morck, R., and B. Yeung, "Internationalization: An event study test," *Journal of International Economics* (33), 1992, pp. 41-56.

NASSCOM (2001) available at http://www.nasscom.org

Natarjan, A. "Whos's afraid of the MNCs?," *Sillicon India*, June 1999, pp. 28-29.

Palvia, S. and M. G. Hunter, "Information systems development: A conceptual mode and a comparison of methods used in Singapore, USA and Europe," *Journal of Global Information Management* (4:3), 1996.

Robilland, P. N. " The role of knowledge in software development," *Communications of the ACM* (42:1), 1999, pp. 87-92.
Schach, S. R., *Software Engineering with JAVA*, McGraw-Hill, Boston, MA, 1997.

Slaughter, S. A., Harter, D. E., and M. S. Krisbran, "Evaluating the Cost of Software Quality," *Communications of the ACM* (41:8), 1998, pp. 67-73

Streeter. L. A., Kraut R. E., Lucas, H. C., and L. Caby, "How open data network influence business performance and Market structure, *Communications of the ACM* (39:7), 1996, pp. 62-73

The World Bank, *World Development Indicator*, 1999.

Tranctinsky, N. and S. L. Jarvenpaa. "Information Systems Design Decisions in a Global Versus Domestic Context," *MIS Quarterly*, 1995, (19:4), pp. 507-529

Vitalari, N. P., and J. C. Wetherbe, "Emerging Best Practice in Global Systems Development," in Palvia, P. C.,

Palvia, S. C., and E. M. Roche, eds*., Global Information Technology and Systems Management: Key Issues and Trends*, Nashua, NH, IVY League Publishing, 1995, pp. 325-351.

Wallace, C. D., "Foreign direct investment in the third world: U.S. corporations and government policy", in Cynthia Day Wallace, editor, *Foreign Direct Investment in the 1990s: A New climate in the Third World*, Boston: Martinus Nijhoff, 1990, pp. 148-202.

Wheeler, D. and A. Mody, 1992. "International investment location decisions," *Journal of International Economics*, (33:1/2), 1992, pp. 57-76.

Woodward, D. P., and R. J. Rolfe, "The location of export-oriented foreign direct investment in the Caribean Basin," *Journal of International Business Studies* (24:1), 1993, pp. 121-144.

SECTION - 6

GLOBAL INFORMATION TECHNOLOGY INFRASTRUCTURE AND OPERATIONS

It should always be kept in mind that the IT infrastructures in multinational corporations are some of the most complex technological systems in the world. In many cases, there are hundreds of smaller data centers, and dozens of large-scale data centers. At all times, this giant infrastructure must be operational, and to do that poses a steep challenge to the IT function. IT after all is a type of ``utility" and just as one does not expect their telephone service or electric power to go out, business users do not expect their IT services to go down.

There are many debates regarding how to organize the IT function---should it be centrally managed, or decentralized, or some combination of the two? What type of management structure should be put in place? For example, more or less all companies have a CIO, but what is the optimal structure of an organization at lower levels (below the CIO level in the enterprise)? How should control and coordination in of IT in the multinational enterprise be managed? Who is to do it and what are best practices in making sure this is successful?

This section presents two chapters that address these issues. The first chapter examines some of the constraints facing the Chief Information Officer (CIO) in a global company. The second chapter presents a methodology for developing, deploying and maintaining infrastructure in the multinational enterprise.

24

Control and Coordination of Information Systems in Multinational Corporations

Madhu T. Rao
Salisbury State University

Carol V. Brown
Indiana University

William Perkins
Indiana University

ABSTRACT

As industries lean collectively ever closer to Kenichi Ohmae's vision of a "borderless world", companies are being forced to re-examine their current operations in order to face the challenge of surviving in a global business environment. Organizations, confronted with the newly emerging imperatives of worldwide markets, have rapidly begun to decompose traditionally domestic value-chain services into ones that have little or no regard for national boundaries. This "stateless" organization is, perhaps, one of the most significant business trends of the 20th century. Globalization's impact has not merely tinted top management's view of long term strategy but has percolated down to functional departments. In this context, no area has been more affected than the Information Systems (IS) function. As more and more multinational corporations seek to expand into emerging markets, senior management is beginning to recognize that global strategies require coordinated global IS options. This chapter examines some of the constraints facing Chief Information Officers (CIOs) in such global companies as well as potential solutions for coordinating worldwide IS activities. The chapter reviews the theoretical concepts of control and coordination in the context of international IS operations, and a framework of mechanisms to deal with the obstacles identified.

INTRODUCTION

Recent years have been witness to the inexorable dissolution of national borders in the face of ever-improving technology. Corporate offices in Bloomington, Indiana communicate as easily with subsidiaries in Bangalore, India or Edinburgh, Scotland as they might with branch offices in Indianapolis. Continent-wide bodies such as the North American Free Trade Agreement (NAFTA) and the European Union allow the free flow of skilled personnel between country units, thus easily transferring knowledge and organizational culture on a worldwide basis. Satellite networks and group software systems make it possible for teams spread around the world to work on collaborative projects. This New World, forged out of complex telecommunication infrastructures and advanced transportation networks, has effectively blurred the borders between countries. The "demise of the nation-state" is in large part due to the imperatives of global business and the proliferation of organizations that have extended their mission-critical operations to countries around the world. Global enterprises, more commonly referred to as Multinational Corporations (or, MNCs), are now legion, and many are worth more than the foreign exchange reserves of small countries. In an astounding statistic published by the Institute for Policy Studies on their Corporate Watch web page (http://www.corpwatch.org), it is noted that:

"Of the 100 largest economies in the world, 51 are corporations; only 49 are countries. Wal-mart, [the 12th largest corporation] is bigger (sic.) than 161 countries."

An MNC is defined by OECD (Organization for Economic Cooperation and Development) and the UNCTC (United Nations Center for Transnational Corporations) to be *"an enterprise that engages in foreign direct investment and owns or controls value-adding activities in more than one country"* (Dunning, 1993; p. 3). In 1997, The United Nations Conference on Trade and Development estimated that the number of MNCs operating worldwide was over 53,000 with nearly 450,000 foreign subsidiaries[1].

Information Technology (IT) has often been viewed as the vehicle that facilitates the global transformation of business (Deans and Karwan, 1994). Advances in telecommunications technology, for example, have contributed greatly to a more integrated style of global operations. Indeed, leading global companies such as ABB Asea Brown Boveri Ltd., Nike Inc., and the Ford Motor Company have invested millions in new IT infrastructures, networks, computer systems, and software in an attempt to stay ahead in global markets[2]. Global information networks at Texas Instruments, for example, allow the company's 76,000 workers to instantly access data from over twenty centers distributed around the world (Eom, 1994). Global information needs global infrastructure, however, and this does not happen without great planning. As Pucik and Katz (1986) note:

"The effectiveness of global sourcing, global marketing, globally rationalized production, and technology transfer are all constrained by the ability of multinational firms to set up an efficient information processing network and coordinate and control its highly complex activities. [The] information processing system in an MNC must be capable of handling multiple types of information, and its control system has to reflect the complexity of its global competitive environment" (p. 121)

This burgeoning of offshore trade and global integration has not, however, been without concomitant difficulties. The crossing of geographic, legal, cultural, and temporal borders has posed complex challenges for Information Systems (IS) managers.

In a roundtable discussion involving IS executives from some of the Netherlands' largest multinationals, Chief Information Officers (CIOs) argued at length about the difficulties of managing decentralized IT installations dispersed across several countries and predicted an increasing emphasis on formulating IS standards and rules[3]. In a study of the global disaggregation of information-intensive services, Apte and Mason (1995) point to a number of potential obstacles in the path of companies attempting "multi-location global insourcing", including communication and coordination, transborder data flows, cultural diversity, and unstable host country environments.

Researchers have suggested that IS managers must ready themselves to radically alter existing technological infrastructures and work processes and adopt a mix of flexibility and structure. IS managers typically acknowledge that there is a critical need to coordinate and control strategic IT-related operations on a global scale.

This chapter examines the issue of control and coordination of IT and IS operations in global enterprises. We first discuss the concept of organizational control and coordination. We then examine some of the key obstacles to achieving global integration of information technology and systems and then describe some mechanisms of coordination. The chapter concludes with a brief discussion of emerging systems of integration.

ORGANIZATIONAL CONTROL AND COORDINATION: DEFINITIONS AND FRAMEWORKS

As organizations grow in size, they tend to differentiate with constituent components exhibiting differences along a variety of dimensions in response to changing environments and goal structures (Lawrence and Lorsch, 1967; Baliga and Jaeger, 1984). In their classic work on organizations and environments, Lawrence and Lorsch (1967) proposed that this differentiation was a critical prerequisite to organizational effectiveness for it allowed functional departments to specialize in dealing with the unique characteristics of their own subenvironments. Though the specialization permitted organizations to undertake complicated tasks otherwise impossible, it required an equally well-developed system to bind sub-units into an integrated operational whole (Lawrence and Lorsch, 1967; Galbraith and Nathanson, 1978; Cray, 1984). Indeed, it has been argued that control of sub-unit behavior is a necessary integrating function in all complex organizations (Baliga and Jaeger, 1984; Doz and Prahalad, 1984; Egelhoff, 1984).

Control and Coordination

The integration of subunits in large organizations is dependent on the manipulation of two processes: control and coordination (Cray, 1984). Broadly, *control* may be viewed as the process of bringing about adherence to a stated goal or policy through the exercise of power or authority (Etzioni, 1965). Though the aim of control in organizations is to curb idiosyncratic behavior and hold individuals and firms to existing policies, its true importance lies in its ability to reduce uncertainty, increase predictability, and ensure behaviors that are consonant with common organizational goals (Egelhoff, 1984). The approach that organizations take in implementing control, of course, varies substantially between firms. Nobel and Birkinshaw (1998), for example, in a study of 15 Swedish multinational companies found significant differences between the control modes used by Alfa Laval, Asea Brown Boveri, and Erriccson.

While control is a more direct intervention into the activities of a subunit's activities, *coordination* is seen as an "enabling process" which allows for linkages between sub-units (Van de Ven, Delbecq, and Koenig, 1976). The coordination of this so-called network of subunits permits an even flow of goods, services, and information among members of the network. While it is possible that coordination may be forcibly imposed through acts of control, its success in integrating diverse subunits lies in placing the member units in a lattice of responsibilities to other units (Cray, 1984).

Classifications of Types of Control

The issue of control has been addressed extensively in organization theory (Jaeger, 1983) and a number of classification schemes have been used to categorize forms of control. Examples include cybernetic and non-cybernetic controls (Egelhoff, 1984), direct and indirect controls (Youssef, 1975), formal and informal controls (Martinez and Jarillo, 1989), bureaucratic controls (Weber, 1946; Child, 1973), behavior and output control (Ouchi and Maguire, 1975; Ouchi, 1977), and cultural control (Edstrom and Galbraith, 1977; Jaeger, 1983; Baliga and Jaeger, 1984). In order to understand various perspectives on the control issue, three major classification schemes that have dominated the literature are discussed below. The relationship between control types is depicted in Figure 1.

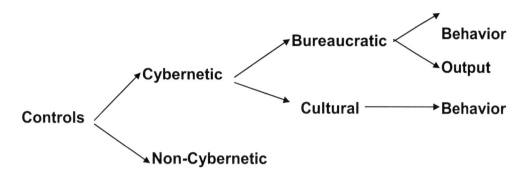

Figure 1: A Framework of Organizational Control Types

<u>Cybernetic Controls</u>: Cybernetics (derived from the Greek. *Kybernetes*, meaning "steersman" or "governor") is a term used to refer to communication and control in a variety of areas. The defining characteristic of cybernetic controls is the integration of monitoring, evaluation, and feedback in determining performance. Cybernetic controls are the most common form of IS controls. Examples are provided below.

1. Behavior and Output Control: Ouchi and Maguire (1975) noted that there are only two phenomena which can be monitored and evaluated by managers to assess the effectiveness of subordinate performance: behavior or the resultant products of a given behavior. Most forms of cybernetic control (in which there is monitoring, evaluation, and feedback) may be classified as either behavior or output controls (Ouchi and Maguire, 1975; Ouchi, 1977).

Behavior controls aim at controlling the process through which inputs are transformed into outputs. It follows, therefore, that in order for an organization to apply behavior controls, it must have some notion of the means-end relationship (Ouchi, 1977). Only then can a manager achieve control by monitoring and guiding subordinate behavior. Examples of this form of control are rules, regulations, and standard procedures.

Output control, on the other hand, requires no knowledge of the transformation process but merely a measure of the desired outputs that the manager perceives to be reliable and valid (Ouchi, 1977). An example of output control is a performance reporting system such as financial reports (Egelhoff, 1984).

In a study of department stores, Ouchi (1977) found that output control and behavior control varied independently of one another, thus indicating that they are not substitutes for each other but merely used in different situations. Ouchi further noted that as organizations grow in size, the number of levels in the hierarchy increase, which in turn leads to loss of control. He argued that the response to such a loss would be a shift from behavior control to output control, which is less susceptible to this form of diminishing control.

2. Bureaucratic and Cultural Control: The concept of bureaucratic control follows from Weber's classic bureaucratic model of the organization (Weber, 1946). In this model, control is achieved through the application of a limited but explicit set of rules and regulations which aim at enforcing specific types of behaviors (Child, 1973). Adherence to policies is monitored by comparing an individual's performance (output) or behavior to those prescribed by the set of rules. Rewards and punishments are based on the result of this comparison. Martinez and Jarillo (1989) equate bureaucratic controls to Ouchi's (1977) "output controls", and Mintzberg's (1979) "performance controls. In all cases, control is based on an evaluation of "files, records, and reports submitted by organizational units to corporate management"

(Martinez and Jarillo, 1989, p. 491). Such a parallelism may be unjustified as Child's (1973) conceptualization of bureaucratic controls was a set of codified rules aimed at ensuring a specific behavior. Further, monitoring under bureaucratic systems of control also included observation of subordinate *behavior* (Jaeger, 1983).

Cultural control systems are perceived to be far more subtle and complex than bureaucratic controls. Such cultural controls must become embedded in a complicated control system consisting of a wide range of "pivotal" and "peripheral" values (Baliga and Jaeger, 1984). The goal of such control systems is to transfer the organization's culture to subunits and firmly establish the culture in said units. Jaeger (1983) notes that cultural controls differ from bureaucratic controls in the nature of personnel interactions which form the basis for control. While bureaucratic control systems utilize formal and impersonal means (such as rules, reports, and written directives), cultural control is achieved through informal interactions of employees. Edstrom and Galbraith (1977), for example, found in a study of three European multinationals that the transfer of subsidiary managers from country to country was a control system aimed at creating an informal personal network of managers. Edstrom and Galbraith referred to this as "control through socialization" and this process is viewed by Baliga and Jaeger (1984) as an example of cultural control. Table 1 summarizes the main types of control in organizations.

Non-Cybernetic Controls: While most control mechanisms can be categorized as "cybernetic", a notable exception is a commonly used method , viz., centralization of decision-making authority. Nobel and Birkinshaw (1998) identify centralization as one of three key control modes in subsidiaries of multinational corporations (in addition to formalization and socialization). Control through this method is unlike any of the other control forms encountered in that it does not involve monitoring, evaluation, or feedback. Centralization of IS decision-making in MNCs should be considered a non-cybernetic form of control.

Table 1: Comparison of Bureaucratic, Cultural, and Non-Cybernetic Controls

Types of Control			
Bureaucratic		**Cultural**	**Non-Cybernetic**
Nature of Control	Output Controls	Behavior Controls	Behavior Controls	Non-cybernetic
Description	Requires no knowledge of the process of converting input to output - only knowledge of desired output. Rewards or punishments decided on basis of comparing actual output to that prescribed.	Aims at controlling the process by which inputs are transformed into outputs. Requires knowledge of the means-end relationship. Mechanisms are used to enforce a limited set of explicit behaviors and are typically formal and impersonal.	All cultural controls are behavior controls. The goal is to transfer and establish a wide range of pivotal "values" (organization culture). Achieved through informal interactions.	Non-cybernetic controls are characterized by a lack of monitoring, evaluation and feedback.
Examples	Financial Reports	Rules, regulations, directives	Manager transfers, socialization, informal communication networks	Centralization of IS decision-making

Classifications of Types of Coordination

As noted earlier, coordination is viewed as an enabling process which permits the smooth flow of goods, services, and information between subunits in a complex organization. In essence, coordination implies the integration of different interdependent parts of the organization to accomplish a collective set of tasks (Van de Ven, Delbecq, and Koenig, 1976). Two major classification schemes exist to organize different types of coordination. The first was proposed by Thompson (1967) who suggested that different types of coordination existed for different forms of interdependence. A second framework is one developed by Van de Ven, Delbecq, and Koenig (1976) who identify three "coordination modes" within organizations based on the manner in which coordination is achieved.

1. The Thompson Coordination Framework: In 1967, James D. Thompson published what is considered by many to be one of the most influential books in the area of organization science. Titled "Organizations in Action", the book was, in essence, a "conceptual inventory" of organization theory.

One of the concepts described in the book is the relationship between interdependence and coordination. Complex organizations such as MNCs are comprised of interdependent parts. Thompson argued that there are various types of interdependence and that the structures of such firms must facilitate the coordinated action of these interdependent components. To this end, Thompson identified three types of interdependence and three associated forms of coordination.

Pooled interdependence is said to exist when branches of an organization do not have contact with one another, but instead, make discrete contributions to the organization as a whole. In return, they are supported by the whole organization. This was the common mode of interdependence in early MNC structures. Thompson suggested that this type of interdependence was best supported by a form of coordination called "Coordination by Standardization" in which branches (or subsidiaries) operate under fairly rigorous set of routines and rules that applied equally to all components of the organization. In later sections of this chapter, examples of IS rules will be presented.

Sequential interdependence is said to exist when branches (or subsidiaries) have direct interaction. This interaction an ordered form of contact. If the Mexico branch of an engine company must provide a specific part to the Brazilian plant before production can proceed, then there is a serial, or "sequential" interdependence between the two sites. Thompson suggested that this type of interdependence would be best matched with a scheme called "coordination by plan". This method of coordination involves the establishment of detailed schedules for the interdependent units through which their operations are managed.

Reciprocal interdependence is said to exist in network organizations where branches (or subsidiaries) exchange goods, services, and information with one another . This is a type of interdependence exhibited in what are sometimes referred to as "transnational corporations". Such organization structures are characterized by high levels of interaction between multiple subsidiaries. Thompson suggested that coordination in such types of interdependence could be achieved through "coordination by mutual adjustment" in which constant communication would be evident between two or more branches during any kind action involving the units.

Figure 1 summarizes the Thompson Coordination Framework.

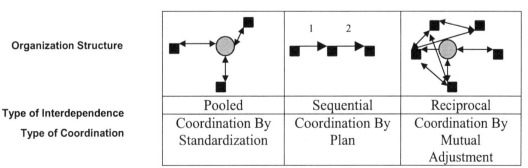

Organization Structure			
Type of Interdependence	Pooled	Sequential	Reciprocal
Type of Coordination	Coordination By Standardization	Coordination By Plan	Coordination By Mutual Adjustment

Figure 1: Thompson Coordination Framework

2. The Van de Ven Coordination Framework: Van de Ven, Delbecq, and Koenig (1976) proposed an alternative framework in which they identified three modes of coordination, viz., impersonal, personal, and group. Unlike the Thompson framework, which is based on the types of mechanisms used to achieve coordination, the Van de Ven framework is based on the nature of the coordination mechanisms.

Impersonal Mode: Plans, schedules, forecasts, rules, policies and procedures are all common means of achieving concerted action in IS departments worldwide. A common characteristic of these mechanisms is that they are independent of the people filling the roles to achieve a given task. The IS programming standards, for example, are codified independent of the actual programmers. Once implemented, minimal communication is needed between task performers to accomplish tasks.

Personal Mode: Often, coordination is achieved through the actions of individuals who occupy certain task roles within the organization. The coordination is typically achieved through vertical or horizontal communications within the firm. Individuals in some integrator roles, project coordinators, for example, may not have direct authority over the individuals who perform the tasks, but their role is to ensure that a project or program runs smoothly. Such individuals would be dependent on horizontal communication channels to accomplish this coordination role.

Group mode: The group mode is commonly seen in global IS projects. In this mode, the mechanisms of adjustment (to achieve coordinated action) are achieved through scheduled or unscheduled meetings. Scheduled meetings are those used for routine, planned communication, such as a monthly or bi-monthly videoconference of subsidiary managers worldwide. Unscheduled meetings are informal, often impromptu, meetings between personnel to deal with a work-related problem. Such meetings are more difficult to arrange in cases where personnel are geographically dispersed in different time zones. Global IS teams are however, becoming increasingly common, and videoconferencing is often used in lieu of travelling for face-to-face meetings.

CONTROL AND COORDINATION OF GLOBAL IS OPERATIONS

There is a certain intuitive appeal to the notion that global organizations would benefit from globally coordinated systems. Asea Brown Boveri, a leader in global operations this decade, has been widely cited as crediting its coordinated and standardized systems base as one of the enablers of its success in the world marketplace.[4] CIOs, however, would be the first to concede that coordination is easier designed than implemented. The frameworks explicated in the previous section provide technology managers an excellent starting point for planning for coordinated systems. They are, however, aware that the internationally dispersed systems face obstacles that are often difficult to maneuver around. This section deals with some of the key factors constraining MNC IS/IT managers in their attempts to integrate systems and operations across foreign subsidiaries.

Obstacles to Coordinating Global IS Operations

Despite the best intentions of IS departments to build and manage global systems, IS managers are constrained by several factors that limit their ability to ensure that systems and IS personnel at subsidiaries around the world operate in a coherent and coordinated manner. Some of these factors are discussed below. Examples are provided in each case.

1. **Telecommunications Infrastructure**: Perhaps more than any other resource, a country's telecommunications infrastructure determines the ability of an MNC to control and coordinate IS and IT activities in a specific location. Infrastructures are not the same around the world. What IS managers in the United States take for granted may be out of reach for subsidiary units. Jerry Corvino, former CIO of Oracle Corporation, provides a telling example[5]. As part of a global IT implementation across 57 subsidiary units worldwide, Corvino requested a

cellular telephone for an IT manager in Mainland China. When the Accounting Department argued that a pager would be less expensive, Corvino was forced to explain that the employee lived in a village that had <u>only one telephone</u>. A pager would be of minimal utility if she could not get access to that telephone.

Telecommunications infrastructure has been shown to be a significant factor in determining changes in the locus of decision-making in MNCs (Chismar and Chidambaram, 1992). In discussing the obstacles confronting organizations attempting the disaggregation of their services, Apte and Mason (1995) identify poor telecommunications infrastructure as one of the crucial barriers to successful communication and coordination. Jarvenpaa and Ives (1993) too found that telecommunications infrastructure impacted the fit between IS and corporate strategies. Certainly, in a situation where the telecommunications infrastructure is poor or costly, the ability of a distant headquarters to direct and control subsidiary IS operations is likely to be limited.

CIOs in MNCs must be aware of the constraints of local operations before committing time and resources to global systems doomed to fail in certain countries. Invariably, international systems projects require some level of data transfer – something that requires sometimes hard-to-get telephone lines. In São Paulo, Brazil, over 400,000 people were still waiting for telephone connections in early 1997.[6] Further, high-speed connections, if available, may be expensive, thus making distributed systems difficult to implement.

2. **Availability of Hardware and Software**: Often, global systems require global platforms. Yet, managers at subsidiary units may have trouble acquiring equipment or software as specified by corporate headquarters due to restrictions or limitations imposed by local vendors, local conditions, or the host country government. Consider the following examples[7].

a. When visiting a Pepsi marketer in Vietnam, an IS executive noticed that employees were using PCs running 386 chips – machines considered obsolete in most US organizations. Pepsi's plans of a global rollout of intranet and enterprise planning software would not be able to include Vietnam unless they could upgrade to the standard used by the rest of the company.
b. Wal-mart discovered the problems of vendor support when they found in China that no local companies could provide technical support for their standard back-office line printers.
c. Until quite recently, government policy in many Latin American countries mandated strict import restrictions on computer-related goods in order to protect local industries. This meant that only locally manufactured PCs would be available to MNCs interested in integrating Latin American operations with the rest of their global IS and IT operations.
d. Mark DuVall, Vice President of Engineering at People-Mover Inc., a human resource software company in California, noted the difficulties in getting contract programmers in the Ukraine or Russia the equipment needed to do the job for US-based firms: "If you send them the latest Dell 300MHz, [the Ukrainian or Russian Mafia] monitors everything that comes into the country and asks you to pay 100% tariff."

3. **Distance and Time Zones**: In an examination of global software teams[8], Professor Erran Carmel of American University, makes the following comment:

"Distance affects all manner of coordination and control...once the team is dispersed... problem solving become more difficult. The socialization of teams becomes agonizing... Managers are reduced to managing through milestone charts and once-a week conference calls and can slowly lose control over the development process" (p.xiv)

Though Carmel writes with specific reference to teams involved in collaborative systems development projects, the comments equally apply to CIOs attempting to integrate other IS and IT operations. With the establishment of specialized software centers in different countries becoming more common in large MNCs, the issue of managing long-distance systems development becomes problematic. As Peggy Scott, a business program manger in Liberty Mutual Insurance Company, comments on her experiences of working with developers based in Belfast, Northern Ireland;

"How do you maintain that knowledge level, that understanding of the big picture, the link between the technical architecture and the business design [with IS part of the team toiling an ocean away]"

Hand in hand with distance problems come the associated time-zone differences. As Carmel writes: *"Time zone differences exacerbate the communication problem. When developers in California and India have no natural overlap of working hours for voice or video conversations, then one side always has to compromise"*(p. xiv).[9]

For this reason, organizations must carefully consider the frequency of required contact when deliberating on where to establish centers for different projects. Consider the case of JP Morgan who chose Barbados over India as an offshore site for systems development.[10] The investment bank routinely outsourced many of its IT projects to sites in India but needed something closer to home for critical projects. As the CIO noted:

"Its [critical projects] a different subset of our work that required time zone compatibility with the United States. For some of our apps (sic), its OK for India to be 10 hours away; we may speak [with developers there] only once a week...but [for critical applications]... we needed more connectivity and closeness to the business during that development cycle."

4. **Culture and Language**: Once the CIO has conquered issues of space and time in his or her attempts at global IS integration, there is still the issue of culture and language of the systems personnel in the foreign subsidiaries.

National culture is, perhaps, one of the most poorly understood issues for IS executives. This is not without reason. Few researchers have been able to provide a single all-inclusive definition of a concept that is often blamed for project setbacks of any kind. However, researchers do seem to agree on certain common aspects to culture – among these are:

a. Culture is learned and shared from generation to generation.
b. Cultural norms may be acquired through parents, schools, religious organizations, and social organizations.
c. Elements of culture include both verbal and non-verbal language, religion, values and attitudes, perceptions, and protocols.

Czinkota, Ronkainen, and Moffet (1996) provide a useful definition of culture:

"...culture is defined as an integrated system of learned behavior patterns that are characteristic of the members of any society. It includes everything a group thinks, says, does, and makes – its customs, language, material artifacts, and shared systems of attitudes and feelings" (p. 298)

While more and more MNCs are embracing the diversity of cultural backgrounds in their global organizations, many senior IS executives are laboring to communicate to their systems teams the subtleties of cross-cultural interaction. A commonly cited example is in the area of conflict resolution. Asian cultures tend to feel uneasy when caught in situations involving dispute. Western cultures, on the other hand, find directness and open arguments useful in clearly defining issues and problems. Mike Cast, Managing director of Mastek UK , for example, comments that Indian programmers tend to be too polite – they are reluctant to warn clients that their expectations are unrealistic, even if it means delaying the project.[11]

Between the years 1967-1978, Dutch researcher, Geert Hofstede, conducted a famous study on the dimensions of culture in which data was collected from over 100,000 IBM employees worldwide. Hofstede found that cultural differences did emerge between countries despite IBM's strong corporate culture, and he classified these variations along four dimensions – power distance, individualism, uncertainty avoidance, and masculinity[12]. These dimensions provide a valuable framework for IS managers in MNCs to understand the impact of cultural differences within their workforce on the management of technology projects. Table 2 briefly outlines Hofstede's dimensions of culture.

Consider, for instance, a multinational systems design team with members drawn from both highly individualistic and collectivist cultures. As per Hofstede's analysis, team members from collectivist cultures tend to value the harmony and well being of the group over individual ambition. Individualistic cultures, on the other hand, place emphasis on the achievements, initiative, and goals of the individual. How does one design a reward scheme for such a group? Rewarding only certain members, though considered acceptable in individualistic cultures, may be considered unjust by the members of the group who expect group rewards and recognition.

Table 2: Hofstede's Dimensions of Culture

Dimension	Description
Uncertainty Avoidance	Reflects a culture's attitude towards risk, ambiguity, predictability, and control. "High avoidance" cultures place emphasis on stability, while "low avoidance" cultures embrace change and innovation.
Individualism vs. Collectivism	The extent to which cultures value the achievements, initiative, and goals of the individual over the goals and well being of the group
Power Distance	The extent to which members of a culture accept that power in organizations is distributed unequally
Masculinity vs. Femininity	Addresses the way in which a culture identifies social roles to the sexes. Cultures high in masculinity tend to have men in assertive roles and women in more nurturing caring roles. High femininity cultures demonstrate less social differentiation between sexes

Language differences also cause problems in trying to get global systems in place and functioning. The term "language" encompasses both verbal and non-verbal aspects of communication. Though English is considered the dominant language of communication in the systems world, colloquialisms are very specific to a given culture. An employee in the IS department of a Hong Kong subsidiary may be very fluent in English but have no idea what is meant when slang or adages are used in meetings. Non-verbal communication can be even be more confusing. Stephen Sprinkle of Deloitte and Touche points out that:

"In Spain... the 'OK' gesture is considered vulgar. In Argentina, the way you clap your hands can be derogatory".[13]

5. **Subsidiary Resistance**:   The 1960s, '70s and '80s were decades dominated by MNCs whose organizational structure was more "multi-domestic" than truly global. Foreign subsidiary units were opened when and where opportunity presented itself. The technology foundations in these country branches were built up country-by-country with little, if any, control from corporate headquarters. Thus, subsidiary IS managers were used to operating autonomously and with absolute power when it came to technology decisions. It comes as no surprise, therefore, that a significant obstacle to integrating and coordinating systems worldwide is wresting some of the individual decision-making powers from subsidiary IS departments.

Subsidiary resistance to these shifts in the locus of decision making and the forced implementation of global standard is often spirited. Data standards held as indispensable by a New York headquarters may be seen as meddlesome and irrelevant by the manufacturing plant in Venezuela. A senior IS executive in Proctor and Gamble states:

"Before, Italy was Italy, Mexico was Mexico, and the U.S. could do as it darn well pleased. Now, we have created an interdependent model where countries depend on other countries."

6. **Transborder Data Flows**:   The past few years have seen rapid improvements in communication technologies, thus making available a new medium for the delivery of goods, services and information across national borders. Transborder data flows (TDF) have allowed MNCs to freely operate on a global level by providing a means by which financial and personnel data can be shared between headquarters and subsidiaries worldwide. As early as 1979, the Organization for Economic Cooperation and Development (OECD) published "Guidelines for Protection of Privacy and Transborder Data Flows" which emphasized the need to maintain free flow of data across national borders.

However, more and more countries have been placing restrictions on TDFs. Some countries require that at least a portion of the data processing be done within the country before the data can moved out of the country through private or leased lines. Others do not allow outbound TDF of personal information on citizens unless the destination countries have equivalent data protection laws. For example, under the European Union Directive on Data Protection, countries doing business with the European Union must have "adequate" privacy policies. The adequacy of the laws would be determined unilaterally by the EU based on an objective assessment of various data protection laws, industry codes, and professional rules of conduct.[14]

Such a directive could be devastating to the operations of MNCs whose transfer of financial and human resources information would be curtailed. Integrating subsidiary IS operations with the rest of the MNC organization would be extremely difficult in such a scenario and such units would be isolated from the rest of a distributed system.

MECHANISMS OF INTEGRATION FOR GLOBAL IS OPERATIONS

Given the breathtaking span of potential hurdles that must be negotiated in order to have globally coordinated IS operations, one may wonder why MNCs even consider such an approach. The returns, however, are immense. Therefore, a key IS headquarters role is to attempt to overcome these obstacles through the creative, often ingenious, use of various mechanisms of integration.

Here we use the term *mechanism of integration* for any administrative device used to achieve integration among different units within an organization (Martinez and Jarillo, 1989).

The term is, therefore, used broadly and includes mechanisms for both control and coordination.

Mechanisms of integration are common to all large organizations, but the complexity of MNCs makes them particularly interesting as a context in which control and coordination processes may be studied (Martinez and Jarillo, 1989). Given the complex environment facing MNCs and the greater physical and cultural distance separating subunits, organizational control and coordination in MNCs is often considered more problematic than in purely domestic companies (Egelhoff, 1984).

The managers of MNCs are continually faced with the challenge of strategically integrating their operations in several countries while simultaneously dealing with needs for national responsiveness and fragmentation (Doz and Prahalad, 1984). Foreign subsidiaries must be differentiated enough to respond to local cultures and customs but this flexibility must be embedded within a structure that contributes maximally to corporate performance (Cray, 1984). This network form of the organization requires an ever-expanding set of integration mechanisms in order to enable the greater level of interdependency of activities between subsidiary units (Neo, 1991).

Table 3: Classification of Integration Mechanisms (from Martinez and Jarillo, 1989)

Mechanism	Description
Formal	
Departmentalization	*This involves the grouping of activities within organizational units. The goal of such mechanisms was to achieve the "right structure" to deal with a given environment.*
Centralization	*A non-cybernetic form of control in which the locus of decision-making is deliberately centralized or decentralized*
Formalization and standardization	*These mechanisms typically indicate the extent to which policies and rules are written down and standard procedures are established through routines.*
Planning	*Planning mechanisms are systems and processes that aim at guiding the activities and actions of subsidiaries. Examples include strategic planning, budgeting, schedules, and goal-setting.*
Output and behavioral	*Output controls are based on the evaluation of subsidiary outputs by the MNC headquarters. Examples of such outputs include records, files, and reports. Behavioral controls are based on direct personal surveillance and aim at monitoring and enforcing certain behaviors in subsidiary units*
Informal	
Lateral relations	*Such mechanisms cut across formal structures and aim at developing direct contact between personnel in various departments and subsidiaries. Examples include task forces, teams, committees, and integrating roles.*
Informal communication	*The goal of these mechanisms is to supplement formal communications through informal and personal contact between managers. Corporate meetings, conferences, management trips, personal visits, and the transfer of managers are typical examples.*
Organizational culture	*These mechanisms aim at imparting a sense of the organization's goals and objectives, how the organization does things, and the style of decision-making. This is achieved through a the socialization of individuals and training and transferring managers across subsidiaries*

A Framework of Integration Mechanisms

A number of frameworks have been devised to organize specific control and coordination mechanisms in a logical manner (Youssef 1975; Galbraith and Nathonson, 1978; Doz and Prahalad, 1981). Perhaps the most comprehensive framework of control and coordination mechanisms is one proposed by Martinez and Jarillo (1989) who, based on an exhaustive literature review of over three decades of MNC coordination research, identified two categories of control and coordination mechanisms: formal and informal mechanisms. Each category is further divided into several specific types of mechanisms. Table 3 identifies and describes the specific mechanisms of integration.

Controlling and coordinating IS in MNCs

Most IS departments in MNCs today use a mix (if not all) of the mechanisms outlined in Martinez and Jarillo's framework. Examples of each are provided for an IS context below.

Formal Mechanisms

1. Departmentalization: The central goal of departmentalization, or the grouping of responsibilities in certain units, is to ensure specialization of certain tasks to fit specific environments. Recently, MNCs have taken departmentalization a step further by creating global departments with global responsibilities that take advantage of location-specific resources. For example, Texas Instruments' Indian subsidiary in Bangalore became the main global center (Center of Excellence) for the design and development of software for CAD systems (Apte and Mason, 1995).

2. Centralization: In an empirical study of IS and IT strategies in 109 MNCs, Jarvenpaa and Ives (1993) noted that an unexpected number of companies leaned towards centralization of the locus of IT-related decision making.   Based on follow-up interviews, they suggested that the primary force behind such centralization was the need to ensure a common global information architecture and systems interface as well as to "minimize the total IT operation, development and maintenance budget worldwide".

3. Formalization and Standardization: Formalization and standardization mechanisms involve the use of codified blueprints for the way systems are developed and managed on a worldwide basis. The idea of coordinated information systems activities across national subsidiaries is certainly appealing, at least one reason being it is better to solve a problem once rather than many times.[15]

Eaton Corporation, for example, manufactures vehicle, industrial, and aerospace parts worldwide. It is attempting to coordinate a heterogeneous base of software applications, parts-numbering systems, and engineering standards in various countries by formulating standards in its enterprise network. [16]Loctite Corporation keeps its subsidiaries in 52 countries on the same page by distributing the "Loctite Worldwide Design Handbook" in nine different languages to all its units.[17]

4. Planning: Worldwide coordination of IS operations can also be accomplished through the development of detailed strategic global IT plans. Typically, these plans strive to align corporate and IT strategies and outline the need for common systems and standards worldwide. A strategic IS plan offers a roadmap for the entire organization and affords subsidiary IS managers to ensure their operations are in line with overall corporate objectives.

Former CIO, Patricia Wallington, for example, developed Xerox Corporation's Information Management 2000 plan whose core intent was one of IS integration.[18]

5. Output and Behavioral: The use of Ouchi's (1977, 1979) output and behavioral control as a category of mechanisms within this framework is not without problems. Ouchi's dichotomy was developed to encompass all forms of cybernetic controls and clearly contains some of the other categories proposed by Martinez and Jarillo.

Centralization, for example, is sometimes used as a means of output control. Centralized resources allow corporate management to monitor systems usage and information access, thus giving them a large degree of control over subsidiary operations.

As seen in Table 3, the emphasis here is on impersonal (records, files, reports) and personal (direct surveillance) mechanisms of control. An example of an impersonal control is a report that keeps track of telecommunications costs and call logs in subsidiary units of an MNC. This may be used to identify patterns of contact between units and the level of coordination between their operations. Personal mechanisms are common in the case of behavioral controls wherein a manager may attempt to maintain quality of output (a systems design or program) by controlling the behavior of the individuals involved. For example, many MNCs have strict program development guidelines in which they specify standards and procedures to be followed when creating global systems. These standards act as behavioral controls that force developers to adhere to certain enterprise-wide guidelines, which, in turn, make it easier to integrate systems across subsidiary units.

The informal mechanisms of integration outlined in the next section fall under the category of behavioral mechanisms of integration, based on Ouchi's definition.

Informal Mechanisms

1. Lateral Relations: As global information systems become more and more complex, a greater number of MNCs are relying on direct contact between subsidiary IS personnel to help ensure coordinated development and management efforts. Examples of such mechanisms include the use of standing committees, multinational project teams, and IS personnel assigned to integrating roles. Companies have utilized the multinational technology committee mechanism to coordinate IT worldwide for many years. In 1993, Coopers and Lybrand, for example, created the International Technology Group, a team of senior executives from Germany, the Netherlands, The United Kingdom, the United States, Canada, and Australia. The team's charter was to devise a global technology strategy that would result in a consistent, coordinated business structure for the firm. Soon after, Coopers and Lybrand implemented an integrated global system based on Lotus Notes.[19]

2. Informal Communication: The goal of informal communications is to supplement formal coordination mechanisms through more personal contact between managers. This can take the form of global IT conferences, regional meetings, personal visits or just simply telephone calls. At Phillips Petroleum Company, global IT executives worldwide gather on a semi-monthly basis.[20] Cummins Engine Company annually invites IT mangers from all its foreign subsidiaries to a conference held in Columbus, Indiana, where global IT issues are redefined and reiterated.

Organizational Culture

A common organization culture is a powerful tool for ensuring a commonality of vision, objectives, and decision-making styles in an MNC. This is often achieved through the international transfer of managers, who take the corporate culture with them to subsidiary units. 3M, for example assigns managers overseas only after having been with the company for at least 10 years, thus ensuring that the individuals have absorbed the corporate culture of the organization. Another common technique is the one used by Motorola Inc. Motorola organizes centralized training for managers worldwide. These executives then take back the knowledge to their home countries and impart it to the people they supervise.

EMERGING TRENDS IN GLOBAL IS SYSTEMS

Missing from Martinez and Jarillo (1989) integration mechanisms framework is the use of common information systems as an integration mechanism.

Technology has advanced tremendously over the past few years and companies have been increasingly turning towards large, specialized information systems packages to help them coordinate their overall worldwide activities. These "megapackages" are comprehensive enterprise software solutions geared toward integrating all business processes and functions "in order to present a holistic view of the business from an information and information architecture [standpoint]" (Gable, 1998; p. 3).

ERP systems, such as those marketed by companies like SAP, Baan, PeopleSoft, and Oracle, are application suites that perform a set of integrated, enterprise-wide "functions" (commonly, purchasing, manufacturing, sales/distribution, finance/accounting, and human resources). These functions are actually executed by sets of associated software "modules." AMR Research Inc., a Boston-based consulting firm estimates the ERP market to soar to $52 billion by the year 2002[21].

ERP systems are designed to integrate business processes, regardless of location. This is their global appeal. It follows, therefore, that every unit in the MNCs network of foreign units may adopt standard processes as part of an ERP implementation, regardless of the subsidiary's strategic role or country environment.

However, a number of anecdotal cases in popular periodicals such as Computerworld, Infoworld, and Computer Reseller suggest that simultaneous global implementation is often infeasible. Corning Inc., for example, has reported an eight-year plan to rollout ERP to all its 10 diversified manufacturing divisions. David L. Johns, former director of global development for Owens Corning, summarized his job as

"[taking] 211 legacy systems that were created to support different businesses in different geographic groups and create a unified global supply chain running on the same software"[22]

AlliedSignal Inc. postponed ERP installation at its Asian sites in order to meet deadlines in the United States.[23] On the other hand, successful global implementations of financial ERP systems have been reported by both manufacturing and service MNCs.[24]

Analysts and industry experts are still debating the future of global ERP implementations, with some heat. Whatever be the case, the implementation of these systems must also be considered as a potential mechanism of coordination and control.

CONCLUSION

Global companies need coordinated IS operations to support global strategies. Multinational Corporations have realized that information technology is not simply the outcome of strategy but can, indeed, be an important driver. However, as discussed in this chapter, conspiring against such systems are a number of factors including scarcity of IT resources and personnel, weak telecommunication infrastructures, cultural barriers, language difficulties, restrictive government policies, and time zone differences. To overcome these obstacles, global CIOs must use innovative combinations of various mechanisms of control and coordination. These mechanisms include the use of traditional, formal means of control, such as centralization, standardization, departmentalization, and planning. In addition, companies may also use informal means of integration such as lateral relations in the form of multinational committees, informal communications between IS managers around the world, and the diffusion of organizational culture through centralized conferences and training.

The future promises an even greater variety of integrating mechanisms to achieve even greater levels of coordination. With ever-improving telecommunications infrastructures in developing countries, the rapid expansion of internet-based intranets (such as virtual private networks), reduced barriers to transborder data flows, and the development of a cadre of "international" IS managers, more and more organizations are likely to begin exploiting their global capabilities to achieve hitherto unimagined economies of scale and scope. The task of global IS coordination in MNCs remains daunting, but the potential returns are enormous.

[1] World Investment Report, United Nations, 1998

[2] "Global Titans", Computerworld: Global 100 Supplement, May 1, 1995

[3] "Dutch Masters", CIO Magazine, November 15, 1995

[4] "Is Standardised Global IS Worth the bother?", Financial Times (London), Survey Edition I, March 1, 1999, p.3.

[5] "Team Heat – Global Efficiency", CIO Magazine, September 1, 1998

[6] "CIOs on the Road-Sud America", CIO Magazine, February 15, 1997

[7] "Emerging Challenges", CIO Magazine, June 15, 1998

[8] Carmel, Erran, "Global Software Teams: Collaborating Across Borders and Time Zones", Prentice Hall PTR, Upper Saddle River, NJ, 1999

[9] See endnote 8.

[10] Abramson, Gary, "IT, Phone Home", CIO Enterprise Magazine, February 15, 1999.

[11] See endnote 6

[12] Hofstede, G., "Culture's Consequences", Sage Publications, Beverly Hills, CA, 1980

[13] See endnote 4

[14] "Battlng over data privacy", Editorial/Opinion, Journal of Commerce, July 30, 1997, p. 8A

[15] See footnote 4

[16] Field, T. "Going for More of the Same", CIO-100: World Leaders, Special Issue" Aug 1996.

[17] Baatz, E.B., "Speaking in Tongues", CIO Magazine, August 1, 1996

[18] Baatz, E.B., "The Cares Up There", CIO, September 15, 1995

[19] See footnote 17

[20] See footnote 3

[21] Melymuka, K., "*An expanding universe*", Computerworld, September 14, 1998.

[22] Stuart, A., "As the World Shrinks", CIO, August 1996.

[23] "Global ERP Rollouts present cross-border problems", Computerworld, November 23, 1998

[24] Conference on "The ERP Revolution", University of Memphis, April 1999.

25

Global Information Technology Infrastructure for Transnational Corporations: Developing, Deploying, and Maintaining

Subhash (Sam) S. Valanju
Johnson Controls, Inc., U.S.A.

Hemant Jain
University of Wisconsin- Milwaukee, USA

ABSTRACT

Over the past decade, global business environment has become significantly more competitive and complex. In most multi-national corporations, Information Technology (IT) is playing significantly important role in formulating global corporate strategy and supporting globalization of business processes and practices. The support of this enhanced role of information technology in providing sustained competitive advantage through effective global processes and practices requires a state-of-the-art technology infrastructure. The objective of this chapter is to present a comprehensive methodology for and issues related to developing, deploying and maintaining global Information Technology infrastructure for multi-national corporations. The process starts with the definition of the business requirements for the infrastructure, identification of infrastructure components, conceptual development and feasibility analysis.

INTRODUCTION

One of the most significant business and economic trends is the stateless corporation. The events of global consolidations, telecommunication deregulation, European common currency, growth of Internet, rapid availability of common technology on a global basis are giving the corporations different economic equations to consider. This environment allows the corporation to embark on strategies such as shared services, centralized call centers, virtual organization, knowledge sharing, global product development, etc. All of these strategies have a common underlying assumption of a global, reliable and cost effective Information Technology infrastructure.

The design, development, implementation and on-going management of this infrastructure is one of the major issues facing the management of large multinational corporations (Ives & Jarvenpaaa, 1991, Brancheau & Wetherbe, 1996). The management of effective infrastructure needs to consider nature of corporation (global, multinational, transnational and international), global business strategy, international data sharing needs, cultural environments and the need for control and coordination. This chapter outlines the linkage between the above factors and IT architecture, defines various components of the architecture and provides guidelines on how to take IT architecture in a global multi-national corporation from concept to an operational and a sustaining reality.

The next Section describes the evolving global business environment and various structures of the multinational corporations. It also summarizes the approaches proposed in the literature for the development of IT infrastructure. Section 3 presents an integrated framework for managing the global Information Technology infrastructure. The process of developing vision for the architecture and obtaining management commitment is discussed in Section 4. Section 5 presents a methodology for architectural planning. The strategies for deployment and global rollout of the architecture are discussed in Section 6. Section 7 identifies the on going issues related to managing the architecture such as performance monitoring, security, auditing and change management.

GLOBAL BUSINESS ENVIRONMENT FOR MNC'S AND IT INFRASTRUCTURE

The evolution in the global expansion has taken place from local to national, international, multi-national to global. Advances in the risk management of capital investments, along with the acceptance of competitive environment by the governments around the world have accelerated this global evolution. As the technology allowed the organizations to realize the economies of scale on a national basis, the movement of local organizations to become national in scope took place in the developed countries in nineteen hundred and sixties. This led to consolidations of similar business organizations.

The next movement in nineteen seventies was to sell products and services beyond the national boundaries by becoming an international organization. There was no international capital investment of any significance in this movement. Most of the arrangements involved either representation in other countries and/or technology transfer arrangements. The technology did not play much of a role other than voice communications technology was extended by transferring older technology to developing countries.

In nineteen eighties North America (mainly the U.S. and Canada) along with Western Europe liberalized regulations to start the evolution of multi-national corporations. In this phase of evolution, capital investment in multiple countries became a norm. Joint ventures became dominant. Data and voice communications became the main technology used by multi-national organizations. The technology gap between developed and developing countries started to become smaller and smaller. As various units of an organization across the world become more integrated, the need for standards in technology become more obvious and gain momentum.

In late eighties and early nineties, the above trend towards multi-national corporations has expanded to cover more countries including developing and under-developed countries to give rise to the global phenomena. The organizations have started to view the world market as one and are developing strategies to make that a reality. The complexity of serving a global customer in terms of geographic, functional and products/services being offered are depicted in Figure 1. For example consider a corporation supplying products such as seats, interiors, engine parts to a global customer like Ford Motor Company. To effectively serve the customer the corporation needs to align its geographic locations (manufacturing facilities around the world, distribution facilities etc.) with the geographic locations of the customer. Similarly, internal functions of the corporation such as sales and marketing, customer service, logistics/manufacturing, accounts receivables etc. needs to align and possibly integrate with appropriate functions within the customer organization. Additionally, products and services offered by the various divisions/business units of the corporation need to map with the divisions/business units of the customer. The above integration allows customer to be more effective in use of its resources and reduces administrative costs and delays.

Economies of scale, availability of natural and human resources all around world and need to compete in the complex global market is resulting in unprecedented consolidation at the global level. Developments in information and communication technologies are serving as the major enabling force in this consolidation. Additionally, the government deregulations around the world are allowing this globalization to succeed. However, true globalization movements are more evident in the developed countries. Other countries have adopted a slower pace of change to allow the impact of globalization on the countries cultures to be as painless, shock-free and trauma-free as possible. This is achieved by controlling the rate of deregulation, allowing for joint ventures with minority ownership of MNC and joint ventures and investment by expatriates.

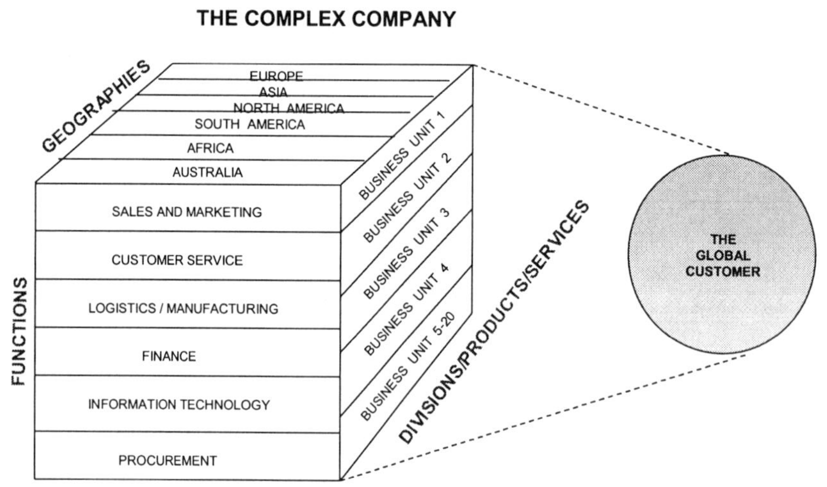

THE COMPLEX COMPANY

Figure 1: Complexities of Serving a Global Customer: Geographies, Functions, Divisions

The global consolidation has taken many forms such as an outright acquisition (Daimler & Chrysler, Ford & Volvo), mergers (City Group & Travelers) and strong alliances (AT&T-BT, United Airlines with six airlines around the world). These global consolidations/alliances have created a tremendous need for tight coupling of business systems and seamless communications, which involve the voice, data, text, graphics and video technology. The technology needs to be readily transferred from one country to other countries.

Apart from this consolidation, the competitive nature of global markets is resulting in the establishment of business partnerships in related industries (called extended enterprise) e.g. between the automotive industry and the emergency service provider industry. The motivation for these partnerships varies from tightening the supply chain management to the outsourcing of some internal business processes to the service providers (i.e., maintenance, repair & operational supplies (MRO), purchases, facility management) on a global basis. Information systems and communications needs of these partnerships vary from tight coupling of the systems to electronic interchange of information. The technology has also given rise to the environment of shared services within a specific region of the world or on a global basis for functions such as Accounts Payable, Accounts Receivable, Call Centers, etc.

The consolidated global corporations are taking many forms. The structure selected may depend on the motivating factors (Vitalari & Wetherbe 1996) such as:

- Economies of scale
- Ability to locate activities to take advantage of lower labor cost, skilled workers, financial markets, customer proximity etc.
- Reduction in the risk of economic down turns in specific countries through diversified markets.

The diverse business environment such as product and market domain, nature of competition, trade barriers, economies of scale in which a corporation operates leads to evolution of various business strategies, which also affect the structure of the corporation varying from highly centralized global environment to dispersed transnational organization. Bartlett and Ghoshal (1989) characterized corporations into the following four strategic structures:

Multinational: In this structure companies have a headquarter base and operating units in various countries and market. This structure can be viewed as classic domestically controlled model, which is an extension of domestic divisional structure. Organizational controls are loose with remote decision-making. Strong financial reporting used to exercise control, results in remote site funneling large quantity of information to headquarters. Since each site performs its own activity, redundancy is a primary disadvantage of this structure. From IT, perspective site autonomy creates difficulty for dissolving cross-functional boundaries.

Global: This structure is characterized by centralized organizational structure with global management perspective. All major decisions about local markets and sites are made at the headquarters. Most information flow outward from headquarters to the sites. This one-way information flow allows little room for remote input; thus, site-specific differences and advantages are ignored.

International: This structure combines international management perspective with an organization of coordinated-federations. Local units have federated relationship with each other. Assets and responsibilities are decentralized to the federations. Formal control systems exist, but the federations are more likely to work together with support and encouragement from headquarters for the good of their common customers.

Transnational: It is the most contemporary structure with promising future. In this case the management has transnational perspective and organization structure is Web-like. Head quarters are highly involved in the complexities of both the coordination and the strategic decision processes. Capabilities, resources, and decision-making are distributed to the remote sites. There are heavy flows of materials, people, information and technology. Internal labor and resource markets, high coordination costs; and absolute dependence on information technology also characterize this structure.

The above structures can be mapped on to different levels of control and coordination. Since Information Technology is primarily used to support the control and coordination activities, the IT strategies and infrastructure should vary according to these four structures (Vitalari & Wetherbe 1996). Jarvenpaa and Ives (1993) empirically examined whether or not information technology structure varies according to Bartlett and Ghoshal's characterization and found some support for it. Additionally, as business environment become globally competitive and firms become more sophisticated to meet the competitive challenges, the organizational model moves to a more loosely coupled, market-coordinated structure. Information technology is required to support this coordinated structure through system integration, e-mail, groupware and World Wide Web. Many researchers (Miles & Snow, 1994; Vitalari, 1992; and Jarvenpaa and Ives, 1994) argue that this technology support will ultimately allow the firms to move to a more networked, loosely coupled structure indicative of the transnational structure.

Steve Simon (1996) proposed a framework for examining the alignment of a multinational corporation's structure and strategy with its information infrastructure. This framework focuses on the processes of co-ordination & control, and discusses the impact of coordination and control strategies on IT infrastructure. Figure 2 depicts the information architecture model proposed by Steve Simon. It shows the relationship between business driven IT factors, control and coordination needs, and the organization's information architecture. The business factors such as corporate structure, strategic predisposition of the firm, organizational culture and personnel practices acts as the independent variables in the model affecting the control and coordination needs. The information architecture defined by the computer location, database structure, telecommunication, and IT organization structure and technology standard acts as the dependent variables affected by coordination and control needs.

Development of IT architecture has been identified as one of the key issues facing the Information Systems Management (Brancheau, Janz, Wetherbe, 1996). The design of the IT architecture becomes much more challenging in transnational corporations because of the various cultural, government regulations and technology incompatibility issues. Nezlek, Jain and Nazareth (1999) present an integrated approach for developing enterprise architecture. The approach allows the designer of an enterprise computing architecture to generate a consistent, technology independent model of the architecture in the context of the information management requirements that it must ultimately satisfy. In deriving this model no assumption regarding existing technologies are made. Figure 3 represents the details of their approach.

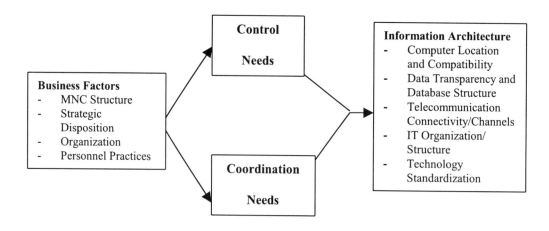

Figure 2: An Information Architecture Model
Source: Simon, S. J. (1996)

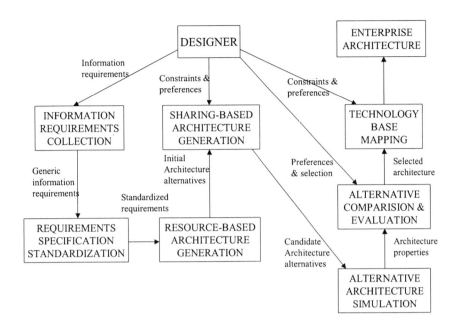

Figure 3: Integrated Design Methodology
(source: Nezlek, Jain & Nazareth (1999))

The approach allows the enterprise computing architecture designer to generate a consistent, technology independent model of the architecture to satisfy a given set of requirements. The approach do not make any assumptions about the underlying technology, thus allowing it be useful in the changing technology environment. A brief description of their approach is presented here.

The designer collects information requirements of various users/user groups located globally by using techniques like interview, questionnaire, study of job functions etc. The requirements are collected in the context of the computer applications and data resources that are or will be used by various users/user groups to support current and future business processes. Their notion of computer and data resources incorporate multi-level schemes of systems, sub-systems and modules as well as the databases, tables, data objects and application specific formats such as spreadsheet files. Depending upon the common requirements the end-users may be considered individually, or in a variety of organizational structures including groups (e.g. accounting, marketing, etc.) or sites (an office in one city). The requirement collected above is generally imprecise and is specified at varied levels of details. For example requirement may say that every user in the group located at location ABC needs Microsoft Access, on the other hand requirements may say that the sales manager in Milwaukee needs to run report A on Friday afternoon. To help in the generation of the architecture the above requirements are converted to lowest possible level of details and put in a standard common form known as atomic form. These standardized requirements are then considered in the resource-based architecture generation process to generate a set of architecture alternatives. The alternative architectures are generated based on various resource allocation strategies. For example, the minimization strategy tries to minimize the redundant copies of the resources (data and/or programs) by encouraging sharing, on the other hand the localization strategy allocates program and data components according to the closest feasible proximity to the potential users. The above set of alternative architectures and designer input goes into generating sharing based architecture. The sharing based architecture considers alternative structure of the application systems such as centralized, thin client, fat client, and decentralized. The designer provides input by specifying constraints and preferences. Few promising alternatives selected by the designer can be used as a basis of inputs to a simulation-based capacity-planning module. The capacity planning tool models the processing, memory, storage and data transmission requirements for an enterprise computing architecture under a frequency weighted set of user demands. The results of the simulation are used by the designer to compare alternative architectures and select the preferred architecture. The architecture is specified in generic terms such as a high-end desktop machine, medium capacity server etc. Based on the designer input, current technology trend and set of products and services available the above architecture is mapped to create the specific enterprise architecture.

FRAMEWORK FOR MANAGING THE
GLOBAL INFORMATION TECHNOLOGY INFRASTRUCTURE

A well-managed Information Technology infrastructure is an essential element for the success of contemporary transnational corporations. The infrastructure needs to support complex coordination and control requirements and should allow smooth flow of information across national boundaries. Figure 4 presents a context diagram showing the relationship of IT infrastructure to other functions. The IT infrastructure is driven by the IT strategy of the corporation, which is determined by the business strategy, IT industry trends and strengths and weaknesses of the corporation's IT function.

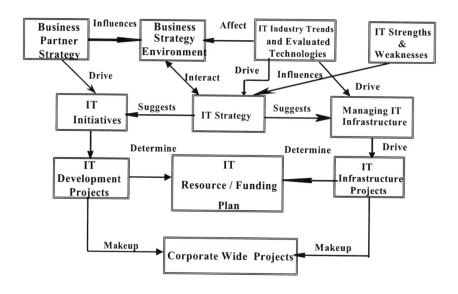

Figure 4: Context Diagram for IT Infrastructure

As shown in figure 4, the IT strategy and strategy of its business partners also drive various IT initiatives. The required IT infrastructure and various IT initiatives determine a set of IT infrastructure projects such as developing global communication network and IT development projects that needs to be funded. The above sets of projects make up the corporate wide projects.

The task of conceptualizing, planning, developing, deploying, and on going management of the IT infrastructure is a complex one. The rapid changes in business environment and technology, and consolidation in various industries makes this a continuous task. There is no unified framework available in the literature to perform this task of managing IT infrastructure. Based on our experience in three large transnational corporations we have developed a framework for on going management of IT infrastructure shown in figure 5. The IT strategy of the corporation which is driven by the business environment of the corporation consisting of type and level of competition, IT industry trends and evaluated technologies and the internal business processes used by the corporation and type and nature of external relationships with supplier and customer's business processes are used to develop a conceptual vision of the IT infrastructure. This conceptual model is used to cost justify the investment in terms of business value and competitive necessity and obtain strong management commitment. The next phase termed as architectural planning phase starts with the creation of an organization structure consisting of internal experts and consultant to facilitate development of detailed architectural plan. This involves technology evaluation, technology selection and vendor selection. Performance simulation and service level agreements are used to ensure the acceptable performance. The architectural planning phase also needs to address issues related to funding for the infrastructure including allocation of cost to local units. The planning phase is followed by deployment, which involve issues related to global rollout, managing the acceptance curve and standard enforcement. On going management of the infrastructure is one of the most important and often ignored phases of the process. The infrastructure's performance needs to be vigilantly monitored on a continuous basis. The whole process of managing the infrastructure although described in multiple phases should be continuous and iterative to allow for changes in technology and strategy.. The next sections describe each of these phases in detail.

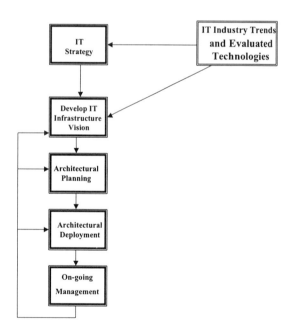

Figure 5: Framework for Managing IT Infrastructure

INFRASTRUCTURE VISION AND LOGICAL DESIGN

This process consists of vision development, cost justification and obtaining management commitment. It must consider the business environment represented by evolving Customer Service Life Cycle; Supply Chain changes such as buying process enabled by Internet/web. The internal business processes need to evolve to support the changes in customer and supplier business processes. These internal processes represent and support the coordination and control needs between various units of the corporation. Figure 6 represents the process of developing an IT infrastructure vision. The overlapping ellipses represent interfaces between processes.

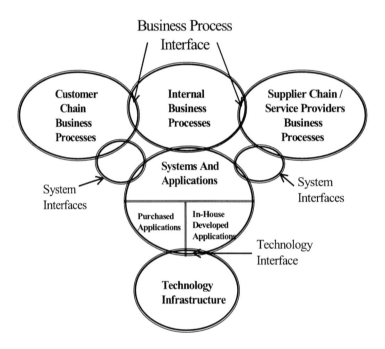

Figure 6: Developing Infrastructure Vision

Vision Development:

The IT infrastructure vision must be based on a sound understanding of the business environment of an organization, which can be analyzed and represented by:
- Mapping business locations of the company around the world to categories such as, wholly owned, majority owned, minority owned and partnerships.
- Identifying business process linkages among all the entities of the organization throughout the customer service life cycle and supply chain management.
- Identifying major application systems required for supporting business processes and their linkages.

A strategic vision statement for the IT Infrastructure needs to align with the strategic business vision statement of the corporation. For example the business vision may be:

"Exceed customer's increasing expectations on a global basis"

An example of IT Infrastructure vision, which aligns with, the business vision may look like:

"The successful execution of the corporate business strategies require that the IT should provide the ability, flexibility, and global cost leverage in supporting the movement and/or collaboration of people, processes and products internally, while participating seamlessly within the overall supply/services chain on a global basis"

Identifying IT Infrastructure Components/Elements

The next step in the conceptual development of the infrastructure includes:

- Development of principles and guidelines, which will govern the business processes, business systems/applications and IT infrastructure. These principles and guidelines may include extent of IT centralization, level of autonomy for each business unit, site, functions and locations, policy on shared services etc.

- Design of Logical IT infrastructure must address the following entities/components at the conceptual level:

    - Client Devices (PCs, Laptops, palmtops, cellular phones, pagers, etc.).
    - Server Devices (File Servers, Application Servers, Database Servers, and Telephony Servers).
    - Local Area Networks (Voice, Data, Video).
    - Wide Area Networks (Voice, Data, Video).
    - Internet, Intranet and Extranet.
    - Performance Monitoring
    - Customer Call Centers.

Cost Justification

The first step in cost justifying the new IT infrastructure is to identify the costs of all components of current IT infrastructure. The cost should include the cost of operating and maintaining the current infrastructure including the cost of voice data and video communication. In the global context, it may be difficult to identify some of the costs of IT infrastructure in developing and underdeveloped countries due to differences in accounting practices and/or government provided services.

It should be recognized that the philosophy of pricing products around the world varies a lot. For example in developed countries, typically a correlation can be drawn between the purchase volume and the price (higher volume leads to lower price). However, in developing and underdeveloped countries infrastructure is often priced based on objective of attaining social balance. Organizations with higher volume of usage are often charged higher per unit price because they can afford it and lower unit prices are charged for lower volume users and poorer population. The cost justification should also take into account the expected price reduction curve per year based on technology trends in various areas of the IT infrastructure.

An aggregate cost/benefit analysis for the organization should be developed based on current state and cost of the infrastructure, technology/price trends in various areas, and the vision of the new IT infrastructure.

Management Commitment

Strong management commitment is vital and essential for making the global IT infrastructure a reality. The logical and strategic IT infrastructure design is presented to the senior management along with appropriate linkage to organization's business vision and strategy.

The emphasis should be on the fact that IT infrastructure is a foundation that is needed for the global business vision to succeed. The cost justification should be explained in a broad sense. The factors that may affect development & implementation of the IT infrastructure negatively should be identified. Some of the example factors are:

- Divisional autonomy
- Local vendor preferences
- Sub-optimization in local market
- Difficulty with cost allocation
- Differing priorities within divisions
- Differences in Technology preferences
- Investments locked in existing technology.

Strategies for dealing with these factors needs to be presented to the management in order to obtain their strong support. After the acceptance of the vision, overall cost/benefit analysis and approach to development of infrastructure by the senior management, the business plan should be communicated to the divisional management of the organization.

IT INFRASTRUCTURE PLANNING

After obtaining the management commitment for the infrastructure vision and communicating the action/project plan to the divisional management of the organization, the formal planning for the infrastructure begins. It involves project planning, technology evaluation and selection and vendor selection. Performance simulation and service level agreements are used to ensure the acceptable performance. This phase also needs to address issues related to the funding for the infrastructure including allocation of costs to local units.

Project Planning

For planning purposes, the entire IT Infrastructure can be divided into logical components such as WAN (voice/data), Video, Telephony Servers (PBXs), Cellular Phones, Pagers, LANs, Intranet, Virtual Private Network desktops and server/mainframe. A planning team consisting of representatives from each division in appropriate geographical regions should be formed. Prioritization of various logical components/segments shown in figure 7 is critical. Preference should be given to highly visible business/IT segments from the point of view of organizational connectivity to cover most business traffic volume.

A good understanding of the organizational vision for global IT infrastructure by the members of the team helps in getting their buy-in and time commitment to the project. Any issues related to cultural barriers, differences of opinion about the vision, priority conflicts need to be resolved before proceeding further. Team leaders, along with sub-teams, need to be formed with proper documentation of roles and responsibilities. Representatives from accounting (for cost analysis), purchasing (negotiations) and legal (contract terms) organizations should be part of the overall team.

Technology Evaluation and Selection

The technology available in various regions of the world and technology trends needs to be investigated and understood by receiving information from:

- Top IT infrastructure vendors (four to five) in the field.
- Research studies from organizations such as Gartner Group, Forrester Research, Burton Group, etc.
- Consulting firms specializing in the IT infrastructure area.

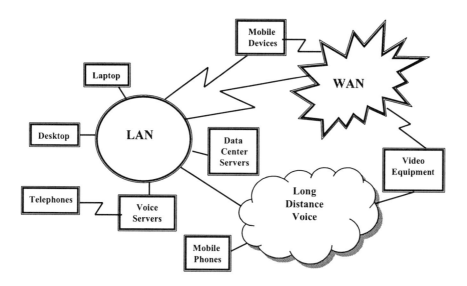

Figure 7: Scope of IT Infrastructure

Alignment of organizational business needs and technology capabilities/trends should lead to the development of tactical and strategic choices of technology for global deployment.

A typical process for technology evaluation and selection in MNCs may consist of following steps.

- Users, technocrats or others may initiate identification of business needs for new technology in the organization.
- The architecture-planning group starts the research on this technology by collecting reports from organizations like Gardner Group, Forester Research and trade publications.
- The next step is to identify companies currently using this technology (if any) and collect information on their experiences.
- If the technology seems promising major vendors providing the technology are invited for demonstration.
- This may result in vendors providing the technology on trial basis for a limited period and/or benchmarking it in the corporation's environment. This allows the company to evaluate the applicability of new technology in their own environment, separate hype from reality and make judgment on ease of implementation.
- The recommendation on the acquisition of technology is made to IT leadership for their final decision.

In MNCs with fairly autonomous business units the representatives form each of the business units are involved throughout this evaluation process. The IT leadership is also kept informed of the progress.

Vendor Selection

Vendor selections process for Global IT infrastructure gets very involved and complicated. There is no single provider that can meet all the needs of global IT infrastructure. Even for individual segments of IT infrastructure (i.e., wide area network), there are no global providers. Various approaches are taken by vendors in order to provide global infrastructure service for MNCs. Some of the approaches are described below:

Vendor Alliances: In this case, contractual agreements are established between two or more companies to provide service to the global customer [Jarvenpaaa & Ives, 1994]. Examples of this are: AT&T and British Telecom's alliance, and United Airlines' alliance with six other airlines. These alliances may involve marketing agreements, technology transfer agreements, product development agreements, etc.

Intermediaries: It involves contractual agreements between the manufacturers & intermediaries (wholesalers, distributors, agencies) for marketing, installing and/or supporting products. These agreements are typically made to cover a specific geographic region of the world or take advantage of already established marketing channels. Intermediaries can also be used in cases where product's competitive margins do not sustain internal sales and marketing overhead. Distributorships can either be confined to a single company and their product along with non-competing products or could be a multi-product and multi-vendor environment.

Factors and Issues: The vendor selection process for the IT infrastructure of an MNC should give adequate consideration to the following factors in addition to the conventional factors like price, and vendor stability:

- Who are the vendors involved (vendor chain) in providing the IT infrastructure during the complete life cycle including sale cycle, solution design cycle, implementation cycle and on-going performance management and support cycle. Identify vendors involved along with their partnerships and alliances.
- Your company's locations in comparison to the locations of the service provider.
- Extent of fit between the technology strategies selected by your company and the technology strategies of the vendor.
- The contractual agreements between various companies in the vendor chain involved in providing IT infrastructure service on a global basis. Impact of these agreements on your company's expectations of service level guarantees.
- How well will the systems used by the vendors in the vendor chain interface and/or integrate with your company's existing information systems?
- Countries/regions that have governmental/political regulations that could prohibit vendors from providing products and services that you require along with their influence on the pricing structure.

Based on our experience in negotiating global contracts with vendors in multiple corporations we found that the following issues need to be considered.

- Price protection during the term of contracts both in upward and downward directions due to technology improvements and/or competitive environment in various regions of the world.
- Flexibility to periodically test/benchmark competitive prices in the marketplace.
- Ability to negotiate based on total revenue given on a global basis.

- One global contract instead of multiple contracts in various countries.
- Global account management organization with proper authority to cut across functional and geographical issues within vendor(s) organization. The vendor needs to consider the whole corporation such as Ford Motor Company as a single account with account manager who has authority to cut across various organizational units and geographical vendor locations.

Performance Evaluation

Performance evaluation provides an ability to predict performance of IT infrastructure by creating various "what if" scenarios in a controlled/lab environment. Performance simulation can be used to tie in the technical approach, technology choices and its economics with the business requirements of today and in the future. Performance simulation also becomes the basis for developing service level agreements. Performance simulation highlights where alternate approaches, redundant infrastructure components or backup plans have to be developed to meet critical business requirements such as "Just-In-Time" mission critical environments.

Contrary to common belief, performance evaluation is an art. Every evaluation requires an intimate knowledge of the system being modeled and a careful selection of the methodology, workload and tools. Raj Jain (Jain, R, 1991) identifies following steps for performance evaluation:

- State Goals and Define the System
- List Services provided by the system and Outcomes
- Select Metrics for comparing performance
- List parameters that affect performance
- Select parameters to be varied and decide on the level of variation
- Select appropriate technique for performance evaluation such as analytical modeling, simulation or measurement from a real system
- Select typical workload
- Design experiments
- Analyze and Interpret results
- Present the results

Service Level Agreements

Service level agreements are critical in establishing contractual linkage between business' expectation of IT infrastructure performance and the vendor's commitment on delivery and ongoing performance. The IT infrastructure service level agreements should cover topics such as:

- Up-time availability such as 99.99% up time. Coverage of service (24x7, 24x365)
- Response time during up time. This may be segmented into categories like peak, off-peak, nights and weekends instead of one general response time.
- Pro-active monitoring to predict potential degradation of the infrastructure.
- Response time on trouble notification and fixing of the problem.
- Analysis reporting of traffic details and patterns of usage.
- Management reporting of important performance statistics on a regular basis (i.e., monthly).

Budgeting/Funding

IT infrastructure in MNC's should be treated as a corporate-wide initiative. Budgeting/Funding for such a crucial and critical initiative needs to be undertaken as one single program, spanning and covering all business units of the MNC. It will be economically and operationally beneficial to negotiate with vendor(s) if it is treated as one program. It is important to identify the budget by geography, category of infrastructure service and sequence of implementation. If gains/savings in one service is going to pay for another service, then the proper priority has to be evaluated based on economics versus urgency of implementation of service. For example, if voice service in Europe is going to pay for data connectivity, then one has to decide between two approaches. One approach will be to budget for voice service first to use the savings from it for the data service. Another approach will be to pay for data connectivity due to its urgency and then take advantage of the voice service savings. Depending on the approach chosen the budget and funding requirements will be different.

The IT infrastructure typically will have two general segments. One that spans across all business units and its usage will be shared across business units. The other segments can be identified with the individual entity of every business unit. Two alternative approaches for funding IT infrastructure of MNCs can be used. One approach is to have the corporate headquarter fund the common portion of the infrastructure e.g. global backbone network, Internet firewalls, and connection to Internet service provider, and the remaining portion to be funded by the individual business units. This approach may involve high internal selling efforts to get the business unit buy-in and could create implementation-timing problems, depending on the economic health of the business unit(s).

The second approach is to fund the entire IT infrastructure for MNC at the corporate headquarter level. This approach gives most advantage in vendor negotiations, program management and minimization for internal politics. This approach needs the understanding, involvement and commitment/support of top/senior management of the MNC.

Cost Allocation

The cost allocation method used will depend on the approach chosen in the budgeting and funding section discussed above.

The billing process for collecting actual costs should align with the approach chosen. For IT infrastructure segments that span multiple business units, all bills should be collected/received centrally and paid centrally. This facilitates audit and validation of charges. The currency in which the payment is going to be made should take into account various tax rules, such as value added tax. Exchange rate of currencies and currency position at the time of payment within MNC should also be considered. Tax and Treasury departments of the MNC should be involved in this process.

The cost for the common portion of the infrastructure can then be allocated to business units based on various factors such as traffic percentage, percentage of locations owned by the business unit, proportion of the number of employees and/or sales. The cost allocation base once agreed upon by corporate and the business units should be fixed for a fiscal year and allocated eventually by month. Attempts to change cost allocation base during a fiscal year should be avoided since it will add administrative burden without any impact on the actual cost incurred. The cost of corporate resources associated with providing infrastructure service should be added to the vendor cost in the allocation method.

Budget segments that are identifiable by individual business unit can either be paid directly by the business unit or they could be paid centrally and then settled through intra-company transfer. The advantage of central payments is leverage in centralized auditing, ease of collecting cost information and the use of appropriate currency in making the payments.

INFRASTRUCTURE DEPLOYMENT

After completing architectural planning, budgeting and funding, the real work of making the architecture a reality starts. The implementation involves developing and managing implementation program, global rollout, enforcement of standards and security. Each of these is discussed here in detail.

Program Management

Once the program for implementing global IT infrastructure is formulated and the MNC management's buy-in is obtained, the difficult task of deployment begins. Organizing for program management is the most important and difficult task. An Office of Program Management, consisting of a steering committee and a program officer/manager should be established. The steering committee should have senior management from corporate, some business units, IT organization and vendor organization.

All entities that will be involved (including sub-contractors or distributors/partners of vendors) should be identified. Initial meetings that include representatives from corporate headquarter, business units, distributors, manufacturers and service providers involved in the deployment should be organized. To accommodate the logistic issues, the initial meeting(s) may be organized on the basis of different regions of the world. The initial meeting should address following issues:

- Purpose, scope and objective of the deployment program.
- Identification of resources involved in the deployment (their skills, full-time and part-time) from all parties. The vendor resources involved in planning and selling activities may not be the ones involved in the deployment.
- Agreement on roles and responsibilities of various parties along with authority levels.
- Commitment to use one project management methodology and tool(s) to be used by all parties.
- Commitment to produce status reports, update and re-plan based on predetermined frequency.
- Creation of a win-win environment for the success of the program.
- Recognition of the fact that problems and issues may arise during the deployment. Environment should be created for the timely identification and notification of these problems & issues.
- Program Management review cycle and method for all projects that make up the deployment program should be identified.
- Scope and plan change management method.

The advent of tools such as MS-Project, Lotus Notes/MS Exchange groupware, video conferencing, net meeting and Intranet should assist in the tasks of program management.

Global Rollout

Global rollout of the IT infrastructure is a challenging undertaking. The number of issues and their severity will depend on the duration of the rollout and associated risks to the business. The anticipated issues related to global rollout can be grouped as:

- Changes in the vendor Environment:
    - Changes in the organization responsible for the MNCs account.

- Acquisition/merger/alliance that involves vendors associated with MNCs rollout.
- Government Policies:
  - Changes in the regulations and pricing policies in the countries involved in the rollout.

- Competitive Pressures:
  - The vendors who lost in the selection process will keep submitting counter proposals to various levels of management within MNC.
  - Uncooperative environment may result when the vendor involved in the rollout has to depend on a local vendor in a country, who has a monopoly in that market. (For example connectivity for the last mile of telecom to MNCs facility).
- Internal Environment at MNCs:
  - Organizational changes, which may undermine the deployment program.
  - Change in support and priority within individual business unit for the program.
  - Local entity may pursue solution, which sub-optimizes the program. This issue will be evident mostly in decentralized organizations with autonomous profit & loss responsibilities.
  - Changes in the economic health of the MNC and/or its selective business unit. This may need subsidizing action on the part of the corporate management during a down cycle.
  - Changes in business needs, which may require performance simulation to run on frequent basis. This may also influence the design philosophy of the IT infrastructure.
  - Language skills required in some entities of MNC and language restrictions placed by unions in rollout of English only versions of applications involved in the infrastructure.
- Technology:
  - Changes in technology may initiate request to review applicability and potential inclusion of new technology in the program.
  - Changes may introduce multiple versions and/or multiple technologies in the program that were not included in the original program plan

Enforcement of Standards

The spread of computing technology at home and abroad, inclusion of information technology in the product offerings such as car seats (memory of settings etc.), building control products of the MNC creates a challenging environment for the enforcement of IT standards.

A large percentage of MNC employees may have computers, Internet access and other technologies at home. Sometimes these technologies may be more advanced and current than the one available in the office. Because of this exposure to home computer technology, employees develop preferences with a given technology and/or vendors. These preferences may contradict with the technology standards chosen by the MNC. Additionally, the employees are looking for commonality between the technology choices they have made for home use and the office and may try to influence the infrastructure at the office. This specifically becomes a serious issue if an employee has significant budget authority. The only viable solution in this situation for MNC will be to stay firm on its course of chosen technology standards and to have:

- Policies/procedures to introduce new/different technologies within MNC.
- A review board to identify the deviations and take appropriate actions to enforce standards.
- IS leadership of business unit accepting the lead responsibility for compliance and assurance.

However, the inclusion of technology in a company's product offerings may require support for multiple technologies and standards to satisfy the requirements of its customer base. Viable solutions in this situation are to create a separate technical environment for supporting the product requirements and identify technical boundaries between product environment and the internal operational environment of the MNC. If the MNC is acquiring products and/or equipment with built-in technology to support the operational environment, standards for compliance and/or interface should be developed. These should be communicated to the purchasing and functional organization units to maintain overall resemblance of technology standards within MNC.

Security

For all segments of IT infrastructure, required security controls should be identified and deployed. The infrastructure segments, such as personal computers, LAN, Servers, WAN and Intranet that are designed for the internal use of the MNC, should have single security scheme such as consistent login procedure and password. The security policies and procedures should be global in scope and allow provision for concepts such as single-sign-on for all computing and application services. The policies should cover access rights, size of passwords, frequency of change, repeatability of passwords along with penalties for non-compliance. The security policies for Extranet should include contractual agreement between MNC and the selective partners it intends to provide with Extranet access. The security provision for Web Technology should include proper firewall protection. The security policies should require a well-defined scheme of global directories to support the authentication process.

ON-GOING MANAGEMENT

Once the architecture is deployed it is natural to declare success and relax a little bit. However, there is a need for well thought out scheme for managing the architecture on an on going basis. It involves monitoring the performance of the architecture, security surveillance, auditing cost performance and change management.

Performance Monitoring

Performance monitoring of IT infrastructure should include the measurement of how each segment of the architecture is doing against Service Level Agreement. There are two major categories of performance management.

1. *Self-Managed Services:* In this case the MNC measures and monitors performance of various segments of its infrastructure internally. In case of performance problems, it may decide to take corrective actions internally or may involve vendor(s) to remedy the situation. This approach requires MNC to select and install the monitoring tools to support automated measurement and detection of performance problem and to provide adequate staff to take corrective action. Some of the characteristics that can be monitored

for performance monitoring are: delivery time, delivered quality, response time, mean time between failure (MTBF), availability (up-time), traffic usage and pattern.

2. *Vendor Managed Services:* In this case, the MNC decides to outsource the infrastructure services inclusive of performance monitoring responsibility. This approach treats infrastructure as a *utility* so that the MNC is interested in paying for its usage but not for its monitoring and maintenance. However, the MNC should understand the tools being used by the vendor for performance monitoring. The monitoring process may involve multiple vendors in the implementation chain. This situation mostly arises during management of infrastructure performance across country / continent boarders. For example a wide area network between a location in the USA and Germany may involve as many as 5 vendors with each one of them using a different tool(s) for monitoring, measurement and recording of customer service information. In this situation, the performance of the weakest link in this chain of vendors is what determines the actual performance seen by the MNC. For example MCI-WorldCom may depend on local postal telephone and telegraph (PTT) organization to provide service within a country. The overall performance seen by the MNC will depend on the performance of the PTT organization, which may be quite different from the performance of MCI-WorldCom.

Documentation of performance becomes very important when there are penalty clauses involved in not meeting the agreed upon expectations. Performance monitoring issues should be typically reviewed with key strategic suppliers on approximately monthly frequency.

Security Surveillance

Security surveillance is very critical for assurance of secured IT infrastructure within MNC. The security surveillance activities can be grouped as:

- *Monitoring*: Any violations and/or unusual activities should be monitored and reported to the proper levels of management depending on their severity. This may also include violations of IT infrastructure standards and policies of MNC.
- *Pro-Active Detection*: The MNC should retain an external company, specializing in detection of security loopholes in the IT infrastructure. This activity should be conducted with complete secrecy and on an unannounced basis. Corrective actions can then be taken before the loophole becomes a problem. This external security assurance testing should normally be done on an annual basis. This should be undertaken at a corporate level.
- *Punishment for Violation*: If the security or policy violations related to IT infrastructure are detected, then prompt actions should be taken without exception.

Auditing Cost Performance

Auditing for cost performance should start with sound baseline information of cost. The unit cost and usage cost should be collected separately. The usage portion is typically business dependent and is within the control of the user organization. The auditing of cost per unit is critical to assure that the initial expectations are fulfilled. The total cost auditing is critical for meeting minimum financial commitments with the vendor along with the re-negotiation or renewal of the current contract.

Auditing the cost performance by conducting a competitive benchmark is also essential. Once or twice a year a competitive pricing analysis of various segments of the IT infrastructure should be done in order to assure the soundness of the current contracts. It would be advisable to include benchmark studies available from major consulting companies or technology trend tracking companies such as the Gartner Group.

Auditing should also include an understanding of the changes in government regulation at local, state, country and regional levels that would impact cost performance of IT infrastructure. MNC may have to take the initiative to bring these changes to the attention of the vendor to take advantage of positive impact on the IT infrastructure cost performance.

Change Management

Change Management is the most critical activity in the on-going support of IT infrastructure. Change Management will assist in assuring high reliability of the infrastructure. Some of the changes in the infrastructure that needs to be properly managed are: increasing bandwidth on one or more segments, rerouting, reallocation of hubs, mergers, acquisition, change of vendors and change of technology.

Change Management requires a well-defined, documented and communicated procedure that includes all internal functional organization of MNC along with the appropriate functional personnel of vendor(s). Related to changes in IT infrastructure, change management involves technical elements and organizational elements.

Based on our experience important technical elements that needs attention to ensure successful Change Management are:

- *Vendor testing of changes*: It is important to understand development, testing and quality check processes within the vendor's organization.
- *Implications*: Understanding all the implications of the proposed changes on the MNC's infrastructure and business environment is essential.
- *Testing in MNC's environment*: It is critical to test the proposed changes in the MNC's own environment. Simulation of the new environment under the stress of the business transaction volumes should be conducted.
- *Back out capability*: The back out capability needs be understood and tested.
- *Support:* On-site or on-call availability of MNC's and vendor's technical support personnel is essential.

The organizational elements are similar to the one recommended by change experts (Kettinger, Teng, and Guha, 1997). Some of these recommendations are:

- The deployment of changes should be planned in detail by involving all relevant people.
- Make constant change part of the culture
- Tell everyone as much as possible and as often as possible.
- Make liberal use of financial incentives abd recognition.
- On-site or on-call availability of MNC's and vendor's technical support personnel is essential.

No change should be introduced within the IT infrastructure of MNC without following a process similar to that outlined above. No changes should be implemented by simply taking the word or assurance of the vendor. Proper change management will assure high availability, reliability and performance of the MNC's IT infrastructure.

SUMMARY AND CONCLUSIONS

Development, deployment and on going management of IT infrastructure for a multinational corporation under fast changing business and technology environment is a major challenge facing most of the MNCs. This chapter provides a brief discussion of the global business environment and its impact on the IT infrastructure. A framework for development, deployment and ongoing management of the IT infrastructure for large multinational corporations was presented. Based on the experience of one of the authors in three multinational corporations, a conceptual framework is developed and some prescriptive suggestions made for managing IT infrastructure. These suggestions are summarized here.

- Understand the business needs, interaction between business units, and complete supply chain of the business and its level of sophistication.
- Understand the government & industry regulations in the countries in which the MNC conduct business.
- Keep track of current technology capabilities and the future trends.
- Identify various segments of IT infrastructure needed to support the business.
- Generate a vision for IT infrastructure and get buy-in from the senior levels of management at corporate and business unit levels. Alignment of infrastructure vision with the business strategies is critical to getting management's buy-in.
- Finalize technology choices and establish company-wide standards with the participation of corporate and all business units.
- Create plan for development and deployment. This includes scoping, sizing and vendor selection. Based on the results of this, baseline expectations can be established.
- The deployment requires detailed plan, understanding of supplier chains and their organization, and government regulations.
- The on-going management requires sound change management, auditing and reporting procedures for assurance of high availability, reliability and performance of global IT infrastructure within MNC.

Mini Case

Congratulations. Your team has been appointed to be the consultant to the Chief Information Officer who directly reports to the CEO of a fortune 500 multinational corporations.

The task you have been assigned is very critical for the success of the company. The company has 5 plants in three mid-western states (Michigan, Illinois, and Wisconsin). Has two plant located in Western Europe (assume exact location), and three plant located in south east Asia (assume exact location). The company has 20 warehouse locations all around the world (assume exact location). Thirty percent of companies business is done inter-nationally. The head office of the company is located in Milwaukee. The head office has centralized marketing, accounting and financial management. The products of the company are sold internationally as OEM product and to customers through distributors. A number of sales persons travel around the country to visit customers and take orders. The company has grown through mergers and acquisitions. Various structures exists in different countries e,g. European operations are wholly owned subsidiary, while the south-east Asia operations are a Joint Venture. Different IT infrastructure components exist at different locations. Fast changing nature of business, competitive pressures, integration needs driven by electronic commerce are forcing the company to re-think its computing strategy.

Use your imagination and information publicly available to assume the existing organizational and other environment of the company as required in your planning (you can visit a company to test the appropriateness of your assumptions). Also assume the exact locations of the plants, warehouses etc. If

Mini Case …. Continued.

you can make strong enough case company is willing to replace all its current hardware software and systems with new Internet based distributed computing environment, which should serve the company well into 21st century. This means that the company is willing to acquire state-of-the-art technology such as: wireless, distributed object technologies etc. Company is also very interested in leveraging Intra Net, extranet and Internet technologies. They plan to be embrace Electronic Commerce in every facet of their business.

Propose a medium term infrastructure strategy (plan), which will allow efficient and effective development and operation of new applications to keep the company competitive. You must specify following in your plan.

1. Specify the standardization effort you will start. Suggest the method you will use to develop hardware architecture of computing for the company.
2. Provide a cost analysis of the architecture recommended by you. Also provide in the justifications for the choices you made.
3. Address the issues related to the implementation of the architecture. Suggest the organizational structure you will create for this.

Also address the cultural and country specific issues.

STUDY QUESTIONS

1. Briefly explain with the help of an example how changing global business environment impact the design of IT infrastructure.
2. Describe and discuss interrelationships and interdependencies within various components of IT infrastructure.
3. Discuss pros and cons of various vendor relationship models or approaches in dealing with multi-vendor, multi-country, multi-division environment.
4. Explain how technical advances in one infrastructure component can influence the modification or obsolescence of other infrastructure component e.g. significant reduction in networking cost may make centralized data centers more cost effective.

REFERENCES

Bartlett, C. A., and Ghoshal, S.(1989), *Managing across borders: The transnational solution*, Harvard Business School Press, 1989, Boston, MA.

Brancheau, J. Janz, B., and Wetherbe, J.(1996), Key Issues in Information Systems Management: 1994-95 SIM Delphi Results, *MIS Quartely*, Vol. 20, No 2, June 1996.

Burn, J. M. and Cheung, H. K. (1996), Information Systems Resources Structure and Management in Multinational Organizations, Chapter in *The Global Issues of Information Technology Management*, Ive League Publishing 1996.

Ghoshal, S., Korine H. and Szulanski G., Interunit (1994), Communication in Multinational Corporations, *Management Science*, Vol 40, No 1, January 1994, pp 96-110.

Gibson, R. (1996), Information Technology Planning and Architectures for Networked Global Organizations, Chapter in *The Global Issues of Information Technology Management*. Ive League Publishing 1996.

Ives, Blake and Jarvenpaa, Sirkka, (1991) Application of Global Information Technology: Key Issues for Management, *MIS Quarterly*, Vol 15, No 1, March 1991, pp 33 - 49.

Jain, Raj, (1991) *The art of Computer System Performance Analysis*, John Wiley & Sons Inc. 1991.

Jarvenpaa, Sirkka and Ives, Blake (1993), Organizing for Global Competition: The Fit of Information technology. *Decision Sciences*, Vol 24, No. 3. 1993, Pp 547- 580.

Jarvenpaa, Sirkka and Ives, Black (1994), The Global Network Organization of the Future: Information Management Opportunities and Challenges, *Journal of Management Information Systems*, Vol 10, No 4, Spring 1994, pp.25-27.

Kettinger, William, Teng, James and Guha, Subashish, "Business Process Change: A Study of Methodologies, Techniques, and Tools." *MIS Quarterly*, March 1997.

Miles, R. and C. Snow, (1994) *Fit, Failure and the Hall of Fame*, Simon and Schuster Inc. 1994.

Nezlek, George, Jain, Hemant and Nazareth, Derek(1999), Enterprise Computing Architecture - An Integrated Approach*, Communications of ACM*.

Simon, S. J. (1996), *An Informational Perspective on the Effectiveness of Headquarters-Subsidiary Relationships: Issues of Control and Coordination*, Ive League Publishing 1996.

Vitalari, N.(1990), Exploring the Type-D Organization: Distributed Work Arrangement, Information Technology and Organizational Design, Research Issues in Information Systems: An Agenda for the 1990's, A. M. Jenkins et. el. (Eds), Wm C. Brown Publishers, 1990.

Vitalari, N. P. and Wetherbe, J.C. (1996), Emerging Best Practices in Global Systems Development, Chapter in *The Global Issues of Information Technology Management*. Ivy League Publishing 1996.

Author Biographies

Dr. Murad Akmanligil (makmanligil@hotmail.com)

Murad Akmanligil is a Senior Technical Analyst at FedEx Corporation where he has been working since 1997. He received his Ph.D. from the University of Memphis in 2000. His primary research interests include global information systems development and software engineering.

Dr. Choton Basu (sbasu@nmu.edu)

Choton Basu is an Assistant Professor of Management (MCS) in the College of Business and Economics at the University of Wisconsin-Whitewater. Earlier he was at the Cisler College of Business at Northern Michigan University. He received his Ph.D. in MIS from the University of Memphis. His primary area of interest is Global Information Technology and Systems Development. He is also interested in areas related to innovation using Technology, Supply Chains, E-business and ERP systems. He has articles published in journals such as Decision Sciences, Information Management and Data Systems, Academy of Marketing Studies Journal (forthcoming), International Journal of Information Management (forthcoming) and other book chapters. He also has several national ad international conference proceedings. He current research includes global business models; e-business, technology implementation in education and global supply chain management.

Dr. Carol V. Brown (cbrown@iupui.edu)

Carol V. Brown is an Associate Professor of Information Systems in the Kelley School of Business at Indiana University, where she has been a member of the faculty since 1990. She also currently serves in the academic liaison position on the executive board of the Society for Information Management. Carol is recognized for her expertise on alternative organizational approaches for achieving strategic alignment of the IT function and effective IT-business partnering. She is the co-author of monographs on IT management topics, an IT management textbook (Prentice Hall), and articles published in major academic journals such as *MIS Quarterly, Organization Science, Information Systems Research,* and *Journal of Management Information Systems*.

Dr. Janice M. Burn (j.burn@cowan.edu.au)

Janice M. Burn is Foundation Professor and Head of School of Management Information Systems at Edith Cowan University in Perth, Western Australia and Director of the We-B Research Centre – Working for e-Business. In 2000 she assumed the role of World President of the Information Resources Management Association (IRMA). She has previously held senior academic posts in Hong Kong and the UK. Her research interests relate to information systems strategy and benefits evaluation in virtual organisations with a particular emphasis on social, political and cultural challenges in an e-business environment. She is recognised as an international researcher with over 150 refereed publications in journals and international conferences. She is on the editorial board of six prestigious IS journals and participates in a number of joint research projects with international collaboration and funding.

Dr. Erran Carmel (ecarmel@american.edu)

Erran Carmel's research deals with global software development. He has been studying software teams and software development for many years. More recently he turned his attention to globally dispersed software team, and is now examining global software human resource issues. His 1999 book *Global Software Teams* was the first on this topic. He has written over 40 articles, reports and manuscripts. He consults and speaks to industry and professional groups. He is an Associate Professor at the business school at American University in Washington D.C where he was co-founder and now shares in the leadership of the program in Management of Global Information Technology (MoGIT).

Dr. Elia Chepaitis (echepaitis@fair1.fairfield.edu)

Elia Chepaitis is an Associate Professor of Information Systems and Operations Management at Fairfield University in Fairfield, Connecticut. Dr. Chepaitis' areas of specialization are emerging economies, information ethics, and ergonomics. She has been awarded several domestic and foreign patents for an alternative to Braille, and has had three Fulbrights to conduct research and to teach IS and quality management in Russia and in Morocco.

Dr. J. Roberto Evaristo (evaristo@uic.edu)

Roberto Evaristo is at the Department of Information and Decision Sciences at the University of Illinois at Chicago. He received his Ph.D. in Management Information Systems from the University of Minnesota. His main research interests include the management of distributed projects, cultural issues in information systems, and competitive intelligence. Dr. Evaristo was the editor of a special issue of *Information, Technology and People* on "Cross-Cultural Research in MIS". He has also published in *Database, Competitive Intelligence Review, International Journal of Project Management, Journal of the Association for Global Strategic Information, Journal of International Information Management, and Information Technology and People.* This chapter was partially developed while Dr. Evaristo was a Visiting Associate Professor at Høgskolen i Agder, in Norway and he expresses his appreciation for their support and insights.

Dr. Roger W. Harris (roger@meranti.fit.unimas.my)

Roger Harris has an MSc. in Business Systems Analysis and Design from the City University of London and a Ph.D. in Information Systems from the City University of Hong Kong. He is a Lecturer in the Faculty of Information Technology at Universiti Malaysia Sarawak (UNIMAS). Dr. Harris has occupied a variety of management and consultancy positions in Africa and Asia, advising organisations on process improvement and organisational effectiveness. He embarked on an academic career in order to pursue his interests in the use of Information Technology in developing countries. He is Vice Chair of the International Federation of Information Processing Working Group 9.4 on IT in Developing Countries, representing the Asian region. In this capacity, Roger launched the group's inaugural Asian regional conference on IT in Asia, held in Kuching, Malaysia, for which he chaired the Programme Committee. Dr. Harris is a member of the editorial advisory boards of the "Journal of End-User Computing", the "Journal of Global Information Management" the "Journal of Global Information Technology Management" and "Computer Personnel". He is Editor-in-Chief of the "Electronic Journal on Information Systems in Developing Countries" and he works with several international conferences that address the particular problems of IT in Asia Pacific and in developing countries.

Dr. Hemant Jain (jain@uwm.edu)

Hemant Jain is Tata Consulting Services Professor of MIS in the School of Business Administration at the University of Wisconsin - Milwaukee. Prof. Jain received his Ph. D. in information system from Lehigh University in 1981, a M. Tech in Industrial Engineering from I.I.T. Kharagpur (India) and B.S. in Mechanical Engineering from University of Indore (India). Dr. Jain specializes in electronic commerce, system development using resuable components, distributed and co-operative computing systems, architecture design, database management and data warehousing, data mining and visulalization. He is currently working on system integration issues within a corporation and across multiple corporations. He has published articles in leading journals like Information Systems Research, MIS Quarterly, IEEE transactions on Software Engineering, Communications of ACM, Navel Research Quarterly, Decision Sciences, Decision Support Systems, Information & Management, etc. Prof. Jain is on the editorial board of Information Technology & Management journal and is book review editor for the Journal of Information Technology Cases & Applications. Prof. Jain has also served as a consultant to several Fortune 500 companies.

Dr. Brian D. Janz (bdjanz@memphis.edu)

Brian Janz is an Assistant Professor of MIS at the Fogelman College of Business and Economics at The University of Memphis where he teaches in the undergraduate, MBA, and Executive MBA programs. In addition, he is the Director of the Institute for Managing Emerging Technology and the Associate Director of the FedEx Center for Cycle Time Research at the University of Memphis. Prior to receiving his Ph.D. in Management Information Systems from the Carlson School of Management at the University of Minnesota in 1995, Dr. Janz spent 12 years in the information systems field working for Fortune 100 companies. Dr. Janz's research interests focus on how information technologies effect organizational strategy, design, and knowledge worker behavior. Specifically, he is interested in the effects that self-direction, cooperation, and organizational learning have on teams of IS system development professionals, development cycle time and systems quality.

Dr. Michelle Lynn Kaarst-Brown (mbrown2@richmond.edu)
Michelle Kaarst-Brown is an Assistant Professor of Management Systems in the E. Claiborne Robins School of Business at the University of Richmond, VA. She received her Ph.D. in Organizational Theory and Management Information Systems from York University in Canada. Building on twenty years in industry and management consulting, her research interests include: strategic risks and opportunities for Internet based firms; the impact of culture on strategic management of IT; and the management of change. Dr. Kaarst-Brown has presented at both national and international conferences and has published in *MIS Quarterly, the Journal of Organizational Change Management, and Information, Technology and People.*

Dr. Kalle Kangas (Kalle.Kangas@tukkk.fi)
Kalle Kangas is currently Professor of Information Systems Science at Pori School of Technology and Economics of Turku School of Economics and Business Administration in Finland. He has extensive industrial experience in company to company sales and contracting in Finland and in the Middle East. His current research focuses on IT package implementation in conglomerates, information technology in global enterprises, information technology and economics in transitional countries, as well as economics of electronic business, and web-based learning and teaching.

Dr. Anil Kumar (kumara@uwwvax.uww.edu)
Anil Kumar is currently an Assistant Professor of Management (MCS) in the College of Business and Economics at the University of Wisconsin-Whitewater. He received the PhD degree from the University of Memphis. His research interests include global IT management, virtual education and group dynamics. His work has been published in several journals such as *Decision Support Systems, Industrial Management & Data Systems, and Information Processing and Management.* His dissertation on Global Executive Information Systems has been published as a book.

Mr. Ned Kumar (nskumar@fedex.com)
Ned Kumar is a Marketing Project Manager with Federal Express Corporation in Memphis, TN. Mr. Kumar's major interests are in the field of Enterprise Customer Relationship Management (ECRM), Internet Marketing, global IT management, E-commerce and virtual organizations. He has published extensively in journals and conference proceedings including Decision Support Systems, European Journal of Operations Research, and Information Processing and Management.

Dr. Jaana Kuula (jaana.kuula@urova.fi)
Jaana Kuula is currently employed by the Regional Council of Lapland, where she is directing the development of the ICT sector in Lapland. Before this position she was a professor at the University of Lapland. Her research interests are electronic commerce, internationalization of business, information society, and digital content production. Ms Kuula has also been working for the University of Jyväskylä, the University of Texas at Austin, Nokia Corporation, and for Kone Corporation.

Mr. Hans Lehmann (h.lehmann@auckland.ac.nz)
Hans Lehmann, Austrian by birth, is a management professional with some 25 years of business experience with information technology. After a career in data processing line management in Austria he worked as an information technology manager in manufacturing and banking in South Africa. After completing an MBA, he joined Deloitte's and worked for some 12 years in their international management consultancy firm. Hans' work experience spans continental Europe, Africa, the United Kingdom, North America and Australasia. He specialised in the development and implementation management of international information systems for a number of blue-chip multi-national companies in the financial and manufacturing sectors. In 1991 Hans changed careers and joined the University of Auckland, New Zealand, where his research focuses on the strategic management of international information systems and electronic commerce.

Mr. David Mason (David.Mason@vuw.ac.nz)

David Mason is a Senior Lecturer with the School of Information Management at Victoria University, Wellington, New Zealand specializing in database design and ecommerce applications. He holds a Masters Degree from the London School of Economics. He has extensive consultanty experience internationally and is the author of numerous articles and books on information systems implementation. His current research interests center on the adoption and application of ICT and community informatics.

Dr. Simon Milne (Simon.Milne@aut.ac.nz)

Simon Milne is Professor of Tourism and Associate Dean of Research in the Business Faculty, Auckland University of Technology. Dr Milne also holds appointments at Derby University (UK) and at McGill University in Canada. Dr Milne coordinates the Tourism Research Institute in New Zealand. His research focuses on creating stronger links between tourism and surrounding economies. He has considerable experience in economic impact assessment, and in formulating tourism-related economic development strategies. In recent years he has become particularly interested in the use of information technology to improve the economic performance and sustainability of tourism firms and destinations.

Dr. Effy Oz (effyoz@psu.edu)

For eleven years, Effy Oz served as an executive for a large aerospace corporation and as the controller of a small company. His practical experience includes financial management, project management, cost accounting, inventory planning, contract administration and negotiation, development of information systems, and strategic planning. Dr. Oz has served on the faculties of Boston University, Boston College, Wayne State University, and The Pennsylvania State University, where he now serves as an associate professor of management science and information systems. He is the author of four books: *Ethics for the Information Age*, *Ethics for the Information Age: Cases*, *Management Information System*, and *The Manager's Bible*. He is currently working on a new textbook titled *Foundations of E*-Commerce. He published articles in academic and professional journals among which are: *MIS Quarterly, Communications of the ACM, Decision Sciences, Information & Management, Omega, Journal of Systems Management, Journal of Business Ethics* and *Journal of Global Information Management*. He has been on the editorial boards of two academic journals and the *Encyclopedia of Information* Systems. His opinions on systems integration and computer ethics have been quoted by print and television media. Dr. Oz is a frequent speaker before corporate and professional groups.

Dr. Prashant C. Palvia (pcpalvia@uncg.edu)

Prashant Palvia is the Joe Rosenthal Excellence Professor of Information Systems and head of the Information Systems & Operations Management department at the University of North Carolina at Greensboro. Earlier he was professor at the University of Memphis for fourteen years. He received his Ph.D., MBA and MS from the University of Minnesota and BS from the University of Delhi, India. In addition to seventeen years in academics, he has nine years in industry. Recently, he chaired the first annual Global Information Technology Management (GITM) World Conference in Memphis in June 2000, and is also chairing the June 2001 conference in Dallas. Prof. Palvia is Editor-in-Chief of *the Journal of Global Information Technology Management (JGITM)*, and is on editorial board of several journals. His research interests include international information systems, electronic commerce, strategic information systems, database design, and software engineering. He has published 60 articles in journals, such as: *MIS Quarterly, Decision Sciences, Communications of the ACM, Information & Management, Decision Support Systems*, and *ACM Transactions on Database Systems*, and over 90 articles in conference proceedings. He has co-edited two previous books on Global Information Technology, this being the third.

Dr. Shailendra Palvia (spalvia@liu.edu)

Professor Shailendra C. Palvia is Professor and Director of Management Information Systems at the Long Island University, New York (USA). He received his Ph.D. from the University of Minnesota. His research publications are in the areas of management of the systems development process, mode of use in problem solving, implementation issues for MIS/DSS, global information technology, software training methods, and global electronic commerce. His work has been published or forthcoming in refereed journals such as Communications of the ACM, MIS Quarterly, Information

& Management, Journal of Global Information Management, International Information Systems, Industrial Management and Data Systems, Journal of Computer Information Systems, and Journal of Information Systems Education. Dr. Palvia is Editor-in-Chief of the Journal of Information Technology Cases and Applications (JITCA) since 1999 and an Associate Editor of the Journal of Global Information Technology Management (JGITM) since 1998. He has been an invited speaker to Boston (USA), Stuttgart (Germany), Singapore, Bombay (India), Bangalore (India), and Anand (India).

Dr. William C. Perkins (perkinsw@indiana.edu)

William C. (Bill) Perkins is Professor and Coordinator of Information Systems in the Kelley School of Business, Indiana University, Bloomington. He received the B.S.C.E. degree (Civil Engineering) from Rose-Hulman Institute of Technology, and the M.B.A. and D.B.A. degrees (Quantitative Business Analysis) from Indiana University. Dr. Perkins has published papers in *Decision Sciences, Journal of Political Economy, Journal of Operations Management, International Journal of Production Research, Decision Support Systems, Group Decision and Negotiation*, and other journals. He has co-authored five books, including Managing Information Systems: What Managers Need to Know (3rd edition, Prentice Hall, 1999). Dr. Perkins has served as President (and other officer positions) of the Decision Sciences Institute, has received the Distinguished Service Award of the Institute, and has been named a Fellow of the Institute.

Dr. Madhu T. Rao (mtrao@ssu.edu)

Madhu T. Rao is currently an Assistant Professor in the Information and Decision Sciences Department of the Perdue School of Business at Salisbury State University. He has been actively involved with the application of technology in business environments for several years. As a Systems Analyst for one of India's largest software firms, he participated in the development of banking systems for clients such as The State Bank of Hyderabad, Deutschebank, and the Royal Bank of Scotland. His current research focuses on the cultural and organizational issues in global IT management. He has presented his research at a number of conferences including DSI, INFORMS, and AIS.

Dr. Edward M. Roche (eroche@mac.com)

Edward M. Roche is Chief Research Officer of The Research Board, and former Chief Scientist at The Concours Group, a management-consulting firm based in Houston, Texas and Watertown, Massachusetts. He received his Ph.D. from Columbia University in 1987, M.Phil. in 1983; M.A. in International Relations from the School of Advanced International Studies (Washington, D.C.), and B.A. from Antioch College. He has taught at New York University, the University of Arizona, and the University of California Berkeley. He is the author of (a) Managing Information Technology in Multinational Corporations, (b) Telecommunication and Business Strategy, and has edited several books including (c) Global Information Technology and Systems Management (with P. and S. Palvia), (d) Information Technology, Development and Policy (with Michael J. Blaine), (e) Information Technology in Multinational Enterprises (with Michael J. Blaine) and (f) Corporate Networks, International Telecommunications and Interdependence (with Henry Bakis).

Dr. Barry Shore (bshore@christa.unh.edu)

Barry Shore is a Professor of Management Information Systems at the Whittemore School of Business and Economics, The University of New Hampshire. He received his Ph.D. from The University of Wisconsin. Professor Shore is the author of four books published by McGraw-Hill and Holt, Rinehart and Winston. He has worked for Boeing Company, General Electric, Hewlett-Packard, and Arthur D. Little. His research Interests are in the area of global information systems and has published in such journals as the Journal of Global Information Management, Information and Management, Journal of Strategic Information Systems, and the Journal of Computer Information Systems.

Dr. Steven John Simon (simons@fiu.edu)

Steven John Simon is an associate professor in the Stetson School of Business and Economics at Mercer University in Atlanta, Georgia. He received his Ph.D. from the University of South Carolina, specializing in MIS and International Business. Before entering the doctoral program he spent eighteen years in the private sector in management/computer operations and was owner/operator of seven McDonalds franchises. His current research interests include information determinants of international business structures, enterprise information systems, supply chain management, electronic commerce in the international environment, and organization change and learning. He has extensive ERP experience having work with companies such as IBM on SAP implementation projects. Dr Simon is also an officer in the United States Naval Reserve formerly assigned to the directorate of logistics for United States Atlantic Command. His past Navy assignments included serving as Information Resource Management Officer to the Commander of the Second Naval Construction Brigade. He has consulted and lectured extensively in Korea, Hong Kong, Malaysia, Singapore, and the People's Republic of China. He has previously published in *Information Systems Research*, *Journal of Applied Psychology*, *Communications of the CAM*, *Database*, *European Journal of Information Systems*, *The Journal of Global Information Technology Management*, *The Journal of Global Information Management*, *Journal* of Information Technology Cases and Applications, and The Information Resources Management Journal.

Mr. Jaeki Song

Jaeki Song is a Ph.D candidate in Management Information Systems at the University of Wisconsin-Milwaukee. His research interests include the implementation of information technology in the area of e-commerce and globalization. His publications have appeared in *IEEE Transactions on Professional Communications* and such conferences as *AMCIS*, *INFORM*, and *DSI*.

Mr. Emmanuel O. Tetteh (etetteh@chmail.ch.ecu.edu.au)

Emmanuel O. Tetteh is a Research Associate of the We-B Research Centre, School of MIS, Edith Cowan University, Western Australia. He is holds a BSc (Hons) in Electrical Engineering (UST) and a MBA in Management Information Systems from the Vrije University Brussel (VUB) Belgium. Emmanuel is completing a PhD in Business Information Systems. His current research interests include electronic business strategies, Internet infrastructures in SMEs, virtual organisations, information and communications technologies (ICT)-enabled business transformation, and national information infrastructures (NII) strategies and case research. Since 1998, he has designed and developed a number of online environments for research and teaching in e-business and virtual organisation. He has over six years experience in ICT policy research at the Science and Technology Policy Research Institute (STEPRI) of the CSIR, Ghana. He has also worked as a computer systems engineer for a leading computer systems vendor in Ghana. Emmanuel has a number of refereed publications on e-business and Internet applications in SMEs.

Mr. Subhash (Sam) S. Valunju

Subhash (Sam) S. Valanju is Vice President and Chief Information Officer for Johnson Controls, Inc. In his position, he oversees Johnson Controls' Information Technology activities. Mr. Valanju joined Johnson Controls in 1996 from Rockwell International, where he had served as Director, Information Systems for their Automotive Businesses. During his 10 year tenure with Rockwell Automotive, Mr. Valanju developed and executed Information Technology strategic plans on a global basis. Prior to Rockwell International, Mr. Valanju worked with Federal-Mogul Corporation. During his 18 year tenure, Mr. Valanju had many different responsibilities, including Production Planning, Warehouse Facility Management and Manufacturing/ Distribution Information Systems. Mr. Valanju earned a BSME degree from the University of Bombay, India; an MSIE degree from the Illinois Institute of Technology and an MBA from the University of Detroit. He also has CPIM and CIRM certifications from the American Production and Inventory Control Society.

Dr. Vijay K. Vemuri (vvemuri@liu.edu)

Vijay Vemuri is an Assistant Professor of Management Information Systems at C.W. Post Campus of Long Island University. He received Ph.D. in Business Administration from University of Illinois at Urbana-Champaign. His research interests include electronic commerce, strategic implications of information technology and networking infrastructure. He has published in European Journal of Operational Research and International Journal of Electronic Commerce.

Dr. Nicholas P. Vitalari

Nicholas P. Vitalari is an international consultant and educator in the strategic application of information technology in corporations and society. He is a co-founder of The Concours Group offering integration of research, consulting and education to assist major corporations in the use of information technology. Dr. Vitalari also co-founded Project NOAH -- a National Science Foundation funded program to assess the impact of microcomputers. Project NOAH predicted many of the technologies emerging today, including the information highway, work at home, consumer use of electronic networks and the rise of electronic commerce.

Dr. James C. Wetherbe

James C. Wetherbe is Stevenson Chair of Information Technology at Texas Tech University as well as Professor of MIS at the University of Minnesota. He was formerly the FedEx Professor of Excellence in MIS at the University of Memphis and a professor of MIS at the University of Houston. He is internationally known as a dynamic and entertaining speaker, author, and leading authority on the use of computers and information systems to improve organizational performance and competitiveness. He is particularly appreciated for his ability to explain complex technology in straightforward, practical terms that can be strategically applied by both executives and general management. He is the author of 18 highly regarded books including the Information Technology for Management (Wiley Publishing), So, What's Your Point? (2nd edition, Mead Publishing, 1996), Systems Analysis and Design: Best Practices (West Publishing, 1994) and The World On Time: 11 Management Principles That Made FedEx an Overnight Sensation (Knowledge Exchange, 1996). His newest book is The Management of Information Technology (Wiley Publishing, 1999). Quoted often in leading business and information system journals, Dr. Wetherbe has also authored over 200 articles, writes regular columns, and serves as a consulting editor for publishing companies.

Dr. James E. Whitworth (jewhitwo@gasou.edu)

James E. Whitworth is currently an assistant professor in the Information Systems and Logistics Department at Georgia Southern University where he teaches a wide variety of systems and information management and development courses. Dr. Whitworth received his Ph.D. in 1999 from the Fogelman College of Business and Economics, University of Memphis, with concentrations in Management Information Systems and International Business. Prior to joining Georgia Southern University in 1998, Dr. Whitworth spent over 38 years working for companies in the information technology industry, the last 14 years with the Federal Express Corporation.

GLOSSARY

ANSI X.12: Acronym for the Amercian National Standards Institute standard for EDI transmission. Used in the U.S.

Application Service Provider (ASP): A vendor who provides turnkey application (now increasingly over the Internet) and sometimes systems integration services to connect the externally-provided applications with back-end applications. Business Services Providers are types of ASP firms.

Architecture: The structure, or structures, of the software system, which comprise software components, the externally visible properties of those components, and the relationships among them.

Arm's-length Model: An interorganizational alliance characterized by: a competitive relationship between the focal firm and its suppliers; little relationship-specific investment; and minimal data sharing

Bandwidth: Communications speed. The greater the bandwidth the more a community is equipped to exchange data with the rest of the world.

Barney's VRIO framework: Value, Rareness, Imitability, and Organization. Depending on the number of how many of these attributes occur in a resource simultaneously, the firm can have competitive disadvantage, competitive parity, competitive advantage, or sustained competitive advantage.

Bartlett and Ghoshal Typology: A classification scheme for multinational strategy-structure. Includes the types – Global, Multinational, International and Transnational.

Browser-ware: Any software that uses as its primary user-interface a web browser.

BSP: Business Services Provider. See ASP.

Business Process Redesign: This refers to the fundamental rethinking and radical redesign of business processes to achieve dramatic improvements in critical, contemporary measures of performance.

Business Process Reengineering: refer to Reengineering; though the focus here is the business process e.g., sales delivery process, order fulfillment or supply chain management.

Business-To-Business (B2B): The use of the Internet (or other electronic means) by a firm for transactions with other businesses (its suppliers, customers, distributors and other value chain partners).

Business-To-Commerce (B2C): The use of the Internet (or other electronic means) by a firm for transactions with its end customers/consumers.

Business-To-Employee (B2E): The use of the Internet (or other electronic means) by a firm for work activities and ransactions with its employees.

Business-To-Government (B2G): Access to information and services using the Internet (or other electronic means) provided by the government to businesses.

Caller-ID: A telecommunications technology that forwards caller information (i.e., name, location, phone number) to the call receiver at the time of call placement.

Capability: Organizational *capabilities* refer to the firm's ability to *use* its competencies. They represent the collective tacit knowledge of the firm in responding to its environment.

Capability Maturity Model (CMM): A model, developed by the Software Engineering Institute at Carnegie Mellon University, to measure the maturity of the processes of an IS department or project.

Collaborative Support Systems: Information systems and software products designed to suuport the needs of a working group, whether at same place/same time or at different places/different times.

Cocooning: Surrounding an existing legacy application with new and improved software that insulates the company from the obsolete legacy applications while providing the ability to interface with an organization's other applications.

Common System: A common system is a computer-based application that utilizes the same software (and hardware) throughout an organization for maintaining consistent and controllable applications.

Community Tourism: Type of tourism where the attraction is the way of life and interaction with the people of a region who share a unique cultural outlook, combined with attractive natural resources.

Competence: Organizational *competencies* refer to the unique knowledge owned by the firm.

Competitive advantage: A firm is said to have a competitive advantage when it is implementing a value creating strategy not simultaneously being implemented by any current or potential competitors.

Competing Values Framework: A framework used to study organizations that emphasizes the competing tensions and conflicts inherent in groups.

Connectivity: The degree to which a community is connected to the Internet; usually measured in number of Internet servers per capita.

Control: Process which brings about adherence to a goal or target through the exercise of power or authority.

Coordination: Administrative tools used for achieving integration among different units within an organization.

CPM: Cost per thousand click-through. It results in charging a designated fee for every 1000 people who visit the website on which a company's banner ad is located.

Critical Success Factors(CSF): Limited number of areas where results, if satisfactory, will ensure successful competitive performance of the organization.

Cultural Differences: Behavioral and other differences among communities as result of tradition, location, and environmental differences.

Culture: An integrated system of learned behavior patterns that are characteristic of the members of any society. It includes everything a group thinks, says, does, and makes – its customs, language, material artifacts, and shared systems of attitudes and feelings

Customer-Centricity: The nature of a firm that provides personalization for each of its customers, and has also adjusted its internal management mechanisms to deliver value to the customer.

Customer Relationship Management (CRM): Systems designed to enable a firm to provide individualized service to each customer. Usually based on two components: customer database and business logic.

Cybersquatting: The illegal use of trademarked names in website addresses

Data Security: An organization's data is a valuable corporate resource and must be secured against abuse advertently or inadvertently.

Disintermediation: The process of eliminating the intermediate steps between producer and consumer.

Distributed Systems: Provision of computer systems (comprising of hardware, software, and /or databases) over local area networks, wide area networks, and the Internet.

Domestic Mindset: Inadequacy in the understanding of international issues and situations.

Economies of Scale: A larger output (of the same product) is associated with a lower production cost per unit.

Economies of Scope: The ability to produce an increasing number of similar products/services at lower marginal costs.

Electronic Business (E-Business): Another term for e-commerce; sometimes used to mean business-to-business electronic commerce.

Electronic Commerce (E-Commerce): is the exchange of business transactions (e.g., purchase orders, funds transfer, etc.) and conduct of business over telecommunications networks (primarily the Internet).

Electronic Data Interchange (EDI): The direct computer-to-computer exchange, between two organizations, of standard business transaction documents.

Ends Means Analysis: A strategy for determining information requirements of executives. The technique separates the definition of ends or outputs from the means (inputs and processes).

Enterprise Resource Planning (ERP) Systems: Large integrated software packages designed to link together multiple functional areas and processes within the firm in order to increase flow-through efficiency from one business process to another. Examples include SAP, Oracle, and BAAN.

eProcess: Business processes that are initiated by or are an integral part in supporting Internet commerce transactions.

e-tailer: A retailer that sells on the web and has no physical retail facilities.

Executive Information Systems (EIS): Information systems designed and developed to support senior executives in an organization.

Extranet: A network that utilizes Internet technologies (i.e., web pages, browsers, etc.) for applications between organizations.

Facsimile (Fax): Transmission in which the source document is scanned and sent over the public switched telephone network to the recipient's fax machine, at which time it is printed on paper.

Family Quadrant: A quadrant into which cultures are placed that are low in uncertainty avoidance and high in power distance.

Focal Firm: The firm in the supply chain relationship that contracts with its suppliers and oversees all of the activities from its suppliers to the delivery of the goods or service to the final customer.

Gilder's Law: Focuses on improvements in telecommunications bandwidth. It holds that the growth (in packets transmitted per second) is exponential - a rate of doubling every 16 months.

GLITS: Global Information Technology Strategic Model – A model and instrument to help identify the various areas for strategic use of information technology in a global business.

Global Business Process Reengineering: Reengineering effort that includes a business process that is global or cuts across at least two national boundaries (countries).

Global Executive Information Systems (Global EIS): A global EIS is for executives that provides easy access to internal and external information (both domestic and international).

Global Information System (GIS): A system that is used in more than one country.

Global IT Outsourcing: Any contribution to a client organization by vendors from a different country of origin in tangible, intangible, human, and/or nonhuman resources related to the IT infrastructure.

Global Trading Web (GTW): It is the world's largest B2B community connecting 58 independently operated B2B portals each designed to serve a specific region or industry. The rate of transactions on GTW exceeded one trillion dollars annually in the year 2000.

Governance (Structure): The set of institutional arrangements in place to make decisions and engage in planning for deployment and operations of large infrastructure systems .

Grounded Theory: A method of analyzing field data (such as case stories) with the declared object of establishing a theory directly related to the facts contained in the field data.

Groupware: Software applications that focus on providing productivity solutions for groups of people. Email, bulletin boards, chat rooms, file sharing, and electronic meetings, are all features of groupware.

G2C (and C2G): Refers to transactions between the Government and the citizens of a country and vice versa.

High-Context & Low-Context Cultures: Language is neutral and explicit for low-context cultures, and emotional and implicit for high context cultures.

Horse-trading: Form of conflict resolution where each party agrees to trade-offs such that each party gets what they want on certain issues.

HTML: Hypertext Mark-Up Language. One of the programming or scripting languages used to develop World-Wide Web (WWW) web pages.

Individualism-Collectivism: The degree to which each individual takes care of himself or herself or relinquishes some of this responsibility to the group.

Infomediary: An intermediary that mainly provides information to facilitate a transaction.

Information Architecture: It is a high level map of the information requirements of an organization. Also called the enterprise model.

Information Culture: A set of information system values and practices shared by those members of an organization.

Information Resource Management (IRM): Management of integrated information in the organization to improve strategic value of resources, such as capital, labor, inventory, plant, know-how.

Information Technology (IT): The hardware and software technologies that permit information gathering, processing, and distribution.

Internet: It is the global network of networks of computers (LANs and WANs) connecting hundreds of thousands of computers and millions of people to communicate, collaborate, and share information from thousands of databases.

Internet-based Firm: Companies that do not have a brick and mortal retail outlet and therefore rely solely on on-line revenue sources

Internet Commerce: Electronic commerce where the main telecommunications channel is the Internet.

Internet Service Provider (ISP): is the company that provides Internet access to users.

Interorganizational Alliance: The nature of relationship between a focal firm and its suppliers, e.g., a close collaborative relationship (partnership) or a limited and competitive one (arm's-length).

Intranet: A network that utilizes Internet technologies (i.e., web pages, browsers, etc.) for applications internal to the organization.

IS Organization Alignment: The organizational positioning of the IS department within the company.

IT Infrastructure: Includes such components as organization's diverse computers, telecommunication networks, databases, operating systems, system software, and business applications.

IT Strategy: Long term plan for selection, acquisition, and deployment of IT to further the business goals and mission of an organization.

Joint application development (JAD): A system development strategy where users and IS staff work together continuously in structured meetings to achieve a shared understanding of business objectives.

Knowledge Based Systems (KBS): A system which represents knowledge in an explicit form, designed for solving a specific problem.

Knowledge Management (KM): Organization of business intelligence concerning customer and competitors, and using this information for formulation of firm strategy, or new product development.

Lateral Relations: Integration mechanisms which cut across formal structures and aim at developing direct contact between personnel in various departments and subsidiaries (e.g., task forces, teams).

Leapfrog computing: A strategy in which an organization that lags its competitors in technology usage makes a quantum leap in the generation of technology.

Legacy systems: Old, typically obsolete computer applications that are typically large, complex, and expensive to maintain.

Line of Business (LOB): A group of similar businesses in a multinational enterprise.

Local Area Network (LAN): A network connecting computers within a short distance (e.g., a building or a campus).

Logistics: The process of obtaining inputs, storing goods, and moving items to their destination.

Loosely Coupled System Model: Distributed applications based on replicated and consequently redundant systems and data storage driven by detailed and specific synchronization rules.

Machine Quadrant: A quadrant into which cultures are placed that are low in power distance and high in uncertainty avoidance.

Management and Control IS Issues: Include among others: communication between IS department and end users, top management support, software development productivity, goal alignment, and security and control.

Market Quadrant: A quadrant into which cultures are placed that are low in uncertainty avoidance and low in power distance.

Masculinity-Femininity: A measure of the difference between the roles played by men and women in a society.

Mass customization: The strategy of customizing a product or service to meet the unique needs of each of the organization's individual customers.

Measurement Standard: The English and metric standards. Units in one must often be converted to the other when exchanging business or technical information.

Metcalfe's Law: States that the value of a network increases as the *square* of the number of devices that it is connect to.

Miles and Snow Typology: A theoretical framework for how organizations define their market domains (strategy) and construct mechanisms (structures and processes). The four types are: Prospector, Reactor, Defender, and Analyzer.

Mixed IS Vendor Shops: When an IS department acquires different hardware, software, and database systems from different IS vendors within a country or worldwide, it results in a mixed IS vendor shop.

Moore's Law: Describes the exponential growth of microprocessor speed - it doubles every 24 months.

Multinational Corporation (MNC): A corporation that has operations in multiple countries other than sales alone.

Multi-Tiered Software: A system that is composed of multiple layers. Strictly speaking a layer interfaces only with the adjacent layer.

National Culture: Shared values of a particular group of people that can affect the way people relate, work, and make decisions.

Off-Shore Services: IT-related services that are provided in another country.

1-Click Ordering: Simplification and streamlining of commerce site so that a customer with an account with the company can complete an order with a single click of the mouse.

Operational IS Issues: Operational issues include among others: management's awareness of MIS capabilities, human resource development for MIS, quality of data, and standards.

Organizational Culture: A pattern of basic assumptions that establishes the correct way to perceive, think and feel about organizational problems.

Outsourcing: Hiring an outside company to perform functions that under other circumstances would be carried out by company employees.

Partnership Model: An interorganizational alliance characterized by a close working relationship, relationship-specific investments, and data sharing.

Pay-Per-Performance: This Internet-based advertising payment method includes pay-per-click, pay-per-lead, and pay-per-sale.

Performance Metrics: A standard of measures used to assess business process and organizational performance.

Personal Digital Assistant (PDA): Small hand-held devices that provide communications and computational support to end-users. Examples are mobile telephones and hand-held organizers.

Personalization: The adjustment of what is delivered to the customer, and the nature of the interaction between the firm and its customer, so that each customer receives a unique experience.

Political Constraints: Laws and regulations that meet political, rather than economic or other, purposes.

Pooled Interdependence: Exists when branches of an organization do not have contact with one another, but instead, make discrete contributions to the organization as a whole.

Portal: is a website or other service that provides an initial point of entry to the Web or to internal company data and provides information on many things like weather and travel.

Power Distance: The (perceived) degree of inequality among people.

Primary Activities: A term attributed to Porter, dividing the activities of the firm into inbound logistics, operations, outbound logistics, marketing and sales, and service.

Privacy: The ability of people to control information about themselves.

Productivity Paradox: is the puzzling lack of observation of productivity gains in macroeconomic data, despite heavy investment in IT by firms.

Prototyping: An iterative development process where applications are broken down into smaller modules that are developed quickly, reviewed by end-users, and enhanced based on feedback.

Provisioning: A term that loosely means "providing", but within the context of IT encompasses the entire cycle of assessment, design, programming, and implementation of a new system.

Proxy Server: A proxy is an interpreter host that acts on behalf of the real user. A proxy server intercepts clients' requests for particular services and evaluates these requests.

Pyramid Quadrant; A quadrant into which cultures are placed that are high in power distance and high in uncertainty avoidance.

Reciprocal Interdependence: Exists in network organizations where branches (or subsidiaries) exchange goods, services, and information and depend on with one another on a constant basis.

Recommenders: Internet commerce systems used to make product recommendations to a customer.

Reengineering: A radical redesign of business processes, challenging traditional assumptions and implementing a "clean-slate" approach to the process, usually with the help to information technology. Also used interchangeably with Redesign in literature.

Relationship-Specific Investment: Investments made in information technology by suppliers to accommodate the information strategy of the focal organization.

Request for a Proposal (RFP): A document distributed by an organization to various vendors asking for their quotation on a group of products or services to be purchased.

Reverse Auction: This is Request For Quotes (RFQ), where the potential suppliers bid to supply the needed products or services. The buyer purchases from the lowest bidder.

Sequential Interdependence: Exists when branches (or subsidiaries) have direct interaction and exchange information. One branch may depend on another but not vice-versa.

Server-Based Web Traffic Analysis: Measurement and analysis of traffic to a website by analyzing the log files of a webserver.

S-M-A-L-L: A framework capturing the five aspects of an SME business environment that may be transformed by an exploitation of an infrastructure management strategy.

SME: Small and medium-sized enterprise.

Software Configuration Management: A software tool used to coordinate the work and assure quality when groups of programmers are dealing with thousands of objects (such as code).

Software Development Productivity: Productivity is measured by the ratio of outputs to inputs – outputs refer to the quality and magnitude of software produced, and inputs refer to total time and effort expended.

Sourcing: See Outsourcing.

Steering Committee: A group of senior executives to provide overall direction for an IS project.

Strategic IS Issues: Strategic issues include among others: nformation architecture, data resource management, strategic planning for MIS, organizational learning.

Strategic Orientation (of an MNC): Explains how the firm is organized. It explains the reporting structures, rules/regulations, and corporate culture as well as how business functions are conducted.

Supply Chain Management (SCM): Integration and management of activities, materials flows, and information flows between suppliers and customers necessary to transform raw materials from suppliers to finished goods to customers or end-users.

Survival IS Issues: The very availability of computer hardware, operating and applications software, human resources for MIS, and availability of foreign currency to buy computer technology components.

Sustainable Tourism: Tourism development that maximises economic benefits while reducing socio-environmental costs.

Synchronizing: A term used in supply chain management to suggest the integration of information and product flow from suppliers through to customers.

TCP/IP: Telecommunications Protocol/Internet Protocol. The original and de facto standard protocol used for data interchange on the Internet.

Theory of the Firm: In micro-economics, theories of the firm try to address two basic questions: "why firms exist", and "what determines their scale and scope". A third question, though less related to economic theory, is also posed: "What is the function of the firm and its managers"?

Three-Click Rule: Simplification and streamlining of commerce site navigation so that a shopper can get to the product she wants within three clicks of a mouse.

Time-Boxing: Breaking a large project down into more manageable sub-tasks with readily achievable time deadlines.

Total Data Quality Management (TDQM): The concept that data quality, defined by integrity, access, and relevance, is the responsibility of all members of an organization

Uncertainty Avoidance: The degree to which a society feels threatened by uncertain situations.

UN/EDIFACT: Acronym for United Nations/Electronic Data Interchange for Administration, Commerce and Transport, the international EDI standard as developed through the United Nations.

User Friendliness of Systems: Are the computer system interfaces easy to understand and use? If yes, such a system is termed user friendly.

Value Added Network (VAN): An intermediary organization in an EDI based network to which EDI encoded messages are sent, stored, and then sent to their final destination.

Value Chain: A term introduced by Porter, suggesting the value added by a firm and including all those activities from suppliers to the final customer.

Vendor-Managed Inventories: The responsibility taken by suppliers to manage the inventories maintained on the shelves of retailers. Requires the use of information technology.

Virtuality (or Virtualness): Characteristic of an organization where it operates as a federation of enterprises through contractual rather than ownership relationships.

Web-Raising: A process of web page development based on participatory community interaction.

Web Server: A computer server primarily used to provide web pages for Internet access.

Wide Area Network (WAN): A network connecting computers that are geographically distributed.

Wireless Application Protocol (WAP): The protocol used to transmit Internet traffic including XML and HTTP information over wireless links, usually to a hand-held device such as a mobile telephone.

World Wide Web (WWW): Vast pool of knowledge residing on the Internet accessible from anywhere by anybody at anytime.

XML: Extensible Markup Language, is a general-purpose language that describes the structure of a document and supports links to multiple documents, allowing data to be manipulated by the computer.

INDEX